DRYDEN

DRYDEN

POETRY, PROSE AND PLAYS

SELECTED BY DOUGLAS GRANT

HARVARD UNIVERSITY PRESS
Cambridge Massachusetts
1965

Printed in Great Britain
by Richard Clay (The Chaucer Press), Ltd.,
Bungay, Suffolk

CONTENTS

CONTENTS

PLAYS

INTRODUCTION

JOHN DRYDEN, in his old age, wrote: 'I think my self as vigorous as ever in the Faculties of my Soul, excepting only my Memory, which is not impair'd to any great degree; and if I lose not more of it, I have no great reason to complain. What Judgment I had, increases rather than diminishes; and Thoughts, such as they are, come crowding in so fast upon me, that my only Difficulty is to chuse or to reject; to run them into Verse, or to give them the other Harmony of Prose; I have so long studied and practis'd both, that they are grown into a Habit, and become familiar to me.' This typical passage is the key to Dryden's genius and character. It could only have been written by a man who had long since scrupulously considered and accurately judged the bent and scope of his abilities; and who had arrived by way of this self-knowledge to a self-confidence which, had it not been entirely justified, would have looked unpleasantly like arrogance. It reveals, in a word, his competence—his most characteristic trait.

Competence has a dull sound in common speech; it suggests a tedious limbo suspended between excellence and incapacity; but it is, nevertheless, the foundation of all art. It is as essential to performance as the dead colours are to a picture—which, if it lacks their solid ground, will vainly glitter with surface brilliance—and can only be reached by study and practice. The qualities needed for its acquisition are primarily reason and judgment, and Dryden possessed these to an unusual degree. His early career shows how entirely he depended on them to master what, it is too often assumed, can only be subdued by force of inspiration. At an age when Coleridge had dwindled into an ineffectual visionary, when Wordsworth was hardening into scriptural form, and when Keats and Shelley, their brief lives run, were secure of fame, he was turning out verses which, had they not his later work to buoy them up, would long ago have sunk into oblivion. If he could write in his old age in a patrician strain, and without fearing contradiction, about his powers and achievements, it was only because he had spent many years labouring to discipline himself and to understand his art. This difficult struggle gave him a profound insight into literary principles.

Once Dryden had grasped these principles, which he did slowly but entirely, he was richly rewarded for his diligence. As long as he kept within their limits, within, that is to say, the scope of his reason and judgment, he was on surer ground than those poets who largely trust themselves to the flux of imagination. Moreover, he pushed out those limits so far by study and practice that he excelled in almost every branch of literature; critic, satirist, lyricist, narrative poet, and translator were all joined in him; and he can only be classed as a man of letters, the English man of letters. But when he understood, he depended upon those principles, and this dependence points out his gravest deficiency. He is, for so great a poet, surprisingly wanting in imagination. He could travel easily to the frontier where reason ends but he could not go beyond where only imagination can make a way. He was too earth-bound and four-square to be able to fly. Often he aspires to flight and sometimes he gives its appearance, but it is only an illusion like the castle which, seen against a flowing skyline of summer clouds, seems to drift through the air.

His reason and judgment are to be seen to the best advantage, in company with their attendant deficiency, in the satires. He knew that satire can only work its most destructive effect when it seems to result from reason, outraged and oppressed by folly and crime, rather than from mere partisan spleen; and his own satires are always a reasoned indictment of his enemies' motives and characters. His enemies were those who offended against his most cherished beliefs; his belief in the necessity of order and authority to the state, and his belief in the dignity of letters; and he had utter contempt for those who stirred up 'the dregs of a democracy', or who debased literary values. He had no need to feign anger or to distort the evidence before he attacked. He reasoned and judged and pronounced sentence. His description of the Popish Plot in *Absalom and Achitophel* is a fairer and clearer-sighted verdict than those passed by later historians, who, in theory at least, had an advantage in knowledge and impartiality; and it is an extraordinary tribute to the strength of his intelligence that he could pierce through that 'unchew'd and crude' mass of monstrous lies to where the truth lay hidden. He could always rescue his mistress from behind the barricades of fear, hypocrisy, stupidity, and malignancy. His satirical portraits are as firmly grounded as his account of the Plot. The follies of Zimri were really the follies of the Duke of Buckingham, and, by avoiding the common tricks of railing and scurrility—tricks which he was not always above—he held him up to ridicule without once stepping beyond probability. His satire gained immeasurably from this strict adherence to reason; it assumed the force and character of justice. His satires, however, for all their greatness, show up his want of imagination. He could not command that harmony which makes all things 'in order to their stations leap', and, lacking that shaping spirit, they are brilliant passages rudely clamped together. Pope took the hint for *The Dunciad* from *Mac Flecknoe*, but on the site of the original structure, a low rambling mansion of wit, he built a flamboyant palace, so aerial and entire that the separate parts are joined and forgotten in the general effect.

The habit of Dryden's mind was ratiocination and it empowered him to impose order on ideas; he understood them immediately and ran them unhesitatingly into either verse or prose. The *Religio Laici* and *The Hind and the Panther* are unparalleled displays of a poet mastering ideas of supreme importance and endless complexity, and rendering them in simple language. The fire of his reason refined the ideal ore into pure gold and surcharged his verse with passionate conviction; or, to choose Coleridge's fine phrase, 'the wheels caught fire from the speed of their own motion'. He brought theological disputation from the solitude of dusty rooms into the crowded arena of common-life, and gave it the interest and excitement of a conflict of flesh-and-blood. His ability to reduce confusion into order might have made him a great narrative poet had he not wanted imagination. He could see at once the logical connection between ideas but he could not distinguish the natural bonds between character and event; and this weakness forced him to take over other men's fables instead of inventing his own. When he had Chaucer or Boccaccio before him as a model, he could write with unfaltering ease, but without their genius to guide him, he could do nothing. He himself claimed that it was lack of time alone which prevented him from beginning his long-projected epic poem, but the real reason was that he knew himself too well to undertake a task for which he had no aptitude.

His style is the body to his thought. The heroic couplet was the complement of his reason and judgment. He could when he chose either emphasise the rhymes to point his expression, or let them sound faintly to carry through and round up his periods. His verses are either compact with significance or eloquent with uninterrupted thought. He gave the couplet a power and dignity to which the apparent simplicity of its regular pattern was admirably suited, and struck out from it a sonorous harmony which 'added length to solemn sounds'. His language is sober and unaffected; the 'soft blight of refinement' never settled on it; but, invigorated by his impassioned thought, it scintillates with a summer-lightning of wit. His style is the broad way of tradition, the golden mean of the English tongue.

Dryden naturally joined to reason and judgment the power of close and critical observation. The portraits in his satires are drawn in the round, and time cannot dim their vitality. Settle still 'faggots his notions as they fall' with the mechanical monotony of a donkey-engine; Shadwell, as 'round as a globe', rolls home from a tavern 'liquored in every chink'; and Slingsby Bethel steps forward clutching his meanness about him like an old coat. This ability to sketch character should have made him a great dramatist, but, at the close of his life, he had to confess, that, in spite of his many plays, his 'genius had never much inclined' towards the stage. Here he failed to achieve greatness because he lacked imagination enough to understand and sympathise with the characters he attempted to create. He could only draw character when the original was before him, as he could only write narrative when the fable was provided. The characters in his plays are shot through with inconsistencies which hamper the action and make a mockery of the noble speeches put into their mouths. It is the measure of his failure that not one of them hangs in that beloved gallery beside, among so many, the portraits of Millamant and Rosalind, of Falstaff and Sir John Brute. His best play, *All for Love*, is, significantly enough, an imitation from Shakespeare, and he frankly owned to his debt: 'I hope I may affirm, and without vanity, that by imitating him, I have excell'd my self throughout the Play'. But if he is not a great, he is often an admirable and always an interesting dramatist. The poetry, whether rhyme or blank verse, frequently rises above the ordinary level of substantial rhetoric to lyrical statement, or, when the chance is offered by the action, to profound and beautiful exposition of some moral or political principle. The action is usually rapid and well-constructed—but this mechanical ability would be expected from a dramatist who had so closely studied his art. He fails only when he is driven to attempt a description of the passions and then, to hide his want of imagination, which alone can treat of those subjects, he descends to such extraordinary bombast that the style should be called the brewery-heroic.

Dryden's remarkable competence is perhaps most obvious in the versatile ease with which he used almost every lyric measure. He could adopt in his odes the martial clangour of *Alexander's*

Feast, or the chaster melody of the *Song for St. Cecilia's Day*, or the moving harmony of the opening verses of the *Ode to Anne Killigrew*, that wells out in a matchless diapason of praise; and whichever he attempted, he succeeded in so well that it would seem he must have devoted himself only to its practice. The songs, tender and bawdy by turns, which are freshly scattered like dew-ponds throughout the plays, are all distinguished by their consummate skill. They have not the aetherial sweetness of the Elizabethans', nor the subtlety of the metaphysicals', nor the cynical grace of his courtly contemporaries'; but they have their own charm and spontaneity, and, once or twice, capture an echo from beyond the frontier:

> Every Nymph mourns me,
> Thus while I languish;
> She only scorns me,
> Who caus'd my anguish.
> No Love returning me, but all hope denying;
> By a dismal Cypress lying,
> Like a *Swan*, so sung he dying:
> Kind is Death that ends my pain,
> But cruel She I lov'd in vain.

Dr. Johnson hailed Dryden as the father of modern criticism, and his acclamation has been accepted without a single dissenting voice. Dryden approached literature by way of reason and judgment; carefully studying the work of earlier writers and mastering their principles before attempting to practise; and his strength in these faculties allowed him to excel in whatever he undertook. He therefore brought to criticism unparalleled resources. His deep understanding of literature was based upon wide knowledge and great experience, and each was continually qualified and illuminated by the other. His habit of mind led him to seek in similar works that principle by which they all were informed, and when he had discovered it running like a common vein below the diversities of style, he announced it in general terms that cannot fail of conviction. His criticism is a great body of literary principles upon which all later criticism has been founded. It is possible to disagree with particular remarks upon poets who have come into fashion since he wrote, but it is difficult to object to the conclusions which he drew from their example. His critical attitude is particularly distinguished by his humility and his devotion to the profession of letters. He is always eager to honour his masters and concerned to rescue their reputations from incompetent critics. He is ever found in the act of crowning some venerable head with laurel, and the action confers as much honour upon his own.

Dryden remains one of the greatest of prose stylists. He wrote what Hazlitt called 'the familiar style'. It depends for its effect upon simple diction and broad rhythm, and it eschews verbal embroidery and curious inversions. It is the common tongue, purged from vulgarity and ennobled by eloquence. His prose has the sonorous harmony of his verse, and its buoyant swell carries on majestically through each period. Its general plainness is set from time to time with images which shed a lustre on his thought, and they shine the more strongly in such a solid and undecorated surround. His description of Chapman's play, *Bussy D'Ambois*, illustrates how economically he could use an image to make clear the whole drift of his thought: 'I have sometimes wonder'd, in the reading, what was become of those glaring Colours which amaz'd me in *Bussy Damboys* upon the Theatre: but when I had taken up what I suppos'd a fallen Star, I found I had been cozen'd with a Jelly: nothing but a cold dull mass, which glitter'd no longer than it was shooting'.

Dryden's career and development were determined by his beliefs. His belief in the dignity of literature made him from the first a man-of-letters, and his belief in the necessity of order and authority made him at the last a Roman Catholic. His opportune conversion, at the time of James II's accession, can be excused by affirming with Dr. Johnson, that there was no reason why his interest and his sudden conviction of the truth of Catholicism should not chance to coincide, but the suspicion cannot be dismissed that the event was partly a result of a fault in his character. The truth is that he was too often a time-server. Buckingham's caricature of him as Bayes in *The Rehearsal* was a palpable hit, and he too easily assumed the obsequious attitude which was paraded as his characteristic across the stage. He found it necessary to dedicate to many patrons but he could have moderated his adulation. It is with unction that he compared the Earl of Dorset to Shakespeare and Homer, and the Earl would doubtless have been willing to have been praised at a lower rate. But this is a blemish which cannot cloud the essential nobility of his character as a man-of-letters. His pre-existing soul, to adapt his praise of Anne Killigrew, had rolled through all the mighty poets 'who Greek or Latin laurels wore', and he worthily carried on their great tradition. His career spans the second half of the seventeenth century. When he began to write the intellectual world was obscured by the struggling wrack of dying beliefs and defeated faiths, and lit by fitful gleams from the new knowledge; but when his industry was stopped by death the sun was rising through a clear sky and shining on more ordered and hopeful times. Dryden anticipated the new century, which was to look constantly back on his example with loving admiration, and sounded the dismissal of his own, which had given him too little peace or delight, in his last verses:

All, all, of a piece throughout;
Thy Chase had a Beast in View;
Thy Wars brought nothing about;
Thy Lovers were all untrue.
'Tis well an Old Age is out,
And time to begin a New.

DOUGLAS GRANT

1951

NOTE ON THE TEXT

THE longer poems, the prose works, and the plays included in this Edition are preceded by a bibliographical note, explaining, where necessary, the choice of text and giving a reference to Mr. Hugh Macdonald's Bibliography of Dryden (Clarendon Press: 1939), which I have found an admirable and invaluable guide. In the case of the shorter pieces—songs, odes, &c.—the bibliographical information is more simply given at the end of each; and, unless otherwise stated, the texts reprinted are always those of the first editions. Thus, the concluding note to 'A Song by Comus and three Peasants' (p. 303), [*King Arthur*, 1691], signifies that the text of the song as it was published in the first edition of the opera has been reprinted I have corrected the printers' errors in these texts and on a very few occasions altered the punctuation when it obscured the sense; otherwise the texts have been exactly reproduced.

I found the choice of plays most difficult to make, and it may require some explanation. I selected *Aureng-Zebe* to represent the heroic plays, believing it to be chaster, more compelling and better constructed than others in this style. *All for Love* was included as a matter of course—it has always been among the most admired of the plays, and has an important place in the history of drama. It appeared to me that the choice of a comedy lay between *Marriage-a-la-Mode* and the tragi-comedy of *The Spanish Fryar*. It was only after much hesitation that I finally decided upon the last. Both Johnson and Scott highly praised the clever construction of its double plot. Scott wrote about it: 'Upon the whole, as the comic part of this play is the author's master-piece in comedy, the tragic plot may be ranked with his very best efforts of that kind, whether in *Don Sebastian*, or *All for Love*.' It also throws considerable light on Dryden's character. I thought *Don Sebastian* both a good example of the dramatist's later skill and an admirable illustration of his reaction to the century's changing sensibility. Its merits are amply stated in Scott's remark, that in it 'the poet was induced . . . to combine, in one effort, the powers of his mighty genius, and the fruits of his long theatrical experience'. I myself am not entirely satisfied with the choice, but since this Edition is intended to represent the poet in all his stages, I was unable to better it.

It would have been impossible in a 'compendious' edition of this kind to give all the annotation necessary to a full understanding of the satires and didactic poems; but I have tried to give in the notes, and in the *Introductory Notes* prefixed to some poems, whatever information I have considered essential. Also, the information is adequate enough to allow anyone to track down quickly and easily in standard works of reference the characters and events which are mentioned.

I am deeply indebted to Mr. D. F. S. Thomson for the translations of the classical quotations, which Dryden used with such skill, and to Mr. Richard Garnett for his kindly help.

D. G.

BIOGRAPHICAL TABLE

1631, 9 *April.*	John Dryden born at Aldwinkle All Saints, Northamptonshire. He was the son of Erasmus Driden (1603–1654), a son of Sir Erasmus Driden, Bart., and of Mary Pickering (*d.* 1671), and the eldest of fourteen children.
164?.	Elected to a King's scholarship at Westminster School. The date of his election is wanting and few details of his school career are known.
1649.	Published an elegy upon the death of Lord Hastings in *Lachrymæ Musarum; The Tears of the Muses*
1650, 18 *May.*	Elected to a scholarship at Trinity College, Cambridge.
	Published some verses to John Hoddesdon in Hoddesdon's collection of epigrams, *Sion and Parnassus.*
1654, *January.*	Graduated B.A. from Cambridge.
1654–9.	Employed in London. He may have served as clerk to his cousin, Sir Gilbert Pickering, Lord Chamberlain to Oliver Cromwell.
1659.	Published an elegy on Oliver Cromwell, *Heroique Stanzas, consecrated to the Glorious Memory of Oliver, late Lord Protector.* These verses were reprinted by his enemies later in his life to remind the public of his early political sympathies.
1660, *June.*	Published *Astræa Redux. A Poem on the happy restoration and return of his sacred Majesty, Charles the Second.*
1661.	Published a poem *To his sacred Majesty, a Panegyrick on his Coronation.* Charles II was crowned on 23 April 1661.
1662, 26 *November*	Elected a Fellow of the newly founded Royal Society.
1663, 3 *February*	*The Wild Gallant,* his first play to be acted. performed; published 1669.
1 *December*	Married Lady Elizabeth Howard (*d.* 1714), the sister of his friend, Sir Robert Howard, and the daughter of the Earl of Berkshire. The marriage was not a success.
1664, *January.*	*The Indian Queen,* written in collaboration with Sir Robert Howard, the first Heroic play to be given in London, performed; published 1665.
c. May.	*The Rival Ladies,* a tragi-comedy, performed and published. It was the first of his plays to be printed.
1665, *Spring.*	*The Indian Emperour,* a sequel to *The Indian Queen,* performed. It was revived on the stage and published in 1667 after the Great Fire.
	Retired from London on account of the Plague to Charlton in Wiltshire. He probably remained there for eighteen months and wrote in his retirement *Annus Mirabilis* and *An Essay of Dramatick Poesie.*
1666.	His eldest son, Charles (*d.* 1704), born.

1667, *January.*	*Annus Mirabilis. The Year of Wonders*, 1666, to commemorate the war with the Dutch and the Fire of London, published.
15 *January.*	*The Indian Emperour* revived on the stage.
2 *March.*	*Secret Love, or, The Maiden Queen* performed; published 1668.
15 *August.*	*Sir Martin Mar-All*, adapted from a translation of Molière's *L'Etourdi* made by the Duke of Newcastle, performed; published 1668.
7 *November.*	*The Tempest*, an alteration of Shakespeare's play made in collaboration with Sir William D'Avenant, performed; published 1670.
	His theatrical successes allowed him to conclude a contract with the company of the King's Theatre by which he agreed to furnish them with three plays a year in return for a share and a quarter out of the twelve and three-quarter shares held by the whole company. It has been estimated that this brought him in profits of £300–£400 a year. His relations with the company, however, were not always happy.
	His second son, John (*d.* 1701), born.
1668, 13 *April.*	Created Poet Laureate by Royal Warrant.
12 *June.*	*An Evening's Love, or, The Mock Astrologer* performed; published 1671.
August.	*An Essay of Dramatick Poesie* published.
September.	*A Defence of an Essay of Dramatique Poesie* published in the second edition of *The Indian Emperour.* Sir Robert Howard, who disagreed with Dryden, had answered the arguments of *An Essay of Dramatick Poesie* in a preface to his play *The Great Favourite, or, The Duke of Lerma. A Defence of an Essay* is a sharp retort to Howard's arguments. The brothers-in-law were later reconciled.
1669, *June.*	*Tyrannick Love, or, The Royal Martyr* performed; published 1670.
	His third son, Erasmus Henry (*d.* 1710), born.
1670, 18 *August.*	Confirmed in the office of Poet Laureate and created Historiographer Royal by patent. His salary was £200, and a butt of canary, a year, but it was irregularly paid.
December.	*The Conquest of Granada, Part One*, performed; published 1672.
1671, *January*	*The Conquest of Granada, Part Two*, performed; published, together with *Part One*, 1672.
7 *December.*	His person and his heroic plays ridiculed by the Duke of Buckingham, and others, in the brilliant comedy of *The Rehearsal.* The name of *Bayes*, given to him in the comedy, stuck to him. He had his revenge by satirising Buckingham as *Zimri* in *Absalom and Achitophel.*
1672, *May.*	*Marriage-a-la-Mode* performed; published 1673.
October.	*The Assignation, or, Love in a Nunnery* performed with ill-success; published 1673.
1673, *Spring.*	*Amboyna: A Tragedy* performed and published. It was intended to rouse popular feeling against the Dutch.
1675, 17 *November.*	*Aureng-Zebe* performed; published 1676.

1677, *February.*	*The State of Innocence*, a rhyming play based upon Milton's *Paradise Lost*, published. Andrew Marvell, in his verses *On Paradise Lost*, slightingly referred to this attempt to change Milton's blank verse into rhyme: While the *Town-Bayes* writes all the while and spells, And like a Pack-horse tires without his bells.
December.	*All for Love*, in imitation of Shakespeare's style, performed; published 1678.
1678, 11 *March.*	*The Kind Keeper, or, Mr. Limberham* performed with ill-success; published 1680.
1679, *January.*	*Œdipus*, written in collaboration with Nathaniel Lee, performed and published.
Spring.	*Troilus and Cressida*, an alteration of Shakespeare's play, performed and published.
18 *December.*	Assaulted and beaten in Rose Alley: 'Last night Mr. *Dryden*, the famous *Dramatic* Poet, going from a Coffee-house in *Covent-Garden*, was set upon by three Persons unknown to him and so rudely by them handled, that it is said, his Life is in no small danger.' It is thought that this attack was instigated by either John Wilmot, Earl of Rochester, the poet, or the Duchess of Portsmouth, Charles II's mistress, who had both been reflected on in the Earl of Mulgrave's *Essay on Satyr*, which was falsely attributed to Dryden.
1680, 8 *March.*	*The Spanish Fryar* performed; published 1681.
1681, 17 *November.*	*Absalom and Architophel* published. This great satire on the Earl of Shaftesbury and the Whigs was an immediate success.
1682, 16 *March.*	*The Medall*, a continuation of the attack on Shaftesbury, published. He carried it to the King and was rewarded with 'a present of a hundred broad pieces for it'.
4 *October.*	*Mac Flecknoe*, a satire against the Whig poet Thomas Shadwell, published. Shadwell had replied to *The Medall* with his abusive *The Medal of John Bayes*, published on 15 May 1683, and Dryden now retaliated by making public this lampoon, which he had written as early as 1678.
10 *November.*	*The Second Part of Absalom and Achitophel* published. This continuation was written by Nahum Tate but Dryden supervised and revised the whole and added the satirical portraits of Thomas Shadwell and Elkanah Settle.
28 *November.*	*Religio Laici*, his great defence of the Church of England, published.
30 *November.*	*The Duke of Guise*, his first play, but re-written at this time in collaboration with Nathaniel Lee, performed; published 1683. It was a political piece written against Shaftesbury, the Duke of Monmouth, and the Whigs.
1683, 17 *December.*	Appointed a collector of customs in the Port of London.
1684, *February.*	The first volume of *Miscellany Poems* published.
July.	His translation from the French of Monsieur Maimbourg's *History of the League* published. He trans-

	lated this work, whose political lessons could be applied to the contemporary situation, at the command of Charles II.
1685, *January.*	*Sylvæ*, the second part of *Miscellany Poems*, published.
6 *February.*	Death of Charles II. Dryden was continued in his offices and pension by James II.
March.	*Thrènodia Augustalia*, a funeral-pindaric poem to the memory of Charles II, published.
6 *June.*	*Albion and Albanius*, an opera set to music by Lewis Grabu, performed and published.
1687, *April.*	*The Hind and the Panther* published. Dryden was received into the Roman Catholic Church after the accession of James II. An acquaintance meeting him 'in a coffee house in London . . . wished him much joy of his *new* religion. "Sir", said Dryden, "you are very much mistaken; my religion is the *old* religion". "Nay", replyed the other, "whatever it be in itself I am sure 'tis new to you for within these 3 days you had no religion at all." ' The sincerity of Dryden's religious beliefs cannot be questioned, but it was unfortunate for his reputation that his interest and his conviction of the truth of Roman Catholicism should so opportunely combine.
	The Hind and the Panther, his apology for his new religion, was parodied by Charles Montague and Matthew Prior in *The Hind and the Panther transvers'd to the Story of the Country-Mouse and the City-Mouse.*
1688, *June.*	*Britannia Rediviva*, a poem written to celebrate the birth of a Prince, the 'Old Pretender', on 10 June, published.
July.	Translation from the French of Dominick Bohour's *Life of St. Francis Xavier* published.
23 *December.*	James II fled the country and was succeeded by William and Mary. Dryden lost his offices of Poet Laureate and Historiographer Royal, being succeeded in them by his old enemy, Thomas Shadwell.
1689, 4 *December.*	*Don Sebastian* performed; published 1690. He was again compelled to write for the stage by the loss of his offices.
1690, *October.*	*Amphitrion* performed and published.
1691, *June.*	*King Arthur, or, The British Worthy*, an opera, performed and published. The music was by Henry Purcell.
1692, 16 *April.*	*Cleomenes, The Spartan Heroe*, performed and published.
1693.	Translation of the *Satires of Juvenal* published. He translated five of the satires himself and chose the translators of the others.
	Examen Poeticum, the third part of *Miscellany Poems*, published.
1694, *c. January.*	*Love Triumphant, or, Nature will Prevail* performed and published. 'It was damned by the universal cry of the town, *nemine contradicente* but the conceited poet.'
	The Annual Miscellany, the fourth part of *Miscellany Poems*, published.

1695.	Translation from the French of Du Fresnoy's *The Art of Painting* published.
1697.	Translation of *The Works of Virgil: containing his Pastorals, Georgics, and Aeneis* published. He probably began this great translation in 1694, and is supposed to have made a considerable profit by it.
1700. *March.*	*The Fables* published.
April.	*The Secular Masque*, an after-piece to an alteration of Fletcher's *The Pilgrim*, which was played for his benefit, performed and published.
1 *May.*	John Dryden died at his house in Gerrard Street. His body, after lying in state at the College of Physicians in Warwick Square, was carried in procession to Westminster Abbey on 13 May, and buried in Poets' Corner.

POETRY

ANNUS MIRABILIS

THE YEAR OF
WONDERS
1666

AN HISTORICAL POEM

CONTAINING

The Progress and various Successes of our Naval War with *HOLLAND*, under the Conduct of His Highness Prince Rupert, and His Grace the Duke of Albemarl. And describing the Fire of *LONDON*.

Multum interest res poscat, an homines latius imperare velint.

Trajan. Imperator. ad Plin.[1]

Urbs antiqua ruit, multos dominata per annos.

Virg.[2]

[1] The case is vastly different, according to whether this action is demanded by the situation or prompted by the desire of men to extend their own powers. (Pliny, *Epistles* 10. 22 (33).)

[2] An ancient city is falling to ruin, a city that for many years has been a mighty mistress. (*Æneid* 2. 363.)

Annus Mirabilis: The Year of Wonders, 1666. An Historical Poem: Containing The Progress and various Successes of our Naval War with Holland, under the Conduct of His Highness Prince Rupert, and His Grace the Duke of Albemarl. And describing The Fire of London. By John Dryden, Esq; [*Latin quot.*] London, Printed for Henry Herringman, at the Anchor in the Lower Walk of the New Exchange. 1667.

SOME corrections were introduced into the third issue of the first edition (Macdonald, 9 a iii), which the present text follows. Dryden's own notes to the poem have been distinguished by a D.

TO THE METROPOLIS OF GREAT BRITAIN

The most renowned and late flourishing city of LONDON, in its representatives the Lord Mayor and Court of Aldermen, the Sheriffs and Common Council of it.

AS perhaps I am the first who ever presented a work of this nature to the Metropolis of any Nation, so is it likewise consonant to Justice, that he who was to give the first Example of such a Dedication should begin it with that City, which has set a pattern to all others of true Loyalty, invincible Courage and unshaken Constancy. Other Cities have been prais'd for the same Virtues, but I am much deceiv'd if any have so dearly purchas'd their reputation; their fame has been won them by cheaper trials then an expensive, though necessary, War, a consuming Pestilence, and a more consuming Fire. To submit your selves with that humility to the Judgments of Heaven, and at the same time to raise your selves with that vigour above all humane Enemies; to be combated at once from above and from below, to be struck down and to triumph; I know not whether such trials have been ever parallel'd in any Nation, the resolution and successes of them never can be. Never had Prince or People more mutual reason to love each other, if suffering for each other can indear affection. You have come together a pair of matchless Lovers, through many difficulties; He, through a long Exile, various traverses of Fortune, and the interposition of many Rivals, who violently ravish'd and with-held You from Him: And certainly you have had your share in sufferings. But Providence has cast upon you want of Trade, that you might appear bountiful to your Country's necessities; and the rest of your afflictions are not more the effects of God's displeasure, (frequent exemples of them having been in the Reign of the most excellent Princes) then occasions for the manifesting of your Christian and Civil virtues. To you therefore this Year of Wonders is justly dedicated, because you have made it so. You who are to stand a wonder to all Years and Ages, and who have built your selves an immortal Monument on your own ruines. You are now a Phœnix *in her ashes, and, as far as Humanity can approach, a great Emblem of the suffering Deity. But Heaven never made so much Piety and Vertue to leave it miserable. I have heard indeed of some vertuous persons who have ended unfortunately, but never of any vertuous Nation: Providence is engag'd too deeply, when the cause becomes so general. And I cannot imagine it has resolv'd the ruine of that people at home, which it has blessed abroad with such successes. I am therefore to conclude, that your sufferings are at an end; and that one part of my Poem has not been more an History of your destruction, then the other a Prophecy of your restoration. The accomplishment of which happiness, as it is the wish of all true* English-men, *so is by none more passionately desired then by*

The greatest of your Admirers,
and most humble of your Servants,
JOHN DRYDEN.

AN ACCOUNT OF THE ENSUING POEM

In a letter to the Honourable Sir ROBERT HOWARD[1]

SIR,

I Am so many ways oblig'd to you, and so little able to return your favours, that, like those who owe too much, I can onely live by getting farther into your debt. You have not onely been careful of my Fortune, which was the effect of your Nobleness, but you have been sollicitous of my Reputation, which is that of your Kindness. It is not long since I gave you the trouble of perusing a Play for me, and now, instead of an acknowledgment, I have given you a greater, in the correction of a Poem. But since you are to bear this persecution, I will at least give you the encouragement of a Martyr, you could never suffer in a nobler cause. For I have chosen the most heroick Subject which any Poet could desire: I have taken upon me to describe the motives, the beginning, progress and successes of a most just and necessary War; in it, the care, management and prudence of our King; the conduct and valour of a Royal Admiral,[2] and of two incomparable Generals; the invincible courage of our Captains and Seamen, and three glorious Victories, the result of all. After this I have, in the Fire, the most deplorable, but withall the greatest Argument that can be imagin'd: the destruction being so swift,

[1] Sir Robert Howard (1626–1698), dramatist, Dryden's brother-in-law, and the *Crites* of *An Essay of Dramatick Poesie*. See also Introductory Note to *A Defence of an Essay*.

[2] James, Duke of York.

so sudden, so vast and miserable, as nothing can parallel in Story. The former part of this Poem, relating to the War, is but a due expiation for my not serving my King and Country in it. All Gentlemen are almost oblig'd to it: And I know no reason we should give that advantage to the Commonalty of *England* to be formost in brave actions, which the Noblesse of *France* would never suffer in their Peasants. I should not have written this but to a Person, who has been ever forward to appear in all employments, whither his Honour and Generosity have call'd him. The latter part of my Poem, which describes the Fire, I owe first to the Piety and Fatherly Affection of our Monarch to his suffering Subjects; and, in the second place, to the courage, loyalty and magnanimity of the City: both which were so conspicuous, that I have wanted words to celebrate them as they deserve. I have call'd my Poem *Historical*, not *Epick*, though both the Actions and Actors are as much Heroick, as any Poem can contain. But since the Action is not properly one, nor that accomplish'd in the last successes, I have judg'd it too bold a Title for a few *Stanza's*, which are little more in number then a single *Iliad*, or the longest of the *Æneids*. For this reason, (I mean not of length, but broken action, ti'd too severely to the Laws of History) I am apt to agree with those who rank *Lucan* rather among Historians in Verse, then Epique Poets: In whose room, if I am not deceiv'd, *Silius Italicus*, though a worse Writer, may more justly be admitted. I have chosen to write my Poem in *Quatrains* or *Stanza's* of four in alternate rhyme, because I have ever judg'd them more noble, and of greater dignity, both for the sound and number, then any other Verse in use amongst us; in which I am sure I have your approbation. The learned Languages have, certainly, a great advantage of us, in not being tied to the slavery of any Rhyme; and were less constrain'd in the quantity of every syllable, which they might vary with *Spondæes* or *Dactiles*, besides so many other helps of Grammatical Figures, for the lengthning or abbreviation of them, then the Modern are in the close of that one Syllable, which often confines, and more often corrupts the sense of all the rest. But in this necessity of our Rhymes, I have always found the couplet Verse most easie, (though not so proper for this occasion) for there the work is sooner at an end, every two lines concluding the labour of the Poet: but in Quattrains he is to carry it farther on; and not onely so, but to bear along in his head the troublesome sense of four lines together. For those who write correctly in this kind must needs acknowledge, that the last line of the Stanza is to be consider'd in the composition of the first. Neither can we give our selves the liberty of making any part of a Verse for the sake of Rhyme, or concluding with a word which is not currant *English*, or using the variety of Female Rhymes, all which our Fathers practis'd; and for the Female Rhymes, they are still in use amongst other Nations: with the *Italian* in every line, with the *Spaniard* promiscuously, with the *French* alternately, as those who have read the *Alarique*, the *Pucelle*,[1] or any of their latter Poems, will agree with me. And besides this, they write in *Alexandrins*, or Verses of six feet, such as amongst us is the old Translation of *Homer*, by *Chapman*; all which, by lengthning of their Chain, makes the sphere of their activity the larger. I have dwelt too long upon the choice of my Stanza, which you may remember is much better defended in the Preface to *Gondibert*,[2] and therefore I will hasten to acquaint you with my endeavours in the writing. In general I will onely say, I have never yet seen the description of any Naval Fight in the proper terms which are us'd at Sea; and if there be any such in another Language, as that of *Lucan* in the third of his *Pharsalia*, yet I could not prevail my self of it in the *English*; the terms of Arts in every Tongue bearing more of the Idiom of it then any other words. We hear, indeed, among our Poets, of the thundring of Guns, the smoke, the disorder and the slaughter; but all these are common notions. And certainly as those who, in a Logical dispute, keep in general terms, would hide a fallacy, so those who do it in any Poetical description would vail their ignorance.

Descriptas servare vices operumque colores
Cur ego, si nequeo ignoroque, poeta salutor?[3]

For my own part, if I had little knowledge of the Sea, yet I have thought it no shame to learn: and if I have made some few mistakes, 'tis onely, as you can bear me witness, because I have wanted opportunity to correct them, the whole Poem being first written, and now sent you from a place, where I have not so much as the converse of any Sea-man. Yet, though the trouble I had in writing it was great, it was more then recompens'd by the pleasure; I found my self so warm in celebrating the praises of military men, two such especially as the *Prince* and *General*, that it is no wonder if they inspir'd me with thoughts above my ordi-

[1] *Alaric* by George de Scudery, and *Pucelle* by Jean Chapelain.
[2] Sir William D'Avenant's (1606–1668) romantic epic of *Gondibert* was published in 1651.
[3] As for me, why should I be hailed as a poet, if my ability and my knowledge do not suffice to preserve forms and styles of writing which are explicitly laid down? (Horace, *Ars Poetica* 86–7.)

nary level. And I am well satisfi'd, that as they are incomparably the best subject I have ever had, excepting onely the *Royal Family*; so also, that this I have written of them is much better then what I have perform'd on any other. I have been forc'd to help out other Arguments, but this has been bountiful to me; they have been low and barren of praise, and I have exalted them, and made them fruitful: but here—*Omnia sponte suâ reddit justissima tellus.*[1] I have had a large, a fair and a pleasant field, so fertile, that, without my cultivating, it has given me two Harvests in a Summer, and in both oppress'd the Reaper. All other greatness in subjects is onely counterfeit, it will not endure the test of danger; the greatness of arms is onely real: other greatness burdens a Nation with its weight, this supports it with its strength. And as it is the happiness of the Age, so is it the peculiar goodness of the best of Kings, that we may praise his Subjects without offending him: doubtless it proceeds from a just confidence of his own vertue, which the lustre of no other can be so great as to darken in him: for the Good or the Valiant are never safely prais'd under a bad or a degenerate Prince. But to return from this digression to a farther account of my Poem, I must crave leave to tell you, that as I have endeavour'd to adorn it with noble thoughts, so much more to express those thoughts with elocution. The composition of all Poems is or ought to be of wit, and wit in the Poet, or wit writing, (if you will give me leave to use a School distinction) is no other then the faculty of imagination in the writer, which, like a nimble Spaniel, beats over and ranges through the field of Memory, till it springs the Quarry it hunted after; or, without metaphor, which searches over all the memory for the species or Idea's of those things which it designs to represent. Wit written, is that which is well defin'd, the happy result of thought, or product of that imagination. But to proceed from wit in the general notion of it, to the proper wit of an Heroick or Historical Poem, I judge it chiefly to consist in the delightful imaging of persons, actions, passions, or things. 'Tis not the jerk or sting of an Epigram, nor the seeming contradiction of a poor Antithesis, (the delight of an ill judging Audience in a Play of Rhyme) nor the gingle of a more poor Paranomasia: neither is it so much the morality of a grave sentence, affected by *Lucan*, but more sparingly used by *Virgil*; but it is some lively and apt description, dress'd in such colours of speech, that it sets before your eyes the absent object, as perfectly and more delightfully then nature. So then, the first happiness of the Poet's imagination

[1] The earth, all-benign, yieldeth every harvest of her own accord.

is properly Invention, or finding of the thought; the second is fancy, or the variation, driving or moulding of that thought, as the judgment represents it proper to the subject; the third is Elocution, or the Art of clothing and adorning that thought so found and varied, in apt, significant and sounding words: the quickness of the Imagination is seen in the Invention, the fertility in the Fancy, and the accuracy in the Expression. For the two first of these *Ovid* is famous amongst the Poets, for the latter, *Virgil*. *Ovid* images more often the movements and affections of the mind, either combating between two contrary passions, or extremely discompos'd by one: his words therefore are the least part of his care, for he pictures Nature in disorder, with which the study and choice of words is inconsistent. This is the proper wit of Dialogue or Discourse, and, consequently, of the *Drama*, where all that is said is to be suppos'd the effect of sudden thought; which, though it excludes not the quickness of wit in repartees, yet admits not a too curious election of words, too frequent allusions, or use of Tropes, or, in fine, anything that shows remoteness of thought, or labour in the Writer. On the other side, *Virgil* speaks not so often to us in the person of another, like *Ovid*, but in his own, he relates almost all things as from himself, and thereby gains more liberty then the other, to express his thoughts with all the graces of elocution, to write more figuratively, and to confess, as well the labour as the force of his imagination. Though he describes his *Dido* well and naturally, in the violence of her passions, yet he must yield in that to the *Myrrha*, the *Biblis*, the *Althæa*, of *Ovid*; for, as great an admirer of him as I am, I must acknowledge, that, if I see not more of their Souls then I see of *Dido*'s, at least I have a greater concernment for them: and that convinces me that *Ovid* has touch'd those tender strokes more delicately then *Virgil* could. But when Action or Persons are to be describ'd, when any such Image is to be set before us, how bold, how masterly are the strokes of *Virgil!* we see the objects he represents us within their native figures, in their proper motions; but we so see them, as our own eyes could never have beheld them so beautiful in themselves. We see the Soul of the Poet, like that universal one of which he speaks, informing and moving through all his Pictures, *Totamque infusa per artus mens agitat molem, & magno se corpore miscet*; [1] we behold him embellishing his Images, as he makes *Venus* breathing beauty upon her son *Æneas*.

[1] An Intelligence deep-set within the members moves the whole mass thereof, everywhere mingling with the mighty frame. (*Æneid* 6. 726–7.)

> ——————————*lumenque juventæ*
> *Purpureum, & lætos oculis afflârat honores:*
> *Quale manus addunt Ebori decus, aut ubi flavo*
> *Argentum, Pariusve lapis circundatur auro.*[1]

See his Tempest, his Funeral Sports, his Combat of *Turnus* and *Æneas*, and in his *Georgicks*, which I esteem the Divinest part of all his writings, the Plague, the Country, the Battel of Bulls, the labour of the Bees, and those many other excellent Images of Nature, most of which are neither great in themselves, nor have any natural ornament to bear them up: but the words wherewith he describes them are so excellent, that it might be well appli'd to him which was said by *Ovid, Materiam superabat opus*:[2] the very sound of his words has often somewhat that is connatural to the subject, and while we read him, we sit, as in a Play, beholding the Scenes of what he represents. To perform this, he made frequent use of Tropes, which you know change the nature of a known word, by applying it to some other signification; and this is it which *Horace* means in his Epistle to the *Pisos*.

> *Dixeris egregie notum si callida verbum*
> *Reddiderit junctura novum.*——————[3]

But I am sensible I have presum'd too far, to entertain you with a rude discourse of that Art, which you both know so well, and put into practice with so much happiness. Yet before I leave *Virgil*, I must own the vanity to tell you, and by you the world, that he has been my Master in this Poem: I have followed him everywhere, I know not with what success, but I am sure with diligence enough: my Images are many of them copied from him, and the rest are imitations of him. My expressions also are as near as the Idioms of the two Languages would admit of in translation. And this, Sir, I have done with that boldness, for which I will stand accomptable to any of our little Criticks, who, perhaps, are not better acquainted with him then I am. Upon your first perusal of this Poem, you have taken notice of some words which I have innovated (if it be too bold for me to say refin'd) upon his *Latin*; which, as I offer not to introduce into *English* prose, so I hope

[1] And she had breathed thereon the roseate glow of youth, and the crown of the eyes which is joy; such a splendour as men's hands bestow upon ivory, or as when silver or the marble of Paros is bordered with bright gold. (*Æneid* 1. 590.)

[2] Finer than the substance itself was its fashioning. (*Metamorphoses* 2. 5.)

[3] You will succeed particularly well in the art of expression if a cunning juxtaposition gives a familiar word fresh significance. (*Ars Poetica* 47–8.)

they are neither improper, nor altogether unelegant in Verse; and, in this, *Horace* will again defend me.

> *Et nova, fictaque nuper habebunt verba fidem, si*
> *Græco fonte cadent, parce detorta*——————[1]

The inference is exceeding plain; for if a *Roman* Poet might have liberty to coin a word, supposing onely that it was derived from the *Greek*, was put into a *Latin* termination, and that he us'd this liberty but seldom, and with modesty: How much more justly may I challenge that privilege to do it with the same prærequisits, from the best and most judicious of *Latin* writers? In some places, where either the fancy, or the words, were his, or any others, I have noted it in the Margin, that I might not seem a Plagiary: in others I have neglected it, to avoid as well the tediousness, as the affectation of doing it too often. Such descriptions or images, well wrought, which I promise not for mine, are, as I have said, the adequate delight of heroick Poesie, for they beget admiration, which is its proper object; as the images of the Burlesque, which is contrary to this, by the same reason beget laughter; for the one shows Nature beautified, as in the picture of a fair Woman, which we all admire; the other shows her deformed, as in that of a Lazar, or of a fool with distorted face and antique gestures, at which we cannot forbear to laugh, because it is a deviation from Nature. But though the same images serve equally for the Epique Poesie, and for the Historique and Panegyrique, which are branches of it, yet a several sort of Sculpture is to be used in them: if some of them are to be like those of *Juvenal, Stantes in curribus Æmiliani*,[2] heroes drawn in their triumphal Chariots, and in their full proportion; others are to be like that of *Virgil, Spirantia mollius æra*:[3] there is somewhat more of softness and tenderness to be shown in them. You will soon find I write not this without concern. Some who have seen a paper of Verses which I wrote last year to her Highness the *Dutchess*, have accus'd them of that onely thing I could defend in them; they have said I did *humi serpere*,[4] that I wanted not onely height of fancy, but dignity of words to set it off; I might well answer with that of *Horace, Nunc non erat hic locus*,[5] I knew I address'd them to a Lady, and accordingly I affected the softness

[1] And new and lately-minted words will carry conviction if, but sparingly altered, they derive from the fountain-head of Greek. (*Ars Poetica* 52–3.)
[2] Men of Æmilius' line displayed on cars of triumph. (8. 3.)
[3] Works of bronze that breathe a tenderer life. (*Æneid* 6. 847.)
[4] Crawl upon the ground. (Cf. Horace, *Ars Poetica* 28).
[5] But there is after all no place here for these things. (*Ars Poetica* 19.)

of expression, and the smoothness of measure, rather then the height of thought; and in what I did endeavour, it is no vanity to say, I have succeeded. I detest arrogance, but there is some difference betwixt that and a just defence. But I will not farther bribe your candour, or the Readers. I leave them to speak for me, and, if they can, to make out that character, not pretending to a greater, which I have given them.

Verses to her Highness *the* DUTCHESS, *on the memorable Victory gain'd by the* DUKE *against the* Hollanders, June *the* 3, 1665, *and on Her Journey afterwards into the North.*

Madam,

When, for our sakes, your Heroe *you resign'd*
To swelling Seas, and every faithless wind;
When you releas'd his courage, and set free
A valour fatal to the Enemy,
You lodg'd your Countries cares within your breast;
(The mansion where soft Love should onely rest:)
And ere our foes abroad were overcome,
The noblest conquest you had gain'd at home.
Ah, what concerns did both your Souls divide!
Your Honour gave us what your Love deni'd:
And 'twas for him much easier to subdue
Those foes he fought with, then to part from you.
That glorious day, which two such Navies saw,
As each, unmatch'd, might to the world give Law,
Neptune, *yet doubtful whom he should obey,*
Held to them both the Trident of the Sea:
The winds were hush'd, the waves in ranks were cast,
As awfully as when God's people past:
Those, yet uncertain on whose sails to blow,
These, where the wealth of Nations ought to flow.
Then with the Duke your Highness rul'd the day:
While all the brave did his command obey.
The fair and pious under you did pray.
How pow'rful are chast vows! the wind and tyde
You brib'd to combat on the English *side.*
Thus to your much lov'd Lord you did convey
An unknown succour, sent the nearest way.
New vigour to his wearied arms you brought;
(So Moses *was upheld while* Israel *fought.)*

While, from afar, we heard the Canon play,
Like distant Thunder on a shiny day,
For absent friends we were asham'd to fear,
When we consider'd what you ventur'd there.
Ships, Men and Arms our Country might restore,
But such a Leader could supply no more.
With generous thoughts of conquest he did burn,
Yet fought not more to vanquish then return.
Fortune and victory he did pursue,
To bring them, as his Slaves, to wait on you.
Thus Beauty ravish'd the rewards of Fame,
And the Fair triumph'd when the Brave o'rcame.
Then, as you meant to spread another way
By Land your Conquests far as his by Sea,
Leaving our Southern Clime, you march'd along
The stubborn North, ten thousand Cupid*'s strong.*
Like Commons the Nobility resort
In crowding heaps, to fill your moving Court:
To welcome your approach the Vulgar run,
Like some new Envoy from the distant Sun.
And Country Beauties by their Lovers go,
Blessing themselves, and wondring at the show.
So when the new-born Phœnix *first is seen,*
Her feather'd Subjects all adore their Queen.
And, while she makes her progress through the East,
From every grove her numerous train 's increast:
Each Poet of the air her glory sings,
And round him the pleas'd Audience clap their wings.

And now, Sir, 'tis time I should relieve you from the tedious length of this account. You have better and more profitable employment for your hours, and I wrong the Publick to detain you longer. In conclusion, I must leave my Poem to you with all its faults, which I hope to find fewer in the printing by your emendations. I know you are not of the number of those, of whom the younger *Pliny* speaks, *Nec sunt parum multi qui carpere amicos suos judicium vocant*;[1] I am rather too secure of you on that side. Your candour in pardoning my errors may make you more remiss in correcting them; if you will not withall consider that they come into the world with your approbation, and through your hands. I beg from you the greatest favor you can confer upon an absent

[1] And there is no great dearth of men who call it judicious appraisal to slander one's friends. (*Epistles* 7. 28.)

person, since I repose upon your management what is dearest to me, my Fame and Reputation; & therefore I hope it will stir you up to make my Poem fairer by many of your blots; if not, you know the story of the Gamester who married the rich man's daughter, and when her father denyed the portion, christned all the children by his sirname, that if, in conclusion, they must beg, they should do so by one name, as well as by the other. But since the reproach of my faults will light on you, 'tis but reason I should do you that justice to the Readers, to let them know that if there be anything tolerable in this Poem, they owe the Argument to your choice, the writing to your encouragement, the correction to your judgment, and the care of it to your friendship, to which he must ever acknowledge himself to owe all things, who is,

SIR,

The most obediant and most
faithful of your Servants,
JOHN DRYDEN.

From *Charlton*, in *Wiltshire*,
Novem. 10. 1666.

ANNUS MIRABILIS

THE YEAR OF
WONDERS

MDCLXVI

1.

In thriving Arts long time had *Holland* grown,
Crouching at home, and cruel when abroad:
Scarce leaving us the means to claim our own.
Our King they courted, & our Merchants aw'd.

2.

Trade, which like bloud should circularly flow,
Stop'd in their Channels, found its freedom lost:
Thither the wealth of all the world did go,
And seem'd but shipwrack'd on so base a Coast.

3.

For them alone the Heav'ns had kindly heat,
In Eastern Quarries ripening precious Dew:
For them the *Idumæan* Balm did sweat,
And in hot Ceilon Spicy Forrests grew.

4.

The Sun but seem'd the Lab'rer of their Year;
Each wexing Moon suppli'd her watry store,
To swell those Tides, which from the Line did bear
Their brim-full Vessels to the *Belg'an* shore.

3 ii. In Eastern Quarries, &c. Precious Stones at first are Dew, condens'd and harden'd by the warmth of the Sun, or Subterranean Fires. D.
4 ii. Each wexing, &c. according to their opinion, who think that great heap of waters under the Line is depressed into Tydes by the Moon, towards the Poles. D.

5.

Thus mighty in her Ships stood *Carthage* long,
And swept the riches of the world from far;
Yet stoop'd to *Rome*, less wealthy, but more strong:
And this may prove our second Punick War.

6.

What peace can be where both to one pretend?
(But they more diligent, and we more strong)
Or if a peace, it soon must have an end
For they would grow too pow'rful were it long.

7.

Behold two Nations then, ingag'd so far,
That each seav'n years the fit must shake each Land:
Where *France* will side to weaken us by War,
Who onely can his vast designs withstand.

8.

See how he feeds th' *Iberian* with delays,
To render us his timely friendship vain;
And, while his secret Soul on *Flanders* preys,
He rocks the Cradle of the Babe of *Spain*.

9.

Such deep designs of Empire does he lay
O're them whose cause he seems to take in hand:
And, prudently, would make them Lords at Sea,
To whom with ease he can give Laws by Land.

10.

This saw our King; and long within his breast
His pensive counsels ballanc'd too and fro;
He griev'd the Land he freed should be oppress'd,
And he less for it then Usurpers do.

5 iv. The first 'Punic' war was Cromwell's defeat of the Dutch in 1654.
8 i. Th' *Iberian*, the *Spaniard*. D.
iv. Louis XIV of France coveted the Spanish Netherlands, to which he had some claim, but at this time, frightened that England and Holland would league against him, he refrained from making war on the infant Charles II of Spain.

11.

His gen'rous mind the fair Idea's drew
  Of Fame and Honour which in dangers lay;
Where wealth, like fruit on precipices, grew,
  Not to be gather'd but by Birds of prey.

12.

The loss and gain each fatally were great;
  And still his Subjects call'd aloud for war:
But peaceful Kings o'r martial people set,
  Each others poize and counter-ballance are.

13.

He, first, survey'd the charge with careful eyes,
  Which none but mighty Monarchs could maintain;
Yet judg'd, like vapours that from Limbecks rise,
  It would in richer showers descend again.

14.

At length resolv'd t' assert the watry Ball,
  He in himself did whole Armado's bring:
Him, aged Sea-men might their Master call,
  And choose for General were he not their King.

15.

It seems as every Ship their Sovereign knows,
  His awful summons they so soon obey;
So here the skaly Herd when *Proteus* blows,
  And so to pasture follow through the Sea.

16.

To see this Fleet upon the Ocean move
  Angels drew wide the Curtains of the skies:
And Heav'n, as if there wanted Lights above,
  For Tapers made two glareing Comets rise.

15 iii. *When* Proteus *blows, or* Caeruleus Proteus immania ponti armenta, & magnas pascit sub gurgite Phocas. *Virg.* D. Sea-green Proteus feeds below the heaving waters his herds of monsters, and his mighty Seals. (*Georgics* 4. 388 and 394–5.)

16 iv. Two comets appeared in 1664 and 1665 and their significance was debated by astrologers and the superstitious.

17.

Whether they unctuous Exhalations are,
  Fir'd by the Sun, or seeming so alone,
Or each some more remote and slippery Star,
  Which looses footing when to Mortals shown.

18.

Or one that bright companion of the Sun,
  Whose glorious aspect seal'd our new-born King;
And now a round of greater years begun,
  New influence from his walks of light did bring.

19.

Victorious *York* did, first, with fam'd success,
  To his known valour make the *Dutch* give place:
Thus Heav'n our Monarch's fortune did confess,
  Beginning conquest from his Royal Race.

20.

But since it was decreed, Auspicious King,
  In *Britain*'s right that thou should'st wed the Main,
Heav'n, as a gage, would cast some precious thing
  And therefore doom'd that *Lawson* should be slain.

21.

Lawson amongst the formost met his fate,
  Whom Sea-green *Syrens* from the Rocks lament:
Thus as an off'ring for the *Grecian* State,
  He first was kill'd who first to Battel went.

22.

Their Chief blown up, in air, not waves expir'd,
  To which his pride presum'd to give the Law:
The *Dutch* confess'd Heav'n present, and retir'd,
  And all was *Britain* the wide Ocean saw.

19 ii. The English fleet under the command of the Duke of York gained a great victory over the Dutch on 3 June 1665.
21 i. Sir John Lawson (*d.* 1665), a Cromwellian admiral who later helped to restore Charles II, was killed in the engagement of 3 June 1665.
22 i. The Admiral of *Holland*. D.

23.

To nearest Ports their shatter'd Ships repair,
  Where by our dreadful Canon they lay aw'd:
So reverently men quit the open air
  Where thunder speaks the angry Gods abroad.

24.

And now approach'd their Fleet from *India*, fraught
  With all the riches of the rising Sun:
And precious Sand from Southern Climates brought,
  (The fatal Regions where the War begun.)

25.

Like hunted *Castors*, conscious of their store,
  Their way-laid wealth to *Norway*'s coasts they bring:
There first the North's cold bosome Spices bore,
  And Winter brooded on the Eastern Spring.

26.

By the rich scent we found our perfum'd prey,
  Which flanck'd with Rocks did close in covert lie:
And round about their murdering Canon lay,
  At once to threaten and invite the eye.

27.

Fiercer then Canon, and then Rocks more hard,
  The *English* undertake th' unequal War:
Seven Ships alone, by which the Port is barr'd,
  Besiege the *Indies*, and all *Denmark* dare.

28.

These fight like Husbands, but like Lovers those:
  These fain would keep, and those more fain enjoy:
And to such height their frantick passion grows,
  That what both love, both hazard to destroy.

29.

Amidst whole heaps of Spices lights a Ball,
  And now their Odours arm'd against them flie:
Some preciously by shatter'd Porc'lain fall,
  And some by Aromatick splinters die.

24. The Attempt at *Berghen*. D. The Dutch merchant fleet from the East Indies took refuge in the harbour at Berghen, in Norway, and the English attempted but failed to capture it on 3 August 1665.
24 iii. Southern Climates, *Guinny*. D.

30.

And though by Tempests of the prize bereft,
In Heavens inclemency some ease we find:
Our foes we vanquish'd by our valour left,
And onely yielded to the Seas and Wind.

31.

Nor wholly lost we so deserv'd a prey;
For storms, repenting, part of it restor'd:
Which, as a tribute from the Balthick Sea,
The British Ocean sent her mighty Lord.

32.

Go, Mortals, now, and vex your selves in vain
For wealth, which so uncertainly must come:
When what was brought so far, and with such pain,
Was onely kept to lose it neerer home.

33.

The Son, who, twice three month's on th' Ocean tost,
Prepar'd to tell what he had pass'd before,
Now sees, in *English* Ships the *Holland* Coast,
And Parents arms in vain stretch'd from the shore.

34.

This carefull Husband had been long away,
Whom his chast wife and little children mourn;
Who on their fingers learn'd to tell the day
On which their Father promis'd to return.

35.

Such are the proud designs of human kind,
And so we suffer Shipwrack every where!
Alas, what Port can such a Pilot find,
Who in the night of Fate must blindly steer!

31 iv. When the Dutch merchant fleet escaped from Berghen it was dispersed by a storm and some of the richest ships were captured by English squadrons.

35 i. *Such are, &c. from* Petronius. Si, bene calculum ponas ubique fit naufragium. D. Shipwreck, if you reckon it fairly, lies all about us. (*Satyricon* 115.)

36.

The undistinguish'd seeds of good and ill
  Heav'n, in his bosom, from our knowledge hides;
And draws them in contempt of human skill,
  Which oft, for friends, mistaken foes provides.

37.

Let *Munster*'s Prelate ever be accurst,
  In whom we seek the *German* faith in vain:
Alas, that he should teach the *English* first
  That fraud and avarice in the Church could reign!

38.

Happy who never trust a Stranger's will,
  Whose friendship's in his interest understood!
Since money giv'n but tempts him to be ill
  When pow'r is too remote to make him good.

39.

Till now, alone the Mighty Nations strove:
  The rest, at gaze, without the Lists did stand:
And threat'ning *France*, plac'd like a painted *Jove*,
  Kept idle thunder in his lifted hand.

40.

That Eunuch Guardian of rich *Hollands* trade,
  Who envies us what he wants pow'r t' enjoy!
Whose noisefull valour does no foe invade,
  And weak assistance will his friends destroy.

41.

Offended that we fought without his leave,
  He takes this time his secret hate to show:
Which *Charles* does with a mind so calm receive
  As one that neither seeks, nor shuns his foe.

37 ii. The *German* faith. *Tacitus* saith of them. *Nullos mortaliam fide aut armis ante Germanos esse*. D. "No men alive (they exclaimed) outdid the Germans in honesty, or in warlike skill." (*Annals* 13. 54.) The Bishop of Munster, whose behaviour is thus contrasted with Tacitus's opinion of the Germans, was subsidised by the English to invade the Dutch provinces, but when France entered the war on the side of the Dutch, the Bishop withdrew his forces and concluded a separate peace.

39. War declar'd by France. D.

42.

With *France*, to aid the *Dutch*, the *Danes* unite:
France as their Tyrant, *Denmark* as their Slave.
But when with one three Nations joyn to fight,
They silently confess that one more brave.

43.

Lewis had chas'd the *English* from his shore;
But *Charles* the *French* as Subjects does invite.
Would Heav'n for each some *Salomon* restore,
Who, by their mercy, may decide their right.

44.

Were Subjects so but onely by their choice,
And not from Birth did forc'd Dominion take,
Our Prince alone would have the publique voice;
And all his Neighbours Realms would desarts make.

45.

He without fear a dangerous War pursues,
Which without rashness he began before.
As Honour made him first the danger choose,
So still he makes it good on virtues score.

46.

The doubled charge his Subjects love supplies,
Who, in that bounty, to themselves are kind:
So glad Egyptians see their *Nilus* rise,
And in his plenty their abundance find.

47.

With equal pow'r he does two Chiefs create,
Two such, as each seem'd worthiest when alone:
Each able to sustain a Nations fate,
Since both had found a greater in their own.

42 i. France declared war on England in January 1666, and in February Denmark joined Holland and France.

43 ii. Charles II extended his protection to all Dutch and French subjects in England who did not correspond with the enemy, and particularly invited the French protestants to seek refuge in England.

47. Prince *Rupert* and Duke *Albemarl* sent to sea. D. Prince Rupert (1619–1682), the great Cavalier General, and George Monk, Duke of Albemarle (1608–1670), the Parliamentary general and principal agent in the restoration of Charles II, were appointed joint-commanders of the English fleet in 1665.

48.

Both great in courage, Conduct and in Fame,
  Yet neither envious of the others praise.
Their duty, faith, and int'rest too the same.
  Like mighty Partners equally they raise.

49.

The Prince long time had courted Fortune's love,
  But once possess'd did absolutely reign;
Thus with their *Amazons* the *Heroes* strove,
  And conquer'd first those Beauties they would gain.

50.

The Duke beheld, like *Scipio*, with disdain
  That *Carthage*, which he ruin'd, rise once more:
And shook aloft the Fasces of the Main,
  To fright those Slaves with what they felt before.

51.

Together to the watry Camp they haste,
  Whom Matrons passing, to their children show:
Infants first vows for them to Heav'n are cast,
  And future people bless them as they go.

52.

With them no riotous pomp, nor *Asian* train,
  T' infect a Navy with their gawdy fears:
To make slow fights, and victories but vain;
  But war, severely, like it self, appears.

53.

Diffusive of themselves, where e'r they pass,
  They make that warmth in others they expect:
Their valour works like bodies on a glass,
  And does its Image on their men project.

51 iv. *Future people*, Examina infantium futurusque populos. Plin. Jun. in pan. ad Traj. D. Swarms of babes, and a people yet to be. (*Panegyric* 26. 1.)

54.

Our Fleet divides, and straight the *Dutch* appear,
 In number, and a fam'd Commander, bold:
The Narrow Seas can scarce their Navy bear,
 Or crowded Vessels can their Soldiers hold.

55.

The Duke, less numerous, but in courage more,
 On wings of all the winds to combat flies:
His murdering Guns a loud defiance roar,
 And bloudy Crosses on his Flag-staffs rise.

56.

Both furl their sails, and strip them for the fight,
 Their folded sheets dismiss the useless air:
Th' *Elean* Plains could boast no nobler sight,
 When strugling Champions did their bodies bare.

57.

Born each by other in a distant Line,
 The Sea-built Forts in dreadful order move:
So vast the noise, as if not Fleets did joyn,
 But Lands unfix'd, and floating Nations, strove.

58.

Now pass'd, on either side they nimbly tack,
 Both strive to intercept and guide the wind:
And, in its eye, more closely they come back
 To finish all the deaths they left behind.

59.

On high-rais'd Decks the haughty *Belgians* ride,
 Beneath whose shade our humble Fregats go:
Such port the Elephant bears, and so defi'd
 By the *Rhinocero's* her unequal foe.

54. *Duke of* Albemarl's *Battel, first day.* D. Prince Rupert was ordered to intercept, with part of the English fleet, a French squadron which, it was reported, was attempting to join up with the Dutch naval forces. While he was absent on this duty, Albemarle, although outnumbered, engaged the Dutch fleet on 1 June.

56 iii. Th' *Elean, &c. Where the Olimpick Games were celebrated.* D.

57 iv. *Lands unfix'd, from* Virgil: *Credas innare revultas Cycladas, &c.* D. One would believe these were islands that floated, uptorn, upon the sea. (*Æneid* 8. 691–2.)

60.

And as the built, so different is the fight;
  Their mounting shot is on our sails design'd:
Deep in their hulls our deadly bullets light,
  And through the yielding planks a passage find.

61.

Our dreaded Admiral from far they threat,
  Whose batter'd rigging their whole war receives.
All bare, like some old Oak which tempests beat,
  He stands, and sees below his scatter'd leaves.

62.

Heroes of old, when wounded, shelter sought,
  But he, who meets all danger with disdain,
Ev'n in their face his ship to Anchor brought,
  And Steeple high stood propt upon the Main.

63.

At this excess of courage, all amaz'd,
  The foremost of his foes a while withdraw.
With such respect in enter'd *Rome* they gaz'd,
  Who on high Chairs the God-like Fathers saw.

64.

And now, as where *Patroclus*' body lay,
  Here *Trojan* Chiefs advanc'd, & there the *Greek*:
Ours o'r the Duke their pious wings display,
  And theirs the noblest spoils of *Britain* seek.

65.

Mean time, his busie Marriners he hasts,
  His shatter'd sails with rigging to restore:
And willing Pines ascend his broken Masts,
  Whose lofty heads rise higher then before.

66.

Straight to the *Dutch* he turns his dreadful prow,
  More fierce th' important quarrel to decide.
Like Swans, in long array his Vessels show,
  Whose creasts, advancing, do the waves divide.

63 iv. When the Gauls took Rome in 387 B.C. they were momentarily awed by the sight of the Roman Fathers seated in chairs of state and dressed in their regalia.

67.

They charge, re-charge, and all along the Sea
They drive, and squander the huge *Belgian* Fleet.
Berkley alone, who neerest Danger lay,
Did a like fate with lost *Creusa* meet.

68.

The night comes on, we eager to pursue
The Combat still, and they asham'd to leave:
Till the last streaks of dying day withdrew,
And doubtful Moon-light did our rage deceive.

69.

In th' *English* Fleet each ship resounds with joy,
And loud applause of their great Lead'rs fame.
In fiery dreams the *Dutch* they still destroy,
And, slumbering, smile at the imagin'd flame.

70.

Not so the *Holland* Fleet, who tir'd and done,
Stretched on their decks like weary Oxen lie:
Faint sweats all down their mighty members run,
(Vast bulks which little souls but ill supply.)

71.

In dreams they fearful precipices tread,
Or, shipwrack'd, labour to some distant shore:
Or in dark Churches walk among the dead:
They wake with horrour & dare sleep no more.

72.

The morn they look on with unwilling eyes,
Till, from their Main-top, joyful news they hear
Of ships, which by their mould bring new supplies,
And in their colours *Belgian* Lions bear.

73.

Our watchful General had discern'd, from far,
This mighty succour which made glad the foe.
He sigh'd, but, like a Father of the War,
His face spake hope, while deep his sorrows flow.

67 iv. Sir William Berkeley (1639–1666), although surrounded by the enemy's forces, fought on until he was overcome and mortally wounded.
72. *Second days Battel.* D. The Dutch were strongly reinforced on the second day and their superiority over the English was increased.
73 iv. *His face, &c.* Spem vultu simulat premit alto corde dolorem. *Virg.* D. He on his countenance sets a look of hope, and checks the grief deep in his heart. (*Æneid* 1. 209.)

74.

His wounded men he first sends off to shore:
  (Never, till now, unwilling to obey.)
They, not their wounds but want of strength deplore,
  And think them happy who with him can stay.

75.

Then, to the rest, Rejoyce (said he) today
  In you the fortune of *Great Britain* lies:
Among so brave a people you are they
  Whom Heav'n has chose to fight for such a Prize.

76.

If number *English* courages could quell,
  We should at first have shun'd, not met our foes;
Whose numerous sails the fearful onely tell:
  Courage from hearts, and not from numbers grows.

77.

He said; nor needed more to say: with hast
  To their known stations chearfully they go:
And all at once, disdaining to be last,
  Sollicite every gale to meet the foe.

78.

Nor did th' incourag'd *Belgians* long delay,
  But, bold in others, not themselves, they stood:
So thick, our Navy scarce could sheer their way,
  But seem'd to wander in a moving wood.

79.

Our little Fleet was now ingag'd so far,
  That, like the Sword-fish in the Whale, they fought.
The Combat onely seem'd a Civil War,
  Till through their bowels we our passage wrought.

80.

Never had valour, no not ours before,
  Done ought like this upon the Land or Main:
Where not to be o'rcome was to do more
  Then all the Conquests former Kings did gain.

81.

The mighty Ghosts of our great *Harries* rose,
  And armed *Edwards* look'd, with anxious eyes,
To see this Fleet among unequal foes,
  By which fate promis'd them their *Charles* should rise.

82.

Mean time the *Belgians* tack upon our Reer,
  And raking Chase-guns through our sterns they send:
Close by, their Fire-ships, like *Jackals*, appear,
  Who on their Lions for the prey attend.

83.

Silent in smoke of Canons they come on:
  (Such vapours once did fiery *Cacus* hide.)
In these the height of pleas'd revenge is shown,
  Who burn contented by another's side.

84.

Sometimes, from fighting Squadrons of each Fleet,
  (Deceiv'd themselves, or to preserve some friend)
Two grapling *Ætna*'s on the Ocean meet,
  And *English* fires with *Belgian* flames contend.

85.

Now, at each Tack, our little Fleet grows less;
  And, like maim'd fowl, swim lagging on the Main.
Their greater loss their numbers scarce confess,
  While they lose cheaper then the *English* gain.

86.

Have you not seen when, whistled from the fist,
  Some Falcon stoops at what her eye design'd,
And, with her eagerness, the quarry miss'd,
  Straight flies at check, and clips it down the wind.

87.

The dastard Crow, that to the wood made wing,
  And sees the Groves no shelter can afford,
With her loud Kaws her Craven kind does bring,
  Who, safe in numbers cuff the noble Bird.

88.

Among the *Dutch* thus *Albemarl* did fare:
He could not conquer, and disdain'd to flie.
Past hope of safety, 'twas his latest care,
Like falling *Cesar*, decently to die.

89.

Yet pity did his manly spirit move
To see those perish who so well had fought:
And, generously, with his despair he strove,
Resolv'd to live till he their safety wrought.

90.

Let other Muses write his prosp'rous fate,
Of conquer'd Nations tell, and Kings restor'd:
But mine shall sing of his eclips'd estate,
Which, like the Sun's, more wonders does afford.

91.

He drew his mighty Fregates all before,
On which the foe his fruitless force employes:
His weak ones deep into his Reer he bore,
Remote from Guns as sick men are from noise.

92.

His fiery Canon did their passage guide,
And foll'wing smoke obscur'd them from the foe.
Thus *Israel* safe from the *Egyptian*'s pride,
By flaming pillars, and by clouds did go.

93.

Elsewhere the *Belgian* force we did defeat,
But here our courages did theirs subdue:
So *Xenophon* once led that fam'd retreat,
Which first the *Asian* Empire overthrew.

94.

The foe approach'd: and one, for his bold sin,
Was sunk, (as he that touch'd the Ark was slain;)
The wild waves master'd him, and suck'd him in,
And smiling Eddies dimpled on the Main.

94 ii. Uzza touched the Ark of God, and the Lord 'smote him, because he had put his hand to the ark; and there he died before God' (*I Chron.*, xiii.10).

95.

This seen, the rest at awful distance stood;
  As if they had been there as servants set,
To stay, or to go on, as he thought good,
  And not pursue, but wait on his retreat.

96.

So *Libian* Huntsmen, on some sandy plain,
  From shady coverts rouz'd, the Lion chace:
The Kingly beast roars out with loud disdain,
  And slowly moves, unknowing to give place.

97.

But if some one approach to dare his force,
  He swings his tail, and swiftly turns him round:
With one paw seizes on his trembling Horse,
  And with the other tears him to the ground.

98.

Amidst these toils succeeds the balmy night,
  Now hissing waters the quench'd guns restore;
And weary waves, withdrawing from the fight,
  Lie lull'd and panting on the silent shore.

99.

The Moon shone clear on the becalmed floud,
  Where, while her beams like glittering silver play,
Upon the Deck our careful General stood,
  And deeply mus'd on the succeeding day.

100.

That happy Sun, said he, will rise again,
  Who twice victorious did our Navy see:
And I alone must view him rise in vain,
  Without one ray of all his Star for me.

96 iv. *The simile is* Virgil's, Vestigia retro improperata refert, &c. D. He paces back upon his way, retracing his steps without haste. (*Æneid* 9. 797–8.)

98 iii. *Weary waves, from* Statius Sylv. Nec trucibus fluviis idem sonus: occidit horror aequoris, ac terris maria acclinata quiescunt. D. And the sound of the threatening floods is not as it was; dead has fallen the sea's unrest; the oceans lean upon the pillow of the land, and are at peace. (*Silvæ* 5. 4. 5–6.)

99. iv. *The third of* June, *famous for two former Victories*. D. England won naval victories over the Dutch on 3 June 1653 and 1665.

101.

Yet, like an *English* Gen'ral will I die,
And all the Ocean make my spatious grave.
Women and Cowards on the Land may lie,
The Sea's a Tomb that's proper for the brave.

102.

Restless he pass'd the remnants of the night,
Till the fresh air proclaim'd the morning nigh,
And burning ships, the Martyrs of the fight,
With paler fires beheld the Eastern sky.

103.

But now, his Stores of Ammunition spent,
His naked valour is his onely guard:
Rare thunders are from his dumb Cannon sent,
And solitary Guns are scarcely heard.

104.

Thus far had Fortune pow'r, here forc'd to stay,
Nor longer durst with vertue be at strife:
This, as a Ransome *Albemarl* did pay
For all the glories of so great a life.

105.

For now brave *Rupert* from afar appears,
Whose waving Streamers the glad General knows:
With full spread Sails his eager Navy steers,
And every Ship in swift proportion grows.

106.

The anxious Prince had heard the Cannon long,
And from that length of time dire *Omens* drew
Of *English* over-match'd, and *Dutch* too strong,
Who never fought three days but to pursue.

107.

Then, as an Eagle, (who, with pious care,
Was beating widely on the wing for prey)
To her now silent Eiry does repair,
And finds her callow Infants forc'd away.

103. *Third day.* D.

108.

Stung with her love she stoops upon the plain,
The broken air loud whistling as she flies:
She stops, and listens, and shoots forth again,
And guides her pinions by her young ones cries.

109.

With such kind passion hastes the Prince to fight,
And spreads his flying canvas to the sound:
Him, whom no danger, were he there, could fright,
Now, absent, every little noise can wound.

110.

As, in a drought, the thirsty creatures cry,
And gape upon the gather'd clowds for rain,
And first the Martlet meets it in the sky,
And, with wet wings, joys all the feather'd train.

111.

With such glad hearts did our despairing men
Salute th' appearance of the Princes Fleet:
And each ambitiously would claim the Ken
That with first eyes did distant safety meet.

112.

The *Dutch*, who came like greedy Hinds before,
To reap the harvest their ripe ears did yield,
Now look like those, when rowling thunders roar,
And sheets of Lightning blast the standing field.

113.

Full in the Princes passage, hills of sand
And dang'rous flats in secret ambush lay,
Where the false tides skim o'r the cover'd Land,
And Sea-men with dissembled depths betray:

114.

The wily *Dutch*, who, like fall'n Angels, fear'd
This new *Messiah*'s coming, there did wait,
And round the verge their braving Vessels steer'd,
To tempt his courage with so fair a bait.

115.

But he, unmov'd, contemns their idle threat,
  Secure of fame when ere he please to fight:
His cold experience tempers all his heat,
  And inbred worth does boasting valour slight.

116.

Heroique virtue did his actions guide,
  And he the substance not th' appearance chose:
To rescue one such friend he took more pride
  Than to destroy whole thousands of such foes.

117.

But, when approach'd, in strict embraces bound,
  Rupert and *Albemarl* together grow:
He joys to have his friend in safety found,
  Which he to none but to that friend would owe.

118.

The chearful Souldiers, with new stores suppli'd,
  Now long to execute their spleenfull will;
And, in revenge for those three days they tri'd,
  Wish one, like *Joshua*'s, when the Sun stood still.

119.

Thus re-inforc'd, against the adverse Fleet
  Still doubling ours, brave *Rupert* leads the way.
With the first blushes of the Morn they meet,
  And bring night back upon the new-born day.

120.

His presence soon blows up the kindling fight,
  And his loud Guns speak thick like angry men:
It seem'd as slaughter had been breath'd all night,
  And death new pointed his dull dart agen.

121.

The *Dutch*, too well his mighty Conduct knew,
  And matchless Courage since the former fight:
Whose Navy like a stiff stretch'd cord did show
  Till he bore in, and bent them into flight.

119. *Fourth days Battel.* D.

122.

The wind he shares while half their Fleet offends
His open side, and high above him shows,
Upon the rest at pleasure he descends,
And, doubly harm'd, he double harms bestows.

123.

Behind, the Gen'ral mends his weary pace;
And sullenly to his revenge he sails:
So glides some trodden Serpent on the grass,
And long behind his wounded vollume trails.

124.

Th' increasing sound is born to either shore,
And for their stakes the throwing Nations fear.
Their passion, double with the Cannons roar,
And with warm wishes each man combats there.

125.

Pli'd thick and close as when the fight begun,
Their huge unwieldy Navy wasts away:
So sicken waning Moons too neer the Sun,
And blunt their crescents on the edge of day.

126.

And now reduc'd on equal terms to fight,
Their Ships like wasted Patrimonies show:
Where the thin scatt'ring Trees admit the light,
And shun each others shadows as they grow.

127.

The warlike Prince had sever'd from the rest
Two giant ships, the pride of all the Main;
Which, with his one, so vigorously he press'd,
And flew so home they could not rise again.

128.

Already batter'd, by his Lee they lay,
In vain upon the passing winds they call:
The passing winds through their torn canvas play,
And flagging sails on heartless Sailors fall.

123 iii. *So glides, &c. from* Virgil. Quum medii nexus, extremaeque agmina caudae solvuntur; tardosque trahit sinus ultimus, &c. D. When the twining middle, and the tail's last columns, are loosed, and the hindmost part thereof circles and writhes in a dragging motion. (*Georgics* 3. 423–4.)

129.

Their open'd sides receive a gloomy light,
Dreadful as day let in to shades below:
Without, grim death rides bare-fac'd in their sight,
And urges ent'ring billows as they flow.

130.

When one dire shot, the last they could supply,
Close by the boar'd the Prince's Main-mast bore:
All three now, helpless, by each other lie,
And this offends not, and those fear no more.

131.

So have I seen some fearful Hare maintain
A Course, till tir'd before the Dog she lay:
Who, stretch'd behind her, pants upon the plain,
Past pow'r to kill as she to get away.

132.

With his loll'd tongue he faintly licks his prey,
His warm breath blows her flix up as she lies:
She, trembling, creeps upon the ground away,
And looks back to him with beseeching eyes.

133.

The Prince unjustly does his Stars accuse,
Which hinder'd him to push his fortune on:
For what they to his courage did refuse,
By mortal valour never must be done.

134.

This lucky hour the wise *Batavian* takes,
And warns his tatter'd Fleet to follow home:
Proud to have so got off with equal stakes,
Where 'twas a triumph not to be o'r-come.

135.

The General's force, as kept alive by fight,
Now, not oppos'd, no longer can persue:
Lasting till Heav'n had done his courage right,
When he had conquer'd he his weakness knew.

134 iv. *From* Horace: Quos opimus fallere & effugere est triumphus. D. Those whom it is a signal triumph to baffle and to evade. (*Odes* 4. 4. 52.)

136.

He casts a frown on the departing foe,
  And sighs to see him quit the watry field:
His stern fix'd eyes no satisfaction show,
  For all the glories which the Fight did yield.

137.

Though, as when Fiends did Miracles avow,
  He stands confess'd ev'n by the boastful *Dutch*,
He onely does his conquest disavow,
  And thinks too little what they found too much.

138.

Return'd, he with the Fleet resolv'd to stay,
  No tender thoughts of home his heart divide:
Domestick joys and cares he puts away,
  For Realms are housholds which the Great must guide.

139.

As those who unripe veins in Mines explore,
  On the rich bed again the warm turf lay,
Till time digests the yet imperfect Ore,
  And know it will be Gold another day.

140.

So looks our Monarch on this early fight,
  Th' essay, and rudiments of great success,
Which all-maturing time must bring to light,
  While he, like Heav'n, does each days labour bless.

141.

Heav'n ended not the first or second day,
  Yet each was perfect to the work design'd:
God and Kings work, when they their work survey,
  And passive aptness in all subjects find.

142.

In burden'd Vessels, first, with speedy care,
  His plenteous Stores do season'd timber send:
Thither the brawny Carpenters repair,
  And as the Surgeons of maim'd ships attend.

142. *His Majesty repairs the Fleet.* D.

143.

With Cord and Canvas from rich *Hamburgh* sent,
His Navies molted wings he imps once more:
Tall *Norway* Fir, their Masts in Battel spent,
And *English* Oak sprung leaks and planks restore.

144.

All hands employ'd, the Royal work grows warm,
Like labouring Bees on a long Summers day,
Some sound the Trumpet for the rest to swarm,
And some on bells of tasted Lillies play:

145.

With gluwy wax some new foundation lay
Of Virgin combs, which from the roof are hung:
Some arm'd within doors, upon duty stay,
Or tend the sick, or educate the young.

146.

So here, some pick out bullets from the sides,
Some drive old Okum through each seam and rift:
Their left-hand does the Calking-iron guide,
The ratling Mallet with the right they lift.

147.

With boiling Pitch another near at hand
(From friendly *Sweden* brought) the seams instops:
Which well paid o'r the salt-Sea waves withstand,
And shakes them from the rising beak in drops.

148.

Some the gall'd ropes with dawby Marling bind,
Or sear-cloth Masts with strong Tarpawling coats:
To try new shrouds one mounts into the wind,
And one, below, their ease or stiffness notes.

149.

Our careful Monarch stands in Person by,
His new-cast Canons firmness to explore:
The strength of big-corn'd powder loves to try,
And Ball and Cartradge sorts for every bore.

144 i. Fervet opus: *the same similitude in* Virgil. D. Warmly glows the work. (*Georgics* 4. 169.)

150.

Each day brings fresh supplies of Arms and Men,
And Ships which all last Winter were abrode:
And such as fitted since the Fight had been,
Or new from Stocks were fall'n into the Road.

151.

The goodly *London* in her gallant trim,
(The *Phœnix* daughter of the vanish'd old:)
Like a rich Bride does to the Ocean swim,
And on her shadow rides in floating gold.

152.

Her Flag aloft spread ruffling to the wind,
And sanguine Streamers seem the floud to fire:
The Weaver charm'd with what his Loom design'd,
Goes on to Sea, and knows not to retire.

153.

With roomy decks, her Guns of mighty strength,
(Whose low-laid mouthes each mounting billow laves:)
Deep in her draught, and warlike in her length,
She seems a Sea-wasp flying on the waves.

154.

This martial Present, piously design'd,
The Loyal City give their best-lov'd King:
And with a bounty ample as the wind,
Built, fitted and maintain'd to aid him bring.

155.

By viewing Nature, Natures Hand-maid, Art,
Makes mighty things from small beginnings grow:
Thus fishes first to shipping did impart
Their tail the Rudder, and their head the Prow.

156.

Some Log, perhaps, upon the waters swam
An useless drift, which, rudely cut within,
And hollow'd, first a floating trough became,
And cross some Riv'let passage did begin.

151. Loyal London *describ'd.* D. This ship, presented to the King by the City of London, replaced another of the same name which had earlier been destroyed by fire.

155. *Digression concerning Shipping and Navigation* D.

157.

In shipping such as this the *Irish Kern*,
And untaught *Indian*, on the stream did glide:
Ere sharp-keel'd Boats to stem the floud did learn,
Or fin-like Oars did spread from either side.

158.

Adde but a Sail, and *Saturn* so appear'd,
When, from lost Empire, he to Exile went,
And with the Golden age to *Tyber* steer'd,
Where Coin & first Commerce he did invent.

159.

Rude as their Ships was Navigation, then;
No useful Compass or Meridian known:
Coasting, they kept the Land within their ken,
And knew no North but when the Pole-star shone.

160.

Of all who since have us'd the open Sea,
Then the bold *English* none more fame have won:
Beyond the Year, and out of Heav'ns high-way,
They make discoveries where they see no Sun.

161.

But what so long in vain, and yet unknown,
By poor man-kinds benighted wit is sought,
Shall in this Age to *Britain* first be shown,
And hence be to admiring Nations taught.

162.

The Ebbs of Tydes, and their mysterious flow,
We, as Arts Elements shall understand:
And as by Line upon the Ocean go,
Whose paths shall be familiar as the Land.

163.

Instructed ships shall sail to quick Commerce;
By which remotest Regions are alli'd:
Which makes one City of the Universe,
Where some may gain, and all may be suppli'd.

160 iii. Extra anni solisque vias. *Virg.* D. Beyond the pathway of the years and of the sun. (*Æneid* 6. 796.)
163 i. *By a more exact knowledge of Longitudes.* D.

164.

Then, we upon our Globes last verge shall go,
And view the Ocean leaning on the sky:
From thence our rolling Neighbours we shall know,
And on the Lunar world securely pry.

165.

This I fore-tel, from your auspicious care,
Who great in search of God and Nature grow:
Who best your wise Creator's praise declare,
Since best to praise his works is best to know.

166.

O truly Royal! who behold the Law,
And rule of beings in your Makers mind,
And thence, like Limbecks, rich Ideas draw,
To fit the levell'd use of humane kind.

167.

But first the toils of war we must endure,
And, from th' Injurious *Dutch* redeem the Seas.
War makes the valiant of his right secure,
And gives up fraud to be chastis'd with ease.

168.

Already were the *Belgians* on our coast,
Whose Fleet more mighty every day became,
By late success, which they did falsely boast,
And now, by first appearing seem'd to claim.

169.

Designing, subtil, diligent, and close,
They knew to manage War with wise delay:
Yet all those arts their vanity did cross,
And, by their pride, their prudence did betray.

170.

Nor staid the *English* long: but, well suppli'd,
Appear as numerous as th' insulting foe.
The Combat now by courage must be tri'd,
And the success the braver Nation show.

165. *Apostrophe to the Royal Society.* D. Dryden was elected to the Royal Society, founded soon after the Restoration, in 1662.

171.

There was the *Plimouth* Squadron new come in,
  Which in the *Straights* last Winter was abroad:
Which twice on *Biscay*'s working Bay had been,
  And on the Mid-land Sea the *French* had aw'd.

172.

Old expert *Allen*, loyal all along,
  Fam'd for his action on the *Smirna* Fleet,
And *Holmes*, whose name shal live in Epique Song,
  While Musick Numbers, or while Verse has Feet.

173.

Holmes, the *Achates* of the Gen'rals fight,
  Who first bewitch'd our eyes with *Guinny* Gold:
As once old *Cato* in the *Roman*'s sight
  The tempting fruits of *Africk* did unfold.

174.

With him went *Sprag*, as bountiful as brave,
  Whom his high courage to command had brought:
Harman, who did the twice fir'd *Harry* save,
  And in his burning ship undaunted fought.

175.

Young *Hollis*, on a *Muse* by *Mars* begot,
  Born, *Cesar*-like, to write and act great deeds:
Impatient to revenge his fatal shot,
  His right hand doubly to his left succeeds.

172 ii. Sir Thomas Allen (1612–1685) attacked the Dutch homeward-bound Smyrna fleet off Cadiz at the beginning of the war, and both inflicted damage and took prizes.

173 ii. Sir Robert Holmes had attacked Dutch trading posts on the African coast in 1663, before hostilities were declared. He is compared to Cato the Censor, who, urging the Romans to declare war on Carthage, displayed in the Senate some figs he had picked three days earlier in that city while on an embassy.

174 ii. Sir Edward Spragge (*d.* 1673) had been knighted for his gallantry in the action of 3 June 1665.

iv. Sir John Harman (*d.* 1673) had his ship, the *Henry*, fired twice by Dutch fire-ships in the battle but each time he was able to save her.

175 iv. Sir Frescheville Hollis (1641–1672) lost an arm in the action of 3 June 1665. His father had been a Cavalier commander during the Civil War and his mother, from the phrase 'on a *Muse* by *Mars* begot', would seem to have been a poetess.

176.

Thousands were there in darker fame that dwell,
Whose deeds some nobler Poem shall adorn:
And, though to me unknown, they, sure, fought well,
Whom *Rupert* led, and who were *British* born.

177.

Of every size an hundred fighting Sail,
So vast the Navy now at Anchor rides,
That underneath it the press'd waters fail,
And, with its weight, it shoulders off the Tydes.

178.

Now Anchors weigh'd, the Sea-men shout so shrill,
That Heav'n & Earth and the wide Ocean rings:
A breeze from Westward waits their sails to fill,
And rests, in those high beds, his downy wings.

179.

The wary *Dutch* this gathering storm foresaw,
And durst not bide it on the *English* coast:
Behind their treach'rous shallows they withdraw,
And there lay snares to catch the *British* Hoast.

180.

So the false Spider, when her Nets are spread,
Deep ambush'd in her silent den does lie:
And feels, far off, the trembling of her thread,
Whose filmy cord should bind the strugling Fly.

181.

Then, if at last, she find him fast beset,
She issues forth, and runs along her Loom:
She joys to touch the Captive in her Net,
And drags the little wretch in triumph home.

182.

The *Belgians* hop'd that, with disorder'd haste,
Our deep-cut keels upon the sands might run:
Or, if with caution leisurely were past,
Their numerous gross might charge us one by one.

183.

But, with a fore-wind pushing them above,
And swelling tyde that heav'd them from below,
O'r the blind flats our warlike Squadrons move,
And, with spread sails, to welcome Battel go.

184.

It seem'd as there the *British Neptune* stood,
With all his host of waters at command,
Beneath them to submit th' officious floud:
And, with his Trident, shov'd them off the sand.

185.

To the pale foes they suddenly draw near,
And summon them to unexpected fight:
They start like Murderers when Ghosts appear,
And draw their Curtains in the dead of night.

186.

Now Van to Van the formost Squadrons meet,
The midmost Battels hasting up behind,
Who view, far off, the storm of falling Sleet,
And hear their thunder ratling in the wind.

187.

At length the adverse Admirals appear:
(The two bold Champions of each Countries right)
Their eyes describe the lists as they come near,
And draw the lines of death before they fight.

188.

The distance judg'd for shot of every size,
The Linstocks touch, the pond'rous ball expires:
The vig'rous Sea-man every port-hole plies,
And adds his heart to every Gun he fires.

184 iv. Levat ipse Tridenti, & vastas aperit Syrtes, &c. *Virg*. D. The sea-god with his trident lifts them up, and opens a way through the great shoals; and he moderates the sea. (*Æneid* 1. 145–6.)

186. *Second Battel*. D. This second engagement was fought off the North Foreland on 25 July 1666.

189.

Fierce was the fight on the proud *Belgians* side,
For honour, which they seldome sought before:
But now they by their own vain boasts were ti'd,
And forc'd, at least in show, to prize it more.

190.

But sharp remembrance on the *English* part,
And shame of being match'd by such a foe:
Rouze conscious vertue up in every heart,
And seeming to be stronger makes them so.

191.

Nor long the *Belgians* could that Fleet sustain,
Which did two Gen'rals fates, and *Cesar*'s bear.
Each several Ship a victory did gain,
As *Rupert* or as *Albemarl* were there.

192.

Their batter'd Admiral too soon withdrew,
Unthank'd by ours for his unfinish'd fight:
But he the minds of his *Dutch* Masters knew,
Who call'd that providence which we call'd flight.

193.

Never did men more joyfully obey,
Or sooner understood the sign to flie:
With such alacrity they bore away,
As if to praise them all the States stood by.

194.

O famous Leader of the *Belgian* Fleet,
Thy Monument inscrib'd such praise shall wear
As *Varro*, timely flying, once did meet,
Because he did not of his *Rome* despair.

190 iv. Possunt quia posse videntur. *Virg.* D. They can; for it seems to them that they can. (*Æneid* 5. 231.)

194 iv. The admiral of the Dutch fleet was Michael Adrien de Ruyter (1607–1676), one of the most renowned seamen of his day; and Dryden compares him to Terentius Varro who, after his defeat by Hannibal at Cannae, was thanked by the Roman Senate for engaging the enemy and not despairing for the State.

195.

Behold that Navy which a while before
Provok'd the tardy *English* to the fight,
Now draw their beaten vessels close to shore,
As Larks lie dar'd to shun the Hobbies flight.

196.

Who ere would *English* Monuments survey,
In other records may our courage know:
But let them hide the story of this day,
Whose fame was blemish'd by too base a foe.

197.

Or if too busily they will enquire
Into a victory which we disdain:
Then let them know, the *Belgians* did retire
Before the Patron Saint of injur'd *Spain.*

198.

Repenting *England* this revengeful day
To *Philip*'s Manes did an off'ring bring.
England, which first, by leading them astray,
Hatch'd up Rebellion to destroy her King.

199.

Our Fathers bent their baneful industry
To check a Monarchy that slowly grew:
But did not *France* or *Hollands* fate foresee,
Whose rising pow'r to swift Dominion flew.

200.

In fortunes Empire blindly thus we go,
And wander after pathless destiny:
Whose dark resorts since prudence cannot know,
In vain it would provide for what shall be.

197 iv. *Patron Saint*: St. James, *on whose day this victory was gain'd.* D.
198 ii. Philip's *Manes*: Philip *the second, of* Spain, *against whom the Hollanders rebelling, were aided by Queen* Elizabeth. D.

201.

But what ere *English* to the bless'd shall go,
And the fourth *Harry* or first *Orange* meet:
Find him disowning of a *Burbon* foe,
And him detesting a *Batavian* Fleet.

202.

Now on their coasts our conquering Navy rides,
Way-lays their Merchants, and their Land besets:
Each day new wealth without their care provides,
They lie asleep with prizes in their nets.

203.

So, close behind some Promontory lie
The huge Leviathans t' attend their prey:
And give no chace, but swallow in the frie,
Which through their gaping jaws mistake the way.

204.

Nor was this all: in Ports and Roads remote,
Destructive Fires among whole Fleets we send:
Triumphant flames upon the water flote,
And out-bound ships at home their voyage end.

205.

Those various Squadrons, variously design'd,
Each vessel fraighted with a several load:
Each Squadron waiting for a several wind,
All find but one, to burn them in the Road.

206.

Some bound for *Guinny*, golden sand to find,
Bore all the gawds the simple Natives wear:
Some for the pride of *Turkish* Courts design'd,
For folded *Turbans* finest *Holland* bear.

201 iv. Dryden imagines that Henry IV of France must disown his war against Henry III, and William of Orange 'detest' the Dutch fleet, by which his country's independence was won from Spain, now that they are among the blessed.

204. *Burning of the Fleet in the* Uly *by Sir* Robert Holmes. D. Immediately after the action on 25 July, Holmes destroyed a Dutch merchant fleet off the island of Uly and burnt the capital city on the island of Schelling.

207.

Some *English* Wool, vex'd in a *Belgian* Loom,
And into Cloth of spungy softness made:
Did into *France* or colder *Denmark* doom,
To ruine with worse ware our staple Trade.

208.

Our greedy Sea-men rummage every hold,
Smile on the booty of each wealthier Chest:
And, as the Priests who with their gods make bold,
Take what they like, and sacrifice the rest.

209.

But ah! how unsincere are all our joys!
Which, sent from Heav'n, like Lightning make no stay:
Their palling taste the journeys length destroys,
Or grief, sent post, o'r-takes them on the way.

210.

Swell'd with our late successes on the Foe,
Which *France* and *Holland* wanted power to cross:
We urge an unseen Fate to lay us low,
And feed their envious eyes with *English* loss.

211.

Each Element his dread command obeys,
Who makes or ruines with a smile or frown;
Who as by one he did our Nation raise,
So now he with another pulls us down.

212.

Yet, *London*, Empress of the Northern Clime,
By an high fate thou greatly didst expire;
Great as the worlds, which at the death of time
Must fall, and rise a nobler frame by fire.

213.

As when some dire Usurper Heav'n provides,
To scourge his Country with a lawless sway:
His birth, perhaps, some petty Village hides,
And sets his Cradle out of Fortune's way:

209. Transitum *to the Fire of* London. D. The Great Fire of London began on 2 September 1666 and, burning for three days, practically destroyed the city.

212 iii. Quum mare quum tellus correptaque regia Coeli, ardeat, &c. *Ovid.* D. When the ocean, and the dry land, and Heaven's palaces, take fire and burn . . . (*Metamorphoses* 1. 257–8.)

214.

Till fully ripe his swelling fate breaks out,
And hurries him to mighty mischiefs on:
His Prince surpriz'd at first, no ill could doubt,
And wants the pow'r to meet it when 'tis known.

215.

Such was the rise of this prodigious fire,
Which in mean buildings first obscurely bred,
From thence did soon to open streets aspire,
And straight to Palaces and Temples spread.

216.

The diligence of Trades and noiseful gain,
And luxury, more late, asleep were laid:
All was the nights, and in her silent reign,
No sound the rest of Nature did invade.

217.

In this deep quiet, from what source unknown,
Those seeds of fire their fatal birth disclose:
And first, few scatt'ring sparks about were blown,
Big with the flames that to our ruine rose.

218.

Then, in some close-pent room it crept along,
And, smouldering as it went, in silence fed:
Till th' infant monster, with devouring strong,
Walk'd boldly upright with exalted head.

219.

Now, like some rich or mighty Murderer,
Too great for prison, which he breaks with gold:
Who fresher for new mischiefs does appear,
And dares the world to tax him with the old.

220.

So scapes th' insulting fire his narrow Jail,
And makes small out-lets into open air:
There the fierce winds his tender force assail,
And beat him down-ward to his first repair.

221.

The winds, like crafty Courtezans, with-held
His flames from burning, but to blow them more:
And, every fresh attempt, he is repell'd
With faint denials, weaker then before.

222.

And now, no longer letted of his prey,
He leaps up at it with inrag'd desire:
O'r-looks the neighbours with a wide survey,
And nods at every house his threatning fire.

223.

The Ghosts of Traitors, from the *Bridge* descend,
With bold Fanatick Spectres to rejoyce:
About the fire into a Dance they bend,
And sing their Sabbath Notes with feeble voice.

224.

Our Guardian Angel saw them where he sate
Above the Palace of our slumbring King,
He sigh'd, abandoning his charge to Fate,
And, drooping, oft looked back upon the wing.

225.

At length the crackling noise and dreadful blaze,
Call'd up some waking Lover to the sight:
And long it was ere he the rest could raise,
Whose heavy eye-lids yet were full of night.

226.

The next to danger, hot pursu'd by fate,
Half cloth'd, half naked, hastily retire:
And frighted Mothers strike their breasts, too late,
For helpless Infants left amidst the fire.

221 i. *Like crafty, &c.* Haec arte tractabat cupidum virum, ut illius animum inopia accenderet. D. With skill did she govern the man's desire, to inflame his passion by starving it.

223 iv. The heads of traitors were shown on London Bridge, and Dryden imagines their spectres celebrating a witches' Sabbath as the City burns.

227.

Their cries soon waken all the dwellers near:
 Now murmuring noises rise in every street:
The more remote run stumbling with their fear,
 And, in the dark, men justle as they meet.

228.

So weary Bees in little Cells repose:
 But if night-robbers lift the well-stor'd Hive,
An humming through their waxen City grows,
 And out upon each others wings they drive.

229.

Now streets grow throng'd and busie as by day:
 Some run for Buckets to the hallow'd Quire:
Some cut the Pipes, and some the Engines play,
 And some more bold mount Ladders to the fire.

230.

In vain: for, from the East, a *Belgian* wind,
 His hostile breath through the dry rafters sent:
The flames impell'd, soon left their foes behind,
 And forward, with a wanton fury went.

231.

A Key of fire ran all along the shore,
 And lighten'd all the River with the blaze:
The waken'd Tydes began again to roar,
 And wond'ring Fish in shining waters gaze.

232.

Old Father *Thames* rais'd up his reverend head,
 But ſear'd the fate of *Simoeis* would return:
Deep in his *Ooze* he sought his sedgy bed,
 And shrunk his waters back into his Urn.

233.

The fire, mean time, walks in a broader gross,
 To either hand his wings he opens wide:
He wades the streets, & straight he reaches cross,
 And plays his longing flames on th' other side.

231 ii. Sigaea igni freta lata relucent. *Virg.* D. The wide straits of Sigeum flash out with fire. (*Æneid* 2. 312.)

234.

At first they warm, then scorch, and then they take:
  Now with long necks from side to side they feed:
At length, grown strong, their Mother fire forsake,
  And a new Collony of flames succeed.

235.

To every nobler portion of the Town,
  The curling billows roul their restless Tyde:
In parties now they straggle up and down,
  As Armies, unoppos'd, for prey divide.

236.

One mighty Squadron, with a side wind sped,
  Through narrow lanes his cumber'd fire does haste:
By pow'rful charms of gold and silver led,
  The *Lombard* Banquers and the *Change* to waste.

237.

Another backward to the *Tow'r* would go,
  And slowly eats his way against the wind:
But the main body of the marching foe
  Against th' Imperial Palace is design'd.

238.

Now day appears, and with the day the King,
  Whose early care had robb'd him of his rest:
Far off the cracks of falling houses ring,
  And shrieks of subjects pierce his tender breast.

239.

Near as he draws, thick harbingers of smoke,
  With gloomy pillars, cover all the place:
Whose little intervals of night are broke
  By sparks that drive against his Sacred Face.

240.

More then his Guards his sorrows made him known,
  And pious tears which down his cheeks did show'r:
The wretched in his grief forgot their own:
  (So much the pity of a King has pow'r.)

241.

He wept the flames of what he lov'd so well,
And what so well had merited his love.
For never Prince in grace did more excel,
Or Royal City more in duty strove.

242.

Nor with an idle care did he behold:
(Subjects may grieve, but Monarchs must redress.)
He chears the fearful, and commends the bold,
And makes despairers hope for good success.

243.

Himself directs what first is to be done,
And orders all the succours which they bring.
The helpful and the good about him run,
And form an Army worthy such a King.

244.

He sees the dire contagion spread so fast,
That where it seizes, all relief is vain:
And therefore must unwillingly lay waste
That Country which would, else, the foe maintain.

245.

The powder blows up all before the fire:
Th' amazed flames stand gather'd on a heap;
And from the precipices brinck retire,
Afraid to venture on so large a leap.

246.

Thus fighting fires a while themselves consume,
But straight, like *Turks*, forc'd on to win or die,
They first lay tender bridges of their fume,
And o'r the breach in unctuous vapours fly.

247.

Part stays for passage till a gust of wind
Ships o'r their forces in a shining sheet:
Part, creeping under ground, their journey blind,
And, climbing from below, their fellows meet.

245 i. Houses in the path of the fire were blown up to prevent the flames from spreading.

248.

Thus, to some desart plain, or old wood side,
  Dire night-hags come from far to dance their round:
And o'r brode Rivers on their fiends they ride,
  Or sweep in clowds above the blasted ground.

249.

No help avails: for, *Hydra*-like, the fire
  Lifts up his hundred heads to aim his way.
And scarce the wealthy can one half retire,
  Before he rushes in to share the prey.

250.

The rich grow suppliant, & the poor grow proud:
  Those offer mighty gain, and these ask more.
So void of pity is th' ignoble crowd,
  When others ruine may increase their store.

251.

As those who live by shores with joy behold
  Some wealthy vessel split or stranded nigh;
And, from the Rocks, leap down for shipwrack'd Gold,
  And seek the Tempest which the others flie:

252.

So these but wait the Owners last despair,
  And what's permitted to the flames invade:
Ev'n from their jaws they hungry morsels tear,
  And, on their backs, the spoils of *Vulcan* lade.

253.

The days were all in this lost labour spent;
  And when the weary King gave place to night;
His Beams he to his Royal Brother lent,
  And so shone still in his reflective light.

254.

Night came, but without darkness or repose,
  A dismal picture of the gen'ral doom:
Where Souls distracted when the Trumpet blows,
  And half unready with their bodies come.

255.

Those who have homes, when home they do repair,
 To a last lodging call their wand'ring friends.
Their short uneasie sleeps are broke with care,
 To look how near their own destruction tends.

256.

Those who have none sit round where once it was,
 And with full eyes each wonted room require:
Haunting the yet warm ashes of the place,
 As murder'd men walk where they did expire.

257.

Some stir up coals and watch the Vestal fire,
 Others in vain from sight of ruine run:
And, while through burning lab'rinths they retire,
 With loathing eyes repeat what they would shun.

258.

The most, in fields, like herded beasts lie down;
 To dews obnoxious on the grassie floor:
And while their Babes in sleep their sorrows drown,
 Sad Parents watch the remnants of their store.

259.

While by the motion of the flames they ghess
 What streets are burning now, & what are near
An Infant, waking, to the paps would press,
 And meets, instead of milk, a falling tear.

260.

No thought can ease them but their Sovereign's care,
 Whose praise th' afflicted as their comfort sing:
Ev'n those whom want might drive to just despair,
 Think life a blessing under such a King.

261.

Mean time he sadly suffers in their grief,
 Out-weeps an Hermite, and out-prays a Saint:
All the long night he studies their relief,
 How they may be suppli'd, and he may want.

262.

O God, said he, thou Patron of my days,
Guide of my youth in exile and distress!
Who me unfriended, broughtst by wondrous ways
The Kingdom of my Fathers to possess.

263.

Be thou my Judge, with what unwearied care
I since have labour'd for my People's good:
To bind the bruises of a Civil War,
And stop the issues of their wasting bloud.

264.

Thou, who hast taught me to forgive the ill,
And recompense, as friends. the good misled;
If mercy be a Precept of thy will,
Return that mercy on thy Servant's head.

265.

Or, if my heedless Youth has stept astray,
Too soon forgetful of thy gracious hand:
On me alone thy just displeasure lay,
But take thy judgments from this mourning Land.

266.

We all have sinn'd, and thou hast laid us low,
As humble Earth from whence at first we came:
Like flying shades before the clowds we show,
And shrink like Parchment in consuming flame.

267.

O let it be enough what thou hast done,
When spotted deaths ran arm'd through every street,
With poison'd darts, which not the good could shun,
The speedy could out-fly, or valiant meet.

268.

The living few, and frequent funerals then,
Proclaim'd thy wrath on this forsaken place:
And now those few who are return'd agen
Thy searching judgments to their dwellings trace.

262. *King's Prayer*. D.
267 iv. The Great Plague of 1665, which had destroyed 100,000 people, was not extinct in 1666.

269.

O pass not, Lord, an absolute decree,
Or bind thy sentence unconditional:
But in thy sentence our remorce foresee,
And, in that foresight, this thy doom recall.

270.

Thy threatnings, Lord, as thine, thou maist revoke:
But, if immutable and fix'd they stand,
Continue still thy self to give the stroke,
And let not foreign foes oppress thy Land.

271.

Th' Eternal heard, and from the Heav'nly Quire,
Chose out the Cherub with the flaming sword:
And bad him swiftly drive th' approaching fire
From where our Naval Magazins were stor'd.

272.

The blessed Minister his wings displai'd,
And like a shooting Star he cleft the night:
He charg'd the flames, and those that disobey'd,
He lash'd to duty with his sword of light.

273.

The fugitive flames, chastis'd, went forth to prey
On pious Structures, by our Fathers rear'd:
By which to Heav'n they did affect the way,
Ere Faith in Church-men without Works was heard.

274.

The wanting Orphans saw, with watry eyes,
Their Founders charity in dust laid low:
And sent to God their ever-answer'd cries,
(For he protects the poor who made them so.)

275.

Nor could thy Fabrick, *Paul*'s, defend thee long,
Though thou wert Sacred to thy Makers praise:
Though made immortal by a Poet's Song;
And Poets Songs the *Theban* walls could raise.

275 iii. An allusion to Edmund Waller's poem *Upon his Majesty's repairing of St. Paul's.*

276.

The dareing flames peept in and saw from far,
  The awful beauties of the Sacred Quire:
But, since it was prophan'd by Civil War,
  Heav'n thought it fit to have it purg'd by fire.

277.

Now down the narrow streets it swiftly came,
  And, widely opening, did on both sides prey.
This benefit we sadly owe the flame,
  If onely ruine must enlarge our way.

278.

And now four days the Sun had seen our woes,
  Four nights the Moon beheld th' incessant fire:
It seem'd as if the Stars more sickly rose,
  And farther from the feav'rish North retire.

279.

In th' Empyrean Heaven, (the bless'd abode)
  The Thrones and the Dominions prostrate lie,
Not daring to behold their angry God:
  And an hush'd silence damps the tuneful sky.

280.

At length th' Almighty cast a pitying eye,
  And mercy softly touch'd his melting breast:
He saw the Town's one half in rubbish lie,
  And eager flames give on to storm the rest.

281.

An hollow chrystal Pyramid he takes,
  In firmamental waters dipt above;
Of it a brode Extinguisher he makes,
  And hoods the flames that to their quarry strove.

282.

The vanquish'd fires withdraw from every place,
  Or full with feeding, sink into a sleep:
Each houshold Genius shows again his face,
  And, from the hearths, the little Lares creep.

283.

Our King this more then natural change beholds;
With sober joy his heart and eyes abound:
To the All-good his lifted hands he folds,
And thanks him low on his redeemed ground.

284.

As when sharp frosts had long constrain'd the earth,
A kindly thaw unlocks it with mild rain:
And first the tender blade peeps up to birth,
And straight the green fields laugh with promis'd grain:

285.

By such degrees, the spreading gladness grew
In every heart, which fear had froze before:
The standing streets with so much joy they view,
That with less grief the perish'd they deplore.

286.

The Father of the people open'd wide
His stores, and all the poor with plenty fed:
Thus God's Anointed God's own place suppli'd,
And fill'd the empty with his daily bread.

287.

This Royal bounty brought its own reward,
And, in their minds, so deep did print the sense:
That if their ruines sadly they regard,
'Tis but with fear the sight might drive him thence.

288.

But so may he live long, that Town to sway,
Which by his Auspice they will nobler make,
As he will hatch their ashes by his stay,
And not their humble ruines now forsake.

289.

They have not lost their Loyalty by fire;
Nor is their courage or their wealth so low,
That from his Wars they poorly would retire,
Or beg the pity of a vanquish'd foe.

288. *Cities request to the King not to leave them.* D.

290.

Not with more constancy the *Jews* of old,
By *Cyrus* from rewarded Exile sent:
Their Royal City did in dust behold,
Or with more vigour to rebuild it went.

291.

The utmost malice of their Stars is past,
And two dire Comets which have scourg'd the Town,
In their own Plague and Fire have breath'd their last,
Or, dimly, in their sinking sockets frown.

292.

Now frequent Trines the happier lights among,
And high-rais'd *Jove* from his dark prison freed:
(Those weights took off that on his Planet hung)
Will gloriously the new laid work succeed.

293.

Me-thinks already, from this Chymick flame,
I see a City of more precious mold,
Rich as the Town which gives the *Indies* name,
With Silver pav'd, and all divine with Gold.

294.

Already, Labouring with a mighty fate,
She shakes the rubbish from her mounting brow,
And seems to have renew'd her Charters date,
Which Heav'n will to the death of time allow.

295.

More great then humane, now, and more *August*,
New deifi'd she from her fires does rise:
Her widening streets on new foundations trust,
And, opening, into larger parts she flies.

296.

Before, she like some Shepherdess did show,
Who sate to bathe her by a River's side:
Not answering to her fame, but rude and low,
Nor taught the beauteous Arts of Modern pride.

292 ii. A trine is an astrological term for a triangular, and supposedly favourable, conjunction of the planets, and Jupiter in the ascension is also a happy omen.

293 iii. *Mexico*. D.

295 i. Augusta, *the old name of* London. D.

297.

Now, like a Maiden Queen, she will behold,
From her high Turrets, hourly Sutors come:
The East with Incense, and the West with Gold,
Will stand, like Suppliants, to receive her doom.

298.

The silver *Thames*, her own domestick Floud,
Shall bear her Vessels, like a sweeping Train;
And often wind (as of his Mistress proud)
With longing eyes to meet her face again.

299.

The wealthy *Tagus*, and the wealthier *Rhine*,
The glory of their Towns no more shall boast:
And *Sein*, That would with *Belgian* Rivers joyn,
Shall find her lustre stain'd, and Traffick lost.

300.

The vent'rous Merchant, who design'd more far,
And touches on our hospitable shore:
Charm'd with the splendour of this Northern Star,
Shall here unlade him, and depart no more.

301.

Our pow'rful Navy shall no longer meet,
The wealth of *France* or *Holland* to invade:
The beauty of this Town, without a Fleet,
From all the world shall vindicate her Trade.

302.

And, while this fam'd Emporium we prepare,
The *British* Ocean shall such triumphs boast,
That those who now disdain our Trade to share,
Shall rob like *Pyrats* on our wealthy Coast.

303.

Already we have conquer'd half the War,
And the less dang'rous part is left behind:
Our trouble now is but to make them dare,
And not so great to vanquish as to find.

299 iii. An allusion to Louis XIV's designs on the Spanish Netherlands.

304.

Thus to the Eastern wealth through storms we go;
  But now, the Cape once doubled, fear no more:
A constant Trade-wind will securely blow,
  And gently lay us on the Spicy shore.

ABSALOM AND ACHITOPHEL

A POEM

——— Si Propiùs stes
Te Capiet Magis ———[1]

[1] One kind will attract you more, if you stand nearer to it. (Horace, *Ars Poetica* 361–2.)

Absalom and Achitophel. A Poem. [*Latin quot.*] The Second Edition; Augmented and Revised. London, Printed for J.T. and are to be Sold by W. Davis in Amen-Corner, 1681.

THE present text is that of the second edition (Macdonald, 12 e i), appearing in the same year as the first edition, to which Dryden made important additions: the twelve lines on Shaftesbury, beginning 'So easie still it proves in Factious Times', and the four on Monmouth, beginning, 'But oh that yet he would repent and live!'.

NOTE TO ABSALOM AND ACHITOPHEL

ENGLAND in 1678 was suddenly plunged into fearful confusion by the Popish Plot. Titus Oates, the perjurer, warned the administration, and deposed on oath before a London magistrate, Sir Edmund Berry Godfrey, that the Roman Catholics were plotting to murder the King and establish the supremacy of their religion by force of foreign arms. Godfrey's murder, a few weeks after Oates's deposition, seemed to confirm the accusations and the country was thrown into a state of panic. The men arraigned by Oates were seized and tried and fifteen of them were executed. Oates's collection of brazen lies was dashed with just enough truth to make it plausible to a bewildered and frightened people.

The Earl of Shaftesbury, the leader of the Whig party, quickly became Oates's patron. He shrewdly realised that the intense popular feeling roused against the Catholics by Oates's disclosures could be used to force the King to exclude his brother, James, Duke of York, an avowed Catholic, from the succession to the throne. He proposed to replace the Duke of York by the King's illegitimate but personable son, James, Duke of Monmouth. He attempted to secure his aim by introducing into Parliament in 1680 the Exclusion Bill. The Bill easily passed the Commons but was narrowly defeated in the Lords. Its defeat was primarily due to the eloquence of the Earl of Halifax—the *Jotham* of this poem—who had supported Shaftesbury until the danger of his extreme policy had become obvious. The Court, who knew that at bottom Halifax was an enemy of the Duke of York, was thankful but not grateful to him for his intervention, and Dryden, faithfully reflecting the Court's sentiments, gave him only cursory praise.

The King prorogued, and then dissolved, Parliament in January 1681, in order to save his brother, but he knew that as soon as he summoned a new Parliament, which he must do quickly were he to obtain supplies essential to government, the Exclusion Bill would be introduced again by the Whigs. He could only defend himself against this threatened attack by finding an alternative source of revenue; and, in March 1681, immediately before the meeting of the new Parliament, he concluded a secret agreement with Louis XIV by which he obtained a subsidy in return for his acquiescence in French foreign policy. Shaftesbury prepared for the new Parliament by stirring up popular agitation and even by plotting an armed rising which, he hoped, would force the King's hand if he still proved recalcitrant. Parliament met at Oxford—a place chosen by the King to prevent Shaftesbury's London mobs from intimidating the members—but after it had sat for a few days, the King, freed from dependence on it by Louis's subsidy, and rightly judging that the Whigs' excesses had alienated every moderate sentiment in the country, dissolved it without warning on 28 March.

This dextrous stroke destroyed Shaftesbury's ascendancy. The Whig leader was arrested and sent to the Tower on 2 July, and while he lay there waiting trial on a charge of high treason, Dryden, it is said at the King's suggestion, wrote this poem. It appeared on about 17 November and its obvious intention was to prejudice the people against Shaftesbury. It was eagerly read but it did not affect the issue. The bill of indictment against Shaftesbury on a charge of high treason was brought before, and thrown out by, a London jury on 24 November 1681.

A KEY TO ABSALOM AND ACHITOPHEL

Aaron's Race, The Clergy.
Abbethdin, Lord Chancellor.
Absalom, James Scott, Duke of Monmouth and Buccleugh (1649–1685), the natural son of Charles II and Lucy Walters, who took the name of Scott upon his marriage with *Annabel.*
Achitophel, Anthony Ashley Cooper, Earl of Shaftesbury (1621–1683).
Adriel, John Sheffield, Earl of Mulgrave (1648–1721).
Agag, Sir Edmund Berry Godfrey (1621–1678).
Amiel, Edward Seymour (1633–1708).
Annabel, Anne Scott, Countess of Buccleugh in her own right, and wife of *Absalom.*
Balaam, Theophilus Hastings, Earl of Huntingdon (1650–1701).
Barzillai, James Butler, Earl of Ormonde (1610–1688).
Bathsheba, Louise Renée de Kéroualle, Duchess of Portsmouth and Aubigny (1649–1734), Charles II's mistress.
Caleb, Forde, Lord Grey of Werke (*d.* 1701).
Corah, Titus Oates (1649–1705).
David, Charles II.
Egypt, France.
Ethnic Plot, Popish Plot.
Gath, Brussels.
Hebrew Priests, Church of England clergy.
Hebron, Scotland.
Hushai, Laurence Hyde, Earl of Rochester (1641–1711).
Ishbosheth, Richard Cromwell (1626–1712).
Israel, England.
Issachar, Thomas Thynne of Longleat (1648–1682), known on account of his wealth as 'Tom of Ten Thousand'.
Jebusites, Roman Catholics.
Jerusalem, London.

Jewish Rabbins, Doctors of the Church of England.
Jonas, Sir William Jones (1631–1682).
Jordan, The English seas or, as '*Jordan's Flood*', the Irish Channel.
Jotham, George Savile, Marquis of Halifax (1633–1695).
Levites, The Presbyterian ministers displaced by the Act of Uniformity.
Michal, Catherine of Braganza (1638–1705), the childless Queen of Charles II.
Nadab, William, Lord Howard of Escrick (1626?–1694).
Pharaoh, Louis XIV of France.
Sagan of Jerusalem, Bishop of London.
Sanhedrin, Parliament.
Saul, Oliver Cromwell.
Shimei, Slingsby Bethel (1617–1697).
Sion, London.
Solymean rout, London mob.
Tyre, Holland.
Zadoc, William Sancroft (1617–1693), Archbishop of Canterbury.
Zimri, George Villiers, Duke of Buckingham (1628–1687).

TO THE READER

'TIS not my intention to make an Apology for my Poem: *Some will think it needs no Excuse; and others will receive none. The Design, I am sure, is honest: but he who draws his Pen for one Party, must expect to make Enemies of the other. For,* Wit *and* Fool, *are Consequents of* Whig *and* Tory: *And every man is a Knave or an Ass to the contrary side. There's a Treasury of Merits in the* Phanatick Church, *as well as in the* Papist; *and a Pennyworth to be had of Saintship, Honesty, and Poetry, for the Leud, the Factious, and the Blockheads: But the longest Chapter in* Deuteronomy, *has not Curses enough for an Anti-*Bromingham.[1] *My Comfort is, their manifest Prejudice to my Cause, will render their Judgment of less Authority against me. Yet if a* Poem *have a* Genius, *it will force its own reception in the World; for there's a sweetness in good Verse, which Tickles even while it Hurts: And no man can be heartily angry with him, who pleases him against his will. The Commendation of Adversaries, is the greatest Triumph of a Writer; because it never comes unless Extorted. But I can be satisfied on more easie terms: If I happen to please the more Moderate sort, I shall be sure of an honest Party; and, in all probability, of the best Judges: for, the least Concern'd, are commonly the least Corrupt. And, I confess, I have laid in for those, by rebating the* Satyre, (*where Justice woud allow it) from carrying too sharp an Edge. They, who can Criticize so weakly, as to imagine I have done my Worst, may be convinc'd, at their own Cost, that I can write Severely, with more ease, than I can Gently. I have but laugh'd at some mens Follies, when I coud have declaim'd against their Vices: and, other mens Vertues I have commended, as freely as I have tax'd their Crimes. And now, if you are a Malicious* Reader, *I expect you should return upon me, that I affect to be thought more Impartial than I am. But, if men are not to be judg'd by their Professions, God forgive you* Commonwealths-men, *for professing so plausibly for the Government. You cannot be so unconscionable, as to charge me for not Subscribing of my Name; for that woud reflect too grosly upon your own Party, who never dare; though they have the advantage of a Jury to secure them. If you like not my* Poem, *the fault may, possibly, be in my Writing:* (*though 'tis hard for an Author to judge against him-*

[1] *Bromingham* was slang for a Whig: Birmingham being notorious for its counterfeit coins.

self;) But, more probably, 'tis in your Morals, which cannot bear the truth of it. The Violent, on both sides, will condemn the Character of Absalom, *as either too favourably, or too hardly drawn. But, they are not the Violent, whom I desire to please. The fault, on the right hand, is to Extenuate, Palliate and Indulge; and, to confess freely, I have endeavour'd to commit it. Besides the respect which I owe his Birth, I have a greater for his Heroick vertues: and,* David *himself, coud not be more tender of the Young-mans Life, than I woud be of his Reputation. But, since the most excellent Natures are always the most easie; and, as being such, are the soonest perverted by ill Counsels, especially when baited with Fame and Glory; 'tis no more a wonder that he withstood not the temptations of* Achitophel, *than it was for* Adam, *not to have resisted the two Devils, the Serpent and the Woman. The conclusion of the Story, I purposely forbore to prosecute: because, I coud not obtain from my self, to shew* Absalom *Unfortunate. The Frame of it, was cut out, but for a Picture to the Waste; and, if the Draught be so far true, 'tis as much as I design'd.*

Were I the Inventor, who am onely the Historian, I shoud certainly conclude the Piece, with the Reconcilement of Absalom *to* David. *And, who knows but this may come to pass? Things were not brought to an Extremity where I left the Story: There seems, yet, to be room left for a Composure; hereafter, there may onely be for Pity. I have not so much as an uncharitable Wish against* Achitophel; *but, am content to be Accus'd of a good natur'd Errour; and, to hope with* Origen, *that the Devil himself may, at last, be sav'd. For which reason, in this* Poem, *he is neither brought to set his House in order, nor to dispose of his Person afterwards, as he in Wisedom shall think fit. God is infinitely merciful; and his Vicegerent is onely not so, because he is not Infinite.*

The true end of Satyre, *is the amendment of Vices by correction. And he who writes Honestly, is no more an Enemy to the Offender, than the Physician to the Patient, when he prescribes harsh Remedies to an inveterate Disease: for those, are onely in order to prevent the Chyrurgeon's work of an* Ense rescindendum,[1] *which I wish not to my very Enemies. To conclude all, If the Body Politique have any Analogy to the Natural, in my weak judgment, an Act of* Oblivion *were as necessary in a Hot, Distemper'd State, as an* Opiate *woud be in a Raging Feavour.*

[1] Something that must be cut away with the sword.

ABSALOM AND ACHITOPHEL

A POEM

IN pious Times, e'r Priest-Craft did begin,
Before *Polygamy* was made a Sin;
When Man, on many, multipli'd his kind,
E'r one to one was, cursedly, confin'd:
When Nature prompted, and no Law deni'd
Promiscuous Use of Concubine and Bride;
Then, *Israel*'s Monarch, after Heavens own heart,
His vigorous warmth did, variously, impart
To Wives and Slaves: And, wide as his Command,
Scatter'd his Maker's Image through the Land.
Michal, of Royal Blood, the Crown did wear;
A Soil ungrateful to the Tiller's care:
Not so the rest; for several Mothers bore
To God-like *David*, several Sons before.
But since like Slaves his Bed they did ascend,
No True Succession could their Seed attend.
Of all this Numerous Progeny was none
So Beautiful so Brave as *Absalon*:
Whether, inspir'd by some diviner Lust,
His Father got him with a greater Gust;
Or that his Conscious Destiny made way,
By manly Beauty to Imperial Sway.
Early in Foreign Fields he won Renown
With Kings and States alli'd to *Israels* Crown: [1]
In Peace the thoughts of War he coud remove,
And seem'd as he were onely born for Love.
Whate'r he did, was done with so much ease,
In him alone, 'twas Natural to please:
His motions all accompani'd with grace;
And *Paradise* was open'd in his face.
With secret Joy, indulgent *David* view'd
His Youthful Image in his Son renew'd:

[1] Monmouth had commanded the British troops serving under the French against the Dutch in 1672–73, and under the Dutch against the French in 1678. He gained distinction in both campaigns.

To all his wishes Nothing he deni'd;
And made the Charming *Annabel* his Bride.
What faults he had (for who from faults is free?)
His Father coud not, or he woud not see.
Some warm excesses, which the Law forbore,
Were constru'd Youth that purg'd by boiling o'r:
And *Amnon*'s Murther, by a specious Name,
Was call'd a Just Revenge for injur'd Fame.[1]
Thus prais'd, and Lov'd, the Noble Youth remain'd,
While *David*, undisturb'd, in *Sion* reign'd.
But Life can never be sincerely blest:
Heav'n punishes the bad, and proves the best.
The *Jews*, a Headstrong, Moody, Murm'ring race,
As ever tri'd th' extent and stretch of grace;
God's pamper'd People whom, debauch'd with ease,
No King could govern, nor no God could please;
(Gods they had tri'd of every shape and size,
That God-smiths could produce, or Priests devise:)
These *Adam*-wits, too fortunately free,
Began to dream they wanted liberty:
And when no rule, no president, was found
Of men, by Laws less circumscrib'd and bound,
They led their wild desires to Woods and Caves,
And thought that all but Savages were Slaves.
They who, when *Saul* was dead, without a blow,
Made foolish *Ishbosheth* the Crown forego;
Who banisht *David* did from *Hebron* bring,[2]
And, with a General shout, proclaim'd him King:
Those very *Jews*, who, at their very best,
Their Humour more than Loyalty exprest,
Now, wondred why, so long, they had obey'd
An Idol-Monarch which their hands had made:
Thought they might ruine him they coud create;
Or melt him to that Golden Calf, a State.
But these were random Bolts: No form'd Design,
Nor Interest made the Factious Croud to join:
The sober part of *Israel*, free from stain,

[1] This is a reference to the attack made on Sir John Coventry (*d.* 1682) in 1670 at the instigation of Monmouth. Coventry reflected on the King's affairs with actresses in a debate in the Commons, and was later waylaid and had his nose slit to the bone with a penknife.

[2] Charles II was crowned King in Scotland in 1651 but not in England until 1661; therefore, although he entered England in 1660 from the Continent, Dryden can say that his people brought him from Scotland.

Well knew the value of a peaceful reign:
And, looking backward with a wise afright,
Saw Seams of wounds, dishonest to the sight:
In contemplation of whose ugly Scars,
They curst the memory of Civil Wars.
The moderate sort of Men, thus qualifi'd,
Inclin'd the Ballance to the better side:
And, *David*'s mildness manag'd it so well,
The bad found no occasion to Rebel.
But, when to Sin our byast Nature leans,
The careful Devil is still at hand with means;
And providently Pimps for ill desires:
The Good Old Cause reviv'd, a Plot requires.
Plots, true or false, are necessary things,
To raise up Common-wealths, and ruine Kings.

Th' Inhabitants of old *Jerusalem*
Were *Jebusites*: the Town so call'd from them;
And their's the Native right—
But when the chosen People grew more strong,
The rightful cause at length became the wrong:
And every loss the men of *Jebus* bore,
They still were thought God's enemies the more.
Thus, worn and weaken'd, well or ill content,
Submit they must to *David*'s Government:
Impoverish't and depriv'd of all Command,
Their Taxes doubled as they lost their Land;
And, what was harder yet to flesh and blood,
Their Gods disgrac'd, and burnt like common Wood.
This set the Heathen Priesthood in a flame;
For Priests of all Religions are the same:
Of whatsoe'r descent their Godhead be,
Stock, Stone, or other homely Pedigree,
In his defence his Servants are as bold,
As if he had been born of beaten Gold.
The *Jewish Rabbins* though their Enemies,
In this conclude them honest men and wise:
For 'twas their duty, all the Learned think,
T' espouse his Cause by whom they eat and drink.
From hence began that Plot, the Nations Curse,
Bad in it self, but represented worse.
Rais'd in extremes, and in extremes decri'd;
With Oaths affirm'd, with dying Vows deni'd.

Not weigh'd, or winnow'd by the Multitude;
But swallow'd in the Mass, unchew'd and crude.
Some Truth there was, but dash'd and brew'd with Lies;
To please the Fools, and puzzle all the Wise.
Succeeding Times did equal Folly call,
Believing nothing, or believing all.
Th' *Egyptian* Rites the *Jebusites* embrac'd;
Where Gods were recommended by their taste.
Such sav'ry Deities must needs be good,
As serv'd at once for Worship and for Food.[1]
By force they could not Introduce these Gods;
For Ten to One, in former days was odds.
So Fraud was us'd, (the Sacrificers trade,)
Fools are more hard to Conquer than Persuade.
Their busie Teachers mingled with the *Jews*;
And rak'd, for Converts, even the Court and Stews:
Which *Hebrew* Priests the more unkindly took,
Because the Fleece accompanies the Flock.
Some thought they God's Anointed meant to slay
By Guns, invented since full many a day:
Our Author swears it not; but who can know
How far the Devil and *Jebusites* may go?
This Plot, which fail'd for want of common Sense,
Had yet a deep and dangerous Consequence:
For, as when raging Fevers boil the Blood,
The standing Lake soon floats into a Floud;
And ev'ry hostile Humour, which before
Slept quiet in its Channels, bubbles o're:
So, several Factions from this first Ferment,
Work up to Foam, and threat the Government.
Some by their Friends, more by themselves thought wise,
Oppos'd the Pow'r, to which they could not rise.
Some had in Courts been Great, and thrown from thence,
Like Fiends, were harden'd in Impenitence.
Some, by their Monarch's fatal mercy grown,
From Pardon'd Rebels, Kinsmen to the Throne;
Were rais'd in Pow'r and publick Office high:
Strong Bands, if Bands ungrateful men coud tie.
Of these the false *Achitophel* was first:
A Name to all succeeding Ages curst.
For close Designs, and crooked Counsels fit;

[1] A gibing reference to the Catholic doctrine of Transubstantiation.

Sagacious, Bold, and Turbulent of wit:
Restless, unfixt in Principles and Place;
In Pow'r unpleas'd, impatient of Disgrace.
A fiery Soul, which working out its way,
Fretted the Pigmy-Body to decay:
And o'r inform'd the Tenement of Clay.[1]
A daring Pilot in extremity;
Pleas'd with the Danger, when the Waves went high
He sought the Storms; but for a Calm unfit,
Would Steer too nigh the Sands, to boast his Wit.
Great Wits are sure to Madness near alli'd;
And thin Partitions do their Bounds divide:
Else, why should he, with Wealth and Honour blest,
Refuse his Age the needful hours of Rest?
Punish a Body which he coud not please;
Bankrupt of Life, yet Prodigal of Ease?
And all to leave, what with his Toil he won,
To that unfeather'd, two-legg'd thing, a Son:
Got, while his Soul did huddled Notions trie;
And born a shapeless Lump, like Anarchy.[2]
In friendship false, implacable in Hate:
Resolv'd to Ruine or to Rule the State.
To Compass this, the Triple Bond he broke;
The Pillars of the Publick safety shook:
And fitted *Israel* for a Foreign Yoke.[3]
Then, seiz'd with Fear, yet still affecting Fame,
Usurp'd a Patriot's All-attoning Name.
So easie still it proves in Factious Times,
With publick Zeal to cancel private Crimes:
How safe is Treason, and how sacred ill,
Where none can sin against the Peoples Will:
Where Crouds can wink; and no offence be known,
Since in anothers guilt they find their own.
Yet, Fame deserv'd, no Enemy can grudge;
The Statesman we abhor, but praise the Judge.[4]

[1] Shaftesbury was a man of poor physique and sickly constitution.

[2] Shaftesbury's son, the second Earl, was entirely without character or ability.

[3] Shaftesbury was a signatory to the second Treaty with France in 1670 which ended the Triple Alliance of 1667 between England, Sweden, and Holland, directed against France. He was ignorant of the first Treaty with France of 1670 by which Charles II pledged himself to re-establish Roman Catholicism in England.

[4] Shaftesbury was Lord Chancellor in 1672–73 but was dismissed from office.

In *Israels* Courts ne'r sat an *Abbethdin*
With more discerning Eyes, or Hands more
  clean:
Unbrib'd, unsought, the Wretched to redress;
Swift of Dispatch, and easie of Access.
Oh, had he been content to serve the Crown,
With vertues onely proper to the Gown;
Or, had the rankness of the Soil been freed
From Cockle, that opprest the Noble Seed:
David, for him his tuneful Harp had strung,
And Heav'n had wanted one Immortal Song.
But wild Ambition loves to slide, not stand;
And Fortunes Ice prefers to Vertues Land:
Achitophel, grown weary to possess
A lawful Fame, and lazie Happiness;
Disdain'd the Golden Fruit to gather free,
And lent the croud his Arm to shake the Tree.
Now, manifest of Crimes, contriv'd long since,
He stood at bold Defiance with his Prince:
Held up the Buckler of the peoples Cause,
Against the Crown; and sculk'd behind the Laws.
The wish'd occasion of the Plot he takes;
Some Circumstances finds, but more he makes.
By buzzing Emissaries, fills the ears
Of listning Crouds, with Jealousies and Fears
Of Arbitrary Counsels brought to light,
And proves the King himself a *Jebusite*.
Weak Arguments! which yet he knew full well,
Were strong with People easie to Rebel.
For, govern'd by the *Moon*, the giddy *Jews*
Tread the same Track when she the Prime renews:
And once in twenty Years, their Scribes Record,
By natural Instinct they change their Lord.
Achitophel still wants a Chief, and none
Was found so fit as Warlike *Absalon*:
Not, that he wish'd his Greatness to create,
(For Polititians neither love nor hate:)
But, for he knew, his Title not allow'd,
Would keep him still depending on the croud:
That Kingly pow'r, thus ebbing out, might be
Drawn to the Dregs of a Democracie.
Him he attempts, with studied Arts to please,
And sheds his Venome, in such words as these.

Auspicious Prince! at whose Nativity
Some Royal Planet rul'd the Southern Sky;
Thy longing Countries Darling and Desire;
Their cloudy Pillar, and their guardian Fire:
Their second *Moses*, whose extended Wand
Divides the Seas, and shews the promis'd Land:
Whose dawning Day, in every distant Age,
Has exercis'd the Sacred Prophets rage:
The Peoples Pray'r, the glad Diviners theam,
The Young mens Vision, and the Old mens Dream!
Thee, *Saviour*, Thee, the Nations Vows confess;
And, never satisfi'd with seeing, bless:
Swift, unbespoken Pomps, thy steps proclaim,
And stammering Babes are taught to lisp thy Name.
How long wilt thou the general Joy detain;
Starve, and defraud the People of thy Reign?
Content ingloriously to pass thy days
Like one of Vertues Fools that Feeds on Praise;
Till thy fresh Glories, which now shine so bright,
Grow Stale and Tarnish with our dayly sight.
Believe me, Royal Youth, thy Fruit must be,
Or gather'd Ripe, or rot upon the Tree.
Heav'n, has to all allotted, soon or late,
Some lucky Revolution of their Fate:
Whose Motions, if we watch and guide with Skill,
(For humane Good depends on humane Will,)
Our fortune rolls, as from a smooth Descent,
And, from the first Impression, takes the Bent:
But, if unseiz'd, she glides away like wind;
And leaves repenting Folly far behind.
Now, now she meets you, with a glorious prize,
And spreads her Locks before her as she flies.
Had thus Old *David*, from whose Loins you spring,
Not dar'd, when Fortune call'd him, to be King,
At *Gath* an Exile he might still remain;
And Heavens Anointing Oil had been in vain.
Let his successful Youth your hopes engage;
But shun th' example of Declining Age:
Behold him setting in his Western Skies,
The Shadows lengthening as the Vapours rise.
He is not now, as when on *Jordan*'s Sand
The Joyful People throng'd to see him Land,
Cov'ring the *Beach*, and blackning all the *Strand*:

But, like the Prince of Angels from his height,
Comes tumbling downward with diminish'd light:
Betray'd by one poor Plot to publick Scorn:
(Our onely blessing since his curst Return:)
Those heaps of People which one Sheaf did bind,
Blown off, and scatter'd by a puff of Wind.
What strength can he to your Designs oppose,
Naked of Friends, and round beset with Foes?
If *Pharaoh*'s doubtful Succour he should use,
A Foreign Aid woud more incense the *Jews*:
Proud *Egypt* woud dissembled Friendship bring;
Foment the War, but not support the King:
Nor woud the Royal Party e'r unite
With *Pharaoh*'s Arms, t' assist the *Jebusite*;
Or if they shoud, their Interest soon woud break,
And, with such odious Aid, make *David* weak.
All sorts of men, by my successful Arts,
Abhorring Kings, estrange their alter'd Hearts
From *David*'s Rule: And 'tis the general Cry,
Religion, Common-wealth, and Liberty.
If you, as Champion of the Publique Good,
Add to their Arms a Chief of Royal Blood;
What may not *Israel* hope, and what Applause
Might such a General gain by such a Cause?
Not barren Praise alone, that Gaudy Flow'r,
Fair onely to the sight, but solid Pow'r:
And Nobler is a limited Command,
Giv'n by the Love of all your Native Land,
Than a Successive Title, Long, and Dark,
Drawn from the Mouldy Rolls of *Noah*'s Ark.

What cannot Praise effect in Mighty Minds,
When Flattery Sooths, and when Ambition Blinds!
Desire of Pow'r, on Earth a vitious Weed,
Yet, sprung from High, is of Cœlestial Seed:
In God 'tis Glory: And when Men Aspire,
'Tis but a Spark too much of Heavenly Fire.
Th' Ambitious Youth, too Covetous of Fame,
Too full of Angels Metal in his Frame;
Unwarily was led from Vertues ways;
Made Drunk with Honour, and debauch'd with Praise.
Half loath, and half consenting to the Ill,
(For Loyal Blood within him strugled still)

He thus repli'd.—And what Pretence have I
To take up Arms for Publick Liberty?
My Father Governs with unquestion'd Right;
The Faiths Defender, and Mankinds Delight:
Good, Gracious, Just, observant of the Laws;
And Heav'n by Wonders has espous'd his Cause.
Whom has he Wrong'd in all his Peaceful Reign?
Who sues for Justice to his Throne in Vain?
What Millions has he Pardon'd of his Foes,
Whom Just Revenge did to his Wrath expose?
Mild, Easie, Humble, Studious of our Good;
Enclin'd to Mercy, and averse from Blood.
If Mildness Ill with Stubborn *Israel* Suit,
His Crime is God's beloved Attribute.
What could he gain, his People to Betray,
Or change his Right, for Arbitrary Sway?
Let Haughty *Pharaoh* Curse with such a Reign,
His Fruitful *Nile*, and Yoak a Servile Train.
If *David*'s Rule *Jerusalem* Displease,
The *Dog-star* heats their Brains to this Disease.
Why then should I, Encouraging the Bad,
Turn Rebel, and run Popularly Mad?
Were he a Tyrant who, by Lawless Might,
Opprest the *Jews*, and rais'd the *Jebusite*,
Well might I mourn; but Natures holy Bands
Woud Curb my Spirits, and Restrain my Hands:
The People might assert their Liberty;
But what was Right in them, were Crime in me.
His Favour leaves me nothing to require;
Prevents my Wishes, and out-runs Desire.
What more can I expect while *David* lives?
All but his Kingly Diadem he gives:
And that: But there he paus'd; then Sighing, said,
Is Justly destin'd for a Worthier Head.
For when my Father from his Toyls shall Rest,
And late Augment the Number of the Blest:
His Lawful Issue shall the Throne ascend;
Or the *Collat'ral* line where that shall end.
His Brother, though Opprest with Vulgar Spight,
Yet Dauntless and Secure of Native Right,
Of every Royal Vertue stands possest;
Still Dear to all the Bravest, and the Best.
His Courage Foes, his Friends his Truth Proclaim;

His Loyalty the King, the World his Fame.
His Mercy ev'n th' Offending croud will find:
For sure he comes of a Forgiving Kind.
Why shoud I then Repine at Heavens Decree;
Which gives me no Pretence to Royalty?
Yet oh that Fate, Propitiously Inclin'd,
Had rais'd my Birth, or had debas'd my Mind;
To my large Soul, not all her Treasure lent,
And then betrai'd it to a mean Descent.
I find, I find my mounting Spirits Bold,
And *David*'s Part disdains my Mothers Mold.
Why am I scanted by a Niggard-Birth?
My Soul Disclaims the Kindred of her Earth:
And made for Empire, Whispers me within;
Desire of Greatness is a God-like Sin.

Him Staggering so when Hells dire Agent found,
While fainting vertue scarce maintain'd her Ground,
He pours fresh Forces in, and thus Replies:
Th' Eternal God, Supreamly Good and Wise,
Imparts not these Prodigious Gifts in vain;
What Wonders are Reserv'd to bless your Reign?
Against your will your Arguments have shown,
Such vertue's only giv'n to guide a Throne.
Not that your Father's Mildness I contemn;
But manly Force becomes the Diadem.
'Tis true, he grants the People all they crave;
And more perhaps than Subjects ought to have:
For lavish Grants suppose a Monarch tame,
And more his Goodness than his Wit proclaim.
But when should People strive their Bonds to break,
If not when Kings are Negligent or Weak?
Let him give on till he can give no more,
The thrifty Sanhedrin shall keep him poor:
And every shekle which he can receive,
Shall cost a Limb of his Prerogative.
To ply him with new Plots, shall be my care;
Or plunge him deep in some Expensive War;
Which, when his Treasure can no more supply,
He must, with the Remains of Kingship, buy.
His faithful Friends, our Jealousies and Fears
Call *Jebusites*; and *Pharaoh*'s Pensioners:
Whom, when our Fury from his Aid has torn,

He shall be naked left to publick Scorn.
The next Successor, whom I fear and hate,
My Arts have made obnoxious to the State;
Turn'd all his Vertues to his Overthrow,
And gain'd our Elders to pronounce a Foe.
His Right, for Sums of necessary Gold,
Shall first be Pawn'd, and afterwards be Sold:
Till time shall Ever-wanting *David* draw,
To pass your doubtful Title into Law:
If not; the People have a Right Supreme
To make their Kings; for Kings are made for them.
All Empire is no more than pow'r in Trust:
Which when resum'd, can be no longer Just.
Succession, for the general Good design'd,
In its own wrong a Nation cannot bind:
If altering that, the People can relieve,
Better one suffer, than a Nation grieve.
The *Jews* well know their pow'r: e'r *Saul* they chose,
God was their King, and God they durst Depose.
Urge now your Piety, your Filial Name,
A Father's Right, and Fear of future Fame;
The Publick Good, that Universal Call,
To which even Heav'n submitted, answers all.
Nor let his Love Enchant your generous Mind;
'Tis Natures trick to propagate her Kind.
Our fond Begetters, who would never die,
Love but themselves in their Posterity.
Or let his Kindness by th' Effects be tri'd,
Or let him lay his vain Pretence aside.
God said he lov'd your Father; coud he bring
A better Proof, than to Anoint him King?
It surely shew'd he lov'd the Shepherd well,
Who gave so fair a Flock as *Israel*.
Woud *David* have you thought his Darling Son?
What means he then, to Alienate the Crown?
The name of Godly he may blush to bear:
'Tis after Gods own heart to Cheat his Heir.
He to his Brother gives Supreme Command;
To you a Legacie of Barren Land:
Perhaps th' old Harp, on which he thrums his Lays:
Or some dull *Hebrew* Ballad in your Praise.
Then the next Heir, a Prince, Severe and Wise
Already looks on you with Jealous Eyes;

Sees through the thin Disguises of your Arts,
And marks your Progress in the Peoples Hearts.
Though now his mighty Soul its Grief contains,
He meditates Revenge who least Complains;
And like a Lion, Slumb'ring in the way,
Or Sleep-dissembling, while he waits his Prey,
His fearless Foes within his Distance draws;
Constrains his Roaring, and Contracts his Paws:
Till at the last, his time for Fury found,
He shoots with sudden Vengeance from the Ground:
The Prostrate Vulgar, passes o'r, and Spares;
But with a Lordly Rage, his Hunters tears.
Your Case no tame Expedients will afford;
Resolve on Death, or Conquest by the Sword,
Which for no less a Stake than Life, you Draw;
And Self-defence is Natures Eldest Law.
Leave the warm People no Considering time;
For then Rebellion may be thought a Crime.
Prevail your self of what Occasion gives,
But trie your Title while your Father lives:
And that your Arms may have a fair Pretence,
Proclaim, you take them in the King's Defence:
Whose Sacred Life each minute woud Expose
To Plots from seeming Friends and secret Foes.
And who can sound the depth of *David*'s Soul?
Perhaps his fear, his kindness may Controul.
He fears his Brother, though he loves his Son,
For plighted Vows too late to be undone.
If so, by Force he wishes to be gain'd;
Like Womens Leachery, to seem Constrain'd:
Doubt not; but when he most affects the Frown,
Commit a pleasing Rape upon the Crown.
Secure his Person to secure your Cause;
They who possess the Prince, possess the Laws.

He said, And this Advice above the rest
With *Absalom*'s Mild Nature suited best;
Unblam'd of Life, (Ambition set aside,)
Not stain'd with Cruelty, nor puft with Pride.
How happy had he been, if Destiny
Had higher plac'd his Birth, or not so high!
His Kingly vertues might have claim'd a Throne;
And blest all other Countries but his own:

But charming Greatness since so few refuse,
'Tis Juster to Lament him, than Accuse.
Strong were his hopes a Rival to remove,
With Blandishments to gain the publick Love;
To Head the Faction while their Zeal was hot,
And Popularly prosecute the Plot.
To farther this, *Achitophel* Unites
The malecontents of all the *Israelites*:
Whose differing Parties he coud wisely Join,
For several Ends, to serve the same Design.
The Best, and of the Princes some were such,
Who thought the pow'r of Monarchy too much:
Mistaken Men, and Patriots in their Hearts;
Not Wicked, but seduc'd by Impious Arts.
By these the Springs of Property were bent,
And wound so high, they Crack'd the Government.
The next for Interest sought t' embroil the State,
To sell their Duty at a dearer rate;
And make their *Jewish* Markets of the Throne;
Pretending Publick Good, to serve their own.
Others thought Kings an useless heavy Load,
Who Cost too much, and did too little Good.
These were for laying Honest *David* by,
On Principles of pure good Husbandry.
With them join'd all th' Haranguers of the Throng,
That thought to get Preferment by the Tongue.
Who follow next, a double danger bring,
Not onely hating *David*, but the King;
The *Solymæan* Rout; well Vers'd of old
In Godly Faction, and in Treason bold;
Cowring and Quaking at a Conqu'ror's Sword,
But Lofty to a Lawful Prince Restor'd;
Saw with Disdain an *Ethnick* Plot begun,
And Scorn'd by *Jebusites* to be Out-done.
Hot *Levites* Headed these; who pul'd before
From th' *Ark*, which in the Judges days they bore,
Resum'd their Cant, and with a Zealous Crie,
Pursu'd their old belov'd Theocracie.
Where Sanhedrin and Priest enslav'd the Nation,
And justifi'd their Spoils by Inspiration:
For who so fit for Reign as *Aaron*'s Race,
If once Dominion they could found in Grace?
These led the Pack; though not of surest scent,

Yet deepest mouth'd against the Government.
A numerous Host of dreaming Saints succeed;
Of the true old Enthusiastick Breed:
'Gainst Form and Order they their Pow'r imploy;
Nothing to Build, and all things to Destroy.
But far more numerous was the Herd of such,
Who think too little, and who talk too much.
These, out of meer instinct, they knew not why,
Ador'd their Father's God, and Property:
And, by the same blind Benefit of Fate,
The Devil and the *Jebusite* did hate:
Born to be sav'd, even in their own despight;
Because they could not help believing right.
Such were the Tools; but a whole Hydra more
Remains, of sprouting heads too long, to score.
Some of their Chiefs were Princes of the Land:
In the first Rank of these did *Zimri* [1] stand:
A man so various, that he seem'd to be
Not one, but all Mankind's Epitome.
Stiff in Opinions, always in the wrong;
Was Every thing by starts, and Nothing long:
But, in the course of one revolving Moon,
Was Chymist, Fidler, States-Man, and Buffoon:
Then all for Women, Painting, Rhiming, Drinking;
Besides ten thousand Freaks that dy'd in thinking.
Blest Madman, who coud every hour employ,
With something New to wish, or to enjoy!
Railing and praising were his usual Theams;
And both (to shew his Judgment) in Extreams:
So over Violent, or over Civil,
That every Man, with him, was God or Devil.
In squandering Wealth was his peculiar Art:
Nothing went unrewarded, but Desert.
Begger'd by Fools, whom still he found too late:
He had his Jest, and they had his Estate.
He laugh'd himself from Court; then sought Relief
By forming Parties, but could ne'r be Chief:
For, spight of him, the weight of Business fell
On *Absalom* and wise *Achitophel*:

[1] The Duke of Buckingham, poet, wit, and politician, was a man of brilliant gifts but of unstable and profligate character. He was at this time a supporter of Shaftesbury. He had superbly ridiculed Dryden and his plays in the comedy of *The Rehearsal*, 1671. Dryden had thus a double reason for satirising him.

Thus, wicked but in Will, of Means bereft,
He left not Faction, but of that was left.

Titles and Names 'twere tedious to reherse
Of Lords, below the Dignity of Verse.
Wits, Warriors, Commonwealths-men, were the best:
Kind Husbands and meer Nobles all the rest.
And, therefore in the name of Dulness, be
The well-hung *Balaam* and cold *Caleb* free.
And Canting *Nadab* let Oblivion damn,
Who made new Porridge for the Paschal Lamb.[1]
Let Friendships holy Band some Names assure:
Some their own Worth, and some let Scorn secure.
Nor shall the Rascal Rabble here have Place,
Whom Kings no Titles gave, and God no Grace:
Not Bull-fac'd *Jonas*,[2] who coud Statutes draw
To mean Rebellion, and make Treason Law.
But he, though bad, is follow'd by a worse,
The Wretch, who Heav'ns Anointed dar'd to Curse.
Shimei,[3] whose Youth did early Promise bring
Of Zeal to God, and Hatred to his King;
Did wisely from Expensive Sins refrain,
And never broke the Sabbath, but for Gain:
Nor ever was he known an Oath to vent,
Or curse, unless against the Government.
Thus, heaping Wealth, by the most ready way
Among the *Jews*, which was to Cheat and Pray;
The City, to reward his pious Hate
Against his Master, chose him Magistrate:
His Hand a Vare [4] of Justice did uphold;
His Neck was loaded with a Chain of Gold.
During his Office, Treason was no Crime.
The Sons of *Belial* had a Glorious Time:
For *Shimei*, though not prodigal of pelf,
Yet lov'd his wicked Neighbour as himself:

[1] Lord Howard was said to have taken the Sacrament in 'lamb's wool', a concoction of ale, sauce, and roasted apples, instead of in wine.

[2] Sir William Jones, as attorney-general, conducted the prosecutions of the Popish Plot but resigned office in order to support Shaftesbury. He secured the passage through the Commons in 1680 of the Bill—which he may have drawn up—to exclude the Duke of York from the succession.

[3] Slingsby Bethel, a wealthy merchant and conspicuous republican, was elected sheriff of London in 1680 but his mean state during his term of office offended many citizens.

[4] Vare, from the Spanish *vara*, means a wand.

When two or three were gather'd to declaim
Against the Monarch of *Jerusalem*,
Shimei was always in the midst of them.
And, if they Curst the King when he was by,
Woud rather Curse, than break good Company.
If any durst his Factious Friends accuse,
He pact a Jury of dissenting *Jews*:
Whose fellow-feeling, in the godly Cause,
Woud free the suff'ring Saint from Humane laws.
For Laws are onely made to Punish those
Who serve the King, and to protect his Foes.
If any leisure time he had from Pow'r,
(Because 'tis Sin to mis-employ an hour;)
His bus'ness was, by Writing, to persuade,
That Kings were Useless, and a Clog to Trade:
And, that his noble Stile he might refine,
No *Rechabite* more shund the fumes of Wine.
Chaste were his Cellars; and his Shrieval Board
The Grossness of a City Feast abhor'd:
His Cooks, with long disuse, their Trade forgot;
Cool was his Kitchin, though his Brains were hot.
Such frugal Vertue Malice may accuse;
But sure 'twas necessary to the *Jews*:
For Towns once burnt, such Magistrates require
As dare not tempt Gods Providence by Fire.
With Spiritual Food he fed his Servants well,
But free from Flesh, that made the *Jews* rebel:
And *Moses*'s Laws he held in more account
For forty days of Fasting in the Mount.
To speak the rest, who better are forgot,
Would tire a well-breath'd Witness of the Plot:
Yet, *Corah*, thou shalt from Oblivion pass;
Erect thy self thou Monumental Brass:
High as the Serpent of thy Metal made,
While Nations stand secure beneath thy shade.
What tho his Birth were base, yet Comets rise
From Earthy Vapours e'r they shine in Skies.
Prodigious Actions may as well be done
By Weaver's issue, as by Prince's Son.
This Arch-Attestor for the Publick Good,
By that one Deed Enobles all his Bloud.
Who ever ask'd the Witnesses high race,
Whose Oath with Martyrdom did *Stephen* grace?

Ours was a *Levite*,[1] and as times went then,
His Tribe were God-almighties Gentlemen.
Sunk were his Eyes, his Voice was harsh and loud,
Sure signs he neither cholerick was, nor Proud:
His long Chin prov'd his Wit; his Saint-like Grace
A Church Vermilion, and a *Moses*'s Face.[2]
His memory, miraculously great,
Coud Plots, exceeding mans belief, repeat;
Which, therefore cannot be accounted Lies,
For humane Wit coud never such devise.
Some future Truths are mingled in his Book;
But, where the Witness fail'd, the Prophet spoke:
Some things like Visionary flights appear;
The Spirit caught him up, the Lord knows where:
And gave him his *Rabbinical* degree,
Unknown to Foreign University.[3]
His Judgment yet his Mem'ry did excel;
Which piec'd his wondrous Evidence so well:
And suited to the temper of the Times;
Then groaning under *Jebusitick* Crimes.
Let *Israels* Foes suspect his Heav'nly call,
And rashly judge his Writ Apocryphal;
Our Laws for such affronts have Forfeits made:
He takes his Life, who takes away his Trade.
Were I my self in Witness *Corah*'s place,
The Wretch who did me such a dire disgrace,
Shoud whet my memory, though once forgot,
To make him an Appendix of my Plot.
His Zeal to Heav'n, made him his Prince despise,
And load his Person with indignities:
But Zeal peculiar priviledge affords,
Indulging latitude to deeds and words.
And *Corah* might for *Agag*'s [4] murther call,
In terms as course as *Samuel* us'd to *Saul*.

[1] Titus Oates had taken orders in the Church of England following his father's lead who, after being a ribbon-weaver and an Anabaptist minister, was also a Church of England clergyman.

[2] The ruddy complexion of a clergyman and a shining expression like Moses's when he came down from Mount Sinai.

[3] Oates claimed to have received the degree of Doctor of Divinity from Salamanca, a place which he is known never to have visited.

[4] Sir Edmund Berry Godfrey, the London Magistrate before whom Oates deposed on oath his story of the Popish Plot, was murdered on Primrose Hill on 12 October 1678. The Protestants accused the Catholics of his murder and the Catholics retaliated by accusing the Whigs of murdering him in order to give substance to the Plot.

What others in his Evidence did join,
(The best that coud be had for love or coin,)
In *Corah*'s own predicament will fall:
For *Witness* is a Common Name to all.

Surrounded thus with Friends of every sort,
Deluded *Absalom* forsakes the Court:
Impatient of high hopes, urg'd with renown,
And Fir'd with near possession of a Crown:
Th' admiring Croud are dazled with surprize,
And on his goodly person feed their eyes:
His joy conceal'd, he sets himself to show;
On each side bowing popularly low:
His looks, his gestures, and his words he frames,
And with familiar ease repeats their Names.
Thus, form'd by Nature, furnish'd out with Arts,
He glides unfelt into their secret hearts:
Then, with a kind compassionating look,
And sighs, bespeaking pity e'r he spoke:
Few words he said; but easie those and fit:
More slow than Hybla drops, and far more sweet.

I mourn, my Country-men, your lost Estate;
Though far unable to prevent your Fate:
Behold a Banish'd man,[1] for your dear cause
Expos'd a prey to Arbitrary Laws!
Yet oh! that I alone coud be undone,
Cut off from Empire, and no more a Son!
Now all your Liberties a spoil are made;
Ægypt and *Tyrus* intercept your Trade,
And *Jebusites* your Sacred Rites invade.
My Father, whom with reverence yet I name,
Charm'd into ease, is careless of his Fame:
And, brib'd with petty sums of Foreign Gold,
Is grown in *Bathsheba*'s Embraces old:
Exalts his Enemies, his Friends destroys:
And all his pow'r against himself imploys.
He gives, and let him give my right away:
But why should he his own, and yours betray?

[1] Monmouth had been sent out of the country by the King in Sept. 1679 but returned without permission in Nov. He was ordered to leave the country again and, when he disobeyed, was deprived of all his offices and banished from the Court.

He, onely he can make the Nation bleed,
And he alone from my revenge is freed.
Take then my tears (with that he wip'd his Eyes)
'Tis all the Aid my present pow'r supplies:
No Court-Informer can these Arms accuse;
These Arms may Sons against their Fathers use;
And, 'tis my wish, the next Successor's Reign
May make no other *Israelite* complain.

Youth, Beauty, Graceful Action, seldom fail:
But Common Interest always will prevail:
And pity never Ceases to be shown
To him, who makes the Peoples wrongs his own.
The croud, (that still believe their Kings oppress,)
With lifted hands their young *Messiah* bless:
Who now begins his Progress to ordain;
With Chariots, Horsemen, and a num'rous train: [1]
From East to West his Glories he displays:
And, like the Sun, the Promis'd Land surveys.
Fame runs before him, as the Morning-Star;
And shouts of Joy salute him from afar:
Each house receives him as a Guardian God;
And Consecrates the Place of his abode:
But hospitable Treats did most commend
Wise *Issachar*, his wealthy Western Friend.
This moving Court, that caught the Peoples Eyes,
And seem'd but Pomp, did other Ends disguise:
Achitophel had form'd it, with intent
To sound the depths, and fathom where it went,
The Peoples hearts; distinguish Friends from Foes;
And trie their strength, before they came to Blows.
Yet all was colour'd with a smooth pretence
Of specious love, and duty to their Prince.
Religion, and redress of Grievances,
Two names, that always cheat and always please,
Are often urg'd; and good King *David*'s life
Endanger'd by a Brother and a Wife.
Thus, in a Pageant Shew, a Plot is made;
And Peace it self is War in Masquerade.
Oh foolish *Israel*! never warn'd by Ill:

[1] Monmouth made a royal progress through Western England after his banishment from Court and his attractive personality gained him and the Whigs many supporters.

Still the same Bait, and circumvented still!
Did ever men forsake their present ease,
In midst of health imagine a Disease;
Take pains Contingent mischiefs to foresee,
Make Heirs for Monarchs, and for God decree?
What shall we think! Can People give away
Both for themselves and Sons, their Native sway?
Then they are left Defenceless to the Sword
Of each unbounded Arbitrary Lord:
And Laws are vain, by which we Right enjoy,
If Kings unquestion'd can those Laws destroy.
Yet, if the Croud be Judge of Fit and Just,
And Kings are onely Officers in Trust,
Then this resuming Cov'nant was declar'd
When Kings were made, or is for ever bar'd:
If those who gave the Scepter, coud not tie
By their own Deed their own Posterity,
How then coud *Adam* bind his future Race?
How coud his Forfeit on Mankind take place?
Or how coud heavenly Justice damn us all,
Who ne'r consented to our Fathers Fall?
Then Kings are Slaves to those whom they command,
And Tenants to their Peoples pleasure stand.
Add, that the Pow'r for Property allow'd,
Is mischievously seated in the croud:
For who can be secure of private Right,
If Sovereign Sway may be dissolv'd by Might?
Nor is the Peoples Judgment always true:
The Most may err as grosly as the Few.
And faultless Kings run down, by Common Cry,
For Vice, Oppression and for Tyranny.
What Standard is there in a fickle rout,
Which, flowing to the Mark, runs faster out?
Nor onely crouds, but Sanhedrins may be
Infected with this publick Lunacy:
And Share the madness of Rebellious Times,
To Murther Monarchs for Imagin'd crimes.
If they may Give and Take when e'r they please,
Not Kings alone, (the Godheads Images,)
But Government it self at length must fall
To Natures state, where all have Right to all.
Yet, grant our lords the people Kings can make,
What prudent men a setled Throne woud shake?

For whatso'er their Sufferings were before,
That change they Covet makes them suffer more.
All other Errors but disturb a State;
But Innovation is the Blow of Fate.
If ancient Fabricks nod, and threat to fall,
To Patch the Flaws, and Buttress up the Wall,
Thus far 'tis Duty; but here fix the Mark:
For all beyond it is to touch our Ark.
To change Foundations, cast the Frame anew,
Is work for Rebels who base Ends pursue:
At once Divine and Humane Laws controul;
And mend the Parts by ruine of the Whole.
The tamp'ring World is subject to this Curse,
To Physick their Disease into a Worse.

Now what Relief can Righteous *David* bring?
How Fatal 'tis to be too good a King!
Friends he has few, so high the madness grows;
Who dare be such, must be the Peoples Foes:
Yet some there were, ev'n in the worst of days;
Some let me name, and Naming is to praise.

In this short File *Barzillai* [1] first appears;
Barzillai crown'd with Honour and with Years:
Long since, the rising Rebels he withstood
In Regions Waste, beyond the *Jordans* Flood:
Unfortunately Brave to buoy the State;
But sinking underneath his Master's Fate:
In Exile with his God-like Prince he Mourn'd;
For him he Suffer'd, and with him Return'd.
The Court he practis'd, not the Courtier's Art:
Large was his Wealth, but larger was his Heart:
Which, well the Noblest Objects knew to chuse,
The Fighting Warriour, and Recording Muse.
His Bed coud once a Fruitful Issue boast:
Now more than half a Father's Name is lost.
His Eldest Hope,[2] with every Grace adorn'd,

[1] The Duke of Ormonde, Lord-Lieutenant of Ireland, was an ardent royalist, and a man of remarkable purity and integrity of character, who, after being defeated in Ireland during the Civil War, was in exile until the Restoration when he was restored to the offices he had held under Charles I.

[2] Ormonde's eldest son was Thomas, Earl of Ossory (1634–1680), who, in John Evelyn's words, 'deserved all that a sincere friend, a brave soldier, a virtuous courtier, a loyal subject, an honest man, a bountiful master, and good christian, could deserve of his prince and country'.

By me (so Heav'n will have it) always Mourn'd,
And always honour'd, snatch'd in Manhoods prime
B' unequal Fates, and Providences crime:
Yet not before the Goal of Honour won,
All Parts fulfill'd of Subject and of Son;
Swift was the Race, but short the Time to run.
Oh Narrow Circle, but of Pow'r Divine,
Scanted in Space, but perfect in thy Line!
By Sea, by Land, thy Matchless Worth was known;
Arms thy Delight, and War was all thy Own:
Thy force, Infus'd, the fainting *Tyrians* prop'd:
And haughty *Pharaoh* found his Fortune stop'd.
Oh Ancient Honour, Oh unconquer'd Hand,
Whom Foes unpunish'd never coud withstand!
But *Israel* was unworthy of thy Name:
Short is the date of all Immoderate Fame.
It looks as Heav'n our Ruine had design'd,
And durst not trust thy Fortune and thy Mind.
Now, free from Earth, thy disencumbred Soul
Mounts up, and leaves behind the Clouds and Starry
Pole:
From thence thy kindred Legions maist thou bring,
To aid the Guardian Angel of thy King.
Here stop my Muse, here cease thy painful flight;
No Pinions can pursue Immortal height:
Tell good *Barzillai* thou canst sing no more,
And tell thy Soul she should have fled before;
Or fled she with his life, and left this Verse
To hang on her departed Patron's Herse?
Now take thy steepy flight from Heav'n, and see
If thou canst find on Earth another *He*;
Another He would be too hard to find,
See then whom thou canst see not far behind.
Zadoc the Priest, whom, shunning Pow'r and Place,
His lowly mind advanc'd to *David*'s Grace:
With him the *Sagan* of *Jerusalem*,[1]
Of hospitable Soul and noble Stem;
Him of the Western dome,[2] whose weighty sense

[1] The Bishop of London was Henry Compton (1632–1713), who had superintended the education of the Duke of York's daughters, Mary and Anne.

[2] A reference to John Dolben (1625–1686), Bishop of Rochester and Dean of Westminster. The 'Western dome' is Westminster Abbey, and the 'Prophets Sons' the boys of Westminster School.

Flows in fit words and heavenly eloquence.
The Prophets Sons by such Example led,
To Learning and to Loyalty were bred:
For *Colleges* on bounteous Kings depend,
And never Rebel was to Arts a Friend.
To these succeed the Pillars of the Laws,
Who best coud plead, and best can judge a Cause.
Next them a train of Loyal Peers ascend:
Sharp judging *Adriel*,[1] the Muses Friend,
Himself a Muse:—in Sanhedrins debate
True to his Prince; but not a Slave of State.
Whom *David*'s love with Honours did adorn,
That from his disobedient Son were torn.[2]
Jotham [3] of piercing Wit and pregnant Thought,
Endew'd by Nature, and by Learning taught
To move Assemblies, who but onely tri'd
The worse awhile, then chose the better side;
Nor chose alone, but turn'd the Balance too;
So much the weight of one brave man can do.
Hushai,[4] the Friend of *David* in distress,
In publick storms of manly stedfastness;
By Foreign Treaties he inform'd his Youth;
And join'd Experience to his Native Truth.
His frugal care suppli'd the wanting Throne;
Frugal for that, but bounteous of his own:
'Tis easie Conduct when Exchequers flow;
But hard the task to manage well the low:
For Sovereign Power is too deprest or high,
When Kings are forc'd to sell, or Crouds to buy.
Indulge one labour more, my weary Muse,
For *Amiel*,[5] who can *Amiel*'s praise refuse?
Of ancient race by birth, but nobler yet

[1] The Earl of Mulgrave was both a poet and a particular friend and patron of Dryden.

[2] Mulgrave was invested with some of the offices taken from Monmouth in 1679.

[3] The Marquis of Halifax had once supported Shaftesbury but, alarmed at his excess, had become a supporter of the Court. It was entirely by his eloquence that the Exclusion Bill was defeated in the Lords in 1680. See also *Introductory Note*.

[4] Laurence Hyde was an ardent royalist, a confidant of the Duke of York, and a patron of Dryden. He was first commissioner of the treasury and an important power in the administration.

[5] Edward Seymour, who had been Speaker of the House of Commons from 1673 to 1678, was re-elected as Speaker in 1679, but the King refused to accept him. A Tory and Churchman, he opposed the Exclusion Bill in 1680.

In his own worth, and without Title great:
The Sanhedrin long time as Chief he rul'd,
Their Reason guided, and their Passion cool'd;
So dexterous was he in the Crown's defence,
So form'd to speak a Loyal Nations Sense,
That as their Band was *Israels* Tribes in small,
So fit was he to represent them all.
Now rasher Charioteers the Seat ascend,
Whose loose Carriers his steady Skill commend:
They, like th' unequal Ruler of the Day,
Misguide the Seasons, and mistake the Way;
While he withdrawn at their mad Labour smiles,
And safe enjoys the Sabbath of his Toils.

These were the chief; a small but faithful Band
Of Worthies, in the Breach who dar'd to stand,
And tempt th' united Fury of the Land.
With grief they view'd such powerful Engines bent,
To batter down the lawful Government.
A numerous Faction with pretended frights,
In Sanhedrins to plume the Regal Rights.
The true Successor from the Court remov'd:
The Plot, by hireling Witnesses improv'd.
These Ills they saw, and as their Duty bound,
They shew'd the King the danger of the Wound:
That no Concessions from the Throne woud please;
But Lenitives fomented the Disease:
That *Absalom*, ambitious of the Crown,
Was made the Lure to draw the People down:
That false *Achitophel*'s pernitious Hate,
Had turn'd the Plot to ruine Church and State:
The Council violent, the Rabble worse:
That *Shimei* taught *Jerusalem* to Curse.

With all these loads of Injuries opprest,
And long revolving in his careful Brest
Th' event of things; at last his patience tir'd,
Thus from his Royal Throne, by Heav'n inspir'd,
The god-like *David* spoke; with awful fear
His Train their Maker in their Master hear.

Thus long have I by Native Mercy sway'd,
My Wrongs dissembl'd, my Revenge delay'd:

So willing to forgive th' Offending Age;
So much the Father did the King asswage.
But now so far my Clemency they slight,
Th' Offenders question my Forgiving Right.
That one was made for many, they contend:
But 'tis to Rule, for that's a Monarch's End.
They call my tenderness of Blood, my Fear:
Though Manly tempers can the longest bear.
Yet, since they will divert my Native Course,
'Tis time to shew I am not Good by Force.
Those heap'd Affronts that haughty Subjects bring,
Are burthens for a Camel, not a King:
Kings are the publick Pillars of the State,
Born to sustain and prop the Nations weight:
If my young *Sampson* will pretend a Call
To shake the Column, let him share the Fall:
But oh that yet he woud repent and live!
How easie 'tis for Parents to forgive!
With how few Tears a Pardon might be won
From Nature, pleading for a Darling Son!
Poor pitied youth, by my Paternal care,
Rais'd up to all the Height his Frame coud bear:
Had God ordain'd his Fate for Empire born,
He woud have giv'n his Soul another turn:
Gull'd with a Patriot's name, whose Modern sense
Is one that woud by Law supplant his Prince:
The People's Brave, the Politicians Tool;
Never was Patriot yet, but was a Fool.
Whence comes it that Religion and the Laws
Should more be *Absalom*'s than *David*'s Cause?
His old Instructor, e'r he lost his Place,
Was never thought endu'd with so much Grace.
Good heav'ns, how Faction can a Patriot Paint!
My Rebel ever proves my People's Saint:
Woud *they* impose an Heir upon the Throne?
Let Sanhedrins be taught to give their Own.
A King's at least a part of Government;
And mine as requisite as their Consent:
Without my leave a future King to choose,
Infers a Right the present to Depose:
True, they Petition me t' approve their Choice:
But *Esau*'s Hands suit ill with *Jacob*'s Voice.
My Pious Subjects for my Safety pray,

Which to Secure they take my Pow'r away.
From Plots and Treasons Heav'n preserve my Years
But save me most from my Petitioners.
Unsatiate as the barren Womb or Grave;
God cannot Grant so much as they can Crave.
What then is left but with a Jealous Eye
To guard the Small remains of Royalty?
The Law shall still direct my peaceful Sway,
And the same Law teach Rebels to obey:
Votes shall no more Establish'd Pow'r controul,
Such Votes as make a Part exceed the Whole:
No groundless Clamours shall my Friends remove,
Nor Crouds have pow'r to Punish e'r they Prove:
For Gods, and God-like Kings their Care express,
Still to defend their Servants in distress.
Oh that my Pow'r to Saving were confin'd:
Why am I forc'd, like Heav'n, against my mind,
To make Examples of another Kind?
Must I at length the Sword of Justice draw?
Oh curst Effects of necessary Law!
How ill my Fear they by my Mercy scan,
Beware the Fury of a Patient Man.
Law they require, let Law then shew her Face;
They could not be content to look on Grace,
Her hinder parts, but with a daring Eye
To tempt the terror of her Front, and Die.
By their own Arts 'tis righteously decreed,
Those dire Artificers of Death shall bleed.
Against themselves their Witnesses will Swear,
Till Viper-like their Mother plot they tear:
And suck for Nutriment that bloudy gore
Which was their Principle of Life before.
Their *Belial* with the *Belzebub* will fight;
Thus on my Foes, my Foes shall do me Right:
Nor doubt th' event: for Factious crouds engage
In their first Onset, all their Brutal Rage;
Then, let 'em take an unresisted Course:
Retire and Traverse, and Delude their Force:
But when they stand all Breathless, urge the fight,
And rise upon 'em with redoubled might:
For Lawful Pow'r is still Superiour found,
When long driv'n back, at length it stands the ground.

He said. Th' Almighty, nodding, gave Consent;
And Peals of Thunder shook the Firmament.
Henceforth a Series of new time began,
The mighty Years in long Procession ran:
Once more the God-like *David* was Restor'd,
And willing Nations knew their Lawful Lord.

THE MEDALL

A SATYRE AGAINST SEDITION

Per Graiûm populos, mediæque per Elidis Urbem
Ibat ovans; Divumque sibi poscebat Honores.[1]

[1] Through the nations of Greece and through the city that is in the midst of Elis he journeyed exultant, and laid claim to divine honours for himself. (Vergil, *Æneid* 6. 588–9.)

The Medall. A Satyre against Sedition. By the Authour of Absalom and Achitophel. [*Latin quot.*] London, Printed for Jacob Tonson at the Judge's Head in Chancery-lane, near Fleet-street. 1682.

THE first issue of the first edition (Macdonald, 13 a i), which the present text follows, ends with Dryden's text. The Latin verses, which were added to the second issue, are reprinted here from the text published in *Miscellany Poems*, 1684.

A bill of indictment for high treason against the Earl of Shaftesbury was presented to a London jury on 24 November 1681. The evidence was not only insufficient but the jury had been packed by the Whig Sheriffs of the City and the bill was rejected. The Whigs' triumph in this victory was unbounded, and they employed an artist, George Bower, to strike a medal in honour of the event. The obverse of this medal depicted a bust of the Earl, with the legend 'Antonio Comiti de Shaftesbury', and the reverse a prospect of London Bridge and the Tower—a sun was shown rising behind a cloud above the Tower to symbolise Shaftesbury's release from imprisonment—with the legend 'Laetamur' and the date '24 Nov. 1681'. The medal was worn in their lapels by the Earl's supporters. It is said that Charles II particularly asked Dryden to ridicule the striking of this medal and even suggested to him the plan for the poem. Dryden accepted the suggestion and *The Medall* was published in March 1682.

EPISTLE TO THE WHIGS

FOR to whom can I dedicate this Poem, with so much justice as to you? 'Tis the representation of your own Heroe: 'tis the Picture drawn at length, which you admire and prize so much in little. None of your Ornaments are wanting; neither the Landscap of the Tower, nor the Rising Sun; nor the Anno Domini *of your New Sovereign's Coronation. This must needs be a gratefull undertaking to your whole Party: especially to those who have not been so happy as to purchase the Original. I hear the* Graver *has made a good Market of it: all his Kings are bought up already; or the value of the remainder so inhanc'd, that many a poor* Polander[1] *who would be glad to worship the Image, is not able to go to the cost of him: But must be content to see him here. I must confess I am no great Artist; but Sign-post painting will serve the turn to remember a Friend by; especially when better is not to be had. Yet for your comfort the lineaments are true: and though he sate not five times to me, as he did to* B.[2] *yet I have consulted History; as the* Italian *Painters doe, when they wou'd draw a* Nero *or a* Caligula; *though they have not seen the Man, they can help their Imagination by a Statue of him, and find out the Colouring from* Suetonius *and* Tacitus. *Truth is, you might have spar'd one side of your Medall: the Head wou'd be seen to more advantage, if it were plac'd on a Spike of the Tower; a little nearer to the Sun. Which wou'd then break out to better purpose. You tell us in your Preface to the* No-protestant Plot,[3] *that you shall be forc'd hereafter to leave off your Modesty: I suppose you mean that little which is left you: for it was worn to rags when you put out this Medall. Never was there practis'd such a piece of notorious Impudence in the face of an Establish'd Government. I believe, when he is dead, you will wear him in Thumb-Rings, as the* Turks *did* Scanderbeg;[4] *as if there were virtue in his Bones to preserve you against Monarchy. Yet all this while you pretend not onely zeal for the Publick good; but a due veneration for the person of the King. But all men who can see an*

[1] It was a joke among the Tories that Shaftesbury aspired to be elected King of Poland in 1675, when John Sobieski was elected. The medal is thus called in the opening verses of the poem the 'Polish Medal'.

[2] George Bower, the engraver of the medal.

[3] A tract written in defence of Shaftesbury, the first part of which is said to have been written by the Earl himself.

[4] The renowned Albanian warrior Scanderbeg (*d.* 1467), whose bones were sought after as charms by his enemies, the Turks.

inch before them, may easily detect those gross fallacies. That it is necessary for men in your circumstances to pretend both, is granted you; for without them there could be no ground to raise a Faction. But I would ask you one civil question, what right has any man among you, or any Association of men, (to come nearer to you,) who out of Parliament, cannot be consider'd in a publick Capacity, to meet, as you daily doe, in Factious Clubs, to vilify the Government, in your Discourses, and to libel it in all your Writings? who made you Judges in Israel? *or how is it consistent with your Zeal of the publick Welfare, to promote Sedition? Does your definition of loyal, which is to serve the King according to the Laws, allow you the licence of traducing the Executive Power, with which you own he is invested? You complain that his Majesty has lost the love and confidence of his People; and by your very urging it, you endeavour what in you lies, to make him lose them. All good Subjects abhor the thought of Arbitrary Power, whether it be in one or many: if you were the Patriots you would seem, you would not at this rate incense the Multitude to assume it; for no sober man can fear it, either from the King's Disposition, or his Practice; or even, where you would odiously lay it, from his Ministers. Give us leave to enjoy the Government and the benefit of Laws under which we were born, and which we desire to transmit to our Posterity. You are not the Trustees of the publick Liberty: and if you have not right to petition in a Crowd,*[1] *much less have you to intermeddle in the management of Affairs; or to arraign what you do not like: which in effect is every thing that is done by the King and Council. Can you imagine that any reasonable man will believe you respect the person of his Majesty, when 'tis apparent that your Seditious Pamphlets are stuff'd with particular Reflexions on him? If you have the confidence to deny this, 'tis easy to be evinc'd from a thousand Passages, which I onely forbear to quote, because I desire they should die and be forgotten. I have perus'd many of your Papers; and to show you that I have, the third part of your* No-protestant Plot *is much of it stolen, from your dead Authour's*[2] *Pamphlet call'd, the* Growth of Popery; *as manifestly as* Milton'*s defence of the* English *People, is from* Buchanan, de jure regni apud Scotos: *or your first Covenant, and new Association,*[3] *from the holy League*

[1] By an Act of 1661 not more than ten persons were allowed to accompany a petition to the King or to the Houses of Parliament.

[2] The dead author was the great Andrew Marvell (1621–1678), poet and politician.

[3] There was found among Shaftesbury's papers when he was seized, a project of an Association for the defence of the Protestant religion and the King's person. It is compared to the Solemn League and Covenant of the Civil War and to the French Holy League of the Guises of the 16th century.

of the French Guisards. *Any one who reads* Davila, *may trace your Practices all along. There were the same pretences for Reformation, and Loyalty, the same Aspersions of the King, and the same grounds of a Rebellion. I know not whether you will take the Historian's word, who says it was reported, that* Poltrot *a* Hugonot, *murther'd* Francis *Duke of* Guise *by the instigations of* Theodore Beza: *or that it was a* Hugonot *Minister, otherwise call'd a* Presbyterian, (*for our Church abhors so devilish a Tenent*) *who first writ a Treatise of the lawfulness of deposing and murthering Kings, of a different Perswasion in Religion: But I am able to prove from the Doctrine of* Calvin, *and Principles of* Buchanan, *that they set the People above the Magistrate; which if I mistake not, is your own Fundamental; and which carries your Loyalty no farther than your likeing. When a Vote of the House of Commons goes on your side, you are as ready to observe it, as if it were pass'd into a Law: But when you are pinch'd with any former, and yet unrepealed* Act of Parliament, *you declare that in some cases, you will not be oblig'd by it. The Passage is in the same third part of the* No-protestant Plot; *and is too plain to be denied. The late Copy of your intended Association, you neither wholly justify nor condemn; But, as the Papists, when they are unoppos'd, fly out into all the Pageantry's of Worship; but in times of War, when they are hard press'd by Arguments, lie close intrench'd behind the* Council of Trent: *So, now, when your Affairs are in a low condition, you dare not pretend that to be a legal Combination, but whensoever you are afloat, I doubt not but it will be maintain'd and justify'd to purpose. For indeed there is nothing to defend it but the Sword: 'tis the proper time to say any thing, when men have all things in their power.*

In the mean time you wou'd fain be nibbling at a parallel betwixt this Association, and that in the time of Queen Elizabeth. *But there is this small difference betwixt them, that the ends of the one are directly opposite to the other: one with the Queen's approbation, and conjunction, as head of it; the other without either the consent, or knowledge of the King, against whose Authority it is manifestly design'd. Therefore you doe well to have recourse to your last Evasion, that it was contriv'd by your Enemies, and shuffled into the Papers that were seiz'd: which yet you see the Nation is not so easy to believe as your own Jury; But the matter is not difficult, to find twelve men in* New-gate, *who wou'd acquit a Malefactour.*

I have one onely favour to desire of you at parting, that when you think of answering this Poem, *you wou'd employ the same Pens against it, who have combated with so much success against* Absalom *and* Achitophel: *for then you may assure your selves of a clear Victory, without the least reply. Raile at me abundantly; and, not to break a Custome, doe it without wit: By this method you will gain a considerable point, which is wholly to wave the answer of my Arguments. Never own the botome of your Principles, for fear they shou'd be Treason. Fall severely on the miscarriages of Government; for if scandal be not allow'd, you are no freeborn subjects. If God has not bless'd you with the Talent of Rhiming, make use of my poor Stock and wellcome: let your Verses run upon my feet: and for the utmost refuge of notorious Block-heads, reduc'd to the last extremity of sense, turn my own lines upon me, and in utter despaire of your own Satyre, make me Satyrize my self. Some of you have been driven to this Bay already; But above all the rest commend me to the Non-conformist Parson, who writ the* Whip and Key. *I am afraid it is not read so much as the Piece deserves, because the Bookseller is every week crying help at the end of his* Gazette, *to get it off. You see I am charitable enough to doe him a kindness, that it may be publish'd as well as printed; and that so much skill in Hebrew Derivations, may not lie for Wast-paper in the Shop. Yet I half suspect he went no farther for his learning, than the Index of Hebrew Names and Etymologies, which is printed at the end of some* English *Bibles. If* Achitophel *signify the Brother of a Fool, the Authour of that Poem will pass with his Readers for the next of kin. And perhaps 'tis the Relation that makes the kindness. Whatever the Verses are; buy 'em up I beseech you out of pity; for I hear the Conventicle is shut up, and the Brother of* Achitophel *out of service.*

Now Footmen, you know, have the generosity to make a Purse, for a Member of their Society, who has had his Livery pull'd over his Ears: and even Protestant Socks are bought up among you, out of veneration to the name. A Dissenter in Poetry from Sense and English, will make as good a Protestant Rhymer, as a Dissenter from the Church of England *a Protestant Parson. Besides, if you encourage a young Beginner, who knows but he may elevate his stile a little, above the vulgar Epithets of prophane, and sawcy Jack, and Atheistick Scribler, with which he treats me, when the fit of Enthusiam is strong upon him: by which well-mannered and charitable Expressions, I was certain of his Sect, before I knew his name. What wou'd you have more of a man? he has damn'd me in your Cause from* Genesis *to the* Revelations: *And has half the Texts of both the* Testaments *against me, if you will be so civil to your selves as to take him for your Interpreter; and not to take them for* Irish *Witnesses. After all, perhaps you will tell me, that you retain'd him onely for the opening of your Cause, and that your main Lawyer is yet behind. Now if it so happen he meet with no more reply than his Predecessours, you may either conclude, that I trust to the goodness of my Cause, or fear my Adversary, or disdain him, or what you please, for the short on't is, 'tis indifferent to your humble servant. whatever your Party says or thinks of him.*

THE MEDALL

A SATYRE AGAINST SEDITION

Of all our Antick Sights, and Pageantry
Which *English* Ideots run in crowds to see,
The *Polish Medall* bears the prize alone:
A Monster, more the Favourite of the Town
Than either Fayrs or Theatres have shown.
Never did Art so well with Nature strive;
Nor ever Idol seem'd so much alive:
So like the Man; so golden to the sight,
So base within, so counterfeit and light.
One side is fill'd with Title and with Face;
And, lest the King shou'd want a regal Place,
On the reverse, a Tow'r the Town surveys;
O'er which our mounting Sun his beams displays.
The Word, pronounc'd aloud by Shrieval voice,
Lætamur, which, in *Polish*, is *rejoyce*.
The Day, Month, Year, to the great Act are join'd:
And a new Canting Holiday design'd.
Five daies he sate, for every cast and look;
Four more than God to finish *Adam* took.
But who can tell what Essence Angels are,
Or how long Heav'n was making *Lucifer?*
Oh, cou'd the Style that copy'd every grace,
And plough'd such furrows for an Eunuch face,
Cou'd it have form'd his ever-changing Will,
The various Piece had tir'd the Graver's Skill!
A Martial Heroe first, with early care,
Blown, like a Pigmee by the Winds, to war.
A beardless Chief, a Rebel, e'r a Man:
(So young his hatred to his Prince began.[1])
Next this, (How wildly will Ambition steer!)
A Vermin, wriggling in th' Usurper's Ear.
Bart'ring his venal wit for sums of gold

[1] Shaftesbury, then Sir Anthony Ashley Cooper, at the age of twenty-two, had raised a regiment in 1643 for the King's service, but he transferred his allegiance to the Parliament a year later.

He cast himself into the Saint-like mould; [1]
Groan'd, sigh'd and pray'd, while Godliness was gain:
The lowdest Bagpipe of the squeaking Train.
But, as 'tis hard to cheat a Juggler's Eyes,
His open lewdness he cou'd ne'er disguise.
There split the Saint: for Hypocritique Zeal
Allows no Sins but those it can conceal.
Whoring to Scandal gives too large a scope:
Saints must not trade; but they may interlope.
Th' ungodly Principle was all the same;
But a gross Cheat betrays his Partner's Game.
Besides, their pace was formal, grave and slack:
His nimble Wit outran the heavy Pack.
Yet still he found his Fortune at a stay;
Whole droves of Blockheads choaking up his way;
They took, but not rewarded, his advice;
Villain and Wit exact a double price.
Pow'r was his aym: but, thrown from that pretence,
The Wretch turn'd loyal in his own defence;
And Malice reconcil'd him to his Prince.
Him, in the anguish of his Soul he serv'd;
Rewarded faster still than he deserv'd.
Behold him now exalted into trust;
His Counsel's oft convenient, seldom just.
Ev'n in the most sincere advice he gave
He had a grudging still to be a Knave.
The Frauds he learnt in his Fanatique years
Made him uneasy in his lawfull gears.
At best as little honest as he cou'd:
And, like white Witches, mischievously good.
To his first byass, longingly he leans;
And *rather* wou'd be great by wicked means.
Thus, fram'd for ill, he loos'd our Triple hold; [2]
(Advice unsafe, precipitous, and bold.)
From hence those tears! that *Ilium* of our woe!
Who helps a pow'rfull Friend, fore-arms a Foe.
What wonder if the Waves prevail so far
When He cut down the Banks that made the bar?
Seas follow but their Nature to invade;

[1] Shaftesbury was appointed a member of the Council of State in 1653, but he was estranged from Cromwell in the following year and ceased to attend.

[2] See *Absalom and Achitophel*, p. 93, n. 3.

But He by Art our native Strength betray'd.
So *Sampson* to his Foe his force confest;
And, to be shorn, lay slumb'ring on her breast.
But, when this fatal Counsel, found too late,
Expos'd its Authour to the publique hate;
When his just Sovereign, by no impious way,
Cou'd be seduc'd to Arbitrary sway;
Forsaken of that hope, he shifts the sayle;
Drives down the Current with a pop'lar gale;
And shews the Fiend confess'd, without a vaile.
He preaches to the Crowd, that Pow'r is lent,
But not convey'd to Kingly Government;
That Claimes successive bear no binding force;
That Coronation Oaths are things of course;
Maintains the Multitude can never err;
And sets the People in the Papal Chair.
The reason's obvious; *Int'rest never lyes*;
The most have still their Int'rest in their eyes;
The pow'r is always theirs, and pow'r is ever wise.
Almighty Crowd, thou shorten'st all dispute;
Pow'r is thy Essence; Wit thy Attribute!
Nor Faith nor Reason make thee at a stay,
Thou leapst o'r all eternal truths, in thy *Pindarique* way!
Athens, no doubt, did righteously decide,
When *Phocion* and when *Socrates* were try'd:
As righteously they did those dooms repent;
Still they were wise, what ever way they went.
Crowds err not, though to both extremes they run;
To kill the Father, and recall the Son.
Some think the Fools were most, as times went then;
But now the World's o'r stock'd with prudent men.
The common Cry is ev'n Religion's Test;
The *Turk*'s is, at *Constantinople*, best;
Idols in *India*, Popery at *Rome*;
And our own Worship onely true at home.
And true, but for the time, 'tis hard to know
How long we please it shall continue so.
This side to day, and that to morrow burns;
So all are God-a'mighties in their turns.
A Tempting Doctrine, plausible and new:
What Fools our Fathers were, if this be true!

Who, to destroy the seeds of Civil War,
Inherent right in Monarchs did declare:
And, that a lawfull Pow'r might never cease,
Secur'd Succession, to secure our Peace.
Thus, Property and Sovereign Sway, at last
In equal Balances were justly cast:
But this new *Jehu* spurs the hot mouth'd horse;
Instructs the Beast to know his native force;
To take the Bit between his teeth and fly
To the next headlong Steep of Anarchy.
Too happy *England*, if our good we knew;
Wou'd we possess the freedom we pursue!
The lavish Government can give no more:
Yet we repine; and plenty makes us poor.
God try'd us once; our Rebel-fathers fought;
He glutted 'em with all the pow'r they sought:
Till, master'd by their own usurping Brave,
The free-born Subject sunk into a Slave.
We loath our Manna, and we long for Quails;
Ah, what is man, when his own wish prevails!
How rash, how swift to plunge himself in ill;
Proud of his Pow'r, and boundless in his Will!
That Kings can doe no wrong we must believe:
None can they doe, and must they all receive?
Help Heaven! or sadly we shall see an hour,
When neither wrong nor right are in their pow'r!
Already they have lost their best defence,
The benefit of Laws, which they dispence.
No justice to their righteous Cause allow'd;
But baffled by an Arbitrary Crowd.
And Medalls grav'd, their Conquest to record,
The Stamp and Coyn of their adopted Lord.

The Man who laugh'd but once, to see an Ass
Mumbling to make the cross-grain'd Thistles pass;
Might laugh again, to see a Jury chaw
The prickles of unpalatable Law.
The Witnesses, that, Leech-like, liv'd on bloud,
Sucking for them were med'cinally good;
But, when they fasten'd on *their* fester'd Sore,
Then, Justice and Religion they forswore;
Their Mayden Oaths debauch'd into a Whore.
Thus Men are rais'd by Factions, and decry'd;

And Rogue and Saint distinguish'd by their Side.[1]
They rack ev'n Scripture to confess their Cause;
And plead a Call to preach, in spight of Laws.
But that's no news to the poor injur'd Page;
It has been us'd as ill in every Age:
And is constrain'd, with patience, all to take;
For what defence can Greek and Hebrew make?
Happy who can this talking Trumpet seize;
They make it speak whatever Sense they please!
'Twas fram'd, at first, our Oracle t' enquire;
But, since our Sects in prophecy grow higher,
The Text inspires not them; but they the Text inspire.

London, thou great *Emporium* of our Isle,
O, thou too bounteous, thou too fruitfull *Nile*,
How shall I praise or curse to thy desert!
Or separate thy sound, from thy corrupted part!
I call'd thee *Nile*; the parallel will stand:
Thy tydes of Wealth o'rflow the fattend Land;
Yet Monsters from thy large increase we find;
Engender'd on the Slyme thou leav'st behind.
Sedition has not wholly seiz'd on thee;
Thy nobler Parts are from infection free.
Of *Israel*'s Tribes thou hast a numerous band;
But still the *Canaanite* is in the Land.
Thy military Chiefs are brave and true;
Nor are thy disinchanted Burghers few.
The Head is loyal which thy Heart commands;
But what's a Head with two such gouty Hands? [2]
The wise and wealthy love the surest way;
And are content to thrive and to obey.
But Wisedom is to Sloath too great a Slave;
None are so busy as the Fool and Knave.
Those let me curse; what vengeance will they urge,
Whose Ordures neither Plague nor Fire can purge;
Nor sharp Experience can to duty bring,
Nor angry Heav'n, nor a forgiving King!
In Gospel phrase their Chapmen they betray:

[1] Several of the witnesses who appeared against Shaftesbury at his trial had earlier appeared as witnesses to the truth of the Popish Plot. The Tories argued that since their testimony against the Catholics had been considered good, their testimony against Shaftesbury should be considered good also.

[2] The 'head' was the Lord Mayor for 1681, a zealous courtier, and the 'two gouty hands' were the Sheriffs, both Whigs.

Their Shops are Dens, the Buyer is their Prey.
The Knack of Trades is living on the Spoyl;
They boast, ev'n when each other they beguile.
Customes to steal is such a trivial thing,
That 'tis their Charter, to defraud their King.
All hands unite of every jarring Sect;
They cheat the Country first, and then infect.
They, for God's Cause their Monarchs dare dethrone;
And they'll be sure to make his Cause their own.
Whether the plotting Jesuite lay'd the plan
Of murth'ring Kings, or the *French* Puritan,
Our Sacrilegious Sects their Guides outgo;
And Kings and Kingly Pow'r wou'd murther too.

What means their Trait'rous Combination less,
Too plain t' evade, too shamefull to confess.
But Treason is not own'd when tis descry'd;
Successfull Crimes alone are justify'd.
The Men, who no Conspiracy wou'd find,
Who doubts, but had it taken, they had join'd.
Joyn'd, in a mutual Cov'nant of defence;
At first without, at last against their Prince.
If Sovereign Right by Sovereign Pow'r they scan,
The same bold Maxime holds in God and Man:
God were not safe, his Thunder cou'd they shun
He shou'd be forc'd to crown another Son.
Thus, when the Heir was from the Vineyard thrown,
The rich Possession was the Murth'rers own.
In vain to Sophistry they have recourse:
By proving theirs no Plot, they prove 'tis worse;
Unmask'd Rebellion, and audacious Force.
Which, though not Actual, yet all Eyes may see
'Tis working, in th' immediate Pow'r to be;
For, from pretended Grievances they rise,
First to dislike, and after to despise.
Then, *Cyclop*-like in humane Flesh to deal;
Chop up a Minister, at every meal:
Perhaps not wholly to melt down the King;
But clip his regal Rights within the Ring.[1]
From thence, t' assume the pow'r of Peace and War;
And ease him by degrees of publique Care.

[1] A reference to the fraudulent practice of clipping unmilled money.

Yet, to consult his Dignity and Fame,
He shou'd have leave to exercise the Name;
And hold the Cards, while Commons play'd the game.
For what can Pow'r give more than Food and Drink,
To live at ease, and not be bound to think?
These are the cooler methods of their Crime;
But their hot Zealots think 'tis loss of time;
On utmost bounds of Loyalty they stand;
And grinn and whet like a *Croatian* Band;
That waits impatient for the last Command.
Thus Out-laws open Villany maintain:
They steal not, but in Squadrons scoure the Plain:
And, if their Pow'r the Passengers subdue;
The Most have right, the wrong is in the Few.
Such impious Axiomes foolishly they show;
For, in some Soyles Republiques will not grow:
Our Temp'rate Isle will no extremes sustain,
Of pop'lar Sway, or Arbitrary Reign:
But slides between them both into the best;
Secure in freedom, in a Monarch blest.
And though the Clymate, vex't with various Winds,
Works through our yielding Bodies, on our Minds,
The wholsome Tempest purges what it breeds;
To recommend the Calmness that succeeds.

But thou, the Pander of the Peoples hearts,
(O Crooked Soul, and Serpentine in Arts,)
Whose blandishments a Loyal Land have whor'd,
And broke the Bonds she plighted to her Lord;
What Curses on thy blasted Name will fall!
Which Age to Age their Legacy shall call;
For all must curse the Woes that must descend on all.
Religion thou hast none: thy *Mercury*
Has pass'd through every Sect, or theirs through Thee.
But what thou giv'st, that Venom still remains;
And the pox'd Nation feels Thee in their Brains.
What else inspires the Tongues, and swells the Breasts
Of all thy bellowing Renegado Priests,[1]
That preach up Thee for God; dispence thy Laws;
And with thy Stumm ferment their fainting Cause?
Fresh Fumes of Madness raise; and toile and sweat
To make the formidable Cripple great.

[1] The dissenting ministers who supported Shaftesbury's cause.

Yet, shou'd thy Crimes succeed, shou'd lawless Pow'r
Compass those Ends thy greedy Hopes devour,
Thy Canting Friends thy Mortal Foes wou'd be;
Thy God and Theirs will never long agree.
For thine, (if thou hast any,) must be one
That lets the World and Humane-kind alone:
A jolly God, that passes hours too well
To promise Heav'n, or threaten us with Hell.
That unconcern'd can at Rebellion sit;
And Wink at Crimes he did himself commit.
A Tyrant theirs; the Heav'n their Priesthood paints
A Conventicle of gloomy sullen Saints;
A Heav'n, like *Bedlam*, slovenly and sad;
Fore-doom'd for Souls, with false Religion, mad.

Without a Vision Poets can fore-show
What all but Fools, by common Sense may know:
If true Succession from our Isle shou'd fail,
And Crowds profane, with impious Arms prevail,
Not Thou, nor those thy Factious Arts ingage
Shall reap that Harvest of Rebellious Rage,
With which thou flatter'st thy decrepit Age.
The swelling Poyson of the sev'ral Sects,
Which wanting vent, the Nations Health infects
Shall burst its Bag; and fighting out their way
The various Venoms on each other prey.
The *Presbyter*, puft up with spiritual Pride,
Shall on the Necks of the lewd Nobles ride:
His Brethren damn, the Civil Pow'r defy;
And parcel out Republique Prelacy.
But short shall be his Reign: his rigid Yoke
And Tyrant Pow'r will puny Sects provoke;
And Frogs and Toads, and all the Tadpole Train
Will croak to Heav'n for help, from this devouring Crane.
The Cut-throat Sword and clamorous Gown shall jar,
In shareing their ill-gotten Spoiles of War:
Chiefs shall be grudg'd the part which they pretend;
Lords envy Lords, and Friends with every Friend
About their impious Merit shall contend.
The surly Commons shall respect deny;
And justle Peerage out with Property.
Their Gen'ral either shall his Trust betray,

And force the Crowd to Arbitrary sway;
Or they suspecting his ambitious Aym,
In hate of Kings shall cast anew the Frame;
And thrust out *Collatine* that bore their Name.[1]

Thus inborn Broyles the Factions wou'd ingage;
Or Wars of Exil'd Heirs, or Foreign Rage,
Till halting Vengeance overtook our Age:
And our wild Labours, wearied into Rest,
Reclin'd us on a rightfull Monarch's Breast.

———————*Pudet hæc opprobria, vobis*
Et dici potuisse, & non potuisse refelli.[2]

[1] A reference to the Duke of Monmouth. Lucius Tarquinius Collatinus, the nephew of the king of Rome, Tarquinius Superbus, after helping to depose his uncle had to go into exile on account of the hatred felt towards his name.

[2] I am ashamed that such an insult could be voiced and ye could not give it the lie. (Ovid, *Metamorphoses* I. 758–9.)

MAC FLECKNOE

OR A SATYR UPON THE

TREW-BLEW PROTESTANT POET

T. S.

Miscellany Poems. Containing a New Translation of Virgills Eclogues, Ovid's Love Elegies, Odes of Horace, And Other Authors; with several Original Poems. By the most Eminent Hands. [*Latin quot.*] London, Printed for Jacob Tonson, at the Judges-head in Chancery-Lane near Fleet-street, 1684.

THE first edition of *Mac Flecknoe* appeared in 1682 but the badness of the text makes it unlikely that it was authorised by Dryden. Consequently, the present text follows that of the 'authorised' edition, first published in *Miscellany Poems*, 1684 (Macdonald, 42 a i).

DRYDEN'S satire on Thomas Shadwell (1642?–1692) would appear to have been written as early as 1678, when the two dramatists were, on the surface at least, on fairly friendly terms. The particular occasion of their quarrel is unknown but it was probably brought about by personal dislike and jealousy aggravated by the political fever of the years following the Popish Plot. Shadwell was a staunch adherent of the Earl of Shaftesbury, and Dryden's dislike of his Whiggish opinions is sufficiently indicated in the title-page to this poem. Shadwell answered Dryden's attack on Shaftesbury in *The Medall* with an abusive satire entitled *The Medal of John Bayes*, published in May 1682; *Mac Flecknoe* appeared in about October of the same year. Dryden also pilloried Shadwell in the second part of *Absalom and Achitophel.*

The idea of *Mac Flecknoe* was suggested by the death of the Irish priest and poet Richard Flecknoe (*d.* 1678). Dryden imagined Flecknoe, the monarch of the 'Realms of *Non-sense*', immediately before death, appointing Shadwell as his worthy successor.

MAC FLECKNOE

ALL humane things are subject to decay,
And, when Fate summons, Monarchs must obey:
This *Fleckno* found, who, like *Augustus*, young
Was call'd to Empire, and had govern'd long:
In Prose and Verse, was own'd, without dispute
Through all the Realms of *Non-sense*, absolute.
This aged Prince now flourishing in Peace,
And blest with issue of a large increase,
Worn out with business, did at length debate
To settle the succession of the State:
And pond'ring which of all his Sons was fit
To Reign, and wage immortal War with Wit;
Cry'd, 'tis resolv'd; for Nature pleads that He
Should onely rule, who most resembles me:
Sh[*adwell*] alone my perfect image bears,
Mature in dullness from his tender years.
Sh[*adwell*] alone, of all my Sons, is he
Who stands confirm'd in full stupidity.
The rest to some faint meaning make pretence,
But *Sh*[*adwell*] never deviates into sense.
Some Beams of Wit on other souls may fall,
Strike through and make a lucid intervall;
But *Sh*[*adwell*]'s genuine night admits no ray,
His rising Fogs prevail upon the Day:
Besides his goodly Fabrick fills the eye,
And seems design'd for thoughtless Majesty:
Thoughtless as Monarch Oakes, that shade the plain,
And, spread in solemn state, supinely reign.
Heywood and *Shirley*[1] were but Types of thee,
Thou last great Prophet of Tautology:
Even I, a dunce of more renown than they,
Was sent before but to prepare thy way;
And coursly clad in *Norwich* Drugget came
To teach the Nations in thy greater name.
My warbling Lute, the Lute I whilom strung

[1] Thomas Heywood (*d.* 1650?) and James Shirley (1596–1666) were both voluminous dramatists but hardly deserving of this disparagement.

When to King *John* of *Portugal* I sung,[1]
Was but the prelude to that glorious day,
When thou on silver *Thames* did'st cut thy way,
With well tim'd Oars before the Royal Barge,
Swell'd with the Pride of thy Celestial charge;
And big with Hymn, Commander of an Host,
The like was ne'er in *Epsom* Blankets tost.[2]
Methinks I see the new *Arion* Sail,
The Lute still trembling underneath thy nail.
At thy well sharpned thumb from Shore to Shore
The Treble squeaks for fear, the Bases roar:
Echoes from *Pissing-Ally*, *Sh*[*adwell*] call,
And *Sh*[*adwell*] they resound from *A*[*ston*] *Hall*.
About thy boat the little Fishes throng,
As at the Morning Toast, that Floats along.
Sometimes as Prince of thy Harmonious band
Thou weild'st thy Papers in thy threshing hand.
St. *Andre*'s [3] feet ne'er kept more equal time,
Not ev'n the feet of thy own *Psyche*'s rhime: [4]
Though they in number as in sense excell;
So just, so like tautology they fell,
That, pale with envy, *Singleton* forswore
The Lute and Sword which he in Triumph bore,
And vow'd he ne'er would act *Villerius* more.[5]
Here stopt the good old *Syre*; and wept for joy
In silent raptures of the hopefull boy.
All arguments, but most his Plays, perswade,
That for anointed dullness he was made.

Close to the Walls which fair *Augusta* bind,
(The fair *Augusta* much to fears inclin'd)
An ancient fabrick, rais'd t' inform the sight,
There stood of yore, and *Barbican* [6] it hight:
A watch Tower once; but now, so Fate ordains,
Of all the Pile an empty name remains.

[1] Flecknoe had lived in Lisbon for some years and been patronised by King John.

[2] Shadwell published his play of *Epsom Wells* in 1673 but the phrase to which Dryden refers, —'Such a fellow as he deserves to be tossed in a blanket'—occurs in another of Shadwell's plays, *The Sullen Lovers*.

[3] A dancing master.

[4] Shadwell's verse opera of *Psyche* was elaborately produced in 1676.

[5] Singleton, a singer, played the part of Villerius in Sir William D'Avenant's opera of *The Seige of Rhodes*.

[6] The Barbican stood in Aldersgate Street.

From its old Ruins Brothel-houses rise,
Scenes of lewd loves, and of polluted joys.
Where their vast Courts the Mother-Strumpets keep,
And, undisturb'd by Watch, in silence sleep.
Near these a Nursery[1] erects its head,
Where Queens are form'd, and future Hero's bred;
Where unfledg'd Actors learn to laugh and cry,
Where infant Punks their tender Voices try,
And little *Maximins*[2] the Gods defy.
Great *Fletcher* never treads in Buskins here,
Nor greater *Johnson* dares in Socks appear;
But gentle *Simkin*[3] just reception finds
Amidst this Monument of vanisht minds:
Pure Clinches, the suburbian Muse affords;
And *Panton*[4] waging harmless War with words.
Here *Fleckno*, as a place to Fame well known,
Ambitiously design'd his *Sh*[*adwell*]'s Throne.
For ancient *Decker*[5] prophesi'd long since,
That in this Pile should Reign a mighty Prince,
Born for a scourge of Wit, and flayle of Sense:
To whom true dulness should some *Psyches* owe,
But Worlds of *Misers* from his pen should flow;
Humorists and Hypocrites it should produce,
Whole *Raymond* families, and Tribes of *Bruce*.[6]

Now Empress *Fame* had publisht the renown,
Of *Sh*[*adwell*]'s Coronation through the Town.
Rows'd by report of Fame, the Nations meet,
From near *Bun-Hill*, and distant *Watling-street*.
No *Persian* Carpets spread th' Imperial way,
But scatter'd Limbs of mangled Poets lay:
From dusty shops neglected Authors come,
Martyrs of Pies, and reliques of the Bum.
Much *Heywood*, *Shirly*, *Ogleby*[7] there lay,
But loads of *Sh*[*adwell*] almost choakt the way.

[1] The Nursery, a theatrical school for training boys and girls for the stage, was established in 1662.
[2] The hero of Dryden's *Tyrannic Love*.
[3] A character of a cobbler in an interlude.
[4] A celebrated punster.
[5] Thomas Dekker (1570?–1632), dramatist and miscellaneous writer.
[6] *The Miser*, and *The Humourists*, are two of Shadwell's less successful plays. Raymond is a character in *The Humourists*, and Bruce a character in another of Shadwell's plays, *The Virtuoso*.
[7] John Ogilby (1600–1676), the translator of Vergil.

Bilk't *Stationers* for Yeomen stood prepar'd,
And *H*[*erringman*][1] was Captain of the Guard.
The hoary Prince in Majesty appear'd,
High on a Throne of his own Labours rear'd.
At his right hand our young *Ascanius* sat
Rome's other hope, and pillar of the State.
His Brows thick fogs, instead of glories, grace,
And lambent dullness plaid arround his face.
As *Hannibal* did to the Altars come,
Sworn by his *Syre* a mortal Foe to *Rome*;
So *Sh*[*adwell*] swore, nor should his Vow bee vain,
That he till Death true dullness would maintain;
And in his father's Right, and Realms defence,
Ne'er to have peace with Wit, nor truce with Sense.
The King himself the sacred Unction made,
As King by Office, and as Priest by Trade:
In his sinister hand, instead of Ball,
He plac'd a mighty Mug of potent Ale;
Love's Kingdom[2] to his right he did convey,
At once his Sceptre and his rule of Sway;
Whose righteous Lore the Prince had practis'd young,
And from whose Loyns recorded *Psyche* sprung,
His Temples last with Poppies were o'erspread,
That nodding seem'd to consecrate his head:
Just at that point of time, if Fame not lye,
On his left hand twelve reverend *Owls* did fly.
So *Romulus*, 'tis sung, by *Tyber*'s *Brook*,
Presage of Sway from twice six Vultures took.
Th' admiring throng loud acclamations make,
And Omens of his future Empire take.
The *Syre* then shook the honours of his head,
And from his brows damps of oblivion shed
Full on the filial dullness: long he stood,
Repelling from his Breast the raging God;
At length burst out in this prophetick mood:

Heavens bless my Son, from *Ireland* let him reign
To farr *Barbadoes* on the Western main;
Of his Dominion may no end be known,
And greater than his Father's be his Throne.

[1] Henry Herringman had been Dryden's publisher.
[2] Flecknoe's pastoral tragi-comedy of *Love's Kingdom* was published in 1664.

Beyond loves Kingdom let him stretch his Pen;
He paus'd, and all the people cry'd *Amen.*
Then thus, continu'd he, my Son advance
Still in new Impudence, new Ignorance.
Success let others teach, learn thou from me
Pangs without birth, and fruitless Industry.
Let *Virtuoso's* in five years be Writ;
Yet not one thought accuse thy toyl of wit.
Let gentle *George*[1] in triumph tread the Stage,
Make *Dorimant* betray, and *Loveit* rage;
Let *Cully*, *Cockwood*, *Fopling*, charm the Pit,
And in their folly shew the Writers wit.
Yet still thy fools shall stand in thy defence,
And justifie their Author's want of sense.
Let 'em be all by thy own model made
Of dullness, and desire no foreign aid:
That they to future ages may be known,
Not Copies drawn, but Issue of thy own.
Nay let thy men of wit too be the same,
All full of thee, and differing but in name;
But let no alien *S*[*e*]*dl*[*e*]*y* interpose
To lard with wit thy hungry *Epsom* prose.[2]
And when false flowers of *Rhetorick* thou would'st cull,
Trust Nature, do not labour to be dull;
But write thy best, and top; and in each line,
Sir *Formal*'s oratory will be thine.[3]
Sir *Formal*, though unsought, attends thy quill,
And does thy *Northern Dedications* fill.[4]
Nor let false friends seduce thy mind to fame,
By arrogating *Johnson*'s Hostile name.[5]
Let Father *Fleckno* fire thy mind with praise,
And Uncle *Ogleby* thy envy raise.
Thou art my blood, where *Johnson* has no part;
What share have we in Nature or in Art?

[1] Sir George Etherege (1634?–1691?), the admirable comic dramatist. The names in the two following lines are characters in his comedies.

[2] Sir Charles Sedley (1639?–1701), dramatist, wit, and profligate, was supposed to have helped Shadwell in the composition of *Epsom Wells*.

[3] Sir Formal Trifle, an oratorical character in Shadwell's comedy of *The Virtuoso*.

[4] A reference to Shadwell's dedications addressed to the Duke of Newcastle (1592–1676), himself a dramatist.

[5] Shadwell was an eulogist of Ben Jonson, whose theory of drama, particularly his conception of 'humours', he copied, and wished to be compared with him in ability and style.

Where did his wit on learning fix a brand,
And rail at Arts he did not understand?
Where made he love in Prince *Nicander*'s[1] vein,
Or swept the dust in *Psyche*'s humble strain?
Where sold he Bargains, Whip-stitch, kiss my Arse,[2]
Promis'd a Play and dwindled to a Farce?
When did his Muse from *Fletcher* scenes purloin,
As thou whole *Eth'ridg* dost transfuse to thine?
But so transfus'd as Oyl on Waters flow,
His always floats above, thine sinks below.
This is thy Province, this thy wondrous way,
New Humours to invent for each new Play:
This is that boasted Byas of thy mind,
By which one way, to dullness, 'tis inclin'd,
Which makes thy writings lean on oneside still,
And in all changes that way bends thy will.
Nor let thy mountain belly make pretence
Of likeness; thine's a tympany of sense.
A Tun of Man in thy Large bulk is writ,
But sure thou 'rt but a Kilderkin of wit.
Like mine thy gentle numbers feebly creep,
Thy Tragick Muse gives smiles, thy Comick sleep.
With whate'er gall thou sett'st thy self to write,
Thy inoffensive Satyrs never bite.
In thy fellonious heart, though Venom lies,
It does but touch thy *Irish* pen, and dyes.
Thy Genius calls thee not to purchase fame
In keen Iambicks, but mild Anagram:
Leave writing Plays, and chuse for thy command
Some peacefull Province in Acrostick Land.
There thou maist wings display and Altars raise,[3]
And torture one poor word Ten thousand ways.
Or if thou would'st thy diff'rent talents suit,
Set thy own Songs, and sing them to thy lute.
He said, but his last words were scarcely heard,
For *Bruce* and *Longvil* had a *Trap* prepar'd,
And down they sent the yet declaiming Bard.[4]

[1] A character in Shadwell's *Psyche*.

[2] The catch-phrase of a character in Shadwell's *The Virtuoso*.

[3] It was a fashion during the earlier years of the 17th century to write verses in such a variety of metres that their shapes on the printed page resembled, among other objects, wings and altars.

[4] Bruce and Longeville, in Shadwell's *The Virtuoso*, dismiss Sir Formal Trifle by opening a trap-door while he is delivering a speech.

Sinking he left his Drugget robe behind,
Born upwards by a subterranean wind.
The Mantle fell to the young Prophet's part,
With double portion of his Father's Art.

THE SECOND PART OF

ABSALOM AND ACHITOPHEL

A POEM

——Si Quis tamen Hæc quoque, Si Quis
Captus Amore Leget.——————[1]

[1] Yet if anyone—if any, I say, victim to love—shall read this too. . . . (Vergil, *Eclogues* 6. 9–10.)

The Second Part of Absalom and Achitophel. A Poem. [*Latin quot.*] The Second Edition. London: Printed for Jacob Tonson, at the Judge's Head in Chancery-Lane, near Fleet-Street. 1682.

THE present text follows that of the second edition (Macdonald, 15 b), which, appearing in the same year as the first edition, included some small corrections.

THE success of *Absalom and Achitophel* was so great that Dryden was pressed by several persons to continue his satirical commentary upon the times. This he declined to do but he engaged his friend Nahum Tate (1652–1715), the poet and dramatist, to write a second part to *Absalom and Achitophel.* He supervised and revised the whole poem and added the verses characterising Thomas Shadwell and Elkanah Settle as *Og* and *Doeg*. Tate's part of the poem is not included here.

THE SECOND PART OF

ABSALOM AND ACHITOPHEL

NEXT these, a Troop of buisy Spirits press,
Of little Fortunes, and of Conscience Less;
With them the Tribe, whose Luxury had drain'd
Their Banks, in former Sequestrations gain'd:
Who Rich and Great by past Rebellions grew,
And long to fish the troubled Streams anew.
Some future Hopes, some present Payment draws,
To sell their Conscience and espouse the Cause,
Such Stipends those vile Hirelings best befit,
Priests without Grace, and Poets without Wit.
Shall that false *Hebronite* escape our Curse,
Judas[1] that keeps the Rebels Pension-Purse;
Judas that pays the Treason-writers Fee,
Judas that well deserves his Namesake's Tree;
Who at *Jerusalem*'s own Gates Erects
His College for a Nursery of Sects.
Young Prophets with an early Care secures,
And with the Dung of his own Arts manures.
What have the Men of *Hebron* here to doe?
What part in *Israel*'s promis'd Land have you?
Here *Phaleg*[2] the Lay-*Hebronite* is come,
'Cause like the rest he cou'd not live at Home;
Who from his own Possessions cou'd not drain
An *Omer* even of *Hebronitish* Grain,
Here Struts it like a Patriot, and talks high
Of Injur'd Subjects, alter'd Property:
An Emblem of that buzzing Insect Just,
That mounts the Wheel, and thinks she raises Dust.

[1] Robert Ferguson (*d.* 1714), the famous plotter, was an Independent preacher and schoolmaster at Islington, 'his Nursery of Sects', and the publisher and chief pamphleteer of the Whig party. He was the trusted confidant of the Earl of Shaftesbury.

[2] James Forbes was sent to Paris as tutor to the young Earl of Derby but he was unable to manage his charge. Eventually, he was beaten at the Earl's instigation. Dryden seems to have misrepresented the affair from political spleen.

Can dry Bones Live? or *Skeletons* produce
The Vital Warmth of Cuckoldizing Juice?
Slim *Phaleg* cou'd, and at the Table fed,
Return'd the gratefull product to the Bed.
A Waiting-man to Trav'ling Nobles chose,
He, his own Laws, wou'd Sawcily impose;
Till Bastinado'd back again he went,
To learn those Manners he to Teach was sent.
Chastiz'd he ought to have retreated Home,
But He reads Politicks to *Absalom.*
For never *Hebronite*, though Kick'd and Scorn'd,
To his own Country willingly return'd.
—But leaving famish'd *Phaleg* to be fed,
And to talk Treason for his daily Bread,
Let *Hebron*, nay let Hell produce a Man
So made for Mischief as *Ben-Jochanan,*[1]
A *Jew* of Humble Parentage was He,
By Trade a Levite, though of low Degree:
His Pride no higher than the Desk aspir'd,
But for the Drudgery of Priests was hir'd
To Reade and Pray in Linen Ephod brave,
And pick up single Shekels from the Grave.
Married at last, and finding Charge come faster,
He cou'd not live by God, but chang'd his Master:
Inspir'd by Want, was made a Factious Tool,
They Got a Villain, and we Lost a Fool.
Still Violent, whatever Cause he took,
But most against the Party he forsook,
For Renegadoes, who ne'er turn by halves,
Are bound in Conscience to be double Knaves.
So this Prose-Prophet took most monstrous Pains,
To let his Masters see he earn'd his Gains.
But as the Dev'l ows all his Imps a Shame,
He Chose th' *Apostate* for his proper Theme;
With little Pains he made the Picture true,
And from Reflexion took the Rogue he drew.
A wondrous Work to prove the *Jewish* Nation,
In every Age a Murmuring Generation;

[1] Samuel Johnson (1649–1703), a Whig divine, published while the Exclusion Bill was depending a learned work proving from the example of the Roman Emperor, Julian the Apostate, that a national religion is threatened when the sovereign adopts a different faith. He was later fined and imprisoned for the opinion expressed in this work. Dryden's lines are a libel on his upright character.

To trace 'em from their Infancy of Sinning,
And shew 'em Factious from their First Beginning.
To prove they cou'd Rebell, and Rail, and Mock,
Much to the Credit of the Chosen Flock;
A strong Authority which must Convince,
That Saints own no Allegiance to their Prince.
As 'tis a Leading-Card to make a Whore,
To prove her Mother had turn'd up before.
But, tell me, did the Drunken Patriarch bless
The Son that shew'd his Father's Nakedness?
Such Thanks the present Church thy Pen will give,
Which proves Rebellion was so Primitive.
Must Ancient Failings be Examples made,
Then Murtherers from *Cain* may learn their Trade?
As thou the Heathen and the Saint hast drawn,
Methinks th' Apostate was the better Man:
And thy hot *Father* (waving my respect)
Not of a Mother Church, but of a Sect.
And Such he needs must be of thy Inditing,
This Comes of drinking Asses Milk and Writing.
If *Balack*[1] should be call'd to leave his place
(As Profit is the loudest call of Grace,)
His Temple, dispossess'd of one, wou'd be
Replenish'd with seven Devils more by thee.

Levi, thou art a load, I'll lay thee down,
And shew Rebellion bare, without a Gown;
Poor Slaves in Metre, Dull and Addle-pated,
Who Rhime below ev'n *David*'s Psalms translated.[2]
Some in my Speedy pace I must out-run,
As lame *Mephibosheth*[3] the Wisard's Son:
To make quick way I'll leap o'er heavy Blocks,
Shun rotten *Uzza* as I wou'd the Pox;
And hasten *Og* and *Doeg* to rehearse,
Two Fools that Crutch their Feeble Sense on Verse;
Who by my Muse to all succeeding times,
Shall live in spight of their own Dogrell Rhimes.

[1] Dr. Gilbert Burnet, whom Dryden satirised as the Buzzard in *The Hind and the Panther*; see p. 244, n. 1 to that poem.
[2] A reference to Sternhold's and Hopkin's verse translation of the Psalms.
[3] Samuel Pordage (1633–1691?) published a poem, *Azaria and Hushai*, 1682, justifying the Whig party and abusing Dryden.

Doeg,[1] though without knowing how or why,
Made still a blundering kind of Melody;
Spurr'd boldly on, and Dash'd through Thick and Thin,
Through Sense and Non-sense, never out nor in;
Free from all meaning, whether Good or Bad,
And in one Word, Heroically Mad:
He was too warm on Picking-work to dwell,
But Faggoted his Notions as they fell,
And if they Rhim'd and rattl'd all was well.
Spightfull he is not, though he wrote a Satyr,
For still there goes some *thinking* to Ill-Nature:
He needs no more than Birds and Beasts to think,
All his occasions are to Eat and Drink.
If he call Rogue and Rascal from a Garrat
He means you no more Mischief than a Parrat:
The words for Friend and Foe alike were made,
To Fetter 'em in Verse is all his Trade.
For Almonds he'll cry Whore to his own Mother:
And call Young *Absalom* King *David*'s Brother.
Let him be Gallows-Free by my Consent,
And nothing Suffer since he nothing Meant;
Hanging supposes Humane Soul and Reason,
This Animal's below committing Treason:
Shall he be hang'd who never cou'd Rebell?
That's a preferment for *Achitophel.*
The Woman that committed Buggary,
Was rightly Sentenc'd by the Law to die;
But 'twas hard Fate that to the Gallows led,
The Dog that never heard the Statute read.
Railing in other Men may be a Crime,
But ought to pass for mere Instinct in him;
Instinct he follows and no farther knows,
For to write Verse with him is to *transprose.*
'Twere pity Treason at his Door to lay,
Who *makes Heaven's Gate a Lock to its own Key*:[2]
Let him Rail on, let his invective Muse
Have four and Twenty Letters to abuse,
Which if he Jumbles to one Line of Sense,
Indict him of a Capital Offence.

[1] Elkanah Settle (1648–1724) had quarrelled with Dryden before he replied to *Absalom and Achitophel* in a satire defending the Whigs, clumsily entitled *Absalom Senior: or, Achitophel Transprosed*, 1682. Dryden makes fun of this title in the line 'For to write Verse with him is to *transprose.*'

[2] A line from Settle's *Absalom Senior: or, Achitophel Transpros'd.*

In Fire-works give him leave to vent his Spight,
Those are the onely Serpents he can write;
The height of his Ambition is we know
But to be Master of a Puppet-show,
On that one Stage his Works may yet appear,
And a Months Harvest keeps him all the Year.

Now stop your Noses, Readers, all and some,
For here's a Tun of Midnight-work to come,
Og[1] from a Treason Tavern rowling Home.
Round as a Globe, and Liquor'd ev'ry chink,
Goodly and great he sayls behind his Link;
With all this bulk ther's nothing lost in *Og*,
For ev'ry inch that is not Fool is Rogue:
A Monstrous mass of foul corrupted matter,
As all the Devils had spew'd to make the batter.
When wine has given him courage to Blaspheme,
He curses God, but God before curst him;
And if man cou'd have reason none has more,
That made his Paunch so rich and him so poor.
With wealth he was not trusted, for Heav'n knew
What 'twas of old to pamper up a *Jew*;
To what wou'd he on Quail and Pheasant swell,
That ev'n on Tripe and Carrion cou'd rebell?
But though Heav'n made him poor, (with rev'rence speaking,)
He never was a Poet of God's making;
The Midwife laid her hand on his thick skull,
With this Prophetick blessing—*Be thou Dull;*
Drink, swear and roar, forbear no lewd delight
Fit for thy bulk, do any thing but write:
Thou art of lasting Make, like thoughtless men,
A strong Nativity—but for the pen;
Eat Opium, mingle Arsenick in thy drink,
Still thou mayst live avoiding pen and ink.
I see, I see, 'tis Counsel given in vain,
For Treason botcht in Rhime will be thy bane;
Rhime is the Rock on which thou art to wreck,
'Tis fatal to thy fame and to thy Neck:
Why shou'd thy metre good King *David* blast?
A Psalm of his will surely be thy last.
Dar'st thou presume in verse to meet thy foes,

[1] Thomas Shadwell, the hero of *Mac Flecknoe*.

Thou whom the penny Pamphlet foil'd in prose?
Doeg, whom God for Mankinds mirth has made,
O'er-tops thy tallent in thy very trade;
Doeg to thee, thy paintings are so course,
A Poet is, though he's the Poets Horse.
A double Noose thou on thy Neck dost pull
For writing Treason, and for writing dull;
To die for Faction is a common evil,
But to be hang'd for Non-sense is the Devil:
Hadst thou the Glories of thy King exprest,
Thy praises had been Satyr at the best;
But thou in clumsie Verse, unlickt, unpointed,
Hast shamefully defi'd the Lord's anointed:
I will not rake the Dung-hill of thy Crimes,
For who would read thy Life that reads thy Rhimes?
But of King *Davids* Foes, be this the Doom,
May all be like the Young-man *Absalom*;
And for my Foes may this their Blessing be,
To talk like *Doeg*, and to write like thee.

RELIGIO LAICI

OR A LAYMANS FAITH

A POEM

Ornari res ipsa negat; contenta doceri [1]

[1] My very subject, content to be taught, spurns adornment. (Manilius, *Astronomica* 3. 39.)

Religio Laici or a Laymans Faith. A Poem. Written by Mr. Dryden. [*Latin quot.*] London, Printed for Jacob Tonson at the Judge's Head in Chancery-Lane, near Fleet-street. 1682.

THE present text follows that of the second issue of the first edition (Macdonald, 16 a ii).

THE PREFACE

A POEM with so bold a Title, and a Name prefix'd, from which the handling of so serious a Subject wou'd not be expected, may reasonably oblige the Author, to say somewhat in defence both of himself, and of his undertaking. In the first place, if it be objected to me that being a *Layman*, I ought not to have concern'd my self with Speculations, which belong to the Profession of *Divinity*; I cou'd Answer, that perhaps, Laymen, with equal advantages of Parts and Knowledge, are not tne most incompetent Judges of Sacred things; But in the due sense of my own weakness and want of Learning, I plead not this; I pretend not to make my self a Judge of Faith, in others, but onely to make a Confession of my own; I lay no unhallow'd hand upon the Ark; but wait on it, with the Reverence that becomes me at a distance: in the next place I will ingeniously confess, that the helps I have us'd in this small Treatise, were many of them taken from the Works of our own Reverend Divines of the Church of *England*; so that the Weapons with which I Combat Irreligion, are already Consecrated; though I suppose they may be taken down as lawfully as the Sword of *Goliah* was by *David*, when they are to be employed for the common Cause, against the Enemies of Piety. I intend not by this to intitle them to any of my errours; which, yet, I hope are only those of Charity to Mankind; and such as my *own* Charity has caus'd me to commit, that of *others* may more easily excuse. Being naturally inclin'd to Scepticism in Philosophy, I have no reason to impose my Opinions, in a Subject which is above it: But whatever they are, I submit them with all reverence to my Mother Church, accounting them no further mine, than as they are Authoriz'd, or at least, uncondemn'd by her. And, indeed, to secure my self on this side, I have us'd the necessary Precaution, of showing this Paper before it was Publish'd to a judicious and learned Friend, a Man indefatigably zealous in the service of the Church and State: and whose Writings, have highly deserv'd of both. He was pleas'd to approve the body of the Discourse, and I hope he is more my Friend, than to do it out of Complaisance: 'Tis true he had too good a tast to like it all; and amongst some other faults recommended to my second view, What I have written, perhaps too boldly on St. *Athanasius*: which he advised me wholly to omit. I am sensible enough that I had done more *prudently* to have follow'd his opinion: But then I could not have satisfied my self, that I had done honestly not to have written what was my own. It has always been my *thought*, that Heathens, who never did, nor without Miracle cou'd hear of the name of Christ, were yet in a possibility of Salvation. Neither will it enter easily into my belief, that before the coming of our Saviour, the whole World excepting only the Jewish Nation, shou'd lye under the inevitable necessity of everlasting Punishment, for want of that Revelation, which was confin'd to so small a spot of ground as that of *Palestine*. Among the Sons of *Noah* we read of one only who was accurs'd; and if a blessing in the ripeness of time was reserv'd for *Japhet*, (of whose Progeny we are,) it seems unaccountable to me, why so many Generations of the same Offspring, as preceeded our Saviour in the Flesh, shou'd be all involv'd in one common condemnation, and yet that their Posterity shou'd be Intitled to the hopes of Salvation: As if a Bill of Exclusion had passed only on the Fathers, which debar'd not the Sons from their Succession. Or that so many Ages had been *deliver'd over* to Hell, and so many *reserv'd* for Heaven, and that the Devil had the first choice, and God the next. Truly I am apt to think, that the revealed Religion which was taught by *Noah* to all his Sons, might continue for some Ages in the whole Posterity. That afterwards it was included wholly in the Family of *Sem* is manifest: but when the Progenies of *Cham* and *Japhet* swarm'd into Colonies, and those Colonies were subdivided into many others; in process of time their Decendants lost by little and little the Primitive and purer Rites of Divine Worship, retaining onely the notion of one Deity; to which succeeding Generations added others: (for Men took their degrees in those Ages from Conquerours to Gods.) Revelation being thus Eclipsed to almost all Mankind, the light of Nature as the next in Dignity was substituted, and that is it which St. *Paul* concludes to be the Rule of the Heathens; and by which they are hereafter to be judg'd. If my supposition be true, then the consequence which I have assum'd in my Poem may be also true; namely, that Deism, or the Principles of Natural Worship are onely the faint remnants or dying flames of reveal'd Religion in the Posterity of *Noah*: And that our Modern Philosophers, nay and some of our Philosophising Divines have too much exalted the faculties of our Souls, when they have maintain'd that by their force, mankind has been able to find out that there is one Supream Agent or Intellectual being which we call God: that Praise and Prayer are his due Worship; and the rest of those deducements, which I am confident are the remote effects of Revelation, and unatainable by our Discourse, I mean as simply considered, and without the benefit of Divine Illumination. So that we have not lifted up our selves to God, by the weak Pinions of our Reason, but he has been pleased to descend to us: and what *Socrates* said of him, what *Plato* writ, and the rest of the Heathen Philosophers of several Nations, is all no more than the Twilight of Revelation, after the Sun of it was set in the Race of *Noah*. That there is some thing above us, some Principle of *motion*, our Reason can apprehend, though it cannot discover what it is, by its own Vertue. And indeed 'tis very improbable, that we, who by the strength of our faculties cannot enter into the knowledge of any *Beeing*, not so much as of our *own*, should be able to find out by them, that Supream Nature, which we cannot otherwise define, than by saying it is Infinite; as if Infinite were definable, or Infinity a Subject for our narrow understanding. They who wou'd prove Religion by Reason, do but weaken the cause which they endeavour to support: 'tis to take away the Pillars from our Faith, and to prop it only with a twig: 'tis to design a Tower like that of *Babel*, which if it were possible (as it is not) to reach Heaven, would come to nothing by the confusion of the Workmen. For every man is Building a several way; impotently conceipted of his own Model, and his own Materials: Reason is always striving, and always at a loss, and of necessity it must so come to pass, while 'tis exercis'd about that which is not its own proper object. Let us be content at last, to know God, by his own Methods; at least so much of him, as he is pleas'd to reveal to us, in the sacred Scriptures; to apprehend them to be the word of God, is all our Reason has to do; for all beyond it is the work of Faith, which is the Seal of Heaven impress'd upon our humane understanding.

And now for what concerns the Holy Bishop *Athanasius*, the Preface of whose Creed seems inconsistent with my opinion; which is, That Heathens may possibly be sav'd; in the first place I desire it may be consider'd that it is the Preface onely, not the Creed it self, which, (till I am better inform'd) is of too hard a digestion for my Charity. 'Tis not that I am ignorant how many several Texts of Scripture seemingly support that Cause; but neither am I ignorant how all those Texts may receive a kinder, and more mollified Interpretation. Every man who is read in Church History, knows *that* Belief was drawn up after a long contestation with *Arrius*, concerning the Divinity of our Blessed Saviour, and his being one Substance with the Father; and that thus compil'd, it was sent abroad among the Christian Churches, as a kind of Test, which whosever took, was look'd on as an Orthodox Believer. 'Tis manifest from hence, that the Heathen part of the Empire was not concerned in it: for its business was not to distinguish betwixt Pagans and Christians, but betwixt Hereticks and true Believers. This, well consider'd, takes off the heavy weight of Censure, which I wou'd willingly avoid from so venerable a Man; for if this Proportion, *whosoever will be sav'd*, be restrained onely, to those to whom it was intended, and for whom it was compos'd, I mean the Christians; then the Anathema reaches not the Heathens, who had never heard of Christ, and were nothing interessed in that dispute. After all, I am far from blaming even that Prefatory addition to the Creed, and as far from cavilling at the continuation of it in the Liturgy of the Church; where on the days appointed, 'tis publickly read: For I suppose there is the same reason for it now, in opposition to the Socinians, as there was then against the Arrians; the one being a Heresy, which seems to have been refin'd out of the other; and with how much more plausibility of Reason it combats our Religion, with so much more caution to be avoided: and therefore the prudence of our Church is to be commended which has interpos'd her Authority for the recommendation of this Creed. Yet to such as are grounded in the true belief, those explanatory Creeds, the *Nicene* and this of *Athanasius* might perhaps be spar'd: for what is supernatural, will always be a mystery in spight of Exposition: and for my own part the plain Apostles Creed, is most suitable to my weak understanding; as the simplest diet is the most easy of Digestion.

I have dwelt longer on this Subject than I intended; and longer than, perhaps, I ought; for having laid down, as my Foundation, that the Scripture is a Rule; that in all things needfull to Salvation, it is clear, sufficient, and ordain'd by God Almighty for that purpose, I have left my self no right to interpret obscure places, such as concern the possibility of eternal happiness to Heathens: because whatsoever is obscure is concluded not necessary to be known.

But, by asserting the Scripture to be the Canon of our Faith, I have unavoidably created to my self two sorts of Enemies: The Papists indeed, more directly, because they have kept the Scripture from us, what they cou'd; and have reserv'd to themselves a right of Interpreting what they have deliver'd under the pretence of Infallibility: and the Fanaticks more collaterally, because they have assum'd what amounts to an Infallibility, in the private Spirit: and have detorted those Texts of Scripture, which are not necessary to Salvation, to the damnable uses of Sedition, disturbance and destruction of the Civil Government. To begin with the Papists, and to speak freely, I think them the less dangerous (at least, in appearance to our present State) for not only the Penal Laws are in force against them, and their number is contemptible; but also their Peerage and Commons are excluded from Parliaments, and consequently those Laws in no probability of being Repeal'd. A General and Uninterrupted Plot of their Clergy, ever since the Reformation, I suppose all Protestants believe. For 'tis not reasonable to think but that so many of their Orders, as were outed from their fat-possessions, wou'd endeavour a re-entrance against those whom they account Hereticks. As for the late design, Mr. *Coleman*s Letters,[1] for aught I know are the best Evidence; and what they discover, without wyre-drawing their Sense, or malicious Glosses, all men of reason conclude credible. If there be any thing more than this requir'd of me, I must believe it as well as I am able, in spight of the Witnesses, and out of a decent conformity to the Votes of Parliament: For I suppose the Fanaticks will not allow the private Spirit in this Case: Here the Infallibility is at least in one part of the Government; and our understandings as well as our wills are represented. But to return to the Roman Catholicks, how can we be secure from the practice of Jesuited Papists in that Religion? For not two or three of that Order, as some of them would impose upon us, but almost the whole Body of them are of opinion, that their Infallible Master has a right over Kings, not only in Spirituals but Temporals. Not to name *Mariana*, *Bellarmine*, *Emanuel Sa*, *Molina*, *Santarel*, *Simancha*,[2] and at least twenty others of Foreign Countries; we can produce of our own Nation, *Champian*, and *Doleman* or *Parsons*,[3] besides many are nam'd whom I have not read, who all of them attest this Doctrine, that the Pope can Depose and give away the Right of any Sovereign Prince, *si vel paulum deflexerit*, if he shall never so little Warp: but if he once comes to be Excommunicated, then the bond of obedience is taken off from Subjects; and they may and ought to drive him like another *Nebuchadnezzar*, *ex hominum Christianorum Dominatu*, from exercising Dominion over Christians: and to this they are bound

[1] Francis Coleman, secretary to the Duke of York, had been engaged in a treasonable correspondence to establish Roman Catholicism in England. His letters proved the existence of a Popish Plot. He was the first of Titus Oates's victims and was executed in 1678.

[2] Jesuit writers of the 16th century.

[3] Edmund Campion (1540–1581) and Robert Parsons (1546–1610) were English Jesuits. Campion was executed and Parsons, fleeing to Rome, published, under the name of Doleman, a work advancing the views to which Dryden refers.

by virtue of Divine Precept, and by all the tyes of Conscience under no less Penalty than Damnation. If they answer me (as a Learned Priest has lately Written,) that this Doctrine of the Jesuits is not *de fide*, and that consequently they are not oblig'd by it, they must pardon me, if I think they have said nothing to the purpose; for 'tis a Maxim in their Church, where Points of Faith are not decided, and that Doctors are of contrary opinions, they may follow which part they please; but more safely the most receiv'd and most Authoriz'd. And their Champion *Bellarmine* has told the World, in his Apology, that the King of *England* is a Vassal to the Pope, *ratione directi Dominii*, and that he holds in Villanage of his Roman Landlord. Which is no new claim put in for *England*. Our Chronicles are his Authentique Witnesses, that King *John* was depos'd by the same Plea, and *Philip Augustus* admitted Tenant. And which makes the more for *Bellarmine*, the French King was again ejected when our King submitted to the Church, and the Crown receiv'd under the sordid Condition of a Vassalage.

'Tis not sufficient for the more moderate and well-meaning Papists (of which I doubt not there are many) to produce the Evidences of their Loyalty to the late King, and to declare their Innocency in this Plot; I will grant their behaviour in the first, to have been as Loyal and as brave as they desire; and will be willing to hold them excus'd as to the second, (I mean when it comes to my turn, and after my betters; for 'tis a madness to be sober alone, while the Nation continues Drunk:) but that saying of their Father *Cres:*[1] is still running in my head, that they may be dispens'd with in their Obedience to an Heretick Prince, while the necessity of the times shall oblige them to it: (for that, (as another of them tells us,) is onely the effect of Christian Prudence,) but when once they shall get power to shake him off, an Heretick is no lawful King, and consequently to rise against him is no Rebellion. I should be glad therefore, that they wou'd follow the advice which was charitably given them by a Reverend Prelate of our Church; namely, that they would joyn in a publick Act of disowning and detesting those Jesuitick Principles; and subscribe to all Doctrines which deny the Popes Authority of deposing Kings, and releasing Subjects from their Oath of Allegiance: to which I shou'd think they might easily be induc'd, if it be true that this present Pope has condemn'd the Doctrine of King-killing (a Thesis of the Jesuites) amongst others *ex Cathedra* (as they call it) or in open Consistory.

[1] Serenus Cressy (1605–1647), Roman Catholic chaplain to Queen Catherine of England.

Leaving them, therefore, in so fair a way (if they please themselves) of satisfying all reasonable Men, of their sincerity and good meaning to the Government, I shall make bold to consider that other extream of our Religion, I mean the Fanaticks, or Schismaticks, of the English Church. Since the Bible has been Translated into our Tongue, they have us'd it so, as if their business was not to be sav'd but to be damn'd by its Contents. If we consider only them, better it had been for the English Nation, that it had still remain'd in the original Greek and Hebrew, or at least in the honest Latine of St. *Jerome*, than that several Texts in it, should have been prevaricated to the destruction of that Government, which put it into so ungrateful hands.

How many Heresies the first Translation of *Tyndal*[1] produced in few years, let my Lord *Herbert*'s History of *Henry* the Eighth inform you;[2] Insomuch that for the gross errours in it, and the great mischiefs it occasion'd, a Sentence pass'd on the first Edition of the Bible, too shameful almost to be repeated. After the short Reign of *Edward* the Sixth (who had continued to carry on the Reformation, on other principles than it was begun) every one knows that not onely the chief promoters of that work, but many others, whose Consciences wou'd not dispence with Popery, were forc'd, for fear of persecution, to change Climates: from whence returning at the beginning of Queen *Elizabeth*'s Reign, many of them who had been in *France*, and at *Geneva*, brought back the rigid opinions and imperious discipline of *Calvin*, to graffe upon our Reformation. Which, though they cunningly conceal'd at first, (as well knowing how nauseously that Drug wou'd go down in a lawful Monarchy, which was prescrib'd for a rebellious Common-wealth) yet they always kept it in reserve; and were never wanting to themselves either in Court or Parliament, when either they had any prospect of a numerous Party of Fanatique Members in the one, or the encouragement of any Favourite in the other, whose Covetousness was gaping at the Patrimony of the Church. They who will consult the Works of our venerable *Hooker*, or the account of his Life,[3] or more particularly the Letter written to him on this Subject, by *George Cranmer*, may see by what gradations they proceeded; from the dislike of Cap and Surplice, the very next step was Admonitions to the

[1] William Tyndal's translation of the New Testament was published in 1525.

[2] Edward, Lord Herbert of Cherbury (1583–1648). His *Life of Henry VIII* was published in 1649.

[3] A reference to Izaak Walton's biography of Richard Hooker, where the letter which Dryden mentions is printed.

Parliament against the whole Government Ecclesiastical: then came out Volumes in English and Latin in defence of their Tenets: and immediately, practices were set on foot to erect their discipline without Authority. Those not succeeding, Satyre and Rayling was the next: And *Martin Mar-Prelate*[1] (the *Marvel*[2] of those times) was the first Presbyterian Scribler, who sanctify'd Libels and Scurrility to the use of the Good Old Cause. Which was done (says my Authour) upon this account; that (their serious Treatises having been fully answered and refuted) they might compass by railing what they had lost by reasoning; and when their Cause was sunk in Court and Parliament, they might at least hedge in a stake amongst the Rabble: for to their ignorance all things are Wit which are abusive; but if Church and State were made the Theme, then the Doctoral Degree of Wit was to be taken at *Billingsgate*: even the most Saintlike of the Party, though they durst not excuse this contempt and villifying of the Government, yet were pleas'd, and grin'd at it with a pious smile: and call'd it a judgment of God against the Hierarchy. Thus Sectaries, we may see, were born with teeth, foul-mouth'd and scurrilous from their Infancy: and if Spiritual Pride, Venome, Violence, Contempt of Superiours and Slander had been the marks of Orthodox Belief; the Presbytery and the rest of our Schismaticks, which are their Spawn, were always the most visible Church in the Christian World.

'Tis true, the Government was too strong at that time for a Rebellion; but to shew what proficiency they had made in *Calvin*'s School, even *Then* their mouths water'd at it: for two of their gifted Brotherhood (*Hacket* and *Coppinger*[3]) as the Story tells us, got up into a Pease-Cart, and harangued the People, to dispose them to an insurrection, and to establish their Discipline by force: so that however it comes about, that now they celebrate Queen *Elizabeth*'s Birth-night, as that of their Saint and Patroness; yet then they were for doing the work of the Lord by Arms against her; and in all probability, they wanted but a Fanatique Lord Mayor and two Sheriffs of their Party to have compass'd it.

Our venerable *Hooker*, after many Admonitions which he had given them, toward the end of his Preface, breaks out into this

[1] Martin Marprelate, the pseudonym of the author of a number of pamphlets attacking the bishops and defending the Presbyterian system which appeared in 1588–9.

[2] Andrew Marvell (1621–1678).

[3] Hacket proclaimed himself the Messiah in the streets of London in 1591; Coppinger announced himself as among his prophets. Hacket was executed and Coppinger starved himself to death in prison.

Prophetick speech. "*There is in every one of these Considerations most just cause to fear lest our hastiness to embrace a thing of so perilous Consequence* (meaning the Presbyterian Discipline) *should cause Posterity to feel those Evils, which as yet are more easy for us to prevent, than they would be for them to remedy.*"

How fatally this *Cassandra* has foretold we know too well by sad experience: the Seeds were sown in the time of Queen *Elizabeth*, the bloudy Harvest ripened in the Reign of King *Charles* the Martyr: and because all the Sheaves could not be carried off, without shedding some of the loose Grains, another Crop is too like to follow; nay I fear 'tis unavoidable if the Conventiclers be permitted still to scatter.

A man may be suffer'd to quote an Adversary to our Religion, when he speaks Truth: and 'tis the observation of *Meimbourg* in his History of Calvinism, that where-ever that Discipline was planted and embrac'd, Rebellion, Civil War and Misery attended it. And how indeed should it happen otherwise? Reformation of Church and State has always been the ground of our Divisions in *England*. While we were Papists, our Holy Father rid us, by pretending authority out of the Scriptures to depose Princes, when we shook off his Authority, the Sectaries furnish'd themselves with the same Weapons; and out of the same Magazine, the Bible. So that the Scriptures, which are in themselves the greatest security of Governours, as commanding express obedience to them, are now turn'd to their destruction: and never since the Reformation has there wanted a Text of their interpreting to authorize a Rebel. And 'tis to be noted by the way, that the Doctrines of King-killing and Deposing, which have been taken up onely by the worst Party of the Papists, the most frontless Flatterers of the Pope's Authority, have been espous'd, defended, and are still maintain'd by the whole Body of Nonconformists and Republicans. 'Tis but dubbing themselves the People of God, which 'tis the interest of their Preachers to tell them they are, and their own interest to believe; and after that, they cannot dip into the Bible, but one Text or another will turn up for their purpose: If they are under Persecution (as they call it) then that is a mark of their Election; if they flourish, then God works Miracles for their Deliverance, and the Saints are to possess the Earth.

They may think themselves to be too roughly handled in this Paper; but I who know best how far I could have gon on this Subject, must be bold to tell them they are spar'd: though at the same time I am not ignorant that they interpret the mildness of a Writer to them, as they do the mercy of the Government; in the one they think it fear, and conclude it weakness in the other. The best way for them to confute me, is, as I before advis'd the Papists, to disclaim their Principles, and renounce their Practices. We shall all be glad to think them true Englishmen when they obey the King, and true Protestants when they conform to the Church Discipline.

It remains that I acquaint the Reader, that the Verses were written for an ingenious young Gentleman my Friend;[1] upon his Translation of *The Critical History of the Old Testament*, compos'd by the learned Father *Simon*: The Verses therefore are address'd to the Translatour of that Work, and the style of them is, what it ought to be, Epistolary.

If any one be so lamentable a Critick as to require the Smoothness, the Numbers and the Turn of Heroick Poetry in this Poem; I must tell him, that if he has not read *Horace*, I have studied him, and hope the style of his Epistles is not ill imitated here. The Expressions of a Poem, design'd purely for Instruction, ought to be Plain and Natural, and yet Majestick: for here the Poet is presum'd to be a kind of Law-giver, and those three qualities which I have nam'd are proper to the Legislative style. The Florid, Elevated and Figurative way is for the Passions; for Love and Hatred, Fear and Anger, are begotten in the Soul by shewing their Objects out of their true proportion; either greater than the Life, or less; but Instruction is to be given by shewing them what they naturally are. A Man is to be cheated into Passion, but to be reason'd into Truth.

[1] The young friend was Henry Dickinson.

RELIGIO LAICI

DIM, as the borrow'd beams of Moon and Stars
To *lonely*, *weary*, *wandring* Travellers,
Is *Reason* to the *Soul*: and as on high,
Those rowling Fires *discover* but the Sky
Not light us *here*; So *Reason*'s glimmering Ray
Was lent not to *assure* our *doubtful* way,
But *guide* us upward to a *better Day*.
And as those nightly Tapers disappear
When Day's bright Lord ascends our Hemisphere
So pale grows *Reason* at *Religions* Sight:
So *dyes*, and so *dissolves* in *Supernatural Light*.
Some few, whose Lamp shone brighter, have been led
From Cause to Cause, to *Natures* secret Head;
And found that *one first Principle* must be:
But *what*, or *who*, that *UNIVERSAL HE*;
Whether some *Soul* incompassing this Ball
Unmade, *unmov'd*; yet *making*, *moving all*;
Or various *Atoms*' interfering Dance
Leapt into *Form* (the Noble work of *Chance*;)
Or this great *All* was from *Eternity*;
Not even the *Stagirite* himself could see;
And *Epicurus Guess'd* as well as He:
As *blindly grop'd* they for a *future State*;
As *rashly Judg'd* of *Providence* and *Fate*:
But least of all could their Endeavours find
What most concern'd the good of Humane kind
For *Happiness* was never to be found;
But vanish'd from 'em, like Enchanted Ground.
One thought *Content* the Good to be enjoy'd:
This, every little *Accident* destroy'd:
The *wiser Madmen* did for *Vertue* toyl:
A Thorny, or at best a barren Soil:
In *Pleasure* some their glutton Souls would steep;
But found their Line too short, the Well too deep;
And leaky Vessels which no *Bliss* cou'd keep.
Thus *anxeous Thoughts* in *endless Circles* roul,
Without a *Centre* where to fix the *Soul*:

Opinions of the several Sects of Philosophers concerning the Summum Bonum.

In this wild Maze their vain Endeavours end
How can the *less* the *Greater* comprehend?
Or *finite Reason* reach *Infinity*?
For what cou'd *Fathom* GOD were *more* than *He*.

Systeme of Deisme.

The *Deist* thinks he stands on firmer ground;
Cries εὕρηκα the mighty Secret's found:
God is that *Spring* of *Good*; *Supreme*, and *Best*;
We, made to *serve*, and in that Service *blest*;
If so, some *Rules* of Worship must be given;
Distributed alike to all by Heaven:
Else *God* were *partial*, and to *some* deny'd
The means his Justice shou'd for all provide.
This *general Worship* is to PRAISE, and PRAY:
One part to *borrow* Blessings, one to *pay*:
And when frail Nature slides into *Offence*,
The *Sacrifice* for *Crimes* is *Penitence*.
Yet, since th' Effects of Providence, we find
Are variously dispens'd to Human kind;
That *Vice Triumphs*, and *Vertue suffers* here,
(A Brand that Sovereign Justice cannot bear;)
Our Reason prompts us to a *future* State:
The *last Appeal* from *Fortune*, and from *Fate*:
Where God's all-righteous ways will be declar'd;
The *Bad* meet *Punishment*, the *Good*, *Reward*.

of Reveal'd Religion.

Thus Man by his own Strength to Heaven wou'd soar:
And wou'd not be Oblig'd to God for more.
Vain, wretched Creature, how art thou misled
To think thy Wit these God-like Notions bred!
These Truths are not the Product of thy Mind,
But dropt from Heaven, and of a Nobler kind.
Reveal'd Religion first inform'd thy Sight,
And *Reason* saw not, till *Faith* sprung the Light.
Hence all thy *Natural Worship* takes the *Source*:
'Tis *Revelation* what thou thinkst *Discourse*.
Else how com'st *Thou* to see these truths so clear,
Which so obscure to *Heathens* did appear?
Not *Plato* these, nor *Aristotle* found:
Nor He whose Wisdom *Oracles* renown'd. *Socrates.*
Hast thou a Wit so deep, or so sublime,
Or canst thou lower dive, or higher climb?

Canst *Thou*, by *reason*, more of *God-head* know
Than *Plutarch*, *Seneca*, or *Cicero*?
Those Gyant Wits, in happier Ages born,
(When *Arms*, and *Arts* did *Greece* and *Rome* adorn)
Knew no such *Systeme*: no such Piles cou'd raise
Of *Natural Worship*, built on *Pray'r* and *Praise*,
To one sole GOD.
Nor did Remorse, to Expiate Sin, prescribe:
But slew their fellow Creatures for a Bribe:
The guiltless *Victim* groan'd for their Offence;
And *Cruelty*, and *Blood* was *Penitence*.
If *Sheep* and *Oxen* cou'd attone for Men
Ah! at how cheap a rate the *Rich* might Sin!
And great Oppressours might Heavens Wrath beguile
By offering his own Creatures for a Spoil!

Dar'st thou, poor Worm, offend *Infinity*?
And must the Terms of Peace be given by *Thee*?
Then *Thou* art *Justice* in the *last Appeal*;
Thy easy God instructs thee to *rebell*:
And, like a King remote, and weak, must take
What Satisfaction *Thou* art pleas'd to make.

But if there be a *Pow'r* too *Just*, and *strong*
To wink at *Crimes*, and bear unpunish'd *Wrong*;
Look humbly upward, see his Will disclose
The *Forfeit* first, and then the *Fine* impose:
A *Mulct thy* Poverty could never pay
Had not *Eternal Wisdom* found the way:
And with Cœlestial Wealth supply'd thy Store:
His Justice makes the *Fine*, *his Mercy* quits the *Score*.
See God descending in thy Humane Frame;
Th' *offended*, suff'ring in th' *Offenders* Name:
All thy Misdeeds to him imputed see;
And all his Righteousness devolv'd on thee.

For granting we have Sin'd, and that th' offence
Of *Man*, is made against *Omnipotence*,
Some Price, that bears *proportion*, must be paid;
And *Infinite* with *Infinite* be weigh'd.
See then the *Deist lost*: *Remorse* for *Vice*,
Not paid, or *paid*, *inadequate* in price:

What farther means can *Reason* now direct,
Or what Relief from *human Wit* expect?
That shews us *sick*; and sadly are we sure
Still to be *Sick*, till *Heav'n* reveal the *Cure*:
If then *Heaven's Will* must needs be understood,
(Which must, if we want *Cure*, and *Heaven*, be *Good*)
Let all Records of *Will reveal'd* be shown;
With *Scripture*, all in equal ballance thrown,
And *our one Sacred Book* will be *That one*.

Proof needs not here, for whether we compare
That Impious, Idle, Superstitious Ware
Of *Rites*, *Lustrations*, *Offerings*, (which before,
In various Ages, various Countries bore)
With *Christian Faith* and *Vertues*, we shall find
None answ'ring the great ends of humane kind,
But *This one Rule of Life*: *That* shews us best
How *God* may be *appeas'd*, and *Mortals blest*.
Whether from length of *Time* its worth we draw,
The *World* is scarce more *Ancient* than the *Law*:
Heav'ns early Care prescrib'd for every Age;
First, in the *Soul*, and after, in the *Page*.
Or, whether more abstractedly we look,
Or on the *Writers*, or the *written Book*,
Whence, but from *Heav'n*, cou'd Men unskill'd in arts,
In several Ages born, in several parts,
Weave such *agreeing Truths*? or *how*, or *why*
Shou'd *all* conspire to cheat us with a *Lye*?
Unask'd their *Pains*, *ungrateful* their *Advice*,
Starving their *Gain*, and *Martyrdom* their *Price*.

If on the Book it self we cast our view,
Concurrent Heathens prove the Story *True*:
The *Doctrine*, *Miracles*; which must convince,
For *Heav'n* in *Them* appeals to *humane Sense*:
And though they *prove* not, they *Confirm* the Cause,
When what is *Taught* agrees with *Natures Laws*.

Then for the *Style*; *Majestick* and *Divine*,
It speaks no less than God in every Line:
Commanding words; whose *Force* is still the same
As the first *Fiat* that produc'd our Frame.

All Faiths *beside*, or did by *Arms* ascend;
Or *Sense* indulg'd has made *Mankind* their *Friend*:
This *only* Doctrin does our *Lusts* oppose:
Unfed by Natures Soil, in which it grows;
Cross to our *Interests*, curbing Sense, and Sin;
Oppress'd without, and undermin'd within,
It thrives through pain; its own Tormentors tires;
And with a stubborn patience still aspires.
To what can *Reason* such Effects assign,
Transcending *Nature*, but to *Laws Divine*:
Which in that Sacred Volume are contain'd;
Sufficient, clear, and for that use ordain'd.

Objection of the Deist.

But stay: the *Deist* here will urge anew,
No *Supernatural Worship* can be *True*:
Because a *general Law* is that alone
Which must to *all*, and every *where* be known:
A Style so large as not *this* Book can claim
Nor ought that bears *reveal'd* Religions *Name*.
'Tis said the sound of a *Messiah*'s *Birth*
Is gone through all the habitable Earth:
But still that Text must be confin'd alone
To what was *Then* inhabited, and known:
And what Provision cou'd from *thence* accrue
To *Indian* Souls, and Worlds discover'd *New*?
In other parts it helps, that Ages past,
The Scriptures there were *known*, and were *imbrac'd*,
Till Sin spread once again the Shades of Night:
What's that to these who never *saw* the Light?

The Objection answered.

Of all Objections this indeed is chief
To startle Reason, stagger frail Belief:
We grant, 'tis true, that Heav'n from humane Sense
Has hid the secret Paths of *Providence*:
But *boundless Wisdom*, *boundless Mercy*, may
Find ev'n for those *be-wildred* Souls, a *way*:
If from his *Nature Foes* may Pity claim,
Much more may *Strangers* who ne'er heard his *Name*.
And though *no Name* be for *Salvation* known,
But that of his *Eternal Sons* alone;
Who knows how far transcending Goodness can
Extend the *Merits* of *that Son* to *Man*?

Who knows what *Reasons* may his *Mercy* lead;
Or *Ignorance invincible* may plead?
Not only *Charity* bids hope the *best*,
But *more* the great Apostle has exprest.
That, if the Gentiles (whom no Law inspir'd,)
By Nature did what was by *Law requir'd*;
They, who the written Rule had never known,
Where to themselves both Rule and Law alone:
To Natures plain Indictment they shall plead;
And, by their Conscience, be condemn'd or freed.
Most righteous Doom! because a *Rule reveal'd*
Is none to *Those*, from whom it was *conceal'd.*
Then those who follow'd *Reasons* Dictates right;
Liv'd up, and lifted high their *Natural Light*;
With *Socrates* may see their Maker's Face,
While Thousand *Rubrick-Martyrs* want a place.

Nor does it baulk my *Charity*, to find
Th' *Egyptian* Bishop of another mind:
For, though his *Creed Eternal Truth* contains,
'Tis hard for *Man* to doom to *endless Pains*
All who believ'd not all, his Zeal requir'd,
Unless he first cou'd prove he was inspir'd.
Then let us either think he meant to say
This faith, where *publish'd*, was the only way;
Or else conclude that, *Arius* to confute,
The good old Man, too eager in dispute,
Flew high; and as his *Christian* Fury rose
Damn'd all for *Hereticks* who durst *oppose.*

Digression to the Translator of Father* Simon's *Critical History of the Old Testament.

Thus far my Charity this path has try'd;
(A much unskilful, but well meaning guide:)
Yet what they are, ev'n these crude thoughts were bred
By reading that, which better thou hast read.
Thy Matchless Author's work: which thou, my Friend,[1]
By well translating better dost commend:
Those youthful hours which, of thy Equals most
In *Toys* have *squander'd*, or in *Vice* have *lost*,
Those hours hast thou to Nobler use employ'd;
And the severe Delights of Truth enjoy'd.
Witness this weighty Book, in which appears
The crabbed Toil of many thoughtful years,

[1] Henry Dickinson, to whom Dryden refers in the *Preface*.

Spent by thy Authour in the Sifting Care
Of *Rabbins* old Sophisticated Ware
From Gold Divine; which he who well can sort
May afterwards make *Algebra* a Sport.
A Treasure, which if *Country-Curates* buy,
They *Junius* and *Tremellius* may defy:[1]
Save pains in various readings, and Translations;
And without *Hebrew* make most learn'd quotations.
A work so full with various Learning fraught,
So nicely pondred, yet so strongly wrought,
As Natures height and Arts last hand requir'd:
As much as Man cou'd compass, uninspir'd.
Where we may see what Errours have been made
Both in the *Copiers* and *Translators Trade*:
How *Jewish*, *Popish*, Interests have prevail'd,
And where *Infallibility* has *fail'd*.

For some, who have his secret meaning *ghes'd*,
Have found our Author not too *much* a *Priest*:
For *Fashion-sake* he seems to have recourse
To *Pope*, and *Councils*, and *Traditions* force:
But he that *old* Traditions cou'd subdue,
Cou'd not but find the weakness of the *New*:
If *Scripture*, though deriv'd from *Heavenly Birth*,
Has been but carelessly preserv'd on *Earth*;
If *God's own People*, who of *God* before
Knew what we know, and had been promis'd more,
In fuller Terms, of Heaven's assisting Care,
And who did neither *Time*, nor *Study* spare
To keep this Book *untainted*, *unperplext*;
Let in gross *Errours* to corrupt the *Text*:
Omitted *Paragraphs*, embroyl'd the *Sense*;
With vain *Traditions* stopt the gaping Fence,
Which every common hand pull'd up with ease:
What Safety from such *brushwood-helps* as these?
If *written words* from time are not secur'd,
How can we think have *oral Sounds* endur'd?
Which *thus* transmitted, if *one* Mouth has fail'd,
Immortal Lyes on *Ages* are intail'd:
And that some such have been, is prov'd too plain;
If we consider *Interest*, *Church*, and *Gain*.

[1] Calvinist translators of the Scriptures.

Of the Infallibility of Tradition, in General.

Oh but says one, *Tradition* set aside,
Where can we hope for an *unerring Guid*?
For since th' *original* Scripture has been lost,
All Copies *disagreeing*, *maim'd* the *most*,
Or *Christian Faith* can have no *certain* ground,
Or *Truth* in *Church Tradition* must be found.

Such an *Omniscient* Church we wish indeed;
'Twere worth *Both Testaments*, and cast in the *Creed*:
But if *this Mother* be a *Guide* so sure,
As can all *doubts resolve*, all *truth secure*;
Then her *Infallibility*, as well
Where Copies are *corrupt*, or *lame*, can tell?
Restore *lost Canon* with as little Pains,
As *truly explicate* what still *remains*:
Which yet no *Council* dare *pretend* to do;
Unless like *Esdras*,[1] they cou'd *write* it new:
Strange Confidence, still to *interpret* true,
Yet not be sure that all they have explain'd,
Is in the blest *Original* contain'd.
More Safe, and much more modest 'tis, to say
God wou'd not leave Mankind without a way:
And that the *Scriptures*, though not *every where*
Free from Corruption, or intire, or clear,
Are uncorrupt, sufficient, clear, intire,
In *all* things which our needful *Faith* require.
If *others* in the *same Glass better* see
'Tis for *Themselves* they look, but not for *me*:
For MY Salvation must it's Doom receive
Not from what OTHERS, but what *I* believe.

Objection in behalf of Tradition urg'd by Father Simon.

Must *all Tradition* then be set aside?
This to affirm were Ignorance, or Pride.
Are there not many points, some needful sure
To saving Faith, that Scripture leaves obscure?
Which every Sect will wrest a several way
(For what *one* Sect Interprets, *all* Sects *may*:)
We hold, and say we prove from Scripture plain,
That *Christ* is *GOD*; the bold *Socinian*
From the *same* Scripture urges he's but *MAN*.

[1] See *Esdras*, viii, 7.

Now what Appeal can end th' important Suit;
Both parts *talk* loudly, but the *Rule* is *mute*?

Shall I speak plain, and in a Nation free
Assume an honest *Layman*'s *Liberty*?
I think (according to my little Skill,
To my own Mother-Church submitting still)
That many have been sav'd, and many may,
Who never heard this Question brought in play.
Th' *unletter'd* Christian, who believes in *gross*,
Plods on to *Heaven*; and ne'er is at a loss:
For the *Streight-gate* wou'd be made *streighter* yet,
Were *none* admitted there but men of *Wit*.
The few, by Nature form'd, with Learning fraught,
Born to instruct, as others to be taught,
Must Study well the Sacred Page; and see
Which Doctrine, this, or that, does best agree
With the whole Tenour of the Work Divine:
And plainlyest points to Heaven's reveal'd Design:
Which Exposition flows from *genuine Sense*;
And which is *forc'd* by *Wit* and *Eloquence*.
Not that Traditions parts are useless here:
When general, old, disinteress'd and clear:
That Antient Fathers thus expound the Page,
Gives *Truth* the reverend Majesty of *Age*:
Confirms its force, by biding every *Test*;
For best *Authority's* next *Rules* are *best*.
And still the nearer to the Spring we go
More limpid, more unsoyl'd the Waters flow.
Thus, *first Traditions* were a proof alone;
Cou'd we be *certain* such they *were*, so *known*:
But since some Flaws in long descent may be,
They make not *Truth* but *Probability*.
Even *Arius* and *Pelagius* durst provoke
To what the *Centuries preceding* spoke.
Such difference is there in an oft-told Tale:
But Truth by its own Sinews will prevail.
Tradition written therefore more commends
Authority, than what from *Voice* descends:
And this, as perfect as its kind can be,
Rouls down to us the Sacred History:
Which, from the *Universal Church receiv'd*,
Is *tri'd*, and *after*, for its *self* believ'd.

The Second Objection.

Answer to the Objection.

The partial *Papists* wou'd infer from hence
Their Church, in last resort, shou'd Judge the *Sense*.
But first they wou'd assume, with wondrous Art,
Themselves to be the *whole*, who are but *part*
Of that vast Frame, the Church; yet grant they were
The handers down, can they from thence infer
A right t' interpret? or wou'd they alone
Who brought the Present, claim it for their own?
The *Book*'s a *Common Largess* to Mankind;
Not more for *them*, than *every* Man design'd:
The *welcome News* is in the *Letter* found;
The *Carrier*'s not Commission'd to *expound*.
It speaks it *Self*, and what it does contain,
In all things *needful* to be known, is plain.

In times o'ergrown with Rust and Ignorance,
A gainful Trade their Clergy did advance:
When want of Learning kept the *Laymen* low,
And none but *Priests* were *Authoriz'd* to *know*:
When what small Knowledg was, in them did dwell;
And he a *God* who could but *Read* or *Spell*;
Then *Mother Church* did mightily prevail:
She parcel'd out the Bible by *retail*:
But still *expounded* what She *sold* or gave;
To keep it in *her Power* to *Damn* and *Save*:
Scripture was *scarce*, and as the Market went,
Poor *Laymen* took *Salvation* on *Content*;
As needy men take Money, good or bad:
God's Word they had not, but the *Priests* they had.
Yet, whate'er *false Conveyances* they made,
The *Lawyer* still was *certain* to be paid.
In those dark times they learn'd their knack so well,
That by long use they grew *Infallible*:
At last, a knowing Age began t' enquire
If *they* the *Book*, or *That* did *them* inspire:
And, making narrower search they found, tho late,
That what they thought the *Priest*'s, was *Their* Estate:
Taught by the *Will produc'd*, (the written Word)
How long they had been *cheated* on *Record*.
Then, every man who saw the Title fair,
Claim'd a Child's part, and put in for a Share:
Consulted Soberly his private good;
And sav'd himself as cheap as e'er he cou'd.

'Tis true, my Friend, (and far be Flattery hence)
This good had full as bad a Consequence:
The Book thus put in every vulgar hand,
Which each presum'd he best cou'd understand,
The *Common Rule* was made the *common Prey*;
And at the mercy of the *Rabble* lay.
The tender Page with horney Fists was gaul'd;
And he was gifted most that loudest baul'd:
The *Spirit* gave the *Doctoral Degree*:
And every member of a *Company*
Was of *his Trade*, and of the *Bible free*.
Plain *Truths* enough for needful *use* they found;
But men wou'd still be itching to *expound*:
Each was ambitious of th' obscurest place,
No measure ta'en from *Knowledg*, all from GRACE.
Study and *Pains* were now no more their Care:
Texts were explain'd by *Fasting*, and by *Prayer*:
This was the Fruit the *private Spirit* brought;
Occasion'd by *great Zeal*, and *little Thought*.
While Crouds unlearn'd, with rude Devotion warm,
About the Sacred Viands buz and swarm,
The *Fly-blown Text* creates a *crawling Brood*;
And turns to *Maggots* what was meant for *Food*.
A Thousand daily Sects rise up, and dye;
A Thousand more the perish'd Race supply:
So all we make of Heavens discover'd Will
Is, not to have it, or to use it ill.
The Danger's much the same; on several Shelves
If *others* wreck *us*, or *we* wreck our *selves*.

What then remains, but, waving each Extreme,
The Tides of Ignorance, and Pride to stem?
Neither so rich a Treasure to forego;
Nor proudly seek beyond our Pow'r to know:
Faith is not built on disquisitions vain;
The things we *must* believe, are *few*, and *plain*:
But since men *will* believe more than they *need*;
And every man will make *himself* a Creed:
In doubtful questions 'tis the safest way
To learn what unsuspected Antients say:
For 'tis not likely *we* shou'd higher Soar
In search of Heav'n, than *all the Church before*:
Nor can we be deceiv'd, unless we see

The *Scripture*, and the *Fathers disagree.*
If after all, they stand suspected still,
(For no man's Faith depends upon his Will;)
'Tis some Relief, that points not clearly known,
Without much hazard may be let alone:
And, after hearing what our Church can say,
If still our Reason runs another way,
That private Reason 'tis more Just to curb,
Than by Disputes the publick Peace disturb:
For points obscure are of small use to learn:
But *Common quiet* is *Mankind*'s *Concern.*

Thus have I made my own Opinions clear:
Yet neither Praise expect, nor Censure fear:
And this unpolish'd, rugged Verse, I chose;
As fittest for Discourse, and nearest Prose:
For, while from *Sacred Truth* I do not swerve,
Tom Sternhold's, or *Tom Sha*[*dwe*]*ll*'s Rhimes will serve.[1]

[1] For Sternhold, see *Dramatick Poesie*, p. 429, n. 3; for Shadwell, see *Mac Flecknoe*.

THE HIND AND THE PANTHER

A POEM
IN THREE PARTS

————Antiquam exquirite matrem.[1]
Et vera, incessu, patuit Dea.————[2]
Virg.

[1] It is your ancient mother that ye are to seek. (*Æneid* 3. 96.)
[2] And in her step stood revealed a true goddess. (*Æneid* 1. 405.)

The Hind and the Panther. A Poem, In Three Parts. [*Latin quot.*] The Second Edition. London, Printed for Jacob Tonson, at the Judges Head in Chancery Lane, near Fleetstreet, 1687.

THE present text follows that of the second edition (Macdonald, 24 d) which, appearing in the same year as the first edition, was corrected and altered.

DRYDEN was converted to the Roman Catholic Church in the first year of James II's reign, 1685. He at once began to compose *The Hind and the Panther*, an apology for his new religion, and the poem was published in April, 1687. A week before it appeared, James II, on the 4th April, issued the Declaration of Indulgence which suspended the penal laws and abrogated the discriminatory acts against both Protestant and Catholic dissenters from the Church of England. James hoped to quieten opposition to the Declaration by including the Protestants in its terms, and if Dryden had known his intention, he would have modified his attack on the Protestant sects in the first book of the poem. His preface was an attempt to soften his severity.

TO THE READER

THE Nation is in too high a Ferment, for me to expect either fair War, or even so much as fair Quarter from a Reader of the opposite Party. All Men are engag'd either on this side or that: and tho' Conscience is the common Word, *which is given by both, yet if a Writer fall among Enemies, and cannot give the Marks of* Their *Conscience, he is knock'd down before the Reasons of his own are heard. A* Preface, *therefore, which is but a bespeaking of Favour, is altogether useless. What I desire the* Reader *should know concerning me, he will find in the Body of the Poem; if he have but the patience to peruse it. Only this Advertisement let him take before hand, which relates to the Merits of the Cause. No general Characters of Parties, (call 'em either Sects or Churches) can be so fully and exactly drawn, as to Comprehend all the several Members of 'em; at least all such as are receiv'd under that Denomination. For example; there are some of the Church by Law Establish'd, who envy not Liberty of Conscience to Dissenters; as being well satisfied that, according to their own Principles, they ought not to persecute them. Yet these, by reason of their fewness, I could not distinguish from the Numbers of the rest with whom they are Embodied in one common Name: On the other side there are many of our Sects, and more indeed then I could reasonably have hop'd, who have withdrawn themselves from the Communion of the* Panther; *and embrac'd this Gracious Indulgence of His Majesty in point of Toleration. But neither to the one nor the other of these is this Satyr any way intended: 'tis aim'd only at the refractory and disobedient on either side. For those who are come over to the Royal Party are consequently suppos'd to be out of Gunshot. Our Physicians have observ'd, that in Process of Time, some Diseases have abated of their Virulence, and have in a manner worn out their Malignity, so as to be no longer Mortal: and why may not I suppose the same concerning some of those who have formerly been Enemies to Kingly Government, As well as Catholick Religion? I hope they have now another Notion of both, as having found, by Comfortable Experience, that the Doctrine of Persecution is far from being an Article of our Faith.*

'Tis not for any Private Man to Censure the Proceedings of a Foreign Prince: but, without suspicion of Flattery, I may praise our own, who has taken contrary Measures, and those more suitable

to the Spirit of Christianity.[1] *Some of the Dissenters in their Addresses to His Majesty have said* That he has restor'd God to his Empire over Conscience: *I Confess I dare not stretch the Figure to so great a boldness: but I may safely say, that Conscience is the Royalty and Prerogative of every Private man. He is absolute in his own Breast, and accountable to no Earthly Power, for that which passes only betwixt God and Him. Those who are driven into the Fold are, generally speaking, rather made Hypocrites then Converts.*

This Indulgence being granted to all the Sects, it ought in reason to be expected, that they should both receive it, and receive it thankfully. For at this time of day to refuse the Benefit, and adhere to those whom they have esteem'd their Persecutors, what is it else, but publickly to own that they suffer'd not before for Conscience sake; but only out of Pride and Obstinacy to separate from a Church for those Impositions, which they now judge may be lawfully obey'd? After they have so long contended for their Classical Ordination, (not to speak of Rites and Ceremonies) will they at length submit to an Episcopal? if they can go so far out of Complaisance to their old Enemies, methinks a little reason should perswade 'em to take another step, and see whether that wou'd lead 'em.

Of the receiving this Toleration thankfully, I shall say no more, than that they ought, and I doubt not they will consider from what hands they receiv'd it. 'Tis not from a Cyrus, *a Heathen Prince, and a Foreigner, but from a Christian King, their Native Sovereign: who expects a Return in* Specie *from them; that the Kindness which He has Graciously shown them, may be retaliated on those of his own perswasion.*

As for the Poem in general, I will only thus far satisfie the Reader: *That it was neither impos'd on me, nor so much as the Subject given me by any man. It was written during the last Winter and the beginning of this Spring; though with long interruptions of ill health, and other hindrances. About a Fortnight before I had finish'd it, His Majesties Declaration for Liberty of Conscience came abroad: which, if I had so soon expected, I might have spar'd my self the labour of writing many things which are contain'd in the third part of it. But I was alwayes in some hope, that the Church of* England *might have been perswaded to have taken off the* Penal Lawes *and the* Test, *which was one Design of the Poem, when I propos'd to my self the writing of it.*

[1] A comparison of Louis XIV's Revocation of the Edict of Nantes and subsequent persecution of his Protestant subjects with James II's Declaration of Indulgence.

'Tis evident that some part of it was only occasional, and not first intended. I mean that defence of my self, to which every honest man is bound, when he is injuriously attacqu'd in Print: and I refer my self to the judgment of those who have read the Answer to the Defence of the late Kings Papers, *and that of the* Dutchess, *(in which last I was concerned) how charitably I have been represented there.*[1] *I am now inform'd both of the Author and Supervisers of his Pamphlet: and will reply when I think he can affront me: for I am of* Socrates's *Opinion that all Creatures cannot. In the mean time let him consider, whether he deserv'd not a more severe reprehension then I gave him formerly; for using so little respect to the Memory of those whom he pretended to answer: and, at his leisure look out for some Original Treatise of Humility, written by any Protestant in English, (I believe I may say in any other Tongue:) for the magnified Piece of* Duncomb *on that Subject, which either he must mean, or none, and with which another of his Fellows has upbraided me, was Translated from the Spanish of* Rodriguez: *tho' with the Omission of the* 17th, *the* 24th, *the* 25th, *and the last Chapter, which will be found in comparing of the Books.*[2]

He would have insinuated to the World that Her late Highness died not a Roman Catholick: He declares himself to be now satisfied to the contrary; in which he has giv'n up the Cause: for matter of Fact was the Principal Debate betwixt us. In the mean time he would dispute the Motives of her Change: how preposterously let all men judge, when he seem'd to deny the Subject of the Controversy, the Change it self. And because I would not take up this ridiculous Challenge, he tells the World I cannot argue: but he may as well infer that a Catholick cannot fast, because he will not take up the Cudgels against Mrs. James, *to confute the Protestant Religion.*[3]

I have but one word more to say concerning the Poem as such, and abstracting from the Matters either Religious or Civil which are

[1] James II published some papers written by Charles II in favour of Roman Catholicism, and a similar paper written by his first wife, Anne Hyde. This publication was answered by Edward Stillingfleet (1635–1699), the Dean of St. Paul's. James caused a defence of the papers to be published, in which Dryden collaborated, and Stillingfleet in his reply severely criticised Dryden's share in this defence.

[2] Dryden in his defence of the papers published by James II asserted that he knew of no Protestant treatise on humility. Stillingfleet in his rejoinder called this assertion 'a bare-faced assertion of a thing known to be false'. Dryden is here assuming that the treatise to which Stillingfleet referred was this translation from the Spanish, but Stillingfleet, in fact, had in mind a treatise written by a Mr. Allen.

[3] Eleanor James (*fl.* 1715) had just published a pamphlet vindicating the Church of England.

handled in it. The first Part, *consisting most in general Characters and Narration, I have endeavour'd to raise, and give it the Majestick Turn of Heroick Poesie. The* second, *being Matter of Dispute, and chiefly concerning Church Authority, I was oblig'd to make as plain and perspicuous as possibly I cou'd: yet not wholly neglecting the Numbers, though I had not frequent occasions for the Magnificence of Verse. The* third, *which has more of the Nature of Domestick Conversation, is, or ought to be more free and familiar than the two former.*

There are in it two Episodes, *or* Fables, *which are interwoven with the main Design; so that they are properly parts of it, though they are also distinct Stories of themselves. In both of these I have made use of the Common Places of* Satyr, *whether true or false, which are urg'd by the Members of the one Church against the other. At which I hope no* Reader *of either Party will be scandaliz'd; because they are not of my Invention: but as old to my knowledge, as the Times of* Boccace *and* Chawcer *on the one side, and as those of the Reformation on the other.*

THE HIND AND THE PANTHER

THE FIRST PART

A MILK white *Hind*,[1] immortal and unchang'd,
Fed on the lawns, and in the forest rang'd;
Without unspotted, innocent within,
She fear'd no danger, for she knew no sin.
Yet had she oft been chas'd with horns and hounds,
And Scythian shafts; and many winged wounds
Aim'd at Her heart; was often forc'd to fly,
And doom'd to death, though fated not to dy.

Not so her young; for their unequal line
Was Heroe's make, half humane, half divine.
Their earthly mold obnoxious was to fate,
Th' immortal part assum'd immortal state.
Of these a slaughtered army lay in bloud,
Extended o'er the *Caledonian* wood,
Their native walk; whose vocal bloud arose,
And cry'd for pardon on their perjur'd foes;[2]
Their fate was fruitful, and the sanguin seed
Endu'd with souls, encreas'd the sacred breed.
So Captive *Israel* multiply'd in chains,
A numerous Exile; and enjoy'd her pains.
With grief and gladness mixt, their mother view'd
Her martyr'd offspring, and their race renew'd;
Their corps to perish, but their kind to last,
So much the deathless plant the dying fruit surpass'd.

Panting and pensive now she rang'd alone,
And wander'd in the kingdoms, once Her own.
The common Hunt, though from their rage restrain'd
By sov'reign pow'r, her company disdain'd:
Grin'd as They pass'd, and with a glaring eye
Gave gloomy signs of secret enmity.

[1] The *Hind*, The Roman Catholic Church.
[2] The Roman Catholic priests executed in England since the Reformation.

'Tis true, she bounded by, and trip'd so light
They had not time to take a steady sight.
For truth has such a face and such a meen
As to be lov'd needs only to be seen.

The bloudy *Bear*[1] an *Independent* beast,
Unlick'd to form, in groans her hate express'd.
Among the timorous kind the *Quaking Hare*[2]
Profess'd neutrality, but would not swear.
Next her the *Buffoon Ape*,[3] as Atheists use,
Mimick'd all Sects, and had his own to chuse:
Still when the Lyon[4] look'd, his knees he bent,
And pay'd at Church a Courtier's Complement.

The bristl'd *Baptist Boar*,[5] impure as He,
(But whitn'd with the foam of sanctity)
With fat pollutions fill'd the sacred place,
And mountains levell'd in his furious race,
So first rebellion founded was in grace.
But since the mighty ravage which he made
In *German* Forests, had his guilt betrayd,
With broken tusks, and with a borrow'd name
He shun'd the vengeance, and conceal'd the shame;
So lurk'd in Sects unseen. With greater guile
False *Reynard*[6] fed on consecrated spoil:
The graceless beast by *Athanasius* first
Was chas'd from *Nice*; then by *Socinus* nurs'd
His impious race their blasphemy renew'd,
And natures King through natures opticks view'd.
Revers'd they view'd him lessen'd to their eye,
Nor in an Infant could a God descry:
New swarming Sects to this obliquely tend,
Hence they began, and here they all will end.

[1] The bloudy *Bear*, The Independents who were an important force in the Puritan ranks during the Civil War.
[2] The *Quaking Hare*, The Quakers.
[3] The *Buffoon Ape*, The Free-thinkers.
[4] The Lyon, The King of England.
[5] The *Baptist Boar*, The Anabaptists, a sect which originated in Germany in the 16th century.
[6] False *Reynard*, The *Arian*. The Arian heresy was condemned at the Council of Nice through the efforts of Athanasius, but the name was also given to the heresy begun by Socinus in the 16th century.

What weight of antient witness can prevail
If private reason hold the publick scale?
But, gratious God, how well dost thou provide
For erring judgments an unerring Guide?
Thy throne is darkness in th' abyss of light,
A blaze of glory that forbids the sight;
O teach me to believe Thee thus conceal'd,
And search no farther than thy self reveal'd;
But her alone for my Directour take
Whom thou hast promis'd never to forsake!
My thoughtless youth was wing'd with vain desires,
My manhood, long misled by wandering fires,
Follow'd false lights; and when their glimps was gone,
My pride struck out new sparkles of her own.
Such was I, such by nature still I am,
Be thine the glory, and be mine the shame.
Good life be now my task: my doubts are done,
(What more could fright my faith, than Three in One?)
Can I believe eternal God could lye
Disguis'd in mortal mold and infancy?
That the great maker of the world could dye?
And after that, trust my imperfect sense
Which calls in question his omnipotence?
Can I my reason to my faith compell,
And shall my sight, and touch, and taste rebell?
Superiour faculties are set aside,
Shall their subservient organs be my guide?
Then let the moon usurp the rule of day,
And winking tapers shew the sun his way;
For what my senses can themselves perceive
I need no revelation to believe.
Can they who say the Host should be descry'd
By sense, define a body glorify'd?
Impassible, and penetrating parts?
Let them declare by what mysterious arts
He shot that body through th' opposing might
Of bolts and barrs impervious to the light,
And stood before his train confess'd in open sight.[1]

For since thus wondrously he pass'd, 'tis plain
One single place two bodies did contain,

[1] A reference to the account in *St. John*, xx, of Christ's appearance to his disciples after the Crucifixion.

And sure the same Omnipotence as well
Can make one body in more places dwell.
Let reason then at Her own quarry fly,
But how can finite grasp Infinity?

'Tis urg'd again that faith did first commence
By miracles, which are appeals to sense,
And thence concluded that our sense must be
The motive still of credibility.
For latter ages must on former wait,
And what began belief, must propagate.

But winnow well this thought, and you shall find,
'Tis light as chaff that flies before the wind.
Were all those wonders wrought by pow'r divine
As means or ends of some more deep design?
Most sure as means, whose end was this alone,
To prove the god-head of th' eternal Son.
God thus asserted: man is to believe
Beyond what sense and reason can conceive.
And for mysterious things of faith rely
On the Proponent, heav'ns authority.
If then our faith we for our guide admit,
Vain is the farther search of human wit,
As when the building gains a surer stay,
We take th' unuseful scaffolding away:
Reason by sense no more can understand,
The game is play'd into another hand.
Why chuse we then like *Bilanders*[1] to creep
Along the coast, and land in view to keep,
When safely we may launch into the deep?
In the same vessel which our Saviour bore
Himself the Pilot, let us leave the shoar,
And with a better guide a better world explore.
Could He his god-head veil with flesh and bloud
And not veil these again to be our food?
His grace in both is equal in extent,
The first affords us life, the second nourishment.
And if he can, why all this frantick pain
To construe what his clearest words contain,
And make a riddle what He made so plain?

[1] *Bilander*, a coasting vessel.

To take up half on trust, and half to try,
Name it not faith, but bungling biggottry.
Both knave and fool the Merchant we may call
To pay great summs, and to compound the small.
For who wou'd break with heav'n, and wou'd not break for all?
Rest then, my soul, from endless anguish freed;
Nor sciences thy guide, nor sense thy creed.
Faith is the best ensurer of thy bliss;
The Bank above must fail before the venture miss.
But heav'n and heav'n-born faith are far from Thee
Thou first Apostate to Divinity.
Unkennel'd range in thy *Polonian* Plains;[1]
A fiercer foe th' insatiate *Wolf*[2] remains.

Too boastful *Britain* please thy self no more,
That beasts of prey are banish'd from thy shoar:
The *Bear*, the *Boar*, and every salvage name,
Wild in effect, though in appearance tame,
Lay waste thy woods, destroy thy blissfull bow'r,
And muzl'd though they seem, the mutes devour.
More haughty than the rest the *wolfish* race,
Appear with belly Gaunt, and famish'd face:
Never was so deform'd a beast of Grace.
His ragged tail betwixt his leggs he wears
Close clapp'd for shame, but his rough crest he rears,
And pricks up his predestinating ears.
His wild disorder'd walk, his hagger'd eyes,
Did all the bestial citizens surprize.
Though fear'd and hated, yet he rul'd a while
As Captain or Companion of the spoil.
Full many a year his hatefull head had been
For tribute paid, nor since in *Cambria* seen:
The last of all the litter scap'd by chance,
And from *Geneva* first infested *France*.
Some Authors thus his pedigree will trace,
But others write him of an upstart Race:
Because of *Wickliff*'s Brood no mark he brings
But his innate Antipathy to Kings.
These last deduce him from th' *Helvetian* kind

[1] An allusion to the Arian or Socinian heresy which was particularly strong among the Polish peasantry.
[2] Th' insatiate *Wolf*, The Presbyterian.

Who near the *Leman lake* his Consort Lin'd.
That fi'ry *Zuynglius* first th' Affection bred,
And Meagre *Calvin* blest the Nuptial Bed.
In *Israel* some believe him Whelp'd long since,
When the proud *Sanhedrim* oppres'd the Prince,[1]
Or, since he will be *Jew*, derive him high'r
When *Corah* with his Brethren did conspire,
From Moyses Hand the Sov'reign sway to wrest,
And *Aaron* of his Ephod to devest:[2]
Till opening Earth made way for all to pass,
And cou'd not bear the Burd'n of a *Class*.
The *Fox*[3] and he came shuffl'd in the Dark,
If ever they were stow'd in *Noah*'s Ark:
Perhaps not made; for all their barking train
The Dog (a common species) will contain.
And some wild currs, who from their masters ran,
Abhorring the supremacy of man,
In woods and caves the rebel-race began.

Vid. Pref. *to* Heyl. *Hist. of Presb.*

O happy pair, how well have you encreas'd,
What ills in Church and State have you redress'd!
With Teeth untry'd, and rudiments of Claws
Your first essay was on your native Laws:
Those having torn with Ease, and trampl'd down,
Your Fangs you fasten'd on the miter'd Crown,
And freed from God and Monarchy your Town.
What though your native kennel still be small
Bounded betwixt a Puddle and a Wall,[4]
Yet your Victorious Colonies are sent
Where the North Ocean girds the Continent.
Quickned with fire below your Monsters Breed,
In Fenny *Holland* and in fruitful *Tweed.*
And like the first the last effects to be
Drawn to the dreggs of a Democracy.
As, where in Fields the fairy rounds are seen,
A rank sow'r herbage rises on the Green;
So, springing where these mid-night Elves advance,
Rebellion Prints the Foot-steps of the Dance.

[1] Dryden refers the reader to Heylyn's *History of the Presbyterians*, as authority for the statements made in these lines.

[2] The rebellious Korah and the sons of Levi, whom Dryden compares to a Presbyterian 'class', were, according to the account in *Numbers*, xvi, punished by being swallowed up in the earth.

[3] The *Fox*, 'false *Reynard*', the Arian.

[4] The territories of Geneva were bounded by ramparts and the lake.

Such are their Doctrines, such contempt they show
To Heaven above, and to their Prince below,
As none but Traytors and Blasphemers know.
God, like the Tyrant of the Skies is plac'd,
And Kings, like slaves, beneath the Croud debas'd.
So fulsome is their food, that Flocks refuse
To bite; and only Dogs for Physick use.
As, where the Lightning runs along the Ground,
No husbandry can heal the blasting Wound,
Nor bladed Grass, nor bearded Corn succeeds,
But Scales of Scurf, and Putrefaction breeds:
Such Warrs, such Waste, such fiery tracks of Dearth
Their Zeal has left, and such a teemless Earth.
But as the Poisons of the deadliest Kind
Are to their own unhappy Coasts confin'd,
As only *Indian* Shades of sight deprive,
And Magick Plants will but in Colchos thrive;
So Presby'try and Pestilential Zeal
Can only flourish in a Common-weal.

From *Celtique* Woods is chas'd the *wolfish* Crew;[1]
But ah! some Pity e'en to Brutes is due,
Their native Walks, methinks, they might enjoy
Curb'd of their native Malice to destroy.
Of all the Tyrannies on humane kind
The worst is that which Persecutes the Mind.
Let us but weigh at what offence we strike,
'Tis but because we cannot think alike.
In punishing of this, we overthrow
The Laws of Nations and of Nature too.
Beasts are the Subjects of Tyrannick sway,
Where still the stronger on the weaker Prey.
Man only of a softer mold is made;
Not for his Fellows ruine, but their Aid.
Created kind, beneficent and free,
The noble Image of the Deity.

One Portion of informing Fire was giv'n
To Brutes, th' inferiour Family of Heav'n:
The Smith Divine, as with a careless Beat,
Struck out the mute Creation at a Heat:

[1] An allusion to Louis XIV's Revocation of the Edict of Nantes and his persecution of the Huguenots.

But when arriv'd at last to humane Race,
The Godhead took a deep consid'ring space:
And, to distinguish Man from all the rest,
Unlock'd the sacred Treasures of his Breast:
And Mercy mixt with reason did impart;
One to his Head, the other to his Heart:
Reason to Rule, but Mercy to forgive:
The first is Law, the last Prerogative.
And like his Mind his outward form appear'd
When issuing Naked, to the wond'ring Herd,
He charm'd their Eyes, and for they lov'd, they fear'd.
Not arm'd with horns of arbitrary might,
Or Claws to seize their furry spoils in Fight,
Or with increase of Feet, t' o'ertake 'em in their flight.
Of easie shape, and pliant ev'ry way;
Confessing still the softness of his Clay,
And kind as Kings upon their Coronation Day:
With open Hands, and with extended space
Of Arms to satisfy a large embrace.
Thus kneaded up with Milk, the new-made Man
His Kingdom o'er his Kindred world began:
Till Knowledg mis-apply'd, mis-understood,
And pride of Empire sour'd his Balmy Blood
Then, first rebelling, his own stamp he coins;
The murth'rer *Cain* was latent in his Loins;
And Blood began its first and loudest Cry
For diff'ring worship of the Deity.
Thus persecution rose, and farther Space
Produc'd the mighty hunter of his Race.[1]
Not so the blessed *Pan*[2] his flock encreas'd,
Content to fold 'em from the famish'd Beast:
Mild were his laws; the Sheep and harmless Hind
Were never of the persecuting kind.
Such pity now the pious Pastor shows,
Such mercy from the *British* Lyon flows,
That both provide protection for their foes.[3]

Oh happy Regions, *Italy* and *Spain*,
Which never did those monsters entertain!
The *Wolfe*, the *Bear*, the *Boar*, can there advance
No native claim of just inheritance.

[1] Nimrod. [2] Jesus Christ.
[3] James II. An allusion to the Declaration of Indulgence.

And self preserving laws, severe in show,
May guard their fences from th' invading foe.
Where birth has plac'd 'em let 'em safely share
The common benefit of vital air.
Themselves unharmful, let them live unharm'd;
Their jaws disabl'd, and their claws disarm'd:
Here, only in nocturnal howlings bold,
They dare not seize the Hind nor leap the fold.
More pow'rful, and as vigilant as they,
The Lyon awfully forbids the prey.
Their rage repress'd, though pinch'd with famine sore,
They stand aloof, and tremble at his roar;
Much is their hunger, but their fear is more.

These are the chief; to number o'er the rest
And stand, like *Adam*, naming ev'ry beast,
Were weary work; nor will the Muse describe
A slimy-born and sun-begotten Tribe:
Who, far from steeples and their sacred sound,
In fields their sullen conventicles found:
These gross, half-animated lumps I leave;
Nor can I think what thoughts they can conceive.
But if they think at all, 'tis sure no high'r,
Than matter, put in motion, may aspire.
Souls that can scarce ferment their mass of clay;
So drossy, so divisible are They,
As wou'd but serve pure bodies for allay:
Such Souls as *shards* produce, such beetle things,
As only buz to heaven with ev'ning wings;
Strike in the dark, offending but by chance,
Such are the blind-fold blows of ignorance.
They know not beings, and but hate a name,
To them the *Hind* and *Panther* are the same.

The *Panther*[1] sure the noblest, next the *Hind*,
And fairest creature of the spotted kind;
Oh, could her in-born stains be wash'd away,
She were too good to be a beast of Prey!
How can I praise, or blame, and not offend,
Or how divide the frailty from the friend!
Her faults and vertues lye so, mix'd, that she
Nor wholly stands condemn'd nor wholly free.
Then, like her injur'd *Lyon*, let me speak,

[1] The *Panther*, The Church of England.

He cannot bend her, and he would not break.
Unkind already, and estrang'd in part,
The *Wolfe* begins to share her wandring heart.
Though unpolluted yet with actual ill,
She half commits, who sins but in Her will.
If, as our dreaming *Platonists* report,
There could be spirits of a middle sort,
Too black for heav'n, and yet too white for hell,
Who just dropt half way down, nor lower fell;
So pois'd, so gently she descends from high,
It seems a soft dismission from the skie.
Her house not ancient, whatsoe'er pretence
Her clergy Heraulds make in her defence.
A second century not half-way run
Since the new honours of her blood begun.
A *Lyon* old, obscene, and furious made
By lust, compress'd her mother in a shade.
Then, by a left-hand marr'age weds the Dame,
Cov'ring adult'ry with a specious name:[1]
So schism begot; and sacrilege and she,
A well-match'd pair, got graceless heresie.
God's and Kings rebels have the same good cause,
To trample down divine and humane laws:
Both wou'd be call'd Reformers, and their hate,
Alike destructive both to Church and State:
The fruit proclaims the plant; a lawless Prince
By luxury reform'd incontinence,
By ruins, charity; by riots, abstinence.
Confessions, fasts and penance set aside;
Oh with what ease we follow such a guide!
Where souls are starv'd, and senses gratify'd!
Where marr'age pleasures, midnight pray'r supply,
And mattin bells (a melancholly cry)
Are tun'd to merrier notes, *encrease* and *multiply*.[2]
Religion shows a Rosie colour'd face;
Not hatter'd out with drudging works of grace;
A down-hill Reformation rolls apace.
What flesh and blood wou'd croud the narrow gate,
Or, till they waste their pamper'd paunches, wait?
All wou'd be happy at the cheapest rate.

[1] Henry VIII's divorce from Catherine of Aragon and marriage to Anne Boleyn led to the Reformation.
[2] The marriage of clergy was allowed by the Reformation.

Though our lean faith these rigid laws has giv'n,
The full fed *Musulman* goes fat to heav'n;
For his *Arabian* Prophet with delights
Of sense, allur'd his eastern Proselytes.
The jolly *Luther*, reading him, began
T' interpret Scriptures by his *Alcoran*;
To grub the thorns beneath our tender feet,
And make the paths of *Paradise* more sweet:
Bethought him of a wife e're half way gone,
(For 'twas uneasie travailing alone,)
And in this masquerade of mirth and love,
Mistook the bliss of heav'n for *Bacchanals* above.
Sure he presum'd of praise, who came to stock
Th' etherial pastures with so fair a flock;
Burnish'd, and bat'ning on their food, to show
The diligence of carefull herds below.

Our *Panther*, though like these she chang'd her head,
Yet, as the mistress of a monarch's bed,
Her front erect with majesty she bore,
The Crozier weilded, and the Miter wore.
Her upper part of decent discipline
Shew'd affectation of an ancient line:
And fathers, councils, church and churches head,
Were on her reverend *Phylacteries* read.
But what disgrac'd and disavow'd the rest,
Was *Calvin*'s brand, that stigmatiz'd the beast.
Thus, like a creature of a double kind,
In her own labyrinth she lives confin'd.
To foreign lands no sound of Her is come,
Humbly content to be despis'd at home.
Such is her faith, where good cannot be had,
At least she leaves the refuse of the bad.
Nice in her choice of ill, though not of best,
And least deform'd, because reform'd the least.
In doubtful points betwixt her diff'ring friends,
Where one for substance, one for sign contends,
Their contradicting terms she strives to joyn.
Sign shall be substance, substance shall be sign.
A real presence all her sons allow,
And yet 'tis flat Idolatry to bow,
Because the God-head's there they know not how.

Her Novices are taught that bread and wine
Are but the visible and outward sign
Receiv'd by those who in communion joyn.
But th' inward grace, or the thing signify'd,
His blood and body, who to save us dy'd;
The faithful this thing signify'd receive.
What is't those faithful then partake or leave?
For what is signify'd and understood,
Is, by her own confession, flesh and blood.
Then, by the same acknowledgement, we know
They take the sign, and take the substance too.[1]
The lit'ral sense is hard to flesh and blood,
But nonsense never can be understood.

Her wild belief on ev'ry wave is tost,
But sure no Church can better morals boast.
True to her King her principles are found;
Oh that her practice were but half so sound!
Stedfast in various turns of state she stood,
And seal'd her vow'd affection with her blood;
Nor will I meanly tax her constancy,
That int'rest or obligement made the tye,
(Bound to the fate of murdr'd Monarchy:)
(Before the sounding Ax so falls the Vine,
Whose tender branches round the Poplar twine.)
She chose her ruin, and resign'd her life,
In death undaunted as an *Indian* wife:
A rare example: but some souls we see
Grow hard, and stiffen with adversity:
Yet these by fortunes favours are undone,
Resolv'd into a baser form they run,
And bore the wind, but cannot bear the sun.
Let this be natures frailty or her fate,
Or **Isgrim*'s counsel, her new chosen mate;
Still she's the fairest of the fallen Crew,
No mother more indulgent but the true.

* *The Wolfe.*

Fierce to her foes, yet fears her force to try,
Because she wants innate auctority;
For how can she constrain them to obey
Who has her self cast off the lawful sway?

[1] A criticism of the Church of England's teaching on the Eucharist.

Rebellion equals all, and those who toil
In common theft, will share the common spoil.
Let her produce the title and the right
Against her old superiours first to fight;
If she reform by Text, ev'n that's as plain
For her own Rebels to reform again.
As long as words a diff'rent sense will bear,
And each may be his own Interpreter,
Our ai'ry faith will no foundation find:
The word's a weathercock for ev'ry wind:
The *Bear*, the *Fox*, the *Wolfe* by turns prevail,
The most in pow'r supplies the present gale.
The wretched *Panther* crys aloud for aid
To church and councils, whom she first betray'd;
No help from Fathers or traditions train,
Those ancient guides she taught us to disdain.
And by that scripture which she once abus'd
To Reformation, stands her self accus'd.[1]
What bills for breach of laws can she prefer,
Expounding which she owns her self may err?
And, after all her winding ways are try'd,
If doubts arise she slips herself aside,
And leaves the private conscience for the guide.
If then that conscience set th' offender free,
It bars her claim to church auctority.
How can she censure, or what crime pretend,
But Scripture may be constru'd to defend?
Ev'n those whom for rebellion she transmits
To civil pow'r, her doctrine first acquits;
Because no disobedience can ensue,
Where no submission to a Judge is due.
Each judging for himself, by her consent,
Whom thus absolv'd she sends to punishment.
Suppose the Magistrate revenge her cause,
'Tis only for transgressing humane laws.
How answ'ring to its end a church is made,
Whose pow'r is but to counsel and perswade?
O solid rock, on which secure she stands!
Eternal house, not built with mortal hands!

[1] Dryden repeats the Roman Catholic argument, that the Church of England, which appealed from tradition to scripture to justify the Reformation, cannot call in tradition's authority to refute the sectaries' criticisms, which are also based upon scriptural interpretation.

O sure defence against th' infernal gate,
A patent during pleasure of the state!

Thus is the *Panther* neither lov'd nor fear'd,
A meer mock Queen of a divided Herd;
Whom soon by lawful pow'r she might controll,
Her self a part submitted to the whole.
Then, as the Moon who first receives the light
By which she makes our nether regions bright,
So might she shine, reflecting from afar
The rays she borrow'd from a better Star:
Big with the beams which from her mother flow
And reigning o'er the rising tides below:
Now, mixing with a savage croud, she goes
And meanly flatters her inveterate foes,
Rul'd while she rules, and losing ev'ry hour
Her wretched remnants of precarious pow'r.

One evening while the cooler shade she sought,
Revolving many a melancholy thought,
Alone she walk'd, and look'd around in vain,
With ruful visage for her vanish'd train:
None of her sylvan subjects made their court;
Leveés and coucheés pass'd without resort.
So hardly can Usurpers manage well
Those, whom they first instructed to rebel:
More liberty begets desire of more,
The hunger still encreases with the store.
Without respect they brush'd along the wood
Each in his clan, and fill'd with loathsome food,
Ask'd no permission to the neighb'ring flood.
The *Panther*, full of inward discontent,
Since they wou'd goe, before 'em wisely went:
Supplying want of pow'r by drinking first,
As if she gave 'em leave to quench their thirst.
Among the rest, the *Hind*, with fearful face
Beheld from far the common wat'ring place,
Nor durst approach; till with an awful roar
The sovereign *Lyon* bad her fear no more.
Encourag'd thus she brought her younglings nigh,
Watching the motions of her Patron's eye,
And drank a sober draught; the rest amaz'd
Stood mutely still, and on the stranger gaz'd:

Survey'd her part by part, and sought to find
The ten-horn'd monster in the harmless *Hind*,
Such as the *Wolfe* and *Panther* had design'd.
They thought at first they dream'd, for 'twas offence
With them, to question certitude of sense,
Their guide in faith; but nearer when they drew,
And had the faultless object full in view,
Lord, how they all admir'd her heav'nly hiew!
Some, who before her fellowship disdain'd,
Scarce, and but scarce, from in-born rage restrain'd,
Now frisk'd about her, and old kindred feign'd.
Whether for love or int'rest, ev'ry sect
Of all the salvage nation shew'd respect:
The Vice-roy *Panther* could not awe the herd,
The more the company the less they fear'd.
The surly *Wolfe* with secret envy burst,
Yet cou'd not howl, the *Hind* had seen him first:[1]
But what he durst not speak, the *Panther* durst.

For when the herd suffis'd, did late repair
To ferney heaths, and to their forest lare,
She made a mannerly excuse to stay,
Proff'ring the *Hind* to wait her half the way:
That since the Skie was clear, an hour of talk
Might help her to beguile the tedious walk.
With much good-will the motion was embrac'd,
To chat awhile on their adventures pass'd:
Nor had the grateful *Hind* so soon forgot
Her friend and fellow-suff'rer in the plot.
Yet wondering how of late she grew estrang'd:
Her forehead cloudy and her count'nance chang'd,
She thought this hour th' occasion would present
To learn her secret cause of discontent,
Which, well she hop'd, might be with ease redress'd,
Consid'ring her a well-bred civil beast,
And more a Gentlewoman than the rest.
After some common talk what rumours ran,
The Lady of the spotted-muff began.

[1] There is a classical superstition that if a wolf saw a man first, the man lost his voice. Dryden reverses the facts.

THE SECOND PART

DAME, said the *Panther*, times are mended well
Since late among the *Philistines* you fell;
The Toils were pitch'd, a spacious tract of ground
With expert Huntsmen was encompass'd round;
Th' Enclosure narrow'd; the sagacious pow'r
Of Hounds, and Death drew nearer ev'ry Hour.[1]
'Tis true, the younger *Lyon* scap'd the snare,[2]
But all your priestly Calves lay strugling there;
As sacrifices on their Altars laid;
While you their careful mother wisely fled
Not trusting destiny to save your head.
For, whate'er Promises you have apply'd,
To your unfailing Church, the surer side
Is four fair Leggs in danger to provide.
And what e'er Tales of *Peter*'s Chair you tell,
Yet saving Reverence of the Miracle,
The better luck was yours to 'scape so well.

As I remember, said the sober *Hind*,
Those Toils were for your own dear self design'd,
As well as me; and, with the self same throw,
To catch the Quarry and the Vermin too,
(Forgive the sland'rous Tongues that call'd you so.)
Howe'er you take it now, the common Cry
Then ran you down for your rank Loyalty;
Besides, in Popery they thought you nurst,
(As evil tongues will ever speak the worst,)
Because some forms, and ceremonies some
You kept, and stood in the main question dumb.
Dumb you were born indeed, but thinking long
The *Test* it seems at last has loos'd your tongue.[3]
And, to explain what your forefathers meant,
By real presence in the Sacrament,

[1] A reference to the proceedings against the Roman Catholics after the Popish Plot.
[2] James II, when Duke of York, escaped being excluded from the succession to the throne by the narrow defeat of the Exclusion Bill in 1680.
[3] The Test Acts of 1672 and 1678 prescribed a Declaration denying the doctrine of transubstantiation, and Dryden asserts that the Church of England's attitude towards this doctrine, which had been purposely concealed in the ambiguous wording of the Article, had now been made plain by its willingness to accept this Declaration.

(After long fencing push'd against a wall,)
Your *salvo* comes, that he's not there at all:
There chang'd your faith, and what may change may
fall.
Who can believe what varies every day,
Nor ever was, nor will be at a stay?

Tortures may force the tongue untruths to tell,
And I ne'er own'd my self infallible,
Reply'd the *Panther*; grant such Presence were,
Yet in your sense I never own'd it there.
A real *vertue* we by faith receive,
And that we in the sacrament believe.

Then, said the *Hind*, as you the matter state
Not only *Jesuits* can equivocate;
For *real*, as you now the Word expound,
From Solid Substance dwindles to a Sound.
Methinks an *Esop*'s fable you repeat,
You know who took the Shadow for the Meat;
Your Churches substance thus you change at will,
And yet retain your former figure still.
I freely grant you spoke to save your Life,
For then you lay beneath the Butchers Knife.
Long time you fought, redoub'd Batt'ry bore,
But, after all, against your self you swore;
Your former self, for ev'ry Hour your form
Is chop'd and chang'd, like Winds before a Storm.
Thus Fear and Int'rest will prevail with some,
For all have not the Gift of Martyrdom.

The *Panther* grin'd at this, and thus reply'd;
That men may err was never yet deny'd.
But, if that common principle be true,
The Cannon, Dame, is level'd full at you.
But, shunning long disputes, I fain wou'd see
That wond'rous Wight Infallibility.
Is he from Heav'n this mighty Champion come,
Or lodg'd below in subterranean *Rome?*[1]
First, seat him somewhere, and derive his Race,
Or else conclude that nothing has no place.

[1] There is a cavern outside Rome called Roma Sotteranea.

Suppose (though I disown it) said the *Hind*,
The certain Mansion were not yet assign'd,
The doubtful residence no proof can bring
Against the plain existence of the thing.
Because *Philosophers* may disagree,
If Sight b' emission or reception be,
Shall it be thence infer'd, I do not see?
But you require an answer positive,
Which yet, when I demand, you dare not give,
For Fallacies in Universals live.[1]
I then affirm that this unfailing guide
In Pope and gen'ral Councils must reside;
Both lawful, both combin'd, what one decrees
By numerous Votes, the other Ratifies:
On this undoubted Sense the Church relies.
Tis true, some Doctors in a scantier space,
I mean in each apart contract the Place.
Some, who to greater length extend the Line,
The Churches after acceptation join.
This last Circumference appears too wide,
The Church diffus'd is by the Council ty'd;
As members by their Representatives
Oblig'd to Laws which Prince and Senate gives:
Thus some contract, and some enlarge the space;
In Pope and Council who denies the place,
Assisted from above with God's unfailing grace?
Those Canons all the needful points contain;
Their sense so obvious, and their words so plain,
That no disputes about the doubtful Text
Have, hitherto, the lab'ring world perplex'd:
If any shou'd in after times appear,
New Councils must be call'd, to make the meaning clear.
Because in them the pow'r supreme resides;
And all the promises are to the Guides.
This may be taught with sound and safe Defence:
But mark how sandy is your own pretence,
Who setting Councils, Pope, and Church aside,
Are ev'ry Man his own presuming Guide.
The sacred Books you say, are full and plain,
And ev'ry needful Point of Truth contain:
All who can read, Interpreters may be:

[1] 'Those who, in a Logical dispute, keep in general terms, would hide a fallacy' (*Annus Mirabilis*, p. 28).

Thus though your several Churches disagree,
Yet ev'ry Saint has to himself alone
The Secret of this Philosophick Stone.
These Principles you jarring Sects unite,
When diff'ring Doctors and Disciples Fight.
Though *Luther*, *Zuinglius*, *Calvin*, holy Chiefs
Have made a Battel Royal of Beliefs;
Or like wild Horses sev'ral ways have whirl'd
The tortur'd Text about the Christian World;
Each *Jehu* lashing on with furious force,
That *Turk* or *Jew* cou'd not have us'd it worse.
No matter what dissention leaders make
Where ev'ry private man may save a stake;
Rul'd by the Scripture and his own advice
Each has a blind-by-path to Paradise;
Where driving in a Circle slow or fast,
Opposing Sects are sure to meet at last.
A wondrous Charity you have in Store
For all reform'd to pass the narrow Door:
So much, that *Mahomet* had scarcely more.
For he, kind Prophet, was for damning none,
But *Christ* and *Moyses* were to save their own:
Himself was to secure his chosen race,
Though reason good for *Turks* to take the place,
And he allow'd to be the better Man
In virtue of his holier *Alcoran*.

True, said the *Panther*, I shall ne'er deny
My Breth'ren may be sav'd as well as I:
Though *Huguenots* contemn our ordination,
Succession, ministerial vocation;
And *Luther*, more mistaking what he read,
Misjoins the sacred Body with the Bread;[1]
Yet, *Lady*, still remember I maintain,
The Word in needfull points is only plain.

Needless or needful I not now contend,
For still you have a loop-hole for a friend,
(Rejoy'ned the Matron) but the rule you lay
Has led whole flocks, and leads them still astray
In weighty points, and full damnation's way.

[1] A reference to Luther's doctrine of consubstantiation.

For did not *Arius* first, *Socinus* now,
The Son's eternal god-head disavow,
And did not these by Gospel Texts alone
Condemn our doctrine, and maintain their own?
Have not all hereticks the same pretence
To plead the Scriptures in their own defence?
How did the *Nicene* council then decide
That strong debate, was it by Scripture try'd?
No sure to those the Rebel would not yield,
Squadrons of Texts he marshall'd in the field;
That was but civil war, an equal set,
Where Piles with piles, and Eagles Eagles met.[1]
With Texts point-blank and plain he fac'd the Foe:
And did not *Sathan* tempt our Saviour so?
The good old Bishops took a simpler way,
Each ask'd but what he heard his Father say,
Or how he was instructed in his youth,
And by tradition's force upheld the truth.

The *Panther* smil'd at this, and when, said she,
Were those first Councils disallow'd by me?
Or where did I at sure tradition strike,
Provided still it were Apostolick?

Friend, said the *Hind*, you quit your former ground,
Where all your Faith you did on Scripture found,
Now, 'tis tradition join'd with holy writ,
But thus your memory betrays your wit.

No, said the *Panther*, for in that I view,
When your tradition's forg'd, and when 'tis true.
I set 'em by the rule, and as they square,
Or deviate from undoubted doctrine there,
This Oral fiction, that old Faith declare.

(*Hind.*) The Council steer'd it seems a diff'rent course,
They try'd the Scripture by tradition's force;
But you tradition by the Scripture try;
Pursu'd, by Sects, from this to that you fly,
Nor dare on one foundation to rely.

[1] An allusion to Lucan's description of the Roman civil war, *Pharsalia*, i, 7.

The word is then depos'd, and in this view,
You rule the Scripture, not the Scripture you.
Thus said the *Dame*, and smiling, thus pursu'd,
I see tradition then is disallow'd,
When not evinc'd by Scripture to be true,
And Scripture, as interpreted by you.
But here you tread upon unfaithfull ground;
Unless you cou'd infallibly expound.
Which you reject as odious Popery,
And throw that doctrine back with scorn on me.
Suppose we on things traditive divide,
And both appeal to Scripture to decide;
By various texts we both uphold our claim,
Nay, often ground our titles on the same:
After long labour lost, and times expence,
Both grant the words, and quarrel for the sense.
Thus all disputes for ever must depend;
For no dumb rule can controversies end.
Thus when you said tradition must be try'd
By Sacred Writ, whose sense your selves decide,
You said no more, but that your selves must be
The judges of the Scripture sense, not we.
Against our church tradition you declare
And yet your Clerks wou'd sit in *Moyses* chair:
At least 'tis prov'd against your argument,
The rule is far from plain, where all dissent.

If not by Scriptures how can we be sure
(Reply'd the *Panther*) what tradition's pure?
For you may palm upon us new for old,
All, as they say, that glitters is not gold.

How but by following her, reply'd the Dame,
To whom deriv'd from sire to son they came;
Where ev'ry age do's on another move,
And trusts no farther than the next above;
Where all the rounds like *Jacob*'s ladder rise,
The lowest hid in earth, the topmost in the skyes.

Sternly the salvage did her answer mark,
Her glowing eye-balls glitt'ring in the dark,
And said but this, since lucre was your trade,
Succeeding times such dreadfull gaps have made

'Tis dangerous climbing: to your sons and you
I leave the ladder, and its omen too.[1]

(*Hind.*) The *Panther*'s breath was ever fam'd for sweet,
But from the *Wolf* such wishes oft I meet:
You learn'd this language from the blatant beast,
Or rather did not speak, but were possess'd.
As for your answer 'tis but barely urg'd;
You must evince tradition to be forg'd;
Produce plain proofs; unblemish'd author's use,
As ancient as those ages they accuse;
Till when 'tis not sufficient to defame:
An old possession stands, till Elder quitts the claim.
Then for our int'rest which is nam'd alone
To load with envy, we retort your own.
For when traditions in your faces fly,
Resolving not to yield, you must decry:
As when the cause goes hard, the guilty man
Excepts, and thins his jury all he can;
So when you stand of other aid bereft,
You to the twelve Apostles would be left.
Your friend the *Wolfe* did with more craft provide
To set those toys traditions quite aside:
And *Fathers* too, unless when reason spent,
He cites 'em but sometimes for ornament.
But, Madam *Panther*, you, though more sincere,
Are not so wise as your Adulterer:
The private spirit is a better blind
Than all the dodging tricks your authours find.
For they, who left the Scripture to the crowd,
Each for his own peculiar judge allow'd;
The way to please 'em was to make 'em proud.
Thus, with full sails, they ran upon the shelf;
Who cou'd suspect a couzenage from himself?
On his own reason safer 'tis to stand,
Than be deceiv'd and damn'd at second hand.
But you who *Fathers* and traditions take,
And garble some, and some you quite forsake,
Pretending church auctority to fix,
And yet some grains of private spirit mix,
Are like a *Mule* made up of diff'ring seed,
And that's the reason why you never breed;

[1] The omen is the gallows. Criminals were 'turned off' a ladder.

At least not propagate your kind abroad,
For home dissenters are by statutes aw'd.
And yet they grow upon you ev'ry day,
While you (to speak the best) are at a stay,
For sects that are extremes, abhor a middle way.
Like tricks of state, to stop a raging flood,
Or mollify a mad-brain'd Senate's mood:
Of all expedients never one was good.
Well may they argue, (nor can you deny)
If we must fix on church auctority,
Best on the best, the fountain, not the flood,
That must be better still, if this be good.
Shall she command, who has her self rebell'd?
Is *Antichrist* by *Antichrist* expell'd?
Did we a lawfull tyranny displace,
To set aloft a bastard of the race?
Why all these wars to win the Book, if we
Must not interpret for our selves, but she?
Either be wholly slaves or wholly free.
For *purging* fires traditions must not fight;
But they must prove Episcopacy's right:
Thus those led horses are from service freed;
You never mount 'em but in time of need.
Like mercenarie's, hir'd for home defence,
They will not serve against their native Prince.
Against domestick foes of *Hierarchy*
These are drawn forth, to make fanaticks fly;
But, when they see their countrey-men at hand,
Marching against 'em under church-command,
Streight they forsake their colours, and disband.

Thus she, nor cou'd the *Panther* well enlarge
With weak defence against so strong a charge;
But said, for what did *Christ* his Word provide,
If still his Church must want a living guide?
And if all saving doctrines are not there,
Or sacred Pen-men cou'd not make 'em clear,
From after-ages we should hope in vain
For truths, which men inspir'd cou'd not explain.

Before the Word was written, said the *Hind*:
Our Saviour preach'd his Faith to humane kind;
From his Apostles the first age receiv'd

Eternal truth, and what they taught, believ'd.
Thus by tradition faith was planted first,
Succeeding flocks succeeding Pastours nurs'd.
This was the way our wise Redeemer chose,
(Who sure could all things for the best dispose,)
To fence his fold from their encroaching foes.
He cou'd have writ himself, but well foresaw
Th' event would be like that of *Moyses* law;
Some difference wou'd arise, some doubts remain,
Like those, which yet the jarring *Jews* maintain.
No written laws can be so plain, so pure,
But wit may gloss, and malice may obscure,
Not those indited by his first command,
A Prophet grav'd the text, an Angel held his hand.
Thus faith was e'er the written word appear'd,
And men believ'd, not what they read, but heard.
But since the Apostles cou'd not be confin'd,
To these, or those, but severally design'd
Their large commission round the world to blow;
To spread their faith they spread their labours too.
Yet still their absent flock their pains did share,
They hearken'd still, for love produces care.
And as mistakes arose, or discords fell,
Or bold seducers taught 'em to rebell,
As charity grew cold, or faction hot,
Or long neglect their lessons had forgot,
For all their wants they wisely did provide,
And preaching by Epistles was supply'd:
So great Physicians cannot all attend,
But some they visit, and to some they send.
Yet all those letters were not writ to all;
Nor first intended, but occasional.
Their absent sermons; nor if they contain
All needfull doctrines, are those doctrines plain.
Clearness by frequent preaching must be wrought,
They writ but seldom, but they daily taught.
And what one Saint has said of holy *Paul*,
He darkly writ, is true appy'd to all.
For this obscurity cou'd heav'n provide
More prudently than by a living guide,
As doubts arose, the difference to decide?
A guide was therefore needfull, therefore made;
And, if appointed, sure to be obey'd.

Thus, with due rev'rence to th' Apostles' writ,
By which my sons are taught, to which, submit;
I think, those truths their sacred works contain,
The church alone can certainly explain;
That following ages, leaning on the past,
May rest upon the Primitive at last.
Nor wou'd I thence the word no rule infer,
But none without the church interpreter.
Because, as I have urg'd before, 'tis mute,
And is it self the subject of dispute.
But what th' Apostles their successours taught,
They to the next, from them to us is brought,
Th' undoubted sense which is in Scripture sought.
From hence the church is arm'd, when errours rise,
To stop their entrance, and prevent surprise;
And safe entrench'd within, her foes without defies.
By these all festering sores her councels heal,
Which time or has discloas'd, or shall reveal,
For discord cannot end without a last appeal.
Nor can a council national decide
But with subordination to her Guide:
(I wish the cause were on that issue try'd.)
Much less the scripture; for suppose debate
Betwixt pretenders to a fair estate,
Bequeath'd by some Legator's last intent;
(Such is our dying Saviour's Testament:)
The will is prov'd, is open'd, and is read;
The doubtfull heirs their diff'ring titles plead:
All vouch the words their int'rest to maintain,
And each pretends by those his cause is plain.
Shall then the testament award the right?
No, that's the *Hungary* for which they fight;[1]
The field of battel, subject of debate;
The thing contended for, the fair estate.
The sense is intricate, 'tis onely clear
What vowels and what consonants are there.
Therefore 'tis plain, its meaning must be try'd
Before some judge appointed to decide.

Suppose, (the fair Apostate said,) I grant,
The faithfull flock some living guide should want,

[1] The possession of Hungary was contested by the Turks and the Germans.

Your arguments an endless chase pursue:
Produce this vaunted Leader to our view,
This mighty *Moyses* of the chosen crew.

The Dame, who saw her fainting foe retir'd,
With force renew'd, to victory aspir'd;
(And looking upward to her kindred sky,
As once our Saviour own'd his Deity,
Pronounc'd his words—*she whom ye seek am I.*)
Nor less amaz'd this voice the *Panther* heard,
Than were those *Jews* to hear a god declar'd.
Then thus the matron modestly renew'd;
Let all your prophets and their sects be view'd,
And see to which of 'em your selves think fit
The conduct of your conscience to submit:
Each Proselyte wou'd vote his Doctor best,
With absolute exclusion to the rest:
Thus wou'd your *Polish Diet* disagree,
And end as it began in Anarchy:[1]
Your self the fairest for election stand,
Because you seem crown-gen'ral of the land;
But soon against your superstitious lawn
Some Presbyterian Sabre wou'd be drawn:
In your establish'd laws of sov'raignty
The rest some fundamental flaw wou'd see,
And call Rebellion gospel-liberty.
To church-decrees your articles require
Submission modify'd, if not entire;
Homage deny'd, to censures you proceed;
But when *Curtana*[2] will not doe the deed,
You lay that pointless clergy-weapon by,
And to the laws, your sword of justice fly.
Now this your sects the more unkindly take
(Those prying varlets hit the blots you make)
Because some ancient friends of yours declare,
Your onely rule of faith the Scriptures are,
Interpreted by men of judgment sound,
Which ev'ry sect will for themselves expound:

[1] The Polish Diet, where unanimity was necessary, was the scene of frequent violence.
[2] The edgeless sword of mercy.

Nor think less rev'rence to their doctours due
For sound interpretation, than to you.
If then, by able heads, are understood
Your brother prophets, who reform'd abroad,
Those able heads expound a wiser way,
That their own sheep their shepherd shou'd obey.
But if you mean your selves are onely sound,
That doctrine turns the reformation round,
And all the rest are false reformers found.
Because in sundry Points you stand alone,
Not in Communion join'd with any one;
And therefore must be all the Church, or none.
Then, till you have agreed whose judge is best,
Against this forc'd submission they protest:
While *sound* and *sound* a diff'rent sense explains
Both play at hard-head till they break their brains:
And from their Chairs each other's force defy,
While unregarded thunders vainly fly.
I pass the rest, because your Church alone
Of all Usurpers best cou'd fill the Throne.
But neither you, nor any Sect beside
For this high Office can be qualify'd
With necessary Gifts requir'd in such a Guide.
For that which must direct the whole, must be
Bound in one Bond of Faith and Unity:
But all your sev'ral Churches disagree.
The *Consubstantiating* Church[1] and Priest
Refuse Communion to the *Calvinist*;
The *French* reform'd, from Preaching you restrain,
Because you judge their Ordination vain;
And so they judge of yours, but Donors must ordain.
In short in Doctrine, or in Discipline
Not one reform'd, can with another join:
But all from each, as from Damnation fly;
No Union they pretend, but in *Non-Popery*.
Nor should their Members in a Synod meet,
Cou'd any Church presume to mount the Seat
Above the rest, their discords to decide;
None wou'd obey, but each wou'd be the Guide:
And face to face Dissensions wou'd encrease;
For only distance now preserves the Peace.
All in their Turns accusers, and accus'd:

[1] The Lutherans.

Babel was never half so much confus'd.
What one can plead, the rest can plead as well;
For amongst equals lies no last appeal,
And all confess themselves are fallible.
Now since you grant some necessary Guide,
All who can err are justly laid aside:
Because a trust so sacred to confer
Shows want of such a sure Interpreter:
And how can he be needful who can err?
Then granting that unerring guide we want,
That such there is you stand oblig'd to grant:
Our Saviour else were wanting to supply
Our needs, and obviate that Necessity.
It then remains that Church can only be
The Guide, which owns unfailing certainty;
Or else you slip your hold, and change your side,
Relapsing from a necessary Guide.
But this annex'd Condition of the Crown,
Immunity from Errours, you disown,
Here then you shrink, and lay your weak pretensions
down.
For petty Royalties you raise debate;
But this unfailing Universal State
You shun: nor dare succeed to such a glorious weight.
And for that cause those Promises detest
With which our Saviour did his Church invest:
But strive t' evade, and fear to find 'em true,
As conscious they were never meant to you:
All which the mother church asserts her own,
And with unrivall'd claim ascends the throne.
So when of old th' Almighty father sate
In Council, to redeem our ruin'd state,
Millions of millions at a distance round,
Silent the sacred Consistory crown'd,
To hear what mercy mixt with Justice cou'd propound.
All prompt with eager pity, to fulfill
The full extent of their Creatour's will:
But when the stern conditions were declar'd,
A mournful whisper through the host was heard,
And the whole hierarchy, with heads hung down,
Submissively declin'd the ponderous proffer'd crown.
Then, not till then, th' eternal Son from high
Rose in the strength of all the Deity;

Stood forth t' accept the terms, and underwent
A weight which all the frame of heav'n had bent,
Nor he Himself cou'd bear, but as omnipotent.
Now, to remove the least remaining doubt,
That ev'n the blear-ey'd sects may find her out,
Behold what heav'nly rays adorn her brows,
What from his Wardrobe her belov'd allows
To deck the wedding-day of his unspotted spouse.
Behold what marks of Majesty she brings;
Richer than antient heirs of Eastern kings:
Her right hand holds the sceptre and the keys,
To shew whom she commands, and who obeys:
With these to bind, or set the sinner free,
With that t' assert spiritual Royalty.

Marks of the Catholick Church from the Nicene *Creed.*

One in herself not rent by Schism, but sound,
Entire, one solid shining Diamond,
Not Sparkles shatter'd into Sects like you,
One is the Church, and must be to be true:
One central principle of unity.
As undivided, so from errours free,
As one in faith, so one in sanctity.
Thus she, and none but she, th' insulting Rage
Of Hereticks oppos'd from Age to Age:
Still when the Giant-brood invades her Throne
She stoops from Heav'n, and meets 'em half way down,
And with paternal Thunder vindicates her Crown.
But like *Egyptian* Sorcerers you stand,
And vainly lift aloft your Magick Wand,
To sweep away the Swarms of Vermin from the Land:
You cou'd like them; with like infernal Force
Produce the Plague, but not arrest the Course.
But when the Boils and Botches, with disgrace
And publick Scandal sat upon the Face,
Themselves attack'd, the *Magi* strove no more,
They saw God's Finger, and their Fate deplore;
Themselves they cou'd not Cure of the dishonest sore.[1]
Thus one, thus pure, behold her largely spread
Like the fair Ocean from her Mother-Bed;
From East to West triumphantly she rides,
All shoars are water'd by her wealthy Tides.

[1] See *Exodus*, viii & ix.

The Gospel-sound diffus'd from Pole to Pole,
Where winds can carry, and where waves can roll.
The self same doctrin of the Sacred Page
Convey'd to ev'ry clime in ev'ry age.

Here let my sorrow give my satyr place,
To raise new blushes on my *British* race;
Our sayling Ships like common shoars we use,
And through our distant Colonies diffuse
The draughts of Dungeons, and the stench of stews.
Whom, when their home-bred honesty is lost,
We disembogue on some far *Indian* coast:
Thieves, Pandars, Palliards, sins of ev'ry sort,
Those are the manufactures we export;
And these the *Missioners* our zeal has made:
For, with my Countrey's pardon be it said,
Religion is the least of all our trade.

Yet some improve their traffick more than we,
For they on gain, their only God, rely:
And set a publick price on piety.
Industrious of the needle and the chart
They run full sail to their *Japponian* Mart:
Prevention fear, and prodigal of fame
Sell all of Christian to the very name;
Nor leave enough of that, to hide their naked shame.[1]

Thus, of three marks which in the Creed we view,
Not one of all can be apply'd to you:
Much less the fourth; in vain alas you seek
Th' ambitious title of Apostolick:
God-like descent! 'tis well your bloud can be
Prov'd noble, in the third or fourth degree:
For all of ancient that you had before,
(I mean what is not borrow'd from our store)
Was Errour fulminated, o'er and o'er.
Old Heresies condemn'd in ages past,
By care and time recover'd from the blast.

'Tis said with ease, but never can be prov'd,
The church her old foundations has remov'd,
And built new doctrines on unstable sands:

[1] Dryden accuses the Dutch of denying their religion in order to trade with Japan, where Christianity was forbidden.

Judge that ye winds and rains; you prov'd her, yet she
stands.
Those ancient doctrines charg'd on her for new,
Shew when, and how, and from what hands they grew.
We claim no pow'r when Heresies grow bold
To coin new faith, but still declare the old.
How else cou'd that obscene disease be purg'd
When controverted texts are vainly urg'd?
To prove tradition new, there's somewhat more
Requir'd, than saying, 'twas not us'd before.
Those monumental arms are never stirr'd
Till Schism or Heresie call down *Goliah*'s sword.

Thus, what you call corruptions, are in truth,
The first plantations of the gospel's youth,
Old standard faith: but cast your eyes again
And view those errours which new sects maintain,
Or which of old disturb'd the churches peaceful reign,
And we can point each period of the time,
When they began, and who begot the crime;
Can calculate how long th' eclipse endur'd,
Who interpos'd, what digits were obscur'd:
Of all which are already pass'd away,
We know the rise, the progress and decay.

Despair at our foundations then to strike
Till you can prove your faith Apostolick;
A limpid stream drawn from the native source;
Succession lawfull in a lineal course.
Prove any church oppos'd to this our head,
So one, so pure, so unconfin'dly spread,
Under one chief of the spiritual state,
The members all combin'd, and all subordinate.
Shew such a seamless coat, from schism so free,
In no communion joyn'd with heresie:
If such a one you find, let truth prevail:
Till when your weights will in the balance fail:
A church unprincipl'd kicks up the scale.

But if you cannot think, (nor sure you can
Suppose in God what were unjust in man,)
That he, the fountain of eternal grace,
Should suffer falshood for so long a space
To banish truth, and to usurp her place:

That seav'n successive ages should be lost
And preach damnation at their proper cost;
That all your erring ancestours should dye,
Drown'd in th' Abyss of deep Idolatry;
If piety forbid such thoughts to rise,
Awake and open your unwilling eyes:
God has left nothing for each age undone,
From this to that wherein he sent his Son:
Then think but well of him, and half your work is done.

See how his church adorn'd with ev'ry grace
With open arms, a kind forgiving face,
Stands ready to prevent her long lost sons embrace.
Not more did *Joseph* o'er his brethren weep,
Nor less himself cou'd from discovery keep,
When in the croud of suppliants they were seen,
And in their crew his best beloved *Benjamin.*
That pious *Joseph* in the church behold,
To feed your famine, and refuse your gold;
The *Joseph* you exil'd, the *Joseph* whom you sold.[1]

The renunciation of the Benedictines to the Abby Lands.

Thus, while with heav'nly charity she spoke,
A streaming blaze the silent shadows broke;
Shot from the skyes: a cheerfull azure light;
The birds obscene to forests wing'd their flight,
And gaping graves receiv'd the wand'ring guilty sprite.

Such were the pleasing triumphs of the sky
For *James* his late nocturnal victory;[2]
The pledge of his Almighty patron's love,
The fire-works which his angel made above.
I saw my self the lambent easie light
Guild the brown horrour and dispell the night;
The messenger with speed the tidings bore;
News which three lab'ring nations did restore,
But heav'ns own *Nuntius* was arriv'd before.

Poëta. loquitur.

By this, the *Hind* had reach'd her lonely cell;
And vapours rose, and dews unwholesome fell.

[1] This renunciation was made in order to prevent the fear that the Roman Catholic Church would claim those lands which had been taken from it at the Reformation if it was re-established.

[2] A reference to James II's victory over Monmouth at Sedgmoor on 6 July 1685. Dryden, judging by the marginal note, had personally seen the phenomenon on the night of the battle which he describes.

When she, by frequent observation wise,
As one who long on heav'n had fix'd her eyes,
Discern'd a change of weather in the skyes.
The Western borders were with crimson spread,
The moon descending look'd all flaming red;
She thought good manners bound her to invite
The stranger Dame to be her guest that night.
'Tis true, course dyet and a short repast,
(She said) were weak inducements to the tast
Of one so nicely bred, and so unus'd to fast.
But what plain fare her cottage cou'd afford,
A hearty welcome at a homely board
Was freely hers; and to supply the rest,
An honest meaning, and an open breast.
Last, with content of mind, the poor man's Wealth;
A grace-cup to their common Patron's health.
This she desir'd her to accept and stay,
For fear she might be wilder'd in her way,
Because she wanted an unerring guide,
And then the dew-drops on her silken hide
Her tender constitution did declare,
Too Lady-like a long fatigue to bear,
And rough inclemencies of raw nocturnal air.
But most she fear'd that travelling so late,
Some evil minded beasts might lye in wait;
And without witness wreak their hidden hate.

The *Panther*, though she lent a list'ning ear,
Had more of *Lyon* in her than to fear:
Yet wisely weighing, since she had to deal
With many foes, their numbers might prevail,
Return'd her all the thanks she cou'd afford;
And took her friendly hostess at her word,
Who ent'ring first her lowly roof, (a shed
With hoary moss and winding Ivy spread,
Honest enough to hide an humble Hermit's head,)
Thus graciously bespoke her welcome guest:
So might these walls, with your fair presence blest
Become your dwelling-place of everlasting rest;
Not for a night, or quick revolving year,
Welcome an owner, not a sojourner.
This peaceful Seat my poverty secures,
War seldom enters but where wealth allures;

Nor yet dispise it, for this poor aboad
Has oft receiv'd, and yet receives a god;
A god victorious of the stygian race
Here laid his sacred limbs, and sanctified the place.
This mean retreat did mighty *Pan* contain;[1]
Be emulous of him, and pomp disdain,
And dare not to debase your soul to gain.

The silent stranger stood amaz'd to see
Contempt of wealth, and wilfull poverty:
And, though ill habits are not soon controll'd,
A while suspended her desire of gold.
But civily drew in her sharpn'd paws,
Not violating hospitable laws,
And pacify'd her tail, and lick'd her frothy jaws.

The *Hind* did first her country Cates provide;
Then couch'd her self securely by her side.

THE THIRD PART

MUCH malice mingl'd with a little wit
Perhaps may censure this mysterious writ:
Because the Muse has peopl'd *Caledon*
With *Panthers*, *Bears* and *Wolves*, and Beasts unknown,
As if we were not stock'd with monsters of our own.
Let *Æsop* answer, who has set to view,
Such kinds as *Greece* and *Phrygia* never knew;
And mother *Hubbard* in her homely dress
Has sharply blam'd a *British Lioness*,
That *Queen*, whose feast the factious rabble keep,
Expos'd obscenely naked and a-sleep.[2]
Led by those great examples, may not I
The wanted organs of their words supply?
If men transact like brutes 'tis equal then
For brutes to claim the privilege of men.

Others our *Hind* of folly will endite,
To entertain a dang'rous guest by night.

[1] Jesus Christ.

[2] Dryden justifies his fable by citing the example of Aesop, and Spenser who, in *Mother Hubbard's Tale*, represents Queen Elizabeth as a lion asleep, while her government is usurped by the Ape and the Fox.

Let those remember that she cannot dye
Till rolling time is lost in round eternity;
Nor need she fear the *Panther*, though untam'd,
Because the *Lyon*'s peace was now proclaim'd;[1]
The wary salvage would not give offence,
To forfeit the protection of her *Prince*;
But watch'd the time her vengeance to compleat,
When all her furry sons in frequent Senate met.
Mean while she quench'd her fury at the floud,
And with a Lenten sallad cool'd her bloud.
Their commons, though but course, were nothing scant,
Nor did their minds an equal banquet want.

For now the *Hind*, whose noble nature strove
T' express her plain simplicity of love,
Did all the honours of her house so well,
No sharp debates disturb'd the friendly meal.
She turn'd the talk, avoiding that extreme,
To common dangers past, a sadly pleasing theam;
Remembring ev'ry storm which toss'd the state,
When both were objects of the publick hate,
And drop'd a tear betwixt for her own childrens fate.

Nor fail'd she then a full review to make
Of what the *Panther* suffer'd for her sake.
Her lost esteem, her truth, her loyal care,
Her faith unshaken to an exil'd Heir,[2]
Her strength t' endure, her courage to defy;
Her choice of honourable infamy.
On these prolixly thankfull, she enlarg'd,
Then with acknowledgments herself she charg'd:
For friendship of it self, an holy tye,
Is made more sacred by adversity.
Now should they part, malicious tongues wou'd say,
They met like chance companions on the way,
Whom mutual fear of robbers had possess'd;
While danger lasted, kindness was profess'd;
But that once o'er, the short-liv'd union ends:
The road divides, and there divide the friends.

[1] A reference to James II's Declaration of Indulgence.
[2] When James II, at the time Duke of York, was exiled to Brussels, the Church of England staunchly supported him and opposed the Exclusion Bill.

The *Panther* nodded when her speech was done,
And thank'd her coldly in a hollow tone.
But said her gratitude had gone too far
For common offices of Christian care.
If to the lawfull Heir she had been true,
She paid but *Cæsar* what was *Cæsar*'s due.
I might, she added, with like praise describe
Your suff'ring sons, and so return your bribe;
But incense from my hands is poorly priz'd,
For gifts are scorn'd where givers are despis'd.
I serv'd a turn, and then was cast away;
You, like the gawdy fly, your wings display,
And sip the sweets, and bask in your Great *Patron*'s day.

This heard, the *Matron* was not slow to find
What sort of malady had seiz'd her mind;
Disdain, with gnawing envy, fell despight,
And canker'd malice stood in open sight.
Ambition, int'rest, pride without controul,
And jealousie, the jaundice of the soul;
Revenge, the bloudy minister of ill,
With all the lean tormenters of the will.
'Twas easie now to guess from whence arose
Her new made union with her ancient foes.
Her forc'd civilities, her faint embrace,
Affected kindness with an alter'd face:
Yet durst she not too deeply probe the wound,
As hoping still the nobler parts were sound;
But strove with Anodynes t' asswage the smart,
And mildly thus her med'cine did impart.

Complaints of Lovers help to ease their pain,
It shows a Rest of kindness to complain;
A friendship loth to quit its former hold,
And conscious merit may be justly bold.
But much more just your jealousie would show,
If others good were injury to you:
Witness ye heav'ns how I rejoice to see
Rewarded worth, and rising loyalty.
Your Warrier Offspring that upheld the crown,
The scarlet honours of your peacefull gown,
Are the most pleasing objects I can find,
Charms to my sight, and cordials to my mind:

When vertue spooms before a prosperous gale
My heaving wishes help to fill the sail;
And if my pray'rs for all the brave were heard,
Cæsar should still have such, and such should still
reward.

The labour'd earth your pains have sow'd and till'd:
'Tis just you reap the product of the field.
Yours be the harvest, 'tis the beggars gain
To glean the fallings of the loaded wain.
Such scatter'd ears as are not worth your care,
Your charity for alms may safely spare,
And alms are but the vehicles of pray'r.
My daily bread is litt'rally implor'd,
I have no barns nor granaries to hoard;
If *Cæsar* to his own his hand extends,
Say which of yours his charity offends:
You know he largely gives, to more than are his friends.
Are you defrauded when he feeds the poor?
Our mite decreases nothing of your store;
I am but few, and by your fare you see
My crying sins are not of luxury.
Some juster motive sure your mind withdraws,
And makes you break our friendships holy laws,
For barefac'd envy is too base a cause.

Show more occasion for your discontent,
Your love, the *Wolf*, wou'd help you to invent;
Some *German* quarrel,[1] or, as times go now,
Some *French*, where force is uppermost, will doe.
When at the fountains head, as merit ought
To claim the place, you take a swilling draught,
How easie 'tis an envious eye to throw,
And tax the sheep for troubling streams below;
Or call her, (when no farther cause you find,)
An enemy profess'd of all your kind.
But then, perhaps, the wicked World wou'd think,
The *Wolf* design'd to eat as well as drink.

This last allusion gaul'd the *Panther* more,
Because indeed it rubb'd upon the sore.

[1] German quarrel, causeless quarrel. Dryden calls it a French quarrel below because Louis XIV picked such quarrels to further his career of conquest.

Yet seem'd she not to winch, though shrewdly pain'd:
But thus her Passive character maintain'd.

I never grudg'd, whate'er my foes report,
Your flaunting fortune in the *Lyon*'s court.
You have your day, or you are much bely'd,
But I am always on the suff'ring side:
You know my doctrine, and I need not say
I will not, but I cannot disobey.
On this firm principle I ever stood:
He of my sons who fails to make it good,
By one rebellious act renounces to my bloud.

Ah, said the *Hind*, how many sons have you
Who call you mother, whom you never knew!
But most of them who that relation plead
Are such ungratious youths as wish you dead.
They gape at rich revenues which you hold,
And fain would nible at your grandame gold;
Enquire into your years, and laugh to find
Your crazy temper shews you much declin'd.
Were you not dim, and doted, you might see
A pack of cheats that claim a pedigree,
No more of kin to you, than you to me.
Do you not know, that for a little coin,
Heralds can foist a name into the line;
They ask you blessing but for what you have,
But once possess'd of what with care you save,
The wanton boyes wou'd piss upon your grave.

Your sons of Latitude[1] that court your grace,
Though most resembling you in form and face,
Are far the worst of your pretended race.
And, but I blush your honesty to blot:
Pray god you prove 'em lawfully begot:
For, in some *Popish* libells I have read,
The *Wolf* has been too busie in your bed.
At least their hinder parts, the belly-piece,
The paunch, and all that *Scorpio* claims are his.

[1] The Church of England divines who wished to broaden the Church's doctrines and comprehend a large body of Dissenters.

Their malice too a sore suspicion brings;
For though they dare not bark, they snarl at kings:
Nor blame 'em for intruding in your line,
Fat Bishopricks are still of right divine.

Think you your new *French* Proselytes are come
To starve abroad, because they starv'd at home?
Your benefices twinckl'd from afar,
They found the new *Messiah* by the star:
Those *Swisses* fight on any side for pay,
And 'tis the living that conforms, not they.
Mark with what management their tribes divide,
Some stick to you, and some to t'other side,
That many churches may for many mouths provide.
More vacant pulpits wou'd more converts make,
All wou'd have Latitude enough to take;
The rest unbenefic'd, your sects maintain:
For ordinations without cures are vain,
And chamber practice is a silent gain.
Your sons of breadth at home, are much like these,
Their soft and yielding metals run with ease;
They melt, and take the figure of the mould:
But harden, and preserve it best in gold.

Your *Delphick* Sword, the *Panther* then reply'd,
Is double edg'd, and cuts on either side.
Some sons of mine who bear upon their shield,
Three steeples Argent in a sable field,[1]
Have sharply tax'd your converts, who unfed
Have follow'd you for miracles of bread;
Such who themselves of no religion are,
Allur'd with gain, for any will declare.
Bare lyes with bold assertions they can face,
But dint of argument is out of place.
The grim Logician puts 'em in a fright,
'Tis easier far to flourish than to fight.
Thus our eighth *Henry*'s marriage they defame;
They say the schism of beds began the game,
Divorcing from the *Church* to wed the Dame.
Though largely prov'd, and by himself profess'd
That conscience, conscience wou'd not let him rest:

[1] A reference to Edward Stillingfleet (see *ante*, p. 179, n. 1 & 2). Stillingfleet, a pluralist, had taxed Dryden with the charge stated below.

I mean, not till possess'd of her he lov'd,
And old, uncharming *Catherine* was remov'd.
For sundry years before did he complain,
And told his ghostly Confessour his pain.
With the same impudence, without a ground,
They say, that look the reformation round,
No *Treatise of Humility* is found.
But if none were, the Gospel does not want,
Our *Saviour* preach'd it, and I hope you grant,
The Sermon in the mount was *Protestant*:

No doubt, reply'd the *Hind*, as sure as all
The writings of Saint *Peter* and Saint *Paul*.
On that decision let it stand or fall.
Now for my converts, who you say unfed
Have follow'd me for miracles of bread,
Judge not by hear-say, but observe at least,
If since their change, their loaves have been increast.
The *Lyon* buyes no Converts, if he did,
Beasts wou'd be sold as fast as he cou'd bid.
Tax those of int'rest who conform for gain,
Or stay the market of another reign.
Your broad-way sons wou'd never be too nice
To close with *Calvin*, if he paid their price;
But rais'd three steeples high'r, wou'd change their note,
And quit the Cassock for the Canting-coat.
Now, if you damn this censure, as too bold,
Judge by your selves, and think not others sold.

Mean-time my sons accus'd, by fames report
Pay small attendance at the *Lyon*'s court,
Nor rise with early crowds, nor flatter late,
(For silently they beg who daily wait.)
Preferment is bestow'd that comes unsought,
Attendance is a bribe, and then 'tis bought.
How they shou'd speed, their fortune is untry'd,
For not to ask, is not to be deny'd.
For what they have, their *God* and *King* they bless,
And hope they shou'd not murmur, had they less.
But, if reduc'd subsistence to implore,
In common prudence they wou'd pass your door;
Unpitty'd *Hudibrass*, your Champion friend,
Has shown how far your charities extend.

This lasting verse shall on his tomb be read,
He sham'd you living, and upbraids you dead.[1]

With odious *Atheist* names you load your foes,
Your lib'ral *Clergy* why did I expose?
It never fails in charities like those.
In climes where true religion is profess'd,
That imputation were no laughing jest.
But *Imprimatur*, with a Chaplain's name,
Is here sufficient licence to defame.[2]
What wonder is't that black detraction thrives,
The Homicide of names is less than lives;
And yet the perjur'd murtherer survives.

This said, she paus'd a little, and suppress'd
The boiling indignation of her breast;
She knew the vertue of her blade, nor wou'd
Pollute her satyr with ignoble bloud:
Her panting foes she saw before her lye,
And back she drew the shining weapon dry:
So when the gen'rous *Lyon* has in sight
His equal match, he rouses for the fight;
But when his foes lyes prostrate on the plain,
He sheaths his paws, uncurls his angry mane;
And, pleas'd with bloudless honours of the day,
Walks over, and disdains th' inglorious Prey,
So *JAMES*, if great with less we may compare,
Arrests his rowling thunder-bolts in air;
And grants ungratefull friends a lengthn'd space,
T' implore the remnants of long suff'ring grace.

This breathing-time the *Matron* took; and then,
Resum'd the thrid of her discourse agen.
Be vengeance wholly left to pow'rs divine,
And let heav'n judge betwixt your sons and mine:
If joyes hereafter must be purchas'd here
With loss of all that mortals hold so dear,

[1] Samuel Butler (1612–1680), the author of *Hudibras*, in spite of the signal service he had rendered the royalist and ecclesiastical cause by his satire, ended his days in want; but Dryden should have blamed James II rather than the Church of England for this neglect.

[2] Stillingfleet's pamphlets against the papers published by James II were licensed by the Archbishop of Canterbury's chaplain.

Then welcome infamy and publick shame,
And, last, a long farewell to worldly fame.
'Tis said with ease, but oh, how hardly try'd
By haughty souls to humane honour ty'd!
O sharp convulsive pangs of agonizing pride!
Down then thou rebell, never more to rise,
And what thou didst, and do'st so dearly prize,
That fame, that darling fame, make that thy sacrifice.
'Tis nothing thou hast giv'n, then add thy tears
For a long race of unrepenting years:
'Tis nothing yet; yet all thou hast to give,
Then add those *may-be* years thou hast to live.
Yet nothing still: then poor, and naked come,
Thy father will receive his unthrift home,
And thy blest Saviour's bloud discharge the mighty sum.

Thus (she pursu'd) I discipline a son
Whose uncheck'd fury to revenge wou'd run:
He champs the bit, impatient of his loss,
And starts a-side, and flounders at the cross.
Instruct him better, gracious God, to know,
As thine is vengeance, so forgiveness too.
That suff'ring from ill tongues he bears no more
Than what his Sovereign bears, and what his Saviour bore.

It now remains for you to school your child,
And ask why *God*'s anointed he revil'd;
A *King* and *Princess* dead! did *Shimei* worse?
The curser's punishment should fright the curse:[1]
Your son was warn'd, and wisely gave it o're,
But he who councell'd him, has paid the score:
The heavy malice cou'd no higher tend,
But wo to him on whom the weights descend:
So to permitted ills the *Dæmon* flyes:
His rage is aim'd at him who rules the skyes;
Constrain'd to quit his cause, no succour found,
The foe discharges ev'ry Tyre around,
In clouds of smoke abandoning the fight,
But his own thund'ring peals proclaim his flight.

[1] Dryden unjustly charges Stillingfleet with reviling the memories of Charles II and the Duchess of York in his answer to their Papers (see *ante*, p. 179, n. 1).

In *Henry*'s change his charge as ill succeeds,
To that long story little answer needs,
Confront but *Henry*'s words with *Henry*'s deeds.
Were space allow'd, with ease it might be prov'd,
What springs his blessed reformation mov'd.
The dire effects appear'd in open sight,
Which from the cause, he calls a distant flight,
And yet no larger leap than from the sun to light.

Now last your sons a double *Pæan* sound,
A *Treatise of Humility* is found.
'Tis found, but better it had ne'er been sought
Than thus in Protestant procession brought.
The fam'd original through *Spain* is known,
Rodriguez work, my celebrated son,
Which yours, by ill-translating made his own;[1]
Conceal'd its authour, and usurp'd the name,
The basest and ignoblest theft of fame.
My Altars kindl'd first that living coal,
Restore, or practice better what you stole:
That vertue could this humble verse inspire,
'Tis all the restitution I require.

Glad was the *Panther* that the charge was clos'd,
And none of all her fav'rite sons expos'd.
For laws of arms permit each injur'd man,
To make himself a saver where he can.
Perhaps the plunder'd merchant cannot tell
The names of Pirates in whose hands he fell:
But at the den of thieves he justly flies,
And ev'ry *Algerine* is lawfull prize.
No private person in the foes estate
Can plead exemption from the publick fate.
Yet Christian laws allow not such redress;
Then let the greater supersede the less.
But let th' Abbetors of the *Panther*'s crime
Learn to make fairer wars another time.
Some characters may sure be found to write
Among her sons; for 'tis no common sight
A spotted Dam, and all her offspring white.

The *Salvage*, though she saw her plea controll'd,
Yet wou'd not wholly seem to quit her hold,

[1] See *ante*, p. 179, n. 2.

But offer'd fairly to compound the strife;
And judge conversion by the convert's life.
'Tis true, she said, I think it somewhat strange
So few shou'd follow profitable change:
For present joys are more to flesh and bloud,
Than a dull prospect of a distant good.
'Twas well alluded by a son of mine,
(I hope to quote him is not to purloin;)
Two magnets, heav'n and earth, allure to bliss;
The larger loadstone that, the nearer this:
The weak attraction of the greater fails,
We nodd a-while, but neighbourhood prevails:
But when the greater proves the nearer too,
I wonder more your converts come so slow.
Methinks in those who firm with me remain,
It shows a nobler principle than gain.

Your inf'rence wou'd be strong (the *Hind* reply'd)
If yours were in effect the suff'ring side:
Your clergy sons their own in peace possess,
Nor are their prospects in reversion less.
My Proselytes are struck with awfull dread,
Your bloudy Comet-laws hang blazing o're their head.
The respite they enjoy but onely lent,
The best they have to hope, protracted punishment.
Be judge your self, if int'rest may prevail,
Which motives, yours or mine, will turn the scale.
While pride and pomp allure, and plenteous ease,
That is, till man's predominant passions cease,
Admire no longer at my slow encrease.

By education most have been misled,
So they believe, because they so were bred.
The *Priest* continues what the nurse began,
And thus the child imposes on the man.
The rest I nam'd before, nor need repeat:
But int'rest is the most prevailing cheat,
The sly seducer both of age and youth;
They study that, and think they study truth:
When int'rest fortifies an argument
Weak reason serves to gain the wills assent;
For souls, already warp'd, receive an easie bent.

Add long prescription of establish'd laws,
And picque of honour to maintain a cause,
And shame of change, and fear of future ill,
And Zeal, the blind conductor of the will;
And chief among the still mistaking crowd,
The fame of teachers obstinate and proud,
And more than all, the private Judge allow'd.
Disdain of Fathers which the daunce began,
And last, uncertain who's the narrower span,
The clown unread, and half-read gentleman.

To this the *Panther*, with a scornfull smile:
Yet still you travail with unwearied toil,
And range around the realm without controll
Among my sons, for Proselytes to prole,
And here and there you snap some silly soul.
You hinted fears of future change in state,
Pray heav'n you did not prophesie your fate;
Perhaps you think your time of triumph near,
But may mistake the season of the year;
The *Swallows* fortune gives you cause to fear.

For charity, (reply'd the Matron) tell
What sad mischance those pretty birds befell.

Nay, no mischance, (the salvage Dame reply'd)
But want of wit in their unerring guide,
And eager haste, and gaudy hopes, and giddy pride.
Yet, wishing timely warning may prevail,
Make you the moral, and I'll tell the tale.

The *Swallow*, privileg'd above the rest
Of all the birds, as man's familiar Guest,
Pursues the Sun in summer brisk and bold,
But wisely shuns the persecuting cold:
Is well to chancels and to chimnies known,
Though 'tis not thought she feeds on smoak alone.
From hence she has been held of heav'nly line,
Endu'd with particles of soul divine.
This merry Chorister had long possess'd
Her summer seat, and feather'd well her nest:
Till frowning skys began to change their chear
And time turn'd up the wrong side of the year;

The shedding trees began the ground to strow
With yellow leaves, and bitter blasts to blow.
Sad auguries of winter thence she drew,
Which by instinct, or Prophecy, she knew:
When prudence warn'd her to remove betimes
And seek a better heav'n, and warmer clymes.

Her sons were summon'd on a steeples height,[1]
And, call'd in common council, vote a flight;
The day was nam'd, the next that shou'd be fair,
All to the gen'ral rendezvous repair,
They try their flutt'ring wings, and trust themselves in air.
But whether upward to the moon they go,
Or dream the winter out in caves below,
Or hawk at flies elsewhere, concerns not us to know.

Southwards, you may be sure, they bent their flight,
And harbour'd in a hollow rock at night:
Next morn they rose and set up ev'ry sail,
The wind was fair, but blew a *mackrel* gale:
The sickly young sat shiv'ring on the shoar,
Abhorr'd salt-water never seen before,
And pray'd their tender mothers to delay
The passage, and expect a fairer day.

With these the *Martyn* readily concurr'd,
A church-begot, and church-believing bird;
Of little body, but of lofty mind,
Round belly'd, for a dignity design'd,
And much a dunce, as *Martyns* are by kind.
Yet often quoted Canon-laws, and *Code*,
And Fathers which he never understood,
But little learning needs in noble bloud.
For, sooth to say, the *Swallow* brought him in,
Her houshold Chaplain, and her next of kin.
In Superstition silly to excess,
And casting Schemes, by planetary guess:

[1] A reference to an assembly of Roman Catholics held in 1686, at which it was proposed that they should petition the King for permission to emigrate to France. Father Edward Petre (1631–1699), the King's confessor, the *Martyn* of this fable, counselled them to remain in England and trust to the King's protection.

In fine, short wing'd, unfit himself to fly,
His fear foretold foul-weather in the sky.

Besides, a *Raven* from a wither'd Oak,
Left of their lodging, was observ'd to croke.
That omen lik'd him not, so his advice
Was present safety, bought at any price:
(A seeming pious care, that cover'd cowardise.)
To strengthen this, he told a boding dream,
Of rising waters, and a troubl'd stream,
Sure signs of anguish, dangers and distress,
With something more, not lawfull to express:
By which he slyly seem'd to intimate
Some secret revelation of their fate.
For he concluded, once upon a time,
He found a leaf inscrib'd with sacred rime,
Whose antique characters did well denote
The *Sibyl*'s hand of the *Cumæan* Grott:
The mad Divineress had plainly writ,
A time should come (but many ages yet,)
In which, sinister destinies ordain,
A *Dame* shou'd drown with all her feather'd train,
And seas from thence be call'd the *Chelidonian* main.
At this, some shook for fear, the more devout
Arose, and bless'd themselves from head to foot.

'Tis true, some stagers of the wiser sort
Made all these idle wonderments their sport:
They said, their onely danger was delay,
And he who heard what ev'ry fool cou'd say,
Wou'd never fix his thoughts, but trim his time away.
The passage yet was good, the wind, 'tis true,
Was somewhat high, but that was nothing new,
Nor more than usual *Equinoxes* blew.
The Sun (already from the scales declin'd)
Gave little hopes of better days behind,
But change from bad to worse of weather and of wind.
Nor need they fear the dampness of the Sky
Should flag their wings, and hinder them to fly,
'Twas onely water thrown on sails too dry.
But, least of all *Philosophy* presumes
Of truth in dreams, from melancholy fumes:

Perhaps the *Martyn* hous'd in holy ground,
Might think of Ghosts that walk their midnight round,
Till grosser atoms tumbling in the stream
Of fancy, madly met and clubb'd into a dream.
As little weight his vain presages bear,
Of ill effect to such alone who fear.
Most prophecies are of a piece with these,
Each *Nostradamus*[1] can foretell with ease:
Not naming persons, and confounding times,
One casual truth supports a thousand lying rimes.

Th' advice was true, but fear had seiz'd the most,
And all good counsel is on cowards lost.
The question crudely put, to shun delay,
'Twas carry'd by the *major* part to stay.

His point thus gain'd, Sir *Martyn* dated thence
His pow'r, and from a Priest become a Prince.
He order'd all things with a busie care,
And cells, and refectories did prepare,
And large provisions laid of winter fare.
But now and then let fall a word or two
Of hope, that heav'n some miracle might show,
And, for their sakes, the sun shou'd backward go;
Against the laws of nature upward climb,
And, mounted on the *Ram*, renew the prime:
For which two proofs in Sacred story lay,
Of *Ahaz* dial, and of *Josuah*'s day.
In expectation of such times as these
A chapel hous'd 'em, truly call'd of ease:
For *Martyn* much devotion did not ask,
They pray'd sometimes, and that was all their task.

It happen'd (as beyond the reach of wit
Blind prophecies may have a lucky hit)
That, this accomplish'd, or at least in part,
Gave great repute to their new *Merlin*'s art.
Some *Swifts*, the Gyants of the *Swallow* kind,[2]
Large limb'd, stout-hearted, but of stupid mind,
(For *Swisses*, or for *Gibeonites* design'd,)

Otherwise call'd Martlets.

[1] Nostradamus (1503–1566), the famous French astrologer.
[2] A reference to the Irish Roman Catholics.

These Lubbers, peeping through a broken pane,
To suck fresh air survey'd the neighbouring plain;
And saw (but scarcely could believe their eyes)
New Blossoms flourish, and new flow'rs arise;
As God had been abroad, and walking there,
Had left his foot-steps, and reform'd the year:
The sunny hills from far were seen to glow
With glittering beams, and in the meads below
The burnish'd brooks appear'd with liquid gold to flow.
At last they heard the foolish *Cuckow* sing,
Whose note proclaim'd the holy-day of spring.

No longer doubting, all prepare to fly,
And repossess their patrimonial sky.
The *Priest* before 'em did his wings display;
And, that good omens might attend their way,
As luck wou'd have it, 'twas St. *Martyn*'s day.

Who but the *Swallow* now triumphs alone,
The Canopy of heaven is all her own,
Her youthfull offspring to their haunts repair;
And glide along in glades, and skim in air,
And dip for insects in the purling springs,
And stoop on rivers to refresh their wings.
Their mothers think a fair provision made,
That ev'ry son can live upon his trade,
And now the carefull charge is off their hands,
Look out for husbands, and new nuptial bands:
The youthfull widow longs to be supply'd;
But first the lover is by Lawyers ty'd
To settle jointure-chimneys on the bride.
So thick they couple, in so short a space,
That *Martyns* marr'age offerings rise apace;
Their ancient houses, running to decay,
Are furbish'd up, and cemented with clay;
They teem already; store of eggs are laid,
And brooding mothers call *Lucina*'s aid.
Fame spreads the news, no foreign fowls appear
In flocks to greet the new returning year,
To bless the founder, and partake the cheer.

And now 'twas time (so fast their numbers rise)
To plant abroad, and people colonies;

The youth drawn forth, as *Martyn* had desir'd,
(For so their cruel destiny requir'd)
Were sent far off on an ill fated day;
The rest wou'd need conduct 'em on their way,
And *Martyn* went, because he fear'd alone to stay.

So long they flew with inconsiderate haste
That now their afternoon began to waste;
And, what was ominous, that very morn
The Sun was entr'd into *Capricorn*;
Which, by their bad Astronomers account,
That week the virgin balance shou'd remount;
An infant moon eclips'd him in his way,
And hid the small remainders of his day:
The crow'd amaz'd, pursu'd no certain mark;
But birds met birds, and justled in the dark;
Few mind the publick in a Panick fright;
And fear increas'd the horrour of the night.
Night came, but unattended with repose,
Alone she came, no sleep their eyes to close,
Alone, and black she came, no friendly stars arose.

What shou'd they doe, beset with dangers round,
No neighb'ring Dorp, no lodging to be found,
But bleaky plains, and bare unhospitable ground.
The latter brood, who just began to fly
Sick-feather'd, and unpractis'd in the sky,
For succour to their helpless mother call,
She spread her wings; some few beneath 'em craul,
She spread 'em wider yet, but cou'd not cover all.
T' augment their woes, the winds began to move
Debate in air, for empty fields above,
Till *Boreas* got the skyes, and powr'd amain
His ratling hail-stones mix'd with snow and rain.

The joyless morning late arose, and found
A dreadfull desolation reign a-round,
Some buried in the Snow, some frozen to the ground:
The rest were strugling still with death, and lay
The *Crows* and *Ravens* rights, an undefended prey;

Excepting *Martyn*'s race, for they and he
Had gain'd the shelter of a hollow tree,
But soon discover'd by a sturdy clown,
He headed all the rabble of a town,
And finish'd 'em with bats, or poll'd 'em down.
Martyn himself was caught a-live, and try'd
For treas'nous crimes, because the laws provide
No *Martyn* there in winter shall abide.
High on an Oak which never leaf shall bear,
He breath'd his last, expos'd to open air,
And there his corps, unbless'd, are hanging still,
To show the change of winds with his prophetick bill.

The patience of the *Hind* did almost fail,
For well she mark'd the malice of the tale:
Which Ribbald art their church to *Luther* owes,
In malice it began, by malice grows,
He sow'd the *Serpent*'s teeth, an iron-harvest rose.
But most in *Martyn*'s character and fate,
She saw her slander'd sons, the *Panther*'s hate,
The people's rage, the persecuting state:
Then said, I take th' advice in friendly part,
You clear your conscience, or at least your heart:
Perhaps you fail'd in your fore-seeing skill,
For *Swallows* are unlucky birds to kill:
As for my sons, the family is bless'd,
Whose ev'ry child is equal to the rest:
No church reform'd can boast a blameless line;
Such *Martyn*'s build in yours, and more than mine:
Or else an old fanatick Authour lyes
Who summ'd their Scandals up by Centuries.[1]
But, through your parable I plainly see
The bloudy laws, the crowds barbarity:
The sun-shine that offends the purblind sight,
Had some their wishes, it wou'd soon be night.
Mistake me not, the charge concerns not you,
Your sons are male-contents, but yet are true,
As far as non-resistance makes 'em so,
But that's a word of neutral sense you know,
A passive term which no relief will bring,
But trims betwixt a rebell and a king.

[1] A reference to John White's (1590–1645) work, *The First Century of Scandalous Malignant Priests*, 1643.

Rest well assur'd the *Pardelis* reply'd,
My sons wou'd all support the regal side,
Though heav'n forbid the cause by battel shou'd be try'd.

The Matron answer'd with a loud Amen,
And thus pursu'd her argument agen.
If as you say, and as I hope no less,
Your sons will practise what your self profess,
What angry pow'r prevents our present peace?
The *Lyon* studious of our common good,
Desires, (and kings desires are ill withstood,)
To join our Nations in a lasting love;
The barrs betwixt are easy to remove,
For sanguinary laws were never made above.
If you condemn that Prince of Tyranny
Whose mandate forc'd your *Gallick* friends to fly,[1]
Make not a worse example of your own,
Or cease to rail at causeless rigour shown,
And let the guiltless person throw the stone.
His blunted sword, your suff'ring brotherhood
Have seldom felt, he stops it short of bloud:
But you have ground the persecuting knife,
And set it to a razor edge on life.
Curs'd be the wit which cruelty refines,
Or to his father's rod the *Scorpion* joins;
Your finger is more gross than the great Monarch's loins.
But you perhaps remove that bloudy note,
And stick it on the first Reformers coat.
Oh let their crime in long oblivion sleep,
'Twas theirs indeed to make, 'tis yours to keep.
Unjust, or just, is all the question now,
'Tis plain, that not repealing you allow.

To name the Test wou'd put you in a rage,
You charge not that on any former age,
But smile to think how innocent you stand
Arm'd by a weapon put into your hand.
Yet still remember that you weild a sword
Forg'd by your foes against your Sovereign Lord.
Design'd to hew th' imperial Cedar down,

[1] Louis XIV.

Defraud Succession, and dis-heir the Crown.[1]
T' abhor the makers, and their laws approve,
Is to hate Traytors, and the treason love.
What means it else, which now your children say,
We made it not, nor will we take away.

Suppose some great Oppressor had by slight
Of law, disseis'd your brother of his right,
Your common sire surrendering in a fright;
Would you to that unrighteous title stand,
Left by the villain's will to heir the land?
More just was *Judas*, who his Saviour sold;
The sacrilegious bribe he cou'd not hold,
Nor hang in peace, before he rendr'd back the gold.
What more could you have done, than now you doe,
Had *Oates* and *Bedlow*, and their Plot been true?[2]
Some specious reasons for those wrongs were found;
The dire Magicians threw their mists around,
And wise men walk'd as on inchanted ground.
But now when time has made th' imposture plain,
(Late though he follow'd truth, & limping held her train,)
What new delusion charms your cheated eyes again?
The painted Harlot might awhile bewitch,
But why the Hag uncas'd, and all obscene with itch?

The first Reformers were a modest race,
Our Peers possess'd in peace their native place:
And when rebellious arms o'return'd the state,
They suffer'd onely in the common fate;
But now the Sov'reign mounts the regal chair
And mitr'd seats are full, yet *David*'s bench is bare:[3]
Your answer is, they were not dispossess'd,
They need but rub their mettle on the Test
To prove their ore: 'twere well if gold alone
Were touch'd and try'd on your discerning stone;
But that unfaithfull Test, unfound will pass
The dross of Atheists, and sectarian brass:

[1] The Test Act of 1678 was designed by the Whigs as the first step in their attack upon the Duke of York. The Church of England opposed it at the time but found it a useful defence against James II's designs to establish Roman Catholicism.

[2] Titus Oates, see *Absalom and Achitophel*: Bedlow was his fellow perjurer.

[3] The Roman Catholic peers were excluded from the House of Lords by the Test Act of 1678.

As if th' experiment were made to hold
For base productions, and reject the gold:
Thus men ungodded may to places rise,
And sects may be preferr'd without disguise:
No danger to the church or state from these,
The Papist onely has his Writ of ease.
No gainfull office gives him the pretence
To grind the Subject or defraud the Prince.
Wrong conscience, or no conscience may deserve
To thrive, but ours alone is privileg'd to sterve.

Still thank your selves you cry, your noble race
We banish not, but they forsake the place.
Our doors are open: true, but e'er they come,
You toss your censing Test, and fume the room;
As if 'twere *Toby*'s rival to expell,
And fright the fiend who could not bear the smell.[1]

To this the *Panther* sharply had reply'd,
But, having gain'd a Verdict on her side,
She wisely gave the loser leave to chide;
Well satisfy'd to have the But and peace,[2]
And for the Plaintiff's cause she car'd the less,
Because she su'd in *formâ Pauperis;*
Yet thought it decent something shou'd be said,
For secret guilt by silence is betray'd:
So neither granted all, nor much deny'd,
But answer'd with a yawning kind of pride.

Methinks such terms of proferr'd peace you bring
As once *Æneas* to th' *Italian* King:
By long possession all the land is mine,
You strangers come with your intruding line,
To share my sceptre, which you call to join.
You plead like him an ancient Pedigree,
And claim a peacefull seat by fates decree.
In ready pomp your Sacrificer stands,
T' unite the *Trojan* and the *Latin* bands,
And that the League more firmly may be ty'd,
Demand the fair *Lavinia* for your bride.

[1] See *Tobit*, viii, 1–3.

[2] A proverbial expression: 'Peace or war?' asks *Trinculo*; 'Peace and the butt', replies *Mustacho* (*Tempest*, iv, 3).

Thus plausibly you veil th' intended wrong,
But still you bring your exil'd gods along;
And will endeavour in succeeding space,
Those houshold Poppits on our hearths to place.
Perhaps some barb'rous laws have been preferr'd,
I spake against the *Test*, but was not heard;
These to rescind, and Peerage to restore,
My gracious Sov'reign wou'd my vote implore:
I owe him much, but owe my conscience more.

Conscience is then your Plea, reply'd the Dame,
Which well-inform'd will ever be the same.
But yours is much of the *Camelion* hew,
To change the dye with ev'ry diff'rent view.
When first the *Lyon* sat with awfull sway
Your conscience taught you duty to obey:
He might have had your Statutes and your Test,
No conscience but of subjects was profess'd.
He found your temper, and no farther try'd,
But on that broken reed your church rely'd.
In vain the sects assay'd their utmost art
With offer'd treasure to espouse their part,
Their treasures were a bribe too mean to move his heart.
But when by long experience you had proov'd,
How far he cou'd forgive, how well he lov'd;
A goodness that excell'd his godlike race,
And onely short of heav'ns unbounded grace:
A floud of mercy that o'erflow'd our Isle,
Calm in the rise, and fruitfull as the *Nile*,
Forgetting whence your *Ægypt* was supply'd,
You thought your Sov'reign bound to send the tide:
Nor upward look'd on that immortal spring,
But vainly deem'd, he durst not be a king:
Then conscience, unrestrain'd by fear, began
To stretch her limits, and extend the span,
Did his indulgence as her gift dispose,
And made a wise Alliance with her foes.
Can conscience own th' associating name,
And raise no blushes to conceal her shame?
For sure she has been thought a bashfull Dame.
But if the cause by battel shou'd be try'd,
You grant she must espouse the regal side:
O *Proteus* Conscience, never to be ty'd!

What *Phœbus* from the *Tripod* shall disclose,
Which are in last resort, your friends or foes?
Homer, who learn'd the language of the sky,
The seeming *Gordian* knot wou'd soon unty;
Immortal pow'rs the term of conscience know,
But int'rest is her name with men below.

Conscience or int'rest be 't, or both in one;
(The *Panther* answer'd in a surly tone,)
The first commands me to maintain the Crown,
The last forbids to throw my barriers down.
Our penal laws no sons of yours admit,
Our *Test* excludes your Tribe from benefit.
These are my banks your ocean to withstand,
Which proudly rising overlooks the land:
And once let in, with unresisted sway
Wou'd sweep the Pastors and their flocks away.
Think not my judgment leads me to comply
With laws unjust, but hard necessity:
Imperious need which cannot be withstood
Makes ill authentick, for a greater good.
Possess your soul with patience, and attend:
A more auspicious Planet may ascend;
Good fortune may present some happier time,
With means to cancell my unwilling crime;
(Unwilling, witness all ye Pow'rs above)
To mend my errours and redeem your love:
That little space you safely may allow,
Your all-dispensing pow'r protects you now.

Hold, said the *Hind*, 'tis needless to explain;
You wou'd *postpone* me to another reign:
Till when you are content to be unjust,
Your part is to possess, and mine to trust.
A fair exchange propos'd of future chance,
For present profit and inheritance:
Few words will serve to finish our dispute,
Who will not now repeal wou'd persecute;
To ripen green revenge your hopes attend,
Wishing that happier Planet wou'd ascend,
For shame let Conscience be your Plea no more,
To will hereafter, proves she might before;
But she's a Bawd to gain, and holds the Door.

Your care about your Banks, infers a fear
Of threat'ning Floods, and inundations near;
If so, a just Reprise would only be
Of what the Land usurp'd upon the Sea;
And all your Jealousies but serve to show
Your Ground is, like your Neighbour-Nation, low.
T' intrench in what you grant unrighteous Laws,
Is to distrust the justice of your Cause;
And argues that the true Religion lyes
In those weak Adversaries you despise.

Tyrannick force is that which least you fear,
The sound is frightfull in a Christian's ear;
Avert it, Heav'n; nor let that Plague be sent
To us from the dispeopled Continent.

But Piety commands me to refrain;
Those Pray'rs are needless in this Monarch's Reign.
Behold! how he protects your Friends opprest,
Receives the Banish'd, succours the Distress'd:[1]
Behold, for you may read an honest open Breast.
He stands in Day-light, and disdains to hide
An Act to which, by Honour he is ty'd,
A generous, laudable, and Kingly Pride.
Your Test he would repeal, his Peers restore,
This when he says he means, he means no more.

Well, said the *Panther*, I believe him just,
And yet——

And yet, 'tis but because you must,
You would be trusted, but you would not trust.
The *Hind* thus briefly; and disdain'd t' inlarge
On Pow'r of *Kings*, and their Superiour charge,
As Heav'ns Trustees before the Peoples choice:
Tho' sure the *Panther* did not much rejoyce
To hear those *Echo*'s giv'n of her once Loyal voice.

The *Matron* woo'd her Kindness to the last,
But cou'd not win; her hour of Grace was past.
Whom, thus persisting, when she could not bring
To leave the *Woolf*, and to believe her King,

[1] James II helped and protected the Huguenot refugees who fled to England to escape Louis XIV's persecution.

She gave Her up, and fairly wish'd her Joy
Of her late Treaty with her new Ally:
Which well she hop'd wou'd more successfull prove,
Than was the *Pigeons*, and the *Buzzards* love.
The *Panther* ask'd, what concord there cou'd be
Betwixt two kinds whose Natures disagree?
The *Dame* reply'd, 'Tis sung in ev'ry Street,
The common chat of Gossips when they meet:
But, since unheard by you, 'tis worth your while
To take a wholesome Tale, tho' told in homely stile.

A Plain good Man, whose Name is understood,[1]
(So few deserve the name of Plain and Good)
Of three fair lineal Lordships stood possess'd,
And liv'd, as reason was, upon the best;
Enur'd to hardships from his early Youth,
Much had he done, and suffer'd for his truth:
At Land, and Sea, in many a doubtfull Fight,
Was never known a more advent'rous Knight,
Who oftner drew his Sword, and always for the right.

As fortune wou'd (his fortune came tho' late)
He took Possession of his just Estate:
Nor rack'd his Tenants with increase of Rent,
Nor liv'd too sparing, nor too largely spent;
But overlook'd his *Hinds*, their Pay was just,
And ready, for he scorn'd to go on trust:
Slow to resolve, but in performance quick;
So true, that he was awkard at a trick.
For little Souls on little shifts rely,
And coward Arts of mean Expedients try:
The noble Mind will dare do any thing but lye.
False Friends, (his deadliest foes,) could find no way
But shows of honest bluntness to betray;
That unsuspected plainness he believ'd;
He look'd into Himself, and was deceiv'd.
Some lucky Planet sure attends his Birth,
Or Heav'n wou'd make a Miracle on Earth;
For prosp'rous Honesty is seldom seen:
To bear so dead a weight, and yet to win.
It looks as Fate with Nature's Law would strive,
To shew Plain dealing once an age may thrive:

[1] James II.

And, when so tough a frame she could not bend,
Exceeded her Commission to befriend.

This gratefull man, as Heav'n encreas'd his Store,
Gave *God* again, and daily fed his Poor;
His House with all convenience was purvey'd;
The rest he found, but rais'd the Fabrick where he pray'd;
And in that Sacred Place, his beauteous Wife
Employ'd Her happiest hours of Holy Life.[1]

Nor did their Alms extend to those alone
Whom common Faith more strictly made their own;
A sort of *Doves*[2] were hous'd too near their Hall,
Who cross the Proverb, and abound with Gall.
Tho' some 'tis true, are passively inclin'd,
The greater Part degenerate from their kind;
Voracious Birds, that hotly Bill and breed,
And largely drink, because on Salt they feed.
Small Gain from them their Bounteous Owner draws;
Yet, bound by Promise, he supports their Cause,
As Corporations priviledg'd by Laws.

That House which harbour to their kind affords
Was built, long since, God knows, for better Birds;
But flutt'ring there they nestle near the Throne,
And lodge in Habitations not their own,
By their high Crops, and Corny Gizzards known.
Like *Harpy's* they could scent a plenteous board,
Then to be sure they never fail'd their Lord.
The rest was form, and bare Attendance paid,
They drunk, and eat, and grudgingly obey'd.
The more they fed, they raven'd still for more,
They drain'd from *Dan*, and left *Beersheba* poor;
All this they had by Law, and none repin'd,
The pref'rence was but due to *Levi*'s Kind,
But when some Lay-preferment fell by chance
The Gourmands made it their Inheritance.
When once possess'd, they never quit their Claim,
For then 'tis sanctify'd to Heav'ns high Name;
And Hallow'd thus they cannot give Consent,
The Gift should be prophan'd by Worldly management.

[1] The Roman Catholic Chapel in Whitehall.
[2] The clergy of the Church of England, particularly those in London.

Their Flesh was never to the Table serv'd,
Tho' 'tis not thence inferr'd the Birds were starv'd;
But that their Master did not like the Food,
As rank, and breeding Melancholy Blood.
Nor did it with His Gracious Nature suite,
Ev'n tho' they were not Doves, to persecute:
Yet He refus'd, (nor could they take Offence)
Their Glutton Kind should teach him abstinence.
Nor Consecrated Grain their Wheat he thought,
Which new from treading in their Bills they brought:
But left his Hinds, each in his Private Pow'r,
That those who like the Bran might leave the Flow'r.
He for himself, and not for others chose,
Nor would He be impos'd on, nor impose;
But in their Faces His Devotion paid,
And Sacrifice with Solemn Rites was made,
And Sacred Incense on His Altars laid.

Besides these jolly Birds, whose Crops impure,
Repay'd their Commons with their Salt Manure;
Another Farm he had behind his House,
Not overstock't, but barely for his use;
Wherein his poor Domestick Poultry fed,
And from His Pious Hands receiv'd their Bread.
Our pamper'd Pigeons with malignant Eyes,
Beheld these Inmates, and their Nurseries:
Tho' hard their fare, at Ev'ning, and at Morn
A Cruise of Water and an Ear of Corn;
Yet still they grudg'd that Modicum, and thought
A Sheaf in ev'ry single Grain was brought;
Fain would they filch that little Food away,
While unrestrain'd those happy Gluttons prey.
And much they griev'd to see so nigh their Hall,
The Bird that warn'd St. *Peter* of his Fall;[1]
That he should raise his miter'd Crest on high,
And clap his Wings, and call his Family
To Sacred Rites; and vex th' Etherial Pow'rs
With midnight Mattins, at uncivil Hours:
Nay more, his quiet Neighbours should molest,
Just in the sweetness of their Morning rest.

Beast of a Bird, supinely when he might
Lye snugg and sleep, to rise before the light:

[1] The Roman Catholic clergy.

What if his dull Forefathers us'd that cry,
Cou'd he not let a Bad Example dye?
The World was fall'n into an easier way;
This Age knew better, than to Fast and Pray.
Good Sense in Sacred Worship would appear
So to begin, as they might end the year.
Such feats in former times had wrought the falls
Of crowing Chanticleers in Cloyster'd Walls.
Expell'd for this, and for their Lands they fled;
And Sister Partlet with her hooded head[1]
Was hooted hence, because she would not pray a Bed.
The way to win the restiff World to God,
Was to lay by the Disciplining Rod,
Unnatural Fasts, and Foreign Forms of Pray'r;
Religion frights us with a meen severe.
'Tis Prudence to reform her into Ease,
And put Her in Undress to make Her pleas:
A lively Faith will bear aloft the Mind,
And leave the Luggage of Good Works behind.

Such Doctrines in the Pigeon-house were taught,
You need not ask how wondrously they wrought;
But sure the common Cry was all for these
Whose Life, and Precept both encourag'd Ease.
Yet fearing those alluring Baits might fail,
And Holy Deeds o're all their Arts prevail:
(For Vice, tho' frontless, and of harden'd Face
Is daunted at the sight of awfull Grace)
An hideous Figure of their Foes they drew,
Nor Lines, nor Looks, nor Shades, nor Colours true;
And this Grotesque design, expos'd to Publick view.
One would have thought it some *Ægyptian* Piece,
With Garden-Gods, and barking Deities,
More thick than *Ptolomey* has stuck the Skies.
All so perverse a Draught, so far unlike,
It was no Libell where it meant to strike:
Yet still the daubing pleas'd, and Great and Small
To view the Monster crowded Pigeon-hall.
There Chanticleer was drawn upon his knees
Adoring Shrines, and Stocks of Sainted Trees,
And by him, a misshapen, ugly Race;

[1] The nuns.

The Curse of God was seen on ev'ry Face:
No *Holland* Emblem could that Malice mend,
But still the worse the look the fitter for a Fiend.

The Master of the Farm displeas'd to find
So much of Rancour in so mild a kind,
Enquir'd into the Cause, and came to know,
The Passive Church had struck the foremost blow:
With groundless Fears, and Jealousies possest,
As if this troublesome intruding Guest
Would drive the Birds of *Venus*, from their nest.
A Deed his inborn Equity abhorr'd,
But Int'rest will not trust, tho' God should plight his Word.

A Law, the Source of many Future harms,
Had banish'd all the Poultry from the Farms;
With loss of Life, if any should be found
To crow or peck on this forbidden Ground.
That Bloody Statute chiefly was design'd
For *Chanticleer* the white, of Clergy kind;
But after-malice did not long forget
The Lay that wore the Robe, and Coronet;
For them, for their Inferiours and Allyes,
Their Foes a deadly *Shibboleth* devise:
By which unrighteously it was decreed,
That none to Trust, or Profit should succeed,
Who would not swallow first a poysonous wicked Weed:
Or that, to which old *Socrates* was curs't,
Or Henbane-Juice to swell 'em till they burst,
The Patron (as in reason) thought it hard
To see this Inquisition in his Yard,
By which the Sovereign was of Subjects use debarr'd.

All gentle means he try'd, which might withdraw
Th' Effects of so unnatural a Law:
But still the Dove-house obstinately stood
Deaf to their own, and to their Neighbours good:
And which was worse, (*if any worse could be*)
Repented of their boasted Loyalty:
Now made the Champions of a cruel Cause,
And drunk with Fumes of Popular Applause;
For those whom God to ruine has design'd,
He fits for Fate, and first destroys their Mind.

New Doubts indeed they daily strove to raise,
Suggested Dangers, interpos'd Delays;
And Emissary Pigeons had in store,
Such as the *Meccan* Prophet us'd of yore,
To whisper Counsels in their Patrons Ear;
And veil'd their false Advice with Zealous Fear.
The Master smil'd to see 'em work in vain,
To wear him out, and make an idle reign:
He saw, but suffer'd their Protractive Arts,
And strove by mildness to reduce their Hearts;
But they abus'd that Grace to make Allyes,
And fondly clos'd with former Enemies;
For Fools are double Fools, endeav'ring to be wise.

After a grave Consult what course were best,
One more mature in Folly than the rest,
Stood up, and told 'em, with his head aside,
That desp'rate Cures must be to desp'rate Ills apply'd:
And therefore since their main impending fear
Was from th' encreasing race of *Chanticleer*:
Some Potent Bird of Prey they ought to find,
A Foe profess'd to him, and all his kind:
Some haggar'd *Hawk*, who had her eyry nigh,
Well pounc'd to fasten, and well wing'd to fly;
One they might trust, their common wrongs to wreak:
The *Musquet*, and the *Coystrel* were too weak,
Too fierce the *Falcon*, but above the rest,
The noble *Buzzard* ever pleas'd me best;
Of small Renown, 'tis true, for not to lye,
We call him but a *Hawk* by courtesie.
I know he haunts the *Pigeon*-House and Farm,
And more, in time of War, has done us harm;
But all his hate on trivial Points depends,
Give up our Forms, and we shall soon be friends.
For *Pigeons* flesh he seems not much to care,
Cram'd *Chickens* are a more delicious fare;
On this high Potentate, without delay,
I wish you would conferr the Sovereign sway:
Petition him t' accept the Government,
And let a splendid Embassy be sent.

This pithy Speech prevail'd, and all agreed,
Old Enmity's forgot, the *Buzzard* should succeed.

Their welcom Suit was granted soon as heard,
His Lodgings furnish'd, and a Train prepar'd,
With *B's* upon their Breast, appointed for his Guard.
He came, and Crown'd with great Solemnity,
God save King *Buzzard*,[1] was the gen'rall cry.

A Portly Prince, and goodly to the sight,
He seem'd a Son of *Anach* for his height:
Like those whom stature did to Crowns prefer;
Black-brow'd, and bluff, like *Homer*'s *Jupiter*:
Broad-back'd, and Brawny built for Loves delight,
A Prophet form'd, to make a female Proselyte.
A Theologue more by need, than genial bent,
By Breeding sharp, by Nature confident.
Int'rest in all his Actions was discern'd;
More learn'd than Honest, more a Wit than learn'd.
Or forc'd by Fear, or by his Profit led,
Or both conjoyn'd, his Native clime he fled:
But brought the Vertues of his Heav'n along;
A fair Behaviour, and a fluent Tongue.
And yet with all his Arts he could not thrive;
The most unlucky Parasite alive.
Loud Praises to prepare his Paths he sent,
And then himself pursu'd his Compliment:
But, by reverse of Fortune chac'd away,
His Gifts no longer than their Author stay:
He shakes the Dust against th' ungrateful race,
And leaves the stench of Ordures in the place.
Oft has he flatter'd, and blasphem'd the same,
For in his Rage, he spares no Sov'raigns name:
The Hero, and the Tyrant change their style
By the same measure that they frown or smile;
When well receiv'd by hospitable Foes,
The kindness he returns, is to expose:
For Courtesies, tho' undeserv'd and great
No gratitude in Fellon-minds beget,
As tribute to his Wit, the churl receives the treat.

[1] The Buzzard is Dr. Gilbert Burnet (1643–1715), afterwards Bishop of Salisbury, a Whig, a broad churchman, and an enemy of James II. He withdrew from England and settled in Holland at the Prince of Orange's court. He was regarded by the clergy as the champion of the Church of England, and he was deep in the counsels of the Prince of Orange, the Protestant heir to the English throne.

His praise of Foes is venomously Nice,
So touch'd, it turns a Vertue to a Vice:
A Greek, *and bountiful forewarns us twice.*
Sev'n Sacraments he wisely do's disown,
Because he knows Confession stands for one;
Where Sins to sacred silence are convey'd,
And not for Fear, or Love, to be betray'd:
But he, uncall'd, his Patron to controul,
Divulg'd the secret whispers of his Soul:
Stood forth th' accusing Sathan of his Crimes,
And offer'd to the *Moloch* of the Times.[1]
Prompt to assayle, and careless of defence,
Invulnerable in his Impudence;
He dares the World, and eager of a name,
He thrusts about, and justles into fame.
Frontless, and satyr-proof he scow'rs the streets,
And runs an *Indian* muck at all he meets.
So fond of loud Report, that not to miss
Of being known (his last and utmost bliss)
He rather would be known, for what he is.

Such was, and is the Captain of the test,[2]
Tho' half his Vertues are not here express't;
The modesty of Fame conceals the rest.
The spleenful *Pigeons* never could create
A Prince more proper to revenge their hate:
Indeed, more proper to revenge, than save;
A King, whom in his wrath, th' Almighty gave:
For all the Grace the Landlord had allow'd,
But made the *Buzzard* and the *Pigeons* proud;
Gave time to fix their Friends, and to seduce the crowd.
They long their Fellow-Subjects to inthrall,
Their Patrons promise into question call,
And vainly think he meant to make 'em Lords of all.

False Fears their Leaders fail'd not to suggest,
As if the *Doves* were to be dispossess't;
Nor Sighs, nor Groans, nor gogling Eyes did want;

[1] Burnet witnessed before a committee of the House of Commons in 1675, that the Duke of Lauderdale, to whom he owed slight obligations, had said, that he wished the Scotch Presbyterians would rise in order that he might bring over Irish Papists to cut their throats.

[2] Burnet supported the Test Act in a number of pamphlets.

For now the *Pigeons* too had learn'd to Cant.
The House of Pray'r is stock'd with large encrease;
Nor Doors, nor Windows can contain the Press:
For Birds of ev'ry feather fill th' abode;
Ev'n Atheists out of envy own a God:
And reeking from the Stews, Adult'rers come,
Like *Goths* and *Vandals* to demolish *Rome*:
That Conscience which to all their Crimes was mute,
Now calls aloud, and cryes to Persecute.
No rigour of the Laws to be releas'd,
And much the less, because it was their Lords request:
They thought it great their Sov'raign to controul,
And nam'd their Pride, Nobility of Soul.

'Tis true, the *Pigeons*, and their Prince Elect
Were short of pow'r their purpose to effect:
But with their Quills, did all the hurt they cou'd,
And cuff'd the tender *Chickens* from their food:
And, much the *Buzzard* in their Cause did stir,
Tho naming not the Patron, to infer,
With all respect, He was a gross Idolater.

But when th' Imperal owner did espy
That thus they turn'd his Grace to villany,
Not suff'ring wrath to discompose his mind,
He strove a temper for th' extreems to find,
So to be just, as he might still be kind.
Then, all Maturely weigh'd, pronounc'd a Doom
Of Sacred Strength for ev'ry Age to come.[1]
By this the Doves their Wealth and State possess,
No rights infring'd, but Licence to oppress:
Such pow'r have they as Factious Lawyers long
To Crowns ascrib'd, that Kings can do no wrong.
But, since His own Domestick Birds have try'd
The dire Effects of their destructive Pride,
He deems that Proof a Measure to the rest,
Concluding well within his Kingly Breast,
His Fowl of Nature too unjustly were opprest.
He therefore makes all Birds of ev'ry Sect
Free of his Farm, with promise to respect
Their sev'ral Kinds alike, and equally protect.

[1] The Declaration of Indulgence.

His gracious Edict the same Franchise yields
To all the wild Encrease of Woods and Fields,
And who in Rocks aloof, and who in Steeples builds.
To *Crows* the like Impartial Grace affords,
And *Choughs* and *Daws*, and such Republick Birds:
Secur'd with ample Priviledge to feed,
Each has his District, and his Bounds decreed:
Combin'd in common Int'rest with his own,
But not to pass the Pigeons *Rubicon*.

Here ends the Reign of this pretended Dove;
All Prophecies accomplish'd from above,
For *Shiloh* comes the Scepter to Remove.
Reduc'd from Her Imperial High Abode,
Like *Dyonysius* to a private Rod:
The Passive Church, that with pretended Grace
Did Her distinctive Mark in Duty place,
Now Touch'd, Reviles her Maker to his Face.

What after happen'd is not hard to guess;
The small Beginnings had a large Encrease,
And Arts and Wealth succeed (the secret spoils of Peace.)
'Tis said th' Doves repented, tho' too late,
Become the Smiths of their own Foolish Fate:
Nor did their Owner hasten their ill hour:
But, sunk in credit, they decreas'd in Pow'r:
Like Snows in warmth that mildly pass away,
Dissolving in the Silence of Decay.

The *Buzzard* not content with equal place,
Invites the feather'd *Nimrods* of his Race,
To hide the thinness of their Flock from Sight,
And all together make a seeming, goodly Flight:
But each have sep'rate Interests of their own,
Two *Czars*, are one too many for a Throne.[1]
Nor can th' Usurper long abstain from Food,
Already he has tasted Pigeons Blood:
And may be tempted to his former fare,
When this Indulgent Lord shall late to Heav'n repair.
Bare benting times, and moulting Months may come,
When lagging late, they cannot reach their home:

[1] Dryden implies that Burnet's authority among the clergy will clash with that of the Archbishop of Canterbury.

Or Rent in Schism, (for so their fate decrees,)
Like the Tumultuous Colledge of the Bees;
They fight their Quarrel, by themselves opprest;
The Tyrant smiles below, and waits the falling feast.

Thus did the gentle *Hind* her fable end,
Nor would the *Panther* blame it, nor commend;
But, with affected Yawnings at the close,
Seem'd to require her natural repose.
For now the streaky light began to peep;
And setting stars admonish'd both to sleep.
The Dame withdrew, and, wishing to her Guest
The peace of Heav'n, betook her self to rest.
Ten thousand Angels on her slumbers waite
With glorious Visions of her future state.

FAMILIAR VERSES
ELEGIES AND
ODES

TO MY HONOUR'D FRIEND

Dr. CHARLETON

ON HIS LEARNED AND USEFUL WORKS AND MORE PARTICULARLY THIS OF STONE-HENG BY HIM RESTORED TO THE TRUE FOUNDERS[1]

THE longest Tyranny that ever sway'd,
Was that wherein our Ancestors betray'd
Their free-born *Reason* to the *Stagirite*,
And made his Torch their universal Light.
So *Truth*, while onely one suppli'd the State,
Grew scarce, and dear, and yet sophisticate.
Until 'twas bought, like Emp'rique Wares, or Charms,
Hard words seal'd up with *Aristotle*'s Armes.
Columbus was the first that shook his Throne;
And found a *Temp'rate* in a *Torrid* Zone:
The fevrish aire fann'd by a cooling breez,
The fruitful Vales set round with shady Trees;
And guiltless *Men*, that danc'd away their time,
Fresh as their *Groves*, and *Happy* as their *Clime*.
Had we still paid that homage to a *Name*,
Which onely *God* and *Nature* justly claim;
The *Western* Seas had been our utmost bound,
Where *Poets* still might dream the *Sun* was drown'd:
And all the *Starrs*, that shine in *Southern* Skies,
Had been admir'd by none but *Salvage* Eyes.

Among th' *Assertors* of free Reason's claim,
Th' *English* are not the least in Worth, or Fame.
The World to *Bacon* does not onely owe
Its *present* Knowledge, but its *future* too.
Gilbert shall live[2] till *Load-stones* cease to draw,
Or *British* Fleets the boundless Ocean awe.

[1] Dr. Walter Charleton (1619–1707), physician to Charles I, proposed Dryden for the Royal Society. These verses were prefixed to his study on Stonehenge, *Chorea Gigantum*, 1663, in which he attempted to show that it was the work of the Danes.

[2] William Gilbert (1540–1603), the author of an important work on magnets.

And noble *Boyle*,[1] not less in *Nature* seen,
Than his great *Brother* read in *States* and *Men*.
The *Circling* streams, once thought but pools, of blood
(Whether Life's fewel, or the Bodie's food)
From dark Oblivion *Harvey*'s name[2] shall save;
While *Ent*[3] keeps all the honour that he gave.
Nor are *You*, Learned Friend, the least renown'd;
Whose Fame, not circumscrib'd with *English* ground,
Flies like the nimble journeys of the Light,
And is, like that, unspent too in its flight.
What ever *Truths* have been, by *Art* or *Chance*,
Redeem'd from *Error*, or from *Ignorance*,
Thin in their *Authors*, (like rich veins in Ore)
Your Works unite, and still discover more.
Such is the healing virtue of Your Pen,
To perfect Cures on *Books* as well as *Men*.
Nor is This Work the least: You well may give
To *Men* new vigour, who make *Stones* to live.
Through You, the *DANES* (their short Dominion lost)
A longer Conquest than the *Saxons* boast.
STONE-HENG, once thought a *Temple*, You have found
A *Throne*, where Kings, our Earthly Gods, were
  Crown'd.
Where by their wondering Subjects They were seen,
Joy'd with their Stature, and their Princely meen.
Our *Soveraign* here above the rest might stand;
And here be chose again to rule the Land.

These Ruines sheltred once *His* Sacred Head,
Then when from *Wor'sters* fatal Field *He* fled;
Watch'd by the Genius of this Royal place,
And mighty Visions of the Danish Race.
His *Refuge* then was for a *Temple* shown:
But, *He* Restor'd, 'tis now become a *Throne*.

[*Chorea Gigantum*, 1663.]

[1] Robert Boyle (1540–1603), the great scientist, was the brother of Roger Boyle, Earl of Orrery (1621–1679), author and statesman.
[2] William Harvey (1578–1657), the discoverer of the circulation of the blood.
[3] George Ent, the friend of Harvey and the editor of his works.

TO MY DEAR FRIEND Mr. CONGREVE

ON HIS COMEDY CALL'D *THE DOUBLE DEALER*

WELL then; the promis'd hour is come at last;
The present Age of Wit obscures the past:
Strong were our Syres; and as they Fought they Writ,
Conqu'ring with force of Arms, and dint of Wit;
Theirs was the Gyant Race, before the Flood;
And thus, when *Charles* Return'd, our Empire stood.
Like *Janus* he the stubborn Soil manur'd,
With Rules of Husbandry the rankness cur'd:
Tam'd us to manners, when the Stage was rude;
And boisterous *English* Wit, with Art endu'd.
Our Age was cultivated thus at length;
But what we gain'd in skill we lost in strength.
Our Builders were, with want of Genius, curst;
The second Temple was not like the first:
Till You, the best *Vitruvius*, come at length;
Our Beauties equal; but excel our strength.
Firm *Dorique* Pillars found Your solid Base:
The Fair *Corinthian* Crowns the higher Space;
Thus all below is Strength, and all above is Grace.
In easie Dialogue is *Fletcher*'s Praise:
He mov'd the mind, but had not power to raise.
Great *Johnson* did by strength of Judgment please:
Yet doubling *Fletcher*'s Force, he wants his Ease.
In differing Tallents both adorn'd their Age;
One for the Study, t'other for the Stage.
But both to *Congreve* justly shall submit,
One match'd in Judgment, both o'er-match'd in Wit.
In Him all Beauties of this Age we see;
Etherege his Courtship, *Southern*'s Purity;
The Satire, Wit, and Strength of Manly *Witcherly*.
All this in blooming Youth you have Atchiev'd;
Nor are your foil'd Contemporaries griev'd;
So much the sweetness of your manners move,
We cannot envy you because we Love.
Fabius might joy in *Scipio*, when he saw
A Beardless Consul made against the Law,

And joyn his Suffrage to the Votes of *Rome*;
Though He with *Hannibal* was overcome.
Thus old *Romano* bow'd to *Raphel*'s Fame;
And Scholar to the Youth he taught, became.

Oh that your Brows my Lawrel had sustain'd,
Well had I been Depos'd, if You had reign'd!
The Father had descended for the Son;
For only You are lineal to the Throne.
Thus when the State one *Edward* did depose;
A Greater *Edward* in his room arose.
But now, not I, but Poetry is curs'd;
For *Tom* the Second reigns like *Tom* the first.[1]
But let 'em not mistake my Patron's part;
Nor call his Charity their own desert.
Yet this I Prophesy; Thou shalt be seen,
(Tho' with some short Parenthesis between:)
High on the Throne of Wit; and seated there,
Not mine (that's little) but thy Lawrel wear.
Thy first attempt an early promise made;
That early promise this has more than paid.
So bold, yet so judiciously you dare,
That Your least Praise, is to be Regular.
Time, Place, and Action, may with pains be wrought,
But Genius must be born; and never can be taught.
This is Your Portion; this Your Native Store;
Heav'n that but once was Prodigal before,
To *Shakespeare* gave as much; she cou'd not give him more.

Maintain Your Post: That's all the Fame You need;
For 'tis impossible you shou'd proceed.
Already I am worn with Cares and Age;
And just abandoning th' Ungrateful Stage:
Unprofitably kept at Heav'ns expence,
I live a Rent-charge on his Providence:
But You, whom ev'ry Muse and Grace adorn,
Whom I foresee to better Fortune born,

[1] Thomas Shadwell, the hero of *Mac Flecknoe*, who succeeded Dryden as Poet Laureate and Historiographer Royal, died in 1692. He was succeeded as Poet Laureate by Nahum Tate and as Historiographer by Thomas Rymer (see also *Preface to Fables*, p. 475, n. 1), the author of a poor tragedy, to whom Dryden refers in this line.

Be kind to my Remains; and oh defend,
Against Your Judgment Your departed Friend!
Let not the Insulting Foe my Fame pursue;
But shade those Lawrels which descend to You:
And take for Tribute what these Lines express:
You merit more; nor cou'd my Love do less.

[*The Double Dealer*, 1694.]

TO
Sir GODFREY KNELLER

ONCE I beheld the fairest of her Kind;
(And still the sweet Idea charms my Mind:)
True she was dumb; for Nature gaz'd so long,
Pleas'd with her work, that she forgot her Tongue:
But, smiling, said, She still shall gain the Prize;
I only have transferr'd it to her Eyes.
Such are thy Pictures, *Kneller*. Such thy Skill,
That Nature seems obedient to thy Will:
Comes out, and meets thy Pencil in the draught:
Lives there, and wants but words to speak her thought.
At least thy Pictures look a Voice; and we
Imagine sounds, deceiv'd to that degree,
We think 'tis somewhat more than just to see.

Shadows are but privations of the Light,
Yet when we walk, they shoot before the Sight;
With us approach, retire, arise and fall;
Nothing themselves, and yet expressing all.
Such are thy Pieces; imitating Life
So near, they almost conquer'd in the strife;
And from their animated Canvass came,
Demanding Souls; and loosen'd from the Frame.

Prometheus, were he here, wou'd cast away
His *Adam*, and refuse a Soul to Clay:
And either wou'd thy Noble Work Inspire;
Or think it warm enough, without his Fire.

But vulgar Hands, may vulgar Likeness raise,
This is the least Attendant on thy Praise:

From hence the Rudiments of Art began;
A Coal, or Chalk, first imitated Man:
Perhaps, the Shadow taken on a Wall,
Gave out-lines to the rude Original:
E're Canvass yet was strain'd: before the Grace
Of blended Colours found their use and place:
Or Cypress Tablets, first receiv'd a Face.

By slow degrees, the Godlike Art advanc'd;
As Man grew polish'd, Picture was inhanc'd;
Greece added posture, shade, and perspective;
And then the Mimick Piece began to Live.
Yet perspective was lame; no distance true;
But all came forward in one common view:
No point of Light was known, no bounds of Art;
When Light was there, it knew not to depart:
But glaring on remoter Objects play'd;
Not languish'd, and insensibly decay'd.

Rome rais'd not Art, but barely kept alive;
And with Old *Greece*, unequally did strive:
Till *Goths* and *Vandals*, a rude *Northern* Race,
Did all the matchless Monuments deface.
Then all the Muses in one ruine lye;
And Rhyme began t' enervate Poetry.
Thus in a stupid Military State,
The Pen and Pencil find an equal Fate.
Flat Faces, such as wou'd disgrace a Skreen,
Such as in *Bantam*'s Embassy were seen,
Unrais'd, unrounded, were the rude delight
Of Brutal Nations, only born to Fight.[1]

Long time the Sister Arts, in Iron sleep,
A heavy Sabbath did supinely keep;
At length, in *Raphael*'s Age, at once they rise;
Stretch all their Limbs, and open all their Eyes.

Thence rose the *Roman*, and the *Lombard* Line;
One colour'd best, and one did best design.
Raphael's like *Homer*'s, was the Nobler part;
But *Titian*'s Painting, look'd like *Virgil*'s Art.

[1] Eight ambassadors from the King of Bantam were in England in 1682. Their appearances would be well known from paintings and engravings.

Thy Genius gives thee both; where true design,
Postures unforc'd, and lively Colours joyn.
Likeness is ever there; but still the best,
Like proper Thoughts in lofty Language drest,
Where Light to Shades descending, plays, not strives;
Dyes by degrees, and by degrees revives.
Of various parts a perfect whole is wrought:
Thy Pictures think, and we Divine their Thought.

Shakespear thy Gift, I place before my sight;
With awe, I ask his Blessing e're I write;
With Reverence look on his Majestick Face;
Proud to be less; but of his Godlike Race.
His Soul Inspires me, while thy Praise I write,
And I like *Teucer*, under *Ajax* Fight;

Shakespear's *Picture drawn by Sir* Godfrey Kneller, *and given to the Author.*

Bids thee through me, be bold; with dauntless breast
Contemn the bad, and Emulate the best.
Like his, thy Criticks in th' attempt are lost;
When most they rail, know then, they envy most.
In vain they snarl a-loof; a noisy Crow'd,
Like Womens Anger, impotent and loud.
While they their barren Industry deplore,
Pass on secure; and mind the Goal before:
Old as she is, my Muse shall march behind;
Bear off the blast, and intercept the wind.
Our Arts are Sisters; though not Twins in Birth:
For Hymns were sung in *Edens* happy Earth,
By the first Pair; while *Eve* was yet a Saint;
Before she fell with Pride, and learn'd to paint.
Forgive th' allusion; 'twas not meant to bite;
But Satire will have room, where e're I write.
For oh, the Painter Muse; though last in place,
Has seiz'd the Blessing first, like *Jacob*'s Race.
Apelles Art, an *Alexander* found;
And *Raphael* did with *Leo*'s Gold abound;
But *Homer*, was with barren *Lawrel* Crown'd.
Thou hadst thy *Charles* a while, and so had I;
But pass we that unpleasing Image by.
Rich in thy self; and of thyself Divine,
All Pilgrims come and offer at thy Shrine.
A graceful truth thy Pencil can Command;
The fair themselves go mended from thy hand:
Likeness appears in every Lineament;

But Likeness in thy Work is Eloquent:
Though Nature, there, her true resemblance bears,
A nobler Beauty in thy Piece appears.
So warm thy Work, so glows the gen'rous frame,
Flesh looks less living in the Lovely Dame.

Thou paint'st as we describe, improving still,
When on wild Nature we ingraft our skill:
But not creating Beauties at our Will.

Some other Hand perhaps may reach a Face;
But none like thee, a finish'd Figure place:
None of this Age; for that's enough for thee,
The first of these Inferiour Times to be:
Not to contend with Heroes Memory.

Due Honours to those mighty Names we grant,
But Shrubs may live beneath the lofty Plant:
Sons may succeed their greater Parents gone;
Such is thy Lott; and such I wish my own.

But Poets are confin'd in Narr'wer space;
To speak the Language of their Native Place:
The Painter widely stretches his command:
Thy Pencil speaks the Tongue of ev'ry Land.
From hence, my Friend, all Climates are your own;
Nor can you forfeit, for you hold of none.
All Nations all Immunities will give
To make you theirs; where e're you please to live;
And not seven Cities; but the World wou'd strive.

Sure some propitious Planet then did Smile,
When first you were conducted to this Isle:
(Our Genius brought you here, t' inlarge our Fame)
(For your good Stars are ev'ry where the same)
Thy matchless hand, of ev'ry Region free,
Adopts our Climate; not our Climate thee.

He travel'd very young into Italy.

Great *Rome* and *Venice* early did impart
To thee th' Examples of their wondrous Art.
Those Masters then but seen, not understood,
With generous Emulation fir'd thy Blood:
For what in Nature's Dawn the Child admir'd,
The Youth endeavour'd, and the Man acquir'd.

TO SIR GODFREY KNELLER

That yet thou hast not reach'd their high Degree
Seems only wanting to this Age, not thee:
Thy Genius bounded by the Times like mine,
Drudges on petty Draughts, nor dare design
A more Exalted Work, and more Divine.
For what a Song, or senceless Opera
Is to the Living Labour of a Play;
Or, what a Play to *Virgil*'s Work wou'd be,
Such is a single Piece to History.

But we who Life bestow, our selves must live;
Kings cannot Reign, unless their Subjects give.
And they who pay the Taxes, bear the Rule:
Thus thou sometimes art forc'd to draw a Fool:
But so his Follies in thy Posture sink,
The senceless Ideot seems at last to think.

Good Heav'n! that Sots and Knaves shou'd be so vain,
To wish their vile Resemblance may remain!
And stand recorded, at their own request,
To future Days, a Libel or a Jeast.
Mean time, while just Incouragement you want,
You only Paint to Live, not Live to Paint.

Else shou'd we see, your Noble Pencil trace
Our Unities of Action, Time, and Place.
A whole compos'd of parts; and those the best;
With ev'ry various Character exprest.
Heroes at large; and at a nearer view;
Less, and at distance, an Ignobler Crew.
While all the Figures in one Action joyne,
As tending to Compleat the main Design.

More cannot be by Mortal Art exprest;
But venerable Age shall add the rest.
For Time shall with his ready Pencil stand;
Retouch your Figures, with his ripening hand.
Mellow your Colours, and imbrown the Teint;
Add every Grace, which Time alone can grant:
To future Ages shall your Fame convey;
And give more Beauties, than he takes away.

[*The Annual Miscellany*, 1694.]

TO MY HONOUR'D KINSMAN

JOHN DRIDEN

OF CHESTERTON IN THE COUNTY OF HUNTINGDON ESQUIRE

How Bless'd is He, who leads a Country Life,
Unvex'd with anxious Cares, and void of Strife!
Who studying Peace, and shunning Civil Rage,
Enjoy'd his Youth, and now enjoys his Age:
All who deserve his Love, he makes his own;
And, to be lov'd himself, needs only to be known.

Just, Good, and Wise, contending Neighbours come
From your Award, to wait their final Doom;
And, Foes before, return in Friendship home.
Without their Cost, you terminate the Cause;
And save th' Expence of long Litigious Laws:
Where Suits are travers'd; and so little won,
That he who conquers, is but last undone:
Such are not your Decrees; but so design'd,
The Sanction leaves a lasting Peace behind;
Like your own Soul, Serene; a Pattern of your Mind.

Promoting Concord, and composing Strife,
Lord of your self, uncumber'd with a Wife;
Where, for a Year, a Month, perhaps a Night,
Long Penitence succeeds a short Delight:
Minds are so hardly match'd, that ev'n the first,
Though pair'd by Heav'n, in Paradise, were curs'd.
For Man and Woman, though in one they grow,
Yet, first or last, return again to Two.
He to God's Image, She to His was made;
So, farther from the Fount, the Stream at random stray'd.

How cou'd He stand, when put to double Pain,
He must a Weaker than himself sustain!
Each might have stood perhaps; but each alone;
Two Wrestlers help to pull each other down.

Not that my Verse wou'd blemish all the Fair;
But yet, if *some* be Bad, 'tis Wisdom to beware;
And better shun the Bait, than struggle in the Snare.

Thus have you shunn'd, and shun the married State,
Trusting as little as you can to Fate.

No Porter guards the Passage of your Door;
T' admit the Wealthy, and exclude the Poor:
For God, who gave the Riches, gave the Heart
To sanctifie the Whole, by giving Part:
Heav'n, who foresaw the Will, the Means has wrought,
And to the Second Son, a Blessing brought:
The First-begotten had his Father's Share;
But you, like *Jacob*, are *Rebecca*'s Heir.

So may your Stores, and fruitful Fields increase;
And ever be you bless'd, who live to bless.
As *Ceres* sow'd, where e'er her Chariot flew;
As Heav'n in Desarts rain'd the Bread of Dew,
So free to Many, to Relations most,
You feed with Manna your own *Israel*-Host.

With Crowds attended of your ancient Race,
You seek the Champain-Sports, or Sylvan-Chace:
With well-breath'd Beagles, you surround the Wood;
Ev'n then, industrious of the Common Good:
And often have you brought the wily Fox
To suffer for the Firstlings of the Flocks;
Chas'd ev'n amid the Folds; and made to bleed,
Like Felons, where they did the murd'rous Deed.
This fiery Game, your active Youth maintain'd;
Not yet, by Years extinguish'd, though restrain'd:
You season still with Sports your serious Hours;
For Age but tastes of Pleasures, Youth devours.
The Hare, in Pastures or in Plains is found,
Emblem of Humane Life, who runs the Round;
And, after all his wand'ring Ways are done,
His Circle fills, and ends where he begun,
Just as the Setting meets the Rising Sun.

Thus Princes ease their Cares: But happier he,
Who seeks not Pleasure thro' Necessity,
Than such as once on slipp'ry Thrones were plac'd;
And chasing, sigh to think themselves are chas'd.

So liv'd our Sires, e'er Doctors learn'd to kill,
And multiply'd with theirs, the Weekly Bill:

The first Physicians by Debauch were made:
Excess began, and Sloth sustains the Trade.
Pity the gen'rous Kind their Cares bestow
To search forbidden Truths; (a Sin to know:)
To which, if Humane Science cou'd attain,
The Doom of Death, pronounc'd by God, were vain.
In vain the Leech wou'd interpose Delay;
Fate fastens first, and vindicates the Prey.
What Help from Arts Endeavours can we have!
Guibbons[1] but guesses, nor is sure to save:
But *Maurus*[2] sweeps whole Parishes, and Peoples
ev'ry Grave,
And no more Mercy to Mankind will use,
Than when he robb'd and murder'd *Maro*'s Muse.
Wou'dst thou be soon dispatch'd, and perish whole?
Trust *Maurus* with thy life, and *M--lb--rn*[3] with thy Soul.

By Chace our long-liv'd Fathers earn'd their Food;
Toil strung the Nerves, and purifi'd the Blood:
But we, their Sons, a pamper'd Race of Men,
Are dwindl'd down to threescore Years and ten.
Better to hunt in Fields, for Health unbought,
Than fee the Doctor for a nauseous Draught.
The Wise, for Cure, on Exercise depend;
God never made his Work, for Man to mend.

The Tree of Knowledge, once in *Eden* plac'd,
Was easie found, but was forbid the Taste:
O, had our Grandsire walk'd without his Wife,
He first had sought the better Plant of Life!
Now, both are lost: Yet, wandring in the dark,
Physicians for the Tree, have found the Bark:
They, lab'ring for Relief of Humane Kind,
With sharpen'd Sight some Remedies may find;
Th' Apothecary-Train is wholly blind.
From Files, a Random-*Recipe* they take,
And Many Deaths of One Prescription make.
Garth,[4] gen'rous as his Muse, prescribes and gives;

[1] Dr. Guibbons, a celebrated physician of the day.
[2] Sir Richard Blackmore, see *Preface to Fables*, p. 491, n. 2.
[3] Luke Milbourne, see *Preface to Fables*, p. 487, n. 1.
[4] Sir Samuel Garth (1661–1719), poet and physician. His well-known poem of *The Dispensary* appeared in 1699.

The Shop-man sells; and by Destruction lives:
Ungrateful Tribe! who, like the Viper's Brood,
From Med'cine issuing, suck their Mother's Blood!
Let These obey; and let the Learn'd prescribe;
That Men may die, without a double Bribe:
Let Them, but under their Superiours kill,
When Doctors first have sign'd the bloody Bill:
He scapes the best, who Nature to repair,
Draws Phisick from the Fields, in Draughts of Vital Air.

You hoard not Health, for your own private Use;
But on the Publick spend the rich Produce.
When, often urg'd, unwilling to be Great,
Your Country calls you from your lov'd Retreat,
And sends to Senates, charg'd with Common Care,
Which none more shuns; and none can better bear.
Where cou'd they find another form'd so fit,
To poise, with solid Sense, a spritely Wit!
Were these both wanting, (as they both abound)
Where cou'd so firm Integrity be found?

Well-born, and Wealthy; wanting no Support,
You steer betwixt the Country and the Court:
Nor gratifie whate'er the Great desire,
Nor grudging give, what Publick Needs require.
Part must be left, a Fund when Foes invade;
And Part employ'd to roll the Watry Trade;
Ev'n *Canaans* happy Land, when worn with Toil,
Requir'd a Sabbath-Year, to mend the meagre Soil.

Good Senators, (and such are you,) so give,
That Kings may be supply'd, the People thrive.
And He, when Want requires, is truly Wise,
Who slights not Foreign Aids, nor over-buys;
But, on our Native Strength, in time of need, relies.
Munster was bought, we boast not the Success;[1]
Who fights for Gain, for greater, makes his Peace.

Our Foes, compell'd by Need, have Peace embrac'd:
The Peace both Parties want, is like to last:
Which, if secure, securely we may trade;
Or, not secure, shou'd never have been made.

[1] See *Annus Mirabilis*, note to *st*. 37. ii.

Safe in our selves, while on our selves we stand,
The Sea is ours, and that defends the Land.
Be, then, the Naval Stores the Nations Care,
New Ships to build, and batter'd to repair.

Observe the War, in ev'ry Annual Course;
What has been done, was done with *British* Force:
Namur Subdu'd, is *England*'s Palm alone;
The Rest Besieg'd; but we Constrain'd the Town:[1]
We saw th' Event that follow'd our Success;
France, though pretending Arms, pursu'd the Peace;
Oblig'd, by one sole Treaty, to restore
What Twenty Years of War had won before.
Enough for *Europe* has our *Albion* fought:
Let us enjoy the Peace our Blood has bought.
When once the *Persian* King was put to Flight,
The weary *Macedons* refus'd to fight:
Themselves their own Mortality confess'd,
And left the Son of *Jove*, to quarrel for the rest.

Ev'n Victors are by Victories undone;
Thus *Hannibal*, with Foreign Laurels won,
To *Carthage* was recall'd, too late to keep his own.
While sore of Battel, while our Wounds are green,
Why shou'd we tempt the doubtful Dye agen?
In Wars renew'd, uncertain of Success,
Sure of a Share, as Umpires of the Peace.

A Patriot, both the King and Country serves;
Prerogative, and Privilege preserves:
Of Each, our Laws the certain Limit show;
One must not ebb, nor t' other overflow:
Betwixt the Prince and Parliament we stand;
The Barriers of the State on either Hand:
May neither overflow, for then they drown the Land.
When both are full, they feed our bless'd Abode;
Like those, that water'd once, the Paradise of God.

Some Overpoise of Sway, by Turns they share;
In Peace the People, and the Prince in War:
Consuls of mod'rate Pow'r in Calms were made;
When the *Gauls* came, one sole Dictator sway'd.

[1] William III took Namur in 1695 after a siege of one month.

TO JOHN DRIDEN

Patriots, in Peace, assert the Peoples Right;
With noble Stubbornness resisting Might:
No Lawless Mandates from the Court receive,
Nor lend by Force; but in a Body give.
Such was your gen'rous Grandsire; free to grant
In Parliaments, that weigh'd their Prince's Want:
But so tenacious of the Common Cause,
As not to lend the King against his Laws.
And, in a lothsom Dungeon doom'd to lie,
In Bonds retain'd his Birthright Liberty,
And sham'd Oppression, till it set him free.[1]

O true Descendant of a Patriot Line,
Who, while thou shar'st their Lustre, lend'st 'em thine,
Vouchsafe this Picture of thy Soul to see;
'Tis so far Good, as it resembles thee:
The Beauties to th' Original I owe;
Which, when I miss, my own Defects I show:
Nor think the Kindred-Muses thy Disgrace;
A Poet is not born in ev'ry Race.
Two of a House, few Ages can afford;
One to perform, another to record.
Praise-worthy Actions are by thee embrac'd;
And 'tis my Praise, to make thy Praises last.
For ev'n when Death dissolves our Humane frame,
The Soul returns to Heav'n, from whence it came;
Earth keeps the Body, Verse preserves the Fame.

[*Fables.* 1700.]

TO THE MEMORY OF
Mr. OLDHAM[2]

Farewel, too little and too lately known,
Whom I began to think and call my own;
For sure our Souls were near ally'd; and thine
Cast in the same Poetick mould with mine.

[1] Sir Erasmus Driden (*d.* 1632), the common grandfather of the poet and his cousin, John Driden, to whom these verses are addressed, was imprisoned for resisting an illegal levy of Charles I.

[2] John Oldham (1653–1683), the satirist. His *Satires on the Jesuits*, published in 1679, made him famous.

One common Note on either Lyre did strike,
And Knaves and Fools we both abhorr'd alike:
To the same Goal did both our Studies drive,
The last set out the soonest did arrive.
Thus *Nisus* fell upon the slippery place,
While his young Friend perform'd and won the Race.
O early ripe! to thy abundant store
What could advancing Age have added more?
It might (what Nature never gives the young)
Have taught the numbers of thy native Tongue.
But Satyr needs not those, and Wit will shine
Through the harsh cadence of a rugged line.
A noble Error, and but seldom made,
When Poets are by too much force betray'd.
Thy generous fruits, though gather'd ere their prime
Still shew'd a quickness; and maturing time
But mellows what we write to the dull sweets of Rime.
Once more, hail and farewel; farewel thou young,
But ah too short, *Marcellus* of our Tongue;
Thy Brows with Ivy, and with Laurels bound;
But Fate and gloomy Night encompass thee around.

[*Remains of John Oldham.* 1684.]

HORACE LIB. I. ODE 9.

I.

Behold yon Mountains hoary height
  Made higher with new Mounts of Snow;
Again behold the Winters weight
  Oppress the lab'ring Woods below:
And streams with Icy fetters bound,
Benum'd and crampt to solid ground.

II.

With well heap'd Logs dissolve the cold
  And feed the genial hearth with fires;
Produce the Wine, that makes us bold,
  And sprightly Wit and Love inspires:
For what hereafter shall betide,
God, if 'tis worth his care, provide.

III.

Let him alone with what he made,
  To toss and turn the World below;
At his command the storms invade;
  The winds by his Commission blow;
Till with a Nod he bids 'em cease,
And then the Calm returns, and all is peace.

IV.

To morrow and her works defie,
  Lay hold upon the present hour,
And snatch the pleasures passing by,
  To put them out of Fortunes pow'r:
Nor love, nor love's delights disdain,
What e're thou get'st to day is gain.

V.

Secure those golden early joyes,
  That Youth unsowr'd with sorrow bears,
E're with'ring time the taste destroyes,
  With sickness and unweildy years!
For active sports, for pleasing rest,
This is the time to be possest;
The best is but in season best.

VI.

The pointed hour of promis'd bliss,
  The pleasing whisper in the dark,
The half unwilling willing kiss,
  The laugh that guides thee to the mark,
When the kind Nymph wou'd coyness feign,
And hides but to be found again,
These, these are joyes the Gods for Youth ordain.

[*Sylvæ*, 1685.]

TO THE PIOUS MEMORY OF THE ACCOMPLISHT YOUNG LADY Mrs. ANNE KILLIGREW[1]

EXCELLENT IN THE TWO SISTER-ARTS OF POËSIE AND PAINTING

AN ODE

1.

THOU youngest Virgin-Daughter of the Skies,
Made in the last Promotion of the *Blest*;
Whose Palms, new pluckt from Paradise,
In spreading *Branches* more sublimely rise,
Rich with Immortal Green above the rest:
Whether, adopted to some Neighbouring Star,
Thou rol'st above us, in thy wand'ring Race,
Or, in Procession fixt and regular,
Mov'd with the Heavens Majestick Pace;
Or, call'd to more Superiour *Bliss*,
Thou treadst, with Seraphims, the vast *Abyss*.
What ever happy Region is thy place,
Cease thy Celestial Song a little space;
(Thou wilt have time enough for Hymns Divine,
Since Heav'ns Eternal Year is thine.)
Hear then a Mortal Muse thy Praise rehearse,
In no ignoble Verse;
But such as thy own voice did practise here,
When thy first Fruits of Poesie were giv'n;
To make thy self a welcome Inmate there:
While yet a young Probationer,
And Candidate of Heav'n.

2.

If by Traduction came thy Mind,
Our Wonder is the less to find
A Soul so charming from a Stock so good;
Thy Father was transfus'd into thy *Blood*:

[1] Anne Killigrew (1660–1685), poetess and painter. She was the daughter of Henry Killigrew (1613–1700), a minor dramatist.

So wert thou born into the tuneful strain,
(An early, rich, and inexhausted Vein.)
But if thy Præexisting Soul
Was form'd, at first, with Myriads more,
It did through all the Mighty Poets roul,
Who *Greek* or *Latine* Laurels wore,
And was that *Sappho* last, which once it was before.
If so, then cease thy flight, *O Heav'n-born Mind!*
Thou hast no *Dross* to purge from thy Rich Ore:
Nor can thy Soul a fairer Mansion find,
Than was the *Beauteous* Frame she left behind:
Return, to fill or mend the Quire, of thy Celestial kind.

3.

May we presume to say, that at thy *Birth*,
New joy was sprung in *Heav'n*, as well as here on *Earth*.
For sure the Milder Planets did combine
On thy *Auspicious* Horoscope to shine,
And ev'n the most Malicious were in Trine.
Thy *Brother-Angels* at thy *Birth*
Strung each his Lyre, and tun'd it high,
That all the People of the Skie
Might know a Poetess was born on Earth;
And then if ever, Mortal Ears
Had heard the Musick of the Spheres!
And if no clust'ring Swarm of *Bees*
On thy sweet Mouth distill'd their golden Dew,
'Twas that, such vulgar Miracles,
Heav'n had not Leasure to renew:
For all the *Blest* Fraternity of Love
Solemniz'd there thy *Birth*, and kept thy Holyday above.

4.

O Gracious God! How far have we
Prophan'd thy Heav'nly Gift of Poesy?
Made prostitute and profligate the Muse,
Debas'd to each obscene and impious use,
Whose Harmony was first ordain'd *Above*
For Tongues of *Angels*, and for *Hymns* of *Love?*
O wretched We! why were we hurry'd down
This lubrique and adult'rate age,
(Nay added fat Pollutions of our own)

T' increase the steaming Ordures of the Stage?
What can we say t' excuse our *Second Fall?*
Let this thy *Vestal*, Heav'n, attone for all!
Her *Arethusian* Stream remains unsoil'd,
Unmixt with Forreign Filth, and undefil'd,
Her Wit was more than Man, her Innocence a Child!

5.

Art she had none, yet wanted none:
For Nature did that Want supply,
So rich in Treasures of her Own,
She might our boasted *Stores* defy:
Such Noble Vigour did her Verse adorn,
That it seem'd borrow'd, where 'twas only born.
Her Morals too were in her *Bosom* bred
By great Examples daily fed,
What in the best of *Books*, her Father's Life, she read.
And to be read her self she need not fear,
Each Test, and ev'ry Light, her Muse will bear,
Though *Epictetus* with his Lamp were there.
Ev'n Love (for Love sometimes her Muse exprest)
Was but a *Lambent-flame* which play'd about her *Breast*:
Light as the Vapours of a Morning Dream,
So cold her self, whilst she such Warmth exprest,
'Twas *Cupid* bathing in *Diana's* Stream.

6.

Born to the Spacious Empire of the *Nine*,
One wou'd have thought, she shou'd have been content
To manage well that Mighty Government;
But what can young ambitious Souls confine?
To the next Realm she stretcht her Sway,
For *Painture* near adjoyning lay,
A plenteous Province, and alluring Prey.
A Chamber of Dependences was fram'd,
(As Conquerors will never want Pretence,
When arm'd, to justifie th' Offence)
And the whole Fief, in right of Poetry she claim'd.
The Country open lay without Defence:
For Poets frequent In-rodes there had made,
And perfectly cou'd represent
The Shape, the Face, with ev'ry Lineament:

And all the large Demains which the *Dumb-sister* sway'd,
All bow'd beneath her Government,
Receiv'd in Triumph wheresoe're she went.
Her Pencil drew, what e're her Soul design'd,
And oft the *happy Draught* surpass'd the *Image* in her
Mind.
The *Sylvan* Scenes of Herds and Flocks,
And fruitful Plains and barren Rocks,
Of shallow *Brooks* that flow'd so clear,
The bottom did the top appear;
Of deeper too and ampler Floods,
Which as in Mirrors, shew'd the Woods;
Of lofty Trees, with Sacred Shades,
And Perspectives of pleasant Glades,
Where Nymphs of brightest Form appear,
And shaggy Satyrs standing near,
Which them at once admire and fear.
The Ruines too of some Majestick Piece,
Boasting the Pow'r of ancient *Rome* or *Greece*,
Whose Statues, Freezes, Columns broken lie,
And tho' defac'd, the Wonder of the Eye,
What *Nature*, *Art*, bold *Fiction* e're durst frame,
Her forming Hand gave Feature to the Name.
So strange a Concourse ne're was seen before,
But when the peopl'd *Ark* the whole Creation bore.

7.

The Scene then chang'd, with bold Erected Look
Our Martial King the sight with Reverence strook:
For not content t' express his Outward Part,
Her hand call'd out the Image of his Heart,
His Warlike Mind, his Soul devoid of fear,
His High-designing *Thoughts*, were figur'd there,
As when, by Magick, Ghosts are made appear.
Our Phenix Queen was portrai'd too so bright,
Beauty alone cou'd *Beauty* take so right:
Her Dress, her Shape, her matchless Grace,
Were all observ'd, as well as heav'nly Face.
With such a Peerless Majesty she stands,
As in that Day she took the Crown from Sacred hands:
Before a Train of Heroins was seen,
In *Beauty* foremost, as in Rank, the Queen!

Thus nothing to her *Genius* was deny'd,
But like a *Ball* of Fire the further thrown,
Still with a greater *Blaze* she shone,
And her bright Soul broke out on ev'ry side.
What next she had design'd, Heaven only knows,
To such Immod'rate Growth her Conquest rose,
That Fate alone its Progress cou'd oppose.

8.

Now all those Charms, that blooming Grace,
The well-proportion'd Shape, and beauteous Face,
Shall never more be seen by Mortal Eyes;
In Earth the much lamented Virgin lies!
Not wit, nor Piety cou'd Fate prevent;
Nor was the cruel *Destiny* content
To finish all the Murder at a blow,
To sweep at once her *Life*, and *Beauty* too;
But, like a hardn'd Fellon, took a pride
To work more Mischievously slow,
And plunder'd first, and then destroy'd.
O double Sacriledge on things Divine,
To rob the Relique, and deface the Shrine!
But thus *Orinda*[1] dy'd:
Heav'n, by the same Disease, did both translate,
As equal were their Souls, so equal was their Fate.

9

Mean time her *Warlike Brother* on the Seas
His waving Streamers to the Winds displays,
And vows for his Return, with vain Devotion, pays.
Ah, Generous Youth, that Wish forbear,
The Winds too soon will waft thee here!
Slack all thy Sails, and fear to come,
Alas, thou know'st not, thou art wreck'd at home!
No more shalt thou behold thy Sister's Face,
Thou hast already had her last Embrace.
But look aloft, and if thou ken'st from far,
Among the *Pleiad*'s, a New-kindl'd Star,
If any sparkles, than the rest, more bright,
'Tis she that shines in that propitious Light.

[1] *Orinda*, the poetic name of the poetess Katherine Philips (1631–1664), who died of the small-pox.

10.

When in mid-Air, the Golden Trump shall sound,
To raise the Nations under ground;
When in the Valley of *Jehosophat*,
The Judging God shall close the book of Fate;
And there the last *Assizes* keep,
For those who Wake, and those who Sleep;
When ratling *Bones* together fly,
From the four Corners of the Skie,
When Sinews o're the Skeletons are spread,
Those cloath'd with Flesh, and Life inspires the Dead;
The Sacred Poets first shall hear the Sound,
And formost from the Tomb shall bound:
For they are cover'd with the lightest Ground,
And streight, with in-born Vigour, on the Wing,
Like mounting Larks, to the New Morning sing.
There *Thou*, sweet Saint, before the Quire shalt go,
As Harbinger of Heav'n, the Way to show,
The Way which thou so well hast learn'd below.

[*Examen Poeticum*, 1693.]

A SONG FOR
St. CECILIA'S DAY, 1687

1.

From Harmony, from Heav'nly Harmony
This Universal Frame began.
When Nature underneath a heap
Of jarring Atoms lay,
And cou'd not heave her Head,
The tuneful Voice was heard from high,
Arise ye more than dead.
Then cold, and hot, and moist, and dry,
In order to their stations leap,
And MUSICK's Pow'r obey.
From Harmony, from Heav'nly Harmony
This Universal Frame began:
From Harmony to Harmony
Through all the compass of the Notes it ran,
The Diapason closing full in Man.

2.

What Passion cannot MUSICK raise and quell!
When *Jubal* struck the corded Shell,
His list'ning Brethren stood around
And wond'ring, on their Faces fell
To worship that Celestial Sound:
Less than a God they thought there cou'd not dwell
Within the hollow of that Shell
That spoke so sweetly and so well.
What Passion cannot MUSICK raise and quell!

3.

The TRUMPETS loud Clangor
Excites us to Arms
With shrill Notes of Anger
And mortal Alarms.
The double double double beat
Of the thundring DRUM
Cries, heark the Foes come;
Charge, Charge, 'tis too late to retreat.

4.

The soft complaining FLUTE
In dying Notes discovers
The Woes of hopeless Lovers,
Whose Dirge is whisper'd by the Warbling LUTE.

5.

Sharp VIOLINS proclaim
Their jealous Pangs, and Desperation,
Fury, frantick Indignation,
Depth of Pains and height of Passion,
For the fair, disdainful Dame.

6.

But oh! what Art can teach
What human Voice can reach
The sacred ORGAN's praise?
Notes inspiring holy Love,
Notes that wing their Heav'nly ways
To mend the Choires above.

7.

Orpheus cou'd lead the savage race;
And Trees unrooted left their place;
Sequacious of the *Lyre*:
But bright *CECILIA* rais'd the wonder high'r;
When to her ORGAN, vocal Breath was giv'n,
An Angel heard, and straight appear'd
Mistaking Earth for Heav'n.

Grand CHORUS.

As from the pow'r of Sacred Lays
The Spheres began to move,
And sung the great Creator's praise
To all the bless'd above;
So when the last and dreadful hour
This crumbling Pageant shall devour,
The TRUMPET *shall be heard on high,*
The Dead shall live, the Living die,
And MUSICK *shall untune the Sky.*

[*Examen Poeticum.* 1693.]

ALEXANDER'S FEAST

OR THE POWER OF MUSIQUE

AN ODE

IN HONOUR OF St. CECILIA'S DAY

1.

'TWAS at the Royal Feast, for *Persia* won,
By *Philip*'s Warlike Son:
Aloft in awful State
The God-like Heroe sate
On his Imperial Throne:
His valiant Peers were plac'd around;
Their Brows with Roses and with Myrtles bound.
(So shou'd Desert in Arms be Crown'd:)
The lovely *Thais* by his side,
Sate like a blooming *Eastern* Bride
In Flow'r of Youth and Beauty's Pride.

Happy, happy, happy Pair!
None but the Brave
None but the Brave
None but the Brave deserves the Fair.

CHORUS.

Happy, happy, happy Pair!
None but the Brave
None but the Brave
None but the Brave deserves the Fair.

II.

Timotheus plac'd on high
Amid the tuneful Quire,
With flying Fingers touch'd the Lyre:
The trembling Notes ascend the Sky,
And Heav'nly Joys inspire.
The Song began from *Jove*;
Who left his blissful Seats above,
(Such is the Pow'r of mighty Love.)
A Dragon's fiery Form bely'd the God:
Sublime on Radiant Spires He rode,
When He to fair *Olympia* press'd:
And while He sought her snowy Breast,
Then, round her slender Waste he curl'd,
And stamp'd an Image of himself, a Sov'raign of the World.
The list'ning Crowd admire the lofty Sound,
A present Deity, they shout around:
A present Deity the vaulted Roofs rebound.
With ravish'd Ears
The Monarch hears,
Assumes the God,
Affects to nod,
And seems to shake the Spheres.

CHORUS.

With ravish'd ears
The Monarch hears,
Assumes the God,
Affects to Nod,
And seems to shake the Spheres.

III.

The Praise of *Bacchus* then, the sweet Musician sung;
Of *Bacchus* ever Fair, and ever Young:
The jolly God in Triumph comes;
Sound the Trumpets; beat the Drums;
Flush'd with a purple Grace
He shews his honest Face,
Now give the Hautboys breath; He comes, He comes.
Bacchus ever Fair and Young,
Drinking Joys did first ordain:
Bacchus Blessings are a Treasure;
Drinking is the Soldiers Pleasure;
Rich the Treasure,
Sweet the Pleasure;
Sweet is Pleasure after Pain.

CHORUS.

Bacchus *Blessings are a Treasure,*
Drinking is the Soldier's Pleasure;
Rich the Treasure,
Sweet the Pleasure;
Sweet is Pleasure after Pain.

IV.

Sooth'd with the Sound the King grew vain;
Fought all his Battails o'er again;
And thrice He routed all his Foes; and thrice He slew the slain.
The Master saw the Madness rise;
His glowing Cheeks, his ardent Eyes;
And while He Heav'n and Earth defy'd,
Chang'd his hand, and check'd his Pride.
He chose a Mournful Muse
Soft Pity to infuse:
He sung *Darius* Great and Good,
By too severe a Fate,
Fallen, fallen, fallen, fallen,
Fallen from his high Estate
And weltring in his Blood:
Deserted at his utmost Need,
By those his former Bounty fed:
On the bare Earth expos'd He lyes,
With not a Friend to close his Eyes.

With down-cast Looks the joyless Victor sate,
Revolveing in his alter'd Soul
The various Turns of Chance below;
And, now and then, a Sigh he stole;
And Tears began to flow.

CHORUS.

Revolveing in his alter'd Soul
The various Turns of Chance below;
And, now and then, a Sigh he stole;
And Tears began to flow.

V.

The Mighty Master smil'd to see
That Love was in the next Degree:
'Twas but a Kindred-Sound to move;
For Pity melts the Mind to Love.
Softly sweet, in *Lydian* Measures,
Soon He sooth'd his Soul to Pleasures.
War, he sung, is Toil and Trouble;
Honour but an empty Bubble.
Never ending, still beginning,
Fighting still, and still destroying,
If the World be worth thy Winning,
Think, O think, it worth Enjoying.
Lovely *Thais* sits beside thee,
Take the Good the Gods provide thee.

The Many rend the Skies, with loud Applause;
So Love was Crown'd, but Musique won the Cause.
The Prince, unable to conceal his Pain,
Gaz'd on the Fair
Who caus'd his Care,
And sigh'd and look'd, sigh'd and look'd,
Sigh'd and look'd, and sigh'd again:
At length, with Love and Wine at once oppress'd,
The vanquish'd Victor sunk upon her Breast.

CHORUS.

The Prince, unable to conceal his Pain,
Gaz'd on the Fair
Who caus'd his Care,

And sigh'd and look'd, sigh'd and look'd,
Sigh'd and look'd, and sigh'd again:
At length, with Love and Wine at once oppress'd,
The vanquish'd Victor sunk upon her Breast.

VI.

Now strike the Golden Lyre again:
A lowder yet, and yet a lowder Strain.
Break his Bands of Sleep asunder,
And rouze him, like a rattling Peal of Thunder.
Hark, hark, the horrid Sound
Has rais'd up his Head,
As awak'd from the Dead,
And amaz'd, he stares around.
Revenge, Revenge, *Timotheus* cries,
See the Furies arise!
See the Snakes that they rear,
How they hiss in their Hair,
And the Sparkles that flash from their Eyes!
Behold a ghastly Band,
Each a Torch in his Hand!
Those are *Grecian* Ghosts, that in Battail were slayn,
And unbury'd remain
Inglorious on the Plain.
Give the Vengeance due
To the Valiant Crew.
Behold how they toss their Torches on high,
How they point to the *Persian* Abodes,
And glitt'ring Temples of their Hostile Gods!
The Princes applaud, with a furious Joy;
And the King seyz'd a Flambeau, with Zeal to destroy:
Thais led the Way,
To light him to his Prey,
And, like another *Hellen*, fir'd another *Troy*.

CHORUS.

And the King seyz'd a flambeau, with Zeal to destroy;
Thais *led the way,*
To light him to his Prey,
And, like another Hellen, *fir'd another* Troy.

VII.

Thus, long ago
'Ere heaving Bellows learn'd to blow,
While Organs yet were mute;
Timotheus, to his breathing Flute,
And sounding Lyre,
Cou'd swell the Soul to rage, or kindle soft Desire.
At last Divine *Cecilia* came,
Inventress of the Vocal Frame;
The sweet Enthusiast, from her Sacred Store,
Enlarg'd the former narrow Bounds,
And added Length to solemn Sounds,
With Nature's Mother-Wit, and Arts unknown before.
Let old *Timotheus* yield the Prize,
Or both divide the Crown;
He rais'd a Mortal to the Skies;
She drew an Angel down.

Grand CHORUS.

At last, Divine Cecilia *came,*
Inventress of the Vocal Frame;
The sweet Enthusiast, from her Sacred Store,
Enlarg'd the former narrow Bounds,
And added Length to solemn Sounds,
With Nature's Mother-Wit, and Arts unknown before.
Let old Timotheus *yield the Prize,*
Or both divide the Crown;
He rais'd a Mortal to the Skies;
She drew an Angel down.

[1697.]

SONGS
AND
THE SECULAR MASQUE

Other songs will be found among the plays
on pages 690 and 748.

SONGS

1.

Ah fading joy, how quickly art thou past?
Yet we thy ruine haste:
As if the cares of Humane Life were few
We seek out new:
And follow Fate that does too fast pursue.

See how on every bough the Birds express
In the sweet notes their happiness.
They all enjoy, and nothing spare;
But on their Mother Nature lay their care:
Why then should Man, the Lord of all below
Such troubles chuse to know
As none of all his Subjects undergo?

Hark, hark, the Waters fall, fall, fall;
And with a Murmuring sound
Dash, dash, upon the ground,
To gentle slumbers call.

[*The Indian Emperour*, 1667.]

2.

I feed a flame within which so torments me
That it both pains my heart, and yet contents me:
'Tis such a pleasing smart, and I so love it,
That I had rather die, then once remove it.

Yet he for whom I grieve shall never know it,
My tongue does not betray, nor my eyes show it:
Not a sigh nor a tear my pain discloses,
But they fall silently like dew on Roses.

Thus to prevent my love from being cruel,
My heart's the sacrifice as 'tis the fuel:

And while I suffer this to give him quiet,
My faith rewards my love, though he deny it.

On his eyes will I gaze, and there delight me;
While I conceal my love, no frown can fright me:
To be more happy I dare not aspire;
Nor can I fall more low, mounting no higher.

[*Secret Love, or, The Maiden Queen*, 1668.]

3.

Ah how sweet it is to love,
Ah how gay is young desire!
And what pleasing pains we prove
When we first approach Loves fire!
  Pains of Love be sweeter far
  Than all other pleasures are.

Sighs which are from Lovers blown,
Do but gently heave the Heart;
Ev'n the tears they shed alone
Cure, like trickling Balm their smart.
  Lovers when they lose their breath,
  Bleed away in easie death.

Love and Time with reverence use,
Treat 'em like a parting friend:
Nor the golden gifts refuse
Which in youth sincere they send:
  For each year their price is more,
  And they less simple than before.

Love, like Spring-tides full and high,
Swells in every youthful vein:
But each Tide does less supply,
Till they quite shrink in again:
  If a flow in Age appear,
  'Tis but rain, and runs not clear.

[*Tyrannick Love*, 1670.]

4.

Damon. *CELIMENA*, of my heart,
None shall e'er bereave you:
If, with your good leave, I may
Quarrel with you once a day,
I will never leave you.

Celimena. Passion's but an empty name
Where respect is wanting:
Damon you mistake your ayme;
Hang your heart, and burn your flame,
If you must be ranting.

Damon. Love as dull and muddy is,
As decaying liquor:
Anger sets it on the lees,
And refines it by degrees,
Till workes it quicker.

Celimena. Love by quarrels to beget
Wisely you endeavour;
With a grave Physician's wit
Who to cure an Ague fit
Put me in a Feavor.

Damon. Anger rouzes love to fight,
And his only bayt is,
'Tis the spurre to dull delight,
And is but an eager bite,
When desire at height is.

Celimena. If such drops of heat can fall
In our wooing weather;
If such drops of heat can fall,
We shall have the Devil and all
When we come together.

[*An Evening's Love*, 1671.]

5.

CALM was the Even, and cleer was the Skie
And the new budding flowers did spring,
When all alone went *Amyntas* and I
To hear the sweet Nightingale sing;
I sate, and he laid him down by me;
But scarcely his breath he could draw;
For when with a fear he began to draw near,
He was dash'd with A ha ha ha ha!

He blush'd to himself, and lay still for a while,
And his modesty curb'd his desire;
But streight I convinc'd all his fear with a smile,
Which added new flames to his fire.
O *Sylvia*, said he, you are cruel,
To keep your poor Lover in awe;
Then once more he prest with his hands to my brest,
But was dash'd with A ha ha ha ha.

I knew 'twas his passion that caus'd all his fear;
And therefore I pity'd his case:
I whisper'd him softly there's no body near,
And layd my cheek close to his face:
But as he grew bolder and bolder,
A Shepherd came by us and saw;
And just as our bliss we began with a kiss,
He laughed out with A ha ha ha ha.

[*An Evening's Love*, 1671.]

6.

AFTER the pangs of a desperate Lover,
When day and night I have sigh'd all in vain,
Ah what a pleasure it is to discover
In her eyes pity, who causes my pain!

When with unkindness our love at a stand is,
And both have punish'd our selves with the pain,
Ah what a pleasure the touch of her hand is,
Ah what a pleasure to press it again!

When the denyal comes fainter and fainter,
And her eyes give what her tongue does deny,
Ah what a trembling I feel when I venture,
Ah what a trembling does usher my joy!

When, with a Sigh, she accords me the blessing,
And her eyes twinkle 'twixt pleasure and pain;
Ah what a joy 'tis beyond all expressing,
Ah what a joy to hear, shall we again!

[*An Evening's Love*, 1671.]

7.

YOU charm'd me not with that fair face
Though it was all divine:
To be anothers is the Grace,
That makes me wish you mine.
The Gods and Fortune take their part
Who like young Monarchs fight;
And boldly dare invade that heart
Which is anothers right.
First mad with hope we undertake
To pull up every barr;
But once possess'd, we faintly make
A dull defensive warr.
Now every friend is turn'd a foe
In hope to get our store:
And passion makes us Cowards grow,
Which made us brave before.

[*An Evening's Love*, 1671.]

8.

WHEREVER I am, and whatever I doe,
My *Phillis* is still in my mind:
When angry I mean not to *Phillis* to goe,
My Feet of themselves the way find:
Unknown to my self I am just at her door,
And when I would raile, I can bring out no more,
Than *Phillis* too fair and unkind!

When *Phillis* I see, my Heart bounds in my Breast,
And the Love I would stifle is shown:
But asleep, or awake, I am never at rest
When from my Eyes *Phillis* is gone!
Sometimes a sad Dream does delude my sad mind,
But, alas, when I wake and no *Phillis* I find
How I sigh to my self all alone.

Should a King be my Rival in her I adore
He should offer his Treasure in vain:
O let me alone to be happy and poor,
And give me my *Phillis* again:
Let *Phillis* be mine, and but ever be kind
I could to a Desart with her be confin'd,
And envy no Monarch his Raign.

Alas, I discover too much of my Love,
And she too well knows her own power!
She makes me each day a new Martyrdom prove,
And makes me grow jealous each hour:
But let her each minute torment my poor mind
I had rather love *Phillis* both False and Unkind,
Then ever be freed from her Pow'r.

[*The Conquest of Granada, Part I*, 1672.]

9.

BENEATH a Myrtle shade
Which Love for none but happy Lovers made,
I slept, and straight my Love before me brought
Phillis the object of my waking thought;
Undress'd she came my flames to meet,
While Love strow'd flow'rs beneath her feet;
Flow'rs, which so press'd by her, became more sweet.

From the bright Visions head
A careless vail of Lawn was loosely spread:
From her white temples fell her shaded hair,
Like cloudy sunshine not too brown nor fair:
Her hands, her lips did love inspire;
Her every grace my heart did fire:
But most her eyes which languish'd with desire.

Ah, Charming fair, said I,
How long can you my bliss and yours deny?
By Nature and by love this lonely shade
Was for revenge of suffring Lovers made:
Silence and shades with love agree:
Both shelter you and favour me;
You cannot blush because I cannot see.

No, let me dye, she said,
Rather than lose the spotless name of Maid:
Faintly me thought she spoke, for all the while
She bid me not believe her, with a smile.
Then dye, said I, she still deny'd:
And, is it thus, thus, thus she cry'd
You use a harmless Maid, and so she dy'd!

I wak'd, and straight I knew
I lov'd so well it made my dream prove true:
Fancy, the kinder Mistress of the two,
Fancy had done what *Phillis* wou'd not do!
Ah, Cruel Nymph, cease your disdain,
While I can dream you scorn in vain;
Asleep or waking you must ease my pain.

[*The Conquest of Granada*, *Part I*, 1672.]

10.

SONG IN TWO PARTS

He. How unhappy a Lover am I
While I sigh for my *Phillis* in vain;
All my hopes of Delight
Are another man's Right,
Who is happy while I am in pain!

She. Since her Honour allows no Relief,
But to pity the pains which you bear,
'Tis the best of your Fate,
(In a hopeless Estate,)
To give o're, and betimes to despair.

He. I have try'd the false Med'cine in vain;
For I wish what I hope not to win:

From without, my desire
Has no Food to its Fire,
But it burns and consumes me within.

She. Yet at least 'tis a pleasure to know
That you are not unhappy alone:
For the Nymph you adore
Is as wretch'd and more,
And accounts all your suff'rings her own.

He. O ye Gods, let me suffer for both;
At the feet of my *Phillis* I'le lye:
I'le resign up my Breath,
And take pleasure in Death,
To be pity'd by her when I dye.

She. What her Honour deny'd you in Life
In her Death she will give to your Love.
Such a Flame as is true
After Fate will renew,
For the Souls to meet closer above.

[*The Conquest of Granada, Part II*, 1672.]

11.

FAREWELL Fair *Arminda*, my joy and my grief,
In vain I have lov'd you, and hope no releif;
Undone by your vertue, too strict and severe,
Your Eyes gave me Love, and you gave me despair.
Now call'd by my Honour, I seek with content,
The Fate which in pitty, you would not prevent:
To languish in Love, were to find by delay,
A death that's more welcome the speedyest way,

On Seas, and in Battles, in Bullets and Fire,
The danger is less, then in hopeless desire;
My Death's-wound you gave [me] though far off I bear,
My fall from your sight, not to cost you a Tear.
But if the kind Flood, on a wave should convey,
And under your Window, my Body would lay.
The wound on my breast, when you happen to see,
You'l say with a sigh—it was given by me.

[*Covent Garden Drolery*, 1672.]

12.

WHY should a foolish Marriage Vow
  Which long ago was made,
Oblige us to each other now
  When Passion is decay'd?
We lov'd, and we lov'd, as long as we cou'd,
  Till our love was lov'd out in us both:
But our Marriage is dead, when the Pleasure is fled:
  'Twas Pleasure first made it an Oath.

If I have Pleasures for a Friend,
  And farther love in store,
What wrong has he whose joys did end,
  And who cou'd give no more?

'Tis a madness that he
Should be jealous of me,
Or that I shou'd bar him of another:
For all we can gain,
Is to give our selves pain,
When neither can hinder the other.

[*Marriage-a-la-Mode*, 1673.]

13.

WHIL'ST *Alexis* lay prest
In her Arms he lov'd best,
With his hands round her neck,
And his head on her breast,
He found the fierce pleasure too hasty to stay,
And his soul in the tempest just flying away.

When *Cælia* saw this,
With a sigh, and a kiss,
She cry'd, Oh my dear, I am robb'd of my bliss;
'Tis unkind to your Love, and unfaithfully done,
To leave me behind you, and die all alone.

The Youth, though in haste,
And breathing his last,

In pity dy'd slowly, while she dy'd more fast;
Till at length she cry'd, Now, my dear, now let us go,
Now die, my *Alexis*, and I will die too.

Thus intranc'd they did lie,
Till *Alexis* did try
To recover new breath, that again he might die:
Then often they di'd; but the more they did so,
The Nymph di'd more quick, and the Shepherd more slow.

[*Marriage-a-la-Mode*, 1673.]

14.

LONG betwixt Love and fear *Phillis* tormented,
Shun'd her own wish yet at last she consented:
But loath that day shou'd her blushes discover,
Come gentle Night She said,
Come quickly to my aid,
And a poor Shamefac'd Maid
Hide from her Lover.

Now cold as Ice I am, now hot as Fire,
I dare not tell my self my own desire;
But let Day fly away, and let Night hast her:
Grant yee kind Powers above,
Slow houres to parting Love,
But when to Bliss we move,
Bid 'em fly faster.

How sweet it is to Love when I discover,
That Fire which burns my Heart, warming my Lover;
'Tis pitty Love so true should be mistaken:
But if this Night he be
False or unkinde to me,
Let me dye ere I see
That I'me forsaken.

[*The Assignation*, 1673.]

15.

EPITHALAMIUM

THE day is come, I see it rise,
Betwixt the Bride's and Bridegroom's Eyes,
That Golden day they wish'd so long,
Love pick'd it out amidst the throng;
He destin'd to himself this Sun,
And took the Reins and drove him on;
In his own Beams he drest him bright,
Yet bid him bring a better night.

The day you wish'd arriv'd at last,
You wish as much that it were past,
One Minute more and night will hide,
The Bridegroom and the blushing Bride.
The Virgin now to Bed do's goe:
Take care oh Youth, she rise not soe;
She pants and trembles at her doom,
And fears and wishes thou wou'dst come.

The Bridegroom comes, He comes apace
With Love and Fury in his Face;
She shrinks away, He close pursues,
And Prayers and Threats, at once do's use,
She softly sighing begs delay,
And with her hand puts his away,
Now out aloud for help she cryes,
And now despairing shuts her Eyes.

[*Amboyna*, 1673.]

16.

CAN life be a blessing,
Or worth the possessing,
Can life be a blessing if love were away?
Ah no! though our love all night keep us waking,
And though he torment us with cares all the day,
Yet he sweetens he sweetens our pains in the taking,
There's an hour at the last, there's an hour to repay.

In every possessing,
The ravishing blessing,
In every possessing the fruit of our pain,
Poor lovers forget long ages of anguish,
Whate're they have suffer'd and done to obtain;
'Tis a pleasure, a pleasure to sigh and to languish,
When we hope, when we hope to be happy again.

[*Troilus and Cressida*, 1679.]

17.

A SONG FROM THE ITALIAN

By a dismal Cypress lying,
Damon cry'd, all pale and dying,
Kind is Death that ends my pain,
But cruel She I lov'd in vain.
The Mossy Fountains
Murmure my trouble,
And hollow Mountains
My groans redouble:
Every Nymph mourns me,
Thus while I languish;
She only scorns me,
Who caus'd my anguish.
No Love returning me, but all hope denying,
By a dismal Cypress lying,
Like a *Swan*, so sung he dying:
Kind is Death that ends my pain,
But cruel She I lov'd in vain.

[*The Kind Keeper*, 1680.]

18.

'Gainst Keepers we petition,
Who wou'd inclose the Common:
'Tis enough to raise Sedition
In the free-born subject Woman.
Because for his gold
I my body have sold,

He thinks I'm a Slave for my life;
He rants, domineers,
He swaggers and swears,
And wou'd keep me as bare as his Wife.

'Gainst Keepers we petition, &c.
'Tis honest and fair,
That a Feast I prepare;
But when his dull appetite's o're,
I'le treat with the rest
Some welcomer Ghest,
For the Reck'ning was paid me before.

[*The Kind Keeper*, 1680.]

19.

Shepherdess. TELL me *Thirsis*, tell your Anguish,
Why you Sigh, and why you Languish;
When the Nymph whom you Adore,
Grants the Blessing of Possessing,
What can Love and I do more?

Shepherd. Think it's Love beyond all measure,
Makes me faint away with pleasure;
Strength of Cordial may destroy,
And the Blessing of Possessing
Kills me with excess of Joy.

Shepherdess. *Thirsis*, how can I believe you?
But confess, and I'le forgive you;
Men are false, and so are you;
Never Nature fram'd a Creature
To enjoy, and yet be true.

Shepherd. Mine's a Flame beyond expiring,
Still possessing, still desiring.
Fit for Love's Imperial Crown;
Ever shining, and refining,
Still the more 'tis melted down.

[*The Duke of Guise, second edition*, 1687.]

20.

THE TEARS OF *AMYNTA* FOR THE DEATH OF *DAMON*

ON a bank, beside a Willow,
Heav'n her Cov'ring, Earth her Pillow,
Sad *Amynta* sigh'd alone:
From the Chearless Dawn of Morning
Till the Dew's of Night returning
Singing thus she made her mone:
    Hope is banish'd
    Joys are vanish'd;
Damon, my belov'd is gone!

Time, I dare thee to discover
Such a Youth, and such a Lover,
Oh so true, so kind was he!
Damon was the Pride of Nature,
Charming in his every Feature;
Damon liv'd alone for me:
    Melting Kisses,
    Murmuring Blisses,
Who so liv'd and lov'd as we!

Never shall we curse the Morning,
Never bless the Night returning,
Sweet Embraces to restore:
Never shall we both ly dying
Nature failing, Love supplying
All the Joyes he drain'd before:
    Death, come end me
    To befriend me;
Love and *Damon* are no more.

[*Miscellany Poems.* 1684.]

21.

A SONG OF THE RIVER *THAMES*

OLD Father Ocean calls my Tyde:
Come away, come away;
The Barks upon the Billows ride,
The Master will not stay;

The merry Boson from his side,
His Whistle takes to check and chide
The lingring Lads delay,
And all the Crew alowd has Cry'd,
Come away, come away.

See the God of Seas attends Thee,
Nymphs Divine, a Beauteous Train:
All the calmer Gales befriend Thee
In thy passage o're the Main:
Every Maid her Locks is binding,
Every *Triton*'s Horn is winding,
Welcome to the watry Plain.

[*Albion and Albanius*, 1685.]

22.

SYLVIA the fair, in the bloom of Fifteen,
Felt an innocent warmth, as she lay on the green;
She had heard of a pleasure, and something she guest
By the towzing & tumbling & touching her Breast;
She saw the men eager, but was at a loss,
What they meant by their sighing, & kissing so close;
By their praying and whining
And clasping and twining,
And panting and wishing,
And sighing and kissing
And sighing and kissing so close.

Ah she cry'd, ah for a languishing Maid
In a Country of Christians to die without aid!
Not a Whig, or a Tory, or Trimmer at least,
Or a Protestant Parson, or Catholick Priest,
To instruct a young Virgin, that is at a loss
What they meant by their sighing, & kissing so close!
By their praying and whining
And clasping and twining,
And panting and wishing,
And sighing and kissing
And sighing and kissing so close.

Cupid in Shape of a Swayn did appear,
He saw the sad wound, and in pity drew near,

Then show'd her his Arrow, and bid her not fear,
For the pain was no more than a Maiden may bear;
When the balm was infus'd, she was not at a loss,
What they meant by their sighing & kissing so close;
By their praying and whining
And clasping and twining,
And panting and wishing,
And sighing and kissing
And sighing and kissing so close.

[*Sylvæ*, 1685.]

23.

I.

Go tell *Amynta* gentle Swain,
I wou'd not die nor dare complain,
Thy tuneful Voice with numbers joyn,
Thy words will more prevail than mine;
To Souls oppress'd and dumb with grief.
The Gods ordain this kind releif;
That Musick shou'd in sounds convey,
What dying Lovers dare not say.

II.

A Sigh or Tear perhaps she'll give,
But love on pitty cannot live.
Tell her that Hearts for Hearts were made,
And love with love is only paid.
Tell her my pains so fast encrease,
That soon they will be past redress;
But ah! the Wretch that speechless lyes,
Attends but Death to close his Eyes.

[*Sylvæ*, 1685.]

24.

MERCURY'S SONG TO *PHAIDRA*

Fair *Iris* I love, and hourly I dye,
But not for a Lip, nor a languishing Eye:
She's fickle and false, and there we agree;
For I am as false, and as fickle as she:

We neither believe what either can say;
And, neither believing, we neither betray.

'Tis civil to swear, and say things of course;
We mean not the taking for better for worse.
When present, we love; when absent, agree:
I think not of *Iris*, nor *Iris* of me:
The Legend of Love no Couple can find
So easie to part, or so equally join'd.

[*Amphitrion*, 1690.]

25.

A PASTORAL DIALOGUE BETWIXT *THYRSIS* AND *IRIS*

Thyrsis. FAIR *Iris* and her Swain
Were in a shady Bow'r;
Where *Thyrsis* long in vain
Had sought the Shepherd's hour:
At length his Hand advancing upon her snowy Breast;
He said, O kiss me longer,
And longer yet and longer,
If you will make me Blest.

Iris. An easie yielding Maid,
By trusting is undone;
Our Sex is oft betray'd,
By granting Love too soon.
If you desire to gain me, your Suff'rings to redress;
Prepare to love me longer,
And longer yet, and longer,
Before you shall possess.

Thyrsis. The little Care you Show,
Of all my Sorrows past;
Makes Death appear too slow,
And Life too long to last.
Fair *Iris* kiss me kindly, in pity of my Fate;
And kindly still, and kindly,
Before it be too late.

Iris. You fondly Court your Bliss,
And no Advances make;
'Tis not for Maids to kiss,
But 'tis for Men to take.
So you may Kiss me kindly, and I will not rebell;
And kindly still, and kindly,
But kiss me not and tell.

A RONDEAU.

Chorus. Thus at the height we love and live,
And fear not to be poor:
We give, and give, and give, and give,
Till we can give no more:
But what to day will take away,
To morrow will restore.
Thus at the height we love and live,
And fear not to be poor.

[*Amphitrion*, 1690.]

26.

CELIA, that I once was blest
Is now the Torment of my Brest;
Since to curse me, you bereave me
Of the Pleasures I possest:
Cruel Creature, to deceive me!
First to love, and then to leave me!

Had you the Bliss refus'd to grant,
Then I had never known the want:
But possessing once the Blessing,
Is the Cause of my Complaint:
Once possessing is but tasting;
'Tis no Bliss that is not lasting.

Celia now is mine no more;
But I am hers; and must adore:
Nor to leave her will endeavour;
Charms, that captiv'd me before,
No unkindness can dissever;
Love that's true, is Love for ever.

[*Amphitrion*, 1690.]

27.

A SONG OF *VENUS*

FAIREST Isle, all Isles Excelling,
  Seat of Pleasures, and of Loves;
Venus here, will chuse her Dwelling,
  And forsake her *Cyprian* Groves.

Cupid, from his Fav'rite Nation,
  Care and Envy will remove;
Jealousie, that poysons Passion,
  And Despair that dies for Love.

Gentle Murmurs, sweet Complaining,
  Sighs that blow the Fire of Love;
Soft Repulses, kind Disdaining,
  Shall be all the Pains you prove.

Every Swain shall pay his Duty,
  Grateful every Nymph shall prove;
And as these Excel in Beauty,
  Those shall be Renown'd for Love.

[*King Arthur*, 1691.]

28.

HOW happy the Lover,
  How easie his Chain,
  How pleasing his Pain?
How sweet to discover!
  He sighs not in vain.
For Love every Creature
Is form'd by his Nature;
No Joys are above
The Pleasures of Love.

In vain are our Graces,
  In vain are your Eyes,
  If Love you despise;
When Age furrows Faces,
  'Tis time to be wise.

Then use the short Blessing,
That Flies in Possessing:
No Joys are above
The Pleasures of Love.

[*King Arthur*, 1691.]

29.

A SONG OF SHEPHERDS AND SHEPHERDESSES

1. *Shepherd sings.*

How blest are Shepherds, how happy their Lasses,
While Drums & Trumpets are sounding Alarms!
Over our Lowly Sheds all the Storm passes;
And when we die, 'tis in each others Arms.
All the Day on our Herds and Flocks employing;
All the Night on our Flutes, and in enjoying.

Chor. All the Day, *&c.*

Bright Nymphs of *Britain*, with Graces attended,
Let not your Days without Pleasure expire;
Honour's but empty, and when Youth is ended,
All Men will praise you, but none wiil desire.
Let not Youth fly away without Contenting;
Age will come time enough, for your Repenting.

Chor. Let not Youth, *&c.*

Here the Men offer their Flutes to the Women, which they refuse.

2. *Shepherdess.*

Shepherd, Shepherd, leave Decoying,
Pipes are sweet, a Summers Day;
But a little after Toying,
Women have the Shot to Pay.

Here are Marriage-Vows for signing,
Set their Marks that cannot write:
After that, without Repining,
Play and Welcom, Day and Night.

Here the Women give the Men Contracts, which they accept.

Chor. of all.

Come, Shepherds, lead up, a lively Measure;
The Cares of Wedlock, are Cares of Pleasure:
But whether Marriage bring Joy, or Sorrow,
Make sure of this Day, and hang to Morrow.

[*King Arthur*, 1691.]

30.

A SONG BY *COMUS* AND THREE PEASANTS

Comus. YOUR Hay it is Mow'd, & your Corn is Reap'd;
Your Barns will be full, and your Hovels heap'd:
Come, my Boys, come;
Come, my Boys, come;
And merrily Roar out Harvest Home;
Harvest Home,
Harvest Home;
And merrily Roar out Harvest Home.

Chorus. Come, my Boys, come, *&c.*

1. *Man.* We ha' cheated the Parson, we'll cheat him agen;
For why shou'd a Blockhead ha' One in Ten?
One in Ten,
One in Ten;
For why shou'd a Blockhead ha' One in Ten?

Chorus. One in Ten,
One in Ten;
For why shou'd a Blockhead ha' One in Ten?

2. *Man.* For Prating so long like a Book-learn'd Sot,
Till Pudding and Dumplin burn to Pot;
Burn to Pot,
Burn to Pot;
Till Pudding and Dumplin burn to Pot.

Chorus. Burn to Pot, *&c.*

3. *Man.* We'll toss off our Ale till we canno' stand,
And Hoigh for the Honour of Old *England*:
Old *England*,
Old *England*;
And Hoigh for the Honour of Old *England.*

Chorus. Old *England*, &c.

[*King Arthur*, 1691.]

31.

No no, poor suff'ring Heart no Change endeavour,
Choose to sustain the smart, rather than leave her;
My ravish'd Eyes behold such Charms about her,
I can dye with her, but not live without her.
One tender Sigh of hers to see me Languish,
Will more than pay the price of my past Anguish:
Beware O cruel Fair, how you smile on me,
'Twas a kind Look of yours that has undone me.

Love has in store for me one happy Minute,
And She will end my pain who did begin it;
Then no Day void of Bliss, or Pleasure leaving,
Ages shall slide away without perceiving:
Cupid shall guard the Door the more to please us,
And keep out Time and Death when they would seize us:
Time and Death shall depart, and say in flying,
Love has found out a way to Live by Dying.

[*Cleomenes*, 1692.]

32.

SONG TO A FAIR, YOUNG LADY, GOING OUT OF THE TOWN IN THE SPRING.

Ask not the Cause, why sullen *Spring*
So long delays her Flow'rs to bear;
Why warbling Birds forget to sing,
And Winter Storms invert the year?
Chloris is gone; and Fate provides
To make it *Spring*, where she resides.

Chloris is gone, the Cruel Fair;
  She cast not back a pitying Eye:
But left her Lover in Despair;
  To sigh, to languish, and to die.
Ah, how can those fair Eyes endure
To give the Wounds they will not cure!

Great God of Love, why hast thou made
  A Face that can all Hearts command,
That all Religions can invade,
  And change the Laws of ev'ry Land?
Where thou hadst plac'd such Pow'r before,
Thou shou'dst have made her Mercy more.

When *Chloris* to the Temple comes,
  Adoring Crowds before her fall;
She can restore the Dead from Tombs,
  And ev'ry Life but mine recall.
I only am by Love design'd
To be the Victim for Mankind.

[*Examen Poeticum*, 1693.]

33.

RONDELAY

CHLOE found *Amyntas* lying
  All in Tears, upon the Plain;
Sighing to himself, and crying,
  Wretched I, to love in vain!
Kiss me, Dear, before my dying;
  Kiss me once, and ease my pain!

Sighing to himself, and crying
  Wretched I, to love in vain:
Ever scorning and denying
  To reward your faithful Swain:
Kiss me, Dear, before my dying;
  Kiss me once, and ease my pain!

Ever scorning, and denying
  To reward your faithful Swain.
Chloe, laughing at his crying,

Told him that he lov'd in vain:
Kiss me, Dear, before my dying;
Kiss me once, and ease my pain!

Chloe, laughing at his crying,
Told him that he lov'd in vain:
But repenting, and complying,
When he kiss'd, she kiss'd again:
Kiss'd him up, before his dying;
Kiss'd him up, and eas'd his pain.

[*Examen Poeticum*, 1693.]

34.

SONG OF *JEALOUSIE*

WHAT State of Life can be so blest
As Love, that warms a Lover's Breast?
Two Souls in one, the same desire
To grant the Bliss, and to require!
'Tis all from thee,
O Jealousie!
'Tis all from thee,
O Jealousie!
Thou Tyrant, Tyrant Jealousie,
Thou Tyrant of the Mind.

All other ills, tho' sharp they prove,
Serve to refine, and perfect Love;
In absence, or unkind disdain,
Sweet Hope relieves the Lover's pain:
But ah, no Cure but Death we find,
To set us free
From Jealousie:
O Jealousie!
Thou Tyrant, Tyrant Jealousie,
Thou Tyrant of the Mind.

False, in thy Glass, all Objects are,
Some set too near, and some too far:

Thou art the Fire of endless Night,
The Fire that burns, and gives no Light.
All Torments of the Damn'd we find
In only thee
O Jealousie!
Thou Tyrant, Tyrant Jealousie,
Thou Tyrant of the Mind!

[*Love Triumphant*, 1694.]

35.

THE *LADY'S SONG.*

I.

A QUIRE of bright Beauties in Spring did appear,
To chuse a *May*-Lady to govern the Year:
All the Nymphs were in White, and the Shepherds in
Green,
The Garland was giv'n, and *Phillis* was Queen:
But *Phillis* refus'd it, and sighing did say,
I'll not wear a Garland while *Pan* is away.

II.

While *Pan*, and fair *Syrinx*, are fled from our Shore,
The Graces are banish'd, and Love is no more:
The soft God of Pleasure that warm'd our Desires,
Has broken his Bow, and extinguish'd his Fires;
And vows that himself, and his Mother, will mourn,
'Till *Pan* and fair *Syrinx* in Triumph return.

III.

Forbear your Addresses, and Court us no more,
For we will perform what the Deity swore:
But if you dare think of deserving our Charms,
Away with your Sheephooks, and take to your Arms;
Then Lawrels and Myrtles your Brows shall adorn,
When *Pan*, and his Son, and fair *Syrinx*, return.

[*Poetical Miscellany. Fifth Part*, 1704.]

36.

FAIR, sweet and young, receive a Prize
Reserv'd for your Victorious Eyes:
From Crowds, whom at your Feet you see,
O pity, and distinguish me;
As I from thousand Beauties more
Distinguish you, and only you adore.

Your Face for Conquest was design'd,
Your ev'ry Motion charms my Mind;
Angels, when you your Silence break,
Forget their Hymns to hear you speak;
But when at once they hear and view,
Are loath to mount, and long to stay with you.

No Graces can your Form improve,
But all are lost, unless you love;
While that sweet Passion you disdain,
Your Veil and Beauty are in vain.
In pity then prevent my Fate,
For after dying all Reprieves too late.

[*Poetical Miscellany. Fifth Part*, 1704.]

37.

HIGH State and Honours to others impart,
   But give me your Heart:
That Treasure, that Treasure alone
   I beg for my own.
So gentle a Love, so fervent a Fire
   My Soul does inspire.
That Treasure, that Treasure alone
   I beg for my own.

Your Love let me crave;
   Give me in Possessing
   So matchless a Blessing,
That Empire is all I wou'd have.

Love's my Petition,
All my Ambition;
If e'er you discover
So faithful a Lover,
So real a Flame,
I'll die, I'll die,
So give up my Game.

[*Poetical Miscellany. Fifth Part*, 1704.]

THE SECULAR MASQUE

Enter JANUS.

Janus. *Chronos, Chronos,* mend thy Pace,
An hundred times the rowling Sun
Around the Radiant Belt has run
In his revolving Race.
Behold, behold, the Goal in sight,
Spread thy Fans, and wing thy flight.

Enter CHRONOS, *with a Scythe in his hand, and a great Globe on his Back, which he sets down at his entrance.*

Chronos. Weary, weary of my weight,
Let me, let me drop my Freight,
And leave the World behind.
I could not bear
Another Year
The Load of Human-kind.

Enter MOMUS *Laughing.*

Momus. Ha! ha! ha! Ha! ha! ha! well hast thou done,
To lay down thy Pack,
And lighten thy Back.
The World was a Fool, e'er since it begun,
And since neither *Janus*, nor *Chronos*, nor I,
Can hinder the Crimes,
Or mend the Bad Times,
'Tis better to Laugh than to Cry.

Cho. of all 3. *'Tis better to Laugh than to Cry.*

Janus. Since *Momus* comes to laugh below,
Old Time begin the Show,
That he may see, in every Scene,
What Changes in this Age have been,

Chronos. Then Goddess of the Silver Bow begin.

Horns, or Hunting-Musique within.

Enter DIANA.

Diana. With Horns and with Hounds I waken the Day,
And hye to my Woodland walks away;

I tuck up my Robe, and am buskin'd soon,
And tye to my Forehead a wexing Moon.
I course the fleet Stagg, unkennel the Fox,
And chase the wild Goats or'e summets of Rocks,
With shouting and hooting we pierce thro' the Sky;
And Eccho turns Hunter, and doubles the Cry.

Cho. of all. *With shouting and hooting, we pierce through the skie,*
And Eccho turns Hunter, and doubles the Cry.

Janus. Then our Age was in it's Prime,
Chronos. Free from Rage,
Diana. ——— And free from Crime.
Momus. A very Merry, Dancing, Drinking,
Laughing, Quaffing, and unthinking Time.

Cho. of all. *Then our Age was in it's Prime,*
Free from Rage, and free from Crime,
A very Merry, Dancing, Drinking,
Laughing, Quaffing, and unthinking Time.

Dance of DIANA'*s Attendants.*

Enter MARS.

Mars. Inspire the Vocal Brass, Inspire;
The World is past its Infant Age:
Arms and Honour,
Arms and Honour,
Set the Martial Mind on Fire,
And kindle Manly Rage.
Mars has lookt the Sky to Red;
And Peace, the Lazy Good, is fled.
Plenty, Peace, and Pleasure fly;
The Sprightly Green
In *Woodland*-Walks, no more is seen;
The Sprightly Green, has drunk the *Tyrian* Dye.

Cho. of all. *Plenty, Peace,* &c.

Mars. Sound the Trumpet, Beat the Drum,
Through all the World around;
Sound a Reveille, Sound, Sound,
The Warrior God is come.

Cho. of all. *Sound the Trumpet,* &c.

Momus. Thy Sword within the Scabbard keep,
And let Mankind agree;
Better the World were fast asleep,

Than kept awake by Thee.
The Fools are only thinner,
With all our Cost and Care;
But neither side a winner,
For Things are as they were.

Cho. of all. *The Fools are only*, &c.

Enter VENUS.

Venus. Calms appear, when Storms are past;
Love will have his Hour at last:
Nature is my kindly Care;
Mars destroys, and I repair;
Take me, take me, while you may,
Venus comes not ev'ry Day.

Cho. of all. *Take her, take her*, &c.

Chronos. The World was then so light,
I scarcely felt the Weight;
Joy rul'd the Day, and Love the Night.
But since the Queen of Pleasure left the Ground,
I faint, I lag,
And feebly drag
The pond'rous Orb around.

Momus, All, all, of a piece throughout;
pointing to *Diana* Thy Chase had a Beast in View;
to *Mars,* Thy Wars brought nothing about;
to *Venus.* Thy Lovers were all untrue.
Janus. 'Tis well an Old Age is out,
Chronus. And time to begin a New.

Cho. of all. *All, all, of a piece throughout;*
Thy Chase had a Beast in View;
Thy Wars brought nothing about;
Thy Lovers were all untrue.
'Tis well an Old Age is out,
And time to begin a New.

Dance of Huntsmen, Nymphs, Warriours and Lovers.

[*The Pilgrim*, 1700.]

PROLOGUES AND EPILOGUES

PROLOGUE TO

SECRET-LOVE

OR *THE MAIDEN QUEEN*

I.

HE who writ this, not without pains and thought
From *French* and *English* Theaters has brought
Th' exactest Rules by which a Play is wrought.

II.

The Unities of Action, Place, and Time;
The Scenes unbroken; and a mingled chime
Of *Johnsons* humour, with *Corneilles* rhyme.

III.

But while dead colours he with care did lay,
He fears his Wit, or Plot he did not weigh,
Which are the living Beauties of a Play.

IV.

Plays are like Towns, which howe're fortifi'd
By Engineers, have still some weaker side
By the o'reseen Defendant unespy'd.

V.

And with that Art you make approaches now;
Such skilful fury in Assaults you show,
That every Poet without shame may bow.

VI.

Ours therefore humbly would attend your doom,
If Souldier-like, he may have termes to come
With flying colours, and with beat of Drum.

[1668.]

PROLOGUE TO
THE TEMPEST
OR *THE ENCHANTED ISLAND*

As when a Tree's cut down the secret root
Lives under ground, and thence new Branches shoot,
So, from old *Shakespear*'s honour'd dust, this day
Springs up and buds a new reviving Play.
Shakespear, who (taught by none) did first impart
To *Fletcher* Wit, to labouring *Johnson* Art.
He Monarch-like gave those his subjects law,
And is that Nature which they paint and draw,
Fletcher reach'd that which on his heights did grow,
Whilst *Johnson* crept and gather'd all below.
This did his Love, and this his Mirth digest:
One imitates him most, the other best.
If they have since out-writ all other men,
'Tis with the drops which fell from *Shakespear*'s Pen.
The Storm which vanish'd on the Neighb'ring shore,
Was taught by *Shakespear*'s Tempest first to roar.
That innocence and beauty which did smile
In *Fletcher*, grew on this *Enchanted Isle*.
But *Shakespear*'s Magick could not copy'd be,
Within that Circle none durst walk but he.
I must confess 'twas bold, nor would you now,
That liberty to vulgar Wits allow,
Which works by Magick supernatural things:
But *Shakespear*'s pow'r is sacred as a King's.
Those Legends from old Priest-hood were receiv'd,
And he then writ, as people then believ'd.
But, if for *Shakespear* we your grace implore,
We for our Theatre shall want it more:
Who by our dearth of Youths are forc'd t' employ
One of our Women to present a Boy;
And that's a transformation you will say
Exceeding all the Magick in the Play.
Let none expect in the last Act to find,
Her Sex transform'd from man to Woman-kind.
What e're she was before the Play began,

All you shall see of her is perfect man.
Or if your fancy will be farther led,
To find her Woman, it must be abed.

[1670.]

PROLOGUE AND EPILOGUE TO TYRANNICK LOVE

OR *THE ROYAL MARTYR*

A TRAGEDY

PROLOGUE

SELF-LOVE (which never rightly understood)
Makes Poets still conclude their Plays are good:
And malice in all Criticks raigns so high,
That for small Errors they whole Plays decry;
So that to see this fondness, and that spite,
You'd think that none but Mad-men judge or write.
Therefore our Poet, as he thinks not fit
T' impose upon you, what he writes for Wit,
So hopes that leaving you your censures free,
You equal Judges of the whole will be:
They judge but half who only faults will see.
Poets like Lovers should be bold and dare,
They spoil their business with an over-care.
And he who servilely creeps after sence,
Is safe, but ne're will reach an Excellence.
Hence 'tis our Poet in his conjuring,
Allow'd his Fancy the full scope and swing.
But when a Tyrant for his Theme he had,
He loos'd the Reins, and bid his Muse run mad:
And though he stumbles in a full career;
Yet rashness is a better fault than fear.
He saw his way; but in so swift a pace,
To chuse the ground, might be to lose the race.
They then who of each trip th' advantage take,
Find but those Faults which they want Wit to make.

EPILOGUE

Spoken by Mrs. Ellen,[1] *when she was to be carried off dead by the Bearers.*

To the Bearer. HOLD, are you mad? you damn'd confounded Dog,
I am to rise, and speak the Epilogue.
To the Audience. I come, kind Gentlemen, strange news to tell ye,
I am the Ghost of poor departed *Nelly*.
Sweet Ladies, be not frighted, I'le be civil,
I'm what I was, a little harmless Devil.
For, after death, we Sprights have just such Natures,
We had for all the World, when humane Creatures;
And therefore I that was an Actress here,
Play all my Tricks in Hell, a Goblin there.
Gallants, look to 't, you say there are no Sprights;
But I'le come dance about your Beds at nights
And faith you'l be in a sweet kind of taking,
When I surprise you between sleep and waking.
To tell you true, I walk because I dye
Out of my Calling in a Tragedy.
O Poet, damn'd dull Poet, who could prove
So senseless! to make *Nelly* dye for Love,
Nay, what's yet worse, to kill me in the prime
Of *Easter*-Term, in Tart and Cheese-cake time!
I'le fit the Fopp; for I'le not one word say
T' excuse his godly out of fashion Play.
A Play which if you dare but twice sit out,
You'l all be slander'd, and be thought devout.
But, farewel Gentlemen, make haste to me,
I'm sure e're long to have your company.
As for my Epitaph when I am gone,
I'll trust no Poet, but will write my own.

Here Nelly *lies, who, though she liv'd a Slater'n,*
Yet dy'd a Princess, acting in S. Cathar'n.[2]

[1670.]

[1] The famous Nell Gwyn. She played the part of Valeria in the play and, having stabbed herself at the close, as she is about to be carried dead off the stage, she rises to deliver this Epilogue.
[2] St. Catherine was 'the Royal Martyr' of the play.

EPILOGUE TO THE SECOND PART OF ALMANZOR AND ALMAHIDE

OR *THE CONQUEST OF GRANADA*

EPILOGUE

THEY who have best succeeded on the Stage,
Have still conform'd their Genius to their Age.
Thus *Jonson* did Mechanique humour show,
When men were dull, and conversation low.
Then Comedy was faultless, but 'twas course:
Cobb's Tankard was a jest, and *Otter*'s horse.[1]
And as their Comedy, their love was mean:
Except, by chance, in some one labour'd Scene,
Which must attone for an ill-written Play.
They rose; but at their height could seldome stay.
Fame then was cheap, and the first commer sped;
And they have kept it since, by being dead.
But were they now to write when Critiques weigh
Each Line, and ev'ry word, throughout a Play,
None of 'em, no not *Jonson*, in his height
Could pass, without allowing grains for weight.
Think it not envy that these truths are told,
Our Poet's not malicious, though he's bold.
'Tis not to brand 'em that their faults are shown,
But, by their errours, to excuse his own.
If Love and Honour now are higher rais'd,
'Tis not the Poet, but the Age is prais'd.
Wit's now ariv'd to a more high degree;
Our native Language more refin'd and free.
Our Ladies and our men now speak more wit
In conversation, than those Poets writ.
Then, one of these is, consequently, true;
That what this Poet writes comes short of you,
And imitates you ill, (which most he fears)
Or else his writing is not worse than theirs.

[1] *Cobb*, the water-bearer in Ben Jonson's *Every Man in his Humour*, and *Captain Otter*, who called his tankards, Horse, Bull, and Bear, in his *Epicene, or, the Silent Woman.*

Yet, though you judge, (as sure the Critiques will)
That some before him writ with greater skill,
In this one praise he has their fame surpast,
To please an Age more Gallant than the last.

[1672].

PROLOGUE AND EPILOGUE

TO THE UNIVERSITY OF OXFORD
1674

PROLOGUE

Spoken by Mr. HART

Poets, your Subjects, have their Parts assign'd
T' unbend, and to divert their Sovereign's mind;
When tyr'd with following Nature, you think fit
To seek repose in the cool shades of Wit,
And from the sweet Retreat, with Joy survey
What rests, and what is conquer'd, of the way.
Here free your selves, from Envie, Care and Strife,
You view the various turns of humane Life:
Safe in our Scene, through dangerous Courts you go,
And Undebauch'd, the Vice of Cities know.
Your Theories are here to Practice brought,
As in Mechanick operations wrought;
And Man the Little world before you set,
As once the Sphere of Chrystal, shew'd the Great:
Blest sure are you above all Mortal kind:
If to your Fortunes you can Suit your Mind.
Content to see, and shun, those Ills we show,
And Crimes, on Theatres alone, to know:
With joy we bring what our dead Authours writ,
And beg from you the value of their Wit.
That *Shakespear*'s, *Fletcher*'s, and great *Johnson*'s claim
May be Renew'd from those, who gave them fame.
None of our living Poets dare appear,
For Muses so severe are worshipt here;

That conscious of their Faults they shun the Eye,
And as Prophane, from Sacred places fly,
Rather than see th' offended God, and dye.
We bring no Imperfections, but our own,
Such Faults as made, are by the Makers shown.
And you have been so kind, that we may boast,
The greatest Judges still can Pardon most.
Poets must stoop, when they would please our Pit,
Debas'd even to the Level of their Wit.
Disdaining that, which yet they know, will Take,
Hating themselves, what their Applause must make:
But when to Praise from you they would Aspire
Though they like Eagles Mount, your *Jove* is Higher.
So far your Knowledge, all their Pow'r transcends,
As what *should* be, beyond what *Is*, extends.

EPILOGUE

Spoken by Mrs. BOUTELL

OFT has our Poet wisht, this happy Seat
Might prove his fading Muses last retreat:
I wonder'd at his wish, but now I find
He sought for quiet, and content of mind;
Which noisfull Towns, and Courts can never know,
And onely in the shades like Laurels grow.
Youth, e'er it sees the World, here studies rest,
And Age returning thence concludes it best.
What wonder if we court that happiness
Yearly to share, which hourly you possess,
Teaching ev'n you, (while the vext World we show,)
Your Peace to value more, and better know?
'Tis all we can return for favours past,
Whose holy Memory shall ever last,
For Patronage from him whose care presides
O'er every noble Art, and every Science guides:
Bathurst, a name the learn'd with reverence know,
And scarcely more to his own *Virgil* owe.[1]
Whose Age enjoys but what his Youth deserv'd,
To rule those Muses whom before he serv'd.

[1] Ralph Bathurst (1620–1704), president of Trinity College, 1664, was vice-chancellor of the University in 1674. He was an accomplished poet in both Latin and English.

His Learning, and untainted Manners too
We find (*Athenians*) are deriv'd to you;
Such Ancient hospitality there rests
In yours, as dwelt in the first *Grecian* Breasts,
Whose kindness was Religion to their Guests.
Such Modesty did to our sex appear,
As had there been no Laws, we need not fear,
Since each of you was our Protector here.
Converse so chast, and so strict Vertue shown,
As might *Apollo* with the Muses own.
Till our return we must despair to find
Judges so just, so knowing, and so kind.

[*Miscellany Poems*, 1684.]

FABLES
ANCIENT AND MODERN

The present text of the *Fables* follows that of the first edition of 1700. For bibliographical note see *Preface to the Fables, post* p. 472. *The Flower and the Leaf*, an anonymous poem of the fifteenth century, is not now considered to be Chaucer's, but it was attributed to him at the time when Dryden wrote.

THE FLOWER AND THE LEAF

OR *THE LADY IN THE ARBOUR*

A VISION

TRANSLATED FROM CHAUCER

Now turning from the wintry Signs, the Sun
His Course exalted through the Ram had run:
And whirling up the Skies, his Chariot drove
Through *Taurus*, and the lightsome Realms of Love;
Where *Venus* from her Orb descends in Show'rs
To glad the Ground, and paint the Fields with Flow'rs:
When first the tender Blades of Grass appear,
And Buds that yet the blast of *Eurus* fear,
Stand at the door of Life; and doubt to cloath the Year;
Till gentle Heat, and soft repeated Rains,
Make the green Blood to dance within their Veins:
Then, at their call, embolden'd out they come,
And swell the Gems, and burst the narrow Room;
Broader and broader yet, their Blooms display,
Salute the welcome Sun, and entertain the Day.
Then from their breathing Souls the Sweets repair
To scent the Skies, and purge th' unwholsome Air:
Joy spreads the Heart, and with a general Song,
Spring issues out, and leads the jolly Months along.

In that sweet Season, as in Bed I lay,
And sought in Sleep to pass the Night away,
I turn'd my weary Side, but still in vain,
Tho' full of youthful Health, and void of Pain:
Cares I had none, to keep me from my Rest,
For Love had never enter'd in my Breast;
I wanted nothing Fortune could supply,
Nor did she Slumber till that hour deny:
I wonder'd then, but after found it true,
Much Joy had dry'd away the balmy Dew:
Sea's wou'd be Pools, without the brushing Air,
To curl the Waves; and sure some little Care
Shou'd weary Nature so, to make her want repair.

When Chaunticleer the second Watch had sung,
Scorning the Scorner Sleep from Bed I sprung;
And dressing, by the Moon, in loose Array,
Pass'd out in open Air, preventing Day,
And sought a goodly Grove as Fancy led my way.
Strait as a Line in beauteous Order stood
Of Oaks unshorn a venerable Wood;
Fresh was the Grass beneath, and ev'ry Tree
At distance planted in a due degree,
Their branching Arms in Air with equal space
Stretch'd to their Neighbours with a long Embrace:
And the new Leaves on ev'ry Bough were seen,
Some ruddy-colour'd, some of lighter green.
The painted Birds, Companions of the Spring,
Hopping from Spray to Spray, were heard to sing;
Both Eyes and Ears receiv'd a like Delight,
Enchanting Musick, and a charming Sight.
On *Philomel* I fix'd my whole Desire;
And list'n'd for the Queen of all the Quire;
Fain would I hear her heav'nly Voice to sing;
And wanted yet an Omen to the Spring.

Attending long in vain; I took the way,
Which through a Path, but scarcely printed, lay;
In narrow mazes oft it seem'd to meet,
And look'd, as lightly press'd, by Fairy Feet.
Wandring I walk'd alone, for still methought
To some strand End so strange a Path was wrought:
At last it led me where an Arbour stood,
The sacred Receptacle of the Wood:
This Place unmark'd though oft I walk'd the Green,
In all my Progress I had never seen:
And seiz'd at once with Wonder and Delight,
Gaz'd all around me, new to the transporting Sight.
'Twas bench'd with Turf, and goodly to be seen,
The thick young Grass arose in fresher Green:
The Mound was newly made, no Sight cou'd pass
Betwixt the nice Partitions of the Grass;
The well-united Sods so closely lay;
And all arround the Shades defended it from Day.
For Sycamours with Eglantine were spread,
A Hedge about the Sides, a Covering over Head.
And so the fragrant Brier was wove between,

The Sycamour and Flow'rs were mix'd with Green.
That Nature seem'd to vary the Delight;
And satisfy'd at once the Smell and Sight.
The Master Work-man of the Bow'r was known
Through Fairy-Lands, and built for *Oberon*;
Who twining Leaves with such Proportion drew,
They rose by Measure, and by Rule they grew:
No mortal Tongue can half the Beauty tell;
For none but Hands divine could work so well.
Both Roof and Sides were like a Parlour made,
A soft Recess, and a cool Summer shade;
The Hedge was set so thick, no Foreign Eye
The Persons plac'd within it could espy:
But all that pass'd without with Ease was seen,
As if nor Fence nor Tree was plac'd between.
'Twas border'd with a Field; and some was plain
With Grass; and some was sow'd with rising Grain.
That (now the Dew with Spangles deck'd the Ground:)
A sweeter spot of Earth was never found.
I look'd, and look'd, and still with new Delight;
Such Joy my Soul, such Pleasures fill'd my Sight:
And the fresh Eglantine exhal'd a Breath;
Whose Odours were of Pow'r to raise from Death:
Nor sullen Discontent, nor anxious Care,
Ev'n tho' brought thither, could inhabit there:
But thence they fled as from their mortal Foe;
For this sweet Place cou'd only Pleasure know.

Thus, as I mus'd, I cast aside my Eye
And saw a Medlar-Tree was planted nigh;
The spreading Branches made a goodly Show,
And full of opening Blooms was ev'ry Bough:
A Goldfinch there I saw with gawdy Pride
Of painted Plumes, that hopp'd from side to side,
Still pecking as she pass'd; and still she drew
The Sweets from ev'ry Flow'r, and suck'd the Dew:
Suffic'd at length, she warbled in her Throat,
And tun'd her Voice to many a merry Note,
But indistinct, and neither Sweet nor Clear,
Yet such as sooth'd my Soul, and pleas'd my Ear.

Her short Performance was no sooner try'd,
When she I sought, the Nightingale reply'd:

So sweet, so shrill, so variously she sung,
That the Grove ecchoed, and the Valleys rung:
And I so ravish'd with her heav'nly Note
I stood intranc'd, and had no room for Thought.
But all o'er-pou'r'd with Exstasy of Bliss,
Was in a pleasing Dream of Paradice;
At length I wak'd; and looking round the Bow'r
Search'd ev'ry Tree, and pry'd on ev'ry Flow'r,
If any where by chance I might espy
The rural Poet of the Melody:
For still methought she sung not far away;
At last I found her on a Lawrel Spray,
Close by my Side she sate, and fair in Sight,
Full in a Line, against her opposite;
Where stood with Eglantine the Lawrel twin'd:
And both their native Sweets were well conjoin'd.

On the green Bank I sat, and listen'd long;
(Sitting was more convenient for the Song!)
Nor till her Lay was ended could I move,
But wish'd to dwell for ever in the Grove.
Only methought the time too swiftly pass'd,
And ev'ry Note I fear'd wou'd be the last.
My Sight, and Smell, and Hearing were employ'd.
And all three Senses in full Gust enjoy'd.
And what alone did all the rest surpass,
The sweet Possession of the Fairy Place;
Single, and conscious to my Self alone,
Of Pleasures to th' excluded World unknown.
Pleasures which no where else, were to be found,
And all *Elysium* in a spot of Ground.

Thus while I sat intent to see and hear,
And drew Perfumes of more than vital Air,
All suddenly I heard th' approaching sound
Of vocal Musick, on th' enchanted Ground:
An Host of Saints it seem'd, so full the Quire;
As if the Bless'd above did all conspire,
To join their Voices, and neglect the Lyre.
At length there issu'd from the Grove behind
A fair Assembly of the Female Kind:
A Train less fair, as ancient Fathers tell,
Seduc'd the Sons of Heaven to rebel.

I pass their Forms, and ev'ry charming Grace,
Less than an Angel wou'd their Worth debase:
But their Attire like Liveries of a kind,
All rich and rare is fresh within my Mind.
In Velvet white as Snow the Troop was gown'd,
The Seams with sparkling Emeralds, set around;
Their Hoods and Sleeves the same: And purfled o'er
With Diamonds, Pearls, and all the shining store
Of Eastern Pomp: Their long descending Train
With Rubies edg'd, and Saphires, swept the Plain:
High on their Heads, with Jewels richly set
Each Lady wore a radiant Coronet.
Beneath the Circles, all the Quire was grac'd
With Chaplets green on their fair Foreheads plac'd,
Of Lawrel some, of Woodbine many more;
And Wreaths of *Agnus castus* others bore:
These last who with those Virgin Crowns were dress'd,
Appear'd in higher Honour than the rest.
They danc'd around, but in the midst was seen
A Lady of a more majestique Mien;
By Stature, and by Beauty mark'd their Sovereign Queen.

She in the midst began with sober Grace;
Her Servants Eyes were fix'd upon her Face:
And as she mov'd or turn'd her Motions view'd,
Her Measures kept, and Step by Step pursu'd.
Methought she trod the Ground with greater Grace,
With more of Godhead shining in her Face;
And as in Beauty she surpass'd the Quire,
So, nobler than the rest, was her Attire.
A Crown of ruddy Gold inclos'd her Brow,
Plain without Pomp, and rich without a Show:
A Branch of *Agnus castus* in her Hand,
She bore aloft (her Scepter of command;)
Admir'd, ador'd by all the circling Crowd,
For wheresoe'er she turn'd her Face, they bow'd:
And as she danc'd, a Roundelay she sung,
In honour of the Lawrel, ever young:
She rais'd her Voice on high, and sung so clear,
The Fawns came scudding from the Groves to hear:
And all the bending Forest lent an Ear.
At ev'ry Close she made, the attending Throng
Reply'd, and bore the Burden of the Song:

So just, so small, yet in so sweet a Note,
It seem'd the Musick melted in the Throat.

Thus dancing on, and singing as they danc'd,
They to the middle of the Mead advanc'd:
Till round my Arbour, a new Ring they made,
And footed it about the secret Shade:
O'erjoy'd to see the jolly Troop so near,
But somewhat aw'd I shook with holy Fear;
Yet not so much, but that I noted well
Who did the most in Song, or Dance excel.

Not long I had observ'd, when from afar
I heard a suddain Symphony of War;
The neighing Coursers, and the Soldiers cry,
And sounding Trumps that seem'd to tear the Sky:
I saw soon after this, behind the Grove
From whence the Ladies did in order move,
Come issuing out in Arms a Warrior-Train,
That like a Deluge pour'd upon the Plain:
On barbed Steeds they rode in proud Array,
Thick as the College of the Bees in *May*,
When swarming o'er the dusky Fields they fly,
New to the Flow'rs, and intercept the Sky.
So fierce they drove, their Coursers were so fleet,
That the Turf trembled underneath their Feet.

To tell their costly Furniture were long,
The Summers Day wou'd end before the Song:
To purchase but the Tenth of all their Store,
Would make the mighty *Persian* Monarch poor.
Yet what I can, I will; before the rest
The Trumpets issu'd in white Mantles dress'd:
A numerous Troop, and all their Heads around
With Chaplets green of Cerrial-Oak were crown'd,
And at each Trumpet was a Banner bound;
Which waving in the Wind display'd at large
Their Master's Coat of Arms, and Knightly Charge.
Broad were the Banners, and of snowy Hue,
A purer Web the Silk-worm never drew.
The chief about their Necks, the Scutcheons wore,
With Orient Pearls and Jewels pouder'd o'er:
Broad were their Collars too, and ev'ry one

Was set about with many a costly Stone.
Next these of Kings at Arms a goodly Train,
In proud Array came prancing o'er the Plain:
Their Cloaks were Cloth of Silver mix'd with Gold,
And Garlands green arround their Temples roll'd:
Rich Crowns were on their royal Scutcheons plac'd
With Saphires, Diamonds, and with Rubies grac'd.
And as the Trumpets their appearance made,
So these in Habits were alike array'd;
But with a Pace more sober, and more slow:
And twenty, Rank in Rank, they rode a-row.
The Pursevants came next, in number more;
And like the Heralds each his Scutcheon bore:
Clad in white Velvet all their Troop they led,
With each an Oaken Chaplet on his Head.

Nine royal Knights in equal Rank succeed,
Each Warrior mounted on a fiery Steed:
In golden Armour glorious to behold;
The Rivets of their Arms were nail'd with Gold.
Their Surcoats of white Ermin-Fur were made;
With Cloth of Gold between that cast a glitt'ring Shade.
The Trappings of their Steeds were of the same;
The golden Fringe ev'n set the Ground on flame;
And drew a precious Trail: A Crown divine
Of Lawrel did about their Temples twine.

Three Henchmen were for ev'ry Knight assign'd,
All in rich Livery clad, and of a kind:
White Velvet, but unshorn, for Cloaks they wore,
And each within his Hand a Truncheon bore:
The foremost held a Helm of rare Device;
A Prince's Ransom wou'd not pay the Price.
The second bore the Buckler of his Knight,
The third of Cornel-Wood a Spear upright,
Headed with piercing Steel, and polish'd bright.
Like to their Lords their Equipage was seen,
And all their Foreheads crown'd with Garlands green.

And after these came arm'd with Spear and Shield
An Host so great, as cover'd all the Field:
And all their Foreheads, like the Knights before,
With Lawrels ever green were shaded o'er,

Or Oak, or other Leaves of lasting kind,
Tenacious of the Stem and firm against the Wind.
Some in their Hands besides the Lance and Shield,
The Boughs of Woodbind or of Hauthorn held,
Or Branches for their mystique Emblems took,
Of Palm, of Lawrel, or of Cerrial Oak.

Thus marching to the Trumpets lofty sound
Drawn in two Lines adverse they wheel'd around,
And in the middle Meadow took their Ground.
Among themselves the Turney they divide,
In equal Squadrons, rang'd on either side.
Then turn'd their Horses Heads, and Man to Man,
And Steed to Steed oppos'd, the Justs began.
They lightly set their Lances in the rest,
And, at the Sign, against each other press'd:
They met, I sitting at my Ease beheld
The mix'd Events, and Fortunes of the Field.
Some broke their Spears, some tumbled Horse and Man,
And round the Fields the lighten'd Coursers ran.
An Hour and more like Tides, in equal sway
They rush'd, and won by turns, and lost the Day:
At length the Nine (who still together held)
Their fainting Foes to shameful Flight compell'd,
And with resistless Force, o'er-ran the Field.
Thus, to their Fame, when finish'd was the Fight,
The Victors from their lofty Steeds alight:
Like them dismounted all the Warlike Train,
And two by two proceeded o'er the Plain:
Till to the fair Assembly they advanc'd,
Who near the secret Arbour sung and danc'd.

The Ladies left their Measures at the Sight,
To meet the Chiefs returning from the Fight,
And each with open Arms embrac'd her chosen Knight.
Amid the Plain a spreading Lawrel stood,
The Grace and Ornament of all the Wood:
That pleasing Shade they sought, a soft retreat,
From suddain *April* Show'rs, a Shelter from the Heat.
Her leavy Arms with such extent were spread,
So near the Clouds was her aspiring Head,
That Hosts of Birds, that wing the liquid Air,
Perch'd in the Boughs, and nightly Lodging there.

And Flocks of Sheep beneath the Shade from far
Might hear the ratling Hail, and wintry War;
From Heav'ns Inclemency here found retreat,
Enjoy'd the cool, and shun'd the scorching Heat:
A hundred Knights might there at Ease abide;
And ev'ry Knight a Lady by his side:
The Trunk it self such Odours did bequeath,
That a Moluccan Breeze to these was common Breath.
The Lords, and Ladies here approaching, paid
Their Homage, with a low Obeisance made:
And seem'd to venerate the sacred Shade.
These Rites perform'd, their Pleasures they pursue,
With Songs of Love, and mix with Measures new;
Around the holy Tree their Dance they frame,
And ev'ry Champion leads his chosen Dame.

I cast my Sight upon the farther Field,
And a fresh Object of Delight beheld:
For from the Region of the West I heard
New Musick sound, and a new Troop appear'd;
Of Knights, and Ladies mix'd a jolly Band,
But all on Foot they march'd, and Hand in Hand.

The Ladies dress'd in rich Symarrs were seen
Of *Florence* Satten, flower'd with White and Green,
And for a Shade betwixt the bloomy Gridelin.
The Borders of their Petticoats below
Were guarded thick with Rubies on a-row;
And ev'ry Damsel wore upon her Head
Of Flow'rs a Garland blended White and Red.
Attir'd in Mantles all the Knights were seen,
That gratify'd the View with chearful Green:
Their Chaplets of their Ladies Colours were
Compos'd of White and Red to shade their shining Hair.
Before the merry Troop the Minstrels play'd,
All in their Master's Liveries were array'd:
And clad in Green, and on their Temples wore,
The Chaplets White and Red their Ladies bore.
Their Instruments were various in their kind,
Some for the Bow, and some for breathing Wind:
The Sawtry, Pipe, and Hautbois noisy band,
And the soft Lute trembling beneath the touching Hand.
A Tuft of Dasies on a flow'ry Lay

They saw, and thitherward they bent their way:
To this both Knights and Dames their Homage made,
And due Obeisance to the Daisy paid.
And then the Band of Flutes began to play,
To which a Lady sung a Virelay;
And still at ev'ry close she wou'd repeat
The Burden of the Song, *The Daisy is so sweet.*
The Daisy is so sweet when she begun,
The Troop of Knights and Dames continu'd on.
The Concert and the Voice so charm'd my Ear,
And sooth'd my Soul, that it was Heav'n to hear.

But soon their Pleasure pass'd: At Noon of Day;
The Sun with sultry Beams began to play:
Not *Syrius* shoots a fiercer Flame from high,
When with his pois'nous Breath he blasts the Sky:
Then droop'd the fading Flow'rs (their Beauty fled)
And clos'd their sickly Eyes, and hung the Head;
And, rivell'd up with Heat, lay dying in their Bed.
The Ladies gasp'd, and scarcely could respire;
The Breath they drew, no longer Air, but Fire;
The fainty Knights were scorch'd; and knew not where
To run for Shelter, for no Shade was near.
And after this the gath'ring Clouds amain,
Pour'd down a Storm of rattling Hail and Rain.
And Lightning flash'd betwixt: The Field, and Flow'rs
Burnt up before, were bury'd in the Show'rs.
The Ladies, and the Knights no Shelter nigh,
Bare to the Weather, and the wintry Sky,
Were dropping wet, disconsolate and wan,
And through their thin Array receiv'd the Rain.

While those in White protected by the Tree
Saw pass the vain Assault, and stood from Danger free.
But as Compassion mov'd their gentle Minds,
When ceas'd the Storm, and silent were the Winds,
Displeas'd at what, not suff'ring they had seen,
They went to chear the Faction of the Green:
The Queen in white Array before her Band,
Saluting, took her Rival by the Hand;
So did the Knights and Dames, with courtly Grace
And with Behaviour sweet their Foes embrace.
Then thus the Queen with Lawrel on her Brow,

Fair sister I have suffer'd in your Woe:
Nor shall be wanting ought within my Pow'r
For your Relief in my refreshing Bow'r.
That other answer'd with a lowly Look,
And soon the gracious Invitation took:
For ill at ease both she and all her Train
The scorching Sun had born, and beating Rain.
Like Courtesy was us'd by all in White,
Each Dame a Dame receiv'd, and every Knight a Knight.
The Lawrel-Champions with their Swords invade,
The neighb'ring Forests where the Justs were made,
And Serewood from the rotten Hedges took,
And Seeds of Latent-Fire from Flints provoke:
A chearful Blaze arose, and by the Fire,
They warm'd their frozen Feet, and dry'd their wet Attire.
Refresh'd with Heat the Ladies sought around
For virtuous Herbs which gather'd from the Ground
They squeez'd the Juice; and cooling Ointment made,
Which on their Sun-burnt Cheeks, and their chapt Skins they
laid:
Then sought green Salads which they bad 'em eat,
A Soveraign Remedy for inward Heat.

The Lady of the Leaf ordain'd a Feast,
And made the Lady of the Flow'r her Guest:
When lo, a Bow'r ascended on the Plain,
With suddain Seats adorn'd, and large for either Train.
This Bow'r was near my pleasant Arbour plac'd,
That I could hear and see whatever pass'd:
The Ladies sat, with each a Knight between
Distinguish'd by their Colours White and Green:
The vanquish'd Party with the Victors join'd,
Nor wanted sweet Discourse, the Banquet of the Mind.
Mean time the Minstrels play'd on either side
Vain of their Art, and for the Mast'ry vy'd:
The sweet Contention lasted for an Hour,
And reach'd my secret Arbour from the Bow'r.

The Sun was set; and Vesper to supply
His absent Beams, had lighted up the Sky:
When *Philomel*, officious all the Day
To sing the Service of th' ensuing *May*,
Fled from her Lawrel Shade, and wing'd her Flight

Directly to the Queen array'd in White:
And hopping sate familiar on her Hand,
A new Musitian, and increas'd the Band.

The Goldfinch, who to shun the scalding Heat,
Had chang'd the Medlar for a safer Seat,
And hid in Bushes scap'd the bitter Show'r,
Now perch'd upon the Lady of the Flow'r,
And either Songster holding out their Throats,
And folding up their Wings renew'd their Notes:
As if all Day, preluding to the Fight,
They only had rehears'd, to sing by Night.
The Banquet ended, and the Battle done,
They danc'd by Star-light and the friendly Moon:
And when they were to part, the Laureat Queen,
Supply'd with Steeds the Lady of the Green.
Her, and her Train conducting on the way
The Moon to follow, and avoid the Day.

This when I saw, inquisitive to know
The secret Moral of the Mystique Show,
I started from my Shade in hopes to find
Some Nymph to satisfy my longing Mind:
And as my fair Adventure fell, I found
A Lady all in White with Lawrel crown'd
Who clos'd the Rear, and softly pac'd along,
Repeating to her self the former Song.
With due respect my Body I inclin'd,
As to some Being of Superiour Kind,
And made my Court, according to the Day,
Wishing her Queen and Her a happy *May*.
Great thanks my Daughter, with a gracious Bow
She said; and I who much desir'd to know
Of whence she was, yet fearful how to break
My Mind, adventur'd humbly thus to speak.
Madam, Might I presume and not offend,
So may the Stars and shining Moon attend
Your Nightly Sports, as you vouchsafe to tell,
What Nymphs they were who mortal Forms excel,
And what the Knights who fought in listed Fields so well.

To this the Dame reply'd: Fair Daughter know
That what you saw, was all a Fairy Show:

And all those airy Shapes you now behold
Were humane Bodies once, and cloath'd with earthly Mold:
Our Souls not yet prepar'd for upper Light,
Till Doomsday wander in the Shades of Night;
This only Holiday of all the Year,
We privileg'd in Sun-shine may appear:
With Songs and Dance we celebrate the Day,
And with due Honours usher in the *May*.
At other Times we reign by Night alone,
And posting through the Skies pursue the Moon:
But when the Morn arises, none are found;
For cruel *Demogorgon* walks the round,
And if he finds a Fairy lag in Light,
He drives the Wretch before; and lashes into Night.

All Courteous are by Kind; and ever proud
With friendly Offices to help the Good.
In every Land we have a larger Space
Than what is known to you of mortal Race:
Where we with Green adorn our Fairy Bow'rs,
And ev'n this Grove unseen before, is ours.
Know farther; Ev'ry Lady cloath'd in White,
And, crown'd with Oak and Lawrel ev'ry Knight,
Are Servants to the Leaf, by Liveries known
Of Innocence; and I my self am one.
Saw you not Her so graceful to behold
In white Attire, and crown'd with Radiant Gold:
The Soveraign Lady of our Land is She,
Diana call'd, the Queen of Chastity:
And, for the spotless Name of Maid she bears,
That *Agnus castus* in her Hand appears:
And all her Train with leavy Chaplets crown'd
Were for unblam'd Virginity renown'd:
But those the chief and highest in Command
Who bear those holy Branches in their Hand:
The Knights adorn'd with Lawrel-crowns, are they
Whom Death nor Danger ever cou'd dismay,
Victorious Names, who made the World obey:
Who while they liv'd, in Deeds of Arms excell'd,
And after Death for Deities were held.
But those who wear the Woodbine on their Brow
Were Knights of Love, who never broke their Vow:
Firm to their plighted Faith, and ever free

From Fears and fickle Chance, and Jealousy.
The Lords and Ladies, who the Woodbine bear,
As true as *Tristram*, and *Isotta* were.

But what are those said I, th' unconquer'd Nine
Who crown'd with Lawrel-Wreaths in golden Armour shine?
And who the Knights in Green, and what the Train
Of Ladies dress'd with Daisies on the Plain?
Why both the Bands in Worship disagree,
And some adore the Flow'r, and some the Tree?

Just is your Suit, fair Daughter, said the Dame,
Those lawrell'd Chiefs were Men of mighty Fame;
Nine Worthies were they call'd of diff'rent Rites,
Three Jews, three Pagans, and three Christian Knights.
These, as you see, ride foremost in the Field,
As they the foremost Rank of Honour held,
And all in Deeds of Chivalry excell'd.
Their Temples wreath'd with Leafs, that still renew;
For deathless Lawrel is the Victor's due:
Who bear the Bows were Knights in *Arthur*'s Reign,
Twelve they, and twelve the Peers of *Charlemain*:
For Bows the Strength of brawny Arms imply,
Emblems of Valour, and of Victory.
Behold an Order yet of newer Date
Doubling their Number, equal in their State;
Our *England*'s Ornament, the Crown's Defence,
In Battle brave, Protectors of their Prince.
Unchang'd by Fortune, to their Sovereign true,
For which their manly Legs are bound with Blue.
These, of the Garter call'd, of Faith unstain'd,
In fighting Fields the Lawrel have obtain'd.
And well repaid those Honours which they gain'd.
The Lawrel-Wreaths were first by *Cæsar* worn,
And still they *Cæsar*'s Successors adorn:
One Leaf of this is Immortality,
And more of Worth, than all the World can buy.

One Doubt remains, said I, the Dames in Green,
What were their Qualities, and who their Queen?
Flora commands, said she, those Nymphs and Knights,
Who liv'd in slothful Ease, and loose Delights:
Who never Acts of Honour durst pursue,

The Men inglorious Knights, the Ladies all untrue:
Who nurs'd in Idleness, and train'd in Courts,
Pass'd all their precious Hours in Plays, and Sports,
Till Death behind came stalking on, unseen,
And wither'd (like the Storm) the freshness of their Green.
These, and their Mates, enjoy the present Hour,
And therefore pay their Homage to the Flow'r.
But Knights in Knightly Deeds should persevere,
And still continue what at first they were;
Continue, and proceed in Honours fair Career.
No room for Cowardise, or dull delay;
From Good to Better they should urge their way.
For this with golden Spurs the Chiefs are grac'd,
With pointed Rowels arm'd to mend their haste;
For this with lasting Leaves their Brows are bound;
For Lawrel is the Sign of Labour crown'd;
Which bears the bitter Blast, nor shaken falls to Ground:
From Winter-Winds it suffers no decay,
For ever fresh and fair, and ev'ry Month is *May*.
Ev'n when the vital Sap retreats below,
Ev'n when the hoary Head is hid in Snow;
The Life is in the Leaf, and still between
The Fits of falling Snows, appears the streaky Green.
Not so the Flow'r, which lasts for little space
A short-liv'd Good, and an uncertain Grace;
This way and that the feeble Stem is driv'n,
Weak to sustain the Storms, and Injuries of Heav'n.
Prop'd by the Spring, it lifts aloft, the Head,
But of a sickly Beauty, soon to shed;
In Summer living, and in Winter dead.
For Things of tender Kind for Pleasure made
Shoot up with swift Increase, and suddain are decay'd.

With humble Words, the wisest I could frame,
And profer'd Service I repaid the Dame:
That of her Grace she gave her Maid to know
The secret meaning of this moral Show.
And she to prove what Profit I had made,
Of mystique Truth, in Fables first convey'd,
Demanded, till the next returning *May*,
Whether the Leaf or Flow'r I would obey?
I chose the Leaf; she smil'd with sober Chear,
And wish'd me fair Adventure for the Year.

And gave me Charms and Sigils, for Defence
Against ill Tongues that scandal Innocence:
But I, said she, my Fellows must pursue,
Already past the Plain, and out of view.

We parted thus; I homeward sped my way,
Bewilder'd in the Wood till Dawn of Day:
And met the merry Crew who danc'd about the *May*.
Then late refesh'd with Sleep I rose to write
The visionary Vigils of the Night:
Blush, as thou may'st, my little Book for Shame,
Nor hope with homely Verse to purchase Fame;
For such thy Maker chose; and so design'd
Thy simple Style to suit thy lowly Kind.

SIGISMONDA AND GUISCARDO

FROM *BOCCACE*

WHILE *Norman Tancred* in *Salerno* reign'd,
The Title of a Gracious Prince he gain'd;
Till turn'd a Tyrant in his latter Days,
He lost the Lustre of his former Praise;
And from the bright Meridian where he stood,
Descending, dipp'd his Hands in Lovers Blood.

This Prince, of Fortunes Favour long possess'd,
Yet was with one fair Daughter only bless'd;
And bless'd he might have been with her alone:
But oh! how much more happy, had he none!
She was his Care, his Hope, and his Delight,
Most in his Thought; and ever in his Sight:
Next, nay beyond his Life, he held her dear;
She liv'd by him, and how he liv'd in her.
For this, when ripe for Marriage, he delay'd
Her Nuptial Bands, and kept her long a Maid,
As envying any else should share a Part
Of what was his, and claiming all her Heart.
At length, as Publick Decency requir'd,
And all his Vassals eagerly desir'd,

With Mind averse, he rather underwent
His Peoples Will, than gave his own Consent:
So was she torn, as from a Lover's Side,
And made almost in his despite a Bride.

Short were her Marriage-Joys; for in the Prime
Of Youth, her Lord expir'd before his time:
And to her Father's Court, in little space
Restor'd anew, she held a higher Place;
More lov'd, and more exalted into Grace.
This Princess fresh and young, and fair, and wise,
The worshipp'd Idol of her Father's Eyes,
Did all her Sex in ev'ry Grace exceed,
And had more Wit beside than Women need.

Youth, Health, and Ease, and most an amorous Mind,
To second Nuptials had her Thoughts inclin'd:
And former Joys had left a secret Sting behind.
But prodigal in ev'ry other Grant,
Her Sire left unsupply'd her only Want;
And she, betwixt her Modesty and Pride,
Her Wishes, which she could not help, would hide.

Resolv'd at last to lose no longer Time,
And yet to please her self without a Crime,
She cast her Eyes around the Court, to find
A worthy Subject suiting to her Mind,
To him in holy Nuptials to be ty'd,
A seeming Widow, and a secret Bride.
Among the Train of Courtiers, one she found
With all the Gifts of bounteous Nature crown'd,
Of gentle Blood; but one whose niggard Fate
Had set him far below her high Estate;
Guiscard his Name was call'd, of blooming Age,
Now Squire to *Tancred*, and before his Page:
To him, the Choice of all the shining Crowd,
Her Heart the noble *Sigismonda* vow'd.

Yet hitherto she kept her Love conceal'd,
And with close Glances ev'ry Day beheld
The graceful Youth; and ev'ry Day increas'd
The raging Fire that burn'd within her Breast:
Some secret Charm did all his Acts attend,

And what his Fortune wanted, hers could mend:
Till, as the Fire will force its outward way,
Or, in the Prison pent, consume the Prey;
So long her earnest Eyes on his were set,
At length their twisted Rays together met;
And he, surpriz'd with humble Joy, survey'd
One sweet Regard, shot by the Royal Maid:
Not well assur'd, while doubtful Hopes he nurs'd,
A second Glance came gliding like the first;
And he who saw the Sharpness of the Dart,
Without Defence receiv'd it in his Heart.
In Publick though their Passion wanted Speech,
Yet mutual Looks interpreted for each:
Time, Ways, and Means of Meeting were deny'd;
But all those Wants ingenious Love supply'd.
Th' inventive God, who never fails his Part,
Inspires the Wit, when once he warms the Heart.

When *Guiscard* next was in the Circle seen,
Where *Sigismonda* held the Place of Queen,
A hollow Cane within her Hand she brought,
But in the Concave had enclos'd a Note:
With this she seem'd to play, and, as in sport,
Toss'd to her Love, in presence of the Court;
Take it, she said; and when your Needs require,
This little Brand will serve to light your Fire.
He took it with a Bow, and soon divin'd
The seeming Toy was not for nought design'd:
But when retir'd, so long with curious Eyes
He view'd the Present, that he found the Prize.
Much was in little writ; and all convey'd
With cautious Care, for fear to be betray'd
By some false Confident, or Fav'rite Maid.
The Time, the Place, the Manner how to meet,
Were all in punctual Order plainly writ:
But since a Trust must be, she thought it best
To put it out of Laymens Pow'r at least,
And for their solemn Vows prepar'd a Priest.

Guiscard (her secret Purpose understood)
With Joy prepar'd to meet the coming Good;
Nor Pains nor Danger was resolv'd to spare,
But use the Means appointed by the Fair.

SIGISMONDA AND GUISCARDO

Near the proud Palace of *Salerno* stood
A Mount of rough Ascent, and thick with Wood;
Through this a Cave was dug with vast Expence,
The Work it seem'd of some suspicious Prince,
Who, when abusing Pow'r with lawless Might,
From Publick Justice would secure his Flight.
The Passage made by many a winding Way,
Reach'd ev'n the Room in which the Tyrant lay.
Fit for his Purpose, on a lower Floor
He lodg'd, whose Issue was an Iron Door,
From whence, by Stairs descending to the Ground,
In the blind Grot a safe Retreat he found.
Its Outlet ended in a Brake o'ergrown
With Brambles, choaked by Time, and now unknown.
A Rift there was, which from the Mountains Height
Convey'd a glimm'ring and malignant Light,
A Breathing-place to draw the Damps away,
A Twilight of an intercepted Day.
The Tyrants den, whose Use though lost to Fame,
Was now th' Apartment of the Royal Dame;
The Cavern only to her Father known,
By him was to his Darling-Daughter shown.

Neglected long she let the Secret rest,
Till Love recall'd it to her lab'ring Breast,
And hinted as the Way by Heav'n design'd
The Teacher, by the Means he taught, to blind.
What will not Women do, when Need inspires
Their Wit, or Love their Inclination fires!
Though Jealousie of State th' Invention found,
Yet Love refin'd upon the former Ground.
That Way, the Tyrant had reserv'd, to fly
Pursuing Hate, now serv'd to bring two Lovers nigh.

The Dame, who long in vain had kept the Key,
Bold by Desire, explor'd the secret Way;
Now try'd the Stairs, and wading through the Night,
Search'd all the deep Recess, and issu'd into Light.
All this her Letter had so well explain'd,
Th' instructed Youth might compass what remain'd:
The Cavern-mouth alone was hard to find,
Because the Path disus'd, was out of mind:

But in what Quarter of the Cops it lay,
His Eye by certain Level could survey:
Yet (for the Wood perplex'd with Thorns he knew)
A Frock of Leather o'er his Limbs he drew:
And thus provided, searched the Brake around,
Till the choak'd Entry of the Cave he found.

Thus, all prepar'd, the promis'd Hour arriv'd,
So long expected, and so well contriv'd:
With Love to Friend, th' impatient Lover went,
Fenc'd from the Thorns, and trod the deep Descent.
The conscious Priest, who was suborn'd before,
Stood ready posted at the Postern-door;
The Maids in distant Rooms were sent to rest,
And nothing wanted but th' invited Guest.
He came, and knocking thrice, without delay,
The longing Lady heard, and turn'd the Key;
At once invaded him with all her Charms,
And the first Step he made, was in her Arms;
The Leathern Out-side, boistrous as it was,
Gave way, and bent beneath her strict Embrace:
On either Side the Kisses flew so thick,
That neither he nor she had Breath to speak.
The holy Man amaz'd at what he saw,
Made haste to sanctifie the Bliss by Law;
And mutter'd fast the Matrimony o're,
For fear committed Sin should get before.
His Work perform'd, he left the Pair alone,
Because he knew he could not go too soon;
His Presence odious, when his Task was done.
What Thoughts he had, beseems not me to say;
Though some surmise he went to fast and pray,
And needed both, to drive the tempting Thoughts away.

The Foe once gone, they took their full Delight;
'Twas restless Rage, and Tempest all the Night:
For greedy Love each Moment would employ,
And grudg'd the shortest Pauses of their Joy.

Thus were their Loves auspiciously begun,
And thus with secret Care were carried on.
The Stealth it self did Appetite restore,
And look'd so like a Sin, it pleas'd the more.

The Cave was now become a common Way,
The Wicket often open'd, knew the Key:
Love rioted secure, and long enjoy'd,
Was ever eager, and was never cloy'd.

But as Extremes are short, of Ill and Good,
And Tides at highest Mark regorge the Flood;
So Fate, that could no more improve their Joy,
Took a malicious Pleasure to destroy.

Tancred, who fondly lov'd, and whose Delight
Was plac'd in his fair Daughters daily Sight,
Of Custom, when his State-Affairs were done,
Would pass his pleasing Hours with her alone:
And, as a Father's Privilege allow'd,
Without Attendance of th' officious Crowd.

It happen'd once, that when in Heat of Day
He try'd to sleep, as was his usual Way,
The balmy Slumber fled his wakeful Eyes,
And forc'd him, in his own despite, to rise:
Of Sleep forsaken, to relieve his Care,
He sought the Conversation of the Fair:
But with her Train of Damsels she was gone,
In shady Walks the scorching Heat to shun:
He would not violate that sweet Recess,
And found besides a welcome Heaviness
That seiz'd his Eyes; and Slumber, which forgot
When call'd before to come, now came unsought.
From Light retir'd, behind his Daughters Bed,
He for approaching Sleep compos'd his Head;
A Chair was ready, for that Use design'd,
So quilted, that he lay at ease reclin'd;
The Curtains closely drawn, the Light to skreen,
As if he had contriv'd to lie unseen:
Thus cover'd with an artificial Night,
Sleep did his Office soon, and seal'd his Sight.

With Heav'n averse, in this ill-omen'd Hour
Was *Guiscard* summon'd to the secret Bow'r,
And the fair Nymph, with Expectation fir'd,
From her attending Damsels was retir'd:

For, true to Love, she measur'd Time so right,
As not to miss one Moment of Delight.
The Garden, seated on the level Floor,
She left behind, and locking ev'ry Door,
Thought all secure; but little did she know,
Blind to her Fate, she had inclos'd her Foe.
Attending *Guiscard*, in his Leathern Frock,
Stood ready, with his thrice-repeated Knock:
Thrice with a doleful Sound the jarring Grate
Rung deaf, and hollow, and presag'd their Fate.
The Door unlock'd, to known Delight they haste,
And panting in each others Arms, embrac'd;
Rush to the conscious Bed, a mutual Freight,
And heedless press it with their wonted Weight.

The sudden Bound awak'd the sleeping Sire,
And shew'd a Sight no Parent can desire:
His opening Eyes at once with odious View
The Love discover'd, and the Lover knew:
He wou'd have cry'd; but hoping that he dreamt,
Amazement ty'd his Tongue, and stopp'd th' Attempt.
Th' ensuing Moment all the Truth declar'd,
But now he stood collected, and prepar'd;
For Malice and Revenge had put him on his Guard.

So, like a Lion that unheeded lay,
Dissembling Sleep, and watchful to betray,
With inward Rage he meditates his Prey.
The thoughtless Pair, indulging their Desires,
Alternate, kindl'd, and then quench'd their Fires;
Nor thinking in the Shades of Death they play'd,
Full of themselves, themselves alone survey'd,
And, too secure, were by themselves betray'd.
Long time dissolv'd in Pleasure thus they lay,
Till Nature could no more suffice their Play;
Then rose the Youth, and through the Cave again
Return'd; the Princess mingl'd with her Train.

Resolv'd his unripe Vengeance to defer
The Royal Spy, when now the Coast was clear,
Sought not the Garden, but retir'd unseen,
To brood in secret on his gather'd Spleen,
And methodize Revenge: To Death he griev'd;
And, but he saw the Crime, had scarce believ'd.

Th' Appointment for th' ensuing Night he heard;
And therefore in the Cavern had prepar'd
Two brawny Yeomen of his trusty Guard.

Scarce had unwary *Guiscard* set his Foot
Within the farmost Entrance of the Grot,
When these in secret Ambush ready lay,
And rushing on the sudden seiz'd the Prey:
Encumber'd with his Frock, without Defence,
An easy Prize, they led the Pris'ner thence,
And, as commanded, brought before the Prince.
The gloomy Sire, too sensible of Wrong
To vent his Rage in Words, restrain'd his Tongue;
And only said, Thus servants are preferr'd,
And trusted, thus their Sov'reigns they reward.
Had I not seen, had not these Eyes receiv'd
Too clear a Proof, I could not have believ'd.

He paus'd, and choaked the rest. The Youth, who saw
His forfeit Life abandoned to the Law,
The Judge th' Accuser, and th' Offence to him
Who had both Pow'r and Will t' avenge the Crime;
No vain Defence prepar'd, but thus reply'd,
The Faults of Love by Love are justifi'd:
With unresisted Might the Monarch reigns,
He levels Mountains, and he raises Plains;
And not regarding Diff'rence of Degree,
Abas'd your Daughter, and exalted me.

This bold Return with seeming Patience heard,
The Pris'ner was remitted to the Guard.
The sullen Tyrant slept not all the Night,
But lonely walking by a winking Light,
Sobb'd, wept, and groan'd, and beat his wither'd Breast,
But would not violate his Daughters Rest;
Who long expecting lay, for Bliss prepar'd,
Listning for Noise, and griev'd that none she heard;
Oft rose, and oft in vain employ'd the Key,
And oft accus'd her Lover of Delay;
And pass'd the tedious Hours in anxious Thoughts away.

The Morrow came; and at his usual Hour
Old *Tancred* visited his Daughters Bow'r;

Her Cheek (for such his Custom was) he kiss'd,
Then bless'd her kneeling, and her Maids dismiss'd.
The Royal Dignity thus far maintain'd,
Now left in private, he no longer feign'd;
But all at once his Grief and Rage appear'd,
And Floods of Tears ran trickling down his Beard.

O *Sigismonda*, he began to say:
Thrice he began, and thrice was forc'd to stay,
Till Words with often trying found their Way:
I thought, O *Sigismonda*, (But how blind
Are Parents Eyes, their Childrens Faults to find!)
Thy Vertue, Birth, and Breeding were above
A mean Desire, and vulgar Sense of Love:
Nor less than Sight and Hearing could convince
So fond a Father, and so just a Prince,
Of such an unforeseen, and unbeliev'd Offence:
Then what indignant Sorrow must I have,
To see thee lie subjected to my Slave!
A Man so smelling of the Peoples Lee,
The Court receiv'd him first for Charity;
And since with no Degree of Honour grac'd,
But only suffer'd, where he first was plac'd:
A grov'ling Insect still; and so design'd
By Natures Hand, nor born of Noble Kind:
A Thing, by neither Man nor Woman priz'd,
And scarcely known enough, to be despis'd.
To what has Heav'n reserv'd my Age? Ah! why
Should Man, when Nature calls, not chuse to die;
Rather than stretch the Span of Life, to find
Such Ills as Fate has wisely cast behind,
For those to feel, whom fond Desire to live
Makes covetous of more than Life can give!
Each has his Share of Good; and when 'tis gone,
The Guest, though hungry, cannot rise too soon.
But I, expecting more, in my own wrong
Protracting Life, have liv'd a Day too long.
If Yesterday cou'd be recall'd again,
Ev'n now would I conclude my happy Reign:
But 'tis too late, my glorious Race is run,
And a dark Cloud o'ertakes my setting Sun.
Hadst thou not lov'd, or loving sav'd the Shame,
If not the Sin, by some Illustrious Name,

This little Comfort had reliev'd my Mind,
'Twas frailty, not unusual to thy Kind:
But thy low Fall beneath thy Royal Blood,
Shews downward Appetite to mix with Mud:
Thus not the least Excuse is left for thee,
Nor the least Refuge for unhappy me.

For him I have resolv'd: whom by Surprize
I took, and scarce can call it, in Disguise:
For such was his Attire, as with Intent
Of Nature, suited to his mean Descent:
The harder Question yet remains behind,
What Pains a Parent and a Prince can find
To punish an Offence of this degenerate Kind.

As I have lov'd, and yet I love thee more
Than ever Father lov'd a Child before;
So, that Indulgence draws me to forgive:
Nature, that gave thee Life, would have thee live.
But, as a Publick-Parent of the State,
My Justice, and thy Crime, requires thy Fate.
Fain would I chuse a middle Course to steer;
Nature's too kind, and Justice too severe:
Speak for us both, and to the Balance bring
On either side, the Father, and the King.
Heav'n knows, my Heart is bent to favour thee;
Make it but scanty weight, and leave the rest to me.

Here stopping with a Sigh, he pour'd a Flood
Of Tears, to make his last Expression good.

She, who had heard him speak, nor saw alone
The secret Conduct of her Love was known;
But he was taken who her Soul possess'd,
Felt all the Pangs of Sorrow in her Breast:
And little wanted, but a Womans Heart
With Cries, and Tears, had testifi'd her Smart:
But in-born Worth, that Fortune can controul,
New strung, and stiffer bent her softer Soul;
The *Heroine* assum'd the Womans Place,
Confirm'd her Mind, and fortifi'd her Face:
Why should she beg, or what cou'd she pretend,
When her stern Father had condemn'd her Friend!

Her Life she might have had; but her Despair
Of saving his, had put it past her Care:
Resolv'd on Fate, she would not lose her Breath,
But rather than not die, sollicit Death.
Fix'd on this Thought, she not as Women use,
Her Fault by common Frailty would excuse;
But boldly justifi'd her Innocence,
And while the Fact was own'd, deny'd th' Offence:
Then with dry Eyes, and with an open Look,
She met his Glance mid-way, and thus undaunted spoke.

Tancred, I neither am dispos'd to make
Request for Life, nor offer'd Life to take:
Much less deny the Deed; but least of all
Beneath pretended Justice weakly fall.
My Words to sacred Truth shall be confin'd,
My Deeds shall shew the Greatness of my Mind.
That I have lov'd, I own; that still I love,
I call to Witness all the Pow'rs above:
Yet more I own: To *Guiscard*'s Love I give
The small remaining Time I have to live;
And if beyond this Life Desire can be,
Not Fate it self shall set my Passion free.

This first avow'd; nor Folly warp'd my Mind,
Nor the frail Texture of the Female Kind
Betray'd my Vertue: For, too well I knew
What Honour was, and Honour had his Due:
Before the Holy Priest my Vows were ty'd,
So came I not a Strumpet, but a Bride;
This for my Fame: and for the Publick Voice:
Yet more, his Merits justifi'd my Choice;
Which had they not, the first Election thine,
That Bond dissolv'd, the next is freely mine:
Or grant I err'd, (which yet I must deny,)
Had Parents pow'r ev'n second Vows to tie,
Thy little Care to mend my Widow'd Nights
Has forc'd me to recourse of Marriage-Rites,
To fill an empty Side, and follow known Delights.
What have I done in this, deserving Blame?
State-Laws may alter: Nature's are the same;
Those are usurp'd on helpless Woman-kind,
Made without our Consent, and wanting Pow'r to bind.

Thou, *Tancred*, better should'st have understood,
That as thy Father gave thee Flesh and Blood,
So gav'st thou me: Not from the Quarry hew'd,
But of a softer Mould, with Sense endu'd;
Ev'n softer than thy own, of suppler Kind,
More exquisite of Taste, and more than Man refin'd.
Nor need'st thou by thy Daughter to be told,
Though now thy spritely Blood with Age be cold,
Thou hast been young; and canst remember still,
That when thou hadst the Pow'r, thou hadst the Will;
And from the past Experience of thy Fires,
Canst tell with what a Tide our strong Desires
Come rushing on in Youth, and what their Rage requires.

And grant thy Youth was exercis'd in Arms,
When Love no leisure found for softer Charms;
My tender Age in Luxury was train'd,
With idle Ease and Pageants entertain'd;
My Hours my own, my Pleasures unrestrain'd.
So bred, no wonder if I took the Bent
That seem'd ev'n warranted by thy Consent;
For, when the Father is too fondly kind,
Such Seed he sows, such Harvest shall he find.
Blame then thy self, as Reason's Law requires,
(Since Nature gave, and thou foment'st my Fires;)
If still those Appetites continue strong,
Thou maist consider, I am yet but young:
Consider too, that having been a Wife,
I must have tasted of a better Life,
And am not to be blam'd, if I renew,
By lawful Means, the Joys which then I knew.
Where was the Crime, if Pleasure I procur'd,
Young, and a Woman, and to Bliss inur'd?
That was my Case, and this is my Defence:
I pleas'd my self, I shunn'd Incontinence,
And, urg'd by strong Desires, indulg'd my Sense.

Left to my self, I must avow, I strove
From publick Shame to screen my secret Love,
And, well acquainted with thy Native Pride,
Endeavour'd, what I could not help, to hide;
For which, a Womans Wit an easie Way supply'd.

How this, so well contriv'd, so closely laid,
Was known to thee, or by what Chance betray'd,
Is not my Care: To please thy Pride alone,
I could have wish'd it had been still unknown.

Nor took I *Guiscard* by blind Fancy led,
Or hasty Choice, as many Women wed;
But with delib'rate Care, and ripen'd Thought,
At leisure first design'd, before I wrought:
On him I rested, after long Debate,
And not without consid'ring, fix'd my Fate:
His Flame was equal, though by mine inspir'd;
(For so the Diff'rence of our Birth requir'd:)
Had he been born like me, like me his Love
Had first begun, what mine was forc'd to move:
But thus beginning, thus we persevere;
Our Passions yet continue what they were,
Nor length of Trial makes our Joys the less sincere.

At this my Choice, though not by thine allow'd,
(Thy Judgment herding with the common Crowd)
Thou tak'st unjust Offence; and, led by them,
Dost less the Merit, than the Man esteem.
Too sharply, *Tancred*, by thy Pride betray'd,
Hast thou against the Laws of Kind inveigh'd;
For all th' Offence is in Opinion plac'd,
Which deems high Birth by lowly Choice debas'd:
This Thought alone with Fury fires thy Breast,
(For Holy Marriage justifies the rest)
That I have sunk the Glories of the State,
And mix'd my Blood with a Plebeian Mate:
In which I wonder thou shouldst oversee
Superiour Causes, or impute to me
The Fault of Fortune, or the Fates Decree.
Or call it Heav'ns Imperial Pow'r alone,
Which moves on Springs of Justice, though unknown;
Yet this we see, though order'd for the best,
The Bad exalted, and the Good oppress'd;
Permitted Laurels grace the Lawless Brow,
Th' Unworthy rais'd, the Worthy cast below.

But leaving that: Search we the secret Springs,
And backward trace the Principles of Things;

There shall we find, that when the World began,
One common Mass compos'd the Mould of Man;
One Paste of Flesh on all Degrees bestow'd,
And kneaded up alike with moistning Blood.
The same Almighty Pow'r inspir'd the Frame
With kindl'd Life, and form'd the Souls the same:
The Faculties of Intellect, and Will,
Dispens'd with equal Hand, dispos'd with equal Skill,
Like Liberty indulg'd with Choice of Good or Ill.
Thus born alike, from Vertue first began
The Diff'rence that distinguish'd Man from Man:
He claim'd no Title from Descent of Blood,
But that which made him Noble, made him Good:
Warm'd with more Particles of Heav'nly Flame,
He wing'd his upward Flight, and soar'd to Fame;
The rest remain'd below, a Tribe without a Name.

This Law, though Custom now diverts the Course,
As Natures Institute, is yet in force;
Uncancell'd, tho disus'd: And he whose Mind
Is Vertuous, is alone of Noble Kind.
Though poor in Fortune, of Celestial Race;
And he commits the Crime, who calls him Base.

Now lay the Line; and measure all thy Court,
By inward Vertue, not external Port,
And find whom justly to prefer above
The Man on whom my Judgment plac'd my Love:
So shalt thou see his Parts, and Person shine;
And thus compar'd, the rest a base degen'rate Line.
Nor took I, when I first survey'd thy Court,
His Valour, or his Vertues on Report;
But trusted what I ought to trust alone,
Relying on thy Eyes, and not my own;
Thy Praise (and Thine was then the Publick Voice)
First recommended *Guiscard* to my Choice:
Directed thus by thee, I look'd, and found
A Man, I thought, deserving to be crown'd;
First by my Father pointed to my Sight,
Nor less conspicuous by his Native Light:
His Mind, his Meen, the Features of his Face,
Excelling all the rest of Humane Race:

These were thy Thoughts, and thou could'st judge aright,
Till Int'rest made a Jaundice in thy Sight.

Or shou'd I grant, thou didst not rightly see;
Then thou wert first deceiv'd, and I deceiv'd by thee.
But if thou shalt alledge, through Pride of Mind,
Thy Blood with one of base Condition join'd,
'Tis false; for 'tis not Baseness to be Poor;
His Poverty augments thy Crime the more;
Upbraids thy Justice with the scant Regard
Of Worth: Whom Princes praise, they shou'd reward.
Are these the Kings intrusted by the Crowd
With Wealth, to be dispens'd for Common Good?
The People sweat not for their King's Delight,
T' enrich a Pimp, or raise a Parasite;
Theirs is the Toil; and he who well has serv'd
His Country, has his Countrys Wealth deserv'd.

Ev'n mighty Monarchs oft are meanly born,
And Kings by Birth, to lowest Rank return;
All subject to the Pow'r of giddy Chance,
For Fortune can Depress, or can advance:
But true Nobility, is of the Mind,
Not giv'n by Chance, and not to Chance resign'd.

For the remaining Doubt of thy Decree,
What to resolve, and how dispose of me,
Be warn'd to cast that useless Care aside,
My self alone, will for my self provide:
If in thy doting, and decrepit Age,
Thy Soul, a Stranger in thy Youth to Rage,
Begins in cruel Deeds to take Delight,
Gorge with my Blood thy barb'rous Appetite;
For I so little am dispos'd to pray
For Life, I would not cast a Wish away,
Such as it is, th' Offence is all my own;
And what to *Guiscard* is already done,
Or to be done, is doom'd by thy Decree,
That, if not executed first by thee,
Shall on my Person be perform'd by me.

Away, with Women weep, and leave me here,
Fix'd, like a Man to die, without a Tear;

Or save, or slay us both this present Hour,
'Tis all that Fate has left within thy Pow'r.

She said: Nor did her Father fail to find,
In all she spoke, the Greatness of her Mind;
Yet thought she was not obstinate to die,
Nor deem'd the Death she promis'd was so nigh:
Secure in this Belief, he left the Dame,
Resolv'd to spare her Life, and save her Shame;
But that detested Object to remove,
To wreak his Vengeance, and to cure her Love.

Intent on this, a secret Order sign'd,
The Death of *Guiscard* to his Guards enjoin'd;
Strangling was chosen, and the Night the Time,
A mute Revenge, and blind as was the Crime:
His faithful Heart, a bloody Sacrifice,
Torn from his Breast, to glut the Tyrant's Eyes,
Clos'd the severe Command: For, (Slaves to Pay)
What Kings decree, the Soldier must obey:
Wag'd against Foes; and, when the Wars are o'er,
Fit only to maintain Despotick Pow'r:
Dang'rous to Freedom, and desir'd alone
By Kings, who seek an Arbitrary Throne:
Such were these Guards; as ready to have slain
The Prince himself, allur'd with greater gain:
So was the Charge perform'd with better Will,
By Men inur'd to Blood, and exercis'd in Ill.

Now, though the sullen Sire had eas'd his Mind,
The Pomp of his Revenge was yet behind,
A Pomp prepar'd to grace the Present he design'd.
A Goblet rich with Gems, and rough with Gold,
Of Depth, and Breadth, the precious Pledge to hold,
With cruel Care he chose; The hollow Part
Inclos'd, the Lid conceal'd the Lover's Heart:
Then of his trusted Mischiefs, one he sent,
And bad him with these Words the Gift present;
Thy Father sends thee this, to cheer thy Breast,
And glad thy Sight with what thou lov'st the best;
As thou hast pleas'd his Eyes, and joy'd his Mind,
With what he lov'd the most of Humane Kind.

E'er this the Royal Dame, who well had weigh'd
The Consequence of what her Sire had said,
Fix'd on her Fate, against th' expected Hour,
Procur'd the Means to have it in her Pow'r:
For this, she had distill'd, with early Care,
The Juice of Simples, friendly to Despair,
A Magazine of Death; and thus prepar'd,
Secure to die, the fatal Message heard:
Then smil'd severe; nor with a troubl'd Look,
Or trembling Hand, the Fun'ral Present took;
Ev'n kept her Count'nance, when the Lid remov'd,
Disclos'd the Heart, unfortunately lov'd:
She needed not be told within whose Breast
It lodg'd; the Message had explain'd the rest.
Or not amaz'd, or hiding her Surprize,
She sternly on the Bearer fix'd her Eyes:
Then thus; Tell *Tancred*, on his Daughters part,
The Gold, though precious, equals not the Heart:
But he did well to give his best; and I,
Who wish'd a worthier Urn, forgive his Poverty.

At this, she curb'd a Groan, that else had come,
And pausing, view'd the Present in the Tomb:
Then, to the Heart ador'd, devoutly glew'd
Her lips, and raising it, her Speech renew'd;
Ev'n from my Day of Birth, to this, the Bound
Of my unhappy Being, I have found
My Father's Care, and Tenderness express'd:
But this last Act of Love excels the rest:
For this so dear a Present, bear him back
The best Return that I can live to make.

The Messenger dispatch'd, again she view'd
The lov'd Remains, and sighing, thus pursu'd;
Source of my Life, and Lord of my Desires,
In whom I liv'd, with whom my Soul expires;
Poor Heart, no more the Spring of Vital Heat,
Curs'd be the Hands that tore thee from thy Seat!
The Course is finish'd, which thy Fates decreed,
And thou, from thy Corporeal Prison freed:
Soon hast thou reach'd the Goal with mended Pace,
A World of Woes dispatch'd in little space:
Forc'd by thy Worth, thy Foe in Death become

Thy Friend, has lodg'd thee in a costly Tomb;
There yet remain'd thy Fun'ral Exequies,
The weeping Tribute of thy Widows Eyes,
And those, indulgent Heav'n has found the way
That I, before my Death, have leave to pay.
My Father ev'n in Cruelty is kind,
Or Heav'n has turn'd the Malice of his Mind
To better Uses than his Hate design'd;
And made th' Insult which in his Gift appears,
The means to mourn thee with my pious Tears;
Which I will pay thee down, before I go,
And save my self the Pains to weep below,
If Souls can weep; though once I meant to meet
My Fate with Face unmov'd, and Eyes unwet,
Yet since I have thee here in narrow Room,
My Tears shall set thee first afloat within thy Tomb:
Then (as I know thy Spirit hovers nigh)
Under thy friendly Conduct will I fly
To Regions unexplor'd, secure to share
Thy State; nor Hell shall Punishment appear;
And Heav'n is double Heav'n, if thou art there.

She said: Her brim-full Eyes, that ready stood,
And only wanted Will to weep a Flood,
Releas'd their watry Store, and pour'd amain,
Like Clouds low hung, a sober Show'r of Rain;
Mute solemn Sorrow, free from Female Noise,
Such as the Majesty of Grief destroys:
For, bending o'er the Cup, the Tears she shed
Seem'd by the Posture to discharge her Head,
O'er-fill'd before; and oft (her Mouth apply'd
To the cold Heart) she kiss'd at once, and cry'd.
Her Maids, who stood amaz'd, nor knew the Cause
Of her Complaining, nor whose Heart it was;
Yet all due Measures of her Mourning kept,
Did Office at the Dirge, and by Infection wept;
And oft enquir'd th' Occasion of her Grief,
(Unanswer'd but by Sighs) and offer'd vain Relief.
At length, her Stock of Tears already shed,
She wip'd her Eyes, she rais'd her drooping Head,
And thus pursu'd: O ever faithful Heart,
I have perform'd the Ceremonial Part,
The Decencies of Grief: It rests behind,

That as our Bodies were, our Souls be join'd:
To thy whate'er abode, my Shade convey,
And as an elder Ghost, direct the way.
She said; and bad the Vial to be brought,
Where she before had brew'd the deadly Draught,
First pouring out the med'cinable Bane,
The Heart, her Tears had rins'd, she bath'd again;
Then down her Throat the Death securely throws,
And quaffs a long Oblivion of her Woes.

This done, she mounts the Genial Bed, and there,
(Her Body first compos'd with honest Care,)
Attends the welcom Rest; Her Hands yet hold
Close to her Heart, the Monumental Gold;
Nor farther Word she spoke, but clos'd her Sight,
And quiet, sought the Covert of the Night.

The Damsels, who the while in Silence mourn'd,
Not knowing, nor suspecting Death suborn'd,
Yet, as their Duty was, to *Tancred* sent,
Who, conscious of th' Occasion, fear'd th' Event.
Alarm'd, and with presaging Heart he came,
And drew the Curtains, and expos'd the Dame
To loathsom Light; then with a late Relief
Made vain Efforts, to mitigate her Grief.
She, what she could, excluding Day, her Eyes
Kept firmly seal'd, and sternly thus replies:

Tancred, restrain thy Tears, unsought by me,
And Sorrow, unavailing now to thee:
Did ever Man before, afflict his Mind,
To see th' Effect of what himself design'd?
Yet if thou hast remaining in thy Heart
Some Sense of Love, some unextinguish'd Part
Of former Kindness, largely once profess'd,
Let me by that adjure thy harden'd Breast,
Not to deny thy Daughters last Request:
The secret Love, which I so long enjoy'd,
And still conceal'd, to gratifie thy Pride,
Thou hast disjoin'd; but, with my dying Breath,
Seek not, I beg thee, to disjoin our Death:
Where-e'er his Corps by thy Command is laid,
Thither let mine in publick be convey'd;

Expos'd in open View, and Side by Side,
Acknowledg'd as a Bridegroom and a Bride.

The Prince's Anguish hinder'd his Reply:
And she, who felt her Fate approaching nigh,
Seiz'd the cold Heart, and heaving to her Breast,
Here, precious Pledge, she said, securely rest:
These Accents were her last; the creeping Death
Benum'd her Senses first, then stopp'd her Breath.

Thus she for Disobedience justly dy'd;
The Sire was justly punish'd for his Pride:
The Youth, least guilty, suffer'd for th' Offence
Of Duty violated to his Prince;
Who late repenting of his cruel Deed,
One common Sepulcher for both decreed;
Intomb'd the wretched Pair in Royal State,
And on their Monument inscrib'd their Fate.

THEODORE AND HONORIA

FROM *BOCCACE*

Of all the Cities in *Romanian* Lands,
The chief, and most renown'd *Ravenna* stands:
Adorn'd in ancient Times with Arms and Arts,
And rich Inhabitants, with generous Hearts.
But *Theodore* the Brave, above the rest,
With Gifts of Fortune, and of Nature bless'd,
The foremost Place, for Wealth and Honour held,
And all in Feats of Chivalry excell'd.

This noble Youth to Madness lov'd a Dame,
Of high Degree, *Honoria* was her Name:
Fair as the Fairest, but of haughty Mind,
And fiercer than became so soft a kind;
Proud of her Birth; (for equal she had none;)
The rest she scorn'd; but hated him alone.
His Gifts, his constant Courtship, nothing gain'd;
For she, the more he lov'd, the more disdain'd:

He liv'd with all the Pomp he cou'd devise,
At Tilts and Turnaments obtain'd the Prize,
But found no favour in his Ladies Eyes:
Relentless as a Rock, the lofty Maid
Turn'd all to Poyson that he did, or said:
Nor Pray'rs, nor Tears, nor offer'd Vows could move;
The Work went backward; and the more he strove
T' advance his Sute, the farther from her Love.

Weary'd at length, and wanting Remedy,
He doubted oft, and oft resolv'd to die.
But Pride stood ready to prevent the Blow,
For who would die to gratify a Foe?
His generous Mind disdain'd so mean a Fate;
That pass'd, his next Endeavour was to Hate.
But vainer that Relief than all the rest,
The less he hop'd with more Desire possess'd;
Love stood the Siege, and would not yield his Breast.

Change was the next, but change deceiv'd his Care,
He sought a Fairer, but found none so Fair.
He would have worn her out by slow degrees,
As Men by Fasting starve th' untam'd Disease:
But present Love requir'd a present Ease.
Looking he feeds alone his famish'd Eyes,
Feeds lingring Death, but looking not he dies.
Yet still he chose the longest way to Fate,
Wasting at once his Life, and his Estate.

His Friends beheld, and pity'd him in vain,
For what Advice can ease a Lover's Pain!
Absence, the best Expedient they could find
Might save the Fortune, if not cure the mind:
This Means they long propos'd, but little gain'd,
Yet after much pursuit, at length obtain'd.

Hard, you may think it was, to give consent,
But, struggling with his own Desires, he went:
With large Expence, and with a pompous Train,
Provided, as to visit *France* or *Spain*,
Or for some distant Voyage o'er the Main.
But Love had clipp'd his Wings, and cut him short,
Confin'd within the purlieus of his Court:

Three Miles he went, nor farther could retreat;
His Travels ended at his Country-Seat:
To *Chassis* pleasing Plains he took his way,
There pitch'd his Tents, and there resolv'd to stay.

The Spring was in the Prime; the neighb'ring Grove,
Supply'd with Birds, the Choristers of Love:
Musick unbought, that minister'd Delight,
The Morning-walks, and lull'd his Cares by Night:
There he discharg'd his Friends; but not th' Expence
Of frequent Treats, and proud Magnificence.
He liv'd as Kings retire, though more at large,
From publick Business, yet with equal Charge;
With House, and Heart still open to receive;
As well content, as Love would give him leave:
He would have liv'd more free; but many a Guest,
Who could forsake the Friend, pursu'd the Feast.

It happ'd one Morning, as his Fancy led,
Before his usual Hour, he left his Bed;
To walk within a lonely Lawn, that stood
On ev'ry side, surrounded by the Wood:
Alone he walk'd, to please his pensive Mind,
And sought the deepest Solitude to find:
'Twas in a Grove of spreading Pines he stray'd;
The Winds, within the quiv'ring Branches plaid,
And Dancing-Trees a mournful Musick made.
The Place it self was suiting to his Care,
Uncouth, and Salvage, as the cruel Fair.
He wander'd on, unknowing where he went,
Lost in the Wood, and all on Love intent:
The Day already half his Race had run,
And summon'd him to due Repast at Noon,
But Love could feel no Hunger but his own.

While list'ning to the murm'ring Leaves he stood,
More than a Mile immers'd within the Wood,
At once the Wind was laid; the whisp'ring sound
Was dumb; a rising Earthquake rock'd the Ground:
With deeper Brown the Grove was overspread:
A suddain Horror seiz'd his giddy Head,
And his Ears tinckled, and his Colour fled.

Nature was in alarm; some Danger nigh
Seem'd threaten'd, though unseen to mortal Eye:
Unus'd to fear, he summon'd all his Soul
And stood collected in himself, and whole;
Not long: For soon a Whirlwind rose around,
And from afar he heard a screaming sound,
As of a Dame distress'd, who cry'd for Aid,
And fill'd with loud Laments the secret Shade.

A Thicket close beside the Grove there stood
With Breers, and Brambles choak'd, and dwarfish Wood:
From thence the Noise: Which now approaching near
With more distinguish'd Notes invades his Ear:
He rais'd his Head, and saw a beauteous Maid,
With Hair dishevell'd, issuing through the Shade;
Stripp'd of her Cloaths, and e'en those Parts reveal'd,
Which modest Nature keeps from Sight conceal'd.
Her Face, her Hands, her naked Limbs were torn,
With passing through the Brakes, and prickly Thorn:
Two Mastiffs gaunt and grim, her Flight pursu'd,
And oft their fasten'd Fangs in Blood imbru'd:
Oft they came up and pinch'd her tender Side,
Mercy, O Mercy, Heav'n, she ran, and cry'd;
When Heav'n was nam'd they loos'd their Hold again,
Then sprung she forth, they follow'd her amain.

Not far behind, a Knight of swarthy Face,
High on a Coal-black Steed pursu'd the Chace;
With flashing Flames his ardent Eyes were fill'd,
And in his Hands a naked Sword he held:
He chear'd the Dogs to follow her who fled,
And vow'd Revenge on her devoted Head.

As *Theodore* was born of noble Kind,
The brutal Action rowz'd his manly Mind:
Mov'd with unworthy Usage of the Maid,
He, though unarm'd, resolv'd to give her Aid.
A Saplin Pine he wrench'd from out the Ground,
The readiest Weapon that his Fury found.
Thus furnish'd for Offence, he cross'd the way
Betwixt the graceless Villain, and his Prey.

The Knight came thund'ring on, but from afar
Thus in imperious Tone forbad the War:
Cease, *Theodore*, to proffer vain Relief,
Nor stop the vengeance of so just a Grief;
But give me leave to seize my destin'd Prey,
And let eternal Justice take the way:
I but revenge my Fate; disdain'd, betray'd,
And suff'ring Death for this ungrateful Maid.

He say'd; at once dismounting from the Steed;
For now the Hell-hounds with superiour Speed
Had reach'd the Dame, and fast'ning on her Side,
The Ground with issuing Streams of Purple dy'd.
Stood *Theodore* surpriz'd in deadly Fright,
With chatt'ring Teeth and bristling Hair upright;
Yet arm'd with inborn Worth, What e'er, said he,
Thou art, who know'st me better than I thee;
Or prove thy rightful Cause, or be defy'd:
The Spectre, fiercely staring, thus reply'd.

Know, *Theodore*, thy Ancestry I claim,
And *Guido Cavalcanti* was my Name.
One common Sire our Fathers did beget,
My Name and Story some remember yet:
Thee, then a Boy, within my Arms I laid,
When for my Sins I lov'd this haughty Maid;
Not less ador'd in Life, nor serv'd by Me,
Than proud *Honoria* now is lov'd by Thee.
What did I not her stubborn Heart to gain?
But all my Vows were answer'd with Disdain;
She scorn'd my Sorrows, and despis'd my Pain.
Long time I dragg'd my Days in fruitless Care,
Then loathing Life, and plung'd in deep Despair,
To finish my unhappy Life, I fell
On this sharp Sword, and now am damn'd in Hell.

Short was her Joy; for soon th' insulting Maid
By Heav'n's Decree in the cold Grave was laid,
And as in unrepenting Sin she dy'd,
Doom'd to the same bad Place, is punish'd for her Pride;
Because she deem'd I well deserv'd to die,
And made a Merit of her Cruelty.

There, then, we met; both try'd and both were cast,
And this irrevocable Sentence pass'd;
That she whom I so long pursu'd in vain,
Should suffer from my Hands a lingring Pain:
Renew'd to Life, that she might daily die,
I daily doom'd to follow, she to fly;
No more a Lover but a mortal Foe,
I seek her Life (for Love is none below:)
As often as my Dogs with better speed
Arrest her Flight, is she to Death decreed:
Then with this fatal Sword on which I dy'd,
I pierce her open'd Back or tender Side,
And tear that harden'd Heart from out her Breast,
Which, with her Entrails, makes my hungry Hounds a Feast.
Nor lies she long, but as her Fates ordain,
Springs up to Life, and fresh to second Pain,
Is sav'd to Day, to Morrow to be slain.

This, vers'd in Death, th' infernal Knight relates,
And then for Proof fulfill'd their common Fates;
Her Heart and Bowels through her Back he drew,
And fed the Hounds that help'd him to pursue.
Stern look'd the Fiend, as frustrate of his Will
Not half suffic'd, and greedy yet to kill.
And now the Soul expiring through the Wound,
Had left the Body breathless on the Ground,
When thus the grisly Spectre spoke again:
Behold the Fruit of ill-rewarded Pain:
As many Months as I sustain'd her Hate,
So many Years is she condemn'd by Fate
To daily Death; and ev'ry several Place,
Conscious of her Disdain, and my Disgrace,
Must witness her just Punishment; and be
A Scene of Triumph and Revenge to me.
As in this Grove I took my last Farewel,
As on this very spot of Earth I fell,
As *Friday* saw me die, so she my Prey
Becomes ev'n here, on this revolving Day.

Thus while he spoke, the Virgin from the Ground
Upstarted fresh, already clos'd the Wound,
And unconcern'd for all she felt before
Precipitates her Flight along the Shore:

The Hell-hounds, as ungorg'd with Flesh and Blood
Pursue their Prey, and seek their wonted Food:
The Fiend remounts his Courser; mends his Pace,
And all the Vision vanish'd from the Place.

Long stood the noble Youth oppress'd with Awe,
And stupid at the wond'rous Things he saw
Surpassing common Faith; transgressing Nature's Law.
He would have been asleep, and wish'd to wake,
But Dreams, he knew, no long Impression make,
Though strong at first: If Vision, to what end,
But such as must his future State portend?
His Love the Damsel, and himself the Fiend.
But yet reflecting that it could not be
From Heav'n, which cannot impious Acts decree,
Resolv'd within himself to shun the Snare
Which Hell for his Distruction did prepare;
And as his better Genius should direct
From an ill Cause to draw a good effect.

Inspir'd from Heav'n he homeward took his way,
Nor pall'd his new Design with long delay:
But of his Train a trusty Servant sent;
To call his Friends together at his Tent.
They came, and usual Salutations paid,
With Words premeditated thus he said:
What you have often counsell'd, to remove
My vain pursuit of unreguarded Love;
By Thrift my sinking Fortune to repair,
Tho' late, yet is at last become my Care:
My Heart shall be my own; my vast Expence
Reduc'd to bounds, by timely Providence:
This only I require; invite for me
Honoria, with her Father's Family,
Her Friends, and mine; the Cause I shall display,
On *Friday* next, for that's th' appointed Day.

Well pleas'd were all his Friends, the Task was light;
The Father, Mother, Daughter they invite;
Hardly the Dame was drawn to this repast;
But yet resolv'd, because it was the last.
The Day was come; the Guests invited came,
And, with the rest, th' inexorable Dame:

A Feast prepar'd with riotous Expence,
Much Cost, more Care, and most Magnificence.
The Place ordain'd was in that haunted Grove,
Where the revenging Ghost pursu'd his Love:
The Tables in a proud Pavilion spred,
With Flow'rs below, and Tissue overhead:
The rest in rank; *Honoria* chief in place,
Was artfully contriv'd to set her Face
To front the Thicket, and behold the Chace.
The Feast was serv'd; the time so well forecast,
That just when the Dessert, and Fruits were plac'd,
The Fiend's Alarm began; the hollow sound
Sung in the Leaves, the Forest shook around,
Air blacken'd; rowl'd the Thunder; groan'd the Ground.

Nor long before the loud Laments arise,
Of one distress'd, and Mastiffs mingled Cries;
And first the Dame came rushing through the Wood,
And next the famish'd Hounds that sought their Food
And grip'd her Flanks, and oft essay'd their Jaws in Blood.
Last came the Fellon on the Sable Steed,
Arm'd with his naked Sword, and urg'd his Dogs to speed:
She ran, and cry'd; her Flight directly bent,
(A Guest unbidden) to the fatal Tent,
The Scene of Death, and Place ordain'd for Punishment.
Loud was the Noise, aghast was every Guest,
The Women shriek'd, the Men forsook the Feast;
The Hounds at nearer distance hoarsly bay'd;
The Hunter close pursu'd the visionary Maid,
She rent the Heav'n with loud Laments, imploring aid.

The Gallants to protect the Ladies right,
Their Fauchions brandish'd at the grisly Spright;
High on his Stirups, he provok'd the Fight.
Then on the Crowd he cast a furious Look,
And wither'd all their Strength before he strook:
Back on your Lives; let be, said he, my Prey,
And let my Vengeance take the destin'd way.
Vain are your Arms, and vainer your Defence,
Against th' eternal Doom of Providence:
Mine is th' ungrateful Maid by Heav'n design'd:
Mercy she would not give, nor Mercy shall she find.

At this the former Tale again he told
With thund'ring Tone, and dreadful to behold:
Sunk were their Hearts with Horror of the Crime,
Nor needed to be warn'd a second time,
But bore each other back; some knew the Face,
And all had heard the much lamented Case,
Of him who fell for Love, and this the fatal Place.

And now th' infernal Minister advanc'd,
Seiz'd the due Victim, and with Fury lanch'd
Her Back, and piercing through her inmost Heart,
Drew backward, as before, th' offending part.
The reeking Entrails next he tore away,
And to his meagre Mastiffs made a Prey:
The pale Assistants, on each other star'd
With gaping Mouths for issuing Words prepar'd;
The still-born sounds upon the Palate hung,
And dy'd imperfect on the faltring Tongue.
The Fright was general; but the Female Band
(A helpless Train) in more Confusion stand;
With Horror shuddring, on a heap they run,
Sick at the sight of hateful Justice done;
For Conscience rung th' Alarm, and made the Case their own.

So spread upon a Lake with upward Eye
A plump of Fowl, behold their Foe on high,
They close their trembling Troop; and all attend
On whom the sowsing Eagle will descend.

But most the proud *Honoria* fear'd th' event,
And thought to her alone the Vision sent.
Her Guilt presents to her distracted Mind
Heav'ns Justice, *Theodore*'s revengeful Kind,
And the same Fate to the same Sin assign'd;
Already sees her self the Monster's Prey,
And feels her Heart, and Entrails torn away.
'Twas a mute Scene of Sorrow, mix'd with fear,
Still on the Table lay th' unfinish'd Cheer:
The Knight, and hungry Mastiffs stood around,
The mangled Dame lay breathless on the Ground:
When on a suddain reinspired with Breath,
Again she rose, again to suffer Death;

Nor stay'd the Hell-hounds, nor the Hunter stay'd,
But follow'd, as before, the flying Maid:
Th' Avenger took from Earth th' avenging Sword,
And mounting light as Air, his Sable Steed he spurr'd:
The Clouds dispell'd, the Sky resum'd her Light,
And Nature stood recover'd of her Fright.

But Fear, the last of Ills, remain'd behind,
And Horror heavy sat on ev'ry Mind.
Nor *Theodore* incourag'd more his Feast,
But sternly look'd, as hatching in his Breast
Some deep Design, which when *Honoria* view'd,
The fresh Impulse her former Fright renew'd:
She thought her self the trembling Dame who fled,
And him the grisly Ghost that spurr'd th' infernal Steed:
The more dismay'd, for when the Guests withdrew
Their courteous Host saluting all the Crew,
Regardless pass'd her o'er; nor grac'd with kind adieu.
That Sting infix'd within her haughty Mind,
The downfal of her Empire she divin'd;
And her proud Heart with secret Sorrow pin'd.
Home as they went, the sad Discourse renew'd,
Of the relentless Dame to Death pursu'd,
And of the Sight obscene so lately view'd.
None durst arraign the righteous Doom she bore,
Ev'n they who pity'd most yet blam'd her more:
The Parallel they needed not to name,
But in the Dead they damn'd the living Dame.

At ev'ry little Noise she look'd behind,
For still the Knight was present to her Mind:
And anxious oft she started on the way,
And thought the Horseman-Ghost came thundring for his Prey.
Return'd, she took her Bed, with little Rest,
But in short Slumbers dreamt the Funeral Feast:
Awak'd, she turn'd her Side; and slept again,
The same black Vapors mounted in her Brain,
And the same Dreams return'd with double Pain.

Now forc'd to wake because afraid to sleep
Her Blood all Fever'd, with a furious Leap

She sprung from Bed, distracted in her Mind,
And fear'd, at every Step, a twitching Spright behind.
Darkling and desp'rate with a stagg'ring pace,
Of Death afraid, and conscious of Disgrace;
Fear, Pride, Remorse, at once her Heart assail'd,
Pride put Remorse to flight, but Fear prevail'd.
Friday, the fatal Day, when next it came,
Her Soul forethought the Fiend would change his Game,
And her pursue, or *Theodore* be slain,
And two Ghosts join their Packs to hunt her o'er the Plain.

This dreadful Image so possess'd her Mind,
That desp'rate any Succour else to find,
She ceas'd all farther hope; and now began
To make reflection on th' unhappy Man.
Rich, Brave, and Young, who past expression lov'd,
Proof to Disdain; and not to be remov'd:
Of all the Men respected, and admir'd,
Of all the Dames, expect her self, desir'd,
Why not of her? Preferr'd above the rest
By him with Knightly Deeds, and open Love profess'd?
So had another been; where he his Vows address'd.
This quell'd her Pride, yet other Doubts remain'd,
That once disdaining she might be disdain'd:
The Fear was just, but greater Fear prevail'd.
Fear of her Life by hellish Hounds assail'd:
He took a low'ring leave; but who can tell,
What outward Hate, might inward Love conceal?
Her Sexes Arts she knew, and why not then,
Might deep dissembling have a place in Men?
Here Hope began to dawn; resolv'd to try,
She fix'd on this her utmost Remedy;
Death was behind, but hard it was to die.
'Twas time enough at last on Death to call,
The Precipice in sight: A Shrub was all,
That kindly stood betwixt to break the fatal fall.

One Maid she had, belov'd above the rest,
Secure of her, the Secret she confess'd:
And now the chearful Light her Fears dispell'd.
She with no winding turns the Truth conceal'd,
But put the Woman off, and stood reveal'd:

With Faults confess'd commission'd her to go,
If Pity yet had place, and reconcile her Foe:
The welcom Message made, was soon receiv'd;
'Twas what he wish'd, and hop'd, but scarce believ'd;
Fate seem'd a fair occasion to present,
He knew the Sex, and fear'd she might repent,
Should he delay the moment of Consent.
There yet remain'd to gain her Friends (a Care
The modesty of Maidens well might spare;)
But she with such a Zeal the Cause embrac'd,
(As Women where they will, are all in hast)
The Father, Mother, and the Kin beside,
Were overborn by fury of the Tide:
With full consent of all, she chang'd her State,
Resistless in her Love, as in her Hate.

By her Example warn'd, the rest beware;
More Easy, less Imperious, were the Fair;
And that one Hunting which the Devil design'd,
For one fair Female, lost him half the Kind.

PROSE

OF DRAMATICK POESIE

AN ESSAY

——————Fungar vice cotis, acutum
Reddere quae ferrum valet, exors ipsa secandi.
Horat. De Arte Poet.[1]

[1] I shall act as a whetstone, which is able to sharpen iron, though of itself it cannot cut. (*Ars Poetica* 304–5.)

Of Dramatick Poesie, An Essay. By John Dreyden, Servant to His Majesty. [*Latin quot.*] London, Printed for Henry Herringman, at the Sign of the Anchor on the Lower-Walk of the New-Exchange. 1684.

THE *Essay* was first published in 1668 and for the second edition (Macdonald, 127 b i), which the present text follows, Dryden made many changes modernising the syntax. It is usual to prefer the style of the first edition—the argument for the preference is that the language is less considered and more spontaneous—but, since this is the poet's most notable contribution to criticism, I have followed the second edition, believing that the revised text, as it received his final stamp, most clearly expresses his opinions.

TO THE RIGHT HONOURABLE

CHARLES LORD BUCKHURST[1]

My LORD,

As I was lately reviewing my loose Papers, amongst the rest I found this Essay, the writing of which in this rude and indigested manner wherein your Lordship now sees it, serv'd as an amusement to me in the Country, when the violence of the last Plague had driven me from the Town. Seeing then our Theaters shut up, I was engag'd in these kind of thoughts with the same delight with which men think upon their absent Mistresses: I confess I find many things in this Discourse which I do not now approve; my Judgment being not a little alter'd since the writing of it, but whether for the better or the worse I know not: Neither indeed is it much material in an Essay, where all I have said is problematical. For the way of writing Plays in Verse, which I have seem'd to favour, I have since that time laid the practice of it aside, till I have more leisure, because I find it troublesome and slow. But I am no way alter'd from my opinion of it, at least with any reasons which have oppos'd it. For your Lordship may easily observe that none are very violent against it, but those who either have not attempted it, or who have succeeded ill in their attempt. 'Tis enough for me to have your Lordships example for my excuse in that little which I have done in it; and I am sure my Adversaries can bring no such Arguments against Verse, as those with which the fourth Act of Pompey[2] *will furnish me in its defence. Yet, my Lord, you must suffer me a little to complain of you, that you too soon withdraw from us a contentment, of which we expected the continuance, because you gave it us so early. 'Tis a revolt without occasion from your Party, where your Merits had already rais'd you to the highest Commands, and where you have not the excuse of other Men that you have been ill us'd, and therefore laid down Arms. I know no other Quarrel you can have to Verse, than that which* Spurina *had to his Beauty, when he tore and mangled the Features of his Face,*

[1] Charles Sackville, Lord Buckhurst (1638–1707), the *Eugenius* of this *Essay*.

[2] Lord Buckhurst had collaborated in a translation of Pierre Corneille's tragedy of *La Mort de Pompée*, which, entitled *Pompey the Great*, was published in 1664.

only because they pleas'd too well the sight. It was an Honour which seem'd to wait for you, to lead out a new Colony of Writers from the Mother Nation: and upon the first spreading of your Ensigns, there had been many in a readiness to have follow'd so fortunate a Leader; if not all, yet the better part of Poets.

Pars, indocili melior grege; mollis & expes
Inominata perprimat cubilia.[1]

I am almost of opinion, that we should force you to accept of the Command, as sometimes the Prætorian *Bands have compell'd their Captains to receive the Empire. The Court, which is the best and surest Judge of writing, has generally allow'd of Verse; and in the Town it has found Favourers of Wit and Quality. As for your own particular, My Lord, you have yet Youth, and time enough to give part of them to the divertisement of the Publick, before you enter into the serious and more unpleasant business of the World. That which the French Poet said of the Temple of Love, may be as well apply'd to the Temple of the Muses. The words, as near as I can remember them, were these :*

Le jeune homme, à mauvaise grace,
N'ayant pas adoré dans le Temple d'Amour:
Il faut qu'il entre; & pour le sage
Si ce n'est pas son vray sejour
C'est un giste sur son passage.

I leave the words to work their effect upon your Lordship in their own Language, because no other can so well express the nobleness of the thought; and wish you may be soon call'd to bear a part in the Affairs of the Nation, where I know the World expects you, and wonders why you have been so long forgotten; there being no Person amongst our young Nobility, on whom the eyes of all men are so much bent. But in the mean time your Lordship may imitate the course of Nature, who gives us the Flower before the Fruit: that I may speak to you in the Language of the Muses, which I have taken from an excellent Poem to the King.

As Nature, when she Fruit designs, thinks fit
By beauteous blossoms to proceed to it;
And while she does accomplish all the Spring,
Birds to her secret Operations sing.

I confess I have no greater reason, in addressing this Essay to your Lordship, than that it might awaken in you the desire of

[1] . . . . Those of us who know better than the unteachable mob; and let the weak-willed and hopeless continue to burden his ill-starred couch. (Horace, *Epodes* 16. 37–8.)

writing something, in whatever kind it be, which might be an Honour to our Age and Country. And me thinks it might have the same effect on you, which Homer *tells us the fight of the* Greeks *and* Trojans *before the Fleet had on the Spirit of* Achilles, *who though he had resolv'd not to ingage, yet found a Martial Warmth to steal upon him, at the sight of Blows, the sound of Trumpets, and the cries of fighting Men. For my own part, if, in treating of this subject, I sometimes dissent from the Opinion of better Wits, I declare it is not so much to combat their Opinions, as to defend my own, which were first made publick. Sometimes, like a Scholar in a Fencing-School, I put forth my self, and shew my own ill play, on purpose to be better taught. Sometimes I stand desperately to my Arms, like the Foot when deserted by their Horse, not in hope to overcome, but only to yield on more honourable terms. And yet, My Lord, this War of Opinions, you well know, has fallen out among the Writers of all Ages, and sometimes betwixt Friends. Only it has been prosecuted by some, like Pedants, with violence of words, and manag'd by others like Gentlemen, with Candour and Civility. Even* Tully *had a Controversie with his dear* Atticus*; and in one of his Dialogues makes him sustain the part of an Enemy in Philosophy, who in his Letters is his Confident of State, and made privy to the most weighty Affairs of the Roman Senate. And the same respect which was paid by* Tully *to* Atticus, *we find return'd to him afterwards by* Cæsar *on a like occasion, who answering his Book in praise of* Cato, *made it not so much his business to condemn* Cato, *as to praise* Cicero.

But that I may decline some part of the Encounter with my Adversaries, whom I am neither willing to combate, nor well able to resist; I will give your Lordship the Relation of a Dispute betwixt some of our Wits on the same subject, in which they did not only speak of Plays in Verse, but mingled, in the freedom of Discourse, some things of the Ancient, many of the Modern ways of Writing; comparing those with these, and the Wits of our Nation with those of others: 'tis true, they differ'd in their Opinions, as 'tis probable they would: neither do I take upon me to reconcile, but to relate them: and that as Tacitus *professes of himself,* Sine studio partium aut irâ:[1] *without Passion or Interest; leaving your Lordship to decide it in favour of which part you shall judge most reasonable, and withal, to pardon the many Errours of,*

Your Lordships

Most obedient humble servant,

JOHN DREYDEN.

[1] Without party-bias or spite. (*Annals* 1. 1.)

TO THE READER

THE drift of the ensuing Discourse was chiefly to vindicate the Honour of our English Writers, from the censure of those who unjustly prefer the French before them. This I intimate, lest any should think me so exceeding vain, as to teach others an Art which they understand much better than my self. But if this incorrect Essay, written in the Country without the help of Books, or advice of Friends, shall find any acceptance in the World, I promise to my self a better success of the Second Part, wherein I shall more fully treat of the Virtues and Faults of the English Poets, who have written either in this, the Epique, or the Lyrique way.

AN ESSAY OF DRAMATICK POESIE

It was that memorable day,[1] in the first Summer of the late War, when our Navy ingag'd the Dutch: a day wherein the two most mighty and best appointed Fleets which any Age had ever seen, disputed the command of the greater half of the Globe, the commerce of Nations, and the riches of the Universe. While these vast floating Bodies, on either side, mov'd against each other in parallel Lines, and our Countrymen, under the happy Conduct of his Royal Highness, went breaking, by little and little, into the Line of the Enemies; the noise of the Cannon from both Navies reach'd our Ears about the City: so that all Men, being alarm'd with it, and in a dreadful suspence of the event, which they knew was then deciding, every one went following the sound as his fancy led him; and leaving the Town almost empty, some took towards the Park, some cross the River, others down it; all seeking the noise in the depth of silence.

Among the rest, it was the fortune of *Eugenius*, *Crites*, *Lisideius*, and *Neander*,[2] to be in company together: three of them persons whom their Wit and Quality have made known to all the Town: and whom I have chose to hide under these borrowed names, that they may not suffer by so ill a relation as I am going to make of their discourse.

Taking then a Barge which a Servant of *Lisideius* had provided for them, they made haste to shoot the Bridge, and left behind them that great fall of waters which hindered them from hearing what they desired: after which, having disingag'd themselves from many Vessels which rodé at Anchor in the *Thames*, and almost blockt up the passage towards *Greenwich*, they order'd the Watermen to let fall their Oares more gently; and then every one favouring his own curiosity with a strict silence, it was not

[1] 3 June 1665. The English fleet won a great victory over the Dutch on that day.

[2] *Eugenius*, *Crites*, *Lisideius*, and *Neander*: Lord Buckhurst, Sir Robert Howard (1626–1698) dramatist and Dryden's brother-in-law, Sir Charles Sedley (*c.* 1639–1701), poet and dramatist, and Dryden. It has been suggested that the identification of *Crites* with Howard is incorrect, and other names, including that of Roscommon, have been put forward.

long ere they perceiv'd the Air to break about them like the noise of distant Thunder, or of Swallows in a Chimney: those little undulations of sound, though almost vanishing before they reach'd them, yet still seeming to retain somewhat of their first horrour which they had betwixt the Fleets: after they had attentively listned till such time as the sound by little and little went from them; *Eugenius*, lifting up his head, and taking notice of it, was the first who congratulated to the rest that happy Omen of our Nations Victory: adding, that we had but this to desire in confirmation of it, that we might hear no more of that noise, which was now leaving the English Coast. When the rest had concur'd in the same opinion, *Crites*, a person of a sharp judgment, and somewhat too delicate a taste in Wit, which the world have mistaken in him for ill nature, said, smiling to us, that if the concernment of this battel had not been so exceeding great, he could scarce have wish'd the Victory at the price he knew he must pay for it, in being subject to the reading and hearing of so many ill verses as he was sure would be made on that Subject. Adding, that no Argument could scape some of those eternal Rhimers, who watch a Battel with more diligence than the Ravens and birds of Prey; and the worst of them surest to be first in upon the quarry, while the better able, either out of modesty writ not at all, or set that due value upon their Poems, as to let them be often desired and long expected! There are some of those impertinent people of whom you speak, answer'd *Lisideius*, who to my knowledge, are already so provided, either way, that they can produce not only a Panegirick upon the Victory, but, if need be, a Funeral Elegy on the Duke: wherein after they have crown'd his valour with many Lawrels, they will at last deplore the odds under which he fell, concluding that his courage deserv'd a better destiny. All the company smil'd at the conceipt of *Lisideius*; but *Crites*, more eager than before, began to make particular exceptions against some Writers, and said the publick Magistrate ought to send betimes to forbid them; and that it concern'd the peace and quiet of all honest people, that ill Poets should be as well silenc'd as seditious Preachers. In my opinion, replyed *Eugenius*, you pursue your point too far; for as to my own particular, I am so great a lover of Poesie, that I could wish them all rewarded who attempt but to do well; at least I would not have them worse us'd than one of their brethren was by *Sylla* the Dictator: *Quem in concione vidimus* (says *Tully*) *cum ei libellum malus poeta de populo subjecisset, quod epigramma in eum fecisset tantummodo alternis versibus longiusculis, statim ex iis rebus quas tunc vendebat jubere ei præmium tribui, sub ea conditione ne quid postea scriberet.*[1] I could wish with all my heart, replied *Crites*, that many whom we know were as bountifully thank'd upon the same condition, that they would never trouble us again. For amongst others, I have a mortal apprehension of two Poets, whom this victory with the help of both her wings will never be able to escape; 'tis easie to guess whom you intend, said *Lisideius*; and without naming them, I ask you if one of them[2] does not perpetually pay us with clenches upon words and a certain clownish kind of raillery? if now and then he does not offer at a Catecresis or Clevelandism,[3] wresting and torturing a word into another meaning: In fine, if he be not one of those whom the French would call *un mauvais buffon*; one who is so much a well-willer to the Satire, that he intends at least, to spare no man; and though he cannot strike a blow to hurt any, yet he ought to be punish'd for the malice of the action; as our Witches are justly hang'd because they think themselves to be such: and suffer deservedly for believing they did mischief, because they meant it. You have described him, said *Crites*, so exactly, that I am affraid to come after you with my other extremity of Poetry: He is one of those who having had some advantage of education and converse, knows better than the other what a Poet should be, but puts it into practice more unluckily than any man; his stile and matter are every where alike; he is the most calm, peaceable Writer you ever read: he never disquiets your passions with the least concernment, but still leaves you in as even a temper as he found you; he is a very Leveller in Poetry, he creeps along with ten little words in every line, and helps out his Numbers with *For to*, and *Unto*, and all the pretty Expletives he can find, till he drags them to the end of another line; while the Sense is left tir'd half way behind it: he doubly starves all his Verses, first for want of thought, and then of expression; his Poetry neither has wit in it, nor seems to have it; like him in *Martial*.

Pauper videri Cinna vult, & est pauper:[4]

[1] We have seen him at a public meeting, when a bad poet, one of the crowd, had simply composed an epigram against him in rather lengthy couplets, order a reward to be paid to the fellow out of the property he was selling at the time—on the condition that he wrote nothing more. (Cicero, *Pro Archia*, 25.)

[2] Robert Wild (1609–1679), a metaphysical poet, whose chief work was *Iter Boreale*, 1660.

[3] John Cleveland (1613–1658), the most extravagant of the metaphysical poets.

[4] Cinna wishes to seem poor, and poor he is, in fact. (*Epigrams* 8. 19.)

He affects plainness, to cover his want of imagination: when he writes the serious way, the highest flight of his fancy is some miserable *Antithesis*, or seeming contradiction; and in the Comick he is still reaching at some thin conceit, the ghost of a Jest, and that too flies before him, never to be caught; these Swallows which we see before us on the *Thames*, are the just resemblance of his Wit: you may observe how near the water they stoop, how many proffers they make to dip, and yet how seldome they touch it: and when they do, 'tis but the surface: they skim over it but to catch a gnat, and then mount into the Air and leave it. Well Gentlemen, said *Eugenius*, you may speak your pleasure of these Authors; but though I and some few more about the Town may give you a peaceable hearing, yet assure your selves, there are multitudes who would think you malicious and them injur'd: especially him whom you first described; he is the very *Withers* of the City: they have bought more Editions of his Works then would serve to lay under all their Pies at the Lord Mayor's *Christmass*. When his famous Poem first came out in the year 1660, I have seen them reading it in the midst of Change-time; nay so vehement they were at it, that they lost their bargain by the Candles ends:[1] but what will you say, if he has been received amongst great Persons; I can assure you he is, this day, the envy of one, who is Lord in the Art of Quibbling; and who does not take it well, that any man should intrude so far into his Province. All I would wish, replied *Crites*, is, that they who love his Writings, may still admire him, and his fellow Poet, *qui Bavium non odit, &c.*[2] is curse sufficient. And farther, added *Lisideius*, I believe there is no man who writes well, but would think he had hard measure, if their Admirers should praise any thing of his: *Nam quos contemnimus eorum quoque laudes contemnimus.*[3] There are so few who write well in this Age, says *Crites*, that methinks any praises should be wellcome; they neither rise to the dignity of the last Age, nor to any of the Ancients; and we may cry out of the Writers of this time, with more reason than *Petronius* of his, *Pace vestrâ liceat dixisse, primi omnium eloquentiam perdidistis:*[4] you have debauched the true old Poetry so far, that Nature, which is the soul of it, is not in any of your Writings.

If your quarrel, (said *Eugenius*) to those who now write, be

[1] A method of auction: bids could be made as long as the candle burnt.

[2] He who hates not Bavius, let him love your poems, Maevius. (Vergil, *Eclogues* 3. 90.)

[3] For if we despise a man, we despise his praises too.

[4] If you will allow me to say so, you have been the very first to ruin the art of speech. (*Satyricon* 2.)

grounded only on your reverence to Antiquity, there is no man more ready to adore those great Greeks and Romans than I am: but on the other side, I cannot think so contemptibly of the Age in which I live or so dishonourably of my own Countrey, as not to judge we equal the Ancients in most kinds of Poesie, and in some surpass them; neither know I any reason why I may not be as zealous for the Reputation of our Age, as we find the Ancients themselves were in reference to those who lived before them. For you hear your *Horace* saying,

> *Indignor quidquam reprehendi, non quia crassé*
> *Compositum, illepidève putetur, sed quia nuper.*[1]

And after,

> *Si meliora dies, ut vina, poemata reddit,*
> *Scire velim pretium chartis quotus arroget annus?*[2]

But I see I am ingaging in a wide dispute, where the arguments are not like to reach close on either side; for Poesie is of so large an extent, and so many both of the Ancients and Moderns have done well in all kinds of it, that in citing one against the other, we shall take up more time this Evening, than each mans occasions will allow him: therefore I would ask *Crites* to what part of Poesie he would confine his Arguments, and whether he would defend the general cause of the Ancients against the Moderns, or oppose any Age of the Moderns against this of ours?

Crites a little while considering upon this Demand, told *Eugenius* that if he pleased, he would limit their Dispute to *Dramatique Poesie*; in which he thought it not difficult to prove, either that the Ancients were superior to the Moderns, or the last Age of this of ours.

Eugenius was somewhat surpriz'd, when he heard *Crites* make choice of that subject; For ought I see, said he, I have undertaken a harder Province than I imagin'd; for though I never judg'd the Plays of the Greek or Roman Poets comparable to ours; yet on the other side those we now see acted, come short of many which were written in the last Age: but my comfort is if we are orecome, it will be onely by our own Countrey-men: and if we yield to them in this one part of Poesie, we more surpass

[1] I think it far from proper that any poem should be censured on the grounds, not that it is deemed to be written rudely or inelegantly, but that it is new. (*Epistles* 2. 1. 76–7.)

[2] If lapse of time improves poetry as it does wines, I should like to know at how many years' end the paper we write on acquires its value. (*Epistles* 2. 1. 34–5.)

them in all the other; for in the Epique or Lyrique way it will be hard for them to shew us one such amongst them, as we have many now living, or who lately were. They can produce nothing so courtly writ, or which expresses so much the Conversation of a Gentleman, as Sir *John Suckling*; nothing so even, sweet, and flowing as Mr. *Waller*; nothing so Majestique, so correct as Sir *John Denham*; nothing so elevated, so copious, and full of spirit, as Mr. *Cowley*; as for the Italian, French, and Spanish plays, I can make it evident, that those who now write, surpass them; and that the *Drama* is wholly ours.

All of them were thus far of *Eugenius* his opinion, that the sweetness of English Verse was never understood or practis'd by our Fathers; even *Crites* himself did not much oppose it: and every one was willing to acknowledge how much our Poesie is improv'd, by the happiness of some Writers yet living; who first taught us to mould our thoughts into easie and significant words; to retrench the superfluities of expression, and to make our Rime so properly a part of the Verse, that it should never mis-lead the sence, but it self be led and govern'd by it.

Eugenius was going to continue this Discourse, when *Lisideius* told him that it was necessary, before they proceeded further, to take a standing measure of their Controversie; for how was it possible to be decided who writ the best Plays, before we know what a Play should be? but, this once agreed on by both Parties, each might have recourse to it, either to prove his own advantages, or to discover the failings of his Adversary.

He had no sooner said this, but all desir'd the favour of him to give the definition of a Play; and they were the more importunate, because neither *Aristotle*, nor *Horace*, nor any other, who had writ of that Subject, had ever done it.

Lisideius, after some modest denials, at last confess'd he had a rude Notion of it; indeed rather a Description than a Definition: but which serv'd to guide him in his private thoughts, when he was to make a judgment of what others writ: that he conceiv'd a Play ought to be, *A just and lively Image of Humane Nature, representing its Passions and Humours, and the Changes of Fortune to which it is subject; for the Delight and Instruction of Mankind.*

This Definition, though *Crites* raised a Logical Objection against it; that it was onely *a genere & fine*,[1] and so not altogether perfect; was yet well received by the rest: and after they had given order to the Water-men to turn their Barge, and row softly, that they might take the cool of the Evening in their return; *Crites*,

[1] By genus and purpose.

being desired by the Company to begin, spoke on behalf of the Ancients, in this manner,

If Confidence presage a Victory, *Eugenius*, in his own opinion, has already triumphed over the Ancients; nothing seems more easie to him, than to overcome those whom it is our greatest praise to have imitated well: for we do not only build upon their foundations; but by their modells. *Dramatique Poesie* had time enough, reckoning from *Thespis* (who first invented it) to *Aristophanes*, to be born, to grow up, and to flourish in Maturity. It has been observed of Arts and Sciences, that in one and the same Century they have arriv'd to great perfection; and no wonder, since every Age has a kind of Universal Genius, which inclines those that live in it to some particular Studies: the Work then being push'd on by many hands, must of necessity go forward.

Is it not evident, in these last hundred years (when the Study of Philosophy has been the business of all the *Virtuosi* in *Christendome*) that almost a New Nature has been reveal'd to us? that more errours of the School have been detected, more useful Experiments in Philosophy have been made, more Noble Secrets in Opticks, Medicine, Anatomy, Astronomy, discover'd, than in all those credulous and doting Ages from *Aristotle* to us? so true it is that nothing spreads more fast than Science, when rightly and generally cultivated.

Add to this the more than common emulation that was in those times of writing well; which though it be found in all Ages and all Persons that pretend to the same Reputation; yet Poesie, being then in more esteem than now it is, had greater Honours decreed to the Professors of it; and consequently the Rivalship was more high between them; they had Judges ordain'd to decide their Merit, and Prizes to reward it: and Historians have been diligent to record of *Eschylus, Euripides, Sophocles, Lycophron*, and the rest of them, both who they were that vanquish'd in these Wars of the Theater, and how often they were crown'd: while the Asian Kings, and Grecian Common-wealths scarce afforded them a Nobler Subject than the unmanly Luxuries of a Debauch'd Court, or giddy Intrigues of a Factious City: *Alit æmulatio ingenia* (says *Paterculus*) *& nunc invidia, nunc admiratio incitationem accendit:* Emulation is the Spur of Wit, and sometimes Envy, sometimes Admiration quickens our Endeavours.

But now since the Rewards of Honour are taken away, that Vertuous Emulation is turn'd into direct Malice; yet so slothful, that it contents it self to condemn and cry down others, without attempting to do better: 'Tis a Reputation too unprofitable, to take the necessary pains for it; yet wishing they had it, that desire is incitement enough to hinder others from it. And this, in short, *Eugenius*, is the reason, why you have now so few good Poets; and so many severe Judges: Certainly, to imitate the Ancients well, much labour and long study is required: which pains, I have already shewn, our Poets would want incouragement to take, if yet they had ability to go through the work. Those Ancients have been faithful Imitators and wise Observers of that Nature which is so torn and ill represented in our Plays; they have handed down to us a perfect resemblance of her; which we, like ill Copyers, neglecting to look on, have rendred monstrous, and disfigur'd. But, that you may know how much you are indebted to those your Masters, and be ashamed to have so ill requited them: I must remember you that all the Rules by which we practise the *Drama* at this day, (either such as relate to the justness and symmetry of the Plot; or the Episodical Ornaments, such as Descriptions, Narrations, and other Beauties, which are not essential to the Play;) were delivered to us from the Observations which *Aristotle* made, of those Poets, who either liv'd before him, or were his Contemporaries: we have added nothing of our own, except we have the confidence to say our wit is better; Of which none boast in this our Age, but such as understand not theirs. Of that Book which *Aristotle* has left us, *περὶ τῆς Ποιητικῆς*,[1] *Horace* his Art of Poetry is an excellent Comment, and, I believe, restores to us that Second Book of his concerning Comedy, which is wanting in him.[2]

Out of these two have been extracted the Famous Rules which the French call, *Des Trois Unitez*, or, The Three Unities, which ought to be observ'd in every Regular Play; namely, of Time, Place, and Action.

The unity of Time they comprehend in 24 hours, the compass of a Natural Day; or as near it as can be contriv'd: and the reason of it is obvious to every one, that the time of the feigned action, or fable of the Play, should be proportion'd as near as can be to the duration of that time in which it is represented; since therefore all Playes are acted on the Theater in a space of time much within the compass of 24 hours, that Play is to be thought the nearest imitation of Nature, whose Plot or Action is confin'd within that time; and, by the same Rule which concludes this

[1] The *Poetics*.

[2] Aristotle discussed Comedy in the *Poetics*, but this section of his work is not extant.

general proportion of time, it follows, that all the parts of it are (as near as may be) to be equally sub-divided; namely, that one act take not up the suppos'd time of half a day; which is out of proportion to the rest: since the other four are then to be straightned within the compass of the remaining half; for it is unnatural that one Act, which being spoke or written, is not longer than the rest, should be suppos'd longer by the Audience; 'tis therefore the Poets duty, to take care that no Act should be imagin'd to exceed the time in which it is represented on the Stage; and that the intervalls and inequalities of time be supposed to fall out between the Acts.

This Rule of Time how well it has been observ'd by the Ancients, most of their Playes will witness; you see them in their Tragedies (wherein to follow this Rule, is certainly most difficult) from the very beginning of their Playes, falling close into that part of the Story which they intend for the action or principal object of it; leaving the former part to be delivered by Narration: so that they set the Audience, as it were, at the Post where the Race is to be concluded: and, saving them the tedious expectation of seeing the Poet set out and ride the beginning of the Course, they suffer you not to behold him, till he is in sight of the Goal, and just upon you.

For the Second Unity, which is that of place, the Ancients meant by it, That the Scene ought to be continu'd through the Play, in the same place where it was laid in the beginning: for the Stage, on which it is represented, being but one and the same place, it is unnatural to conceive it many; and those far distant from one another. I will not deny but by the variation of painted Scenes, the fancy (which in these cases will contribute to its own deceit) may sometimes imagine it several places, with some appearance of probability; yet it still carries the greater likelihood of Truth, if those places be suppos'd so near each other, as in the same Town or City; which may all be comprehended under the larger Denomination of one place: for a greater distance will bear no proportion to the shortness of time, which is allotted in the acting, to pass from one of them to another; for the Observation of this, next to the Antients, the French are to be most commended. They tie themselves so strictly to the unity of place, that you never see in any of their Plays, a Scene chang'd in the middle of an Act: if the Act begins in a Garden, a Street, or Chamber, 'tis ended in the same place; and that you may know it to be the same, the Stage is so supplied with persons that it is never empty all the time: he who enters second has business with him who was on before; and before the second quits the Stage, a third appears who has business with him.

This *Corneille* calls *La Liaison des Scenes*, the continuity or joyning of the Scenes; and 'tis a good mark of a well contriv'd Play when all the Persons are known to each other, and every one of them has some affairs with all the rest.

As for the third Unity which is that of Action, the Ancients meant no other by it than what the Logicians do by their *Finis*, the end or scope of any action: that which is the first in Intention, and last in Execution: now the Poet is to aim at one great and compleat action, to the carrying on of which all things in his Play, even the very obstacles, are to be subservient; and the reason of this is as evident as any of the former.

For two Actions equally labour'd and driven on by the Writer, would destroy the unity of the Poem; it would be no longer one Play, but two: not but that there may be many actions in a Play, as *Ben. Jonson* has observ'd in his *Discoveries*; but they must be all subservient to the great one, which our language happily expresses in the name of under-plots: such as in *Terences Eunuch* is the difference and reconcilement of *Thais* and *Phædria*, which is not the cheif business of the Play, but promotes the marriage of *Chærea* and *Chremes's* Sister, principally intended by the Poet. There ought to be but one action, says *Corneille*, that is one compleat action which leaves the mind of the Audience in a full repose: But this cannot be brought to pass but by many other imperfect actions which conduce to it, and hold the Audience in a delightful suspence of what will be.

If by these Rules (to omit many other drawn from the Precepts and Practice of the Ancients) we should judge our modern Plays, 'tis probable, that few of them would endure the tryal: that which should be the business of a day, takes up in some of them an age; instead of one action they are the Epitomes of a mans life; and for one spot of ground (which the Stage should represent) we are sometimes in more Countries than the Map can shew us.

But if we allow the Ancients to have contriv'd well, we must acknowledge them to have written better; questionless we are depriv'd of a great stock of wit in the loss of *Menander* among the Greek Poets, and of *Cæcilius*, *Affranius*, and *Varius*, among the Romans: we may guess at *Menanders* Excellency by the Plays of *Terence*, who translated some of them: and yet wanted so much of him that he was call'd by *C. Cæsar* the Half-*Menander*; and may judge of *Varius*, by the Testimonies of *Horace*, *Martial*, and *Velleius Paterculus*: 'Tis probable that these, could they be recover'd, would decide the controversie; but so long as *Aristophanes* and *Plautus* are extant; while the Tragedies of *Euripides, Sophocles,* and *Seneca* are in our hands, I can never see one of those Plays which are now written, but it encreases my admiration of the Ancients; and yet I must acknowledge further, that to admire them as we ought, we should understand them better than we do. Doubtless many things appear flat to us, the wit of which depended on some custome or story which never came to our knowledge, or perhaps on some Criticism in their language, which being so long dead, and only remaining in their Books, 'tis not possible they should make us understand perfectly. To read *Macrobius,* explaining the propriety and elegancy of many words in *Virgil,* which I had before pass'd over without consideration, as common things, is enough to assure me that I ought to think the same of *Terence*; and that in the purity of his style (which *Tully* so much valued that he ever carried his works about him) there is yet left in him great room for admiration, if I knew but where to place it. In the mean time I must desire you to take notice, that the greatest man of the last age (*Ben. Johnson*) was willing to give place to them in all things: He was not only a professed Imitator of *Horace,* but a learned Plagiary of all the others; you track him every where in their Snow: if *Horace, Lucan, Petronius Arbiter, Seneca,* and *Juvenal,* had their own from him, there are few serious thoughts which are new in him; you will pardon me therefore if I presume he lov'd their fashion when he wore their cloaths. But since I have otherwise a great veneration for him, and you, *Eugenius,* prefer him above all other Poets, I will use no farther argument to you than his example: I will produce before you Father *Ben.* dress'd in all the ornaments and colours of the Ancients, you will need no other guide to our Party if you follow him; and whether you consider the bad Plays of our Age, or regard the good Plays of the last, both the best and worst of the Modern Poets will equally instruct you to admire the Ancients.

Crites had no sooner left speaking, but *Eugenius,* who had waited with some impatience for it, thus began:

I have observ'd in your Speech that the former part of it is convincing as to what the Moderns have profited by the rules of the Ancients, but in the latter you are careful to conceal how much they have excell'd them: we own all the helps we have from them, and want neither Veneration nor Gratitude while we acknowledge that to overcome them we must make use of the advantages we have receiv'd from them; but to these Assistances we have joyned our own industry; for (had we sate down with a dull imitation of them) we might then have lost somewhat of the old perfection, but never acquir'd any that was new. We draw not therefore after their lines, but those of Nature; and having the life before us, besides the experience of all they knew, it is no wonder if we hit some airs and features which they have miss'd; I deny not what you urge of Arts and Sciences, that they have flourish'd in some ages more than others; but your instance in Philosophy makes for me: for if Natural Causes be more known now than in the time of *Aristotle*, because more studied, it follows that Poesie and other Arts may with the same pains arrive still neerer to perfection, and, that granted, it will rest for you to prove that they wrought more perfect Images of humane life than we; which, seeing in your Discourse you have avoided to make good, it shall now be my task to shew you some part of their defects, and some few Excellencies of the Moderns; and I think there is none among us can imagine I do it enviously, or with purpose to detract from them; for what interest of Fame or Profit can the living lose by the reputation of the dead? on the other side, it is a great truth which *Velleius Paterculus* affirms, *Audita visis libentius laudamus; & præsentia invidiâ, præterita admiratione prosequimur; & his nos obrui, illis instrui credimus*:[1] That praise or censure is certainly the most sincere which unbrib'd posterity shall give us.

Be pleased then in the first place to take notice, that the Greek Poesie, which *Crites* has affirm'd to have arriv'd to perfection in the Reign of the old Comedy, was so far from it, that the distinction of it into Acts was not known to them; or if it were, it is yet so darkly deliver'd to us that we cannot make it out.

All we know of it is from the singing of their Chorus, and that too is so uncertain that in some of their Plays we have reason to conjecture they sung more than five times: *Aristotle* indeed divides the integral parts of a Play into four: First, The *Protasis* or entrance, which gives light only to the Characters of the persons, and proceeds very little into any part of the action: Secondly, The *Epitasis*, or working up of the Plot where the Play grows warmer: the design or action of it is drawing on, and you see something promising that it will come to pass: Thirdly, the *Catastasis*, call'd by the Romans, *Status*, the heighth, and full growth of the Play:

[1] We are readier to praise things we have heard of than things we have seen: upon those of the present we bestow malice, on those of the past, admiration; and we consider ourselves to be oppressed by the former, but instructed by the latter. (2. 92.)

we may call it properly the Counterturn, which destroys that expectation, imbroyls the action in new difficulties, and leaves you far distant from that hope in which it found you, as you may have observ'd in a violent stream resisted by a narrow passage; it runs round to an eddy, and carries back the waters with more swiftness than it brought them on: Lastly, the *Catastrophe*, which the Grecians call'd λύσις[1] the French *le denouement*, and we the discovery or unravelling of the Plot: there you see all things setling again upon their first foundations, and the obstacles which hindred the design or action of the Play once remov'd, it ends with that resemblance of truth and nature, that the audience are satisfied with the conduct of it. Thus this great man deliver'd to us the image of a Play, and I must confess it is so lively that from thence much light has been deriv'd to the forming it more perfectly into Acts [and] Scenes; but what Poet first limited to five the number of the Acts I know not; only we see it so firmly establish'd in the time of *Horace*, that he gives it for a rule in Comedy; *Neu brevior quinto, neu sit productior actu:*[2] So that you see the Grecians cannot be said to have consummated this Art; writing rather by Entrances than by Acts, and having rather a general indigested notion of a Play, than knowing how and where to bestow the particular graces of it.

But since the Spaniards at this day allow but three Acts, which they call *Jornadas*, to a Play; and the Italians in many of theirs follow them, when I condemn the Ancients, I declare it is not altogether because they have not five Acts to every Play, but because they have not confin'd themselves to one certain number; 'tis building an House without a Model: and when they succeeded in such undertakings, they ought to have sacrific'd to Fortune, not to the Muses.

Next, for the Plot, which *Aristotle* called τὸ μῦθος,[3] and often τῶν πραγμάτων σύνθεσις,[4] and from him the Romans *Fabula*, it has already been judiciously observ'd by a late Writer, that in their Tragedies it was only some Tale deriv'd from *Thebes* or *Troy*, or at least some thing that happen'd in those two Ages; which was worn so thred bare by the Pens of all the Epique Poets, and even by tradition itself of the Talkative Greeklings (as *Ben. Johnson* calls them) that before it came upon the Stage, it was already known to all the Audience: and the people so soon as ever they

[1] Literally, 'untying'.

[2] Let it not be shorter than five acts, nor yet prolonged beyond that number. (*Ars Poetica* 189.)

[3] The plot.

[4] The composition of the story.

heard the Name of *Oedipus*, knew as well as the Poet, that he had kill'd his Father by a mistake, and committed Incest with his Mother, before the Play; that they were now to hear of a great Plague, an Oracle, and the Ghost of *Laius*: so that they sate with a yawning kind of expectation, till he was to come with his eyes pull'd out, and speak a hundred or more verses in a Tragick tone, in complaint of his misfortunes. But one *Oedipus*, *Hercules*, or *Medea*, had been tolerable; poor people they scap'd not so good cheap: they had still the *Chapon Bouillé* set before them, till their appetites were cloy'd with the same dish, and the Novelty being gone, the pleasure vanish'd: so that one main end of *Dramatique Poesie* in its Definition, which was to cause Delight, was of consequence destroy'd.

In their Comedies, The Romans generally borrow'd their Plots from the Greek Poets; and theirs was commonly a little Girl stollen or wandred from her Parents, brought back unknown to the City, there got with child by some lewd young fellow; who, by the help of his servant, cheats his father, and when her time comes, to cry *Juno Lucina fer opem*;[1] one or other sees a little Box or Cabinet which was carried away with her, and so discovers her to her friends, if some God do not prevent it, by coming down in a Machine, and taking the thanks of it to himself.

By the Plot you may guess much of the Characters of the Persons. An Old Father who would willingly before he dies see his Son well married; his Debauch'd Son, kind in his Nature to his Mistres, but miserably in want of Money; a Servant or Slave, who has so much wit to strike in with him, and help to dupe his Father; a Braggadochio Captain, a Parasite, and a Lady of Pleasure.

As for the poor honest Maid, on whom the Story is built, and who ought to be one of the principal Actors in the Play, she is commonly a Mute in it: She has the breeding of the Old *Elizabeth* way, which was for Maids to be seen and not to be heard; and it is enough you know she is willing to be married, when the Fifth Act requires it.

These are Plots built after the Italian Mode of Houses, you see thorow them all at once; the Characters are indeed the Imitations of Nature, but so narrow as if they had imitated only an Eye or an Hand, and did not dare to venture on the lines of a Face, or the Proportion of a Body.

But in how straight a compass soever they have bounded their Plots and Characters, we will pass it by, if they have regularly pursued them, and perfectly observ'd those three Unities of Time,

[1] Juno, goddess of childbirth, lend thine aid!

Place, and Action: the knowledge of which you say is deriv'd to us from them. But in the first place give me leave to tell you, that the Unity of Place, how ever it might be practised by them, was never any of their Rules: We neither find it in *Aristotle*, *Horace*, or any who have written of it, till in our age the French Poets first made it a Precept of the Stage. The unity of time, even *Terence* himself (who was the best and most regular of them) has neglected: his *Heautontimoroumenos* or Self-Punisher takes up visibly two days; says *Scaliger*, the two first Acts concluding the first day, the three last the day ensuing; and *Eurypides*, in tying himself to one day, has committed an absurdity never to be forgiven him: for in one of his Tragedies he has made *Theseus* go from *Athens* to *Thebes*, which was about 40 English miles, under the walls of it to give battel, and appear victorious in the next Act; and yet from the time of his departure to the return of the *Nuntius*, who gives the relation of his Victory, *Æthra* and the Chorus have but 36 Verses; which is not for every Mile a Verse.

The like errour is as evident in *Terence* his Eunuch, when *Laches*, the old man, enters by mistake into the house of *Thais*, where betwixt his Exit and the entrance of *Pythias*, who comes to give ample relation of the disorders he has rais'd within, *Parmeno*, who was left upon the Stage, has not above five lines to speak: *C'est bien employer un temps si court*, says the French Poet, who furnish'd me with one of the observations; And almost all their Tragedies will afford us examples of the like nature.

'Tis true, they have kept the continuity, or as you call'd it, *Liaison des Scenes* somewhat better: two do not perpetually come in together, talk, and go out together; and other two succeed them, and do the same throughout the Act, which the English call by the name of single Scenes; but the reason is, because they have seldom above two or three Scenes, properly so call'd, in every act; for it is to be accounted a new Scene, not only every time the Stage is empty, but every person who enters, though to others, makes it so; because he introduces a new business: Now the Plots of their Plays being narrow, and the persons few, one of their Acts was written in a less compass than one of our well wrought Scenes; and yet they are often deficient even in this: To go no further than *Terence*, you find in the Eunuch *Antipho* entring single in the midst of the third Act, after *Chremes* and *Pythias* were gone off: In the same Play you have likewise *Dorias* beginning the fourth Act alone; and after she has made a relation of what was done at the Souldiers entertainment (which by the way was very inartificial) because she was presum'd to speak directly to the Audience, and to acquaint them with what was necessary to be known, but yet should have been so contriv'd by the Poet as to have been told by persons of the *Drama* to one another, (and so by them to have come to the knowledge of the people) she quits the Stage, and *Phædria* enters next, alone likewise: He also gives you an account of himself, and of his returning from the Country in *Monologue*, to which unnatural way of narration *Terence* is subject in all his Plays: In his *Adelphi* or Brothers, *Syrus* and *Demea* enter; after the Scene was broken by the departure of *Sostrata*, *Geta*, and *Canthara;* and indeed you can scarce look into any of his Comedies, where you will not presently discover the same interruption.

But as they have fail'd both in laying of their Plots, and in the management, swerving from the Rules of their own Art, by mis-representing Nature to us, in which they have ill satisfied one intention of a Play, which was delight, so in the instructive part they have err'd worse: instead of punishing Vice and rewarding Virtue, they have often shewn a Prosperous Wickedness, and an Unhappy Piety: They have set before us a bloudy image of revenge in *Medea*, and given her Dragons to convey her safe from punishment. A *Priam* and *Astyanax* murder'd, and *Cassandra* ravish'd, and the lust and murder ending in the victory of him who acted them: In short, there is no indecorum in any of our modern Plays, which if I would excuse, I could not shaddow with some Authority from the Ancients.

And one farther note of them let me leave you: Tragedies and Comedies were not writ then as they are now, promiscuously, by the same person; but he who found his genius bending to the one, never attempted the other way. This is so plain, that I need not instance to you, that *Aristophanes*, *Plautus*, *Terence*, never any of them writ a Tragedy; *Æschylus*, *Eurypides*, *Sophocles*, and *Seneca*, never medled with Comedy: the Sock and Buskin were not worn by the same Poet: having then so much care to excel in one kind, very little is to be pardon'd them if they miscarried in it; and this would lead me to the consideration of their wit, had not *Crites* given me sufficient warning not to be too bold in my judgment of it; because the languages being dead, and many of the Customs and little accidents on which it depended, lost to us, we are not competent judges of it. But though I grant that here and there we may miss the application of a Proverb or a Custom, yet a thing well said will be wit in all Languages; and though it may lose something in the Translation, yet to him who reads it in the Original, 'tis still the same; He has an Idea of its excellency, though it cannot pass from his mind into any other expression or words than those in which he finds it. When *Phædria*—in the Eunuch—had a command from his Mistress to be absent two days; and encouraging himself to go through with it, said; *Tandem ego non illâ caream, si opus sit, vel totum triduum?*[1] *Parmeno* to mock the softness of his Master, lifting up his hands and eyes, cryes out as it were in admiration; *Hui! universum triduum!*[2] the elegancy of which *universum*, though it cannot be rendred in our language, yet leaves an impression on our souls: but this happens seldom in him, in *Plautus* oftner; who is infinitely too bold in his Metaphors and coyning words; out of which many times his wit is nothing, which questionless was one reason why *Horace* falls upon him so severely in those Verses:

> *Sed proavi nostri Plautinos & numeros, &*
> *Laudavere sales, nimium patienter utrumque*
> *Ne dicam stolidè.*[3]

For *Horace* himself was cautious to obtrude a new word on his Readers, and makes custom and common use the best measure of receiving it into our writings.

> *Multa renascentur quæ nunc cecidere, cadentq;*
> *Quæ nunc sunt in honore vocabula, si volet usus,*
> *Quem penes, arbitrium est, & jus, & norma loquendi.*[4]

The not observing this Rule is that which the world has blam'd in our Satyrist, *Cleveland*; to express a thing hard and unnaturally, is his new way of Elocution: 'Tis true, no Poet but may sometimes use a *Catachresis*; *Virgil* does it;

> *Mistaque ridenti Colocasia fundet Acantho.*[5]

In his Eclogue of *Pollio*, and in his 7th *Æneid.*

> *Mirantur & undæ,*
> *Miratur nemus, insuetum fulgentia longe,*
> *Scuta virum fluvio, pictasq; innare carinas.*[6]

[1] Wouldn't I be prepared to be without her for a whole week-end, even, if necessary? (Terence, *Eunuchus* 2. 1. 17.)

[2] What! An entire week-end! (*Ibid.* 2. 1. 18.)

[3] But our great-grandfathers praised Plautus' verse-rhythms and his wit; in both cases too complacently—not to say with excessive stupidity. (*Ars Poetica* 270–72.)

[4] Many words which have now fallen out of use will be reborn, and many now prominent will disappear, if usage (which owns the right to decide, and the law, and the canons of speech) so chooses. (*Ars Poetica* 70–2.)

[5] The earth will yield, together and in profusion, the bean and the smiling acanthus. (*Eclogues* 4. 20.)

[6] The waves, and the woods too, wonder at the unaccustomed sight of men's shields flashing far over the stream, and man-made craft afloat thereon. (*Æneid* 8. 91–3.)

And *Ovid* once so modestly, that he asks leave to do it;

> *Si verbo audacia detur*
> *Haud metuam summi dixisse Palatia cœli.*[1]

Calling the Court of *Jupiter* by the name of *Augustus* his Pallace, though in another place he is more bold, where he says, *Et longas visent Capitolia pompas.*[2] But to do this always, and never be able to write a line without it, though it may be admir'd by some few Pedants, will not pass upon those who know that wit is best convey'd to us in the most easie language; and is most to be admir'd when a great thought comes drest in words so commonly receiv'd that it is understood by the meanest apprehensions, as the best meat is the most easily digested: but we cannot read a verse of *Cleveland's* without making a face at it, as if every word were a Pill to swallow: he gives us many times a hard Nut to break our Teeth, without a Kernel for our pains. So that there is this difference betwixt his *Satyres* and Doctor Donne's, That the one gives us deep thoughts in common language; though rough cadence; the other gives us common thoughts in abstruse words: 'tis true, in some places his wit is independent of his words, as in that of the Rebel *Scot*:

> *Had Cain been Scot God would have chang'd his doom;*
> *Not forc'd him wander, but confin'd him home,*

Si sic, omnia dixisset![3] This is wit in all languages: 'tis like Mercury, never to be lost or kill'd; and so that other;

> *For beauty, like White-powder, makes no noise,*
> *And yet the silent Hypocrite destroys.*

You see the last line is highly Metaphorical, but it is so soft and gentle that it does not shock us as we read it.

But, to return from whence I have digress'd, to the consideration of the Ancients Writing and their Wit (of which by this time you will grant us in some measure to be fit judges,) Though I see many excellent thoughts in *Seneca*, yet he, of them who had a Genius most proper for the Stage, was *Ovid*; he had a way of writing so fit to stir up a pleasing admiration and concernment, which are the objects of a Tragedy, and to shew the various movements of a Soul combating betwixt two different Passions, that, had he liv'd in our Age, or in his own could have writ with our

[1] If I may speak so boldly, I should not hesitate to call it the Palace of the highest heaven. (*Metamorphoses* 1. 176.)
[2] And the Capitol shall behold long processions. (*Metamorphoses* 1. 561.)
[3] Had he but expressed everything thus!

advantages, no man but must have yeilded to him; and therefore I am confident the *Medea* is none of his: for, though I esteem it for the gravity and sententiousness of it, which he himself concludes to be suitable to a Tragedy, *Omne genus scripti gravitate Tragœdia vincit,*[1] yet it moves not my soul enough to judge that he, who in the Epique way wrote things so near the *Drama*, as the Story of *Myrrha*, of *Caunus* and *Biblis*, and the rest, should stir up no more concernment where he most endeavour'd it. The Master-piece of *Seneca* I hold to be that Scene in the *Troades*, where *Ulysses* is seeking for *Astyanax* to kill him; There you see the tenderness of a Mother, so represented in *Andromache*, that it raises compassion to a high degree in the Reader, and bears the nearest resemblance of any thing in the Tragedies of the Ancients, to the excellent Scenes of Passion in *Shakespeare*, or in *Fletcher*: for Love-Scenes you will find few among them, their Tragique Poets dealt not with that soft passion, but with Lust, Cruelty, Revenge, Ambition, and those bloody actions they produc'd; which were more capable of raising horrour than compassion in an audience: leaving Love untoucht, whose gentleness would have temper'd them, which is the most frequent of all the passions, and which being the private concernment of every person, is sooth'd by viewing its own image in a publick entertainment.

Among their Comedies, we find a Scene or two of tenderness, and that where you would least expect it, in *Plautus*; but to speak generally, their Lovers say little, when they see each other, but *anima mea, vita mea*;[2] Ζωὴ καὶ ψυχή,[3] as the women in *Juvenal*'s time us'd to cry out in the fury of their kindness: Any sudden gust of passion (as an extasie of love in an unexpected meeting) cannot better be express'd than in a word and a sigh, breaking one another. Nature is dumb on such occasions, and to make her speak, would be to represent her unlike her self. But there are a thousand other concernments of Lovers, as jealousies, complaints, contrivances and the like, where not to open their minds at large to each other, were to be wanting to their own love, and to the expectation of the Audience; who watch the movements of their minds, as much as the changes of their fortunes. For the imaging of the first is properly the work of a Poet, the latter he borrows from the Historian.

Eugenius was proceeding in that part of his Discourse, when *Crites* interrupted him. I see, said he, *Eugenius* and I are never

[1] Of all kinds of literature, Tragedy is the most solemn and elevated. (Ovid, *Tristia* 2. 381.)

[2] My soul; my life.

[3] Life and Soul. (*Juvenal* 6. 195.)

like to have this Question decided betwixt us; for he maintains the Moderns have acquir'd a new perfection in writing, I can only grant they have alter'd the mode of it. *Homer* describ'd his Heroes men of great appetites, lovers of beef broild upon the coals, and good fellows; contrary to the practice of the French Romances, whose Heroes neither eat, nor drink, nor sleep, for love. *Virgil* makes *Æneas* a bold Avower of his own virtues,

Sum pius Æneas, famâ super æthera notus; [1]

which in the civility of our Poets is the Character of a Fanfaron or Hector: for with us the Knight takes occasion to walk out, or sleep, to avoid the vanity of telling his own Story, which the trusty Squire is ever to perform for him. So in their Love Scenes, of which *Eugenius* spoke last, the Ancients were more hearty, we more talkative: they writ love as it was then the mode to make it, and I will grant thus much to *Eugenius*, that perhaps one of their Poets, had he liv'd in our Age,

Si foret hoc nostrum fato delapsus in ævum [2]

(as *Horace* says of *Lucilius*) he had alter'd many things; not that they were not natural before, but that he might accommodate himself to the Age in which he liv'd; yet in the mean time, we are not to conclude any thing rashly against those great men, but preserve to them the dignity of Masters, and give that honour to their memories, (*Quos libitina sacravit;*)[3] part of which we expect may be paid to us in future times.

This moderation of *Crites*, as it was pleasing to all the company, so it put an end to that dispute; which, *Eugenius*, who seem'd to have the better of the Argument, would urge no farther: but *Lisideius*, after he had acknowledg'd himself of *Eugenius* his opinion concerning the Ancients, yet told him he had forborn, till his Discourse were ended, to ask him why he prefer'd the English Plays above those of other Nations? and whether we ought not to submit our Stage to the exactness of our next Neighbours?

Though, said *Eugenius*, I am at all times ready to defend the honour of my Country against the French, and to maintain, we are as well able to vanquish them with our Pens as our Ancestors have been with their swords; yet, if you please, added he, looking upon *Neander*, I will commit this cause to my friend's manage-

[1] I am Æneas the Dutiful, known by repute even beyond the skies. (*Æneid* 1. 378–9.)

[2] If he had been fated to come down to this age of ours. (*Satires* 1. 10.68.)

[3] Consecrated by decease. (Horace, *Epistles* 2. 1. 49.)

ment; his opinion of our Plays is the same with mine: and besides, there is no reason, that *Crites* and I, who have now left the Stage, should re-enter so suddenly upon it; which is against the Laws of Comedie.

If the Question had been stated, replied *Lisideius*, who had writ best, the French or English forty years ago, I should have been of your opinion, and adjud'g'd the honour to our own Nation; but since that time, (said he, turning towards *Neander*) we have been so long together bad Englishmen, that we had not leisure to be good Poets. *Beaumont*, *Fletcher*, and *Johnson* (who were only capable of bringing us to that degree of perfection which we have) were just then leaving the world; as if in an Age of so much horrour, wit and those milder studies of humanity, had no farther business among us. But the Muses, who ever follow Peace, went to plant in another Countrey; it was then, that the great Cardinal of *Richlieu* began to take them into his protection; and that, by his encouragement, *Corneil* and some other French-men reform'd their Theatre, (which before was as much below ours as it now surpasses it and the rest of *Europe*;) but because *Crites*, in his Discourse for the Ancients, has prevented me, by observing many Rules of the Stage, which the Moderns have borrow'd from them; I shall only, in short, demand of you, whether you are not convinc'd that of all Nations the French have best observ'd them? In the unity of time you find them so scrupulous, that it yet remains a dispute among their Poets, whether the artificial day of twelve hours more or less, be not meant by *Aristotle*, rather than the natural one of twenty four; and consequently whether all Plays ought not to be reduc'd into that compass? This I can testifie, that in all their *Drama*'s writ within these last 20 years and upwards, I have not observ'd any that have extended the time to thirty hours: in the unity of place they are full as scrupulous, for many of their Criticks limit it to that very spot of ground where the Play is suppos'd to begin; none of them exceed the compass of the same Town or City.

The unity of Action in all their plays is yet more conspicuous, for they do not burden them with under-plots, as the English do; which is the reason why many Scenes of our Tragi-comedies carry on a design that is nothing of kin to the main Plot; and that we see two distinct webbs in a Play, like those in ill wrought stuffs; and two actions, that is, two Plays carried on together, to the confounding of the Audience; who, before they are warm in their concernments for one part, are diverted to another; and by that means espouse the interest of neither. From hence likewise it arises that the one half of our Actors are not known to the other. They keep their distances as if they were *Mountagues* and *Capulets*, and seldom begin an acquaintance till the last Scene of the Fifth Act, when they are all to meet upon the Stage. There is no Theatre in the world has any thing so absurd as the English Tragi-comedie, 'tis a *Drama* of our own invention, and the fashion of it is enough to proclaim it so; here a course of mirth, there another of sadness and passion; And a third of honour, and a Duel: Thus in two hours and a half we run through all the fits of *Bedlam*. The French affords you as much variety on the same day, but they do it not so unseasonably, or *mal a propos* as we: Our Poets present you the Play and the farce together; and our Stages still retain somewhat of the Original civility of the Red-Bull;[1]

Atque ursum & pugiles media inter carmina poscunt.[2]

The end of Tragedies or serious Plays, says *Aristotle*, is to beget admiration, compassion, or concernment; but are not mirth and compassion things incompatible? and is it not evident that the Poet must of necessity destroy the former by intermingling of the latter? that is, he must ruine the sole end and object of his Tragedy to introduce somewhat that is forced into it; and is not of the body of it: Would you not think that Physician mad, who having prescribed a Purge, should immediately order you to take restringents?

But to leave our Playes, and return to theirs, I have noted one great advantage they have had in the Plotting of their Tragedies; that is, they are always grounded upon some known History: according to that of *Horace*, *Ex noto fictum carmen sequar*;[3] and in that they have so imitated the Ancients that they have surpass'd them. For the Ancients, as was observ'd before, took for the foundation of their Plays some Poetical Fiction, such as under that consideration could move but little concernment in the Audience, because they already knew the event of it. But the French goes farther;

Atque ita mentitur; sic veris falsa remiscet,
Primo ne medium, medio ne discrepet imum:[4]

[1] The *Red Bull* in St. John's Street, Clerkenwell, was used for plays, drolls, and other diversions.

[2] And in the middle of a poetic play, call for boxers and a bear. (Horace, *Epistles* 2. 1. 186.)

[3] I should pursue my poetic invention upon a basis of known themes. (*Ars Poetica* 240.)

[4] And thus he spins fictions; so does he mingle the false with the true, that the middle may not clash with the beginning, nor the end with the middle. (*Ars Poetica* 151–2.)

He so interweaves Truth with probable Fiction, that he puts a pleasing Fallacy upon us; mends the intrigues of Fate, and dispenses with the severity of History, to reward that vertue which has been rendred to us there unfortunate. Sometimes the story has left the success so doubtful, that the Writer is free, by the priviledge of a Poet, to take that which of two or more relations will best sute with his design: As for example, in the death of *Cyrus*, whom *Justin* and some others report to have perish'd in the *Scythian* war, but *Xenophon* affirms to have died in his bed of extream old age. Nay more, when the event is past dispute, even then we are willing to be deceiv'd, and the Poet, if he contrives it with appearance of truth, has all the audience of his Party; at least during the time his Play is acting: so naturally we are kind to vertue, when our own interest is not in question, that we take it up as the general concernment of Mankind. On the other side, if you consider the Historical Plays of *Shakespeare*, they are rather so many Chronicles of Kings, or the business many times of thirty or forty years, crampt into a representation of two hours and a half, which is not to imitate or paint Nature, but rather to draw her in miniature, to take her in little; to look upon her through the wrong end of a Perspective, and receive her Images not only much less, but infinitely more imperfect than the life: this, instead of making a Play delightful, renders it ridiculous.

Quodcunque ostendis mihi sic, incredulus odi.[1]

For the Spirit of man cannot be satisfied but with truth, or at least verisimility; and a Poem is to contain, if not τὰ ἔτυμα,[2] yet ἐτύμοισιν ὁμοῖα,[3] as one of the Greek Poets has express'd it.

Another thing in which the French differ from us and from the Spaniards, is, that they do not embarass, or cumber themselves with too much Plot: they only represent so much of a Story as will constitute one whole and great action sufficient for a Play; we, who undertake more, do but multiply adventures; which, not being produc'd from one another, as effects from causes, but barely following, constitute many actions in the Drama, and consequently make it many Plays.

But by pursuing closely one argument, which is not cloy'd with many turns, the French have gain'd more liberty for verse, in which they write: they have leisure to dwell on a subject which

[1] I disbelieve and loathe whatever is exhibited to me in this fashion. (Horace, *Ars Poetica* 188.)

[2] The truth. [3] Things similar to the truth.

deserves it; and to represent the passions (which we have acknowledg'd to be the Poets work) without being hurried from one thing to another, as we are in the Plays of *Calderon*, which we have seen lately upon our Theaters, under the name of Spanish Plots.[1] I have taken notice but of one Tragedy of ours, whose Plot has that uniformity and unity of design in it which I have commended in the French; and that is *Rollo*,[2] or rather, under the name of *Rollo*, The Story of *Bassianus* and *Geta* in *Herodian*; there indeed the Plot is neither large nor intricate, but just enough to fill the minds of the Audience, not to cloy them. Besides, you see it founded upon the truth of History, only the time of the action is not reduceable to the strictness of the Rules; and you see in some places a little farce mingled, which is below the dignity of the other parts; and in this all our Poets are extreamly peccant, even *Ben. Johnson* himself in *Sejanus* and *Cataline* has given us this Oleo of a Play: this unnatural mixture of Comedy and Tragedy, which to me sounds just as ridiculously as the History of *David* with the merry humours of *Golia's*. In *Sejanus* you may take notice of the Scene betwixt *Livia* and the Physician, which is a pleasant Satyre upon the artificial helps of beauty: In *Catiline* you may see the Parliament of Women; the little envies of them to one another; and all that passes betwixt *Curio* and *Fulvia*: Scenes admirable in their kind, but of an ill mingle with the rest.

But I return again to the French Writers; who, as I have said, do not burden themselves too much with Plot, which has been reproach'd to them by an *ingenious person* of our Nation as a fault, for he says they commonly make but one person considerable in a Play; they dwell on him, and his concernments, while the rest of the persons are only subservient to set him off. If he intends this by it, that there is one person in the Play who is of greater dignity than the rest, he must tax, not only theirs, but those of the Ancients, and which he would be loth to do, the best of ours; for 'tis impossible but that one person must be more conspicuous in it than any other, and consequently the greatest share in the action must devolve on him. We see it so in the management of all affairs; even in the most equal Aristocracy, the ballance cannot be so justly poys'd, but some one will be superiour to the rest; either in parts, fortune, interest, or the consideration of

[1] Sir Samuel Tuke's comedy of *The Adventures of Five Hours*, 1663, and the Earl of Bristol's *Elvira, or the Worst not always True*, 1667, were both adaptations from plays by Calderon.

[2] John Fletcher's tragedy of *The Bloody Brother, or, Rollo, Duke of Normandy*, 1616 (?).

some glorious exploit; which will reduce the greatest part of business into his hands.

But, if he would have us to imagine that in exalting one character the rest of them are neglected, and that all of them have not some share or other in the action of the Play, I desire him to produce any of *Corneilles* Tragedies, wherein every person (like so many servants in a well govern'd Family) has not some employment, and who is not necessary to the carrying on of the Plot, or at least to your understanding it.

There are indeed some protatick persons [1] in the Ancients, whom they make use of in their Plays, either to hear, or give the Relation: but the French avoid this with great address, making their narrations only to, or by such, who are some way interessed in the main design. And now I am speaking of Relations, I cannot take a fitter opportunity to add this in favour of the French, that they often use them with better judgment and more *a propos* than the English do. Not that I commend narrations in general, but there are two sorts of them; one of those things which are antecedent to the Play, and are related to make the conduct of it more clear to us, but, 'tis a fault to choose such subjects for the Stage as will force us on that Rock; because we see they are seldom listned to by the Audience, and that is many times the ruin of the Play: for, being once let pass without attention, the Audience can never recover themselves to understand the Plot; and indeed it is somewhat unreasonable that they should be put to so much trouble, as, that to comprehend what passes in their sight, they must have recourse to what was done, perhaps, ten or twenty years ago.

But there is another sort of Relations, that is, of things hapning in the Action of the Play, and suppos'd to be done behind the Scenes: and this is many times both convenient and beautiful: for, by it the French avoid the tumult, to which we are subject in *England*, by representing Duells, Battels, and the like; which renders our Stage too like the Theaters where they fight Prizes. For what is more ridiculous than to represent an Army with a Drum and five men behind it; all which, the Heroe of the other side is to drive in before him, or to see a Duel fought, and one slain with two or three thrusts of the foyles, which we know are so blunted, that we might give a man an hour to kill another in good earnest with them.

I have observ'd that in all our Tragedies, the Audience cannot forbear laughing when the Actors are to die; 'tis the most Comick

[1] Characters who appear only in the introductory part of a play.

part of the whole Play. All *passions* may be lively represented on the Stage, if to the well-writing of them the Actor supplies a good commanded voice, and limbs that move easily, and without stifness; but there are many *actions* which can never be imitated to a just height: dying especially is a thing which none but a Roman Gladiator could naturally perform on the Stage when he did not imitate or represent, but do it; and therefore it is better to omit the representation of it.

The words of a good Writer which describe it lively, will make a deeper impression of belief in us than all the Actor can insinuate into us, when he seems to fall dead before us; as a Poet in the description of a beautiful Garden, or a Meadow, will please our imagination more than the place itself can please our sight. When we see death represented we are convinc'd it is but Fiction; but when we hear it related, our eyes (the strongest witnesses) are wanting, which might have undeceiv'd us; and we are all willing to favour the sleight when the Poet does not too grosly impose on us. They therefore who imagine these relations would make no concernment in the Audience, are deceiv'd, by confounding them with the other, which are of things antecedent to the Play; those are made often in cold blood (as I may say) to the audience; but these are warm'd with our concernments, which were before awaken'd in the Play. What the Philosophers say of motion, that, when it is once begun, it continues of it self, and will do so to Eternity without some stop put to it, is clearly true on this occasion; the soul being already mov'd with the Characters and Fortunes of those imaginary persons, continues going of its own accord, and we are no more weary to hear what becomes of them when they are not on the Stage, than we are to listen to the news of an absent Mistress. But it is objected, That if one part of the Play may be related, then why not all? I answer, Some parts of the action are more fit to be represented, some to be related. *Corneille* says judiciously, that the Poet is not oblig'd to expose to view all particular actions which conduce to the principal: he ought to select such of them to be seen which will appear with the greatest beauty, either by the magnificence of the show, or the vehemence of passions which they produce, or some other charm which they have in them, and let the rest arrive to the audience by narration. 'Tis a great mistake in us to believe the French present no part of the action on the Stage: every alteration or crossing of a design, every new sprung passion, and turn of it, is a part of the action, and much the noblest, except we conceive nothing to be action till the Players come to blows; as if the painting of the Heroes mind were not more properly the Poets work than the strength of his body. Nor does this any thing contradict the opinion of *Horace*, where he tells us,

> *Segnius irritant animos demissa per aurem*
> *Quam quæ sunt oculis subjecta fidelibus.*——[1]

For he says immediately after,

> ——————*Non tamen intus*
> *Digna geri promes in scenam, Multaq; tolles*
> *Ex oculis, quæ mox narret facundia præsens.*[2]

Among which many he recounts some.

> *Nec pueros coram populo Medea trucidet,*
> *Aut in avem Progne mutetur, Cadmus in anguem, &c.*[3]

That is, those actions which by reason of their cruelty will cause aversion in us, or by reason of their impossibility unbelief, ought either wholly to be avoided by a Poet, or only deliver'd by narration. To which, we may have leave to add such as to avoid tumult, (as was before hinted) or to reduce the Plot into a more reasonable compass of time, or for defect of Beauty in them, are rather to be related than presented to the Eye. Examples of all these kinds are frequent, not only among all the Ancients, but in the best receiv'd of our English Poets. We find *Ben. Johnson* using them in his Magnetick Lady, where one comes out from Dinner, and relates the quarrels and disorders of it to save the undecent appearance of them on the Stage, and to abbreviate the Story; and this in express imitation of *Terence*, who had done the same before him in his Eunuch, where *Pythias* makes the like relation of what had happen'd within at the Soldiers entertainment. The relations likewise of *Sejanus's* death, and the prodigies before it are remarkable; the one of which was hid from sight to avoid the horrour and tumult of the representation; the other to shun the introducing of things impossible to be believ'd. In that excellent Play, the King and no King, *Fletcher* goes yet farther; for the whole unravelling of the Plot is done by narration in the fifth Act, after the manner of the Ancients; and it moves great concernment in the Audience, though it be only a relation

[1] That which we hear instilled into the ears arouses our minds more slowly than what is presented before our eyes, which we trust. (*Ars Poetica* 180–1.)

[2] Yet you will not bring upon the scene actions that ought to be performed behind the scenes, and you will remove from sight many things which can be presently related by the eloquence of a witness. (*Ibid.* 182–3.)

[3] Nor must Medea slay her children in the sight of the audience, or Procne be changed to a bird thus, or Cadmus to a serpent. (*Ibid.* 185, 187.)

of what was done many years before the Play. I could multiply other instances, but these are sufficient to prove that there is no errour in choosing a subject which requires this sort of narrations; in the ill management of them, there may.

But I find I have been too long in this discourse since the French have many other excellencies not common to us; as that you never see any of their Plays end with a conversion, or simple change of will, which is the ordinary way which our Poets use to end theirs. It shews little art in the conclusion of a Dramatick Poem, when they who have hinder'd the felicity during the four Acts, desist from it in the fifth without some powerful cause to take them off their design; and though I deny not but such reasons may be found, yet it is a path that is cautiously to be trod, and the Poet is to be sure he convinces the Audience that the motive is strong enough. As for example, the conversion of the Usurer in the Scornful Lady seems to me a little forc'd; for being an Usurer, which implies a lover of Money to the highest degree of covetousness, (and such the Poet has represented him) the account he gives for the sudden change is, that he has been dup'd by the wild young fellow, which in reason might render him more wary another time, and make him punish himself with harder fare and courser cloaths to get up again what he had lost: but that he should look on it as a Judgment, and so repent, we may expect to hear in a Sermon, but I should never indure it in a play.

I pass by this; neither will I insist on the care they take, that no person after his first entrance shall ever appear, but the business which brings him upon the Stage shall be evident: which rule if observ'd, must needs render all the events in the Play more natural; for there you see the probability of every accident, in the cause that produc'd it; and that which appears chance in the Play, will seem so reasonable to you, that you will there find it almost necessary; so that in the exit of the Actor you have a clear account of his purpose and design in the next entrance: (though, if the Scene be well wrought, the event will commonly deceive you) for there is nothing so absurd, says *Corneille*, as for an Actor to leave the Stage only because he has no more to say.

I should now speak of the beauty of their Rhime, and the just reason I have to prefer that way of writing in Tragedies before ours in Blanck-verse; but because it is partly receiv'd by us, and therefore not altogether peculiar to them, I will say no more of it in relation to their Plays. For our own, I doubt not but it will exceedingly beautifie them, and I can see but one reason why it should not generally obtain, that is, because our Poets write so ill in it. This indeed may prove a more prevailing argument than all others which are us'd to destroy it, and therefore I am only troubled when great and judicious Poets, and those who are acknowledg'd such, have writ or spoke against it; as for others they are to be answered by that one sentence of an ancient Authour.

Sed ut primo ad consequendos eos quos priores ducimus accendimur, ita ubi aut præteriri, aut æquari eos posse desperavimus, studium cum spe senescit: quod, scilicet, assequi non potest, sequi desinit; præteritoque eo in quo eminere non possumus, aliquid in quo nitamur, conquirimus.[1]

Lisideius concluded in this manner; and *Neander* after a little pause thus answer'd him.

I shall grant *Lisideius*, without much dispute, a great part of what he has urg'd against us; for I acknowledge that the French contrive their Plots more regularly, and observe the Laws of Comedy, and decorum of the Stage (to speak generally) with more exactness than the English. Farther, I deny not but he has tax'd us justly in some irregularities of ours which he has mention'd; yet, after all, I am of opinion that neither our faults nor their virtues are considerable enough to place them above us.

For the lively imitation of Nature being in the definition of a Play, those which best fulfil that law ought to be esteem'd superiour to the others. 'Tis true, those beauties of the French-poesie are such as will raise perfection higher where it is, but are not sufficient to give it where it is not: they are indeed the Beauties of a Statue, but not of a Man, because not animated with the Soul of Poesie, which is imitation of humour and passions: and this *Lisideius* himself, or any other, however byassed to their Party, cannot but acknowledge, if he will either compare the humours of our Comedies, or the Characters of our serious Plays with theirs. He who will look upon theirs which have been written till these last ten years or thereabouts, will find it a hard matter to pick out two or three passable humours amongst them. *Corneille* himself, their Arch-Poet, what has he produc'd except *the Lier*, and you know how it was cryd up in *France*; but when it came upon the English Stage, though well translated, and that part of *Dorant* acted to so much advantage as I am confident

[1] But as at the beginning we are fired to follow those whom we take to be the leaders, so, when we have despaired of the possibility of outrunning or even drawing level with them, our enthusiasm fades along with our hopes; what plainly cannot be overtaken ceases even to be followed; and forgoing that in which we are unable to distinguish ourselves, we look for something else to strive at. (Velleius Paterculus 1. 17.)

it never receiv'd in its own Country, the most favourable to it would not put it in competition with many of *Fletchers* or *Ben. Johnsons*. In the rest of *Corneilles* Comedies you have little humour; he tells you himself his way is first to shew two Lovers in good intelligence with each other; in the working up of the Play to embroyl them by some mistake, and in the latter end to clear it, and reconcile them.

But of late years *Moliere*, the younger *Corneille*, *Quinault*, and some others, have been imitating afar off the quick turns and graces of the English Stage. They have mix'd their serious Plays with mirth, like our Tragicomedies since the death of Cardinal *Richlieu*, which *Lisideius* and many others not observing, have commended that in them for a virtue which they themselves no longer practise. Most of their new Plays are like some of ours, deriv'd from the Spanish Novells. There is scarce one of them without a veil, and a trusty *Diego*, who drolls much after the rate of the *Adventures*.[1] But their humours, If I may grace them with that name, are so thin sown that never above one of them comes up in any Play: I dare take upon me to find more variety of them in some one Play of *Ben. Johnsons* than in all theirs together: as he who has seen the Alchymist, the Silent Woman, or *Bartholomew*-Fair, cannot but acknowledge with me.

I grant the French have performed what was possible on the ground-work of the Spanish Plays; what was pleasant before, they have made regular; but there is not above one good Play to be writ on all those Plots; they are too much alike to please often, which we need not the experience of our own Stage to justifie. As for their new way of mingling mirth with serious Plot, I do not with *Lysideius* condemn the thing, though I cannot approve their manner of doing it: He tells us we cannot so speedily recollect our selves after a Scene of great passion and concernment, as to pass to another of mirth and humour, and to enjoy it with any relish: but why should he imagine the soul of man more heavy than his Senses? Does not the eye pass from an unpleasant object to a pleasant in a much shorter time than is requir'd to this? and does not the unpleasantness of the first commend the beauty of the latter; The old Rule of Logick might have convinc'd him, that contraries when plac'd near, set off each other. A continued gravity keeps the spirit too much bent; we must refresh it sometimes, as we bait in a journey, that we may go on with greater ease. A Scene of mirth mix'd with Tragedy has the same effect upon us which our musick has betwixt the Acts, which we

[1] See *ante*, p. 402, n. 1.

find a relief to us from the best Plots and language of the Stage, if the discourses have been long. I must therefore have stronger arguments ere I am convinc'd that compassion and mirth in the same subject destroy each other, and in the mean time cannot but conclude, to the honour of our Nation, that we have invented, increas'd, and perfected a more pleasant way of writing for the Stage than was ever known to the Ancients or Moderns of any Nation, which is Tragicomedie.

And this leads me to wonder why *Lisideius* and many others should cry up the barrenness of the French Plots above the variety and copiousness of the English. Their Plots are single, they carry on one design which is push'd forward by all the Actors, every Scene in the play contributing and moving towards it: Our Plays besides the main design, have under-plots or by-concernments, of less considerable Persons, and Intrigues, which are carried on with the motion of the main Plot: as they say the Orb of the fix'd Stars, and those of the Planets, though they have motions of their own, are whirl'd about by the motion of the *primum mobile*, in which they are contain'd: that similitude expresses much of the English Stage: for if contrary motions may be found in Nature to agree; if a Planet can go East and West at the same time; one way by virtue of his own motion, the other by the force of the first mover; it will not be difficult to imagine how the under-Plot, which is only different, not contrary to the great design, may naturally be conducted along with it.

Eugenius has already shewn us, from the confession of the French Poets, that the Unity of Action is sufficiently preserv'd if all the imperfect actions of the Play are conducing to the main design: but when those petty intrigues of a Play are so ill order'd, that they have no coherence with the other, I must grant that *Lisideius* has reason to tax that want of due connexion; for Coordination in a Play is as dangerous and unnatural as in a State. In the mean time he must acknowledge our variety, if well order'd, will afford a greater pleasure to the audience.

As for his other argument, that by pursuing one single Theme they gain an advantage to express and work up the passions, I wish any example he could bring from them would make it good: for I confess their verses are to me the coldest I have ever read: Neither indeed is it possible for them, in the way they take, so to express passion, as that the effects of it should appear in the concernment of an Audience, their Speeches being so many declamations, which tire us with the length; so that instead of perswading us to grieve for their imaginary Heroes, we are concern'd for our own trouble, as we are in tedious visits of bad company; we are in pain till they are gone. When the French Stage came to be reform'd by Cardinal *Richelieu*, those long Harangues were introduc'd to comply with the gravity of a Churchman. Look upon the *Cinna* and the *Pompey*, they are not so properly to be called Plays, as long discourses of reason of State; and *Polieucte* in matters of Religion is as solemn as the long stops upon our Organs.[1] Since that time it is grown into a custome, and their Actors speak by the Hour-glass, like our Parsons; nay, they account it the grace of their parts, and think themselves disparag'd by the Poet, if they may not twice or thrice in a Play entertain the Audience with a Speech of an hundred lines. I deny not but this may sute well enough with the French; for as we, who are a more sullen people, come to be diverted at our Plays; so they who are of an aiery and gay temper come thither to make themselves more serious: And this I conceive to be one reason why Comedy's are more pleasing to us, and Tragedies to them. But to speak generally, it cannot be deny'd that short Speeches and Replies are more apt to move the passions, and beget concernment in us than the other: for it is unnatural for any one in a gust of Passion to speak long together, or for another in the same condition, to suffer him, without interruption. Grief and Passion are like floods rais'd in little Brooks by a sudden rain; they are quickly up, and if the concernment be pour'd unexpectedly in upon us, it overflows us: But a long sober shower gives them leisure to run out as they came in, without troubling the ordinary current. As for Comedy, Repartee is one of its chiefest graces; the greatest pleasure of the Audience is a chase of wit kept up on both sides, and swiftly manag'd. And this our forefathers, if not we, have had in *Fletchers* Plays, to a much higher degree of perfection than the French Poets can, reasonably, hope to reach.

There is another part of *Lisideius* his Discourse, in which he has rather excus'd our neighbours than commended them; that is, for aiming only to make one person considerable in their Plays. 'Tis very true what he has urged, that one character in all Plays, even without the Poets care, will have advantage of all the others; and that the design of the whole *Drama* will chiefly depend on it. But this hinders not that there may be more shining characters in the Play; many persons of a second magnitude, nay, some so very near, so almost equal to the first, that greatness may be oppos'd to greatness, and all the persons be made considerable,

[1] These three plays, *Cinna*, 1643, *La Mort de Pompee*, 1644, and *Polyceute Martyr*, 1643, were by Pierre Corneille.

not only by their quality, but their action. 'Tis evident that the more the persons are, the greater will be the variety of the Plot. If then the parts are manag'd so regularly that the beauty of the whole be kept intire, and that the variety become not a perplex'd and confus'd mass of accidents, you will find it infinitely pleasing to be led in a labyrinth of design, where you see some of your way before you, yet discern not the end till you arrive at it. And that all this is practicable, I can produce for examples many of our English Plays: as the Maids Tragedy, the Alchymist, the Silent Woman; I was going to have named the Fox, but that the unity of design seems not exactly observ'd in it; for there appear two actions in the Play; the first naturally ending with the fourth Act; the second forc'd from it in the fifth: which yet is the less to be condemn'd in him, because the disguise of *Volpone*, though it suited not with his character as a crafty or covetous person, agreed well enough with that of a voluptuary: and by it the Poet gain'd the end at which he aym'd, the punishment of Vice, and the reward of Virtue, both which that disguise produc'd. So that to judge equally of it, it was an excellent fifth Act, but not so naturally proceeding from the former.

But to leave this, and pass to the latter part of *Lisideius* his discourse, which concerns relations, I must acknowledge with him, that the French have reason to hide that part of the action which would occasion too much tumult on the Stage, and to choose rather to have it made known by narration to the Audience. Farther I think it very convenient, for the reasons he has given, that all incredible actions were remov'd; but, whither custome has so insinuated it self into our Country-men, or nature has so form'd them to fierceness, I know not; but they will scarcely suffer combats and other objects of horrour to be taken from them. And indeed, the indecency of tumults is all which can be objected against fighting: For why may not our imagination as well suffer it self to be deluded with the probability of it, as with any other thing in the Play? For my part, I can with as great ease perswade myself that the blows are given in good earnest, as I can, that they who strike them are Kings or Princes, or those persons which they represent. For objects of incredibility I would be satisfied from *Lisideius*, whether we have any so remov'd from all appearance of truth, as are those of *Corneilles Andromède*?[1] A Play which has been frequented the most of any he has writ? If the *Perseus*, or the Son of a Heathen God, the *Pegasus* and the Monster were

[1] Pierre Corneille's tragedy of *Andromede*, an elaborately staged festival piece, was published in 1651.

not capable to choak a strong belief, let him blame any representation of ours hereafter. Those indeed were objects of delight; yet the reason is the same as to the probability: for he makes it not a Ballette or Masque, but a Play, which is to resemble truth. But for death, that it ought not to be represented, I have besides the Arguments alledg'd by *Lisideius*, the authority of *Ben. Johnson*, who has forborn it in his Tragedies; for both the death of *Sejanus* and *Catiline* are related: though in the latter I cannot but observe one irregularity of that great Poet; he has remov'd the Scene in the same Act, from *Rome* to *Catiline*'s Army, and from thence again to *Rome*; and besides, has allow'd a very inconsiderable time, after *Catiline*'s Speech, for the striking of the battle, and the return of *Petreius*, who is to relate the event of it to the Senate: which I should not animadvert on him, who was otherwise a painful observer of τὸ πρέπον, or the *decorum* of the Stage, if he had not us'd extream severity in his judgment on the incomparable *Shakespeare* for the same fault. To conclude on this subject of Relations, if we are to be blam'd for shewing too much of the action, the French are as faulty for discovering too little of it: a mean betwixt both should be observed by every judicious Writer, so as the audience may neither be left unsatisfied by not seeing what is beautiful, or shock'd by beholding what is either incredible or undecent. I hope I have already prov'd in this discourse, that though we are not altogether so punctual as the French, in observing the Laws of Comedy; yet our errours are so few, and little, and those things wherein we excel them so considerable, that we ought of right to be prefer'd before them. But what will *Lisideius* say if they themselves acknowledge they are too strictly bounded by those Laws, for breaking which he has blam'd the English? I will alledge *Corneille*'s words, as I find them in the end of his Discourse of the three Unities: *Il est facile aux speculatifs d'estre severes, &c.* 'Tis easy for speculative persons to judge severely; but if they would produce to publick view ten or twelve pieces of this nature, they would perhaps give more latitude to the Rules than I have done, when by experience they had known how much we are limited and constrain'd by them, and how many beauties of the Stage they banish'd from it. To illustrate a little what he has said; By their servile observations of the unities of time and place, and integrity of Scenes, they have brought on themselves that dearth of Plot, and narrowness of Imagination, which may be observ'd in all their Plays. How many beautiful accidents might naturally happen in two or three days, which cannot arrive with any probability in the compass of 24 hours? There is time to be allowed also for maturity of design, which amongst great and prudent persons, such as are often represented in Tragedy, cannot, with any likelihood of truth, be brought to pass at so short a warning. Farther, by tying themselves strictly to the unity of place, and unbroken Scenes, they are forc'd many times to omit some beauties which cannot be shown where the Act began; but might, if the Scene were interrupted, and the Stage clear'd for the persons to enter in another place; and therefore the French Poets are often forc'd upon absurdities: for if the Act begins in a Chamber, all the persons in the Play must have some business or other to come thither, or else they are not to be shewn that Act; and sometimes their characters are very unfitting to appear there; As, suppose it were the Kings Bed-chamber, yet the meanest man in the Tragedy must come and dispatch his business there, rather than in the Lobby or Court-yard (which is fitter for him) for fear the Stage should be clear'd, and the Scenes broken. Many times they fall by it in a greater inconvenience; for they keep their Scenes unbroken, and yet change the place; as in one of their newest Plays,[1] where the Act begins in the Street. There a Gentleman is to meet his Friend; he sees him with his man, coming out from his Fathers house; they talk together, and the first goes out: the second, who is a Lover, has made an appointment with his Mistress; she appears at the window, and then we are to imagine the Scene lies under it. This Gentleman is call'd away, and leaves his servant with his Mistress; presently her father is heard from within; the young Lady is affraid the Serving-man should be discover'd, and thrusts him into a place of safety, which is suppos'd to be her Closet. After this, the Father enters to the Daughter, and now the Scene is in a House: for he is seeking from one room to another for this poor *Philipin*, or French *Diego*, who is heard from within, drolling and breaking many a miserable conceit on the subject of his sad condition. In this ridiculous manner the Play goes forward, the Stage being never empty all the while: so that the Street, the Window, the Houses, and the Closet, are made to walk about, and the Persons to stand still. Now what I beseech you is more easie than to write a regular French Play, or more difficult than to write an irregular English one, like those of *Fletcher*, or of *Shakespeare*?

If they content themselves as *Corneille* did, with some flat design, which, like an ill Riddle, is found out e're it be half propos'd; such Plots we can make every way regular as easily as

[1] Thomas Corneille's comedy of *L'Amour à la Mode*, 1651.

they: but when e're they endeavour to rise to any quick turns and counterturns of Plot, as some of them have attempted, since *Corneille*'s Plays have been less in vogue, you see they write as irregularly as we, though they cover it more speciously. Hence the reason is perspicuous, why no French Plays, when translated, have, or ever can succeed on the English Stage. For, if you consider the Plots, our own are fuller of variety; if the writing, ours are more quick and fuller of spirit: and therefore 'tis a strange mistake in those who decry the way of writing Plays in Verse, as if the English therein imitated the French. We have borrowed nothing from them; our Plots are weav'd in English Looms: we endeavour therein to follow the variety and greatness of characters which are derived to us from *Shakespeare* and *Fletcher*: the copiousness and well-knitting of the intrigues we have from *Johnson*, and for the Verse it self we have English Presidents of elder date than any of *Corneilles*'s Plays: (not to name our old Comedies before Shakespeare, which were all writ in verse of six feet, or *Alexandrin's*, such as the French now use) I can shew in *Shakespeare* many Scenes of rhyme together, and the like in *Ben. Johnsons* Tragedies: in *Catiline* and *Sejanus* sometimes thirty or forty lines; I mean besides the Chorus, or the Monologues, which by the way, shew'd *Ben.* no enemy to this way of writing, especially if you read his Sad Shepherd, which goes sometimes on rhyme, sometimes on blank Verse, like an Horse who eases himself on Trot and Amble. You find him likewise commending *Fletchers* Pastoral of the Faithful Shepherdess; which is for the most part Rhyme, though not refin'd to that purity to which it hath since been brought: And these examples are enough to clear us from a servile imitation of the French.

But to return whence I have digress'd, I dare boldly affirm these two things of the English *Drama*: First, That we have many Plays of ours as regular as any of theirs; and which, besides, have more variety of Plot and Characters: And secondly, that in most of the irregular Plays of *Shakespeare* or *Fletcher*, (for *Ben. Johnson*'s are for the most part regular) there is a more masculine fancy and greater spirit in the writing, than there is in any of the French. I could produce even in *Shakespeare*'s and *Fletcher*'s Works, some Plays which are almost exactly form'd; as the Merry Wives of *Windsor*, and the Scornful Lady: but because (generally speaking) *Shakespeare*, who writ first, did not perfectly observe the Laws of Comedy, and *Fletcher*, who came nearer to perfection, yet through carelessness made many faults; I will take the pattern of a perfect Play from *Ben. Johnson*, who was a careful and learned Observer of the Dramatique Laws, and from all his Comedies I shall select *The Silent Woman*; of which I will make a short Examen, according to those Rules which the French observe.

As *Neander* was beginning to examine *The Silent Woman*, *Eugenius*, earnestly regarding him; I beseech you, *Neander*, said he, gratifie the company and me in particular so far, as before you speak of the Play, to give us a Character of the Author; and tell us frankly your opinion, whether you do not think all Writers, both French and English, ought to give place to him?

I fear, replied *Neander*, That in obeying your Commands I shall draw some envy on my self. Besides, in performing them, it will be first necessary to speak somewhat of *Shakespeare* and *Fletcher*, his Rivals in Poesie; and one of them, in my opinion, at least his equal, perhaps his superiour.

To begin then with *Shakespeare*; he was the Man who of all Modern, and perhaps Ancient Poets, had the largest and most comprehensive Soul. All the Images of Nature were still present to him, and he drew them not laboriously, but luckily; when he describes anything, you more than see it, you feel it too. Those who accuse him to have wanted learning, give him the greater commendation: he was naturally learn'd; he needed not the Spectacles of Books to read Nature; he look'd inwards, and found her there. I cannot say he is every where alike; were he so, I should do him injury to compare him with the greatest of Mankind. He is many times flat, insipid; his Comick Wit degenerating into Clenches, his serious Swelling into Bombast. But he is always great, when some great occasion is presented to him: no Man can say he ever had a fit subject for his Wit, and did not then raise himself as high above the rest of Poets,

Quantum lenta solent, inter viburna cupressi.[1]

The consideration of this made Mr. *Hales* of *Eaton*[2] say, That there was no subject of which any Poet ever writ, but he would produce it much better done in *Shakespeare*; and however others are now generally preferr'd before him, yet the Age wherein he liv'd, which had Contemporaries with him, *Fletcher* and *Johnson*, never equall'd them to him in their esteem: And in the last Kings Court, when *Ben*'s reputation was at highest, Sir *John Suckling*, and with him the greater part of the Courtiers, set our *Shakespeare* far above him.

[1] As the cypresses are wont to tower above the yielding osiers. (Vergil, *Eclogues* 1. 26.)

[2] John Hales (1584–1656), a Fellow of Eton.

Beaumont and *Fletcher* of whom I am next to speak, had with the advantage of *Shakespeare*'s Wit, which was their precedent, great natural gifts, improv'd by study. *Beaumont* especially being so accurate a Judge of Plays, that *Ben. Johnson* while he liv'd, submitted all his Writings to his Censure, and 'tis thought, used his Judgment in correcting, if not contriving all his Plots. What value he had for him, appears by the Verses he writ to him; and therefore I need speak no farther of it. The first Play that brought *Fletcher* and him in esteem was their *Philaster*: for before that, they had written two or three very unsuccesfully: as the like is reported of *Ben. Johnson*, before he writ *Every Man in his Humour*. Their Plots were generally more regular than *Shakespeare*'s, especially those which were made before *Beaumont*'s death; and they understood and imitated the Conversation of Gentlemen much better; whose wild debaucheries, and quickness of wit in reparties, no Poet before them could paint as they have done. Humour which *Ben. Johnson* deriv'd from particular persons, they made it not their business to describe: they represented all the passions very lively, but above all, Love. I am apt to believe the English Language in them arriv'd to its highest perfection; what words have since been taken in, are rather superfluous than ornamental. Their Plays are now the most pleasant and frequent entertainments of the Stage; two of theirs being acted through the year for one of *Shakespeare*'s or *Johnson*'s: the reason is, because there is a certain gayety in their Comedies, and Pathos in their more serious Plays, which suits generally with all mens humours. *Shakespeare*'s Language is likewise a little obsolete, and *Ben. Johnson*'s Wit comes short of theirs.

As for *Johnson*, to whose Character I am now arriv'd, if we look upon him while he was himself, (for his last Plays were but his dotages) I think him the most learned and judicious Writer which any Theater ever had. He was a most severe Judge of himself as well as others. One cannot say he wanted wit, but rather that he was frugal of it. In his Works you find little to retrench or alter. Wit and Language, and Humour also in some measure we had before him; but something of Art was wanting to the *Drama* till he came. He manag'd his strength to more advantage than any who preceded him. You seldom find him making Love in any of his Scenes, or endeavouring to move the Passions; his Genius was too sullen and saturnine to do it gracefully, especially when he knew he came after those who had performed both to such an height. Humour was his proper Sphere, and in that he delighted most to represent Mechanick people. He was deeply conversant in the Ancients, both Greek and Latine, and he borrow'd boldly from them: there is scarce a Poet or Historian among the Roman Authors of those times whom he has not translated in *Sejanus* and *Catiline*. But he has done his Robberies so openly, that one may see he fears not to be taxed by any Law. He invades Authors like a Monarch, and what would be theft in other Poets, is only victory in him. With the spoils of these Writers he so represents old *Rome* to us, in its Rites, Ceremonies and Customs, that if one of their Poets had written either of his Tragedies, we had seen less of it than in him. If there was any fault in his Language, 'twas that he weav'd it too closely and laboriously, in his Comedies especially: perhaps, too, he did a little too much Romanize our Tongue, leaving the words which he translated almost as much Latine as he found them: wherein though he learnedly followed their Language, he did not enough comply with the Idiom of ours. If I would compare him with *Shakespeare*, I must acknowledge him the more correct Poet, but *Shakespeare* the greater Wit. *Shakespeare* was the *Homer*, or Father of our Dramatick Poets; *Johnson* was the *Virgil*, the pattern of elaborate Writing; I admire him, but I love *Shakespeare*. To conclude of him, as he has given us the most correct Plays, so in the precepts which he has laid down in his Discoveries, we have as many and profitable Rules for perfecting the Stage as any wherewith the French can furnish us.

Having thus spoken of the Author, I proceed to the examination of his Comedy, *The Silent Woman*.

Examen of the Silent Woman.

To begin first with the length of the Action, it is so far from exceeding the compass of a Natural day, that it takes not up an Artificial one. 'Tis all included in the limits of three hours and an half, which is no more than is requir'd for the presentment on the Stage. A beauty perhaps not much observ'd; if it had, we should not have look'd on the Spanish Translation of five hours [1] with so much wonder. The Scene of it is laid in *London*; the latitude of place is almost as little as you can imagine: for it lies all within the compass of two Houses, and after the first Act, in one. The continuity of Scenes is observ'd more than in any of our Plays, except his own Fox and Alchymist. They are not broken above twice or thrice at most in the whole Comedy, and in the two best of *Corneille*'s Plays, the *Cid* and *Cinna*, they are inter-

[1] See *ante*, p. 402, n. 1.

rupted once. The action of the Play is intirely one; the end or aim of which is the setling *Morose*'s Estate on *Dauphine*. The Intrigue of it is the greatest and most noble of any pure unmix'd Comedy in any Language: you see in it many persons of various characters and humours, and all delightful: As first, *Morose*, or an old Man, to whom all noise but his own talking is offensive. Some who would be thought Criticks, say this humour of his is forc'd: but to remove that objection, we may consider him first to be naturally of a delicate hearing, as many are to whom all sharp sounds are unpleasant; and secondly, we may attribute much of it to the peevishness of his Age, or the wayward authority of an old Man in his own house, where he may make himself obeyed; and to this the Poet seems to allude in his name *Morose*. Beside this, I am assur'd from divers persons, that *Ben. Johnson* was actually acquainted with such a man, one altogether as ridiculous as he is here represented. Others say it is not enough to find one man of such an humour; it must be common to more, and the more common the more natural. To prove this, they instance in the best of Comical Characters, *Falstaffe*: There are many men resembling him; Old, Fat, Merry, Cowardly, Drunken, Amorous, Vain, and Lying: But to convince these people, I need but tell them, that humour is the ridiculous extravagance of conversation, wherein one man differs from all others. If then it be common, or communicated to many, how differs it from other mens? or what indeed causes it to be ridiculous so much as the singularity of it? As for *Falstaffe*, he is not properly one humour, but a Miscellany of Humours or Images, drawn from so many several men; that wherein he is singular is his wit, or those things he says *præter expectatum*,[1] unexpected by the Audience; his quick evasions when you imagine him surpriz'd, which as they are extreamly diverting of themselves, so receive a great addition from his person; for the very sight of such an unweildy old de-bauch'd Fellow is a Comedy alone. And here having a place so proper for it, I cannot but enlarge somewhat upon this subject of humour into which I am fallen. The Ancients had little of it in their Comedies; for the τὸ γελοῖον,[2] of the old Comedy, of which *Aristophanes* was chief, was not so much to imitate a man, as to make the people laugh at some odd conceit, which had commonly somewhat of unnatural or obscene in it. Thus when you see *Socrates* brought upon the Stage, you are not to imagine him made ridiculous by the imitation of his actions, but rather by making him perform something very unlike himself: something

[1] Contrary to expectation. [2] The ridiculous.

so childish and absurd, as by comparing it with the gravity of the true *Socrates*, makes a ridiculous object for the Spectators. In their new Comedy which succeeded, the Poets sought indeed to express the ἦθος,[1] as in their Tragedies the πάθος[2] of Mankind. But this ἦθος contain'd only the general Characters of Men and Manners; as Old Men, Lovers, Servingmen, Courtizans, Parasites, and such other persons as we see in their Comedies; all which they made alike: that is, one Old Man or Father; one Lover, one Courtizan so like another, as if the first of them had begot the rest of every sort: *Ex homine hunc natum dicas*.[3] The same custom they observ'd likewise in their Tragedies. As for the *French*, though they have the word *humeur* among them, yet they have small use of it in their Comedies, or Farces; they being but ill imitations of the *ridiculum*, or that which stirr'd up laughter in the old Comedy. But among the *English* 'tis otherwise: where by humour is meant some extravagant habit, passion, or affection; particular (as I said before) to some one person: by the oddness of which, he is immediately distinguish'd from the rest of men; which being lively and naturally represented, most frequently begets that malicious pleasure in the Audience which is testified by laughter: as all things which are deviations from customs are ever the aptest to produce it: though by the way this laughter is only accidental, as the person represented is Fantastick or Bizarre; but pleasure is essential to it, as the imitation of what is natural. The description of these humours, drawn from the knowledge and observation of particular persons, was the peculiar genius and talent of *Ben. Johnson*; to whose Play I now return.

Besides *Morose*, there are at least nine or ten different Characters and humours in the *Silent Woman*, all which persons have several concernments of their own, yet are all us'd by the Poet, to the conducting of the main design to perfection. I shall not waste time in commending the writing of this Play, but I will give you my opinion, that there is more wit and acuteness of Fancy in it than in any of *Ben. Johnson*'s. Besides, that he has here describ'd the Conversation of Gentlemen in the persons of *True-Wit*, and his Friends, with more gayety, air and freedom, than in the rest of his Comedies. For the contrivance of the Plot, 'tis extream elaborate, and yet withal easie; for the λύσις, or untying of it, 'tis so admirable, that when it is done, no one of the Audience would think the Poet could have miss'd it; and yet it was conceal'd so much before the last Scene, that any other way would

[1] Character. [2] Experience.
[3] One would say this fellow was born of a human being.

sooner have enter'd into your thoughts. But I dare not take upon me to commend the Fabrick of it, because it is altogether so full of Art, that I must unravel every Scene in it to commend it as I ought. And this excellent contrivance is still the more to be admir'd, because 'tis Comedy where the persons are only of common rank, and their business private, not elevated by passions or high concernments as in serious Plays. Here every one is a proper Judge of all he sees; nothing is represented but that with which he daily converses: so that by consequence all faults lie open to discovery, and few are pardonable. 'Tis this which Horace has judiciously observ'd:

> *Creditur ex medio quia res arcessit habere*
> *Sudoris minimum, sed habet Comedia tanto*
> *Plus oneris, quanto veniæ minus.*——[1]

But our Poet, who was not ignorant of these difficulties, has made use of all advantages; as he who designs a large leap takes his rise from the highest ground. One of these advantages is that which *Corneille* has laid down as the greatest which can arrive to any Poem, and which he himself could never compass above thrice in all his Plays, *viz.* the making choice of some signal and long-expected day, whereon, the action of the Play is to depend. This day was that design'd by *Dauphine* for the setling of his Uncles Estate upon him; which to compass he contrives to marry him: That the marriage had been plotted by him long beforehand is made evident by what he tells *True-Wit* in the second Act, that in one moment he had destroy'd what he had been raising many months.

There is another artifice of the Poet, which I cannot here omit, because by the frequent practice of it in his Comedies, he has left it to us almost as a Rule, that is, when he has any Character or humour wherein he would shew a *Coup de Maistre*, or his highest skill; he recommends it to your observation by a pleasant description of it before the person first appears. Thus, in *Bartholomew-Fair* he gives you the Pictures of *Numps* and *Cokes*, and in this those of *Daw*, *Lafoole*, *Morose*, and the *Collegiate Ladies*; all which you hear describ'd before you see them. So that before they come upon the Stage you have a longing expectation of them, which prepares you to receive them favourably; and when they are there, even from their first appearance you are so far acquainted with them, that nothing of their humour is lost to you.

[1] Comedy is thought to involve least effort, since it draws its plots from ordinary life; but in fact it involves a heavier responsibility in proportion as it is allowed less indulgence. (*Epistles* 2. 1. 169.)

I will observe yet one thing further of this admirable Plot; the business of it rises in every Act. The second is greater than the first; the third than the second, and so forward to the fifth. There too you see, till the very last Scene, new difficulties arising to obstruct the action of the Play; and when the Audience is brought into despair that the business can naturally be effected, then, and not before, the discovery is made. But that the Poet might entertain you with more variety all this while, he reserves some new Characters to show you, which he opens not till the second and third Act. In the second *Morose*, *Daw*, the *Barber* and *Otter*; in the third the *Collegiat Ladies*: All which he moves afterwards in by-walks, or underplots, as diversions to the main design, lest it should grow tedious, though they are still naturally joyned with it, and somewhere or other subservient to it. Thus, like a skilful Chess-player, by little and little he draws out his men, and makes his pawns of use to his greater persons.

If this Comedy, and some others of his, were translated into French Prose (which would now be no wonder to them, since *Moliere* has lately given them Plays out of Verse which have not displeas'd them) I believe the controversie would soon be decided betwixt the two nations, even making them the Judges. But we need not call our Hero's to our aid; Be it spoken to the honour of the English, our Nation can never want in any Age such who are able to dispute the Empire of Wit with any people in the Universe. And though the fury of a Civil War, and Power, for twenty years together, abandon'd to a barbarous race of men, Enemies of all good Learning, had buried the Muses under the ruines of Monarchy; yet with the restoration of our happiness, we see reviv'd Poesie lifting up its head, and already shaking off the rubbish which lay so heavy on it. We have seen since his Majesties return, many Dramatick Poems which yield not to those of any forreign Nation, and which deserve all Lawrels but the English. I will set aside Flattery and Envy: it cannot be deny'd but we have had some little blemish either in the Plot or writing of all those Plays which have been made within these seven years: (and perhaps there is no Nation in the world so quick to discern them, or so difficult to pardon them, as ours:) yet if we can perswade our selves to use the candour of that Poet, who (though the most severe of Criticks) has left us this caution by which to moderate our censures;

——*Ubi plura nitent in carmine non ego paucis offendar maculis.*[1]

[1] Where in a poem there are several excellences, I am not one to be offended at a few blemishes. (Horace, *Ars Poetica* 351–2.)

If in consideration of their many and great beauties, we can wink at some slight, and little imperfections; if we, I say, can be thus equal to our selves, I ask no favour from the French. And if I do not venture upon any particular judgment of our late Plays, 'tis out of the consideration which an Ancient Writer gives me; *Vivorum, ut magna admiratio, ita censura difficilis:*[1] betwixt the extreams of admiration and malice, 'tis hard to judge upright of the living. Only I think it may be permitted me to say, that as it is no less'ning to us to yeild to some Plays, and those not many of our own Nation in the last Age, so can it be no addition to pronounce of our present Poets that they have far surpass'd all the Ancients, and the Modern Writers of other Countreys.

This, was the substance of what was then spoke on that occasion; and *Lisideius*, I think was going to reply, when he was prevented thus by *Crites*: I am confident, said he, that the most material things that can be said, have been already urg'd on either side; if they have not, I must beg of *Lisideius* that he will defer his answer till another time: for I confess I have a joynt quarrel to you both, because you have concluded, without any reason given for it, that Rhyme is proper for the Stage. I will not dispute how ancient it hath been among us to write this way; perhaps our Ancestours knew no better till *Shakespeare's* time. I will grant it was not altogether left by him, and that *Fletcher* and *Ben. Johnson* us'd it frequently in their Pastorals, and sometimes in other Plays. Farther, I will not argue whether we receiv'd it originally from our own Countrymen, or from the French; for that is an inquiry of as little benefit, as theirs who in the midst of the great Plague were not so sollicitous to provide against it, as to know whether we had it from the malignity of our own air, or by transportation from *Holland.* I have therefore only to affirm, that it is not allowable in serious Plays; for Comedies I find you already concluding with me. To prove this, I might satisfie my self to tell you, how much in vain it is for you to strive against the stream of the peoples inclination; the greatest part of which are prepossess'd so much with those excellent Plays of *Shakespeare*, *Fletcher*, and *Ben. Johnson*, (which have been written out of Rhyme) that except you could bring them such as were written better in it, and those too by persons of equal reputation with them, it will be impossible for you to gain your cause with them, who will still be judges. This it is to which in

[1] Living writers are highly admired and correspondingly hard to judge. (Velleius Paterculus 2. 36.)

fine all your reasons must submit. The unanimous consent of an Audience is so powerful, That even *Julius Cæsar* (as *Macrobius* reports of him) when he was perpetual Dictator, was not able to ballance it on the other side. But when *Laberius*, a *Roman* Knight, at his request contended in the *Mime* with another Poet, he was forc'd to cry out, *Etiam favente me victus es Laberi.*[1] But I will not on this occasion, take the advantage of the greater number, but only urge such reasons against Rhyme, as I find in the Writings of those who have argu'd for the other way. First then I am of opinion, that Rhyme is unnatural in a Play, because Dialogue there is presented as the effect of sudden thought. For a Play is the imitation of Nature; and since no man, without premeditation speaks in Rhyme, neither ought he to do it on the Stage; this hinders not but the Fancy may be there elevated to an higher pitch of thought than it is in ordinary discourse: for there is a probability that men of excellent and quick parts may speak noble things *ex tempore*: but those thoughts are never fetter'd with the numbers or sound of Verse without study, and therefore it cannot be but unnatural to present the most free way of speaking, in that which is the most constrain'd. For this Reason, says *Aristotle*; 'Tis best to write Tragedy in that kind of Verse which is the least such, or which is nearest Prose: and this amongst the Ancients was the Iambique, and with us is blank verse, or the measure of verse, kept exactly without Rhyme. These numbers therefore are fittest for a Play; the others for a paper of Verses, or a Poem. Blank verse being as much below them, as Rhyme is improper for the *Drama*. And if it be objected that neither are blank verses made *ex tempore*, yet as nearest Nature, they are still to be preferr'd. But there are two particular exceptions which many besides my self have had to verse; by which it will appear yet more plainly, how improper it is in Plays. And the first of them is grounded on that very reason for which some have commended Rhyme: they say the quickness of repartees in argumentative Scenes receives an ornament from verse. Now what is more unreasonable than to imagine that a man should not only imagine the Wit, but the Rhyme too upon the sudden? This nicking of him who spoke before both in sound and measure, is so great an happiness, that you must at least suppose the persons of your Play to be born Poets, *Arcades omnes & cantare pares & respondere parati*,[2] they must have arriv'd to the degree of *quicquid*

[1] You were worsted, Laberius, even though you had my support. (*Saturnalia* 2. 7. 8.)

[2] Arcadians all, ready to sing and to reply in equal contest. (Cf. Vergil, *Eclogues* 7. 4–5.)

conabar dicere:[1] to make Verses almost whether they will or no: if they are any thing below this, it will look rather like the design of two, than the answer of one: it will appear that your Actors hold intelligence together, that they perform their tricks like Fortune-tellers, by confederacy. The hand of Art will be too visible in it against that maxim of all Professions; *Ars est celare artem*,[2] That it is the greatest perfection of Art to keep it self undiscover'd. Nor will it serve you to object, that however you manage it, 'tis still known to be a Play; and consequently the Dialogue of two persons understood to be the labour of one Poet. For a Play is still an imitation of Nature; we know we are to be deceiv'd, and we desire to be so; but no man ever was deceiv'd but with a probability of truth, for who will suffer a gross lie to be fasten'd on him? Thus we sufficiently understand that the Scenes which represent Cities and Countries to us, are not really such, but only painted on boards and Canvas: But shall that excuse the ill Painture or designment of them; Nay rather ought they not to be labour'd with so much the more diligence and exactness to help the imagination? since the mind of man does naturally tend to truth: and therefore the nearer any thing comes to the imitation of it, the more it pleases.

Thus, you see, your Rhyme is uncapable of expressing the greatest thoughts naturally, and the lowest it cannot with any grace: for what is more unbefitting the Majesty of Verse, than to call a Servant, or bid a door be shut in Rhime? And yet you are often forc'd on this miserable necessity. But Verse, you say, circumscribes a quick and luxuriant fancy, which would extend it self too far on every subject, did not the labour which is requir'd to well turn'd and polish'd Rhyme, set bounds to it. Yet this Argument, if granted, would only prove that we may write better in Verse, but not more naturally. Neither is it able to evince that; for he who wants judgment to confine his fancy in blank Verse, may want it as much in Rhyme; and he who has it will avoid errours in both kinds. Latine verse was as great a confinement to the imagination of those Poets, as Rhyme to ours: and yet you find *Ovid* saying too much on every subject *Nescivit* (says *Seneca*) *quod bene cessit relinquere:*[3] of which

[1] Whatever I strove to say was verse ('I lisped in numbers, for the numbers came'). (Cf. Ovid, *Tristia* 4. 10. 26.)

[2] To conceal one's art, is art itself. (Cf. *Disticha Catonis* 126. 2: 'sic ars deluditur arte'.)

[3] He knew not how to let alone a thing done well enough already. (Seneca the Elder, *Controversiæ* 28.)

he gives you one famous instance in his Description of the Deluge:

Omnia pontus erat, deerant quoque Litora Ponto.

Now all was Sea, Nor had that Sea a shore. Thus *Ovid's* fancy was not limited by verse, and *Virgil* needed not verse to have bounded his.

In our own language we see *Ben. Johnson* confining himself to what ought to be said, even in the liberty of blank Verse; and yet *Corneile*, the most judicious of the *French* Poets, is still varying the same sense an hundred ways, and dwelling eternally on the same subject, though confin'd by Rhyme. Some other exceptions I have to Verse, but since these I have nam'd are for the most part already publick, I conceive it reasonable they should first be answer'd.

It concerns me less than any, said *Neander*, (seeing he had ended) to reply to this Discourse; because when I should have prov'd that Verse may be natural in Plays, yet I should always be ready to confess, that those which I have written in this kind come short of that perfection which is requir'd. Yet since you are pleas'd I should undertake this Province, I will do it, though with all imaginable respect and deference, both to that person from whom you have borrow'd your strongest Arguments, and to whose judgment when I have said all, I finally submit. But before I proceed to answer your objections, I must first remember you, that I exclude all Comedy from my defence; and next that I deny not but blank verse may be also us'd, and content my self only to assert, that in serious Plays where the subject and characters are great, and the Plot unmix'd with mirth, which might allay or divert these concernments which are produc'd, Rhyme is there as natural, and more effectual than blank Verse.

And now having laid down this as a foundation, to begin with *Crites*, I must crave leave to tell him, that some of his Arguments against Rhyme reach no farther than from the faults or defects of ill Rhyme, to conclude against the use of it in general. May not I conclude against blank verse by the same reason? If the words of some Poets who write in it, are either ill chosen, or ill placed (which makes not only Rhime, but all kind of verse in any language unnatural;) Shall I, for their vitious affectation condemn those excellent lines of *Fletcher*, which are written in that kind? Is there any thing in Rhyme more constrain'd than this line in blank verse? *I Heav'n invoke, and strong resistance make*; where you see both the clauses are plac'd unnaturally; that is, contrary to the common way of speaking, and that without the excuse of a Rhyme to cause it: yet you would think me very ridiculous, if I should accuse the stubbornness of blank Verse for this, and not rather the stifness of the Poet. Therefore, *Crites*, you must either prove that words, though well chosen, and duly plac'd, yet render not Rhyme natural in it self; or that however natural and easie the Rhyme may be, yet it is not proper for a Play. If you insist on the former part, I would ask you what other conditions are requir'd to make Rhyme natural in it self, besides an election of apt words, and a right disposition of them? For the due choice of your words expresses your sense naturally, and the due placing them adapts the Rhyme to it. If you object that one verse may be made for the sake of another, though both the words and Rhyme be apt; I answer it cannot possibly so fall out; for either there is a dependance of sense betwixt the first line and the second, or there is none: if there be that connection, then in the natural position of the words, the latter line must of necessity flow from the former: if there be no dependance, yet still the due ordering of words makes the last line as natural in it self as the other: so that the necessity of a Rhyme never forces any but bad or lazy Writers to say what they would not otherwise. 'Tis true, there is both care and Art requir'd to write in Verse; A good Poet never establishes the first line, till he has sought out such a Rhime as may fit the sense, already prepar'd to heighten the second: many times the close of the sense falls into the middle of the next verse, or farther off, and he may often prevail himself of the same advantages in English which *Virgil* had in Latine, he may break off in the *Hemystich*, and begin another line: indeed, the not observing these two last things, makes Plays which are writ in verse, so tedious: for though, most commonly, the sense is to be confin'd to the Couplet, yet nothing that does *perpetuo tenore fluere*, run in the same channel, can please always. 'Tis like the murmuring of a stream, which not varying in the fall, causes at first attention, at last drowsiness. Variety of cadences is the best rule, the greatest help to the Actors, and refreshment to the Audience.

If then Verse may be made natural in it self, how becomes it unnaturall in a Play? You say the Stage is the representation of Nature, and no man in ordinary conversation speaks in Rhime. But you foresaw when you said this, that it might be answer'd; neither does any man speak in blank verse, or in measure without Rhime. Therefore you concluded, that which is nearest Nature is still to be preferr'd. But you took no notice that

Rhime might be made as natural as blank verse, by the well placing of the words, *&c.* All the difference between them when they are both correct, is the sound in one, which the other wants; and if so, the sweetness of it, and all the advantage resulting from it, which are handled in the Preface to the *Rival Ladies*, will yet stand good. As for that place of *Aristotle*, where he says Plays should be writ in that kind of Verse which is nearest Prose; it makes little for you, blank verse being properly but measur'd Prose. Now measure alone in any modern Language, does not constitute verse; those of the ancients in Greek and Latine, consisted in quantity of words, and a determinate number of feet. But when, by the inundation of the *Goths* and *Vandals* into *Italy* new Languages were introduced, and barbarously mingled with the Latine (of which the *Italian*, *Spanish*, *French*, and ours (made out of them and the *Teutonick*) are Dialects:) a new way of Poesie was practis'd; new, I say in those Countries, for in all probability it was that of the Conquerors in their own Nations: at least we are able to prove, that the Eastern people have us'd it from all Antiquity, *Vid. Dan. his Defence of Rhyme.*[1] This new way consisted in measure or number of feet and Rhyme. The sweetness of Rhyme, and observation of Accent, supplying the place of quantity in words, which could neither exactly be observ'd by those *Barbarians* who knew not the Rules of it, neither was it suitable to their tongues as it had been to the Greek and Latine. No man is tied in modern Poesie to observe any farther rule in the feet of his verse, but that they be dissyllables; whether *Spondee*, *Trochee*, or *Iambique*, it matters not; only he is obliged to Rhyme: neither do the *Spanish*, *French*, *Italian*, or *Germans* acknowledge at all, or very rarely any such kind of Poesie as blank verse amongst them. Therefore at most 'tis but a Poetick Prose, a *Sermo pedestris*,[2] and as such most fit for Comedies, where I acknowledge Rhyme to be improper. Farther, as to that quotation of *Aristotle*, our Couplet Verses may be rendred as near Prose as blank verse it self, by using those advantages I lately nam'd, as breaks in an Hemystick, or running the sense into another line, thereby making Art and Order appear as loose and free as Nature; or not tying our selves to Couplets strictly, we may use the benefit of the Pindarique way practis'd in the Siege of *Rhodes*; where the numbers vary and the Rhyme is dispos'd carelesly, and far from often chyming. Neither is that

[1] The reference is to Samuel Daniel's (1552–1619) *Defence of Rhyme*, 1602.

[2] Prose discourse.

other advantage of the Ancients to be despis'd, of changing the kind of verse when they please with the change of the Scene, or some new entrance: for they confine not themselves always to Iambiques, but extend their liberty to all Lyrick numbers, and sometimes, even to Hexameter. But I need not go so far to prove that Rhyme, as it succeeds to all other offices of Greek and Latine Verse, so especially to this of Plays, since the custome of Nations at this day confirms it, the *French*, *Italian*, and *Spanish* Tragedies are generally writ in it, and sure the Universal consent of the most civiliz'd parts of the world, ought in this, as it doth in other customs, to include the rest.

But perhaps you may tell me I have propos'd such a way to make Rhyme natural, and consequently proper to Plays, as is unpracticable, and that I shall scarce find six or eight lines together in any Play, where the words are so plac'd and chosen as is requir'd to make it natural. I answer, no Poet need constrain himself at all times to it. It is enough he makes it his general Rule; for I deny not but sometimes there may be a greatness in placing the words otherwise; and sometimes they may sound better, sometimes also the variety it self is excuse enough. But if, for the most part, the words be plac'd as they are in the negligence of Prose, it is sufficient to denominate the way practicable; for we esteem that to be such, which in the Tryal oftner succeeds than misses. And thus far you may find the practice made good in many Plays; where you do not, remember still, that if you cannot find six natural Rhymes together, it will be as hard for you to produce as many lines in blank Verse, even among the greatest of our Poets, against which I cannot make some reasonable exception.

And this, Sir, calls to my remembrance the beginning of your discourse, where you told us we should never find the Audience favourable to this kind of writing, till we could produce as good Plays in Rhyme, as *Ben. Johnson*, *Fletcher*, and *Shakespeare*, had writ out of it. But it is to raise envy to the living, to compare them with the dead. They are honour'd, and almost ador'd by us, as they deserve; neither do I know any so presumptuous of themselves as to contend with them. Yet give me leave to say thus much, without injury to their Ashes, that not only we shall never equal them, but they could never equal themselves, were they to rise and write again. We acknowledge them our Fathers in wit, but they have ruin'd their Estates themselves before they came to their childrens hands. There is scarce an Humour, a Character, or any kind of Plot, which they have not us'd. All comes sullied or wasted to us: and were they to entertain this Age, they could not now make so plenteous treatments out of such decay'd Fortunes. This therefore will be a good Argument to us either not to write at all, or to attempt some other way. There is no Bays to be expected in their Walks; *Tentanda via est, quà me quoque possum tollere humo.*[1]

This way of writing in Verse, they have only left free to us; our age is arriv'd to a perfection in it, which they never knew; and which (if we may guess by what of theirs we have seen in Verse (as the *Faithful Shepherdess*, and *Sad Shepherd*:)[2] 'tis probable they never could have reach'd. For the Genius of every Age is different; and though ours excel in this, I deny not but that to imitate Nature in that perfection which they did in Prose, is a greater commendation than to write in verse exactly. As for what you have added, that the people are not generally inclin'd to like this way; if it were true, it would be no wonder, that betwixt the shaking off an old habit, and the introducing of a new, there should be difficulty. Do we not see them stick to *Hopkins* and *Sternholds* Psalms,[3] and forsake those of *David*, I mean *Sandys* his Translation of them?[4] If by the people you understand the multitude, the οἱ πολλοί.[5] 'Tis no matter what they think; they are sometimes in the right, sometimes in the wrong; their judgment is a meer Lottery. *Est ubi plebs rectè putat, est ubi peccat.*[6] *Horace* says it of the vulgar, judging Poesie. But if you mean the mix'd audience of the populace and the Noblesse, I dare confidently affirm that a great part of the latter sort, are already favourable to verse; and that no serious Plays written since the Kings return have been more kindly receiv'd by them, than the Seige of *Rhodes*, the *Mustapha*, the *Indian* Queen, and *Indian* Emperor.

But I come now to the inference of your first Argument. You said that the Dialogue of Plays is presented as the effect of sudden thought, but no man speaks suddenly, or *ex tempore* in Rhyme: And you inferr'd from thence, that Rhyme, which you acknowledge to be proper to Epique Poesie cannot equally be proper to

[1] I must try some way to raise myself from the earth, like these. (Vergil, *Georgics* 3. 8.)

[2] John Fletcher's pastoral play of *The Faithful Shepherdess* was published in 1610; Ben Jonson's unfinished pastoral play of *The Sad Shepherd* was published in 1641.

[3] John Hopkin's (*d.* 1549) and Thomas Sternhold's (*d.* 1570) famous collection of versified psalms first appeared in 1549.

[4] George Sandys's (1578–1644) *Paraphrase upon the Psalmes* was published in 1636.

[5] The many.

[6] There are times when the common people is right in its opinions, times when it errs. (*Epistles* 2. 1. 63.)

Dramatick, unless we could suppose all men born so much more than Poets, that verses should be made in them, not by them.

It has been formerly urg'd by you, and confess'd by me, that since no man spoke any kind of verse *ex tempore*, that which was nearest Nature was to be preferr'd. I answer you therefore, by distinguishing betwixt what is nearest to the nature of Comedy, which is the imitation of common persons and ordinary speaking, and what is nearest the nature of a serious Play; this last is indeed the representation of Nature, but 'tis Nature wrought up to an higher pitch. The Plot, the Characters, the Wit, the Passions, the Descriptions, are all exalted above the level of common converse, as high as the imagination of the Poet can carry them, with proportion to verisimility. Tragedy we know is wont to image to us the minds and fortunes of noble persons, and to portray these exactly; Heroick Rhime is nearest Nature, as being the noblest kind of modern verse.

> *Indignatur enim privatis, & prope socco,*
> *Dignis carminibus, narrari cœna Thyestæ.* (Says *Horace*.)[1]

And in another place,

> *Effutire levis indigna tragœdia versus.*[2]

Blank Verse is acknowledg'd to be too low for a Poem; nay more, for a paper of verses; but if too low for an ordinary Sonnet, how much more for Tragedy, which is by *Aristotle* in the dispute betwixt the Epique Poesie and the Dramatick, for many reasons he there alledges, rank'd above it?

But setting this defence aside, your Argument is almost as strong against the use of Rhyme in Poems as in Plays; for the Epique way is every where interlac'd with Dialogue, or discoursive Scenes; and therefore you must either grant Rhyme to be improper there, which is contrary to your assertion, or admit it into Plays by the same title which you have given it to Poems. For though Tragedy be justly preferr'd above the other, yet there is a great affinity between them, as may easily be discover'd in that definition of a Play which *Lisideius* gave us. The Genus of them is the same, a just and lively Image of humane nature, in its Actions, Passions, and traverses of Fortune: so is the end, namely, for the delight and benefit of Mankind. The Characters and Persons are still the same, *viz.* the greatest of both sorts, only the manner of acquainting us with those Actions, Passions and Fortunes is

[1] For the tale of Thyestes' banquet cannot be told adequately in verses of a humdrum sort, fit almost for comedy. (*Ars Poetica* 90–1.)

[2] Tragedy is unfitted to prate in frivolous lines. (*Ibid.* 231.)

different. Tragedy performs it *viva voce*, or by action, in Dialogue, wherein it excels the Epique Poem which does it chiefly by narration, and therefore is not so lively an Image of Humane Nature. However, the agreement betwixt them is such, that if Rhyme be proper for one, it must be for the other. Verse 'tis true is not the effect of sudden thought; but this hinders not that sudden thought may be represented in verse, since those thoughts are such as must be higher than Nature can raise them without premeditation, especially to a continuance of them even out of verse, and consequently you cannot imagine them to have been sudden either in the Poet, or in the Actors. A Play, as I have said to be like Nature, is to be set above it; as Statues which are plac'd on high are made greater than the life, that they may descend to the sight in their just proportion.

Perhaps I have insisted too long on this objection; but the clearing of it will make my stay shorter on the rest. You tell us *Crites*, that Rhyme appears most unnatural in repartees, or short replyes: when he who answers, (it being Presum'd he knew not what the other would say, yet) makes up that part of the verse which was left incompleat, and supplies both the sound and measure of it. This you say looks rather like the confederacy of two, than the answer of one.

This, I confess, is an objection which is in every mans mouth who loves not Rhyme: but suppose, I beseech you, the repartee were made only in blank verse, might not part of the same argument be turn'd against you? for the measure is as often supply'd there as it is in Rhyme. The latter half of the Hemystich as commonly made up, or a second line subjoyn'd as a reply to the former; which any one leaf in *Johnson's* Plays will sufficiently clear to you. You will often find in the Greek Tragedians, and in *Seneca*, that when a Scene grows up into the warmth of repartees (which is the close fighting of it) the latter part of the Trimeter is supply'd by him who answers; and yet it was never observ'd as a fault in them by any of the Ancient or Modern Criticks. The case is the same in our verse as it was in theirs; Rhyme to us being in lieu of quantity to them. But if no latitude is to be allow'd a Poet, you take from him not only his licence of *quidlibet audendi*,[1] but you tie him up in a straighter compass than you would a Philosopher. This is indeed *Musas colere severiores*:[2] You would have him follow Nature, but he must follow her on foot: you have dismounted him from his *Pegasus*. But you tell us this supplying

[1] Venturing anything he pleases. (*Ibid.* 10.)
[2] To cultivate the more exacting Muses. (Cf. Horace, *Odes* 2. 1. 9.)

the last half of a verse, or adjoyning a whole second to the former, looks more like the design of two than the answer of one. Suppose we acknowledge it: how comes this confederacy to be more displeasing to you than in a Dance which is well contriv'd? You see there the united design of many persons to make up one Figure: after they have separated themselves in many petty divisions, they rejoyn one by one into a gross: the confederacy is plain amongst them; for chance could never produce any thing so beautiful, and yet there is nothing in it, that shocks your sight. I acknowledge the hand of Art appears in repartee, as of necessity it must in all kind of verse. But there is also the quick and poynant brevity of it (which is an high imitation of Nature in those sudden gusts of passion) to mingle with it: and this joyn'd with the cadency and sweetness of the Rhyme, leaves nothing in the soul of the hearer to desire. 'Tis an Art which appears; but it appears only like the shadowings of Painture, which being to cause the rounding of it, cannot be absent; but while that is consider'd they are lost: so while we attend to the other beauties of the matter, the care and labour of the Rhyme is carry'd from us, or at least drown'd in its own sweetness, as Bees are sometimes bury'd in their Honey. When a Poet has found the repartee, the last perfection he can add to it, is to put it into verse. However good the thought may be; however apt the words in which 'tis couch'd, yet he finds himself at a little unrest while Rhyme is wanting: he cannot leave it till that comes naturally, and then is at ease, and sits down contented.

From Replies, which are the most elevated thoughts of Verse, you pass to those which are most mean and which are common with the lowest of houshold conversation. In these, you say, the Majesty of Verse suffers. You instance in the calling of a servant, or commanding a door to be shut in Rhyme. This, *Crites*, is a good observation of yours, but no argument: for it proves no more but that such thoughts should be wav'd, as often as may be, by the address of the Poet. But suppose they are necessary in the places where he uses them, yet there is no need to put them into Rhyme. He may place them in the beginning of a Verse, and break it off, as unfit, when so debas'd for any other use: or granting the worst, that they require more room than the Hemystich will allow; yet still there is a choice to be made of the best words, and least vulgar (provided they be apt) to express such thoughts. Many have blam'd Rhyme in general, for this fault, when the Poet, with a little care, might have redress'd it. But they do it with no more justice, than if English Poesie should be made ridiculous for the sake of the Water Poet's Rhymes.[1] Our language is noble, full and significant; and I know not why he who is Master of it may not cloath ordinary things in it as decently as the Latine; if he use the same diligence in his choice of words.

Delectus verborum Origo est Eloquentiæ.[2]

It was the saying of *Julius Cæsar*, one so curious in his, that none of them can be chang'd but for a worse. One would think unlock the door was a thing as vulgar as could be spoken; and yet *Seneca* could make it sound high and lofty in his Latine.—

Reserate clusos Regii postes Laris.

Set wide the Palace gates.

But I turn from this exception, both because it happens not above twice or thrice in any Play that those vulgar thoughts are us'd; and then too (were there no other Apology to be made, yet) the necessity of them (which is alike in all kind of writing) may excuse them. For if they are little and mean in Rhyme, they are of consequence such in Blank Verse. Besides that the great eagerness and precipitation with which they are spoken makes us rather mind the substance than the dress; that for which they are spoken, rather than what is spoke. For they are always the effect of some hasty concernment, and something of consequence depends on them.

Thus, *Crites*, I have endeavour'd to answer your objections; it remains only that I should vindicate an Argument for Verse, which you have gone about to overthrow. It had formerly been said, that the easiness of blank verse, renders the Poet too luxuriant; but that the labour of Rhyme bounds and circumscribes an over-fruitful fancy. The scene there being commonly confin'd to the couplet, and the words so order'd that the Rhyme naturally follows them, not they the Rhyme. To this you answer'd, that it was no Argument to the question in hand, for the dispute was not which way a man may write best; but which is most proper for the subject on which he writes.

First, give me leave, Sir, to remember you that the Argument against which you rais'd this objection, was only secondary: it was built on this *Hypothesis*, that to write in verse was proper

[1] John Taylor (1580–1653), known as the Water Poet, was a Thames waterman with a remarkable gift for writing fluent rhyme. He published his collected works in 1630.

[2] Choice of words is the beginning of eloquence. (Julius Cæsar, quoted by Cicero, *Brutus* 72. 253.)

for serious Plays. Which supposition being granted (as it was briefly made out in that discourse, by shewing how verse might be made natural) it asserted, that this way of writing was an help to the Poets judgment, by putting bounds to a wilde over-flowing Fancy. I think therefore it will not be hard for me to make good what it was to prove on that supposition. But you add, that were this let pass, yet he who wants judgment in the liberty of his fancy, may as well shew the defect of it when he is confin'd to verse: for he who has judgment will avoid errours, and he who has it not, will commit them in all kinds of writing.

This Argument, as you have taken it from a most acute person, so I confess it carries much weight in it. But by using the word Judgment here indefinitely, you seem to have put a fallacy upon us: I grant he who has Judgment, that is, so profound, so strong, or rather so infallible a judgment, that he needs no helps to keep it always pois'd and upright, will commit no faults either in Rhyme or out of it. And on the other extream, he who has a judgment so weak and craz'd that no helps can correct or amend it, shall write scurvily out of Rhyme, and worse in it. But the first of these judgments is no where to be found, and the latter is not fit to write at all. To speak therefore of judgment as it is in the best Poets; they who have the greatest proportion of it, want other helps than from it within. As for example, you would be loth to say, that he who is endued with a sound judgment has no need of History, Geography, or Moral Philosophy, to write correctly. Judgment is indeed the Master-workman in a Play: but he requires many subordinate hands, many tools to his assistance. And verse I affirm to be one of these: 'tis a Rule and line by which he keeps his building compact and even, which otherwise lawless imagination would raise either irregularly or loosly. At least if the Poet commits errours with this help, he would make greater and more without it: 'tis (in short) a slow and painful, but the surest kind of working. *Ovid* whom you accuse for luxuriancy in Verse, had perhaps been farther guilty of it had he writ in Prose. And for your instance of *Ben. Johnson*, who you say, writ exactly without the help of Rhyme; you are to remember 'tis only an aid to a luxuriant Fancy, which his was not: As he did not want imagination, so none ever said he had much to spare. Neither was verse then refin'd so much to be an help to that Age as it is to ours. Thus then the second thoughts being usually the best, as receiving the maturest digestion from judgment, and the last and most mature product of those thoughts being artful and labour'd verse, it may well be inferr'd, that verse is a great help to a luxuriant Fancy; and this is what that Argument which you oppos'd was to evince.

Neander was pursuing this Discourse so eagerly, that *Eugenius* had call'd to him twice or thrice ere he took notice that the Barge stood still, and that they were at the foot of *Somerset*-Stairs,[1] where they had appointed it to land. The company were all sorry to separate so soon, though a great part of the evening was already spent; and stood a while looking back on the water, upon which the Moon-beams play'd, and made it appear like floating quick-silver: at last they went up through a crowd of French people who were merrily dancing in the open air, and nothing concern'd for the noise of Guns which had allarm'd the Town that afternoon. Walking thence together to the *Piazze*,[2] they parted there; *Eugenius* and *Lysideius* to some pleasant appointment they had made, and *Crites* and *Neander* to their several Lodgings.

[1] Somerset Stairs led from below Somerset House to the river.
[2] The *Piazza* stood in front of Somerset House.

A DEFENCE
OF AN ESSAY OF
DRAMATIQUE POESIE

The Indian Emperour, or, The Conquest of Mexico by the Spaniards. Being the Sequel of the Indian Queen. By John Dryden Esq; The Second Edition. [*Latin quot.*] London, Printed for H. Herringman, at the Sign of the Blew Anchor in the Lower walk of the New Exchange. 1668.

SIR Robert Howard sharply answered the arguments which Dryden had advanced in favour of rhyming plays in *An Essay of Dramatick Poesie* in the Preface to his play of *The Great Favourite, or, The Duke of Lerma*, 1668. Dryden as sharply replied to this attack on his opinions in the *Defence of an Essay*, prefixed to the second edition of *The Indian Emperour*, published a few weeks after Howard's Preface. The brothers-in-law were quickly reconciled to each other, and Dryden omitted the *Defence* from later editions of the play.

THE present text follows that of the second edition of *The Indian Emperour* (Macdonald, 69 b).

A DEFENCE

OF AN ESSAY OF

DRAMATIQUE POESIE

BEING AN ANSWER TO

THE GREAT FAVOURITE OR *THE DUKE OF LERMA*

THE former Edition of the *Indian Emperour* being full of faults which had escaped the Printer, I have been willing to over-look this second with more care: and though I could not allow my self so much time as was necessary, yet by that little I have done, the Press is freed from some gross errours which it had to answer for before. As for the more material faults of writing, which are properly mine, though I see many of them, I want leisure to amend them. 'Tis enough for those who make one Poem the business of their lives, to leave that correct: yet, excepting *Virgil*, I never met with any which was so in any Language.

But while I was thus employ'd about this Impression, there came to my hands a new printed Play, called, *The Great Favourite, or the Duke of* Lerma. The Author of which, a noble and most ingenious Person, has done me the favour to make some Observations and Animadversions upon my *Dramatique Essay*. I must confess he might have better consulted his Reputation, than by matching himself with so weak an Adversary. But if his Honour be diminished in the choice of his Antagonist, it is sufficiently recompens'd in the election of his Cause: which being the weaker, in all appearance, as combating the received Opinions of the best Ancient and Modern Authors, will add to his glory, if he overcome; and to the opinion of his generosity, if he be vanquished, since he ingages at so great odds; and, so like a Cavalier, undertakes the protection of the weaker party. I have only to fear on my own behalf, that so good a cause as mine may not suffer by my ill management, or weak defence; yet I cannot in Honour but take the Glove when 'tis offer'd me: though I am only a Champion by succession; and no more able to defend the right of *Aristotle* and *Horace*, than an Infant *Dimock* [1] to maintain the Title of a King.

For my own concernment in the Controversie, it is so small, that I can easily be contented to be driven from a few Notions of Dramatique Poesie; especially by one, who has the reputation of understanding all things: and I might justly make that excuse for my yielding to him, which the Philosopher made to the Emperour; why should I offer to contend with him who is Master of more than twenty Legions of Arts and Sciences? But I am forc'd to fight, and therefore it will be no shame to be overcome.

Yet I am so much his Servant as not to meddle with any thing which does not concern me in his Preface: therefore I leave the good sense and other excellencies of the first twenty lines, to be consider'd by the Critiques. As for the Play of the Duke of *Lerma*, having so much alter'd and beautifi'd it, as he has done, it can justly belong to none but him. Indeed they must be extream ignorant as well as envious, who would rob him of that Honour; for you see him putting in his claim to it, even in the first two lines.

Repulse upon repulse like waves thrown back,
That slide to hang upon obdurate rocks.

After this let detraction do its worst; for if this be not his, it deserves to be. For my part I declare for distributive Justice, and from this and what follows he certainly deserves *those advantages, which he acknowledges to have received from the opinion of sober men.*

In the next place I must beg leave to observe his great Address in courting the Reader to his party. For intending to assault all Poets, both Ancient and Modern, he discovers not his whole design at once, but seems only to aim at me, and attacques me on my weakest side, my defence of Verse.

To begin with me, he gives me the Compellation of *The Author of a Dramatique Essay*; which is a little Discourse in Dialogue, for the most part borrowed from the observations of others: therefore, that I may not be wanting to him in civility, I return his Complement by calling him *The Author of the Duke of* Lerma.

But (that I may pass over his salute) he takes notice of my great pains to prove Rhyme as natural in a serious Play, and more

[1] The hereditary Champion of England; Dymock is the family name of the Lords of the Manor of Scrivelsby.

effectual than blanck Verse. Thus indeed I did state the question; but he tells me, *I pursue that which I call Natural in a wrong application: for 'tis not the question whether Rhyme or not Rhyme be best or most natural for a serious subject, but what is nearest the nature of that it represents.*

If I have formerly mistaken the Question, I must confess my ignorance so far, as to say I continue still in my mistake: But he ought to have prov'd that I mistook it; for it is yet but *gratis dictum*; I still shall think I have gain'd my point, if I can prove that Rhyme is best or most natural for a serious subject. As for the question as he states it, whether Rhyme be nearest the nature of what it represents, I wonder he should think me so ridiculous as to dispute whether Prose or Verse be nearest to ordinary Conversation?

It still remains for him to prove his inference; that, since Verse is granted to be more remote than Prose from ordinary Conversation, therefore no serious Plays ought to be writ in Verse: and when he clearly makes that good, I will acknowledge his Victory as absolute as he can desire it.

The question now is which of us two has mistaken it, and if it appear I have not, the world will suspect *what Gentleman that was, who was allowed to speak twice in Parliament, because he had not yet spoken to the Question*; and perhaps conclude it to be the same, who, as 'tis reported, maintain'd a contradiction *in terminis*, in the face of three hundred persons.

But to return to Verse, whether it be natural or not in Plays, is a Problem which is not demonstrable of either side: 'tis enough for me that he acknowledges he had rather read good Verse than Prose: for if all the Enemies of Verse will confess as much, I shall not need to prove that it is natural. I am satisfied if it cause delight: for delight is the chief, if not the only end of Poesie; instruction can be admitted but in the second place, for Poesie only instructs as it delights. 'Tis true that to imitate well is a Poets work; but to affect the Soul, and excite the Passions, and above all to move admiration (which is the delight of serious Plays) a bare imitation will not serve. The converse therefore which a Poet is to imitate, must be heighten'd with all the Arts and Ornaments of Poesie; and must be such, as, strictly consider'd, could never be supposed spoken by any without premeditation.

As for what he urges, that *a Play will still be supposed to be a composition of several Persons speaking* ex tempore; *and that good Verses are the hardest things which can be imagin'd to be so spoken*: I must crave leave to dissent from his opinion, as to the former part of it: for, if I am not deceiv'd, a Play is suppos'd to be the work of the Poet, imitating, or representing the conversation of several persons: and this I think to be as clear, as he thinks the contrary.

But I will be bolder, and do not doubt to make it good, though a Paradox, that one great reason why Prose is not to be us'd in serious Plays, is because it is too near the nature of converse: there may be too great a likeness; as the most skilful Painters affirm, that there may be too near a resemblance in a Picture: to take every lineament and feature, is not to make an excellent piece, but to take so much only as will make a beautiful Resemblance of the whole; and, with an ingenious flattery of Nature, to heighten the beauties of some parts, and hide the deformities of the rest. For so says *Horace*,

> *Ut pictura poesis erit, &c. . . .*
> *Hæc amat obscurum, vult hæc sub luce videri,*
> *Judicis argutum quæ non formidat acumen.*[1]
> *. . . et quæ*
> *Desperat, tractata nitescere posse, relinquit.*[2]

In *Bartholomew-Fair*, or the Lowest kind of Comedy, that degree of heightning is used, which is proper to set off that Subject: 'tis true the Author was not there to go out of Prose, as he does in his higher Arguments of Comedy, *The Fox* and *Alchymist*; yet he does so raise his matter in that Prose, as to render it delightful; which he could never have performed, had he only said or done those very things that are daily spoken or practised in the Fair: for then the Fair it self would be as full of pleasure to an ingenious person as the Play; which we manifestly see it is not. But he hath made an excellent Lazar of it; the Copy is of price, though the Original be vile. You see in *Catiline* and *Sejanus*, where the Argument is great, he sometimes ascends to Verse, which shews he thought it not unnatural in serious Plays: and had his Genius been as proper for Rhyme, as it was for Humour; or had the Age in which he liv'd, attain'd to as much knowledge in Verse, as ours, 'tis probable he would have adorn'd those Subjects with that kind of Writing.

Thus Prose, though the rightful Prince, yet is by common

[1] It is with painting as with poetry; . . . one work likes the shadows, another demands to be seen in the light, not dreading keen-edged criticism. . . . (*Ars Poetica*, 361, 363–4.)

[2] And abandons whatever he thinks his treatment cannot aspire to adorn. (*Ibid.*, 149–50.)

consent depos'd, as too weak for the Government of serious Plays; and he failing, there now start up two Competitors; one the nearer in blood, which is blanck Verse; the other more fit for the ends of Government, which is Rhyme. Blanck Verse is, indeed, the nearer Prose, but he is blemish'd with the weakness of his Predecessor. Rhyme (for I will deal clearly) has somewhat of the Usurper in him, but he is brave, and generous, and his Dominion pleasing. For this reason of delight, the Ancients (whom I will still believe as wise as those who so confidently correct them) wrote all their Tragedies in Verse, though they knew it most remote from Conversation.

But I perceive I am falling into the danger of another rebuke from my Opponent: for when I plead that the Ancients used Verse, I prove not that they would have admitted Rhyme, had it then been written: all I can say is only this, That it seems to have succeeded Verse by the general consent of Poets in all Modern Languages: for almost all their serious Plays are written in it: which, though it be no demonstration that therefore they ought to be so, yet, at least the practice first, and then the continuation of it, shews that it attain'd the end, which was to please; and if that cannot be compass'd here, I will be the first who shall lay it down. For I confess my chief endeavours are to delight the Age in which I live. If the humour of this, be for low Comedy, small Accidents, and Raillery, I will force my Genius to obey it, though with more reputation I could write in Verse. I know I am not so fitted by Nature to write Comedy: I want that gaiety of humour which is required to it. My Conversation is slow and dull, my humour Saturnine and reserv'd: In short, I am none of those who endeavour to break Jests in Company, or make repartees. So that those who decry my Comedies do me no injury, except it be in point of profit: reputation in them is the last thing to which I shall pretend. I beg pardon for entertaining the Reader with so ill a Subject; but before I quit that Argument, which was the cause of this digression, I cannot but take notice how I am corrected for my quotation of *Seneca*, in my defence of Plays in Verse. My words are these. Our language is Noble, Full, and Significant; and I know not why he who is Master of it, may not cloath ordinary things in it as decently as the Latine, if he use the same diligence in his *choice of Words.* One would think *Unlock a door* was a thing as vulgar as could be spoken; yet *Seneca* could make it sound high and lofty in his Latine.

Reserate Clusos Regii postes Laris.

But he says of me, *That being fill'd with the Precedents of the Ancients who writ their Plays in Verse, I commend the thing, declaring our Language to be Full, Noble, and Significant, and charging all defects upon the* ill placing of words, *which I prove by quoting* Seneca *loftily expressing such an ordinary thing as* shutting a door.

Here he manifestly mistakes; for I spoke not of the placing, but of the choice of words: for which I quoted that Aphorism of *Julius Cæsar, Delectus verborum est origo Eloquentiæ*: but *delectus verborum* is no more Latine for the placing of words, than *Reserate* is Latine for shut the door, as he interprets it, which I ignorantly construed unlock or open it.

He supposes I was highly affected with the sound of those words; and I suppose I may more justly imagine it of him: for if he had not been extreamly satisfied with the sound, he would have minded the sense a little better.

But these are now to be no faults; for ten days after his Book is publish'd, and that his mistakes are grown so famous, that they are come back to him, he sends his *Errata* to be printed, and annexed to his Play: and desires that instead of *shutting* you would read *opening*; which it seems, was the Printers fault. I wonder at his modesty, that he did not rather say it was *Seneca*'s or mine, and that in some Authors *Reserare* was to *shut* as well as to *open*, as the word *Barach*, say the Learned, is both to *bless* and *curse*.

Well, since it was the Printer, he was a naughty man to commit the same mistake twice in six lines: I warrant you *delectus verborum* for placing of words was his mistake too, though the Author forgot to tell him of it: if it were my Book I assure you I should. For those Rascals ought to be the Proxies of every Gentleman Author, and to be chastis'd for him, when he is not pleas'd to own an Errour. Yet since he has given the *Errata*, I wish he would have inlarged them only a few sheets more, and then he would have spar'd me the labour of an Answer: for this cursed Printer is so given to mistakes, that there is scarce a sentence in the Preface, without some false Grammar or hard sence in it: which will all be charg'd upon the Poet, because he is so good natur'd as to lay but three Errours to the Printers account, and to take the rest upon himself, who is better able to support them. But he needs not apprehend that I should strictly examine those little faults, except I am call'd upon to do it: I shall return therefore to that quotation of *Seneca*, and answer not to what he writes, but to what he means. I never intended it as an Argument, but only as an illustration of what I had said before concerning the election of words; and all he can charge me with is only this, that if *Seneca* could make an ordinary thing sound well in Latine by the choice of words, the same with the like care might be perform'd in English: if it cannot, I have committed an Errour on the right hand, by commending too much the copiousness and well sounding of our Language, which I hope my Country men will pardon me. At least the words which follow in my Dramatique Essay will plead somewhat in my behalf; for I say there, that this Objection happens but seldom in a Play, and then too either the meanness of the expression may be avoided, or shut out from the Verse by breaking it in the midst.

But I have said too much in the defence of Verse; for after all 'tis a very indifferent thing to me, whether it obtain or not. I am content hereafter to be ordered by his rule, that is, to write it sometimes because it pleases me, and so much the rather, because he has declared that it pleases him. But he has taken his last farewel of the Muses, and he has done it civilly, by honouring them with the name of *his long acquaintances*, which is a Complement they have scarce deserved from him. For my own part I bear a share in the publick loss, and how emulous soever I may be of his fame and reputation, I cannot but give this testimony of his Style, that it is extream poetical, even in Oratory; his Thoughts elevated, sometimes above common apprehension; his Notions politick and grave, and tending to the instruction of Princes, and reformation of States; that they are abundantly interlac'd with variety of Fancies, Tropes, and Figures, which the Criticks have enviously branded with the name of obscurity and false Grammar.

Well he is now fetter'd in business of more unpleasant nature: the Muses have lost him, but the Commonwealth gains by it; The corruption of a Poet is the Generation of a Statesman.

He will not venture again into the civil Wars of Censure, ubi . . . nullos habitura triumphos:[1] if he had not told us he had left the Muses, we might have half suspected it by that word, *ubi*, which does not any way belong to them in that place; the rest of the Verse is indeed *Lucans*, but that *ubi* I will answer for it, is his own. Yet he has another reason for this disgust of Poesie; for he says immediately after, that *the manner of Plays which are now in most esteem, is beyond his power to perform:* to perform the manner of a thing I confess is new English to me.

[1] Where those wars will contain no triumphs. (Lucan 1. 12.)

However, he condemns not the satisfaction of others, but rather their unnecessary understanding, who, like Sancho Panca's *Doctor, prescribe too strictly to our appetites; for, says he, in the difference of* Tragedy *and* Comedy, *and of* Farce *it self, there can be no determination but by the taste, nor in the manner of their composure.*

We shall see him now as great a Critick as he was a Poet, and the reason why he excell'd so much in Poetry will be evident, for it will appear to have proceeded from the exactness of his judgment. *In the difference of* Tragedy, Comedy, *and* Farce *itself, there can be no determination but by the taste.* I will not quarrel with the obscurity of his Phrase, though I justly might; but beg his pardon if I do not rightly understand him: if he means that there is no essential difference betwixt *Comedy, Tragedy*, and *Farce*, but what is only made by the peoples taste, which distinguishes one of them from the other, that is so manifest an Errour, that I need not lose time to contradict it. Were there neither Judge, Taste, nor Opinion in the world, yet they would differ in their natures; for the action, character, and language of *Tragedy*, would still be great and high; that of *Comedy* lower and more familiar; Admiration would be the Delight of one, and Satyr of the other.

I have but briefly touch'd upon these things, because, whatever his words are, I can scarce imagine, that *he who is always concern'd for the true honour of reason, and would have no spurious issue father'd upon her*, should mean anything so absurd as to affirm, *that there is no difference betwixt* Comedy *and* Tragedy, *but what is made by the taste only*: Unless he would have us understand the Comedies of my Lord *L.*[1] where the first Act should be Pottages, the second Fricassees, *&c.*, and the Fifth a *Chere entiere* of Women.

I rather guess he means that betwixt one *Comedy* or *Tragedy* and another, there is no other difference but what is made by the liking or disliking of the Audience. This is indeed a less errour than the former, but yet it is a great one. The liking or disliking of the peoples gives the Play the denomination of good or bad, but does not really make, or constitute it such. To please the people ought to be the Poets aim, because Plays are made for their delight; but it does not follow that they are always pleas'd with good Plays, or that the Plays which please them are always good. The humour of the people is now for *Comedy*; therefore in hope to please them, I write *Comedies*

[1] John Maitland, 2nd Duke of Lauderdale (1616–1682).

rather than serious Plays: and so far their taste prescribes to me: but it does not follow from that reason, that *Comedy* is to be preferr'd before *Tragedy* in its own nature: for that which is so in its own nature cannot be otherwise; as a man cannot but be a rational creature: but the opinion of the people may alter, and in another Age, or perhaps in this, serious Plays may be set up above Comedies.

This I think a sufficient Answer; if it be not, he has provided me of an Excuse; it seems in his wisdom, he foresaw my weakness, and has found out this expedient for me, *That it is not necessary for Poets to study strict reason, since they are so used to a greater latitude than is allowed by that severe inquisition; that they must infringe their own jurisdiction to profess themselves oblig'd to argue well.*

I am obliged to him for discovering to me this back door; but I am not yet resolv'd on my retreat: For I am of opinion that they cannot be good Poets who are not accustomed to argue well. False Reasonings and colours of Speech, are the certain marks of one who does not understand the Stage: For Moral Truth is the Mistress of the Poet as much as of the Philosopher: Poesie must resemble Natural Truth, but it must *be* Ethical. Indeed the Poet dresses Truth, and adorns Nature, but does not alter them:

Ficta voluptatis causâ sint proxima veris.[1]

Therefore that is not the best Poesie which resembles notions of things that are not, to things that are: though the fancy may be great and the words flowing, yet the Soul is but half satisfied when there is not Truth in the foundation. This is that which makes *Virgil* be preferred before the rest of Poets: In variety of fancy and sweetness of expression, you see *Ovid* far above him: for *Virgil* rejected many of those things which *Ovid* wrote. *A great Wits great Work is to refuse*, as my worthy Friend Sir *John Berkenhead* has ingeniously express'd it: [2] you rarely meet with any thing in *Virgil* but Truth, which therefore leaves the strongest impression of pleasure in the Soul. This I thought my self oblig'd to say in behalf of Poesie: and to declare, though it be against my self, that when Poets do not argue well, the defect is in the Work-men, not in the Art.

And now I come to the boldest part of his Discourse, wherein

[1] Things invented to give pleasure should be as like the truth as possible. (Horace, *Ars Poetica*, 338.)

[2] The line is a quotation from Sir John Berkenhead's (1616–1679) verses *In Memory of Mr. William Cartwright*, 1651.

he attacques not me, but all the Ancients and Moderns; and undermines, as he thinks, the very foundations on which Dramatique Poesie is built. I could wish he would have declin'd that envy which must of necessity follow such an undertaking, and contented himself with triumphing over me in my opinions of Verse, which I will never hereafter dispute with him; but he must pardon me if I have that Veneration for *Aristotle*, *Horace*, *Ben. Johnson*, and *Corneille*, that I dare not serve him in such a Cause, and against such Heroes, but rather fight under their protection, as *Homer* reports of little *Teucer*, who shot the Trojans from under the large Buckler of *Ajax Telamon*.

Στῆ δ' ἄρ' ὑπ' Αἴαντος σάκεϊ Τελαμωνιάδαο, &c.

He stood beneath his Brothers ample shield;
And, cover'd there, shot death through all the field.

The words of my noble Adversary are these:

But if we examine the general Rules laid down for Plays by strict reason, we shall find the errours equally gross; for the great foundation which is laid to build upon, is nothing as it is generally stated, as will appear upon the examination of the Particulars.

These Particulars in due time shall be examin'd: in the mean while let us consider what this great foundation is, which he says is nothing, as it is generally stated. I never heard of any other foundation of Dramatique Poesie than the imitation of Nature; neither was there ever pretended any other by the Ancients or Moderns, or me, who endeavour to follow them in that Rule. This I have plainly said in my definition of a Play; that it is a just and lively image of humane Nature, &c. Thus the Foundation, as it is generally stated, will stand sure, if this definition of a Play be true; if it be not, he ought to have made his exception against it, by proving that a Play is not an imitation of Nature, but somewhat else which he is pleas'd to think it.

But 'tis very plain, that he has mistaken the foundation for that which is built upon it, though not immediately: for the direct and immediate consequence is this; if Nature be to be imitated, then there is a Rule for imitating Nature rightly, otherwise there may be an end, and no means conducing to it. Hitherto I have proceeded by demonstration; but as our Divines, when they have prov'd a Deity, because there is order, and have infer'd that this Deity ought to be worshipped, differ afterwards in the manner of the Worship; so having laid down, that Nature is to be imitated, and that Proposition proving the next, that then there are means which conduce to the imitating of

Nature, I dare proceed no farther positively: but have only laid down some opinions of the Ancients and Moderns, and of my own, as means which they used, and which I thought probable for the attaining of that end. Those means are the same which my Antagonist calls the Foundations, how properly the world may judge; and to prove that this is his meaning, he clears it immediately to you, by enumerating those Rules or Propositions against which he makes his particular exceptions; as namely, those of time and place, in these words: *First we are told the plot should not be so ridiculously contrived, as to crowd two several Countries into one Stage; secondly, to cramp the Accidents of many years or days into the representation of two hours and an half; and lastly, a Conclusion drawn, that the only remaining Dispute is, concerning time, whether it should be contained in* 12 *or* 24 *hours; and the place to be limited to that spot of ground where the Play is supposed to begin: and this is called nearest Nature; for that is concluded most natural, which is most probable, and nearest to that which it presents.*

Thus he has only made a small mistake of the means conducing to the end, for the end itself, and of the superstructure for the foundation: but he proceeds. *To shew therefore upon what ill grounds they dictate Laws for Dramatique Poesie, &c.* He is here pleased to charge me with being Magisterial, as he has done in many other places of his Preface. Therefore in vindication of my self, I must crave leave to say, that my whole Discourse was Sceptical, according to that way of reasoning which was used by *Socrates*, *Plato*, and all the Academiques of old, which *Tully* and the best of the Ancients followed, and which is imitated by the modest Inquisitions of the Royal Society. That it is so, not only the name will shew, which is *an Essay*, but the frame and Composition of the Work. You see, it is a Dialogue sustain'd by persons of several opinions, all of them left doubtful, to be determined by the Readers in general; and more particularly deferr'd to the accurate Judgment of my Lord *Buckhurst*, to whom I made a Dedication of my Book. These are my words in my Epistle, speaking of the persons whom I introduc'd in my Dialogue: 'tis true they differ'd in their opinions, as 'tis probable they would; neither do I take upon me to reconcile, but to relate them, leaving your Lordship to decide it in favour of that part which you shall judge most reasonable. And after that in my Advertisement to the Reader I said this; The drift of the ensuing Discourse is chiefly to vindicate the Honour of our English Writers from the Censure of those who unjustly prefer the French before them. This I intimate, lest any should think me so exceeding vain, as to teach others an Art which they understand much better than my self. But this is more than necessary to clear my modesty in that point: & I am very confident that there is scarce any man who has lost so much time, as to read that trifle, but will be my Compurgator as to that arrogance whereof I am accus'd. The truth is, if I had been naturally guilty of so much vanity as to dictate my opinions; yet I do not find that the Character of a positive or self-conceited person is of such advantage to any in this Age, that I should labour to be publickly admitted of that Order.

But I am not now to defend my own Cause, when that of all the Ancients and Moderns is in question: for this Gentleman who accuses me of arrogance, has taken a course not to be taxed with the other extream of modesty. Those propositions which are laid down in my Discourse as helps to the better imitation of Nature, are not mine (as I have said) nor were ever pretended so to be, but derived from the Authority of *Aristotle* and *Horace*, and from the Rules and Examples of *Ben. Johnson* and *Corneille*. These are the men with whom properly he contends, and against *whom he will endeavour to make it evident, that there is no such thing as what they All pretend.*

His Argument against the Unities of place and time, is this: *That 'tis as impossible for one Stage to present two Rooms or Houses truly, as two Countries or Kingdoms, & as impossible that five hours or twenty four hours should be two hours, as that a thousand hours or years should be less than what they are, or the greatest part of time to be comprehended in the less: for all of them being impossible, they are none of them nearest the Truth or Nature of what they present; for impossibilities are all equal, and admit of no degree.*

This Argument is so scattered into parts, that it can scarce be united into a Syllogism; yet, in obedience to him, *I will abbreviate* and comprehend as much of it as I can in few words, that my Answer to it may be more perspicuous. I conceive his meaning to be what follows as to the unity of place: (if I mistake, I beg his pardon, professing it is not out of any design to play the *Argumentative Poet.*) If one Stage cannot properly present two Rooms or Houses, much less two Countries or Kingdoms, then there can be no Unity of place: but one Stage cannot properly perform this; therefore there can be no Unity of place.

I plainly deny his minor Proposition; the force of which, if I mistake not, depends on this; that the Stage being one place, cannot be two. This indeed is as great a Secret, as that we are all mortal; but to requite it with another, I must crave leave to tell him, that though the Stage cannot be two places, yet it may properly represent them, successively, or at several times. His Argument is indeed no more than a meer fallacy, which will evidently appear when we distinguish place, as it relates to Plays, into real and imaginary. The real place is that Theater, or piece of ground on which the Play is acted. The imaginary, that House, Town, or Country where the action of the *Drama* is supposed to be; or more plainly, where the Scene of the Play is laid. Let us now apply this to that Herculean Argument, *which if strictly and duely weighed, is to make it evident, that there is no such thing as what they all pretend.* 'Tis impossible, he says, for one Stage to present two Rooms or Houses: I answer, 'tis neither impossible, nor improper, for one real place to represent two or more imaginary places, so it be done successively, which in other words is no more than this; That the imagination of the Audience, aided by the words of the Poet, and painted Scenes, may suppose the Stage to be sometimes one place, sometimes another, now a Garden, or Wood, and immediately a Camp: which I appeal to every mans imagination, if it be not true. Neither the Ancients nor Moderns, as much Fools as he is pleased to think them, ever asserted that they could make one place two; but they might hope by the good leave of this Author, that the change of a Scene might lead the imagination to suppose the place alter'd: So that he cannot fasten those absurdities upon this Scene of a Play, or imaginary place of Action, that it is one place and yet two. And this being so clearly proved, that 'tis past any shew of a reasonable denial, it will not be hard to destroy that other part of his Argument which depends upon it, namely, that 'tis as impossible for a Stage to represent two Rooms or Houses, as two Countries or Kingdoms: for his reason is already overthrown, which was, because both were alike impossible. This is manifestly otherwise; for 'tis proved, that a Stage may properly represent two Rooms or Houses; for the imagination being Judge of what is represented, will in reason be less chocqu'd with the appearance of two rooms in the same house, or two houses in the same City, than with two distant Cities in the same Country, or two remote Countries in the same Universe. Imagination in a man, or reasonable Creature, is supposed to participate of reason, and when that governs, as it does in the belief of fiction, reason is not destroyed, but misled, or blinded: that can prescribe to the reason, during the time of the representation, somewhat like a weak belief of what it sees and hears; and reason suffers it self to be so hood-wink'd, that it may better enjoy the pleasures of the fiction: but it is never so wholly made a captive, as to be drawn head-long into a perswasion of those things which are most remote from probability: 'tis in that case a free-born Subject, not a Slave, it will contribute willingly its assent, as far as it sees convenient, but will not be forc'd. Now there is a greater vicinity in Nature, betwixt two Rooms than betwixt two Houses, betwixt two Houses than betwixt two Cities, and so of the rest: reason therefore can sooner be led by imagination to step from one room into another, than to walk to two distant houses, and yet rather to go thither, than to flye like a Witch through the Air, and be hurried from one Region to another. Fancy and Reason go hand in hand, the first cannot leave the last behind; and though Fancy, when it sees the wide Gulph, would venture over, as the nimbler; yet it is with-held by Reason, which will refuse to take the leap, when the distance over it appears too large. If *Ben. Johnson* himself will remove the Scene from *Rome* into *Tuscany* in the same Act, and from thence return to *Rome*, in the Scene which immediately follows; reason will consider there is no proportionable allowance of time to perform the journey, and therefore will chuse to stay at home. So then the less change of place there is, the less time is taken up in transporting the persons of the *Drama*, with Analogy to reason; and in that Analogy, or resemblance of Fiction to Truth, consists the excellency of the Play.

For what else concerns the Unity of place, I have already given my opinion of it in my *Essay*, that there is a latitude to be allowed to it, as several places in the same Town or City, or places adjacent to each other in the same Country; which may all be comprehended under the larger denomination of one place; yet with this restriction, that the nearer and fewer those imaginary places are, the greater resemblance they will have to Truth: and Reason which cannot make them one, will be more easily led to suppose them so.

What has been said of the Unity of place, may easily be applyed to that of time: I grant it to be impossible, that the greater part of time should be comprehended in the less, that twenty four hours should be crowded into three: but there is no necessity of that Supposition. For as *Place*, so *Time* relating to a Play, is either imaginary or real: The real is comprehended in those three hours, more or less, in the space of which the

Play is represented: The imaginary is that which is supposed to be taken up in the Representation, as twenty four hours more or less. Now no man ever could suppose that twenty four real hours could be included in the space of three: but where is the absurdity of affirming that the feigned business of twenty four imagin'd hours, may not more naturally be represented in the compass of three real hours, than the like feigned business of twenty four years in the same proportion of real time? For the proportions are always real, and much nearer, by his permission, of twenty four to three, than of four thousand to it.

I am almost fearful of illustrating anything by similitude, lest he should confute it for an Argument; yet I think the comparison of a Glass will discover very aptly the fallacy of his Argument, both concerning time and place. The strength of his Reason depends on this, That the less cannot comprehend the greater. I have already answered, that we need not suppose it does; I say not that the less can comprehend the greater, but only that it may represent it: As in a Glass or Mirrour of half a yard Diameter, a whole room and many persons in it may be seen at once: not that it can comprehend that room or those persons, but that it represents them to the sight.

But the Author of the Duke of *Lerma* is to be excus'd for his declaring against the Unity of time: for if I be not much mistaken, he is an interessed person; the time of that Play taking up so many years as the favour of the Duke of *Lerma* continued; nay, the second and third Act including all the time of his Prosperity, which was a great part of the Reign of *Philip* the Third: for in the beginning of the second Act he was not yet a Favourite, and before the end of the Third, was in disgrace. I say not this with the least design of limiting the Stage too servilely to 24 hours, however he be pleased to tax me with dogmatizing in that point. In my Dialogue, as I before hinted, several persons maintained their several opinions: one of them, indeed, who supported the Cause of the French Poesie, said how strict they were in that Particular: but he who answered in behalf of our Nation, was willing to give more latitude to the Rule; and cites the words of *Corneille* himself, complaining against the severity of it, and observing what Beauties it banish'd from the Stage, *pag.* 44 of my *Essay*. In few words my own opinion is this, (and I willingly submit it to my Adversary, when he will please impartially to consider it,) that the imaginary time of every Play ought to be contrived into as narrow a compass, as the nature of the Plot, the quality of the Persons, and variety of Accidents will allow. In Comedy I would not exceed 24 or 30 hours: for the Plot, Accidents, and Persons of Comedy are small, and may be naturally turn'd in a little compass: But in Tragedy the Design is weighty, and the Persons great, therefore there will naturally be required a greater space of time in which to move them. And this, though *Ben. Johnson* has not told us, yet 'tis manifestly his opinion: for you see that to his Comedies he allows generally but 24 hours; to his two Tragedies, *Sejanus* and *Catiline*, a much larger time: though he draws both of them into as narrow a compass as he can: For he shews you only the latter end of *Sejanus* his Favour, and the Conspiracy of Catiline already ripe, and just breaking out into action.

But as it is an errour on the one side, to make too great a disproportion betwixt the imaginary time of the Play, and the real time of its representations; so on the other side, 'tis an oversight to compress the accidents of a Play into a narrower compass than that in which they could naturally be produc'd. Of this last errour the French are seldom guilty, because the thinness of their Plots prevents them from it: but few English men, except *Ben. Johnson*, have ever made a Plot with variety of design in it, included in 24 hours which was altogether natural. For this reason, I prefer the *Silent Woman* before all other Plays, I think justly, as I do its Author in Judgment, above all other Poets. Yet of the two, I think that errour the most pardonable, which in too straight a compass crowds together many accidents; since it produces more variety, and consequently more pleasure to the Audience: and because the nearness of proportion betwixt the imaginary and real time, does speciously cover the compression of the Accidents.

Thus I have endeavoured to answer the meaning of his Argument; for as he drew it, I humbly conceive that it was none: as will appear by his Proposition, and the proof of it. His Proposition was this.

If strictly and duely weighed, 'tis as impossible for one Stage to present two Rooms or Houses, as two Countries or Kingdoms, &c. And his Proof this: *For all being impossible, they are none of them nearest the Truth or Nature of what they present.*

Here you see, instead of a Proof or Reason, there is only a *Petitio principii*: for in plain words, his sense is this; Two things are as impossible as one another, because they are both equally impossible: but he takes those two things to be granted as impossible, which he ought to have prov'd such before he had proceeded to prove them equally impossible: he should have made out first that it was impossible for one Stage to represent two Houses, & then have gone forward to prove that it was as equally impossible for a Stage to present two Houses, as two Countries.

After all this, the very absurdity to which he would reduce me, is none at all: for he only drives at this, That if his Argument be true, I must then acknowledge that there are degrees in impossibilities, which I easily grant him without dispute: and if I mistake not, *Aristotle* and the *School* are of my opinion. For there are some things which are absolutely impossible, and others which are only so *ex parte*; as 'tis absolutely impossible for a thing *to be*, and *not be* at the same time; but for a Stone to move naturally upward, is only impossible *ex parte materiæ*; but it is not impossible for the first Mover, to alter the Nature of it.

His last Assault, like that of a French man, is most feeble: for whereas I have observed, that none have been violent against Verse, but such only as have not attempted it, or have succeeded ill in their attempt, he will needs, according to his usual custom, improve my Observation to an Argument, that he might have the glory to confute it. But I lay my Observation at his feet, as I do my Pen, which I have often employ'd willingly in his deserved commendations, and now most unwillingly against his Judgment. For his person and parts, I honour them as much as any man living, and have had so many particular Obligations to him, that I should be very ungrateful, if I did not acknowledge them to the World. But I gave not the first occasion of this difference in opinions. In my Epistle Dedicatory, before my *Rival Ladies*, I had said somewhat in behalf of Verse, which he was pleased to answer in his Preface to his Plays: that occasioned my Reply in my Essay, and that Reply begot this rejoynder of his in his Preface to the Duke of *Lerma*. But as I was the last who took up Arms, I will be the first to lay them down. For what I have here written, I submit it wholly to him; and if I do not hereafter answer what may be objected against this Paper, I hope the World will not impute it to any other reason, than only the due respect which I have for so noble an Opponent.

DEDICATION
OF
EXAMEN POETICUM
BEING THE THIRD PART OF
MISCELLANY POEMS

Examen Poeticum: Being the Third Part of Miscellany Poems. Containing Variety of New Translations of the Ancient Poets. Together with many Original Copies, By the Most Eminent Hands. [*Latin quot.*] London: Printed by R. E. for Jacob Tonson, at the Judges Head in Chancery-Lane, near Fleet-street. M DC XCIII.

JACOB TONSON published four volumes of miscellany poems during Dryden's life, 1684, 1685, 1693 and 1694—a fifth volume appeared in 1704—, and the poet would seem to have acted as an occasional adviser; all the volumes containing much of his work. The present text of the Dedication of the third part of *Miscellany Poems* is that of the first edition (Macdonald, 45 a i).

DEDICATION OF

EXAMEN POETICUM

TO THE RIGHT HONOURABLE

MY LORD RADCLIFFE[1]

MY LORD, These Miscellany Poems, are by many Titles yours. The first they claim from your acceptance of my Promise to present them to you; before some of them were yet in being. The rest are deriv'd from your own Merit, the exactness of your Judgment in Poetry, and the candour of your Nature; easie to forgive some trivial faults when they come accompanied, with countervailing Beauties. But after all, though these are your equitable claims to a Dedication from other Poets, yet I must acknowledge a Bribe in the case, which is your particular liking of my Verses. 'Tis a vanity common to all Writers, to overvalue their own Productions; and 'tis better for me to own this failing in my self, than the World to do it for me. For what other Reason have I spent my Life in so unprofitable a Study? Why am I grown Old, in seeking so barren a Reward as Fame? The same Parts and Application, which have made me a Poet, might have rais'd me to any Honours of the Gown, which are often given to Men of a little Learning and less Honesty than my self. No Government has ever been, or ever can be, wherein Time-servers and Blockheads will not be uppermost. The Persons are only chang'd, but the same juglings in State, the same Hypocrisie in Religion, the same Self-Interest, and Mis-mannagement, will remain for ever. Blood and Mony will be lavish'd in all Ages, only for the Preferment of new Faces, with old Consciences. There is too often a Jaundise in the Eyes of Great Men; they see not those whom they raise, in the same Colours with other Men. All whom they affect, look Golden to them; when the Gilding is only in their own distemper'd Sight. These Considerations, have given me a kind of Contempt for those who have risen by unworthy ways. I am

[1] Edward Lord Radcliffe (1655–1705), succeeded as 2nd Earl of Derwentwater in 1696.

not asham'd to be Little, when I see them so Infamously Great. Neither, do I know, why the Name of Poet should be Dishonourable to me; if I am truly one, as I hope I am; for I will never do any thing, that shall dishonour it. The Notions of Morality are known to all Men: None can pretend Ignorance of those Idea's which are In-born in Mankind: and if I see one thing, and practise the contrary, I must be Disingenuous, not to acknowledge a clear Truth, and Base to Act against the light of my own Conscience. For the Reputation of my Honesty, no Man can question it, who has any of his own: For that of my Poetry, it shall either stand by its own Merit; or fall for want of it. Ill Writers are usually the sharpest Censors: For they (as the best Poet, and the best Patron said), when in the full perfection of decay, turn Vinegar, and come again in Play.[1] Thus the corruption of a Poet, is the Generation of a Critick: I mean of a Critick in the general acceptation of this Age: For formerly they were quite another Species of Men. They were Defendors of Poets, and Commentators on their Works: to Illustrate obscure Beauties; to place some passages in a better light, to redeem others from malicious Interpretations: to help out an Author's Modesty, who is not ostentatious of his Wit; and, in short, to shield him from the Ill-Nature of those Fellows, who were then call'd *Zoili*, and *Momi*, and now take upon themselves the Venerable Name of Censors. But neither *Zoilus*, nor he who endeavour'd to defame *Virgil*, were ever Adopted into the Name of Criticks by the *Ancients*: what their Reputation was then, we know; and their Successours in this Age deserve no better. Are our Auxiliary Forces turn'd our Enemies? Are they, who, at best, are but Wits of the Second Order, and whose only Credit amongst Readers, is what they obtain'd by being subservient to the Fame of Writers, are these become Rebels of Slaves, and Usurpers of Subjects; or to speak in the most Honourable Terms of them, are they from our Seconds, become Principals against us? Does the Ivy undermine the Oke, which supports its weakness? What labour wou'd it cost them to put in a better Line, than the worst of those which they expunge in a True Poet? *Petronius*, the greatest Wit perhaps of all the *Romans*, yet when his Envy prevail'd upon his Judgment, to fall on *Lucan*, he fell himself in his attempt: He perform'd worse in his Essay of the Civil War, than the Authour of the *Pharsalia*: and avoiding his Errours, has made greater of his own. *Julius Scaliger*, wou'd needs turn down

[1] These verses are quoted from a poem by Charles Sackville, Lord Buckhurst, to whom *An Essay of Dramatick Poesie* is dedicated.

Homer, and Abdicate him, after the possession of Three Thousand Years: Has he succeeded in his Attempt? He has indeed shown us some of those Imperfections in him, which are incident to Humane Kind: But who had not rather be that *Homer* than this *Scaliger*? You see the same Hypercritick, when he endeavours to mend the beginning of *Claudian*, (a faulty Poet, and Living in a Barbarous Age;) yet how short he comes of him, and substitutes such Verses of his own, as deserve the *Ferula*. What a Censure has he made of *Lucan*, that he rather seems to Bark than Sing? Wou'd any but a Dog, have made so snarling a Comparison? One wou'd have thought, he had Learn'd Latin, as late as they tell us he did Greek. Yet he came off, with a *pace tuâ*, by your good leave, *Lucan*; he call'd him not by those outrageous Names, of Fool, Booby, and Blockhead: He had somewhat more of good Manners, than his Successours, as he had much more Knowledge. We have two sorts of those Gentlemen, in our Nation: Some of them proceeding with a seeming moderation and pretence of Respect, to the Dramatick Writers of the last Age, only scorn and vilifie the present Poets, to set up their Predecessours. But this is only in appearance; for their real design is nothing less, than to do Honour to any Man, besides themselves. *Horace* took notice, of such Men in his Age: *Non Ingeniis favet ille, Sepultis; nostra sed impugnat; nos nostraque lividus odit*.[1] 'Tis not with an ultimate intention to pay Reverence to the Manes of *Shakespear*, *Fletcher*, and *Ben Johnson*, that they commend their Writings, but to throw Dirt on the Writers of this Age: Their *Declaration* is one thing, and their Practice is another. By a seeming veneration to our Fathers, they wou'd thrust out us their Lawful Issue, and Govern us themselves, under a specious pretence of Reformation. If they could compass their intent, what wou'd Wit and Learning get by such a change? If we are bad Poets, they are worse, and when any of their woful pieces come abroad, the difference is so great betwixt them and good Writers, that there need no Criticisms on our part to decide it. When they describe the Writers of this Age, they draw such monstrous figures of them, as resemble none of us: Our pretended Pictures are so unlike, that 'tis evident we never sate to them: They are all Grotesque: the products of their wild Imaginations, things out of Nature, so far from being Copy'd from us, that they resemble nothing that ever was, or ever can be. But there is another sort of Insects, more venomous than

[1] Not that he is really devoted to dead and buried geniuses: what he desires is to attack us, for he hates—and envies—both ourselves and our work. (*Epistles* 2. 1. 89.)

the former. Those who manifestly aim at the destruction of our Poetical Church and State. Who allow nothing to their Country-Men, either of this or of the former Age. These attack the Living by raking up the Ashes of the Dead. Well knowing that if they can subvert their Original Title to the Stage, we who claim under them, must fall of course. Peace be to the Venerable Shades of *Shakespear*, and *Ben Johnson*: None of the Living will presume to have any competition with them: as they were our Predecessours, so they were our Masters. We Trayl our Plays under them: but, (as at the Funerals of a *Turkish* Emperour,) our Ensigns are furl'd, or dragg'd upon the ground, in Honour to the Dead; so we may lawfully advance our own, afterwards, to show that we succeed: If less in Dignity, yet on the same Foot and Title, which we think too, we can maintain, against the Insolence of our own Janizaries. If I am the Man, as I have Reason to believe, who am seemingly Courted, and secretly Undermin'd: I think I shall be able to defend my self, when I am openly Attacqu'd. And to shew besides, that the *Greek* Writers only gave us the Rudiments of a Stage, which they never finish'd. That many of the Tragedies in the former Age amongst us, were without Comparison beyond those of *Sophocles* and *Euripides*. But at present, I have neither the leisure nor the means for such an Undertaking. 'Tis ill going to Law for an Estate, with him who is in possession of it, and enjoys the present Profits, to feed his Cause. But the *quantum mutatus* [1] may be remember'd in due time. In the mean while I leave the World to judge, who gave the Provocation.

This, my Lord, is, I confess, a long digression, from *Miscellany Poems* to *Modern Tragedies*: But I have the ordinary Excuse of an Injured Man, who will be telling his Tale unseasonably to his Betters. Though at the same time, I am certain you are so good a Friend as to take a Concern in all things which belong to one who so truly Honours you. And besides, being your self a Critick of the Genuine sort, who have Read the best Authours, in their own Languages, who perfectly distinguish of their several Merits, and in general prefer them to the Moderns, yet, I know, you judge for the *English* Tragedies, against the *Greek* and *Latin*, as well as against the *French*, *Italian*, and *Spanish*, of these latter Ages. Indeed there is a vast difference, betwixt arguing like *Perault*, [2] in behalf of the *French* Poets, against *Homer* and *Virgil*,

[1] How changed! (Vergil, *Æneid* 2. 274.)
[2] Charles Perrault (1628–1703), the French critic, had maintained in his *Parallèle des Anciens et des Modernes*, the superiority of contemporary French poets to the classical poets.

and betwixt giving the *English* Poets their undoubted due, of excelling *Æschylus*, *Euripides*, and *Sophocles*. For if we or our greater Fathers, have not yet brought the *Drama* to an absolute Perfection, yet at least we have carried it much farther than those Ancient Greeks; who beginning from a *Chorus*, cou'd never totally exclude it, as we have done, who find it an unprofitable incumbrance, without any necessity of Entertaining it amongst us; and without the possibility of establishing it here, unless it were supported by a Publick Charge. Neither can we accept of those Lay-Bishops, as some call them, who under pretence of reforming the Stage, wou'd intrude themselves upon us, as our Superiours, being indeed incompetent Judges of what is Manners, what Religion, and least of all, what is Poetry and Good Sense. I can tell them in behalf of all my Fellows, that when they come to Exercise a Jurisdiction over us, they shall have the Stage to themselves, as they have the Lawrel. As little can I grant, that the *French* Dramatick Writers, excel the *English*: Our Authours as far surpass them in Genius, as our Souldiers Excel theirs in Courage: 'Tis true, in conduct they surpass us either way: Yet that proceeds not so much from their greater Knowledge, as from the difference of Tasts in the two Nations. They content themselves with a thin Design, without Episodes, and manag'd by few Persons. Our Audience will not be pleas'd, but with variety of Accidents, an Underplot, and many Actours. They follow the Ancients too servilely, in the Mechanick Rules, and we assume too much Licence to our selves, in keeping them only in view, at too great a distance. But if our Audience had their Tasts, our Poets could more easily comply with them, than the *French* Writers cou'd come up to the Sublimity of our Thoughts, or to the difficult variety of our Designs. However it be, I dare establish it for a Rule of Practice on the Stage, that we are bound to please those, whom we pretend to Entertain: And that at any price, Religion and Good Manners only excepted. And I care not much, if I give this handle, to our bad Illiterate Poetasters, for the defence of their *SCRIPTIONS* as they call them. There is a sort of Merit in delighting the Spectatours; which is a Name more proper for them, than that of Auditours: Or else *Horace* is in the wrong, when he commends *Lucilius* for it. But these common places I mean to Treat at greater leisure: In the mean time, submitting that little I have said, to your Lordship's Approbation, or your Censure, and chusing rather to Entertain you this way, as you are a Judge of Writing, than to oppress your Modesty, with other Commendations; which though they are your due, yet wou'd not be equally receiv'd, in this Satirical, and Censorious Age. That which cannot without Injury be deny'd to you, is the easiness of your Conversation, far from Affectation or Pride: not denying even to Enemies, their just Praises. And this, if I wou'd dwell on any Theme of this Nature, is no vulgar Commendation to your Lordship. Without Flattery, my Lord, you have it in your Nature, to be a Patron and Encourager of Good Poets, but your Fortune has not yet put into your Hands the opportunity of expressing it. What you will be hereafter, may be more than guess'd, by what you are at present. You maintain the Character of a Nobleman, without that Haughtiness which generally attends too many of the Nobility, and when you Converse with Gentlemen, you forget not that you have been of their Order. You are Marryed to the Daughter of a King,[1] who, amongst her other high Perfections, has deriv'd from him a Charming Behaviour, a winning Goodness, and a Majestick Person. The Muses and the Graces are the Ornaments of your Family. While the Muse Sings, the Grace accompanies her Voice: even the Servants of the Muses have sometimes had the Happiness to hear her; and to receive their Inspirations from her.

I will not give my self the liberty of going farther; for 'tis so sweet to wander in a pleasing way, that I shou'd never arrive at my Journeys end. To keep my self from being belated in my Letter, and tiring your Attention, I must return to the place where I was setting out. I humbly Dedicate to your Lordship, my own Labours in this Miscellany: At the same time, not arrogating to my self the Priviledge, of Inscribing to you, the Works of others who are join'd with me, in this undertaking; over which I can pretend no right. Your Lady and You have done me the favour to hear me Read my Translations of *Ovid*: And you both seem'd not to be displeas'd with them. Whether it be the partiality of an Old Man to his Youngest Child, I know not: But they appear to me the best of all my Endeavours in this kind. Perhaps this Poet, is more easie to be Translated, than some others, whom I have lately attempted: Perhaps too, he was more according to my Genius. He is certainly more palatable to the Reader, than any of the *Roman* Wits, though some of them are more lofty, some more Instructive, and others more Correct. He had Learning enough to make him equal to the best. But as his Verse came easily, he wanted the toyl of Application to amend it. He is often luxuriant, both in his Fancy and Expressions; and

[1] Lady Radcliffe was the natural daughter of Charles II.

as it has lately been observ'd, not always Natural. If Wit be pleasantry, he has it to excess: but if it be propriety, *Lucretius*, *Horace*, and above all *Virgil* are his Superiours. I have said so much of him already, in my Preface to his Heroical Epistles, that there remains little to be added in this place. For my own part, I have endeavour'd to Copy his Character what I cou'd in this Translation, even perhaps, farther than I shou'd have done; to his very Faults. Mr. *Chapman* in his Translation of *Homer*, professes to have done it somewhat paraphrastically; and that on set purpose; his Opinion being, that a good Poet is to be Translated in that manner. I remember not the Reason which he gives for it: But I suppose it is, for fear of omitting any of his Excellencies: sure I am, that if it be a Fault, 'tis much more pardonable, than that of those who run into the other extream, of a litteral, and close Translation, where the Poet is confin'd so streightly to his Author's Words, that he wants elbow-room, to express his Elegancies. He leaves him obscure; he leaves him Prose, where he found him Verse. And no better than thus has *Ovid* been serv'd by the so much admir'd *Sandys*.[1] This is at least the Idea which I have remaining of his Translation; for I never Read him since I was a Boy. They who take him upon Content, from the Praises which their Fathers gave him; may inform their Judgment by Reading him again: And see (if they understand the Original) what is become of *Ovid's* Poetry, in his Version; whether it be not all, or the greatest part of it evaporated. But this proceeded from the wrong Judgment of the Age in which he liv'd: They neither knew good Verse, nor lov'd it; they were Scholars 'tis true, but they were Pedants. And for a just Reward of their Pedantick pains, all their Translations want to be Translated into *English*.

If I Flatter not my self, or if my Friends have not Flatter'd me, I have given my Author's Sense, for the most part truly: for to mistake sometimes, is incident to all Men: And not to follow the *Dutch* Commentatours alwaies, may be forgiven to a Man, who thinks them, in the general, heavy gross-witted Fellows; fit only to gloss on their own dull Poets. But I leave a farther Satire on their Wit, till I have a better opportunity to shew how much I Love and Honour them. I have likewise attempted to restore *Ovid* to his Native sweetness, easiness, and smoothness; and to give my Poetry a kind of Cadence, and, as we call it, a run of Verse, as like the Original, as the *English* can come up to the

[1] George Sandys's translation of Ovid's *Metamorphoses* was published in 1626.

Latin. As he seldom uses any *Synalephas*, so I have endeavour'd to avoid them, as often as I cou'd. I have likewise given him his own turns, both on the Words and on the Thought: Which I cannot say are inimitable, because I have Copyed them: and so may others, if they use the same diligence: But certainly they are wonderfully Graceful in this Poet. Since I have Nam'd the *Synalepha*, which is the cutting off one Vowel, immediately before another, I will give an Example of it, from *Chapman's Homer*, which lyes before me; for the benefit of those who understand not the *Latine Prosodia.* 'Tis in the first Line of the Argument to the First *Iliad.*

Apollo's *Priest to th'* Argive *Fleet doth bring*, &c.

There we see he makes it not the *Argive*, but th' *Argive*, to shun the shock of the two Vowels, immediately following each other. But in his Second Argument, in the same Page, he gives a bad Example of the quite contrary kind:

> Alpha *the Pray'r of* Chryses *Sings:*
> *The Army's Plague, the strife of Kings.*

In these words the *Armies, the* ending with a Vowel, and *Armies* beginning with another Vowel, without cutting off the first, which by it had been th' Armies, there remains a most horrible ill-sounding-gap betwixt those Words. I cannot say, that I have every way observ'd the Rule of this *Synalepha* in my Translation; but wheresoever I have not, 'tis a fault in sound. The *French* and the *Italians* have made it an inviolable Precept in their versification; therein following the severe Example of the *Latin* Poets. Our Countrymen have not yet Reform'd their Poetry so far; but content themselves with following the Licentious Practice of the *Greeks*; who though they sometimes use *Synalepha's*, yet make no difficulty very often, to sound one Vowel upon another; as *Homer* does, in the very first line of *Alpha.* Μῆνιν ἄειδε, θεά, Πηληϊάδεω 'Αχιλῆος.[1] 'Tis true, indeed, that in the second line, in these words, μυρί' 'Αχαιοῖς and ἄλγε' ἔθηκε, the *Synalepha* in revenge is twice observ'd. But it becomes us, for the sake of *Euphony*, rather *Musas colere severiores*,[2] with the *Romans*; than to give into the looseness of the *Grecians.*

[1] Sing, O goddess, the wrath of Peleus' son Achilles. (Many griefs did he bring to the Achaeans.) (*Iliad* 1. 1–2.)

[2] To cultivate the more exacting Muses. (Cf. Horace, *Odes* 2. 1. 9.)

I have tir'd my self, and have been summon'd by the Press to send away this Dedication; otherwise I had expos'd some other faults, which are daily committed by our *English* Poets; which, with care and observation, might be amended. For after all, our Language is both Copious, Significant, and Majestical; and might be reduc'd into a more harmonious sound. But for want of Publick Encouragement, in this *Iron Age*, we are so far from making any progress in the improvement of our Tongue, that in few years, we shall Speak and Write as Barbarously as our Neighbours.

Notwithstanding my haste, I cannot forbear to tell your Lordship, that there are two fragments of *Homer* Translated in this *Miscellany*, one by Mr. *Congreve* (whom I cannot mention without the Honour which is due to his Excellent Parts, and that entire affection which I bear him;) and the other by my self. Both the Subjects are pathetical; and I am sure my Friend has added to the Tenderness which he found in the Original; and, without Flattery, surpass'd his Author. Yet I must needs say this in reference to *Homer*, that he is much more capable of exciting the Manly Passions, than those of Grief and Pity. To cause Admiration is indeed the proper and adequate design of an Epick Poem; And in that he has Excell'd even *Virgil*. Yet, without presuming to Arraign our Master, I may venture to affirm, that he is somewhat too Talkative, and more than somewhat too digressive. This is so manifest, that it cannot be deny'd, in that little parcel which I have Translated, perhaps too literally: There *Andromache* in the midst of her Concernment, and Fright for *Hector*, runs off her Bias, to tell him a Story of her Pedigree, and of the lamentable Death of her Father, her Mother, and her Seven Brothers. The Devil was in *Hector*, if he knew not all this matter, as well as she who told it him; for she had been his Bed-fellow for many Years together: And if he knew it, then it must be confess'd, that *Homer* in this long digression, has rather given us his own Character, than that of the Fair Lady whom he Paints. His Dear Friends the Commentators, who never fail him at a pinch, will needs excuse him, by making the present Sorrow of *Andromache*, to occasion the remembrance of all the past: But others think that she had enough to do with that Grief which now oppress'd her, without running for assistance to her Family. *Virgil*, I am confident, wou'd have omitted such a work of supererrogation. But *Virgil* had the Gift of expressing much in little, and sometimes in silence: For though he yielded much to *Homer* in Invention, he more Excell'd him in his Admirable

Judgment. He drew the Passion of *Dido* for *Eneas* in the most lively and most natural Colours that are imaginable: *Homer* was ambitious enough of moving pity; for he has attempted twice on the same subject of *Hector's* death: First, when *Priam*, and *Hecuba* beheld his Corps, which was drag'd after the Chariot of *Achilles*; and then in the Lamentation which was made over him, when his Body was redeem'd by *Priam*; and the same Persons again bewail his death with a Chorus of others to help the cry. But if this last excite Compassion in you, as I doubt not but it will, you are more oblig'd to the Translatour than the poet. For *Homer*, as I observ'd before, can move rage better than he can pity: He stirs up the irascible appetite, as our Philosophers call it, he provokes to Murther, and the destruction of God's Images; he forms and equips those ungodly Man-killers, whom we Poets, when we flatter them, call Heroes; a race of Men who can never enjoy quiet in themselves, till they have taken it from all the World. This is *Homer's* Commendation, and such as it is, the Lovers of Peace, or at least of more moderate Heroism, will never Envy him. But let *Homer* and *Virgil* contend for the Prize of Honour, betwixt themselves, I am satisfied they will never have a third Concurrent. I wish Mr. *Congreve* had the leisure to Translate him, and the World the good Nature and Justice, to Encourage him in that noble Design, of which he is more capable than any Man I know. The Earl of *Mulgrave*, and Mr. *Waller*, two of the best Judges of our Age, have assur'd me, that they cou'd never read over the Translation of *Chapman*, without incredible Pleasure, and extream Transport. This Admiration of theirs, must needs proceed from the Author himself: for the Translator has thrown him down as low, as harsh Numbers, improper *English*, and a monstrous length of Verse cou'd carry him. What then wou'd he appear in the Harmonious Version, of one of the best Writers, Living in a much better Age than was the last? I mean for versification, and the Art of Numbers; for in the *Drama* we have not arriv'd to the pitch of *Shakespear* and *Ben Johnson*. But here, my Lord, I am forc'd to break off abruptly, without endeavouring at a Compliment in the close. This *Miscellany*, is without dispute one of the best of the kind, which has hitherto been extant in our Tongue. At least, as Sir *Samuel Tuke* has said before me, a Modest Man may praise what's not his own.[1] My Fellows have no need of any Protection, but I humbly recommend my part of it, as much as it deserves,

[1] Tuke made this remark in the Prologue to *The Adventures of Five Hours*, see *Dramatick Poesie*, p. 402, n.1.

to your Patronage and Acceptance, and all the rest to your Forgiveness.

I am,

My Lord,

Your Lordship's most Obedient Servant,

JOHN DRYDEN.

PREFACE
TO THE
FABLES

Fables Ancient and Modern; Translated into Verse, from Homer, Ovid, Boccace, & Chaucer: with Original Poems. By M[r] Dryden. [*Latin quot.*] London: Printed for Jacob Tonson, within Gray's Inn Gate next Gray's Inn Lane. MDCC.

THE present text of the Preface to the *Fables* follows that of the first edition (Macdonald, 37 a).

PREFACE
TO THE FABLES

'TIS with a Poet, as with a Man who designs to build, and is very exact, as he supposes, in casting up the Cost beforehand: But, generally speaking, he is mistaken in his Account, and reckons short of the Expense he first intended: He alters his Mind as the Work proceeds, and will have this or that Convenience more, of which he had not thought when he began. So has it hapned to me; I have built a House, where I intended but a Lodge: Yet with better Success than a certain Nobleman, who beginning with a Dog-kennil, never liv'd to finish the Palace he had contriv'd.[1]

From translating the First of *Homer*'s *Iliads*, (which I intended as an Essay to the whole Work) I proceeded to the Translation of the Twelfth Book of *Ovid*'s *Metamorphoses*, because it contains, among other Things, the Causes, the Beginning, and Ending, of the *Trojan* War: Here I ought in reason to have stopp'd; but the Speeches of *Ajax* and *Ulysses* lying next in my way, I could not balk 'em. When I had compass'd them, I was so taken with the former Part of the Fifteenth Book, (which is the Master-piece of the whole *Metamorphoses*) that I enjoyn'd my self the pleasing Task of rendring it into *English*. And now I found, by the Number of my Verses, that they began to swell into a little Volume; which gave me an Occasion of looking backward on some Beauties of my Author, in his former Books: There occurr'd to me the Hunting of the Boar, *Cinyras* and *Myrrha*, the good-natur'd Story of *Baucis* and *Philemon*, with the rest, which I hope I have translated closely enough, and given them the same Turn of Verse which they had in the Original; and this, I may say without vanity, is not the Talent of every Poet: He who has arriv'd the nearest to it, is the Ingenious and Learned *Sandys*,[2] the best Versifier of the former Age; if I may properly call it by that Name, which was the former Part of this concluding Century. For *Spenser* and *Fairfax* both flourish'd in the Reign of Queen

[1] George Villiers, 2nd Duke of Buckingham (1628–1687); the unfinished palace was Cliveden. He is the *Zimri* of *Absalom and Achitophel*.
[2] See *Examen Poeticum*, p. 465, n. 1.

Elizabeth: Great Masters in our Language; and who saw much farther into the Beauties of our Numbers, than those who immediately followed them. *Milton* was the Poetical Son of *Spenser*, and Mr. *Waller* of *Fairfax*; for we have our Lineal Descents and Clans, as well as other Families: *Spenser* more than once insinuates, that the Soul of *Chaucer* was transfus'd into his Body; and that he was begotten by him Two hundred years after his Decease. *Milton* has acknowledg'd to me, that *Spenser* was his Original; and many besides my self have heard our famous *Waller* own, that he deriv'd the Harmony of his Numbers from the *Godfrey of Bulloign*, which was turn'd into *English* by Mr. *Fairfax*. But to return: Having done with *Ovid* for this time, it came into my mind, that our old *English* Poet *Chaucer* in many Things resembled him, and that with no disadvantage on the Side of the Modern Author, as I shall endeavour to prove when I compare them: And as I am, and always have been studious to promote the Honour of my Native Country, so I soon resolv'd to put their Merits to the Trial, by turning some of the *Canterbury* Tales into our Language, as it is now refin'd: For by this Means both the Poets being set in the same Light, and dress'd in the same *English* Habit, Story to be compar'd with Story, a certain Judgment may be made betwixt them, by the Reader, without obtruding my Opinion on him: Or if I seem partial to my Country-man, and Predecessor in the Laurel, the Friends of Antiquity are not few: And besides many of the Learn'd, *Ovid* has almost all the *Beaux*, and the whole Fair Sex his declar'd Patrons. Perhaps I have assum'd somewhat more to my self than they allow me; because I have adventur'd to sum up the Evidence: But the Readers are the Jury; and their Privilege remains entire to decide according to the Merits of the Cause: Or, if they please to bring it to another Hearing, before some other Court. In the mean time, to follow the Thrid of my Discourse, (as Thoughts, according to Mr. *Hobbs*, have always some Connexion) so from *Chaucer* I was led to think on *Boccace*, who was not only his Contemporary, but also pursu'd the same Studies; wrote Novels in Prose, and many Works in Verse; particularly is said to have invented the Octave Rhyme, or *Stanza* of Eight Lines, which ever since has been maintain'd by the Practice of all *Italian* Writers, who are, or at least assume the Title of *Heroick Poets*: He and *Chaucer*, among other Things, had this in common, that they refin'd their Mother-Tongues; but with this difference, that *Dante* had begun to file their Language, at least in Verse, before the time of *Boccace*, who likewise receiv'd no little Help from his Master *Petrarch*: But the

Reformation of their Prose was wholly owing to *Boccace* himself; who is yet the Standard of Purity in the *Italian* Tongue; though many of his Phrases are become obsolete, as in process of Time it must needs happen. *Chaucer* (as you have formerly been told by our learn'd Mr. *Rhymer*[1]) first adorn'd and amplified our barren Tongue from the *Provencall*, which was then the most polish'd of all the Modern Languages: But this Subject has been copiously treated by that great Critick, who deserves no little Commendation from us his Countrymen. For these Reasons of Time, and Resemblance of Genius, in *Chaucer* and *Boccace*, I resolv'd to join them in my present Work; to which I have added some Original Papers of my own; which whether they are equal or inferiour to my other Poems, an Author is the most improper Judge; and therefore I leave them wholly to the Mercy of the Reader: I will hope the best, that they will not be condemn'd; but if they should, I have the Excuse of an old Gentleman, who mounting on Horseback before some Ladies, when I was present, got up somewhat heavily, but desir'd of the Fair Spectators, that they would count Fourscore and eight before they judg'd him. By the Mercy of God, I am already come within Twenty Years of his Number, a Cripple in my Limbs, but what Decays are in my Mind, the Reader must determine. I think my self as vigorous as ever in the Faculties of my Soul, excepting only my Memory, which is not impair'd to any great degree; and if I lose not more of it, I have no great reason to complain. What Judgment I had, increases rather than diminishes; and Thoughts, such as they are, come crowding in so fast upon me, that my only Difficulty is to chuse or to reject; to run them into Verse, or to give them the other Harmony of Prose; I have so long studied and practis'd both, that they are grown into a Habit, and become familiar to me. In short, though I may lawfully plead some part of the old Gentleman's Excuse; yet I will reserve it till I think I have greater need, and ask no Grains of Allowance for the Faults of this my present Work, but those which are given of course to Humane Frailty. I will not trouble my Reader with the shortness of Time in which I writ it; or the several Intervals of Sickness: They who think too well of their own Performances, are apt to boast in their Prefaces how little Time their Works have cost them; and what other Business of more importance interfer'd: But the Reader will be as apt to ask the Question, Why they allow'd not a longer Time to make their Works more perfect? and why they had so

[1] Thomas Rymer (1641–1713), critic and historian; he advanced the opinion to which Dryden refers below in his *Short View of Tragedy*, 1692.

despicable an Opinion of their Judges, as to thrust their indigested Stuff upon them, as if they deserv'd no better?

With this Account of my present Undertaking, I conclude the first Part of this Discourse: In the second Part, as at a second Sitting, though I alter not the Draught, I must touch the same Features over again, and change the Dead-colouring of the Whole. In general I will only say, that I have written nothing which savours of Immorality or Profaneness; at least, I am not conscious to myself of any such Intention. If there happen to be found an irreverent Expression, or a Thought too wanton, they are crept into my Verses through my Inadvertency: If the Searchers find any in the Cargo, let them be stav'd or forfeited, like Counterbanded Goods; at least, let their Authors be answerable for them, as being but imported Merchandise, and not of my own Manufacture. On the other Side, I have endeavour'd to chuse such Fables, both Ancient and Modern, as contain in each of them some instructive Moral, which I could prove by Induction, but the Way is tedious; and they leap foremost into sight, without the Reader's Trouble of looking after them. I wish I could affirm with a safe Conscience, that I had taken the same Care in all my former Writings; for it must be own'd, that supposing Verses are never so beautiful or pleasing, yet if they contain any thing which shocks Religion, or Good Manners, they are at best, what *Horace* says of good Numbers without good Sense, *Versus inopes rerum, nugæque canoræ*:[1] Thus far, I hope, I am Right in Court, without renouncing to my other Right of Self-defence, where I have been wrongfully accus'd, and my Sense wire-drawn into Blasphemy or Bawdry, as it has often been by a Religious Lawyer, in a late Pleading against the Stage; in which he mixes Truth with Falshood, and has not forgotten the old Rule, of calumniating strongly, that something may remain.[2]

I resume the Thrid of my Discourse with the first of my Translations, which was the First *Iliad* of *Homer*. If it shall please God to give me longer Life, and moderate Health, my Intentions are to translate the whole *Ilias*; provided still, that I meet with those Encouragements from the Publick, which may enable me to proceed in my Undertaking with some Chearfulness. And this I dare assure the World before-hand, that I have found by Trial, *Homer* a more pleasing Task than *Virgil*, (though I say not the Translation will be less laborious.) For the *Grecian* is more according to

[1] Lines lacking substance, melodious trifles. (*Ars Poetica*, 322.)

[2] A reference to Jeremy Collier's (1650–1726), *Short View of the Immorality and Profaneness of the English Stage*, 1698, in which Dryden was criticised.

my Genius, than the *Latin* Poet. In the Works of the two Authors we may read their Manners, and natural Inclinations, which are wholly different. *Virgil* was of a quiet, sedate Temper; *Homer* was violent, impetuous, and full of Fire. The chief Talent of *Virgil* was Propriety of Thoughts, and Ornament of Words: *Homer* was rapid in his Thoughts, and took all the Liberties both of Numbers, and of Expressions, which his Language, and the Age in which he liv'd allow'd him: *Homer*'s Invention was more copious, *Virgil*'s more confin'd: So that if *Homer* had not led the Way, it was not in *Virgil* to have begun Heroick Poetry: For, nothing can be more evident, than that the *Roman* Poem is but the Second Part of the *Ilias*; a Continuation of the same Story: And the Persons already form'd: The Manners of *Æneas*, are those of *Hector* superadded to those which *Homer* gave him. The Adventures of *Ulysses* in the *Odysseis*, are imitated in the first Six Books of *Virgil*'s *Æneis*: And though the Accidents are not the same, (which would have argu'd him of a servile, copying, and total Barrenness of Invention) yet the Seas were the same, in which both the *Heroes* wander'd; and *Dido* cannot be deny'd to be the Poetical Daughter of *Calypso*. The Six latter Books of *Virgil*'s Poem, are the Four and twenty *Iliads* contracted: A Quarrel occasion'd by a Lady, a Single Combate, Battels fought, and a Town besieg'd. I say not this in derogation to *Virgil*, neither do I contradict any thing which I have formerly said in his just Praise: For his *Episodes* are almost wholly of his own Invention; and the Form which he has given to the Telling, makes the Tale his own, even though the Original Story had been the same. But this proves, however, that *Homer* taught *Virgil* to design: And if Invention be the first Vertue of an Epick Poet, then the *Latin* Poem can only be allow'd the second Place. Mr. *Hobbs*,[1] in the Preface to his own bald Translation of the *Ilias*, (studying Poetry as he did Mathematicks, when it was too late) Mr. *Hobbs*, I say, begins the Praise of *Homer* where he should have ended it. He tells us, that the first Beauty of an Epick Poem consists in Diction, that is, in the Choice of Words, and Harmony of Numbers: Now, the Words are the Colouring of the Work, which in the Order of Nature is last to be consider'd. The Design, the Disposition, the Manners, and the Thoughts, are all before it: Where any of those are wanting or imperfect, so much wants or is imperfect in the Imitation of Humane Life; which is in the very Definition of a Poem. Words indeed, like glaring Colours, are

[1] Thomas Hobbes (1588–1679), the philosopher, published a translation of Homer in 1676.

the first Beauties that arise, and strike the Sight; but if the Draught be false or lame, the Figures ill dispos'd, the Manners obscure or inconsistent, or the Thoughts unnatural, then the finest Colours are but Dawbing, and the Piece is a beautiful Monster at the best. Neither *Virgil* nor *Homer* were deficient in any of the former Beauties: but in this last, which is Expression, the *Roman* Poet is at least equal to the *Grecian*, as I have said elsewhere; supplying the Poverty of his Language, by his Musical Ear, and by his Diligence. But to return: our two Great Poets, being so different in their Tempers, one Cholerick and Sanguin, the other Phlegmatick and Melancholick; that which makes them excel in their several Ways, is, that each of them has follow'd his own natural Inclination, as well in Forming the Design, as in the Execution of it. The very *Heroes* shew their *Authors*: *Achilles* is hot, impatient, revengeful, *Impiger*, *iracundus*, *inexorabilis*, *acer*, *&c.*[1] *Æneas* patient, considerate, careful of his People, and merciful to his Enemies; ever submissive to the Will of Heaven, *quo fata trahunt retrahuntque, sequamur*.[2] I could please my self with enlarging on this Subject, but am forc'd to defer it to a fitter Time. From all I have said, I will only draw this Inference, That the Action of *Homer* being more full of Vigour than that of *Virgil*, according to the Temper of the Writer, is of consequence more pleasing to the Reader. One warms you by Degrees; the other sets you on fire all at once, and never intermits his Heat. 'Tis the same Difference which *Longinus* makes betwixt the Effects of Eloquence in *Demosthenes*, and *Tully*. One persuades; the other commands. You never cool while you read *Homer*, even not in the Second Book, (a graceful Flattery to his Countrymen;) but he hastens from the Ships, and concludes not that Book till he has made you an Amends by the violent playing of a new Machine. From thence he hurries on his Action with Variety of Events, and ends it in less Compass than Two Months. This Vehemence of his, I confess, is more suitable to my Temper: and therefore I have translated his First Book with greater Pleasure than any Part of *Virgil*: But it was not a Pleasure without Pains: The continual Agitations of the Spirits, must needs be a Weakning of any Constitution, especially in Age: and many Pauses are required for Refreshment betwixt the Heats; the *Iliad* of its self being a third part longer than all *Virgil*'s Works together.

This is what I thought needful in this Place to say of *Homer*.

[1] Energetic, hot-tempered, unyielding and vehement. (*Ars Poetica*, 121.)
[2] Where the fates convey us, be it forth or back, let us obey and go. (Vergil, *Æneid* 5. 709.)

I proceed to *Ovid*, and *Chaucer*; considering the former only in relation to the latter. With *Ovid* ended the Golden Age of the *Roman* Tongue: From *Chaucer* the Purity of the *English* Tongue began. The Manners of the Poets were not unlike: Both of them were well-bred, well-natur'd, amorous, and Libertine, at least in their Writings, it may be also in their Lives. Their Studies were the same, Philosophy, and Philology. Both of them were knowing in Astronomy, of which *Ovid*'s Books of the *Roman* Feasts, and *Chaucer*'s Treatise of the *Astrolabe*, are sufficient Witnesses. But *Chaucer* was likewise an Astrologer, as were *Virgil, Horace, Persius*, and *Manilius*. Both writ with wonderful Facility and Clearness; neither were great Inventors: For *Ovid* only copied the *Grecian* Fables; and most of *Chaucer*'s Stories were taken from his *Italian* Contemporaries, or their Precedessors: *Boccace* his *Decameron* was first publish'd; and from thence our *Englishman* has borrow'd many of his *Canterbury* Tales: Yet that of *Palamon* and *Arcite* was written in all probability by some *Italian* Wit, in a former Age; as I shall prove hereafter: The Tale of *Grizild* was the Invention of *Petrarch*; by him sent to *Boccace*; from whom it came to *Chaucer*: *Troilus* and *Cressida* was also written by a *Lombard* Author; but much amplified by our *English* Translatour, as well as beautified; the Genius of our Countrymen in general being rather to improve an invention, than to invent themselves; as is evident not only in our Poetry, but in many of our Manufactures. I find I have anticipated already, and taken up from *Boccace* before I come to him: But there is so much less behind; and I am of the Temper of most Kings, *who love to be in Debt*, are all for present Money, no matter how they pay it afterwards: Besides, the Nature of a Preface is rambling; never wholly out of the Way, nor in it. This I have learn'd from the Practice of honest *Montaign*, and return at my pleasure to *Ovid* and *Chaucer*, of whom I have little more to say. Both of them built on the Inventions of other Men; yet since *Chaucer* had something of his own, as *The Wife of Baths Tale, The Cock and the Fox*, which I have translated, and some others, I may justly give our Countryman the Precedence in that Part; since I can remember nothing of *Ovid* which was wholly his. Both of them understood the Manners; under which Name I comprehend the Passions, and, in a larger Sense, the Descriptions of Persons, and their very Habits: For an Example, I see *Baucis* and *Philemon* as perfectly before me, as if some ancient Painter had drawn them; and all the Pilgrims in the *Canterbury* Tales, their Humours, their Features, and the very Dress, as distinctly as if I had supp'd with them at the *Tabard* in *Southwark*: Yet even there too the Figures of *Chaucer* are much more lively, and set in a better Light: Which though I have not time to prove; yet I appeal to the Reader, and am sure he will clear me from Partiality. The Thoughts and Words remain to be consider'd, in the Comparison of the two Poets; and I have sav'd my self one half of that Labour, by owning that *Ovid* liv'd when the *Roman* Tongue was in its Meridian; *Chaucer*, in the Dawning of our Language: Therefore that Part of the Comparison stands not on an equal Foot, any more than the Diction of *Ennius* and *Ovid*; or of *Chaucer*, and our present *English*. The Words are given up as a Post not to be defended in our Poet, because he wanted the Modern Art of Fortifying. The Thoughts remain to be consider'd: And they are to be measur'd only by their Propriety; that is, as they flow more or less naturally from the Persons describ'd, on such and such Occasions. The Vulgar Judges, which are Nine Parts in Ten of all Nations, who call Conceits and Jingles Wit, who see *Ovid* full of them, and *Chaucer* altogether without them, will think me little less than mad, for preferring the *Englishman* to the *Roman*: Yet, with their leave, I must presume to say, that the Things they admire are only glittering Trifles, and so far from being Witty, that in a serious Poem they are nauseous, because they are unnatural. Wou'd any Man who is ready to die for Love, describe his Passion like *Narcissus*? Wou'd he think of *inopem me copia fecit*,[1] and a Dozen more of such Expressions, pour'd on the Neck of one another, and signifying all the same Thing? If this were Wit, was this a Time to be witty, when the poor Wretch was in the Agony of Death? This is just *John Littlewit* in *Bartholomew Fair*, who had a Conceit (as he tells you) left him in his Misery; a miserable Conceit. On these Occasions the Poet shou'd endeavour to raise Pity: But instead of this, *Ovid* is tickling you to laugh. *Virgil* never made use of such Machines, when he was moving you to commiserate the Death of *Dido*: He would not destroy what he was building. *Chaucer* makes *Arcite* violent in his Love, and unjust in the Pursuit of it: Yet when he came to die, he made him think more reasonably: He repents not of his Love, for that had alter'd his Character; but acknowledges the Injustice of his Proceedings, and resigns *Emilia* to *Palamon*. What would *Ovid* have done on this Occasion? He would certainly have made *Arcite* witty on his Death-bed. He had complain'd he was farther off from Possession, by being so near, and a thousand such Boyisms, which *Chaucer* rejected as below the Dignity of the Subject.

[1] Abundance has rendered me needy. (Ovid, *Metamorphoses* 3. 466.)

They who think otherwise, would by the same Reason prefer *Lucan* and *Ovid* to *Homer* and *Virgil*, and *Martial* to all Four of them. As for the Turn of Words, in which *Ovid* particularly excels all Poets; they are sometimes a Fault, and sometimes a Beauty, as they are us'd properly or improperly; but in strong Passions always be to shunn'd, because Passions are serious, and will admit no Playing. The *French* have a high Value for them; and I confess, they are often what they call Delicate, when they are introduc'd with Judgment; but *Chaucer* writ with more Simplicity, and follow'd Nature more closely, than to use them. I have thus far, to the best of my Knowledge, been an upright Judge betwixt the Parties in Competition, not medling with the Design nor the Disposition of it; because the Design was not their own; and in the disposing of it they were equal. It remains that I say somewhat of *Chaucer* in particular.

In the first place, As he is the Father of *English* Poetry, so I hold him in the same Degree of Veneration as the *Grecians* held *Homer*, or the *Romans Virgil*: He is a perpetual Fountain of good Sense; learn'd in all Sciences; and therefore speaks properly on all Subjects: As he knew what to say, so he knows also when to leave off; a Continence which is practis'd by few Writers, and scarcely by any of the Ancients, excepting *Virgil* and *Horace*. One of our late great Poets [1] is sunk in his Reputation, because he cou'd never forgive any Conceit which came in his way; but swept like a Drag-net, great and small. There was plenty enough, but the Dishes were ill sorted; whole Pyramids of Sweet-meats, for Boys and Women; but little of solid Meat, for Men: All this proceeded not from any want of Knowledge, but of Judgment; neither did he want that in discerning the Beauties and Faults of other Poets; but only indulg'd himself in the Luxury of Writing; and perhaps knew it was a Fault, but hop'd the Reader would not find it. For this Reason, though he must always be thought a great Poet, he is no longer esteem'd a good Writer: And for Ten Impressions, which his Works have had in so many successive Years, yet at present a hundred Books are scarcely purchas'd once a Twelvemonth: For, as my last Lord *Rochester* said, though somewhat profanely, *Not being of God, he could not stand.*

Chaucer follow'd Nature every where; but was never so bold to go beyond her: And there is a great Difference of being *Poeta* and *nimis Poeta*,[2] if we may believe *Catullus*, as much as betwixt a modest Behaviour and Affectation. The Verse of *Chaucer*, I confess, is not Harmonious to us; but 'tis like the Eloquence of

[1] Abraham Cowley (1618–1667). [2] A poet. Poetical to excess.

one whom *Tacitus* commends, it was *auribus istius temporis accommodata:*[1] They who liv'd with him, and some time after him, thought it Musical; and it continues so even in our Judgment, if compar'd with the Numbers of *Lidgate* and *Gower* his Contemporaries: There is the rude Sweetness of a *Scotch* Tune in it, which is natural and pleasing, though not perfect. 'Tis true, I cannot go so far as he who publish'd the last Edition of him;[2] for he would make us believe the Fault is in our Ears, and that there were really Ten Syllables in a Verse where we find but Nine: But this Opinion is not worth confuting; 'tis so gross and obvious an Errour, that common Sense (which is a Rule in every thing but Matters of Faith and Revelation) must convince the Reader, that Equality of Numbers in every Verse which we call *Heroick*, was either not known, or not always practis'd in *Chaucer*'s Age. It were an easie Matter to produce some thousands of his Verses, which are lame for want of half a Foot, and sometimes a whole one, and which no Pronunciation can make otherwise. We can only say, that he liv'd in the Infancy of our Poetry, and that nothing is brought to Perfection at the first. We must be Children before we grow Men. There was an *Ennius*, and in process of Time a *Lucilius*, and a *Lucretius*, before *Virgil* and *Horace*; even after *Chaucer* there was a *Spenser*, a *Harrington*, a *Fairfax*, before *Waller* and *Denham* were in being: And our Numbers were in their Nonage till these last appear'd. I need say little of his Parentage, Life, and Fortunes: They are to be found at large in all the Editions of his Works. He was employ'd abroad, and favour'd by *Edward* the Third, *Richard* the Second, and *Henry* the Fourth, and was Poet, as I suppose, to all Three of them. In *Richard*'s Time, I doubt, he was a little dipt in the Rebellion of the Commons; and being Brother-in-Law to *John of Ghant*, it was no wonder if he follow'd the Fortunes of that Family; and was well with *Henry* the Fourth when he had depos'd his Predecessor. Neither is it to be admir'd, that *Henry*, who was a wise as well as a valiant Prince, who claim'd by Succession, and was sensible that his Title was not sound, but was rightfully in *Mortimer*, who had married the Heir of *York*; it was not to be admir'd, I say, if that great Politician should be pleas'd to have the greatest Wit of those Times in his Interests, and to be the Trumpet of his Praises. *Augustus* had given him the Example, by the Advice of

[1] Suited to the ears of that generation. (*Annals* 13. 3.)

[2] Thomas Speght's edition of Chaucer appeared in 1597 and 1602. He advanced in his Preface the opinion, to which Dryden here mistakenly objects, that Chaucer's verse could be scanned.

Mæcenas, who recommended *Virgil* and *Horace* to him; whose Praises help'd to make him Popular while he was alive, and after his Death have made him Precious to Posterity. As for the Religion of our Poet, he seems to have some little Byas towards the Opinions of Wickliff, after *John of Ghant* his Patron; somewhat of which appears in the Tale of *Piers Plowman*: Yet I cannot blame him for inveighing so sharply against the Vices of the Clergy in his Age: Their Pride, their Ambition, their Pomp, their Avarice, their Worldly Interest, deserv'd the Lashes which he gave them, both in that, and in most of his *Canterbury Tales*: Neither has his Contemporary *Boccace*, spar'd them. Yet both those Poets liv'd in much esteem, with good and holy Men in Orders: For the Scandal which is given by particular Priests, reflects not on the Sacred Function. *Chaucer*'s *Monk*, his *Chanon*, and his *Fryar*, took not from the Character of his *Good Parson*. A Satyrical Poet is the Check of the Laymen, on bad Priests. We are only to take care, that we involve not the Innocent with the Guilty in the same Condemnation. The Good cannot be too much honour'd, nor the Bad too coursly us'd: For the Corruption of the Best, becomes the Worst. When a Clergy-man is whipp'd, his Gown is first taken off, by which the Dignity of his Order is secur'd: If he be wrongfully accus'd, he has his Action of Slander; and 'tis at the Poet's Peril, if he transgress the Law. But they will tell us, that all kind of Satire, though never so well deserv'd by particular Priests, yet brings the whole Order into Contempt. Is then the Peerage of *England* any thing dishonour'd, when a Peer suffers for his Treason? If he be libell'd, or any way defam'd, he has his *Scandalum Magnatum* to punish the Offender. They who use this kind of Argument, seem to be conscious to themselves of somewhat which has deserv'd the Poet's Lash; and are less concern'd for their Publick Capacity, than for their Private: At least, there is Pride at the bottom of their Reasoning. If the Faults of Men in Orders are only to be judg'd among themselves, they are all in some sort Parties: For, since they say the Honour of their Order is concern'd in every Member of it, how can we be sure, that they will be impartial Judges? How far I may be allow'd to speak my Opinion in this Case, I know not: But I am sure a Dispute of this Nature caus'd Mischief in abundance betwixt a King of *England* and an Archbishop of *Canterbury*; one standing up for the Laws of his Land, and the other for the Honour (as he call'd it) of God's Church; which ended in the Murther of the Prelate, and in the whipping of his Majesty from Post to Pillar for his Penance. The Learn'd and Ingenious Dr.

Drake[1] has sav'd me the Labour of inquiring into the Esteem and Reverence which the Priests have had of old; and I would rather extend than diminish any part of it: Yet I must needs say, that when a Priest provokes me without any Occasion given him, I have no Reason, unless it be the Charity of a *Christian*, to forgive him: *Prior læsit* is Justification sufficient in the Civil Law. If I answer him in his own Language, Self-defence, I am sure, must be allow'd me; and if I carry it farther, even to a sharp Recrimination, somewhat may be indulg'd to Humane Frailty. Yet my Resentment has not wrought so far, but that I have follow'd *Chaucer* in his Character of a Holy Man, and have enlarg'd on that Subject with some Pleasure, reserving to my self the Right, if I shall think fit hereafter, to describe another sort of Priests, such as are more easily to be found than the Good Parson; such as have given the last Blow to Christianity in this Age, by a Practice so contrary to their Doctrine. But this will keep cold till another time. In the mean while, I take up *Chaucer* where I left him. He must have been a Man of a most wonderful comprehensive Nature, because, as it has been truly observ'd of him, he has taken into the Compass of his *Canterbury Tales* the various Manners and Humours (as we now call them) of the whole *English* Nation, in his Age. Not a single Character has escap'd him. All his Pilgrims are severally distinguish'd from each other; and not only in their Inclinations, but in their very Phisiognomies and Persons. *Baptista Porta*[2] could not have describ'd their Natures better, than by the Marks which the Poet gives them. The Matter and Manner of their Tales, and of their Telling, are so suited to their different Educations, Humours, and Callings, that each of them would be improper in any other Mouth. Even the grave and serious Characters are distinguish'd by their several sorts of Gravity: Their Discourses are such as belong to their Age, their Calling, and their Breeding; such as are becoming of them, and of them only. Some of his Persons are Vicious, and some Vertuous; some are unlearn'd, or (as *Chaucer* calls them) Lewd, and some are Learn'd. Even the Ribaldry of the Low Characters is different: The *Reeve*, the *Miller*, and the *Cook*, are several Men, and distinguish'd from each other, as much as the mincing Lady Prioress, and the broad-speaking gap-tooth'd Wife of *Bathe*. But enough of this: There is such a Variety of Game springing up before me, that I am distracted in my Choice, and know not which

[1] James Drake (1667–1707) published an answer to Collier's condemnation of the immorality of the stage.

[2] An Italian physiognomist.

to follow. 'Tis sufficient to say according to the Proverb, that here is God's Plenty. We have our Fore-fathers and Great grand-dames all before us, as they were in *Chaucer*'s Days; their general Characters are still remaining in Mankind, and even in *England*, though they are call'd by other Names than those of *Moncks*, and *Fryars*, and *Chanons*, and *Lady Abbesses*, and *Nuns*: For Mankind is ever the same, and nothing lost out of Nature, though every thing is alter'd. May I have leave to do my self the Justice, (since my Enemies will do me none, and are so far from granting me to be a good Poet, that they will not allow me so much as to be a Christian, or a Moral Man) may I have leave, I say, to inform my Reader, that I have confin'd my Choice to such Tales of *Chaucer*, as savour nothing of Immodesty. If I had desir'd more to please than to instruct, the *Reve*, the *Miller*, the *Shipman*, the *Merchant*, the *Sumner*, and above all, the *Wife of Bathe*, in the Prologue to her Tale, would have procur'd me as many Friends and Readers, as there are *Beaux* and Ladies of Pleasure in the Town. But I will no more offend against Good Manners: I am sensible as I ought to be of the Scandal I have given by my loose Writings; and make what Reparation I am able, by this Publick Acknowledgment. If any thing of this Nature, or of Profaneness, be crept into these Poems, I am so far from defending it, that I disown it. *Totum hoc indictum volo.*[1] *Chaucer* makes another manner of Apologie for his broad-speaking, and *Boccace* makes the like; but I will follow neither of them. Our Country-man, in the end of his Characters, before the *Canterbury Tales*, thus excuses the Ribaldry, which is very gross, in many of his Novels.

But first, I pray you, of your courtesy,
That ye ne arrete it nought my villany,
Though that I plainly speak in this mattere
To tellen you her words, and eke her chere:
Ne though I speak her words properly,
For this ye knowen as well as I,
Who shall tellen a tale after a man
He mote rehearse as nye, as ever He can:
Everich word of it been in his charge,
All speke he, never so rudely, ne large.
Or else he mote tellen his tale untrue,
Or feine things, or find words new:
He may not spare, altho he were his brother,
He mote as well say o word as another.

[1] I would have all this unsaid.

Christ *spake himself full broad in holy Writ,*
And well I wote no Villany is it.
Eke Plato *saith, who so can him rede,*
The words mote been Cousin to the dede.

Yet if a Man should have enquir'd of *Boccace* or of *Chaucer*, what need they had of introducing such Characters, where obscene Words were proper in their Mouths, but very undecent to be heard; I know not what Answer they could have made: For that Reason, such Tales shall be left untold by me. You have here a *Specimen* of *Chaucer*'s Language, which is so obsolete, that his Sense is scarce to be understood; and you have likewise more than one Example of his unequal Numbers, which were mention'd before. Yet many of his Verses consist of Ten Syllables, and the Words not much behind our present *English*: As for Example, these two Lines, in the Description of the Carpenter's Young Wife:

Wincing she was, as is a jolly Colt,
Long as a Mast, and upright as a Bolt.

I have almost done with *Chaucer*, when I have answer'd some Objections relating to my present Work. I find some People are offended that I have turn'd these Tales into modern *English*; because they think them unworthy of my Pains, and look on *Chaucer* as a dry, old-fashion'd Wit, not worth receiving. I have often heard the late Earl of *Leicester* [1] say, that Mr. *Cowley* himself was of that opinion; who having read him over at my Lord's Request, declar'd he had no Taste of him. I dare not advance my Opinion against the Judgment of so great an Author; But I think it fair, however, to leave the Decision to the Publick. Mr. *Cowley* was too modest to set up for a Dictatour; and being shock'd perhaps with his old Style, never examin'd into the depth of his good Sense. *Chaucer*, I confess, is a rough Diamond, and must first be polish'd e're he shines. I deny not likewise, that living in our early Days of Poetry, he writes not always of a piece; but sometimes mingles trivial Things, with those of greater Moment. Sometimes also, though not often, he runs riot, like *Ovid*, and knows not when he has said enough. But there are more great Wits, beside *Chaucer*, whose Fault is their Excess of Conceits, and those ill sorted. An Author is not to write all he can, but only all he ought. Having observ'd this Redundancy in *Chaucer*, (as it is an easie Matter for a Man of ordinary Parts to find a Fault in one of

[1] Philip Sidney, 3rd Earl of Leicester, to whom *Don Sebastian* is dedicated.

greater) I have not ty'd my self to a Literal Translation; but have often omitted what I judg'd unnecessary, or not of Dignity enough to appear in the Company of better Thoughts. I have presum'd farther in some Places, and added somewhat of my own where I thought my Author was deficient, and had not given his Thoughts their true Lustre, for want of Words in the Beginning of our Language. And to this I was the more embolden'd, because (if I may be permitted to say it of my self) I found I had a Soul congenial to his, and that I had been conversant in the same Studies. Another Poet, in another Age, may take the same Liberty with my Writings; if at least they live long enough to deserve Correction. It was also necessary sometimes to restore the Sense of *Chaucer*, which was lost or mangled in the Errors of the Press: Let this Example suffice at present in the Story of *Palamon* and *Arcite*, where the Temple of *Diana* is describ'd, you find these Verses, in all the Editions of our Author:

> *There saw I* Danè *turned unto a Tree,*
> *I mean not the Goddess* Diane,
> *But* Venus *Daughter, which that hight* Danè.

Which after a little Consideration I knew was to be reform'd into this Sense, that *Daphne* the Daughter of *Peneus* was turn'd into a Tree. I durst not make thus bold with *Ovid*, lest some future *Milbourn* [1] should arise, and say, I varied from my Author, because I understood him not.

But there are other Judges who think I ought not to have translated *Chaucer* into *English*, out of a quite contrary Notion: They suppose there is a certain Veneration due to his old Language; and that it is little less than Profanation and Sacrilege to alter it. They are farther of opinion, that somewhat of his good Sense will suffer in this Transfusion, and much of the Beauty of his Thoughts will infallibly be lost, which appear with more Grace in their old Habit. Of this Opinion was that excellent Person, whom I mention'd, the late Earl of *Leicester*, who valu'd *Chaucer* as much as Mr. *Cowley* despis'd him. My Lord dissuaded me from this Attempt, (for I was thinking of it some Years before his Death) and his Authority prevail'd so far with me, as to defer my Undertaking while he liv'd, in deference to him: Yet my Reason was not convinc'd with what he urg'd against it. If the first End of a

[1] Luke Milbourne (1649–1720), a clergyman, who had published an unsuccessful translation of Virgil in 1688, jealously criticised Dryden's translation in a pamphlet which appeared in 1698.

Writer be to be understood, then as his Language grows obsolete, his Thoughts must grow obscure, *multa renascuntur, quæ nunc cecidere; cadentque quæ nunc sunt in honore vocabula, si volet usus, quem penes arbitrium est & jus & norma loquendi.*[1] When an ancient Word for its Sound and Significancy deserves to be reviv'd, I have that reasonable Veneration for Antiquity, to restore it. All beyond this is Superstition. Words are not like Land-marks, so sacred as never to be remov'd: Customs are chang'd, and even Statutes are silently repeal'd, when the Reason ceases for which they were enacted. As for the other Part of the Argument, that his Thoughts will lose of their original Beauty, by the innovation of Words; in the first place, not only their Beauty, but their Being is lost, where they are no longer understood, which is the present Case. I grant, that something must be lost in all Transfusion, that is, in all Translations; but the Sense will remain, which would otherwise be lost, or at least be maim'd, when it is scarce intelligible; and that but to a few. How few are there who can read *Chaucer*, so as to understand him perfectly? And if imperfectly, then with less Profit, and no Pleasure. 'Tis not for the Use of some old *Saxon* Friends, that I have taken these Pains with him: Let them neglect my Version, because they have no need of it. I made it for their sakes who understand Sense and Poetry, as well as they; when that Poetry and Sense is put into Words which they understand. I will go farther, and dare to add, that what Beauties I lose in some Places, I give to others which had them not originally: But in this I may be partial to my self; let the Reader judge, and I submit to his Decision. Yet I think I have just Occasion to complain of them, who because they understand *Chaucer*, would deprive the greater part of their Countrymen of the same Advantage, and hoord him up, as Misers do their Grandam Gold, only to look on it themselves, and hinder others from making use of it. In sum, I seriously protest, that no Man ever had, or can have, a greater Veneration for *Chaucer*, than my self. I have translated some part of his Works, only that I might perpetuate his Memory, or at least refresh it, amongst my Countrymen. If I have alter'd him any where for the better, I must at the same time acknowledge, that I could have done nothing without him: *Facile est inventis addere*,[2] is no great Commendation; and I am not so vain to think I have deserv'd a greater. I will conclude

[1] Many words which have now fallen out of use will be reborn, and many now prominent will disappear, if usage (which owns the right to decide, and the law, and the canons of speech) so chooses. (Horace, *Ars Poetica* 70–72.)

[2] To add to another man's discoveries, is easy.

what I have to say of him singly, with this one Remark: A Lady of my Acquaintance, who keeps a kind of Correspondence with some Authors of the Fair Sex in *France*, has been inform'd by them, that *Mademoiselle de Scudery*,[1] who is as old as *Sibyl*, and inspir'd like her by the same God of Poetry, is at this time translating *Chaucer* into modern *French*. From which I gather, that he has been formerly translated into the old *Provencall*, (for, how she should come to understand Old *English*, I know not.) But the Matter of Fact being true, it makes me think, that there is something in it like Fatality; that, after certain Periods of Time, the Fame and Memory of Great Wits should be renew'd, as *Chaucer* is both in *France* and *England*. If this be wholly Chance, 'tis extraordinary; and I dare not call it more, for fear of being tax'd with Superstition.

Boccace comes last to be consider'd, who living in the same Age with *Chaucer*, had the same Genius, and follow'd the same Studies: Both writ Novels, and each of them cultivated his Mother-Tongue: But the greatest Resemblance of our two Modern Authors being in their familiar Style, and pleasing way of relating Comical Adventures, I may pass it over, because I have translated nothing from *Boccace* of that Nature. In the serious Part of Poetry, the Advantage is wholly on *Chaucer*'s Side, for though the *Englishman* has borrow'd many Tales from the *Italian*, yet it appears, that those of *Boccace* were not generally of his own making, but taken from Authors of former Ages, and by him only modell'd: So that what there was of Invention in either of them, may be judg'd equal. But *Chaucer* has refin'd on *Boccace*, and has mended the Stories which he has borrow'd, in his way of telling; though Prose allows more Liberty of Thought, and the Expression is more easie, when unconfin'd by Numbers. Our Countryman carries Weight, and yet wins the Race at disadvantage. I desire not the Reader should take my Word; and therefore I will set two of their Discourses on the same Subject, in the same Light, for every Man to judge betwixt them. I translated *Chaucer* first, and amongst the rest, pitch'd on the Wife of *Bath's* Tale; not daring, as I have said, to adventure on her Prologue; because 'tis too licentious: There *Chaucer* introduces an old Woman of mean Parentage, whom a youthful Knight of Noble Blood was forc'd to marry, and consequently loath'd her: The Crone being in bed with him on the wedding Night, and finding his Aversion, endeavours to win his Affection by Reason, and

[1] Madeleine de Scudéry (1607–1701), a voluminous author of heroic romances.

speaks a good Word for her self, (as who could blame her?) in hope to mollifie the sullen Bridegroom. She takes her Topiques from the Benefits of Poverty, the Advantages of old Age and Ugliness, the Vanity of Youth, and the silly Pride of Ancestry and Titles without inherent Vertue, which is the true Nobility. When I had clos'd *Chaucer*, I returned to *Ovid*, and translated some more of his Fables; and by this time had so far forgotten the Wife of *Bath's* Tale, that when I took up *Boccace*, unawares I fell on the same Argument of preferring Virtue to Nobility of Blood, and Titles, in the Story of *Sigismonda*; which I had certainly avoided for the Resemblance of the two Discourses, if my Memory had not fail'd me. Let the Reader weigh them both; and if he thinks me partial to *Chaucer*, 'tis in him to right *Boccace*.

I prefer in our Countryman, far above all his other Stories, the Noble Poem of *Palamon* and *Arcite*, which is of the *Epique* kind, and perhaps not much inferiour to the *Ilias* or the *Æneis*: the Story is more pleasing than either of them, the Manners as perfect, the Diction as poetical, the Learning as deep and various; and the Disposition full as artful: only it includes a greater length of time; as taking up seven years at least; but *Aristotle* has left undecided the Duration of the Action; which yet is easily reduc'd into the Compass of a year, by a Narration of what preceded the Return of *Palamon* to *Athens*. I had thought for the Honour of our Nation, and more particularly for his, whose Laurel, tho' unworthy, I have worn after him, that this Story was of *English* Growth, and *Chaucer*'s own: But I was undeceiv'd by *Boccace*; for casually looking on the End of his seventh *Giornata*, I found *Dioneo* (under which name he shadows himself) and *Fiametta* (who represents his Mistress, the natural Daughter of *Robert* King of *Naples*) of whom these Words are spoken. *Dioneo e Fiametta gran pezza cantarono insieme d'Arcita, e di Palemone*: by which it appears that this Story was written before the time of *Boccace*; but the Name of its Author being wholly lost, *Chaucer* is now become an Original; and I question not but the Poem has receiv'd many Beauties by passing through his Noble Hands. Besides this Tale, there is another of his own Invention, after the manner of the *Provencalls*, call'd *The Flower and the Leaf*; with which I was so particularly pleas'd, both for the Invention and the Moral; that I cannot hinder my self from recommending it to the Reader.

As a Corollary to this Preface, in which I have done Justice to others, I owe somewhat to my self: not that I think it worth my time to enter the Lists with one *M*——,[1] and one *B*——,[2] but barely to take notice, that such Men there are who have written scurrilously against me without any Provocation. *M*——, who is in Orders, pretends amongst the rest this Quarrel to me, that I have fallen foul on Priesthood: If I have, I am only to ask Pardon of good Priests, and am afraid his part of the Reparation will come to little. Let him be satisfied that he shall not be able to force himself upon me for an Adversary. I contemn him too much to enter into Competition with him. His own Translations of *Virgil* have answer'd his Criticisms on mine. If (as they say, he has declar'd in Print) he prefers the Version of *Ogilby*[3] to mine, the World has made him the same Compliment: For 'tis agreed on all hands, that he writes even below *Ogilby*. That, you will say, is not easily to be done; but what cannot *M*—— bring about? I am satisfy'd however, that while he and I live together, I shall not be thought the worst Poet of the Age. It looks as if I had desir'd him underhand to write so ill against me: But upon my honest Word I have not brib'd him to do me this Service, and am wholly guiltless of his Pamphlet. 'Tis true I should be glad, if I could persuade him to continue his good Offices, and write such another Critique on any thing of mine: For I find by Experience he has a great Stroke with the Reader, when he condemns any of my Poems to make the World have a better Opinion of them. He has taken some Pains with my Poetry; but no body will be persuaded to take the same with his. If I had taken to the Church (as he affirms, but which was never in my Thoughts) I should have had more Sense, if not more Grace, than to have turn'd my self out of my Benefice by writing Libels on my Parishioners. But his Account of my Manners and my Principles, are of a Piece with his Cavils and his Poetry: And so I have done with him for ever.

As for the City Bard, or Knight Physician, I hear his Quarrel to me is, that I was the author of *Absalom* and *Achitophel*, which he thinks is a little hard on his Fanatick Patrons in *London*.

But I will deal the more civilly with his two Poems, because nothing ill is to be spoken of the Dead: And therefore Peace be to the *Manes* of his *Arthurs*. I will only say that it was not for this Noble Knight that I drew the Plan of an Epick Poem on King *Arthur* in my Preface to the Translation of *Juvenal*. The Guardian

[1] Luke Milbourne, see *ante*, p. 487, n. 1.

[2] Sir Richard Blackmore (*d.* 1729), 'the City Bard, or Knight Physician' (see below); he published his epic poems, 'his *Arthurs*' (see below), *Prince Arthur* and *King Arthur*, in 1695 and 1697. Blackmore reflected unfavourably on Dryden in the first of these two poems.

[3] John Ogilby's (1600–1676) translation of Virgil first appeared in 1654.

Angels of Kingdoms were Machines too ponderous for him to manage; and therefore he rejected them as *Dares* did the Whirl-bats of *Eryx* when they were thrown before him by *Entellus*: Yet from that Preface he plainly took his Hint: For he began immediately upon the Story; though he had the Baseness not to acknowledge his Benefactor; but in stead of it, to traduce me in a Libel.

I shall say the less of Mr. *Collier*, because in many Things he has tax'd me justly; and I have pleaded Guilty to all Thoughts and Expressions of mine, which can be truly argu'd of Obscenity, Profaneness, or Immorality; and retract them. If he be my Enemy, let him triumph; if he be my Friend, as I have given him no Personal Occasion to be otherwise, he will be glad of my Repentance. It becomes me not to draw my Pen in the Defence of a bad Cause, when I have so often drawn it for a good one. Yet it were not difficult to prove, that in many Places he has perverted my Meaning by his Glosses; and interpreted my Words into Blasphemy and Baudry, of which they were not guilty. Besides that, he is too much given to Horse-play in his Raillery; and comes to Battel, like a Dictatour from the Plough. I will not say, *The Zeal of Gods House has eaten him up*; but I am sure it has devour'd some Part of his Good Manners and Civility. It might also be doubted, whether it were altogether Zeal, which prompted him to this rough manner of Proceeding; perhaps it became not one of his Function to rake into the Rubbish of Ancient and Modern Plays; a Divine might have employ'd his Pains to better purpose, than in the Nastiness of *Plautus* and *Aristophanes*; whose Examples, as they excuse not me, so it might be possibly suppos'd, that he read them not without some Pleasure. They who have written Commentaries on those Poets, or on *Horace*, *Juvenal*, and *Martial*, have explain'd some Vices, which without their Interpretation had been unknown to Modern Times. Neither has he judg'd impartially betwixt the former Age and us.

There is more Baudry in one Play of *Fletcher*'s, call'd *The Custom of the Country*, than in all ours together. Yet this has been often acted on the Stage in my remembrance. Are the Times so much more reform'd now, than they were Five and twenty Years ago? If they are, I congratulate the Amendment of our Morals. But I am not to prejudice the Cause of my Fellow-Poets, though I abandon my own Defence: They have some of them answer'd for themselves, and neither they nor I can think Mr. *Collier* so formidable an Enemy, that we should shun him. He has lost Ground at the latter end of the Day, by pursuing his Point too far, like the

Prince of *Condé* at the Battel of *Senneph*[1]: From Immoral Plays, to No Plays, *ab abusu ad usum, non valet consequentia.*[2] But being a Party, I am not to erect my self into a Judge. As for the rest of those who have written against me, they are such Scoundrels, that they deserve not the least Notice to be taken of them. *B*—— and *M*—— are only distinguish'd from the Crowd, by being remember'd to their Infamy.

> Demetri, Teque Tigelli
> Discipularum inter jubeo plorare cathedras.[3]

[1] The battle was fought on 11 August 1674.
[2] No valid inference can be made from the abuse of a thing to its use.
[3] As for you, Demetrius and Tigellius, I bid you go howl amidst the chairs of your lady-pupils. (Horace, *Satires* 1. 10. 90–1.)

PLAYS

AURENG-ZEBE

A TRAGEDY

——Sed, cum fregit subsellia versu,
Esurit, intactam *Paridi* nisi vendat Agaven.

JUV.[1]

[1] But even when an author has brought down the house with his lines, he must go hungry if he is not prepared to sell his Agave unspotted to his Paris (i.e. to his chief actor). (Juvenal 6. 87.)

Aureng-Zebe: A Tragedy. Acted at the Royal Theatre. Written by John Dryden, Servant to his Majesty. [*Latin quot.*] Licensed, Roger L'Estrange. London, Printed by T.N. for Henry Herringman, at the Anchor in the Lower Walk of the New Exchange. 1676.

Aureng-Zebe was first performed at the Theatre Royal, Drury Lane, on 17 November 1675. The present text follows that of the first edition (Macdonald, 80 a). The speech headings have been expanded and, in the interests of clarity, the stage directions have occasionally been rearranged.

TO THE RIGHT HONOURABLE

JOHN, EARL OF MULGRAVE[1]

GENTLEMAN OF HIS MAJESTY'S BEDCHAMBER AND KNIGHT OF THE MOST NOBLE ORDER OF THE GARTER

My Lord,

'TIS a severe Reflection which Montaign *has made on Princes, That we ought not, in reason, to have any expectations of Favour from them; and that 'tis kindness enough, if they leave us in possession of our own. The boldness of the Censure shows the free Spirit of the Author: And the Subjects of* England *may justly congratulate to themselves, that both the Nature of our Government, and the Clemency of our King, secure us from any such Complaint. I, in particular, who subsist wholely by his Bounty, am oblig'd to give posterity a far other account of my Royal Master, than what* Montaign *has left of his. Those Accusations had been more reasonable, if they had been plac'd on inferiour Persons. For in all Courts, there are too many, who make it their business to ruine Wit: And* Montaign, *in other places, tells us, what effects he found of their good Natures. He describes them such, whose Ambition, Lust, or private Interest, seem to be the onely end of their Creation. If good accrue to any from them, 'tis onely in order to their own designs: conferr'd most commonly on the base and infamous; and never given, but onely* hapning *sometimes on well deservers. Dulness has brought them to what they are; and Malice secures them in their Fortunes. But somewhat of Specious they must have, to recommend themselves to Princes, (for Folly will not easily go down in its own natural form with discerning Judges.) And diligence in waiting, is their gilding of the Pill; for that looks like Love, though 'tis onely Interest. 'Tis that which gains 'em their advantage over witty Men; whose love of Liberty and Ease, makes them willing too often to discharge their burden of Attendance on these officious Gentlemen. 'Tis true, that the nauseousness of such Company is enough to disgust a reasonable Man; when he sees, he can hardly approach*

[1] John Sheffield, 3rd Earl of Mulgrave (1648–1721), soldier, politician, and poet; the *Adriel* of *Absalom and Achitophel.*

Greatness, but as a Moated Castle; he must first pass through the Mud and Filth with which it is encompass'd. These are they, who wanting Wit, affect Gravity, and go by the name of Solid men: and a solid man is, in plain English, a solid, solemn Fool. Another disguise they have, (for Fools, as well as Knaves, take other names, and pass by an Alias) *and that is the Title of honest Fellows. But this honesty of theirs ought to have many Grains for its Allowance; for certainly they are no farther honest, than they are silly: They are naturally mischievous to their power; and if they speak not maliciously, or sharply, of witty men, 'tis onely because God has not bestow'd on them the gift of utterance. They fawn and crouch to men of parts, whom they cannot ruine: quote their Wit when they are present, and when they are absent, steal their Jests: But to those who are under 'em, and whom they can crush with ease, they show themselves in their natural Antipathy; there they treat Wit like the common Enemy, and give it no more quarter, than a Dutch-man would to an English Vessel in the* Indies; *they strike Sail where they know they shall be master'd, and murder where they can with safety.*

This, my Lord, is the Character of a Courtier without Wit; and therefore that which is a Satyre to other men, must be a Panegyrick to your Lordship, who are a Master of it. If the least of these Reflections could have reach'd your Person, no necessity of mine could have made me to have sought so earnestly, and so long to have cultivated your kindness. As a Poet, I cannot but have made some observations on Mankind: The lowness of my Fortune has not yet brought me to flatter Vice; and 'tis my duty to give testimony to Virtue. 'Tis true, your Lordship is not of that nature, which either seeks a Commendation, or wants it. Your mind has always been above the wretched affectation of Popularity. A popular man is, in truth, no better than a Prostitute to common Fame, and to the People. He lies down to every one he meets for the hire of praise; and his Humility is onely a disguis'd Ambition. Even Cicero *himself, whose Eloquence deserv'd the admiration of Mankind; yet by his insatiable thirst of Fame, he has lessen'd his Character with succeeding Ages: His action against* Catiline *may be said to have ruin'd the Consul, when it sav'd the City: for it so swell'd his Soul, which was not truly great, that ever afterwards it was apt to be over-set with vanity. And this made his Virtue so suspected by his Friends, that* Brutus, *whom of all men he ador'd, refus'd him a place in his Conspiracy. A Modern Wit has made this Observation on him, That coveting to recommend himself to Posterity, he begg'd it as an Alms of all his Friends, the Historians, to remember his Consulship: And observe, if you please, the odness of the event;*

all their Histories are lost, and the vanity of his request stands yet recorded in his own Writings. How much more great and manly in your Lordship, is your contempt of popular applause, and your retir'd Virtue, which shines onely to a few; with whom you live so easily and freely, that you make it evident, you have a Soul which is capable of all the tenderness of Friendship; and that you onely retire your self from those, who are not capable of returning it. Your kindness, where you have once plac'd it, is inviolable: And 'tis to that onely I attribute my happiness in your love. This makes me more easily forsake an Argument, on which I could otherwise delight to dwell: I mean, your Judgment in your choice of Friends; because I have the honour to be one. After which, I am sure you will more easily permit me to be silent, in the care you have taken of my Fortune; which you have rescu'd, not onely from the power of others, but from my worst of Enemies, my own modesty and Laziness. Which favour, had it been employ'd on a more deserving Subject, had been an effect of Justice in your Nature; but, as plac'd on me, is onely Charity. Yet, withal, 'tis conferr'd on such a man, as prefers your kindness it self, before any of its Consequences; and who values, as the greatest of your Favours, those of your Love, and of your Conversation. From this constancy to your Friends, I might reasonably assume, that your Resentments would be as strong and lasting, if they were not restrain'd by a nobler Principle of good Nature and Generosity. For certainly, 'tis the same composition of Mind, the same Resolution and Courage, which makes the greatest Friendships, and the greatest Enmities. And he who is too lightly reconcil'd, after high Provocations, may recommend himself to the World for a Christian, but I should hardly trust him for a Friend. The Italians have a Proverb to that purpose, To forgive the first time shows me a good Catholic, the second time a Fool. *To this firmness in all your Actions (though you are wanting in no other Ornaments of Mind and Body, yet to this) I principally ascribe the Interest your Merits have acquir'd you in the Royal Family. A Prince, who is constant to himself, and steady in all his undertakings; one with whom that Character of* Horace *will agree,*

Si fractus illabatur orbis
Impavidum ferient ruinæ,[1]

such an one cannot but place an esteem, and repose a confidence on him, whom no Adversity, no change of Courts, no Bribery of

[1] Should the world's sphere be rent and fall upon him, he will be undismayed when smitten by the wreck. (*Odes* 3. 3. 7–8.)

Interests, or Cabals of Factions, or Advantages of Fortune, can remove from the solid foundations of Honour and Fidelity.

Ille meos, primus qui me sibi junxit, amores
Abstulit; ille habeat secum, servetque sepulcro.[1]

How well your Lordship will deserve that praise, I need no inspiration to foretel. You have already left no room for Prophecy: your early undertakings have been such, in the service of your King and Countrey, when you offer'd your self to the most dangerous employment, that of the Sea; when you chose to abandon those delights, to which your Youth and Fortune did invite you, to undergo the hazards, and, which was worse, the company of common Seamen, that you have made it evident, you will refuse no opportunity of rendring your self useful to the Nation, when either your Courage or Conduct shall be requir'd. The same zeal and faithfulness continues in your Bloud, which animated one of your Noble Ancestors to sacrifice his life in the Quarrel of his Sovereign: though, I hope, both for your sake, and for the publick Tranquillity, the same occasion will never be offer'd to your Lordship, and that a better Destiny will attend you. But I make haste to consider you as abstracted from a Court, which (if you will give me leave to use a term of Logick) is onely an Adjunct, not a Propriety of Happiness. The Academicks, I confess, were willing to admit the Goods of Fortune into their Notion of Felicity; but I do not remember, that any of the Sects of old Philosophers did ever leave a room for Greatness. Neither am I form'd to praise a Court, who admire and covet nothing, but the easiness and quiet of retirement. I naturally withdraw my sight from a Precipice; and admit the Prospect be never so large and goodly, can take no pleasure even in looking on the downfall, though I am secure from the danger. Methinks there's something of a malignant joy in that excellent description of Lucretius,

Suave mari magno turbantibus æquora ventis
E terrâ magnum alterius spectare laborem;
Non quia vexari quenquam est jucunda voluptas
Sed quibus ipse malis careas, quiâ cernere suave est.[2]

I am sure his Master Epicurus, *and my better Master* Cowley, *prefer'd the solitude of a Garden, and the conversation of a friend to any consideration, so much as a regard, of those unhappy People,*

[1] He who first united me to himself, and the same has reft away my love; let him possess that love, and guard it in the tomb. (Vergil, *Æneid* 4. 28–9.)

[2] Sweet it is, when the winds whip the great seas's surface into turmoil, to observe from the land the mighty struggles of another man; not because it gives joyous pleasure that anyone should be in distress, but because it is agreeable to perceive what troubles thou thyself hast not to endure. (2. 1–4.)

whom in our own wrong, we call the great. True greatness, if it be any where on Earth, is in a private Virtue; remov'd from the notion of Pomp and Vanity, confin'd to a contemplation of it self, and centring on it self:

> Omnis enim per se Divum natura, necesse est
> Immortali ævo summâ cum pace fruatur;
> ———Curâ semota, metuque
> Ipsa suis pollens opibus——[1]

If this be not the life of a Deity, because it cannot consist with Providence, 'tis at least a godlike life: I can be contented, (and I am sure I have your Lordship of my opinion) with an humbler station in the Temple of Virtue, than to be set on the Pinnacle of it.

> Despicere unde queas alios, passimque videre
> Errare, atque viam palantes quærere vitæ.[2]

The truth is, the consideration of so vain a Creature as man, is not worth our pains. I have fool enough at home without looking for it abroad; and am a sufficient Theater to my self of ridiculous actions, without expecting company, either in a Court, a Town, or a Play-house. 'Tis on this account that I am weary with drawing the deformities of Life, and Lazars of the People, where every figure of imperfection more resembles me than it can do others. If I must be condemn'd to Rhyme, I should find some ease in my change of punishment. I desire to be no longer the Sisyphus *of the Stage; to rowl up a Stone with endless labour (which to follow the proverb,* gathers no Mosse) *and which is perpetually falling down again. I never thought my self very fit for an Employment, where many of my Predecessors have excell'd me in all kinds; and some of my Contemporaries, even in my own partial Judgement, have out-done me in* Comedy. *Some little hopes I have yet remaining, and those too, considering my abilities, may be vain, that I may make the world some part of amends, for many ill Playes, by an Heroick Poem. Your Lordship has been long acquainted with my design; the subject of which you know is great, the story English, and neither too far distant from the present Age, nor too near approaching it. Such it is in my opinion that I could not have wish'd a nobler occasion to do honour by it to my King, my Country, and my friends; most of our antient Nobility being concern'd in the Action. And your Lordship*

[1] For it must be that the whole nature of the gods enjoys immortality in the most perfect peace . . . remote from care, and from fear, and possessed of a power furnished by its own resources. (*Ibid.* 1. 44–5, and cf. 46–8.)

[2] Whence thou mayest look down and behold others, and see them wander hither and yon seeking, with straggling steps, a way of life. (*Ibid.* 2. 9–10.)

has one particular reason to promote this undertaking, because you were the first who gave me the opportunity of discoursing it to his Majesty, and his Royal Highness: They were then pleas'd, both to commend the Design, and to encourage it by their Commands. But the unsettl'dness of my condition has hitherto put a stop to my thoughts concerning it. As I am no successor to Homer *in his Wit, so neither do I desire to be in his Poverty. I can make no Rhapsodies, nor go a begging at the* Græcian *doors, while I sing the praises of their Ancestors. The times of* Virgil *please me better, because he had an* Augustus *for his Patron. And to draw the Allegory nearer you, I am sure I shall not want a* Mecenas *with him. 'Tis for your Lordship to stir up that remembrance in his Majesty, which his many avocations of business have caus'd him, I fear, to lay aside. And, (as himself and his Royal Brother are the Heroes of the Poem) to represent to them the Images of their Warlike Predecessors; as* Achilles *is said to be rous'd to Glory, with the sight of the Combat before the Ships. For my own part, I am satisfi'd to have offer'd the Design; and it may be to the advantage of my Reputation to have it refus'd me.*

In the mean time, my Lord, I take the confidence to present you with a Tragedy; the Characters of which are the nearest to those of an Heroick Poem. 'Twas dedicated to you in my heart, before 'twas presented on the Stage. Some things in it have pass'd your approbation, and many your amendment. You were likewise pleas'd to recommend it to the King's perusal, before the last hand was added to it, when I receiv'd the favour from him, to have the most considerable event of it modell'd by his Royal Pleasure. It may be some vanity in me to add his Testimony then, and which he graciously confirm'd afterwards, that it was the best of all my Tragedies; in which he has made Authentick my private opinion of it; at least, he has given it a value by his Commendation, which it had not by my Writing.

That which was not pleasing to some of the fair Ladies in the last Act of it, as I dare not vindicate, so neither can I wholly condemn, till I find more reason for their Censures. The procedure of Indamora *and* Melesinda, *seems yet, in my judgment, natural, and not unbecoming of their Characters. If they who arraign them fail not more, the World will never blame their conduct; And I shall be glad, for the honour of my Countrey, to find better Images of Virtue drawn to the life in their behaviour, than any I could feign to adorn the Theatre. I confess, I have onely represented a practical Virtue, mix'd with the frailties and imperfections of humane life. I have made my* Heroine *fearful of death, which neither* Cassandra *nor*

Cleopatra *would have been; and they themselves, I doubt it not, would have outdone Romance in that particular. Yet their* Mandana (*and the* Cyrus *was written by a Lady*) *was not altogether so hard-hearted: for she sat down on the cold ground by the King of* Assyria, *and not onely piti'd him, who dy'd in her defence; but allow'd him some favours, such, perhaps, as they would think, should onely be permitted to her* Cyrus.[1] *I have made my* Melesinda, *in opposition to* Nourmahal, *a Woman passionately loving of her Husband, patient of injuries and contempt, and constant in her kindness, to the last: and in that, perhaps, I may have err'd, because it is not a Virtue much in use. Those* Indian *Wives are loving Fools, and may do well to keep themselves in their own Countrey, or, at least, to keep company with the* Arria's *and* Portia's *of old* Rome*: some of our Ladies know better things. But, it may be, I am partial to my own Writings: yet I have labour'd as much as any man, to divest my self of the self-opinion of an Author; and am too well satisfi'd of my own weakness, to be pleas'd with any thing I have written. But on the other side, my reason tells me, that, in probability, what I have seriously and long consider'd, may be as likely to be just and natural, as what an ordinary Judge (if there be any such amongst those Ladies) will think fit, in a transient Presentation, to be plac'd in the room of that which they condemn. The most judicious Writer is sometimes mistaken, after all his care: but the hasty Critick, who judges on a view, is full as liable to be deceiv'd. Let him first consider all the Arguments, which the Author had, to write this, or to design the other, before he arraigns him of a fault: and then, perhaps, on second thoughts, he will find his Reason oblige him to revoke his Censure. Yet, after all, I will not be too positive.* Homo sum, humani à me nihil alienum puto.[2] *As I am a Man, I must be changeable: and sometimes the gravest of us all are so, even upon ridiculous accidents. Our minds are perpetually wrought on by the temperament of our Bodies: which makes me suspect, they are nearer alli'd, than either our Philosophers or School-Divines will allow them to be. I have observ'd, says* Montaign, *that when the Body is out of Order, its Companion is seldom at his ease. An ill Dream, or a Cloudy day, has power to change this wretched Creature, who is so proud of a reasonable Soul, and make him think what he thought not yesterday. And* Homer *was of this opinion, as* Cicero *is pleas'd to translate him for us:*

[1] An incident from *Le Grand Cyrus*, an heroic romance by Madeleine de Scudéry: see also *Preface to Fables*, p. 489, n. 1.

[2] I am human, and nothing that is human do I deem alien to myself. (Terence, *Heautontimorumenos* 1. 1. 25.)

Tales sunt hominum mentes quali pater ipse
Jupiter, auctiferâ lustravit lampade terras.[1]

Or as the same Author, in his Thusculane Questions, speaks with more modesty than usual of himself: Nos in diem vivimus; quodcunque animos nostros probabilitate percussit, id dicimus.[2] *'Tis not therefore impossible, but that I may alter the conclusion of my Play, to restore my self into the good Graces of my fair Criticks. And your Lordship, who is so well with them, may do me the Office of a Friend and Patron, to intercede with them on my promise of amendment. The Impotent Lover in* Petronius, *though his was a very unpardonable crime, yet was receiv'd to mercy on the terms I offer.* Summa excusationis meæ hæc est: placebo tibi, si culpam emendare permiseris.[3]

But I am conscious to my self of offering at a greater boldness, in presenting to your view what my meanness can produce, than in any other error of my Play. And therefore make haste to break off this tedious Address, which has, I know not how, already run it self into so much of Pedantry, with an excuse of Tully's, *which he sent with his Books* De Finibus, *to his Friend* Brutus, De ipsis rebus autem, sæpenumerò Brute vereor ne reprehendar, cum hæc ad te scribam, qui tum in Poesi, (*I change it from* Philosophiâ) tum in optimo genere Poeseos tantum processeris. Quod si facerem quasi te erudiens, jure reprehenderer. Sed ab eo plurimùm absum: nec, ut ea cognoscas quæ tibi notissima sunt ad te mitto; sed quià facillimè in nomine tuo acquiesco, & quia te habeo æquissimum eorum studiorum, quæ mihi communia tecum sunt, æstimatorem & judicem.[4] *Which you may please, my Lord, to apply to your self, from him, who is*

Your Lordship's most obedient humble Servant,
DRYDEN.

[1] The minds of men are such as the light that giveth increase, wherewith Father Jove himself doth traverse the earth. (Cicero, quoted by Augustine, *De Civitate Dei* 5. 8.)

[2] As for us, we live from day to day, and what we assert is merely that which has impressed us at the time as being credible. (5. 11. 33.)

[3] The sole apology I will make is this: if you will permit me to mend my fault, I am ready to do your will. (*Satyricon* 130.)

[4] Now as to the subjects themselves, I often fear, Brutus, I may be open to reproach for writing thus about them to you, who have made such progress not only in poetry but in the best kind of poetry. Indeed I should earn a reproach if I were to do this as if I were seeking to instruct you; but I am very far from doing so, nor do I send you these pages in order that you may gain acquaintance with what is perfectly familiar to you, but because I find it very easy to yield to my confidence in you, and believe you to be the fairest appraiser of my efforts in the pursuits which we have in common. (Cicero, *De Finibus* 3. 2. 6.)

PROLOGUE

Our Author by experience finds it true,
'Tis much more hard to please himself than you:
And out of no feign'd modesty, this day,
Damns his laborious Trifle of a Play:
Not that its worse than what before he writ,
But he has now another taste of Wit;
And to confess a truth, (though out of time)
Grows weary of his long-lov'd Mistris, Rhyme.
Passion's too fierce to be in Fetters bound,
And Nature flies him like Enchanted Ground.
What Verse can do, he has perform'd in this,
Which he presumes the most correct of his:
But spite of all his pride a secret shame,
Invades his breast at Shakespear's *sacred name:*
Aw'd when he hears his Godlike Romans *rage,*
He, in a just despair, would quit the Stage.
And to an Age less polish'd, more unskill'd,
Does, with disdain the foremost Honours yield.
As with the greater Dead he dares not strive,
He wou'd not match his Verse with those who live:
Let him retire, betwixt two Ages cast,
The first of this, and hindmost of the last.
A losing Gamester, let him sneak away;
He bears no ready Money from the Play.
The Fate which governs Poets, thought it fit,
He shou'd not raise his Fortunes by his Wit.
The Clergy thrive, and the litigious Bar;
Dull Heroes fatten with the spoils of War:
All Southern Vices, Heav'n be prais'd, are here;
But Wit's a luxury you think too dear.
When you to cultivate the Plant are loath,
'Tis a shrewd sign 'twas never of your growth:
And Wit in Northern Climates will not blow,
Except, like Orange-trees, *'tis hous'd from Snow.*
There needs no care to put a Play-house down,
'Tis the most desart place of all the Town.
We and our Neighbours, to speak proudly, are
Like Monarchs, ruin'd with expensive War.
While, like wise English, *unconcern'd, you sit,*
And see us play the Tragedy of Wit.

PERSONS REPRESENTED

	BY
The Old Emperor.	Mr. *Mohun.*
Aureng-Zebe his Son.	Mr. *Hart.*
Morat, his younger Son.	Mr. *Kynaston.*
Arimant, Governour of Agra.	Mr. *Wintershal.*
Dianet. *Solyman.* *Mir Baba.* *Abas.* *Asaph Chan.* *Fazel Chan.* — *Indian* Lords, or *Omrahs*, of several Factions.	
Nourmahal, the Empress.	Mrs. *Marshal.*
Indamora, a Captive Queen.	Mrs. *Cox.*
Melesinda, Wife to Morat.	Mrs. *Corbet.*
Zayda, favourite Slave to the Empress.	Mrs. *Uphil.*

SCENE, *Agra*, in the Year 1660.

AURENG-ZEBE

A TRAGEDY

ACT I

ARIMANT, ASAPH CHAWN, FAZEL CHAWN.

ARIMANT: Heav'n seems the Empire of the East to lay
On the success of this important day:
Their Arms are to the last decision bent,
And Fortune labours with the vast event:
She now has in her hand the greatest stake,
Which for contending Monarchs she can make.
What e'r can urge ambitious Youth to fight,
She pompously displays before their sight:
Laws, Empire, All permitted to the Sword,
And Fate could ne'r an ampler Scene afford.

ASAPH CHAWN: Four several Armies to the Field are led,
Which, high in equal hopes four Princes Head:
Indus and *Ganges*, our wide Empires Bounds,
Swell their dy'd Currents with their Natives wounds:
Each purple River winding, as he runs,
His bloudy arms about his slaughter'd Sons.

FAZEL CHAWN: I well remember you foretold the Storm,
When first the Brothers did their Factions form:
When each, by curs'd Cabals of Women, strove
To draw th' indulgent King to partial Love.

ARIMANT: What Heav'n decrees, no prudence can prevent.
To cure their mad Ambition, they were sent
To rule a distant Province each alone.
What could a careful Father more have done?
He made provision against all, but Fate;
While, by his health, we held our peace of State.
The weight of seventy Winters prest him down,
He bent beneath the burthen of a Crown:
Sickness, at last, did his spent Body seize,
And life almost sunk under the disease:

Mortal 'twas thought, at least by them desir'd,
Who, impiously, into his years inquir'd:
As at a Signal, streight the Sons prepare
For open force, and rush to sudden War:
Meeting, like Winds broke loose upon the Main,
To prove, by Arms, whose Fate it was to Reign.

ASAPH CHAWN: Rebels and Parricides!

ARIMANT: Brand not their actions with so foul a name:
Pity, at least, what we are forc'd to blame.
When Death's cold hand has clos'd the Father's eye,
You know the younger Sons are doom'd to die.
Less ills are chosen greater to avoid,
And Nature's Laws are by the States destroy'd.
What courage tamely could to death consent,
And not, by striking first, the blow prevent?
Who falls in fight, cannot himself accuse,
And he dies greatly who a Crown pursues.

To them, SOLYMAN AGAH.

SOLYMAN AGAH: A new Express all *Agra* does afright:
Darah and *Aureng-Zebe* are joyn'd in Fight;
The Press of people thickens to the Court,
Th' impatient crowd devouring the report.

ARIMANT: T' each changing news they chang'd affections bring,
And servilely from Fate expect a King.

SOLYMAN: The Ministers of State, who gave us Law,
In corners, with selected Friends, withdraw:
There, in deaf murmurs, solemnly are wise;
Whisp'ring, like Winds, ere Hurricanes arise.
The most corrupt are most obsequious grown,
And those they scorn'd, officiously they own.

ASAPH CHAWN: In change of Government,
The Rabble rule their great Oppressors Fate:
Do Sovereign Justice, and revenge the State.

SOLYMAN: The little Courtiers, who ne'r come to know
The depth of Factions, as in Mazes go,
Where Int'rests meet and cross so oft, that they
With too much care are wilder'd in their way.

ARIMANT: What of the Emperor?

SOLYMAN: Unmov'd, and brave, he like himself appears,
And, meriting no ill, no danger fears:
Yet mourns his former vigour lost so far,
To make him now spectator of a War:

Repining that he must preserve his Crown
By any help or courage but his own:
Wishes, each minute, he could unbeget
Those Rebel-Sons, who dare t' usurp his Seat:
To sway his Empire with unequal skill,
And mount a Throne, which none but he can fill.

ARIMANT: Oh! had he still that Character maintain'd,
Of Valour, which in blooming Youth he gain'd!
He promis'd in his East a glorious Race;
Now, sunk from his Meridian, sets apace.
But as the Sun, when he from Noon declines,
And with abated heat, less fiercely shines,
Seems to grow milder as he goes away,
Pleasing himself with the remains of Day:
So he who, in his Youth, for Glory strove,
Would recompence his Age with Ease and Love.

ASAPH CHAWN: The name of Father hateful to him grows,
Which, for one Son, produces him three Foes.

FAZEL CHAWN: *Darah*, the eldest, bears a generous mind;
But to implacable revenge inclin'd.
Too openly does Love and hatred show:
A bounteous Master, but a deadly Foe.

SOLYMAN: From *Sujah*'s valour I should much expect,
But he's a *Bigot* of the *Persian* sect:
And, by a Foreign Int'rest seeks to Reign,
Hopeless by Love the Sceptre to obtain.

ASAPH CHAWN: *Morat*'s too insolent, too much a Brave,
His Courage to his Envy is a Slave.
What he attempts, if his endeavours fail
T' effect, he is resolv'd no other shall.

ARIMANT: But *Aureng-Zebe*, by no strong passion sway'd,
Except his Love, more temp'rate is, and weigh'd:
This *Atlas* must our sinking State uphold;
In Council cool, but in Performance bold:
He sums their Virtues in himself alone,
And adds the greatest, of a Loyal Son:
His Father's Cause upon his Sword he wears,
And with his Arms, we hope, his Fortune bears.

SOLYMAN: Two vast Rewards may well his courage move,
A Parent's Blessing, and a Mistris Love.
If he succeed, his recompence, we hear,
Must be the Captive Queen of *Cassimere*.

To them, ABAS.

ABAS: Mischiefs on mischiefs, greater still, and more:
The neighb'ring Plain with Arms is cover'd o'r:
The Vale an Iron-Harvest seems to yield
Of thick-sprung Lances in a waving Field.
The pollish'd Steel gleams terribly from far,
And every moment nearer shows the War.
The Horses Neighing by the Wind is blown,
And Castl'd-Elephants o'r-look the Town.

ARIMANT: If, as I fear, *Morat* these Pow'rs commands,
Our Empire on the brink of ruine stands:
Th' ambitious Empress with her Son is joyn'd,
And, in his Brother's absence, has design'd
The unprovided Town to take with ease,
And then, the Person of the King to seize.

SOLYMAN: To all his former Issue she has shown
Long hate, and labour'd to advance her own.

ABAS: These Troops are his.
Surat he took; and thence, preventing Fame,
By quick and painful Marches hither came.
Since his approach, he to his Mother sent,
And two long hours in close debate were spent.

ARIMANT: I'll to my Charge, the Cittadel, repair,
And show my duty by my timely care.

To them the EMPEROR *with a letter in his hand: after him, an* AMBASSADOR, *with a Train following.*

ASAPH CHAWN: But see, the Emperor! a fiery red
His Brows and glowing Temples does o'erspread,
Morat has some displeasing Message sent.

AMBASSADOR: Do not, great Sir, misconstrue his intent;
Nor call Rebellion what was prudent care,
To guard himself by necessary War:
While he believ'd you living, he obey'd:
His Governments but as your Vice-Roy sway'd:
But, when he thought you gone,
T' augment the number of the Bless'd above,
He deem'd 'em Legacies of Royal love:
Nor arm'd his Brothers Portions to invade,
But to defend the present you had made.

EMPEROR: By frequent Messages, and strict Commands,

He knew my pleasure to discharge his Bands:
Proof of my life my Royal Signet made;
Yet still he arm'd, came on, and disobey'd.

AMBASSADOR: He thought the *Mandat* forg'd, your death conceal'd:
And but delay'd, till truth should be reveal'd.

EMPEROR: News of my death from Rumor he receiv'd;
And what he wish'd, he easily believ'd:
But long demurr'd, though from my hand he knew
I liv'd, so loath he was to think it true.
Since he pleads ignorance to that command,
Now let him show his duty, and disband.

AMBASSADOR: His Honour, Sir, will suffer in the Cause,
He yields his Arms unjust if he withdraws:
And begs his Loyalty may be declar'd,
By owning those he leads to be your guard.

EMPEROR: I, in myself, have all the Guard I need;
Bid the presumptuous Boy draw off with speed:
If his audacious Troops one hour remain,
My Cannon from the Fort shall scour the Plain.

AMBASSADOR: Since you deny him entrance, he demands
His Wife, whom cruelly you hold in Bands:
Her, if unjustly you from him detain,
He justly will by force of arms regain.

EMPEROR: O'r him and his, a right from Heav'n I have;
Subject, and Son, he's doubly born my Slave.
But whatsoe'r his own demerits are,
Tell him, I shall not make on Women, War.
And yet I'll do her Innocence the grace,
To keep her here, as in the safer place.
But thou, who dar'st this bold defiance bring,
May'st feel the rage of an offended King.
Hence from my sight, without the least reply:
One word, nay, one look more, and thou shalt die.

[*Exit* AMBASSADOR.

Re-enter ARIMANT.

ARIMANT: May Heav'n, great Monarch, still augment your bliss
With length of days, and every day like this.
For, from the Banks of *Gemna* news is brought,
Your Army has a bloudy Battel fought;
Darah from Loyal *Aureng-Zebe* is fled;

And fourty thousand of his Men lie dead.
To *Sujah* next your conquering Army drew;
Him they surpris'd, and easily o'r-threw.
EMPEROR: 'Tis well.
ARIMANT: But well! what more could at your wish be done,
Than two such Conquests gain'd by such a Son?
Your pardon, mighty Sir;
You seem not high enough your Joys to rate;
You stand indebted a vast sum to Fate:
And should large thanks for the great Blessing pay.
EMPEROR: My fortune owes me greater every day.
And, should my joy more high for this, appear,
It would have argu'd me before of fear.
How is Heav'n kind, where I have nothing won,
And Fortune onely pays me with my own?
ARIMANT: Great *Aureng-Zebe* did duteous care express:
And durst not push too far his good success.
But lest *Morat* the City should attack,
Commanded his victorious Army back;
Which, left to march as swiftly as they may,
Himself comes first, and will be here this day,
Before a close-form'd Siege shut up his way.
EMPEROR: Prevent his purpose, hence, hence with all thy speed.
Stop him; his entrance to the Town forbid.
ARIMANT: How, Sir? your Loyal, your Victorious Son?
EMPEROR: Him would I, more than all the Rebels, shun.
ARIMANT: Whom with your pow'r and fortune, Sir, you trust;
Now to suspect is vain, as 'tis unjust.
He comes not with a Train to move your fear,
But trusts himself, to be a pris'ner here.
You knew him brave, you know him faithful now:
He aims at Fame, but Fame from serving you.
'Tis said, Ambition in his breast does rage:
Who would not be the *Hero* of an Age?
All grant him prudent: prudence interest weighs,
And interest bids him seek your love and praise.
I know you grateful; When he march'd from hence,
You bad him hope an ample recompence:
He conquer'd in that hope; and from your hands,
His Love, the precious pledge he left, demands.
EMPEROR: No more; you search too deep my wounded mind:
And show me what I fear, and would not find.
My Son has all the debts of duty paid:

Our Prophet sends him to my present aid.
Such virtue to distrust were base and low:
I'm not ungrateful—or I was not so!
Inquire no farther, stop his coming on:
I will not, cannot, dare not see my Son.

ARIMANT: 'Tis now too late his entrance to prevent:
Nor must I to your ruine give consent.
At once your Peoples heart and Son's you lose:
And give him all, when you just things refuse.

EMPEROR: Thou lov'st me sure; thy faith has oft been tri'd,
In ten pitch'd Fields, not shrinking from my side,
Yet giv'st me no advice to bring me ease.

ARIMANT: Can you be cur'd, and tell not your disease?
I ask'd you, sir.

EMPEROR: ——Thou should'st have ask'd again:
There hangs a secret shame on guilty men.
Thou shouldst have pull'd the secret from my breast,
Torn out the bearded Steel to give me rest:
At least, thou should'st have ghess'd——
Yet thou art honest, thou could'st near have ghess'd.
Hast thou been never base? did Love ne'r bend
Thy frailer Virtue, to betray thy Friend?
Flatter me, make thy Court, and say, It did:
Kings in a Crowd would have their Vices hid.
We would be kept in count'nance, sav'd from shame:
And own'd by others who commit the same.
Nay, now I have confess'd.————
Thou seest me naked, and without disguise:
I look on *Aureng-Zebe* with Rivals eyes.
He has abroad my enemyes o'recome,
And I have sought to ruin him at home.

ARIMANT: This free confession showes you long did strive:
And virtue, though opprest, is still alive.
But what success did your injustice find?

EMPEROR: What it deserv'd, and not what I design'd.
Unmov'd she stood, and deaf to all my prayers,
As Seas and Winds to sinking Mariners.
But Seas grow calm, and Winds are reconcil'd:
Her Tyrant beauty never grows more mild.
Pray'rs, promises, and threats were all in vain.

ARIMANT: Then cure your self by generous disdain.

EMPEROR: Virtue, disdain, despair, I oft have tri'd,
And foil'd, have with new Arms my Foe defi'd.

This made me with so little joy to hear
The Victory, when I the Victor fear.

ARIMANT: Something you swiftly must resolve to do,
Lest *Aureng-Zebe* your secret Love should know.
Morat without does for your ruine wait;
And would you lose the Buckler of your State?
A jealous Empress lies within your Arms,
Too haughty to endure neglected Charms.
Your Son is duteous, but (as Man) he's frail.
And just revenge o'r vertue may prevail.

EMPEROR: Go then to *Indamora*, say from me,
Two Lives depend upon her secresie.
Bid her conceal my passion from my Son:
Though *Aureng-Zebe* return a Conqueror,
Both he and she are still within my pow'r.
Say, I'm a Father, but a Lover too:
Much to my Son, more to my self I owe.
When she receives him, to her words give Law:
And even the kindness of her glances awe.
See, he appears!

[*After a short whisper*, ARIMANT *departs.*

Enter AURENG-ZEBE, DIANET, *and Attendants.*—AURENG-ZEBE *kneels to his Father, and kisses his hand.*

AURFNG-ZEBE: My Vows have been successful as my Sword:
My pray'rs are heard, you have your health restor'd.
Once more 'tis given me to behold your face:
The best of Kings and Fathers to embrace.
Pardon my tears; 'tis joy which bids 'em flow,
A joy which never was sincere till now.
That which my Conquest gave I could not prize;
Or 'twas imperfect till I saw your eyes.

EMPEROR: Turn the discourse: I have a reason why
I would not have you speak so tenderly.
Knew you what shame your kind expressions bring,
You would in pity spare a wretched King.

AURENG-ZEBE: A King! you rob me, Sir, of half my due:
You have a dearer name, a Father too.

EMPEROR: I had that name.

AURENG-ZEBE: ——What have I said or done,
That I no longer must be call'd your Son?
'Tis in that name, Heav'n knows, I glory more,
Than that of Prince, or that of Conqueror.

EMPEROR: Then you upbraid me; I am pleas'd to see
You're not so perfect, but can fail, like me.
I have no God to deal with.

AURENG-ZEBE: ————Now I find
Some slie Court-Devil has seduc'd your mind:
Fill'd it with black suspicions, not your own:
And all my actions through false Optics shown.
I ne'r did Crowns ambitiously regard:
Honour I sought, the generous mind's reward.
Long may you live! while you the Sceptre sway
I shall be still most happy to obey.

EMPEROR: Oh, *Aureng-Zebe!* thy virtues shine too bright,
They flash too fierce: I, like the Bird of Night,
Shut my dull eyes, and sicken at the sight.
Thou hast deserv'd more love than I can show:
But 'tis thy fate to give, and mine to owe.
Thou seest me much distemper'd in my mind:
Pull'd back, and then push'd forward to be kind.
Virtue, and——fain I would my silence break,
But have not yet the confidence to speak.
Leave me, and to thy needful rest repair.

AURENG-ZEBE: Rest is not suiting with a Lover's care.
I have not yet my *Indamora* seen. [*Is going.*

EMPEROR: Somewhat I had forgot; come back again:
So weary of a Father's company!

AURENG-ZEBE: Sir, you were pleas'd your self to license me.

EMPEROR: You made me no relation of the Fight.
Besides, a Rebel's Army is in sight.
Advise me first: yet go——
He goes to *Indamora*; I should take [*Aside.*
A kind of envious joy to keep him back.
Yet to detain him makes my love appear:
I hate his presence, and his absence fear. [*Exit.*

AURENG-ZEBE: To some new Clime, or to thy native Sky,
Oh friendless and forsaken Virtue flie.
Thy *Indian* Air is deadly to thee grown:
Deceit and canker'd malice rule thy Throne.
Why did my Arms in Battel prosp'rous prove,
To gain the barren praise of Filial love?
The best of Kings by Women is misled,
Charm'd by the Witchcraft of a second Bed.
Against my self I Victories have wonn,
And by my fatal absence am undone.

To him INDAMORA, *with* ARIMANT.

But here she comes!
In the calm Harbour of whose gentle breast,
My Tempest-beaten Soul may safely rest.
Oh, my heart's joy! whate'r my sorrows be,
They cease and vanish, in beholding thee!
Care shuns thy walks; as at the cheerful light,
The groaning Ghosts, and Birds obscene take flight.
By this one view, all my past pains are paid:
And all I have to come more easie made.

INDAMORA: Such sullen Planets at my Birth did shine,
They threaten every Fortune mixt with mine.
Fly the pursuit of my disastrous love,
And from unhappy Neighbourhood remove.

AURENG-ZEBE: Bid the laborious Hind,
Whose hardned hands did long in Tillage toil,
Neglect the promis'd Harvest of the Soil.
Should I, who cultivated Love with Bloud,
Refuse possession of approaching good?

INDAMORA: Love is an aery good Opinion makes:
Which he who onely thinks he has, partakes.
Seen by a strong Imagination's Beam;
That tricks and dresses up the gaudy Dream.
Presented so, with rapture 'tis enjoy'd:
Rais'd by high Fancy, and by low destroy'd.

AURENG-ZEBE: If Love be Vision, mine has all the fire
Which, in first Dreams, young Prophets does inspire:
I dream, in you, our promis'd Paradice:
An Ages tumult of continu'd bliss.
But you have still your happiness in doubt:
Or else 'tis past, and you have dream't it out.

INDAMORA: Perhaps not so.

AURENG-ZEBE:——————Can *Indamora* prove
So alter'd? Is it but, Perhaps you Love?
Then farewell all! I thought in you to find
A Balm, to cure my much distemper'd mind.
I came to grieve a Father's heart estrang'd;
But little thought to find a Mistris chang'd.
Nature her self is chang'd to punish me:
Virtue turn'd Vice, and Faith Inconstancy.

INDAMORA: You heard me not Inconstancy confess:
'Twas but a Friend's advice to love me less.
Who knows what adverse Fortune may befall?

Arm well your mind: hope little, and fear all.
Hope, with a goodly prospect, feeds your Eye:
Shows, from a rising ground, possession nigh:
Shortens the distance, or o'r-looks it quite:
So easie 'tis to travel with the sight.

AURENG-ZEBE: Then to despair you would my Love betray,
By taking hope, its last kind Friend, away.
You hold the Glass, but turn the Perspective;
And farther off the lessen'd Object drive.
You bid me fear: in that your change I know:
You would prepare me for the coming blow.
But, to prevent you, take my last Adieu;
I'll sadly tell my self you are untrue,
Rather than stay to hear it told by you. [*Going*.

INDAMORA: Stay, *Aureng-Zebe*, I must not let you go.
And yet believe your self, your own worst Foe,
Think I am true, and seek no more to know.
Let in my breast the fatal Secret lie,
'Tis a sad Riddle, which, if known, we die.
[*Seeming to pause.*

AURENG-ZEBE: Fair Hypocrite, you seek to cheat in vain;
Your silence argues you ask time to feign.
Once more, farewel: the snare in sight is laid,
'Tis my own fault if I am now betray'd. [*Going again.*

INDAMORA: Yet once more stay; you shall believe me true,
Though in one Fate I wrap my self and you.
Your absence————

ARIMANT: ——Hold; you know the hard Command
I must obey: you onely can withstand
Your own mishap. I beg you on my Knee,
Be not unhappy by your own Decree.

AURENG-ZEBE: Speak, Madam, by (if that be yet an Oath)
Your Love, I'm pleas'd we should be ruin'd both.
Both is a sound of joy.
In Death's dark Bow'rs our Bridals we will keep:
And his cold hand
Shall draw the Curtain when we go to sleep.

INDAMORA: Know then, that Man whom both of us did trust,
Has been to you unkind, to me unjust.
The Guardian of my Faith so false did prove,
As to sollicit me with lawless Love:
Pray'd, promis'd, threaten'd, all that Man could do,
Base as he's great; and need I tell you who?

AURENG-ZEBE: Yes; for I'll not believe my Father meant:
Speak quickly, and my impious thoughts prevent.
INDAMORA: You've said; I wish I could some other name!
ARIMANT: My duty must excuse me, Sir, from blame.
A Guard there.

Enter Guards.

AURENG-ZEBE: ——Slave, for me?
ARIMANT: ——My Orders are
To seize this Princess, whom the Laws of War
Long since made Prisoner.
AURENG-ZEBE:—Villain.
ARIMANT:—Sir, I know
Your Birth, nor durst another call me so.
AURENG-ZEBE: I have redeem'd her; and as mine she's free.
ARIMANT: You may have right to give her liberty:
But with your Father, Sir, that right dispute;
For his commands to me were absolute;
If she disclos'd his love, to use the right
Of War, and to secure her from your sight.
AURENG-ZEBE: I'll rescue her, or die. [*Draws.*
And you, my friends, though few, are yet too brave
To see your Gen'rals Mistris made a Slave. [*All draw.*
INDAMORA: Hold, my dear Love! if so much pow'r there lies,
As once you own'd, in *Indamora*'s Eyes,
Lose not the Honour you have early wonn;
But stand the blameless pattern of a Son.
My love your claim inviolate secures:
'Tis writ in Fate, I can be onely yours.
My suff'rings for you make your heart my due:
Be worthy me, as I am worthy you.
AURENG-ZEBE *putting up his sword*: I've thought, and bless'd be you who gave me time:
My Virtue was surpris'd into a Crime.
Strong Virtue, like strong Nature, struggles still:
Exerts it self, and then throws off the ill.
I to a Son's and Lover's praise aspire:
And must fulfil the parts which both require.
How dear the cure of jealousie has cost!
With too much care and tenderness y'are lost.
So the fond Youth from Hell redeem'd his Prize,
Till, looking back, she vanish'd from his eyes!
[*Exeunt severally.*

ACT II

Betwixt the Acts, a Warlike Tune is plaid, shooting off Guns, and shouts of Souldiers are heard, as in an Assault.

AURENG-ZEBE, ARIMANT, ASAPH CHAWN, FAZEL CHAWN, SOLYMAN.

AURENG-ZEBE: What man could do, was by *Morat* perform'd:
The Fortress thrice himself in person storm'd.
Your valour bravely did th' Assault sustain;
And fill'd the Moats and Ditches with the Slain.
Till, mad with rage, into the Breach he fir'd:
Slew Friends and Foes, and in the Smoak retir'd.

ARIMANT: To us you give what praises are not due:
Morat was thrice repuls'd, but thrice by you.
High, over all, was your great conduct shown:
You sought our safety, but forgot your own.

ASAPH CHAWN: Their Standard, planted on the Battlement,
Despair and death among the Souldiers sent:
You, the bold *Omrah* tumbled from the Wall;
And shouts of Victory pursu'd his fall.

FAZEL CHAWN: To you, alone, we owe this prosp'rous day:
Our Wives and Children rescu'd from the prey:
Know your own int'rest Sir, where'r you lead,
We joyntly vow to own no other Head.

SOLYMAN: Your wrongs are known. Impose but your commands;
This hour shall bring you twenty thousand hands.

AURENG-ZEBE: Let them who truly would appear my friends,
Employ their Swords, like mine, for noble ends.
No more: remember you have bravely done:
Shall Treason end, what Loyalty begun?
I own no wrongs; some grievance I confess,
But Kings, like Gods, at their own time redress.
Yet, some becoming boldness I may use:
I've well deserv'd, nor will he now refuse. [*Aside.*
I'll strike my Fortunes with him at a heat:
And give him not the leisure to forget.

[*Exit, attended by the* OMRAHS.

ARIMANT: Oh! *Indamora*, hide these fatal Eyes;
Too deep they wound whom they too soon surprise:
My Virtue, Prudence, Honour, Interest, all

Before this Universal Monarch fall.
Beauty, like Ice, our footing does betray;
Who can tread sure on the smooth slippery way?
Pleas'd with the passage, we slide swiftly on:
And see the dangers which we cannot shun.

To him, INDAMORA.

INDAMORA: I hope my liberty may reach thus far:
These Terras Walks within my limits are.
I came to seek you, and to let you know,
How much I to your generous Pity owe.
The King, when he design'd you for my Guard,
Resolv'd he would not make my Bondage hard:
If otherwise, you have deceiv'd his end;
And whom he meant a Guardian, made a Friend.
ARIMANT: A Guardian's Title I must own with shame:
But should be prouder of another Name.
INDAMORA: And therefore 'twas I chang'd that Name before:
I call'd you Friend, and could you wish for more?
ARIMANT: I dare not ask for what you would not grant:
But wishes, Madam, are extravagant.
They are not bounded with things possible:
I may wish more then I presume to tell:
Desire's the vast extent of humane mind,
It mounts above, and leaves poor hope behind.
I could wish——— ———
INDAMORA: What?
ARIMANT: Why did you speak? you've dashed my Fancy quite:
Ev'n in th' approaching minute of delight.
I must take breath ————————
Ere I the Rapture of my wish renew,
And tell you then, It terminates in you.
INDAMORA: Have you consider'd what th' event would be?
Or know you, *Arimant*, your self, or me?
Were I no Queen, did you my beauty weigh,
My Youth in bloom, your Age in its decay?
ARIMANT: I my own Judge, condemn'd my self before:
For pity aggravate my crime no more.
So weak I am, I with a frown am slain;
You need have us'd but half so much disdain.
INDAMORA: I am not cruel yet to that degree:
Have better thoughts both of your self, and me.
Beauty a Monarch is,

Which Kingly power magnificently proves,
By crouds of Slaves, and peopled Empire loves.
And such a Slave as you, what Queen would lose?
Above the rest, I *Arimant* would chuse:
For counsel, valour, truth, and kindness too,
All I could wish in man, I find in you.

ARIMANT: What Lover could to greater joy be rais'd!
I am, methinks, a God, by you thus prais'd.

INDAMORA: To what may not desert, like yours, pretend?
You have all qualities—that fit a Friend.

ARIMANT: So Mariners mistake the promis'd Coast:
And, with ful Sails, on the blind Rocks are lost.
Think you my aged veins so faintly beat,
They rise no higher than to Friendships heat?
So weak your Charms, that, like a Winter's night,
Twinkling with Stars, they freez me while they light?

INDAMORA: Mistake me not, good *Arimant*, I know
My Beauty's pow'r, and what my charms can do.
You your own Talent have not learn'd so well;
But practise one, where you can ne'r excel.
You can at most,
To an indiff'rent Lover's praise pretend:
But you would spoil an admirable Friend.

ARIMANT: Never was Amity so highly priz'd;
Nor ever any Love so much despis'd.
Ev'n to myself ridiculous I grow;
And would be angry, if I knew but how.

INDAMORA: Do not. Your Anger, like your Love, is vain:
When e'r I please, you must be pleas'd again.
Knowing what pow'r I have your will to bend,
I'll use it; for I need just such a Friend.
You must perform, not what you think is fit:
But, to whatever I propose, submit.

ARIMANT: Madam, you have a strange Ascendant gain'd;
You use me like a Courser, spurr'd and rein'd:
If I fly out, my fierceness you command,
Then sooth, and gently stroke me with your hand.
Impose; but use your pow'r of Taxing well:
When Subjects cannot Pay, they soon Rebel.

Enter the EMPEROR, *unseen by them.*

INDAMORA: My Rebels punishment would easie prove:
You know y'are in my pow'r by making Love.

ARIMANT: Would I, without dispute, your will obey,
And could you, in return, my life betray?
EMPEROR: What danger, *Arimant*, is this you fear?
Or what Love-secret which I must not hear?
These alter'd looks some inward motion show.
His cheeks are pale, and yours with blushes glow. [*To her.*
INDAMORA: 'Tis what, with justice, may my anger move:
He has been bold, and talk'd to me of Love.
ARIMANT: I am betray'd, and shall be doom'd to die. [*Aside.*
EMPEROR: Did he, my Slave, presume to look so high?
That crawling Insect, who from Mud began,
Warm'd by my Beams, and kindl'd into Man?
Durst he, who does but for my pleasure live,
Intrench on Love, my great Prerogative?
Print his base Image on his Sovereign's Coin?
'Tis Treason if he stamp his Love with mine.
ARIMANT: 'Tis true, I have been bold; but if it be
A crime——
INDAMORA: ——He means, 'tis onely so to me.
You, Sir, should praise, what I must disapprove:
He insolently talk'd to me of Love:
But, Sir, 'twas yours, he made it in your name:
You, if you please, may all he said disclaim.
EMPEROR: I must disclaim whate'r he can express:
His groveling sense will show my passion less.
But stay, if what he said my message be,
What fear, what danger could arrive from me?
He said, He feard you would his life betray.
INDAMORA: Should he presume again, perhaps I may.
Though in your hands he hazard not his life,
Remember, Sir, your fury of a Wife;
Who, not content to be reveng'd on you,
The Agents of your passion will pursue.
EMPEROR: If I but hear her nam'd, I'm sick that day;
The sound is mortal, and frights life away.
Forgive me, *Arimant*, my jealous thought:
Distrust in Lovers is the tender'st fault.
Leave me, and tell thy self in my excuse,
Love, and a Crown, no Rivalship can bear;
And precious things are still possess'd with fear.
[*Exit* ARIMANT *bowing.*
This, Madam, my excuse to you may plead;
Love should forgive the faults which Love has made.

INDAMORA: From me, what pardon can you hope to have,
Robb'd of my Love, and treated as a Slave?
EMPEROR: Force is the last relief which Lovers find:
And 'tis the best excuse of Woman-kind.
INDAMORA: Force never yet a generous Heart did gain:
We yield on parley, but are storm'd in vain.
Constraint, in all things, makes the pleasure less;
Sweet is the Love which comes with willingness.
EMPEROR: No; 'tis resistance that inflames desire:
Sharpens the Darts of Love, and blows his Fire.
Love is disarm'd that meets with too much ease:
He languishes, and does not care to please.
And therefore 'tis your golden Fruit you guard
With so much care, to make possession hard.
INDAMORA: Was't not enough you took my Crown away,
But cruelly you must my Love betray?
I was well pleas'd to have transferr'd my right,
And better chang'd your Claim of Lawless might,
By taking him, whom you esteem'd above
Your other Sons, and taught me first to love.
EMPEROR: My Son, by my command his course must steer:
I bad him love, I bid him now forbear.
If you have any kindness for him still,
Advise him not to shock a Father's will.
INDAMORA: Must I advise?
Then let me see him, and I'll try t' obey.
EMPEROR: I had forgot, and dare not trust your way.
But send him word,
He has not here an Army to command:
Remember he and you are in my hand.
INDAMORA: Yes, in a Father's hand, whom he has serv'd;
And, with the hazard of his life, preserv'd.
But piety to you, unhappy Prince,
Becomes a crime, and duty an offence:
Against your self, you with your Foes combine,
And seem your own destruction to design.
EMPEROR: You may be pleas'd your Politiques to spare:
I'm old enough, and can my self take care.
INDAMORA: Advice from me was, I confess, too bold:
Y'are old enough it may be, Sir, too old.
EMPEROR: You please your self with your contempt of Age:
But Love, neglected, will convert to Rage.
If on your head my fury does not turn,

Thank that fond dotage which so much you scorn.
But, in another's person, you may prove,
There's warmth for Vengeance left, though not for Love.

Re-enter ARIMANT.

ARIMANT: The Empress has the Anti-chambers past,
And this way moves with a disorder'd haste:
Her brows, the stormy marks of anger bear.
EMPEROR: Madam, retire: she must not find you here.
[*Exit* INDAMORA *with* ARIMANT.

Enter NOURMAHAL *hastily*.

NOURMAHAL: What have I done, that *Nourmahal* must prove
The scorn and triumph of a Rival's Love?
My eyes are still the same, each glance, each grace,
Keep their first lustre, and maintain their place;
Not second yet to any other face.
EMPEROR: What rage transports you? are you well awake?
Such Dreams distracted minds in Feavers make.
NOURMAHAL: Those Feavers you have giv'n, those Dreams have bred,
By broken Faith, and an abandon'd Bed.
Such Visions hourly pass before my sight;
Which from my eyes their Balmy slumbers fright,
In the severest silence of the night.
Visions, which in this Cittadel are seen;
Bright, glorious Visions of a Rival Queen.
EMPEROR: Have patience, my first flames can ne'r decay:
These are but Dreams, and soon will pass away.
Thou know'st, my Heart, my Empire, all is thine:
In thy own Heav'n of Love serenely shine:
Fair as the face of Nature did appear,
When Flowers first peep'd, and Trees did Blossoms bear,
And Winter had not yet deform'd th' inverted year.
Calm as the Breath which fans our Eastern Groves,
And bright as when thy Eyes first lighted up our Loves.
Let our eternal Peace be seal'd by this,
With the first ardour of a Nuptial Kiss. [*Offers to kiss her*.
NOURMAHAL: Me would you have, me your faint kisses prove,
The dregs and droppings of enervate Love?
Must I your cold long-labouring age sustain,
And be to empty joys provok'd in vain?

Receive you sighing after other Charms,
And take an absent Husband in my Arms?

EMPEROR: Even these reproaches I can bear from you:
You doubted of my Love, believe it true.
Nothing but Love this patience could produce;
And I allow your rage that kind excuse.

NOURMAHAL: Call it not patience; 'tis your guilt stands mute:
You have a cause too foul to bear dispute.
You wrong me first, and urge my rage to rise,
Then I must pass for mad; you, meek and wise,
Good man, plead merit by your soft replies.
Vain priviledge poor Women have of tongue:
Men can stand silent, and resolve on wrong.

EMPEROR: What can I more? my friendship you refuse,
And even my mildness, as my crime, accuse.

NOURMAHAL: Your sullen silence cheats not me, false Man;
I know you think the bloudiest things you can.
Could you accuse me, you would raise your voice:
Watch for my crimes, and in my guilt rejoyce.
But my known virtue is from scandal free,
And leaves no shadow for your calumny.

EMPEROR: Such virtue is the plague of humane life:
A virtuous Woman, but a cursed Wife.
In vain of pompous chastity y'are proud:
Virtue's adultery of the Tongue, when loud,
I, with less pain, a Prostitute could bear,
Than the shrill sound of Virtue, virtue hear.
In unchaste Wives ——
There's yet a kind of recompensing ease:
Vice keeps 'em humble, gives 'em care to please:
But against clamorous Virtue, what defence?
It stops our mouthes, and gives your noise pretence.

NOURMAHAL: Since Virtue does your indignation raise,
'Tis pity but you had that Wife you praise.
Your own wild appetites are prone to range,
And then you tax our humours with your change.

EMPEROR: What can be sweeter than our native home!
Thither for ease, and soft repose, we come:
Home is the sacred refuge of our life:
Secur'd from all approaches, but a Wife.
If thence we fly, the cause admits no doubt:
None but an Inmate Foe could force us out.
Clamours, our privacies uneasie make:

Birds leave their Nests disturb'd, and Beasts their Haunts forsake.

NOURMAHAL: Honour's my crime that has your loathing bred:
You take no pleasure in a virtuous Bed.

EMPEROR: What pleasure can there be in that estate,
Which your unquietness has made me hate?
I shrink far off ——————
Dissembling sleep, but wakeful with the fright.
The day takes off the pleasure of the night.

NOURMAHAL: My thoughts no other joys but pow'r pursue;
Or, if they did, they must be lost in you.
And yet the fault's not mine——————
Though Youth and Beauty cannot warmth command;
The Sun in vain shines on the barren Sand.

EMPEROR: 'Tis true, of Marriage-bands I'm weary grown.
Love scorns all ties, but those that are his own.
Chains that are dragg'd, must needs uneasie prove:
For there's a God-like liberty in Love.

NOURMAHAL: What's Love to you?
The bloom of Beauty other years demands;
Nor will be gather'd by such wither'd hands:
You importune it with a false desire:
Which sparkles out, and makes no solid fire.
This impudence of Age, whence can it spring?
All you expect, and yet you nothing bring.
Eager to ask, when you are past a grant;
Nice in providing what you cannot want.
Have conscience; give not her you love this pain:
Sollicit not your self, and her, in vain.
All other Debts may compensation find:
But Love is strict, and will be paid in kind.

EMPEROR: Sure of all ills, Domestic are the worst;
When most secure of blessings, we are curst.
When we lay next us what we hold most dear,
Like *Hercules*, envenom'd Shirts we wear;
And cleaving mischiefs.

NOURMAHAL:——————What you merit, have:
And share, at least, the miseries you gave.
Your days, I will alarm, I'll haunt your nights:
And, worse than Age, disable your delights.
May your sick Fame still languish, till it die:
All Offices of Pow'r neglected lie,
And you grow cheap in every Subject's eye.

Then, as the greatest Curse that I can give;
Unpiti'd, be depos'd; and after live. [*Going off.*

EMPEROR: Stay; and now learn,
How criminal soe'r we Husbands are,
'Tis not for Wives to push our crimes too far.
Had you still Mistris of your temper been,
I had been modest, and not own'd my Sin.
Your fury hardens me: and what e'r wrong
You suffer, you have cancell'd by your tongue.
A Guard there; seize her: she shall know this hour,
What is a Husband's and a Monarch's pow'r.
[*Guard seizes her.*

Enter AURENG-ZEBE.

NOURMAHAL: I see for whom your Charter you maintain:
I must be fetter'd, and my Son be slain,
That *Zelyma*'s ambitious Race may reign.
Not so you promis'd, when my Beauty drew
All *Asia*'s Vows; when *Persia* left for you,
The Realm of *Candahar* for Dow'r I brought:
That long contended Prize for which you fought.

AURENG-ZEBE: The name of Step-mother, your practis'd Art,
By which you have estrang'd my Father's heart,
All you have done against me, or design,
Shows your aversion, but begets not mine.
Long may my Father *India*'s Empire guide:
And may no breach your Nuptial Vows divide.

EMPEROR: Since Love obliges not, I from this hour,
Assume the right of Man's Despotic pow'r:
Man is by Nature form'd your Sexes head:
And is himself the Canon of his Bed.
In Bands of Iron fetter'd you shall be:
An easier yoke than what you put on me.

AURENG-ZEBE: Though much I fear my int'rest is not great,
[*Kneeling.*
Let me your Royal Clemency intreat.
Secrets of Marriage still are Sacred held:
Their sweet and bitter by the wise conceal'd.
Errors of Wives reflect on Husbands still:
And, when divulg'd, proclaim you've chosen ill.
And the mysterious pow'r of Bed and Throne,
Should always be maintain'd, but rarely shown.

EMPEROR: To so perverse a Sex all Grace is vain:

It gives 'em courage to offend again:
For with feign'd tears they penitence pretend:
Again are pardon'd, and again offend.
Fathom our pity when they seem to grieve;
Onely to try how far we can forgive.
Till lanching out into a Sea of strife,
They scorn all pardon, and appear all Wife.
But be it as you please: for your lov'd sake,
This last and fruitless trial I will make.
In all requests, your right of merit use:
And know, There is but one I can refuse.

[*He signs to the Guards, and they remove from the Empress.*

NOURMAHAL: You've done enough, for you design'd my Chains:
The Grace is vanish'd, but th' Affront remains.
Nor is't a Grace, or for his merit done;
You durst no farther, for you fear'd my Son.
This you have gain'd by the rough course you prove;
I'm past Repentance, and you past my Love. [*Exit.*

EMPEROR: A Spirit so untam'd the world ne'r bore.

AURENG-ZEBE: And yet worse usage had incens'd her more.
But since by no obligement she is ti'd,
You must betimes for your defence provide.
I cannot idle in your danger stand;
But beg once more I may your Arms command:
Two Battels your auspicious Cause has wonn;
My Sword can perfect what it has begun,
And, from your Walls, dislodge that haughty Son.

EMPEROR: My Son, your valour has, this day, been such,
None can enough admire, or praise too much.
But now, with reason, your success I doubt:
Her Faction's strong within, his Arms without.

AURENG-ZEBE: I left the City in a Panic fright:
Lions they are in Council, Lambs in Fight.
But my own Troops, by *Mirzah* led, are near:
I, by to morrow's dawn, expect 'em here:
To favour 'em, I'll Sally out ere day,
And through our slaughter'd Foes enlarge their way.

EMPEROR: Age has not yet
So shrunk my Sinews, or so chill'd my Veins,
But conscious Virtue in my breast remains.
But had I now

That strength, with which my boiling Youth was fraught;
When in the Vale of *Balasor* I fought,
And from *Bengale* their Captive Monarch brought;
When Elephant 'gainst Elephant did rear
His Trunck, and Castles justl'd in the Air;
My Sword thy way to Victory had shown:
And ow'd the Conquest to it self alone.

AURENG-ZEBE: Those fair Idea's to my aid I'll call,
And emulate my great Original.
Or, if they fail, I will invoke in Arms,
The pow'r of Love, and *Indamora*'s Charms.

EMPEROR: I doubt the happy influence of your Star:
T' invoke a Captives name bodes ill in War.

AURENG-ZEBE: Sir, give me leave to say, What ever now
The Omen prove, it boded well to you.
Your Royal Promise, when I went to fight,
Oblig'd me to resign a Victor's right.
Her liberty I fought for, and I wonn:
And claim it as your General, and your Son.

EMPEROR: My ears still ring with noise, I'm vext to death:
Tongue-kill'd, and have not yet recover'd breath.
Nor will I be prescrib'd my time by you:
First end the War, and then your Claim renew.
While to your Conduct I my Fortune trust,
To keep this pledge of duty is but just.

AURENG-ZEBE: Some hidden cause your jealousie does move,
Or you could ne'r suspect my Loyal Love.

EMPEROR: What love soever by an Heir is shown,
He waits but time to step into the Throne.
You're neither justifi'd, nor yet accus'd:
Mean while, the Pris'ner with respect is us'd.

AURENG-ZEBE: I know the kindness of her Guardian such,
I need not fear too little, but too much.
But how, Sir, how have you from virtue swerv'd?
Or what so ill return have I deserv'd?
You doubt not me, nor have I spent my bloud,
To have my faith no better understood:
Your Soul's above the baseness of distrust:
Nothing but Love could make you so unjust.

EMPEROR: You know your Rival then; and know 'tis fit,
The Son's should to the Father's Claim submit.

AURENG-ZEBE: Sons may have right, which they can never quit.

Your self first made that Title which I claim:
First bid me love, and authoris'd my flame.

EMPEROR: The value of my gift I did not know:
If I could give, I can resume it too.

AURENG-ZEBE: Recal your gift, for I your power confess:
But first, take back my life, a gift that's less.
Long life would now but a long burthen prove:
You're grown unkind, and I have lost your love.
My grief lets unbecoming speeches fall:
I should have di'd, and not complain'd at all.

EMPEROR: Witness yee Pow'rs,
How much I suffer'd, and how long I strove
Against th' assaults of this imperious Love!
I represented to my self the shame
Of perjur'd Faith, and violated Fame.
Your great deserts, how ill they were repay'd;
All arguments, in vain, I urg'd and weigh'd:
For mighty Love, who Prudence does despise,
For Reason, show'd me *Indamora*'s Eyes.
What would you more, my crime I sadly view,
Acknowledge, am asham'd, and yet pursue.

AURENG-ZEBE: Since you can love, and yet your error see,
The same resistless pow'r may plead for me.
With no less ardor I my claim pursue:
I love, and cannot yield her even to you.

EMPEROR: Your elder Brothers, though o'rcome, have right:
The youngest yet in Arms prepar'd to fight.
But, yielding her, I firmly have decreed,
That you alone to Empire shall succeed.

AURENG-ZEBE: To after Ages let me stand a shame,
When I exchange for Crowns my Love or Fame.
You might have found a mercenary Son,
To profit of the Battels he had won:
Had I been such, what hinder'd me to take
The Crown? nor had th' exchange been yours to make.
While you are living, I no right pretend;
Wear it, and let it where you please descend.
But from my Love, 'tis Sacrilege to part:
There, there's my Throne in *Indamora*'s heart.

EMPEROR: 'Tis in her heart alone that you must Reign:
You'll find her person difficult to gain.
Give willingly what I can take by force:
And know, Obedience is your safest course.

AURENG-ZEBE: I'm taught, by Honour's precepts, to obey:
Fear to Obedience is a slavish way.
If ought my want of duty could beget;
You take the most prevailing means, to threat.
Pardon your Bloud that boils within my veins;
It rises high, and menacing disdains.
Even death's become to me no dreadful name:
I've often met him, and have made him tame:
In fighting fields, where our acquaintance grew,
I saw him, and contemn'd him first for you.

EMPEROR: Of formal duty make no more thy boast:
Thou disobey'st where it concerns me most.
Fool, with both hands thus to push back a Crown:
And headlong cast thy self from Empire down.
Though *Nourmahal* I hate, her Son shall Reign:
Inglorious thou, by thy own fault remain.
Thy younger Brother I'll admit this hour:
So mine shall be thy Mistris, his thy Pow'r. [*Exit.*

AURENG-ZEBE: How vain is Virtue which directs our ways
Through certain danger to uncertain praise!
Barren, and aery name! thee Fortune flies;
With thy lean Train, the Pious and the Wise.
Heav'n takes thee at thy word, without regard;
And lets thee poorly be thy own reward.
The World is made for the bold impious man;
Who stops at nothing, seizes all he can.
Justice to merit does weak aid afford;
She trusts her Ballance, and neglects her Sword.
Virtue is nice to take what's not her own;
And, while she long consults, the Prize is gone.

To him, DIANET.

DIANET: Forgive the Bearer of unhappy news:
Your alter'd Father openly pursues
Your ruine; and, to compass his intent,
For violent *Morat* in haste has sent.
The Gates he order'd all to be unbarr'd:
And from the Market-place to draw the Guard.

AURENG-ZEBE: How look the People in this turn of State?

DIANET: They mourn your ruine as their proper Fate.
Cursing the Empress: for they think it done
By her procurement, to advance her Son.
Him too, though aw'd, they scarcely can forbear:

His pride they hate, his violence they fear.
All bent to rise, would you appear their Chief,
Till your own Troops come up to your relief.

AURENG-ZEBE: Ill treated, and forsaken, as I am,
I'll not betray the glory of my name:
'Tis not for me, who have preserv'd a State,
To buy an Empire at so base a rate.

DIANET: The points of Honour Poets may produce;
Trappings of life, for Ornament, not Use:
Honour, which onely does the name advance,
Is the meer raving madness of Romance.
Pleas'd with a word, you may sit tamely down;
And see your younger Brother force the Crown.

AURENG-ZEBE: I know my fortune in extremes does lie;
The Sons of *Indostan* must Reign, or die;
That desperate hazard Courage does create,
As he plays frankly, who has least Estate;
And that the World the Coward will despise,
When Life's a Blank, who pulls not for a Prize.

DIANET: Of all your knowledge, this vain fruit you have,
To walk with eyes broad open to your Grave.

AURENG-ZEBE: From what I've said, conclude, without reply,
I neither would Usurp, nor tamely die.
Th' attempt to flie, would guilt betray, or fear:
Besides, 'twere vain; the Fort's our Prison here.
Somewhat I have resolv'd———
Morat, perhaps, has Honour in his breast:
And, in extremes, bold Counsels are the best.
Like Emp'ric Remedies, they last are tri'd;
And by th' event condemn'd, or justifi'd.
Presence of mind and courage in distress,
Are more than Armies to procure success. [*Exit.*

ACT III

ARIMANT, *with a Letter in his hand:* INDAMORA.

ARIMANT: And I the Messenger to him from you?
Your Empire you to Tyranny pursue:
You lay commands, both cruel and unjust,
To serve my Rival, and betray my trust.

INDAMORA: You first betray'd your trust in loving me,
And should not I my own advantage see?

Serving my Love, you may my Friendship gain,
You know the rest of your pretences vain.
You must, my *Arimant*, you must be kind:
'Tis in your Nature, and your Noble Mind.

ARIMANT: I'll to the King, and streight my trust resign.

INDAMORA: His trust you may, but you shall never mine.
Heav'n made you love me for no other end,
But to become my Confident and Friend:
As such, I keep no Secret from your sight,
And therefore make you judge how ill I write:
Read it, and tell me freely then your mind:
If 'tis indited as I meant it, kind.

ARIMANT *reading*: I ask not Heav'n my freedom to restore,
But onely for your sake——I'll read no more:
And yet I must——
[*Reading*] Less for my own, than for your sorrow, sad——
Another line, like this, would make me mad——
[*As reading*] Heav'n! she goes on—yet more—and yet more kind!
Each Sentence is a Dagger to my mind.
(*Reading*) See me this night——
Thank Fortune, who did such a Friend provide,
For faithful *Arimant* shall be your Guide.
Not onely to be made an Instrument,
But preingag'd without my own consent!

INDAMORA: Unknown t' ingage you still augments my score,
And gives you scope of meriting the more.

ARIMANT: The best of men
Some int'rest in their actions must confess;
None merit but in hope they may possess.
The fatal Paper rather let me tear,
Than, like *Bellerophon*, my own Sentence bear.

INDAMORA: You may; but 'twill not be your best advice:
'Twill onely give me pains of writing twice.
You know you must obey me, soon or late:
Why should you vainly struggle with your Fate?

ARIMANT: I thank thee, Heav'n, thou hast been wondrous kind!
Why am I thus to slavery design'd,
And yet am cheated with a free-born mind?
Or make thy Orders with my reason sute,
Or let me live by Sense a glorious Brute—— [*She frowns.*
You frown, and I obey with speed, before
That dreadful Sentence comes, *See me no more:*

See me no more! that sound, methinks, I hear
Like the last Trumpet thund'ring in my ear.

Enter SOLYMAN.

SOLYMAN: The Princess *Melesinda*, bath'd in tears,
And toss'd alternately with hopes and fears,
If your affairs such leisure can afford,
Would learn from you the fortunes of her Lord.

ARIMANT: Tell her, that I some certainty may bring;
I go this minute to attend the King.

INDAMORA: This lonely Turtle I desire to see:
Grief, though not cur'd, is eas'd by Company.

ARIMANT *to* SOLYMAN: Say, if she please, she hither may repair,
And breathe the freshness of the open Air.

[*Exit* SOLYMAN.

INDAMORA: Poor Princess! how I pity her estate,
Wrapt in the ruines of her Husbands Fate!
She mourn'd *Morat* should in Rebellion rise;
Yet he offends, and she's the Sacrifice.

ARIMANT: Not knowing his design, at Court she staid;
Till, by command, close pris'ner she was made.
Since when,
Her Chains with *Roman* Constancy she bore;
But that, perhaps, an *Indian* Wife's is more.

INDAMORA: Go, bring her comfort; leave me here alone.

ARIMANT: My love must still be in obedience shown.

[*Exit* ARIMANT.

Enter MELESINDA, *led by* SOLYMAN, *who retires afterwards.*

INDAMORA: When graceful sorrow in her pomp appears,
Sure she is dress'd in *Melesinda*'s tears.
Your head reclin'd, (as hiding grief from view,)
Droops, like a Rose surcharg'd with morning Dew.

MELESINDA: Can Flow'rs but droop in absence of the Sun,
Which wak'd their sweets? and mine, alas! is gone.
But you the noblest Charity express:
For they who shine in Courts still shun distress.

INDAMORA: Distress'd my self, like you, confin'd I live:
And therefore can compassion take, and give.
We're both Love's Captives, but with Fate so cross,
One must be happy by the others loss.
Morat, or *Aureng-Zebe* must fall this day.

MELESINDA: Too truly *Tamerlain*'s Successors they,
Each thinks a World too little for his sway.

Could you and I the same pretences bring,
Mankind should with more ease receive a King:
I would to you the narrow World resign,
And want no Empire while *Morat* was mine.

INDAMORA: Wish'd freedom I presage you soon will find;
If Heav'n be just, and be to Virtue kind.

MELESINDA: Quite otherwise my mind foretels my Fate:
Short is my life, and that unfortunate.
Yet should I not complain, would Heav'n afford
Some little time, ere death, to see my Lord.

INDAMORA: These thoughts are but your melancholy's food;
Rais'd from a lonely life, and dark abode:
But whatsoe'r our jarring fortunes prove,
Though our Lords hate, me-thinks we two may love.

MELESINDA: Such be our Loves as may not yield to Fate:
I bring a heart more true than fortunate.
[*Giving their hands.*

To them ARIMANT.

ARIMANT: I come with haste surprising news to bring:
In two hours time, since last I saw the King,
Th' affairs of Court have wholely chang'd their face:
Unhappy *Aureng-Zebe* is in disgrace:
And your *Morat*, (proclaim'd the Successor)
Is call'd, to awe the City with his power.
Those Trumpets his triumphant Entry tell.
And now the Shouts waft near the Cittadel.

INDAMORA: See, Madam, see th' event by me foreshown:
I envy not your chance, but grieve my own.

MELESINDA: A change so unexpected must surprise:
And more, because I am unus'd to joys.

INDAMORA: May all your wishes ever prosp'rous be.
But I'm too much concern'd th' event to see.
My eyes too tender are ————
To view my Lord become the publick scorn.
I came to comfort, and I go to mourn. [*Taking her leave.*

MELESINDA: Stay, I'll not see my Lord,
Before I give your sorrow some relief;
And pay the charity you lent my grief.
Here he shall see me first with you confin'd:
And, if your virtue fail to move his mind,
I'll use my int'rest that he may be kind.
Fear not, I never mov'd him yet in vain.

INDAMORA: So fair a Pleader any Cause may gain.
MELESINDA: I have no taste, methinks, of coming joy;
For black presages all my hopes destroy.
Die, something whispers, *Melesinda*, die;
Fulfil, fulfil, thy mournful Destiny.
Mine is a gleam of bliss, too hot to last,
Watry it shines, and will be soon o'r-cast.

INDAMORA *and* MELESINDA *re-enter, as into the Chamber.*

ARIMANT: Fortune seems weary grown of *Aureng-Zebe,*
While to her new-made Favourite, *Morat,*
Her lavish hand is wastefully profuse:
With Fame and flowing Honours tided in,
Born on a swelling Current smooth beneath him.
The King and haughty Empress, to our wonder,
If not atton'd, yet seemingly at peace.
As Fate for him that Miracle reserv'd.

Enter in Triumph, EMPEROR, MORAT, *and Train.*

EMPEROR: I have confess'd I love.
As I interpret fairly your design,
So look not with severer eyes on mine.
Your Fate has call'd you to th' Imperial Seat:
In duty be, as you in Arms are, great.
For *Aureng-Zebe* a hated name is grown,
And Love less bears a Rival than the Throne.
MORAT: To me, the cries of fighting Fields are Charms:
Keen be my Sabre, and of proof my Arms,
I ask no other blessing of my Stars:
No prize but Fame, nor Mistris but the Wars.
I scarce am pleas'd I tamely mount the Throne:
Would *Aureng-Zebe* had all their Souls in one:
With all my elder Brothers I would fight,
And so from partial Nature force my right.
EMPEROR: Had we but lasting Youth, and time to spare,
Some might be thrown away on Fame and War:
But Youth, the perishing good, runs on too fast:
And unenjoy'd will spend it self to waste;
Few know the use of life before 'tis past.
Had I once more thy vigour to command,
I would not let it die upon my hand:
No hour of pleasure should pass empty by;
Youth should watch joys, and shoot 'em as they flie.

MORAT: Me-thinks all pleasure is in greatness found.
Kings, like Heav'n's Eye, should spread their beams around,
Pleas'd to be seen while Glory's race they run:
Rest is not for the Chariot of the Sun.
Subjects are stiff-neck'd Animals, they soon
Feel slacken'd Reins, and pitch their Rider down.

EMPEROR: To thee that drudgery of Pow'r I give:
Cares be thy lot: Reign thou, and let me live.
The Fort I'll keep for my security,
Bus'ness, and public State resign to thee.

MORAT: Luxurious Kings are to their People lost;
They live, like Drones, upon the Public cost.
My Arms, from Pole to Pole, the World shall shake:
And, with my self, keep all Mankind awake.

EMPEROR: Believe me, Son, and needless trouble spare;
'Tis a base World, and is not worth our care.
The Vulgar, a scarce animated Clod,
Ne'r pleas'd with aught above 'em, Prince or God.
Were I a God, the drunken Globe should roul:
The little Emmets with the humane Soul
Care for themselves, while at my ease I sat,
And second Causes did the work of Fate.
Or, if I would take care, that care should be
For Wit that scorn'd the World, and liv'd like me.

To them, NOURMAHAL, ZAYDA, *and Attendants.*

NOURMAHAL: My dear *Morat,* [*Embracing her Son.*
This day propitious to us all has been:
You're now a Monarch's Heir, and I a Queen.
Your faithful Father now may quit the State,
And find the ease he sought, indulg'd by Fate.
Cares shall not keep him on the Throne awake,
Nor break the golden Slumbers he would take.

EMPEROR: In vain I struggl'd to the Gaol of Life,
While Rebel-Sons, and an imperious Wife
Still dragg'd me backward into noise and strife.

MORAT: Be that remembrance lost; and be't my pride
To be your pledge of peace on either side.

To them, AURENG-ZEBE.

AURENG-ZEBE: With all th' assurance Innocence can bring,
Fearless without, because secure within,

Arm'd with my courage, unconcern'd I see
This pomp; a shame to you, a pride to me.
Shame is but where with wickedness 'tis joyn'd
And, while no baseness in this breast I find,
I have not lost the birth-right of my mind.

EMPEROR: Children (the blind effect of Love and Chance,
Form'd by their sportive Parents ignorance)
Bear from their birth th' impressions of a Slave:
Whom Heav'n for play-games first, and then for service gave.
One then may be displac'd, and one may Reign:
And want of Merit, render Birth-right vain.

MORAT: Comes he t' upbraid us with his innocence?
Seize him, and take the preaching *Brachman* hence.

AURENG-ZEBE: Stay, Sir; I, from my years, no merit plead:
[*To his Father*.
All my designs and acts to duty lead.
Your Life and Glory are my onely end;
And for that Prize I with *Morat* contend.

MORAT: Not him alone; I all Mankind defie.
Who dares adventure more for both than I?

AURENG-ZEBE: I know you brave, and take you at your word:
That present service which you vaunt, afford.
Our two Rebellious Brothers are not dead:
Though vanquish'd, yet again they gather head.
I dare you, as your Rival in renown,
March out your Army from th' imperial Town:
Chuse whom you please, the other leave to me:
And set our Father absolutely free.
This, if you do, to end all future strife,
I am content to lead a private life:
Disband my Army to secure the State,
Nor aim at more, but leave the rest to Fate.

MORAT: I'll do't. Draw out my Army on the Plain:
War is to me a pastime, Peace a pain.

EMPEROR *to* MORAT: Think better first.
[*To* AURENG-ZEBE] You see your self inclos'd beyond escape,
And therefore, *Proteus*-like, you change your shape.
Of promise prodigal, while pow'r you want,
And preaching in the Self-denying Cant.

MORAT: Plot better; for these Arts too obvious are,
Of gaining time, the Masterpiece of War:
Is *Aureng-Zebe* so known?

AURENG-ZEBE:——If Acts like mine,
So far from int'rest, profit, or design,
Can show my heart, by those I would be known:
I wish you could as well defend your own.
My absent Army for my Father fought:
Yours, in these Walls, is to inslave him brought.
If I come singly, you an armed guest,
The World with ease may judge whose Cause is best.
MORAT: My Father saw you ill designs Pursue:
And my admission show'd his fear of you.
AURENG-ZEBE: Himself best knows why he his Love withdraws:
I owe him more than to declare the cause.
But still I press our duty may be shown
By Arms.
MORAT: ——I'll vanquish all his foes alone.
AURENG-ZEBE: You speak as if you could the Fates command,
And had no need of any other hand.
But, since my Honour you so far suspect,
'Tis just I should on your designs reflect.
To prove your self a Loyal Son, declare
You'll lay down Arms when you conclude the War.
MORAT: No present answer your demand requires;
The War once done, I'll do what Heav'n inspires.
And while the Sword this Monarchy secures,
'Tis manag'd by an abler Arm than yours.
EMPEROR: *Morat*'s design a doubtful meaning bears: [*Apart.*
In *Aureng-Zebe* true Loyalty appears.
He, for my safety, does his own despise;
Still, with his wrongs, I find his duty rise.
I feel my Virtue strugling in my Soul,
But stronger Passion does its pow'r controul.
Yet be advis'd your ruine to prevent.
[*To* AURENG-ZEBE *apart.*
You might be safe, if you would give consent.
AURENG-ZEBE: So to your welfare I of use may be,
My life or death are equal both to me.
EMPEROR: The Peoples hearts are yours; the Fort yet mine:
Be wise, and *Indamora*'s love resign.
I am observ'd: remember that I give
This my last proof of kindness, die, or live.
AURENG-ZEBE: Life, with my *Indamora*, I would chuse;
But, losing her, the end of living lose.
I had consider'd all I ought before;

And fear of death can make me change no more.
The Peoples love so little I esteem,
Condemn'd by you, I would not live by them.
May he who must your favour now possess,
Much better serve you, and not love you less.

EMPEROR: I've heard you; and, to finish the debate, [*Aloud.*
Commit that Rebel pris'ner to the State.

MORAT: The deadly draught he shall begin this day:
And languish with insensible decay.

AURENG-ZEBE: I hate the lingring summons to attend,
Death all at once would be the nobler end.
Fate is unkind! me-thinks a General
Should warm, and at the head of Armies fall.
And my ambition did that hope pursue,
That so I might have di'd in fight for you. [*To his Father.*

MORAT: Would I had been disposer of thy Stars;
Thou shouldst have had thy wish, and di'd in Wars.
'Tis I, not thou, have reason to repine,
That thou shouldst fall by any hand, but mine.

AURENG-ZEBE: When thou wert form'd, Heav'n did a Man begin;
But the brute Soul, by chance, was shuffl'd in.
In Woods and Wilds thy Monarchy maintain:
Where valiant Beasts, by force and rapine, reign,
In Life's next Scene, if Transmigration be,
Some Bear or Lion is reserv'd for thee.

MORAT: Take heed thou com'st not in that Lion's way:
I prophecy thou wilt thy Soul convey
Into a Lamb, and be again my Prey.
Hence with that dreaming Priest.

NOURMAHAL: ——Let me prepare
The pois'nous draught: his death shall be my care.
Near my Apartment let him pris'ner be:
That I his hourly ebbs of life may see.

AURENG-ZEBE: My life I would not ransome with a pray'r:
'Tis vile, since 'tis not worth my Father's care.
I go not, Sir, indebted to my grave:
You pai'd your self, and took the life you gave. [*Exit.*

EMPEROR: O that I had more sense of vertue left, [*Aside.*
Or were of that, which yet remains, bereft.
I've just enough to know how I offend,
And, to my shame, have not enough to mend.
Lead to the Mosque——

MORAT: Love's pleasures why should dull devotion stay?
Heav'n to my *Melesinda*'s but the way.
[*Exeunt* EMPEROR, MORAT, *and Train.*
ZAYDA: Sure *Aureng-Zebe* has somewhat of Divine,
Whose virtue through so dark a clowd can shine.
Fortune has from *Morat* this day remov'd
The greatest Rival, and the best belov'd.
NOURMAHAL: He is not yet remov'd.
ZAYDA: ——He lives, 'tis true;
But soon must die, and, what I mourn, by you.
NOURMAHAL: My *Zayda*, may thy words prophetic be: {*Embracing her eagerly.*
I take the Omen, let him die by me.
He stifl'd in my arms shall lose his breath:
And Life itself shall envious be of Death.
ZAYDA: Bless me, you Pow'rs above!
NOURMAHAL: ——Why dost thou start?
Is Love so strange? or have not I a heart?
Could *Aureng-Zebe* so lovely seem to thee,
And I want eyes that noble worth to see?
Thy little Soul was but to wonder mov'd:
My sense of it was higher, and I lov'd.
That Man, that God-like Man, so brave, so great;
But these are thy small praises I repeat.
I'm carri'd by a Tide of Love away:
He's somewhat more than I my self can say.
ZAYDA: Though all th' Ideas you can form be true,
He must not, cannot be possess'd by you.
If contradicting int'rests could be mixt,
Nature her self has cast a bar betwixt.
And, ere you reach to this incestuous Love,
You must Divine and Humane Rights remove.
NOURMAHAL: Count this among the Wonders Love has done:
I had forgot he was my Husband's Sone!
ZAYDA: Nay, more; you have forgot who is your own:
For whom your care so long design'd the Throne.
Morat must fall, if *Aureng-Zebe* should rise.
NOURMAHAL: 'Tis true; but who was ere in love, and wise?
Why was that fatal knot of Marriage ti'd,
Which did, by making us too near, divide?
Divides me from my Sex! for Heav'n, I find
Excludes but me alone of Woman-kind.
I stand with guilt confounded, lost with shame,

And yet made wretched onely by a name,
If names have such command on humane Life,
Love sure's a name that's more Divine than Wife.
That Sovereign power all guilt fròm action takes,
At least the stains are beautiful it makes.

ZAYDA: Th' incroaching ill you early should oppose:
Flatter'd 'tis worse, and by indulgence grows.

NOURMAHAL: Alas! and what have I not said or done?
I fought it to the last: and Love has wonn.
A bloudy Conquest; which destruction brought,
And ruin'd all the Countrey where he fought.
Whether this Passion from above was sent
The Fate of him Heav'n favours to prevent,
Or as the curse of Fortune in excess;
That, stretching, would beyond its reach possess:
And, with a taste which plenty does deprave,
Loaths lawful good, and lawless ill does crave?

ZAYDA: But yet consider———

NOURMAHAL: ——No, 'tis loss of time:
Think how to farther, not divert my crime.
My artful Engines instantly I'll move:
And chuse the soft and gentlest hour of Love.
The Under-Provost of the Fort is mine.
But see, *Morat!* I'll whisper my design.

Enter MORAT *with* ARIMANT, *as talking: Attendants.*

ARIMANT: And for that cause was not in public seen:
But stays in Prison with the captive Queen.

MORAT: Let my Attendants wait; I'll be alone:
Where least of State, there most of Love is shown.

NOURMAHAL: My Son, your bus'ness is not hard to ghess; [*To* MORAT.
Long absence makes you eager to possess:
I will not importune you by my stay;
She merits all the Love which you can pay. [*Exit with* ZAYDA.

Re-enter ARIMANT, *with* MELESINDA; *then Exit.*
MORAT *runs to* MELESINDA, *and embraces her.*

MORAT: Should I not chide you, that you chose to stay
In gloomy shades, and lost a glorious day?
Lost the first fruits of joy you should possess

In my return, and made my Triumph less?

MELESINDA: Should I not chide, that you could stay and see
Those joys, preferring public Pomp to me?
Through my dark Cell your shouts of Triumph rung:
I heard with pleasure; but I thought 'em long.

MORAT: The Public will in Triumphs rudely share.
And Kings the rudeness of their joys must bear:
But I made haste to set my Captive free:
And thought that work was onely worthy me.
The Fame of antient Matrons you pursue;
And stand a blameless pattern to the new.
I have not words to praise such Acts as these:
But take my Heart, and mold it as you please.

MELESINDA: A trial of your kindness I must make,
Though not for mine so much as Virtue's sake.
The Queen of *Cassimeer*——

MORAT: ——No more, my love;
That onely suit I beg you not to move.
That she's in Bonds for *Aureng-Zebe* I know,
And should, by my consent, continue so.
The good old man, I fear, will pity show.
My Father dotes, and let him still dote on;
He buys his Mistris dearly with his Throne.

MELESINDA: See her; and then be cruel if you can.

MORAT: 'Tis not with me as with a private Man.
Such may be sway'd by Honour, or by Love;
But Monarchs, onely by their int'rest move.

MELESINDA: Heav'n does a Tribute for your pow'r demand:
He leaves th' opprest and poor upon your hand.
And those, who Stuards of his pity prove,
He blesses, in return, with public Love.
In his distress, some Miracle is shown:
If exil'd, Heav'n restores him to his Throne.
He needs no Guard while any Subject's near:
Nor, like his Tyrant Neighbours, lives in fear:
No Plots th' Alarm to his retirements give:
'Tis all Mankinds concern that he should live.

MORAT: You promis'd friendship in your low estate,
And should forget it in your better Fate;
Such Maxims are more plausible than true;
But somewhat must be given to Love and you.
I'll view this Captive Queen; to let her see,
Pray'rs and complaints are lost on such as me.

MELESINDA: I'll bear the news: Heav'n knows how much I'm pleas'd,
That, by my care, th' afflicted may be eas'd.

As she is going off, Enter INDAMORA.

INDAMORA: I'll spare your pains, and venture out alone,
Since you, fair Princess, my protection own.
But you, brave Prince, a harder task must find;
[*To* MORAT *kneeling, who takes her up.*
In saving me, you would but half be kind.
An humble Suppliant at your feet I lie;
You have condemn'd my better part to die.
Without my *Aureng-Zebe* I cannot live;
Revoke his Doom, or else my Sentence give.
MELESINDA: If *Melesinda* in your love have part,
Which, to suspect, would break my tender heart:
If Love, like mine, may for a Lover plead,
By the chaste pleasures of our Nuptial Bed,
By all the int'rest my past suff'rings make,
And all I yet would suffer for your sake;
By you your self, the last and dearest tie—
MORAT: You move in vain; for *Aureng-Zebe* must die.
INDAMORA: Could that Decree from any Brother come?
Nature her self is sentenc'd in your doom.
Piety is no more, she sees her place
Usurp'd by Monsters, and a savage Race.
From her soft Eastern Climes you drive her forth,
To the cold Mansions of the utmost North.
How can our Prophet suffer you to Reign,
When he looks down, and sees your Brother slain?
Avenging Furies will your life pursue:
Think there's a Heav'n, *Morat*, though not for you.
MELESINDA: Her words imprint a terror on my mind.
What if this death, which is for him design'd,
Had been your Doom, (far be that Augury!)
And you, not *Aureng-Zebe*, condemn'd to die?
Weigh well the various turns of Humane Fate,
And seek, by Mercy, to secure your State.
INDAMORA: Had Heav'n the Crown for *Aureng-Zebe* design'd,
Pity, for you, had pierc'd his generous mind.
Pity does with a Noble Nature suit:
A Brother's life had suffer'd no dispute.
All things have right in life, our Prophet's care

Commands the beings ev'n of Brutes to spare.
Though int'rest his restraint has justifi'd,
Can life, and to a Brother, be deni'd?

MORAT: All Reasons for his safety urg'd, are weak:
And yet, me-thinks, 'tis Heav'n to hear you speak.

MELESINDA: 'Tis part of your own being to invade——

MORAT: Nay, if she fail to move, would you perswade?
[*Turning to* INDAMORA.
My Brother does a glorious Fate pursue.
I envy him, that he must fall for you.
He had been base had he releas'd his right:
For such an Empire none but Kings should fight.
If with a Father, he disputes this prize,
My wonder ceases when I see these Eyes.

MELESINDA: And can you then deny those Eyes you praise?
Can Beauty wonder, and not pity raise?

MORAT: Your intercession now is needless grown:
Retire, and let me speak with her alone.
[MELESINDA *retires, weeping, to the side of the Theatre.*
Queen, that you may not fruitless tears employ,
[*Taking* INDAMORA'*s hand.*
I bring you news to fill your heart with joy:
Your Lover King of all the East shall Reign:
For *Aureng-Zebe* tomorrow shall be slain.

INDAMORA: The hopes you rais'd, y'ave blasted with a breath:
[*Starting back.*
With Triumphs you began, but end with Death.
Did you not say, my Lover should be King?

MORAT: I, in *Morat*, the best of Lovers bring?
For one forsaken both of Earth and Heav'n,
Your kinder Stars a nobler choice have given:
My Father, while I please, a King appears;
His Pow'r is more declining than his Years.
An Emperor and Lover, but in show:
But you, in me, have Youth and Fortune too.
As Heav'n did to your eyes and form Divine,
Submit the Fate of all th' Imperial Line;
So was it order'd by its wise Decree,
That you should find 'em all compris'd in me.

INDAMORA: If, Sir, I seem not discompos'd with rage,
Feed not your fancy with a false presage.
Farther to press your Courtship is but vain:
A cold refusal carries more disdain.

Unsettled Virtue stormy may appear;
Honour, like mine, serenely is severe.
To scorn your person, and reject your Crown,
Disorder not my face into a frown. [*Turns from him.*

MORAT: Your Fortune you should rev'rently have us'd:
Such offers are not twice to be refus'd.
I go to *Aureng-Zebe*, and am in haste:
For your Commands, they're like to be the last.

INDAMORA: Tell him,
With my own death I would his life redeem;
But, less than Honour, both our Lives esteem.

MORAT: Have you no more?

INDAMORA: ——What shall I do or say? [*Aside.*
He must not in this fury go away.
Tell him, I did in vain his Brother move;
And yet he falsly said, he was in love.
Falsly; for had he truly lov'd, at least,
He would have giv'n one day to my request.

MORAT: A little yielding may my love advance:
She darted from her eyes a sidelong glance,
Just as she spoke; and, like her words, it flew:
Seem'd not to beg, what yet she bid me do.
A Brother, Madam, cannot give a day; [*To her.*
A Servant, and who hopes to merit, may.

MELESINDA: If, Sir—— —— [*coming to him.*

MORAT: No more—set speeches, and a formal tale,
With none but States-men and grave Fools prevail.
Dry up your tears, and practise every Grace,
That fits the Pageant of your Royal place. [*Exit.*

MELESINDA: Madam, the strange reverse of Fate you see:
[*To* INDAMORA.
I piti'd you, now you may pity me. [*Exit after him.*

INDAMORA: Poor Princess! thy hard Fate I could bemoan,
Had I not nearer sorrows of my own.
Beauty is seldom fortunate, when great:
A vast Estate, but overcharg'd with Debt.
Like those whom want to baseness does betray:
I'm forc'd to flatter him I cannot pay.
O would he be content to seize the Throne:
I beg the life of *Aureng-Zebe* alone.
Whom Heav'n would bless, from Pomp it will remove,
And make their wealth in privacy and Love. [*Exit.*

ACT IV

AURENG-ZEBE *solus.*

Distrust, and darkness, of a future state,
Make poor Mankind so fearful of their Fate.
Death, in itself, is nothing; but we fear
To be we know not what, we know not where.
[*Soft music.*
This is the Ceremony of my Fate:
A parting Treat; and I'm to die in State.
They lodge me, as I were the *Persian* King:
And with luxurious Pomp my death they bring.

To him NOURMAHAL.

NOURMAHAL: I thought, before you drew your latest breath,
To smooth your passage, and to soften death;
For I would have you, when you upward move,
Speak kindly of me, to our Friends above:
Nor name me there th' occasion of your Fate;
Or what my Interest does, impute to Hate.
AURENG-ZEBE: I ask not for what end your Pomp's design'd;
Whether t' insult, or to compose my mind:
I mark'd it not;
But, knowing Death would soon th' Assault begin,
Stood firm collected in my Strength within:
To guard that breach did all my Forces guide,
And left unmann'd the quiet Senses side.
NOURMAHAL: Because *Morat* from me his being took,
All I can say will much suspected look:
'Tis little to confess your Fate I grieve;
Yet more than you would easily believe.
AURENG-ZEBE: Since my inevitable death you know,
You safely unavailing pity show:
'Tis Popular to mourn a dying Foe.
NOURMAHAL: You made my Liberty your late request:
Is no return due from a grateful breast?
I grow impatient, till I find some way
Great Offices, with greater, to repay.
AURENG-ZEBE: When I consider Life, 'tis all a cheat;
Yet, fool'd with hope, men favour the deceit;
Trust on, and think tomorrow will repay:
Tomorrow's falser than the former day;

Lies worse; and while it says, We shall be blest
With some new joys, cuts off what we possest.
Strange couzenage! none would live past years again,
Yet all hope pleasure in what yet remain;
And, from the dregs of Life, think to receive
What the first sprightly running could not give.
I'm tir'd with waiting for this Chymic Gold,
Which fools us young, and beggars us when old.

NOURMAHAL: 'Tis not for nothing that we life pursue;
It pays our hopes with something still that's new:
Each day's a Mistris, unenjoy'd before;
Like Travellers, we're pleas'd with seeing more.
Did you but know what joys your way attend,
You would not hurry to your journeys end.

AURENG-ZEBE: I need not haste the end of Life to meet;
The precipice is just beneath my feet.

NOURMAHAL: Think not my sense of Virtue is so small:
I'll rather leap down first, and break your fall.
My *Aureng-Zebe*, (may I not call you so?)
[*Taking him by the hand.*
Behold me now no longer for your Foe;
I am not, cannot be your Enemy:
Look, is there any malice in my eye?
Pray sit—— ———— [*Both sit.*
That distance shows too much respect, or fear:
You'll find no danger in approaching near.

AURENG-ZEBE: Forgive th' amazement of my doubtful state:
This kindness from the Mother of *Morat!*
Or is't some Angel, pitying what I bore,
Who takes that shape, to make my wonder more?

NOURMAHAL: Think me your better *Genius* in disguise;
Or any thing that more may charm your eyes.
Your Guardian Angel never could excel
In care, nor could he love his charge so well.

AURENG-ZEBE: Whence can proceed so wonderful a change?

NOURMAHAL: Can kindness to desert, like yours, be strange?
Kindness by secret Sympathy is ty'd;
For Noble Souls in Nature are alli'd.
I saw with what a brow you brav'd your Fate;
Yet with what mildness bore your Father's hate.
My Virtue, like a String wound up by Art,
To the same sound, when yours was touch'd, took part,
At distance shook, and trembled at my heart.

AURENG-ZEBE: I'll not complain my Father is unkind,
Since so much pity from a Foe I find.
Just Heav'n reward this act.
NOURMAHAL: 'Tis well the debt no payment does demand,
You turn me over to another hand.
But happy, happy she,
And with the Bless'd above to be compar'd,
Whom you your self would, with your self, reward:
The greatest, nay, the fairest of her kind,
Would envy her that Bliss which you design'd.
AURENG-ZEBE: Great Princes thus, when Favourites they raise,
To justifie their Grace, their Creatures praise.
NOURMAHAL: As Love the Noblest Passion we account,
So to the highest Object it should mount.
It shows you brave when mean desires you shun.
An Eagle onely can behold the Sun:
And so must you; if yet, presage Divine
There be in Dreams, or was't a Vision mine?
AURENG-ZEBE: Of me?
NOURMAHAL: ——And who could else employ my thought?
I dream'd, your Love was by Love's Goddess sought;
Officious Cupids, hov'ring o'r your head,
Held Myrtle wreaths: beneath your feet were spread
What Sweets soe'r *Sabean* Springs disclose,
Our *Indian* Jasmine, or the *Syrian* Rose:
The wanton Ministers around you strove
For service, and inspir'd their Mother's Love:
Close by your side, and languishing, she lies,
With blushing cheeks, short breath, and wishing eyes;
Upon your breast supinely lay her head,
While, on your face, her famish'd sight she fed.
Then, with a sigh, into these words she broke,
(And gather'd humid kisses as she spoke.)
Dull, and ingrateful! must I offer love?
Desir'd of Gods, and envi'd ev'n by *Jove*:
And dost thou ignorance or fear pretend?
Mean Soul! and dar'st not gloriously offend?
Then, pressing thus his hand——
AURENG-ZEBE: ——I'll hear no more. [*Rising up.*
'Twas impious to have understood before;
And I, till now, endeavour'd to mistake
Th' incestuous meaning which too plain you make.
NOURMAHAL: And why this niceness to that pleasure shown,

Where Nature sums up all her joys in one;
Gives all she can, and labouring still to give,
Makes it so great, we can but taste and live:
So fills the Senses, that the Soul seems fled,
And thought it self does, for the time, lie dead;
Till, like a String scru'd up with eager haste,
It breaks, and is too exquisite to last?

AURENG-ZEBE: Heav'ns! can you this, without just vengeance, hear?
When will you thunder, if it now be clear?
Yet her alone let not your Thunder seize:
I, too, deserve to die, because I please.

NOURMAHAL: Custom our Native Royalty does awe;
Promiscuous Love is Nature's general Law:
For whosoever the first Lovers were,
Brother and Sister made the second Pair,
And doubled, by their love, their piety.

AURENG-ZEBE: Hence, hence, and to some barbarous Climate fly,
Which onely Brutes in humane form does yield,
And Man grows wild in Nature's common Field.
Who eat their Parents, piety pretend;
Yet there no Sons their Sacred Bed ascend.
To vail great Sins, a greater Crime you chuse;
And, in your Incest, your Adult'ry lose.

NOURMAHAL: In vain this haughty fury you have shown.
How I adore a Soul so like my own!
You must be mine, that you may learn to live:
Know joys, which onely she who loves can give.
Nor think that action you upbraid, so ill:
I am not chang'd; I love my Husband still;
But love him as he was, when youthful grace,
And the first down began to shade his face:
That Image does my Virgin-flames renew,
And all your Father shines more bright in you.

AURENG-ZEBE: In me a horrour of my self you raise;
Curs'd by your love, and blasted by your praise.
You find new ways to prosecute my Fate;
And your least-guilty passion was your Hate.

NOURMAHAL: I beg my death, if you can Love deny.
[*Offering him a Dagger.*

AURENG-ZEBE: I'll grant you nothing; no, not ev'n to die.

NOURMAHAL: Know then, you are not half so kind as I.
[*Stamps with her foot.*

Enter Mutes, some with Swords drawn, one with a Cup.

You've chosen, and may now repent too late.
Behold th' effect of what you wish'd, my Hate.
[*Taking the Cup to present him.*
This Cup, a cure for both our ills has brought:
You need not fear a Philtre in the Draught.

AURENG-ZEBE: All must be poison which can come from thee;
[*Receiving it from her.*
But this the least. T' immortal Liberty
This first I pour—like dying *Socrates*;
[*Spilling a little of it.*
Grim though he be, Death pleases when he frees.

As he is going to drink, Enter MORAT *attended.*

MORAT: Make not such haste, you must my leisure stay:
Your Fate's deferr'd, you shall not die to day.
[*Taking the Cup from him.*

NOURMAHAL: What foolish pity has possess'd your mind,
To alter what your prudence once design'd?

MORAT: What if I please to lengthen out his date
A day, and take a pride to cozen Fate?

NOURMAHAL: 'Twill not be safe to let him live an hour.

MORAT: I'll do't, to show my Arbitrary pow'r.

NOURMAHAL: Fortune may take him from your hands again,
And you repent th' occasion lost in vain.

MORAT: I smile at what your Female fear foresees:
I'm in Fate's place, and dictate her Decrees.
Let *Arimant* be call'd. [*Exit one of his Attendants.*

AURENG-ZEBE: Give me the poison, and I'll end your strife:
I hate to keep a poor precarious life.
Would I my safety on base terms receive,
Know, Sir, I could have liv'd without your leave.
But those I could accuse, I can forgive:
By my disdainful silence, let 'em live.

NOURMAHAL: What am I, that you dare to bind my hand?
[*To* MORAT.
So low, I've not a Murder at command!
Can you not one poor Life to her afford,
Her who gave up whole Nations to your Sword?
And from th' abundance of whose Soul and Heat,
Th' o'rflowing serv'd to make your mind so great.

MORAT: What did that greatness in a Woman's mind?

Ill lodg'd, and weak to act what it design'd.
Pleasure's your portion, and your slothful ease:
When Man's at leisure, study how to please.
Soften his angry hours with servile care,
And when he calls, the ready Feast prepare.
From Wars, and from affairs of State abstain:
Women Emasculate a Monarch's Reign;
And murmuring Crouds, who see 'em shine with Gold,
That pomp, as their own ravish'd Spoils behold.

NOURMAHAL: Rage choaks my words: 'tis Womanly to weep: [*Aside.*
In my swoll'n breast my close revenge I'll keep;
I'll watch his tender'st part, and there strike deep. [*Exit.*

AURENG-ZEBE: Your strange proceeding does my wonder move;
Yet seems not to express a Brother's love.
Say to what Cause my rescu'd life I owe.

MORAT: If what you ask would please, you should not know.
But since that knowledge, more than Death, will grieve,
Know, *Indamora* gain'd you this Reprieve.

AURENG-ZEBE: And whence had she the pow'r to work your change?

MORAT: The pow'r of Beauty is not new or strange.
Should she command me more, I could obey;
But her request was bounded with a day.
Take that; and, if you'll spare my farther crime,
Be kind, and grieve to death against your time.

Enter ARIMANT.

Remove this Pris'ner to some safer place:
He has, for *Indamora*'s sake, found grace:
And, from my Mother's rage must guarded be,
Till you receive a new Command from me.

ARIMANT: Thus Love, and Fortune, Persecute me still,
And make me Slave to every Rivals will. [*Aside.*

AURENG-ZEBE: How I disdain a Life, which I must buy
With your contempt, and her inconstancy!
For a few hours, my whole content I pay:
You shall not force on me another day.
[*Exit with* ARIMANT.

Enter MELESINDA.

MELESINDA: I have been seeking you this hour's long space,
And fear'd to find you in another place;

But, since you're here, my jealousie grows less:
You will be kind to my unworthiness.
What shall I say? I love to that degree,
Each glance another way is robb'd from me.
Absence, and Prisons, I could bear again;
But sink, and die, beneath your least disdain.

MORAT: Why do you give your mind this needless care,
And, for your self, and me, new pains prepare?
I ne'r approv'd this passion in excess:
If you would show your love, distrust me less.
I hate to be pursu'd from place to place:
Meet, at each turn, a stale domestic face.
Th' approach of jealousie Love cannot bear,
He's wild, and soon on wing, if watchful eyes come
near.

MELESINDA: From your lov'd presence, how can I depart?
My eyes pursue the object of my heart.

MORAT: You talk as if it were our Bridal night:
Fondness is still th' effect of new delight;
And Marriage but the pleasure of a day:
The Metall's base the Gilding worn away.

MELESINDA: I fear I'm guilty of some great offence,
And that has bred this cold indifference.

MORAT: The greatest in the world to flesh and bloud:
You fondly love much longer than you shou'd.

MELESINDA: If that be all which makes your discontent,
Of such a crime I never can repent.

MORAT: Would you force Love upon me, which I shun?
And bring course fare, when appetite is gone?

MELESINDA: Why did I not, in Prison, die before
My fatal freedom made me suffer more?
I had been pleas'd to think I dy'd for you,
And doubly pleas'd, because you then were true:
Then I had hope; but now, alas, have none.

MORAT: You say you love me; let that love be shown.
'Tis in your power to make my happiness.

MELESINDA: Speak quickly: to command me is to bless.

MORAT: To *Indamora* you my Suit must move:
You'll sure speak kindly of the man you love.

MELESINDA: Oh! rather let me perish by your hand,
Than break my heart, by this unkind command:
Think 'tis the onely one I could deny;
And that 'tis harder to refuse than die.

Try, if you please, my Rival's heart to win:
I'll bear the pain, but not promote the sin.
You own what e'r perfections man can boast,
And if she view you with my eyes, she's lost.

MORAT: Here I renounce all love, all Nuptial ties:
Henceforward live a stranger to my eyes:
When I appear, see you avoid the place,
And haunt me not with that unlucky face.

MELESINDA: Hard, as it is, I this command obey,
And haste, while I have life, to go away:
In pity stay some hours, till I am dead,
That blameless you may court my Rival's Bed.
My hated face I'll not presume to show;
Yet I may watch your steps where e'r you go.
Unseen, I'll gaze; and with my latest breath,
Bless, while I die, the Author of my death. [*Weeping.*

Enter EMPEROR

EMPEROR: When your Triumphant Fortune high appears,
What cause can draw these unbecoming tears?
Let cheerfulness on happy Fortune wait,
And give not thus the Counter-time to Fate.

MELESINDA: Fortune long frown'd, and has but lately smil'd:
I doubt a Foe so newly reconcil'd.
You saw but sorrow in its waning form,
A working Sea remaining from a Storm;
When the now weary Waves roul o'r the Deep,
And faintly murmur ere they fall asleep.

EMPEROR: Your inward griefs you smother in your mind;
But Fame's loud voice proclaims your Lord unkind.

MORAT: Let Fame be busie where she has to do:
Tell of fought Fields, and every pompous Show.
Those Tales are fit to fill the People's ears;
Monarchs, unquestion'd, move in higher Spheres.

MELESINDA: Believe not Rumor, but your self; and see
The kindness 'twixt my plighted Lord and me.
[*Kissing* MORAT.
This is our State; thus happily we live;
These are the quarrels which we take and give.
[*Aside to* MORAT] I had no other way to force a Kiss.
Forgive my last Farewel to you, and Bliss. [*Exit.*

EMPEROR: Your haughty carriage shows too much of scorn,
And love, like hers, deserves not that return.

MORAT: You'll please to leave me judge of what I do,
And not examine by the outward show.
Your usage of my Mother might be good:
I judg'd it not.
EMPEROR: ——Nor was it fit you shou'd.
MORAT: Then, in as equal Ballance weigh my deeds.
EMPEROR: My Right, and my Authority, exceeds.
Suppose (what I'll not grant) Injustice done;
Is judging me the duty of a Son?
MORAT: Not of a Son, but of an Emperor:
You cancell'd Duty when you gave me pow'r.
If your own Actions on your Will you ground,
Mine shall hereafter know no other bound.
What meant you when you call'd me to a Throne?
Was it to please me with a Name alone?
EMPEROR: 'Twas that I thought your gratitude would know
What to my partial kindness you did owe:
That what your Birth did to your Claim deny,
Your merit of Obedience might supply.
MORAT: To your own thoughts such hopes you might propose;
But I took Empire not on terms like those.
Of business you complain'd; now take your ease:
Enjoy whate're decrepid Age can please:
Eat, Sleep, and tell long Tales of what you were
In flow'r of Youth, if any one will hear.
EMPEROR: Pow'r like new Wine, does your weak Brain surprise,
And its mad fumes, in hot discourses, rise;
But time these giddy vapours will remove;
Mean while, I'll taste the sober joys of Love.
MORAT: You cannot Love, nor pleasures take, or give;
But life begin, when 'tis too late to live.
On a tir'd Courser you pursue delight,
Let slip your morning and set out at night.
If you have liv'd, take thankfully the past:
Make, as you can, the sweet remembrance last.
If you have not enjoy'd what Youth could give,
But life sunk through you like a leaky Sieve,
Accuse your self you liv'd not while you might;
But, in the Captive Queen resign your right.
I've now resolv'd to fill your useless place;
I'll take that Post to cover your disgrace,
And love her, for the honour of my Race.
EMPEROR: Thou dost but try how far I can forbear,

Nor art that Monster which thou wouldst appear:
But do not wantonly my passion move;
I pardon nothing that relates to Love.
My fury does, like jealous Forts, pursue
With death, ev'n Strangers who but come to view.

MORAT: I did not onely view, but will invade:
Could you shed venom from your reverend shade,
Like Trees, beneath whose arms 'tis death to sleep;
Did rouling Thunder your fenc'd Fortress keep,
Thence would I snatch my *Semele*, like *Jove*,
And midst the dreadful Rack enjoy my Love.

EMPEROR: Have I for this, ungrateful as thou art,
When Right, when Nature, struggl'd in my heart;
When Heav'n call'd on me for thy Brother's claim,
Broke all, and sulli'd my unspotted Fame?
Wert thou to Empire, by my baseness, brought,
And wouldst thou ravish what so dear I bought?
Dear! for my Conscience and its peace I gave:
Why was my Reason made my passion's slave?
I see Heav'ns Justice; thus the Pow'rs Divine,
Pay Crimes with Crimes and punish mine by thine.

MORAT: Crimes let them pay, and punish as they please:
What Pow'r makes mine, by Pow'r I mean to seize.
Since 'tis to that they their own greatness owe
Above, why should they question mine below? [*Exit.*

EMPEROR: Prudence, thou vainly in our Youth art sought,
And with Age purchas'd art too dearly bought:
We're past the use of Wit, for which we toil;
Late Fruit, and planted in too cold a Soil.
My Stock of Fame is lavish'd and decay'd;
No profit of the vast profusion made.
Too late my folly I repent; I know
My *Aureng-Zebe* would ne'r have us'd me so.
But, by his ruine I prepar'd my own;
And, like a naked Tree, my shelter gone,
To Winds and Winter-storms must stand expos'd alone.
[*Exit.*

AURENG-ZEBE, ARIMANT.

ARIMANT: Give me not thanks, which I will ne'r deserve;
But know, 'tis for a Noble Price I serve.
By *Indamora*'s will you're hither brought:
All my reward, in her command I sought.

The rest your Letter tells you.——See, like Light,
She comes; and I must vanish, like the Night. [*Exit.*

Enter INDAMORA.

INDAMORA: 'Tis now that I begin to live again:
Heav'ns, I forgive you all my fear and pain:
Since I behold my *Aureng-Zebe* appear,
I could not buy him at a Price too dear.
His name alone afforded me relief,
Repeated as a charm to cure my grief.
I that lov'd name did, as some God, invoke,
And printed kisses on it while I spoke.

AURENG-ZEBE: Short ease; but long, long pains from you I find:
Health, to my eyes; but poison, to my mind.
Why are you made so excellently fair?
So much above what other Beauties are,
That, ev'n in cursing, you new form my breath;
And make me bless those Eyes which give me death?

INDAMORA: What reason for your curses can you find?
My Eyes your conquest, not your death, design'd.
If they offend, 'tis that they are too kind.

AURENG-ZEBE: The ruines they have wrought, you will not see:
Too kind they are, indeed, but not to me.

INDAMORA: Think you base Interest Souls, like mine, can sway?
Or that, for Greatness, I can Love betray?
No, *Aureng-Zebe*, you merit all my heart,
And I'm too Noble but to give a part.
Your Father, and an Empire! am I known
No more? Or have so weak a judgment shown,
In chusing you, to change you for a Throne?

AURENG-ZEBE: How, with a Truth, you would a Falshood blind!
'Tis not my Father's love you have design'd;
Your choice is fix'd where Youth and Pow'r are joyn'd.

INDAMORA: Where Youth and Power are joyn'd! has he a name?

AURENG-ZEBE: You would be told; you glory in your shame:
There's Music in the Sound; and, to provoke
Your pleasure more, by me it must be spoke.
Then, then it ravishes, when your pleas'd ear
The sound does from a wretched Rival hear.
Morat's the name your heart leaps up to meet,
While *Aureng-Zebe* lies dying at your feet.

INDAMORA: Who told you this?

AURENG-ZEBE: ——Are you so lost to shame?
Morat, *Morat*, *Morat:* You love the name
So well, your ev'ry question ends in that;
You force me still to answer you, *Morat*.
Morat, who best could tell what you reveal'd;
Morat, too proud to keep his joy conceal'd.

INDAMORA: Howe'r unjust your jealousie appear,
It shows the loss, of what you love, you fear;
And does my pity, not my anger move:
I'll fond it, as the froward Child of Love.
To show the truth of my unalter'd breast,
Know, that your life was given at my request:
At least Repriev'd. When Heav'n deni'd you aid,
She brought it; she, whose falshood you upbraid.

AURENG-ZEBE: And 'tis by that you would your falshood hide;
Had you not ask'd, how happy had I dy'd!
Accurst Reprieve! not to prolong my breath,
It brought a ling'ring, and more painful death.
I have not liv'd since first I heard the news;
The gift the guilty giver does accuse.
You knew the price, and the request did move,
That you might pay the Ransome with your love.

INDAMORA: Your accusation must, I see, take place;
And I am guilty, infamous, and base!

AURENG-ZEBE: If you are false, those Epithets are small;
You're then the things, the abstract of 'em all.
And you are false: you promis'd him your love.
No other price a heart so hard could move.
Do not I know him? could his Brutal mind
Be wrought upon? could he be just, or kind?
Insultingly, he made your love his boast;
Gave me my life, and told me what it cost.
Speak; answer. I would fain yet think you true:
Lie; and I'll not believe my self, but you.
Tell me you love; I'll pardon the deceit,
And, to be fool'd, my self assist the cheat.

INDAMORA: No; 'tis too late: I have no more to say.
If you'll believe I have been false, you may.

AURENG-ZEBE: I would not; but your crimes too plain appear:
Nay, even that I should think you true, you fear.
Did I not tell you, I would be deceiv'd?

INDAMORA: I'm not concern'd to have my truth believ'd.
You would be cozin'd! would assist the cheat!

But I'm too plain to joyn in the deceit:
I'm pleas'd you think me false———
And, whatsoe'r my Letter did pretend,
I made this meeting for no other end.

AURENG-ZEBE: Kill me not quite, with this indifference:
When you are guiltless, boast not an offence.
I know you better than your self you know:
Your heart was true, but did some frailty show:
You promis'd him your Love, that I might live;
But promis'd what you never meant to give.
Speak, was't not so? confess; I can forgive.

INDAMORA: Forgive what dull excuses you prepare!
As if your thoughts of me were worth my care.

AURENG-ZEBE: Ah Traitress! Ah ingrate! Ah faithless mind!
Ah Sex, invented first to damn Mankind!
Nature took care to dress you up for sin:
Adorn'd, without; unfinish'd left, within.
Hence, by no judgment you your loves direct;
Talk much, ne'r think, and still the wrong affect.
So much self-love in your composures mix'd,
That love to others still remains unfix'd:
Greatness, and Noise, and Show, are your delight;
Yet wise men love you, in their own despight:
And, finding in their native Wit no ease,
Are forc'd to put your folly on to please.

INDAMORA: Now you shall know what cause you have to rage;
But to increase your fury, not asswage:
I found the way your Brother's heart to move,
Yet promis'd not the least return of Love.
His Pride, and Brutal fierceness I abhor;
But scorn your mean suspitions of me more.
I ow'd my Honour and my Fame this care:
Know what your folly lost you, and despair.
[*Turning from him.*

AURENG-ZEBE: Too cruelly your innocence you tell;
Show Heav'n, and damn me to the pit of Hell.
Now I believe you; 'tis not yet too late:
You may forgive, and put a stop to Fate;
Save me, just sinking, and no more to rise. [*She frowns.*
How can you look with such relentless eyes?
Or let your mind by penitence be mov'd,
Or I'm resolv'd to think you never lov'd.

You are not clear'd, unless you mercy speak:
I'll think you took th' occasion thus to break.

INDAMORA: Small jealousies, 'tis true, inflame desire;
Too great, not Fan, but quite blow out the Fire:
Yet I did love you, till such pains I bore,
That I dare trust my self and you no more.
Let me not love you; but here end my pain:
Distrust may make me wretched once again.
Now, with full Sails, into the Port I move,
And safely can unlade my breast of Love;
Quiet, and calm: why should I then go back,
To tempt the second hazard of a Wrack?

AURENG-ZEBE: Behold these dying eyes, see their submissive awe;
These tears, which fear of death could never draw:
Heard you that sigh? from my heav'd heart it past,
And said, If you forgive not, 'tis my last.
Love mounts, and rowls about my stormy mind,
Like Fire, that's born by a tempestuous Wind.
Oh, I could stifle you, with eager haste!
Devour your kisses with my hungry taste!
Rush on you! eat you! wander o'r each part,
Raving with pleasure, snatch you to my heart!
Then hold you off, and gaze! then, with new rage,
Invade you, till my conscious Limbs presage
Torrents of joy, which all their banks o'rflow!
So lost, so blest, as I but then could know!

INDAMORA: Be no more jealous. [*Giving him her hand.*

AURENG-ZEBE: ——Give me cause no more:
The danger's greater after, than before,
If I relapse; to cure my jealousie
Let me (for that's the easiest parting) die.

INDAMORA: My life!

AURENG-ZEBE:——My Soul!

INDAMORA:——————My all that Heav'n can give!
Death's life with you; without you, death to live.

To them ARIMANT *hastily.*

ARIMANT: Oh, we are lost, beyond all humane aid!
The Citadel is to *Morat* betraid.
The Traitor, and the Treason, known too late;
The false *Abas* deliver'd up the Gate.
Ev'n, while I speak, we're compass'd round with Fate.

The Valiant cannot fight, or Coward flie;
But both in undistinguish'd Crouds must die.

AURENG-ZEBE: Then my Prophetic fears are come to pass:
Morat was always bloudy; now, he's base:
And has so far in Usurpation gone,
He will by Paricide secure the Throne.

To them the EMPEROR.

EMPEROR: Am I forsaken, and betray'd, by all?
Not one brave man dare, with a Monarch, fall?
Then, welcome death, to cover my disgrace;
I would not live to Reign o'r such a Race.
My *Aureng-Zebe!* [*Seeing* AURENG-ZEBE.
But thou no more art mine; my cruelty
Has quite destroy'd the right I had in thee.
I have been base,
Base ev'n to him from whom I did receive
All that a Son could to a Parent give:
Behold me punish'd in the self-same kind,
Th' ungrateful does a more ungrateful find.

AURENG-ZEBE: Accuse your self no more; you could not be
Ungrateful: could commit no crime to me:
I onely mourn my yet uncancell'd score:
You put me past the pow'r of paying more:
That, that's my grief, that I can onely grieve,
And bring but pity, where I would relieve;
For had I yet ten thousand lives to pay,
The mighty sum should go no other way.

EMPEROR: Can you forgive me? 'tis not fit you shou'd.
Why will you be so excellently good?
'Twill stick too black a brand upon my name:
The Sword is needless; I shall die with shame.
What had my age to do with Love's delight,
Shut out from all enjoyments but the sight?

ARIMANT: Sir, you forget the danger's imminent:
This minute is not for excuses lent.

EMPEROR: Disturb me not——————
How can my latest hour be better spent?
To reconcile my self to him is more,
Than to regain all I possess'd before.
Empire, and Life are now not worth a pray'r:
His love, alone, deserves my dying care.

AURENG-ZEBE: Fighting for you, my death will glorious be.

INDAMORA: Seek to preserve your self, and live for me.
ARIMANT: Lose then no farther time.
Heav'n has inspir'd me with a sudden thought,
Whence your unhop'd for safety may be wrought,
Though with the hazard of my bloud 'tis bought.
But, since my life can ne'r be fortunate,
'Tis so much sorrow well redeem'd from Fate.
You, Madam, must retire;
Your Beauty is its own security,
And leave the conduct of the rest to me.
Glory will crown my life, if I succeed;
If not, she may afford to love me dead. [*Aside.*
AURENG-ZEBE: My Father's kind; and, Madam, you forgive:
Were Heav'n so pleas'd, I now could wish to live.
And, I shall live.
With Glory, and with Love, at once I burn:
I feel th' inspiring heat, and absent God return. [*Exeunt.*

ACT V

INDAMORA *alone.*

THe night seems doubled with the fear she brings,
And, o'r the Cittadel, new spreads her wings.
The Morning, as mistaken, turns about,
And all her early fires again go out.
Shouts, cries, and groans, first pierce my ears, and then
A flash of Lightning draws the guilty Scene,
And shows me Arms, and Wounds, and Dying men.
Ah, should my *Aureng-Zebe* be fighting there,
And envious Winds distinguish'd to my ear,
His dying groans, and his last accents bear!

To her MORAT, *attended.*

MORAT: The bloudy bus'ness of the Night is done,
And, in the Cittadel, an Empire wonn.
Our Swords so wholly did the Fates employ,
That they, at length, grew weary to destroy:
Refus'd the work we brought; and, out of breath,
Made Sorrow and Despair attend for Death.

But what of all my Conquest can I boast?
My haughty pride, before your eyes, is lost:
And Victory but gains me to present
That Homage, which our Eastern World has sent.

INDAMORA: Your Victory, alas, begets my fears:
Can you not then triumph without my tears?
Resolve me; (for you know my Destiny
In *Aureng-Zebe*'s) say, do I live, or die?

MORAT: Urg'd by my Love, by hope of Empire fir'd;
'Tis true, I have perform'd what both requir'd:
What Fate decreed; for when great Souls are giv'n,
They bear the marks of Sov'reignty from Heav'n.
My Elder Brothers my fore-runners came;
Rough-draughts of Nature, ill design'd, and lame:
Blown off, like Blossoms, never made to bear;
Till I came, finish'd; her last-labour'd care.

INDAMORA: This Prologue leads to your succeeding sin:
Bloud ended what Ambition did begin.

MORAT: 'Twas rumor'd, but by whom I cannot tell,
My Father 'scap'd from out the Cittadel:
My Brother too may live.

INDAMORA: ——————He may.

MORAT: ————————He must:
I kill'd him not: and a less Fate's unjust.
Heav'n owes it me, that I may fill his room;
A Phœnix-Lover, rising from his Tomb.
In whom you'll lose your sorrows for the dead;
More warm, more fierce, and fitter for your Bed.

INDAMORA: Should I from *Aureng-Zebe* my heart divide,
To love a Monster, and a Paricide?
These names your swelling Titles cannot hide.
Severe Decrees may keep our Tongues in awe;
But to our thoughts, what Edict can give Law?
Ev'n you your self, to your own breast, shall tell
Your crimes; and your own Conscience be your Hell.

MORAT: What bus'ness has my Conscience with a Crown?
She sinks in Pleasures, and in Bowls will drown.
If mirth should fail, I'll busie her with cares;
Silence her clamorous voice with louder Wars:
Trumpets and Drums shall fright her from the Throne,
As sounding Cymbals aid the lab'ring Moon.

INDAMORA: Repell'd by these, more eager she will grow;
Spring back more strongly than a *Scythian* Bowe:

Amidst your Train, this unseen Judge will wait;
Examine how you came by all your State;
Upbraid your impious Pomp; and, in your ear,
Will hallow, *Rebel, Tyrant, Murderer*.
Your ill-got Pow'r wan looks and care shall bring:
Known but by discontent to be a King.
Of crouds afraid, yet anxious when alone;
You'l sit and brood your sorrows on a Throne.

MORAT: Birthright's a vulgar road to Kingly sway;
'Tis ev'ry dull-got Elder Brother's way.
Dropt from above, he lights into a Throne;
Grows of a piece with that he sits upon,
Heav'ns choice, a low, inglorious, rightful Drone.
But who by force a Scepter does obtain,
Shows he can govern that which he could gain.
Right comes of course, what e'r he was before;
Murder and Usurpation are no more.

INDAMORA: By your own Laws you such Dominion make,
As ev'ry stronger Pow'r has right to take:
And Paricide will so deform your name,
That dispossessing you will give a claim.
Who next Usurps, will a just Prince appear;
So much your ruine will his Reign endear.

MORAT: I without guilt, would mount the Royal Seat;
But yet 'tis necessary to be great.

INDAMORA: All Greatness is in Virtue understood:
'Tis onely necessary to be good.
Tell me, what is't at which great Spirits aim,
What most your self desire?

MORAT: ————————Renown, and Fame,
And Pow'r, as uncontrol'd as is my will.

INDAMORA: How you confound desires of good and ill!
For true renown is still with Virtue joyn'd;
But lust of Pow'r lets loose th' unbridl'd mind.
Yours is a Soul irregularly great,
Which wanting temper, yet abounds with heat:
So strong, yet so unequal pulses beat.
A Sun which does, through vapours dimnly shine;
What pity 'tis you are not all Divine!
New molded, thorow lighten'd, and a breast
So pure, to bear the last severest test;
Fit to command an Empire you should gain
By Virtue, and without a blush to Reign.

MORAT: You show me somewhat I ne'r learnt before;
But 'tis the distant prospect of a Shore,
Doubtful in mists; which, like inchanted ground,
Flies from my sight, before 'tis fully found.
INDAMORA: Dare to be great, without a guilty Crown;
View it, and lay the bright temptation down:
'Tis base to seize on all, because you may;
That's Empire, that which I can give away:
There's joy when to wild Will you Laws prescribe,
When you bid Fortune carry back her Bribe:
A joy, which none but greatest minds can taste;
A Fame, which will to endless Ages last.
MORAT: Renown, and Fame, in vain, I courted long;
And still pursu'd 'em, though directed wrong.
In hazard, and in toils, I heard they lay;
Sail'd farther than the Coast, but miss'd my way:
Now you have giv'n me Virtue for my guide;
And, with true Honour, ballasted my Pride.
Unjust Dominion I no more pursue;
I quit all other claims but those to you.
INDAMORA: Oh be not just to halves! pay all you owe:
Think there's a debt to *Melesinda* too.
To leave no blemish on your after life;
Reward the virtue of a Suff'ring Wife.
MORAT: To love once past, I cannot backward move;
Call yesterday again, and I may love.
'Twas not for nothing I the Crown resign'd;
I still must own a Mercenary mind:
I, in this venture, double gains pursue,
And laid out all my Stock to purchase you.

To them ASAPH CHAN.

Now, what success? does *Aureng-Zebe* yet live?
ASAPH CHAWN: Fortune has giv'n you all that she can give
Your Brother———
MORAT: ———Hold; thou show'st an impious joy,
And think'st I still take pleasure to destroy:
Know, I am chang'd, and would not have him slain.
ASAPH CHAWN: 'Tis past; and you desire his life in vain.
He prodigal of Soul, rush'd on the stroke
Of lifted Weapons, and did wounds provoke:
In scorn of Night, he would not be conceal'd;
His Souldiers, where he fought, his name reveal'd:

In thickest crouds, still *Aureng-Zebe* did sound:
The vaulted Roofs did *Aureng-Zebe* rebound,
Till late, and in his fall, the name was drown'd.

INDAMORA: Wither that hand which brought him to his fate,
And blasted be the tongue which did relate.

ASAPH CHAWN: His Body——————————

MORAT:——————————Cease to inhanse her misery:
Pity the Queen, and show respect to me.
'Tis ev'ry Painters Art to hide from sight,
And cast in shades, what seen would not delight.
Your grief, in me such sympathy has bred, [*To her.*
I mourn; and wish I could recall the dead.
Love softens me; and blows up fires, which pass
Through my tough heart, and melt the stubborn Mass.

INDAMORA: Break, heart; or choak, with sobs, my hated breath;
Do thy own work: admit no forreign death.
Alas! why do I make this useless moan?
I'm dead already, for my Soul is gone.

To them, MIR BABA.

MIR BABA: What tongue the terror of this night can tell,
Within, without, and round the Citadel!
A new-form'd Faction does your pow'r oppose;
The Fight's confus'd, and all who meet are foes:
A second clamour, from the Town, we hear;
And the far noise so loud, it drowns the near.
Abas, who seem'd our Friend, is either fled;
Or, what we fear, our Enemies does head:
Your frighted Soldiers scarce their ground maintain.

MORAT: I thank their fury; we shall fight again:
They rouse my rage; I'm eager to subdue:
'Tis fatal to with-hold my eyes from you.
[*Exit with the two* OMRAHS.

Enter MELESINDA.

MELESINDA: Can misery no place of safety know?
The noise pursues me wheresoe'r I go,
As Fate sought onely me, and where I fled,
Aim'd all its Darts at my devoted head.
And let it; I am now past care of life;
The last of Women; an abandon'd Wife.

INDAMORA: Whether Design or Chance has brought you here,
I stand oblig'd to Fortune, or to Fear:
Weak Women should, in danger, herd like Deer.

But say, from whence this new combustion springs?
Are there yet more *Morats?* more fighting Kings?

MELESINDA: Him from his Mother's love your eyes divide,
And now her Arms the cruel strife decide.

INDAMORA: What strange misfortunes my vext life attend?
Death will be kind, and all my sorrows end.
If *Nourmahal* prevail, I know my fate.

MELESINDA: I pity, as my own, your hard estate;
But what can my weak charity afford?
I have no longer int'rest in my Lord:
Nor in his Mother, He: she owns her hate
Aloud, and would her self Usurp the State.

INDAMORA: I'm stupifi'd with sorrow, past relief
Of tears: parch'd up, and wither'd with my grief.

MELESINDA: Dry mourning will decays more deadly bring,
As a North Wind burns a too forward Spring.
Give sorrow vent, and let the sluces go.

INDAMORA: My tears are all congeal'd, and will not flow.

MELESINDA: Have comfort; yield not to the blows of Fate.

INDAMORA: Comfort, like Cordials after death, comes late.
Name not so vain a word; my hopes are fled:
Think your *Morat* were kind, and think him dead.

MELESINDA: I can no more———
Can no more arguments, for comfort, find:
Your boding words have quite o'r-whelmed my mind.

[*Clattering of weapons within.*

INDAMORA: The noise increases, as the Billows rore,
When rowling from afar they threat the Shore.
She comes; and feeble Nature now I find
Shrinks back in danger, and forsakes my mind.
I wish to die, yet dare not death endure;
Detest the Med'cine, yet desire the Cure.
I would have death; but mild, and at command:
I dare not trust him in another's hand.
In *Nourmahal*'s, he would not mine appear;
But arm'd with terror, and disguis'd with fear.

MELESINDA: Beyond this place you can have no retreat:
Stay here, and I the danger will repeat.
I fear not death, because my life I hate:
And envious death will shun th' unfortunate.

INDAMORA: You must not venture.

MELESINDA: ———————Let me: I may do
My self a kindness, in obliging you.

In your lov'd name, I'll seek my angry Lord;
And beg your safety from his conqu'ring Sword:
So his protection all your fears will ease,
And I shall see him once, and not displease. [*Exit.*

INDAMORA: O wretched Queen! what pow'r thy life can save?
A stranger, and unfriended, and a slave!

Enter NOURMAHAL, ZAYDA, *and* ABAS, *with Souldiers.*

Alas, she's here!
[INDAMORA *withdraws to the inner part of the Scene.*

NOURMAHAL: Heartless they fought, and quitted soon their ground,
While ours with easie victory were crown'd.
To you, *Abas*, my Life and Empire too,
And, what's yet dearer, my Revenge, I owe.

ABAS: The vain *Morat*, by his own rashness wrought,
Too soon discover'd his ambitious thought;
Believ'd me his, because I spoke him fair,
And pitch'd his head into the ready snare:
Hence 'twas I did his Troops at first admit;
But such, whose numbers could no fears beget;
By them th' Emperor's Party first I slew,
Then turn'd my Arms the Victors to subdue.

NOURMAHAL: Now let the head-strong Boy my will controul:
Virtue's no slave of Man; no Sex confines the Soul:
I, for my self, th' Imperial Seat will gain,
And he shall wait my leisure for his Reign.
But *Aureng-Zebe* is no where to be found.
And now perhaps in Death's cold arms he lies:
I fought, and conquer'd, yet have lost the prize.

ZAYDA: The chance of War determin'd well the strife,
That rack'd you, 'twixt the Lover and the Wife.
He's dead, whose love had sulli'd all your Reign,
And made you Empress of the World in vain.

NOURMAHAL: No; I my pow'r and pleasure would divide:
The Drudge had quench'd my flames, and then had di'd.
I rage, to think without that Bliss I live;
That I could wish what Fortune would not give:
But, what Love cannot, Vengeance must supply;
She, who bereav'd me of his heart, shall die.

ZAYDA: I'll search: far distant hence she cannot be. [*Goes in.*

NOURMAHAL: This wondrous Master-piece I fain would see;

This fatal *Helen*, who can Wars inspire,
Make Kings her Slaves, and set the World on fire.
My Husband lock'd his Jewel from my view;
Or durst not set the false one by the true.

Re-enter ZAYDA, *leading* INDAMORA.

ZAYDA: Your frighted Captive, ere she dies, receive;
Her Soul's just going else, without your leave.

NOURMAHAL: A fairer Creature did my eyes ne'r see!
Sure she was form'd by Heav'n in spite to me!
Some Angel copi'd, while I slept, each grace,
And molded ev'ry feature from my face.
Such Majesty does from her forehead rise,
Her cheeks such blushes cast, such rays her eyes,
Nor I, nor Envy, can a blemish find;
The Palace is, without, too well design'd:
Conduct me in, for I will view thy mind. [*To her.*
Speak, if thou hast a Soul, that I may see,
If Heav'n can make throughout another Me.

INDAMORA: My tears and miseries must plead my cause; [*Kneeling.*
My words, the terror of your presence awes:
Mortals, in sight of Angels, mute become;
The Nobler Nature strikes th' Inferiour dumb.

NOURMAHAL: The Palm is, by the Foes confession, mine;
But I disdain what basely you resign.
Heav'n did, by me, the outward model build:
Its inward work, the Soul, with rubbish fill'd.
Yet, Oh! th' imperfect Piece moves more delight;
'Tis gilded o'r with Youth, to catch the sight.
The Gods have poorly robb'd my Virgin bloom,
And what I am, by what I was, o'rcome.
Traitress, restore my Beauty and my Charms,
Nor steal my Conquest with my proper Arms.

INDAMORA: What have I done, thus to inflame your hate?
I am not guilty, but unfortunate.

NOURMAHAL: Not guilty, when thy looks my pow'r betray,
Seduce Mankind, my Subject, from my Sway,
Take all my Hearts, and all my Eyes away?
My Husband first; but that I could forgive:
He onely mov'd, and talk'd, but did not live.
My *Aureng-Zebe*, for I dare own the name,
The glorious sin, and the more glorious flame;

Him, from my beauty, have thy eyes misled,
And starv'd the joys of my expected Bed.

INDAMORA: His love, so sought, he's happy that he's dead.
O had I courage but to meet my Fate;
That short dark passage to a future state;
That melancholly Riddle of a breath.

NOURMAHAL: That something, or that nothing, after death:
[*Giving a Dagger*.
Take this, and teach thy self.

INDAMORA: Alas!

NOURMAHAL: ————Why dost thou shake?
Dishonour not the vengeance I design'd:
A Queen, and own a base Plebeian mind!
Let it drink deep in thy most vital part:
Strike home, and do me reason in thy heart.

INDAMORA: I dare not.

NOURMAHAL:————Do't, while I stand by and see,
At my full gust, without the drudgery.
I love a Foe, who dares my stroke prevent,
Who gives me the full Scene of my content,
Shows me the flying Soul's convulsive strife,
And all the anguish of departing life:
Disdain my mercy, and my rage defie;
Curse me with thy last breath; and make me see
A Spirit worthy to have Rival'd me.

INDAMORA: Oh, I desire to die; but dare not yet:
Give me some respite, I'll discharge the debt.
Without my *Aureng-Zebe* I would not live.

NOURMAHAL: Thine, Traitress! thine! that word has wing'd thy fate,
And put me past the tedious forms of hate.
I'll kill thee with such eagerness and haste,
As Fiends, let loose, would lay all Nature waste.

[INDAMORA *runs back: as* NOURMAHAL *is running to her. Clashing of Swords is heard within.*

SOLDIER: Yield, y'are o'rpow'r'd: resistance is in vain. [*Within.*

MORAT: Then death's my choice: submission I disdain. [*Within.*

NOURMAHAL: Retire, you Slaves! Ah whither does he run
[*At the door.*
On pointed Swords? Disarm, but save my Son.

ACT FIVE

Enter MORAT *staggering, and upheld by Souldiers.*

MORAT: She lives! and I shall see her once again!
I have not thrown away my life in vain.
[*Catches hold of* INDAMORA'S *Gown, and falls by her: she sits.*
I can no more; yet, ev'n in death, I find
My fainting body byass'd by my mind:
I fall toward you; still my contending Soul
Points to your breast, and trembles to its Pole.

To them MELESINDA, *hastily, casting her self on the other side of* MORAT.

MELESINDA: Ah wo, wo, wo! the worst of woes I find!
Live still; Oh live; live ev'n to be unkind.
With half-shut eyes he seeks the doubtful day;
But, Ah! he bends his sight another way.
He faints! and in that sigh his Soul is gone;
Yet Heaven's unmov'd, yet Heav'n looks careless on.

NOURMAHAL: Where are those Pow'rs which Monarchs should defend?
Or do they vain Authority pretend,
O'r humane Fates, and their weak Empire show,
Which cannot guard their Images below?
If, as their Image, he was not Divine,
They ought to have respected him as mine.
I'll waken them with my revenge; and she
Their *Indamora* shall my Victim be,
And Helpless Heav'n shall mourn in vain, like me.
[*As she is going to stab* INDAMORA, MORAT *raises himself, and holds her hand.*

MORAT: Ah, what are we,
Who dare maintain with Heav'n this wretched strife,
Puft with the pride of Heav'ns own gift, frail life?
That blast which my ambitious Spirit swell'd,
See by how weak a Tenure it was held!
I onely stay to save the Innocent:
Oh envy not my Soul its last content.

INDAMORA: No, let me die; I'm doubly summon'd now;
First, by my *Aureng-Zebe*; and, since, by you.
My Soul grows hardy, and can death endure:
Your Convoy makes the dang'rous way secure.

MELESINDA: Let me, at least, a Funeral Marriage crave;
Nor grudge my cold embraces in the Grave.

I have too just a Title in the strife:
By me, unhappy me, he lost his life:
I call'd him hither; 'twas my fatal breath;
And I the Screech-Owl that proclaim'd his death.
[*Shout within.*

ABAS: What new Alarms are these? I'll haste and see. [*Exit.*

NOURMAHAL: Look up, and live: an Empire shall be thine.

MORAT: That I contemn'd, ev'n when I thought it mine.
Oh, I must yield to my hard Destinies, [*To* INDAMORA.
And must for ever cease to see your eyes.

MELESINDA: Ah turn your sight to me, my dearest Lord!
Can you not one, one parting look afford?
Ev'n so unkind in death? but 'tis in vain;
I lose my breath, and to the Winds complain:
Yet 'tis as much in vain your cruel scorn;
Still I can love, without this last return.
Nor Fate, nor You, can my vow'd faith controul;
Dying, I'll follow your disdainful Soul:
A Ghost, I'll haunt your Ghost; and, where you go,
With mournful murmurs fill the Plains below.

MORAT: Be happy, *Melesinda*, cease to grieve,
And, for a more deserving Husband, live:
Can you forgive me?

MELESINDA: ————Can I! Oh my heart!
Have I heard one kind word before I part?
I can, I can forgive: is that a task
To love, like mine? Are you so good to ask?
One kiss—Oh 'tis too great a blessing this; [*Kisses him.*
I would not live to violate the bliss.

Re-enter ABAS.

ABAS: Some envious Devil has ruin'd us yet more:
The Fort's revolted to the Emperor;
The Gates are open'd, the Portcullis drawn;
And deluges of Armies, from the Town,
Come pow'ring in: I heard the mighty flaw,
When first it broke; the crowding Ensigns saw,
Which choak'd the passage; and, (what least I fear'd,)
The waving Arms of *Aureng-Zebe* appear'd,
Display'd with your *Morat*'s:
In either's Flag the golden Serpents bear,
Erected Crests alike, like Volumes rear,
And mingle friendly hissings in the Air.

Their Troops are joyn'd, and our destruction nigh.

NOURMAHAL: 'Tis vain to fight, and I disdain to flie.
I'll mock the Triumphs which our Foes intend;
And, spite of Fortune, make a glorious end.
In pois'nous draughts my liberty I'll find:
And from the nauseous World set free my mind. [*Exit.*

At the other end of the Stage, Enter AURENG-ZEBE, DIANET, *and Attendants.* AURENG-ZEBE *turns back, and speaks, entring.*

AURENG-ZEBE: The lives of all, who cease from combat, spare;
My Brother's be your most peculiar care:
Our impious use no longer shall obtain;
Brothers no more, by Brothers, shall be slain.
[*Seeing* INDAMORA *and* MORAT.
Ha! do I dream? is this my hop'd success?
I grow a Statue, stiff, and motionless.
Look, *Dianet*; for I dare not trust these eyes;
They dance in mists, and dazle with surprise.

DIANET: Sir, 'tis *Morat*; dying he seems, or dead;
And *Indamora*'s hand——

AURENG-ZEBE:————Supports his head. [*Sighing.*
Thou shalt not break yet heart, nor shall she know
My inward torments, by my outward show;
To let her see my weakness were too base;
Dissembled Quiet sit upon my face:
My sorrow to my eyes no passage find,
But let it inward sink, and drown my mind.
Falshood shall want its Triumph: I begin
To stagger; but I'll prop my self within.
The specious Tow'r no ruine shall disclose,
Till down, at once, the mighty Fabrick goes.

MORAT: In sign that I die yours, reward my love,
[*To* INDAMORA.
And seal my Pasport to the Bless'd above.
[*Kissing her hand.*

INDAMORA: Oh stay; or take me with you when you go:
There's nothing now worth living for below.

MORAT: I leave you not; for my expanded mind
Grows up to Heav'n, while it to you is joyn'd:
Not quitting, but enlarg'd! A blazing Fire,
Fed from the Brand. [*Dies.*

MELESINDA: Ah me! he's gone! I die! [*Swoons.*

INDAMORA: ————————Oh, dismal day!

Fate, thou hast ravish'd my last hope away.
O Heav'n! my *Aureng-Zebe*————
————————What strange surprise!
[*She turns, and sees* AURENG-ZEBE *standing by her, and starts.*
Or does my willing mind delude my eyes,
And shows the Figure always present there?
Or liv'st thou? am I bless'd, and see thee here?

AURENG-ZEBE: My Brother's body see convey'd with care,
[*Turning from her, to his Attendants.*
Where we may Royal Sepulture prepare.
With speed to *Melesinda* bring relief:
Recal her spirits, and moderate her grief.——
[*Half turning to* INDAMORA.
I go, to take for ever from your view
Both the lov'd Object, and the hated too.
[*Going away after the Bodies, which are carried off.*

INDAMORA: Hear me; yet think not that I beg your stay:
[*Laying hold of him.*
I will be heard, and after take your way.
Go; but your late repentance shall be vain:
[*He struggles still: She lets him go.*
I'll never, never see your face again. [*Turning away.*

AURENG-ZEBE: Madam, I know what ever you can say:
You might be pleas'd not to command my stay.
All things are yet disorder'd in the Fort;
I must crave leave your audience may be short.

INDAMORA: You need not fear I shall detain you long;
Yet you may tell me your pretended wrong.

AURENG-ZEBE: Is that the bus'ness? then my stay is vain.

INDAMORA: How are you injur'd?

AURENG-ZEBE:————When did I complain?

INDAMORA: Leave off your forc'd respect————
And show your rage in its most furious form:
I'm arm'd with innocence to brave the Storm.
You heard, perhaps, your Brother's last desire;
And after saw him in my arms expire:
Saw me, with tears, so great a loss bemoan:
Heard me complaining my last hopes were gone.

AURENG-ZEBE: Oh stay, and take me with you when you go,
There's nothing now worth living for below.
Unhappy Sex! whose Beauty is your snare;
Expos'd to trials; made too frail to bear.

I grow a fool, and show my rage again:
'Tis Nature's fault; and why should I complain?
INDAMORA: Will you yet hear me?
AURENG-ZEBE: ——————Yes, till you relate
What pow'rful Motives did your change create.
You thought me dead, and prudently did weigh
Tears were but vain, and brought but Youths decay.
Then, in *Morat*, your hopes a Crown design'd;
And all the Woman work'd within your mind.
I rave again, and to my rage return,
To be again subjected to your scorn.
INDAMORA: I wait till this long storm be over-blown.
AURENG-ZEBE: I'm conscious of my folly: I have done.
I cannot rail; but silently I'll grieve.
How did I trust! and how did you deceive!
Oh, *Arimant*, would I had di'd for thee!
I dearly buy thy generosity.
INDAMORA: Alas, is he then dead?
AURENG-ZEBE: ——————Unknown to me,
He took my Arms; and while I forc'd my way,
Through Troops of Foes, which did our passage stay,
My Buckler o'r my aged Father cast,
Still fighting, still defending as I past,
The noble *Arimant* usurp'd my name;
Fought, and took from me, while he gave me, fame.
To *Aureng-Zebe*, he made his Souldiers cry,
And seeing not, where he heard danger nigh,
Shot, like a Star, through the benighted Sky.
A short, but mighty aid: at length he fell.
My own adventures 'twere lost time to tell;
Or how my Army, entring in the night,
Surpris'd our Foes: the dark disorder'd fight:
How my appearance, and my Father shown,
Made peace; and all the rightful Monarch own.
I've summ'd it briefly, since it did relate
Th' unwelcome safety of the man you hate.
INDAMORA: As briefly will I clear my innocence:
Your alter'd Brother di'd in my defence.
Those tears you saw, that tenderness I show'd,
Were just effects of grief and gratitude.
He di'd my Convert.
AURENG-ZEBE:————But your Lover too:
I heard his words, and did your actions view;

You seem'd to mourn another Lover dead:
My sighs you gave him, and my tears you shed.
But worst of all,
Your gratitude for his defence was shown:
It prov'd you valu'd life when I was gone.

INDAMORA: Not that I valu'd life but fear'd to die:
Think that my weakness, not inconstancy.

AURENG-ZEBE: Fear show'd you doubted of your own intent:
And she who doubts becomes less innocent.
Tell me not you could fear;
Fear's a large promiser, who subject live
To that base passion, know not what they give.
No circumstance of grief you did deny;
And what could she give more who durst not die?

INDAMORA: My love, my faith.

AURENG-ZEBE: ————Both so adult'rate grown,
When mix'd with fear, they never could be known.
I wish no ill might her I love befall;
But she ne'r lov'd who durst not venture all.
Her life and fame should my concernment be;
But she should onely be afraid for me.

INDAMORA: My heart was yours; but, Oh! you left it here,
Abandon'd to those Tyrants, Hope and Fear:
If they forc'd from me one kind look or word,
Could you not that, not that small part afford?

AURENG-ZEBE: If you had lov'd, you nothing yours could call:
Giving the least of mine, you gave him all.
True love's a Miser; so tenacious grown,
He weighs to the least grain of what's his own.
More delicate than Honour's nicest sense:
Neither to give nor take the least offence.
With, or without you, I can have no rest:
What shall I do? y'are lodg'd within my breast:
Your Image never will be thence displac'd;
But there it lies, stabb'd, mangled, and defac'd.

INDAMORA: Yet, to restore the quiet of your heart,
There's one way left.

AURENG-ZEBE: ————Oh name it.

INDAMORA: ————————'Tis to part.
Since perfect bliss with me you cannot prove,
I scorn to bless by halves the man I love.

AURENG-ZEBE: Now you distract me more: shall then the day,
Which views my Triumph, see our loves decay?

Must I new bars to my own joy create?
Refuse, my self, what I had forc'd from Fate?
What though I am not lov'd?
Reason's nice taste does our delights destroy:
Brutes are more bless'd, who grossly feed on joy.

INDAMORA: Such endless jealousies your love pursue,
I can no more be fully bless'd than you.
I therefore go, to free us both from pain:
I pris'd your Person, but your Crown disdain.
Nay, ev'n my own——
I give it you; for since I cannot call
Your heart my Subject, I'll not Reign at all. [*Exit.*

AURENG-ZEBE: Go: though thou leav'st me tortur'd on the Rack,
'Twixt Shame and Pride, I cannot call thee back.
She's guiltless, and I should submit; but Oh!
When she exacts it, can I stoop so low?
Yes; for she's guiltless;—but she's haughty too.
Great Souls long struggle ere they own a crime:
She's gone; and leaves me no repenting time.
I'll call her now; sure, if she loves, she'll stay;
Linger at least, or not go far away.
[*Looks to the door, and returns.*
For ever lost, and I repent too late.
My foolish pride, would set my whole Estate,
Till, at one throw, I lost all back to Fate.

To him the Emperor, drawing in INDAMORA: *Attendants.*

EMPEROR: It must not be, that he, by whom we live,
Should no advantage of his gift receive.
Should he be wholly wretched? he alone,
In this bless'd day, a day so much his own?
[*To* INDAMORA.
I have not quitted yet a Victor's right:
I'll make you happy in your own despight.
I love you still; and if I struggle hard
To give, it shows the worth of the reward.

INDAMORA: Suppose he has o'rcome; must I find place
Among his conquer'd Foes, and sue for grace?
Be pardon'd, and confess I lov'd not well?
What though none live my innocence to tell?
I know it: Truth may own a gen'rous pride:
I clear my self, and care for none beside.

AURENG-ZEBE: Oh, *Indamora*, you would break my heart!
Could you resolve, on any terms, to part?
I thought your love eternal: was it ti'd
So loosely, that a quarrel could divide?
I grant that my suspitions were unjust;
But would you leave me for a small distrust?
Forgive those foolish words—— [*Kneeling to her.*
They were the froth my raging folly mov'd,
When it boil'd up: I knew not then I lov'd;
Yet then lov'd most.

INDAMORA *to* AURENG-ZEBE: You would but half be blest!
[*Giving her hand, smiling.*

AURENG-ZEBE:————Oh do but try
My eager love: I'll give my self the lie.
The very hope is a full happiness;
Yet scantly measures what I shall possess.
Fancy it self, ev'n in enjoyment, is
But a dumb Judge, and cannot tell its bliss.

EMPEROR: Her eyes a secret yielding do confess,
And promise to partake your happiness.
May all the joys I did my self pursue,
Be rais'd by her, and multipli'd on you!

A Procession of Priests, Slaves following, and last MELESINDA *in white.*

INDAMORA: Alas! what means this Pomp?

AURENG-ZEBE: 'Tis the Procession of a Funeral Vow,
Which cruel Laws to *Indian* Wives allow,
When fatally their Virtue they approve;
Chearful in flames, and Martyrs of their Love.

INDAMORA: Oh my foreboding heart! th' event I fear;
And see! sad *Melesinda* does appear.

MELESINDA: You wrong my love; what grief do I betray?
This is the Triumph of my Nuptial day.
My better Nuptials; which, in spight of Fate,
For ever joyn me to my dear *Morat*.
Now I am pleas'd; my jealousies are o'r:
He's mine; and I can lose him now no more.

EMPEROR: Let no false show of Fame your reason blind.

INDAMORA: You have no right to die; he was not kind.

MELESINDA: Had he been kind, I could no love have shown:
Each vulgar Virtue would as much have done.
My love was such, it needed no return;

But could, though he suppli'd no fuel, burn.
Rich in it self, like Elemental fire,
Whose pureness does no Aliment require.
In vain you would bereave me of my Lord;
For I will die: die is too base a word;
I'll seek his breast, and kindling by his side,
Adorn'd with flames, I'll mount a glorious Bride. [*Exit.*

Enter NOURMAHAL *distracted, with* ZAYDA.

ZAYDA: She's lost, she's lost! but why do I complain
For her, who generously did life disdain!
Poison'd, she raves——
Th' invenom'd Body does the Soul attack;
Th' invenom'd Soul works its own poison back.

NOURMAHAL: I burn, I more than burn; I am all fire:
See how my mouth and nostrils flame expire.
I'll not come near my self——
Now I'm a burning Lake, it rowls and flows;
I'll rush, and pour it all upon my Foes.
Pull, pull that reverend piece of Timber near:
Throw't on—'tis dry—'twill burn—
Ha, ha! how my old Husband crackles there!
Keep him down, keep him down, turn him about:
I know him; he'll but whiz, and strait go out.
Fan me, you Winds: what, not one breath of Air?
I burn 'em all, and yet have flames to spare.
Quench me: pour on whole Rivers. 'Tis in vain:
Morat stands there to drive 'em back again:
With those huge Bellows in his hands, he blows
New fire into my head: my Brain-pan glows.
See, see! there's *Aureng-Zebe* too takes his part;
But he blows all his fire into my heart.

AURENG-ZEBE: Alas, what fury's this?

NOURMAHAL: ——————————That's he, that's he!
[*Staring upon him, and catching at him.*
I know the dear man's voice:
And this my Rival, this the cursed she.
They kiss; into each others arms they run:
Close, close, close! must I see, and must have none?
Thou art not hers: give me that eager kiss.
Ingrateful! have I lost *Morat* for this?
Will you?—before my face?—poor helpless I
See all; and have my Hell before I die! [*Sinks down.*

EMPEROR: With thy last breath thou hast thy crimes confest:
Farewel; and take, what thou ne'er gav'st me, rest.
But you, my Son, receive it better here:
[*Giving him* INDAMORA'*s hand.*
The just rewards of Love and Honour wear.
Receive the Mistris you so long have serv'd;
Receive the Crown your Loialty preserv'd.
Take you the Reins, while I from cares remove,
And sleep within the Chariot which I drove.

EPILOGUE

A pretty task! and so I told the Fool,
Who needs would undertake to please by Rule:
He thought that, if his Characters were good,
The Scenes entire, and freed from noise and bloud;
The Action great, yet circumscrib'd by Time,
The Words not forc'd, but sliding into Rhime,
The Passions rais'd and calm'd by just Degrees,
As Tides are swell'd, and then retire to Seas;
He thought, in hitting these, his bus'ness done,
Though he, perhaps, has fail'd in ev'ry one:
But, after all, a Poet must confess,
His Art's like Physick, but a happy ghess.
Your Pleasure on your Fancy must depend:
The Lady's pleas'd, just as she likes her Friend.
No Song! no Dance! no Show! he fears you'l say,
You love all naked Beauties, but a Play.
He much mistakes your methods to delight;
And, like the French, abhors our Target-fight:
But those damn'd Dogs can never be i' th' right.
True English hate your Monsieur's paltry Arts;
For you are all Silk-weavers,[1] *in your hearts.*
Bold Brittons, at a brave Bear-garden Fray,
Are rouz'd: and, clatt'ring Sticks, cry, Play, play, play.
Mean time, your filthy Forreigner will stare,
And mutter to himself, Ha gens Barbare!
And, Gad, 'tis well he mutters; well for him;
Our Butchers else would tear him limb from limb.

[1] The London silk-weavers were always threatened with unemployment by the import of French silks.

EPILOGUE

'Tis true, the time may come, your Sons may be
Infected with this French civility;
But this in After-ages will be done:
Our Poet writes a hundred years too soon.
This Age comes on too slow, or he too fast:
And early Springs are subject to a blast!
Who would excel, when few can make a Test
Betwixt indiff'rent Writing and the best?
For Favours cheap and common, who wou'd strive,
Which, like abandon'd Prostitutes, you give?
Yet scatter'd here and there I some behold,
Who can discern the Tinsel from the Gold:
To these he writes; and, if by them allow'd,
'Tis their Prerogative to rule the Crowd.
For he more fears (like a presuming Man)
Their Votes who cannot judge, than theirs who can.

ALL FOR LOVE

OR, THE WORLD WELL LOST

A TRAGEDY

WRITTEN IN IMITATION
OF SHAKESPEARE'S STILE

Facile est verbum aliquod ardens (ut ita dicam) notare: idque restinctis animorum incendiis irridere. Cicero.[1]

[1] It is easy to mark down some word that reflects, as it were, the heat of an emotion, and subsequently to deride the same word once the fires of passion are quenched.

All for Love: or, The World well Lost. A Tragedy, As it is Acted at the Theatre-Royal; And Written in Imitation of Shakespeare's Stile. By John Dryden, Servant to His Majesty. [*Latin quot.*] In the Savoy: Printed by Tho. Newcomb, for Henry Herringman, at the Blew Anchor in the Lower Walk of the New-Exchange. 1678.

All for Love was first performed at the Theatre Royal, Drury Lane, *c.* 12 December 1677. The present text follows that of the first edition (Macdonald, 82 a). The speech headings have been expanded and, in the interests of clarity, the stage directions have occasionally been rearranged.

TO THE RIGHT HONOURABLE

THOMAS, EARL OF DANBY

VISCOUNT LATIMER AND BARON OSBORNE
OF KIVETON IN YORKSHIRE
LORD HIGH TREASURER OF ENGLAND
ONE OF HIS MAJESTIES MOST HONOURABLE PRIVY-COUNCIL, AND KNIGHT OF THE MOST NOBLE
ORDER OF THE GARTER, &c.

MY LORD,

The Gratitude of Poets is so troublesome a Virtue to Great Men, that you are often in danger of your own Benefits: for you are threaten'd with some Epistle, and not suffer'd to do good in quiet, or to compound for their silence whom you have oblig'd. Yet, I confess, I neither am nor ought to be surpriz'd at this Indulgence: for your Lordship has the same right to favour Poetry which the Great and Noble have ever had.

Carmen amat, quisquis carmine digna gerit.[1]

There is somewhat of a tye in Nature betwixt those who are born for Worthy Actions, and those who can transmit them to Posterity: And though ours be much the inferiour part, it comes at least within the Verge of Alliance; nor are we unprofitable Members of the Commonwealth, when we animate others to those Virtues, which we copy and describe from you.

'Tis indeed their Interest, who endeavour the Subversion of Governments, to discourage Poets and Historians; for the best which can happen to them is to be forgotten: But such who, under KINGS, *are the Fathers of their Country, and by a just and prudent ordering of affairs preserve it, have the same reason to cherish the Chroniclers of their Actions, as they have to lay up in safety the Deeds and Evidences of their Estates: For such Records are their undoubted Titles to the love and reverence of After-Ages. Your* lordships *Administration has already taken up a considerable part of the* English Annals; *and many of its most happy years are owing to it. His* MAJESTY, *the most knowing Judge of Men, and the*

[1] Whoever does deeds worthy of poetry is a lover of poetry.

best Master, has acknowledg'd the Ease and Benefit he receives in the Incomes of His Treasury, which You found not only disorder'd, but exhausted. All things were in the confusion of a Chaos, *without Form or Method, if not reduc'd beyond it, even to Annihilation: so that you had not only to separate the Jarring Elements, but (if that boldness of expression might be allow'd me) to Create them. Your Enemies had so embroyl'd the management of your Office, that they look'd on your Advancement as the Instrument of your Ruine. And as if the clogging of the Revenue, and the Confusion of Accounts, which you found in your entrance, were not sufficient, they added their own weight of malice to the Publick Calamity, by forestalling the Credit which shou'd cure it: your Friends on the other side were only capable of pitying, but not of aiding you: no farther help or counsel was remaining to you, but what was founded on your Self: and that indeed was your Security: For your Diligence, your Constancy, and your Prudence, wrought more surely within, when they were not disturb'd by any outward Motion. The highest Virtue is best to be trusted with it Self, for Assistance only can be given by a* Genius *Superiour to that which it assists. And 'tis the Noblest kind of Debt, when we are only oblig'd to God and Nature. This then,* My Lord, *is your just Commendation, That you have wrought out your Self a way to Glory, by those very Means that were design'd for your Destruction: You have not only restor'd, but advanc'd the Revenues of your Master without grievance to the Subject: and as if that were little yet, the Debts of the* Exchequer, *which lay heaviest both on the* Crown, *and on* Private Persons, *have by your Conduct been establish'd in a certainty of satisfaction. An Action so much the more Great and Honourable, because the case was without the ordinary relief of Laws; above the Hopes of the Afflicted, and beyond the Narrowness of the Treasury to redress, had it been manag'd by a less able Hand. 'Tis certainly the happiest, and most unenvy'd part of all your Fortune, to do good to many, while you do injury to none: to receive at once the Prayers of the Subject, and the Praises of the Prince: and by the care of your Conduct, to give Him Means of exerting the chiefest, (if any be the chiefest) of His Royal Virtues, His Distributive Justice to the Deserving, and his Bounty and Compassion to the Wanting. The Disposition of Princes towards their People, cannot better be discover'd than in the choice of their Ministers: who, like the Animal Spirits betwixt the Soul and Body, participate somewhat of both Natures, and make the Communication which is betwixt them. A King, who is just and moderate in his Nature, who Rules according to the Laws, whom God made happy by forming the Temper of his Soul to the Constitution of his Government, and who makes us happy, by assuming over us no other Soveraignty than that wherein our Welfare and Liberty consists; a Prince, I say, of so excellent a Character, and so suitable to the Wishes of all Good Men, could not better have convey'd Himself into his Peoples Apprehensions, than in your Lordships Person: who so lively express the same Virtues, that you seem not so much a Copy, as an Emanation of Him. Moderation is doubtless an Establishment of Greatness; but there is a steadiness of temper which is likewise requisite in a Minister of State: so equal a mixture of both Virtues, that he may stand like an* Isthmus *betwixt the two encroaching Seas of Arbitrary Power, and Lawless Anarchy. The Undertaking would be difficult to any but an extraordinary* Genius, *to stand at the Line, and to divide the Limits; to pay what is due to the Great Representative of the Nation, and neither to inhance, nor to yield up the undoubted Prerogatives of the Crown. These,* My Lord, *are the proper Virtues of a Noble Englishman, as indeed they are properly English Virtues: No People in the World being capable of using them, but we who have the happiness to be born under so equal, and so well pois'd a Government. A Government which has all the Advantages of Liberty beyond a Commonwealth, and all the Marks of Kingly Sovereignty without the danger of a Tyranny. Both my Nature, as I am an Englishman, and my Reason, as I am a Man, have bred in me a loathing to that specious Name of a Republick: that mock-appearance of a Liberty, where all who have not part in the Government, are Slaves: and Slaves they are of a viler note than such as are Subjects to an absolute Dominion. For no Christian Monarchy is so absolute, but 'tis circumscrib'd with Laws: But when the Executive Power is in the Law-makers, there is no farther check upon them; and the People must suffer without a remedy, because they are oppress'd by their Representatives. If I must serve, the number of my Masters, who were born my Equals, would but add to the ignominy of my Bondage. The Nature of our Government above all others, is exactly suited both to the Situation of our Country, and the Temper of the Natives: An Island being more proper for Commerce and for Defence, than for extending its Dominions on the Continent: for what the Valour of its Inhabitants might gain, by reason of its remoteness, and the casualties of the Seas, it cou'd not so easily preserve: and therefore, neither the Arbitrary Power of one in a Monarchy, nor of many in a Commonwealth, could make us greater than we are. 'Tis true, that vaster and more frequent Taxes might be gather'd, when the consent of the People was not ask'd or needed, but this were only by Conquering abroad to be poor at home:*

And the Examples of our Neighbours teach us, that they are not always the happiest Subjects whose Kings extend their Dominions farthest. Since therefore we cannot win by an Offensive War, at least a Land-War, the Model of our Government seems naturally contriv'd for the Defensive part: and the consent of a People is easily obtain'd to contribute to that Power which must protect it. Felices nimium bona si sua nôrint, Angligenæ![1] *And yet there are not wanting Malecontents amongst us, who surfeiting themselves on too much happiness, wou'd perswade the People that they might be happier by a change. 'Twas indeed the policy of their old Forefather, when himself was fallen from the station of Glory, to seduce Mankind into the same Rebellion with him, by telling him he might yet be freer than he was: that is, more free than his Nature wou'd allow, or (if I may so say) than God cou'd make him. We have already all the Liberty which Free-born Subjects can enjoy; and all beyond it is but Licence. But if it be Liberty of Conscience which they pretend, the Moderation of our Church is such, that its practice extends not to the severity of Persecution, and its Discipline is withal so easie, that it allows more freedom to Dissenters than any of the Sects wou'd allow to it. In the mean time, what right can be pretended by these Men to attempt Innovations in Church or State? Who made them the Trustees, or (to speak a little nearer their own Language) the Keepers of the Liberty of* England? *If their Call be extraordinary, let them convince us by working Miracles; for ordinary Vocation they can have none to disturb the Government under which they were born, and which protects them. He who has often chang'd his Party, and always has made his Interest the Rule of it, gives little evidence of his sincerity for the Publick Good: 'Tis manifest he changes but for himself, and takes the People for Tools to work his Fortune. Yet the experience of all Ages might let him know, that they who trouble the Waters first, have seldom the benefit of the Fishing: As they who began the late Rebellion, enjoy'd not the fruit of their undertaking, but were crush'd themselves by the Usurpation of their own Instrument. Neither is it enough for them to answer that they only intend a Reformation of the Government, but not the Subversion of it: On such pretences all Insurrections have been founded: 'Tis striking at the Root of Power, which is Obedience. Every Remonstrance of private Men, has the seed of Treason in it; and Discourses which are couch'd in ambiguous Terms, are therefore the more dangerous, because they do all the Mischief of open sedition, yet are safe from the punishment of the*

[1] Too happy the sons of England, did they but recognise their good fortune! (Adapted from Vergil, *Georgics* 2. 458–9.)

Laws. These, My Lord, *are Considerations which I should not pass so lightly over, had I room to manage them as they deserve : for no Man can be so inconsiderable in a Nation, as not to have a share in the welfare of it; and if he be a true Englishman, he must at the same time be fir'd with Indignation, and revenge himself as he can on the Disturbers of his Country. And to whom could I more fitly apply my self, than to your Lordship, who have not only an inborn, but an hereditary Loyalty? The memorable constancy and sufferings of your Father, almost to the ruine of his Estate for the Royal Cause, were an earnest of that, which such a Parent and such an Institution wou'd produce in the Person of a Son. But so unhappy an occasion of manifesting your own Zeal in suffering for his present* MAJESTY, *the Providence of God, and the Prudence of your Administration, will, I hope, prevent. That as your Fathers Fortune waited on the unhappiness of his* Sovereign, *so your own may participate of the better Fate which attends his* Son. *The Relation which you have by Alliance to the Noble Family of your Lady, serves to confirm to you both this happy Augury. For what can deserve a greater place in the English Chronicle, than the Loyalty and Courage, the Actions and Death of the General of an Army Fighting for his Prince and Country? The Honour and Gallantry of the Earl of* Lindsey, *is so illustrious a Subject, that 'tis fit to adorn an Heroique Poem; for He was the Proto-Martyr of the Cause, and the Type of his unfortunate Royal Master.*[1]

Yet, after all, My Lord, *if I may speak my thoughts, you are happy rather to us than to your self: for the Multiplicity, the Cares, and the Vexations of your Imployment, have betray'd you from your self, and given you up into the Possession of the Publick. You are robb'd of your Privacy and Friends, and scarce any hour of your Life you can call your own. Those who envy your Fortune, if they wanted not good Nature, might more justly pity it; and when they see you watch'd by a Croud of Suitors, whose importunity 'tis impossible to avoid, would conclude with Reason, that you have lost much more in true content, than you have gain'd by Dignity; and that a private Gentleman is better attended by a single Servant, than your Lordship with so clamorous a Train. Pardon me,* My Lord, *If I speak like a Philosopher on this Subject; the Fortune which makes a Man uneasie, cannot make him happy: and a Wise Man must think himself uneasie, when few of his Actions are in his choice.*

This last Consideration has brought me to another, and a very

[1] Robert Bertie, 1st Earl of Lindsey (1582–1642), high admiral of England, fought for the King in the Civil War and died of wounds received at Edgehill.

seasonable one for your relief; which is, That while I pity your want of leisure, I have impertinently Detain'd you so long a time. I have put off my own Business, which was my Dedication, till 'tis so late, that I am now asham'd to begin it: And therefore I will say nothing of the Poem, which I Present to you, because I know not if you are like to have an Hour, which, with a good Conscience, you may throw away in perusing it: And for the Author, I have only to beg the continuance of your Protection to him, who is,

MY LORD,

Your Lordships, most Oblig'd,

most Humble, and most

Obedient Servant,

JOHN DRYDEN.

PREFACE

THE death of *Anthony* and *Cleopatra*, is a Subject which has been treated by the greatest Wits of our Nation, after *Shakespeare*; and by all so variously, that their example has given me the confidence to try my self in this Bowe of *Ulysses* amongst the Crowd of Sutors; and, withal, to take my own measures, in aiming at the Mark. I doubt not but the same Motive has prevailed with all of us in this attempt; I mean the excellency of the Moral: for the chief persons represented, were famous patterns of unlawful love; and their end accordingly was unfortunate. All reasonable men have long since concluded, That the Heroe of the Poem, ought not to be a character of perfect Virtue, for, then, he could not, without injustice, be made unhappy; nor yet altogether wicked, because he could not then be pitied: I have therefore steer'd the middle course; and have drawn the character of *Anthony* as favourably as *Plutarch*, *Appian*, and *Dion Cassius* wou'd give me leave: the like I have observ'd in *Cleopatra.* That which is wanting to work up the pity to a greater heighth, was not afforded me by the story: for the crimes of love which they both committed, were not occasion'd by any necessity, or fatal ignorance, but were wholly voluntary; since our passions are, or ought to be, within our power. The Fabrick of the Play is regular enough, as to the inferior parts of it; and the Unities of Time, Place and Action, more exactly observ'd, than, perhaps, the English Theater requires. Particularly, the Action is so much one, that it is the only of the kind without Episode, or Underplot; every Scene in the Tragedy conducing to the main design, and every Act concluding with a turn of it. The greatest errour in the contrivance seems to be in the person of *Octavia*: For, though I might use the priviledge of a Poet, to introduce her into *Alexandria*, yet I had not enough consider'd, that the compassion she mov'd to her self and children, was destructive to that which I reserv'd for *Anthony* and *Cleopatra*; whose mutual love being founded upon vice, must lessen the favour of the Audience to them, when Virtue and Innocence were oppress'd by it. And, though I justified *Anthony* in some measure, by making *Octavia*'s departure, to proceed wholly from her self; yet the force of the first Machine still remain'd; and the dividing of pity, like the cutting of a River into many Channels, abated the strength of the natural stream. But this is an Objection which none of my Critiques have urg'd against me; and therefore I might have let it pass, if I could have resolv'd to have been partial to my self. The faults my Enemies have found, are rather cavils concerning little, and not essential Decencies; which a Master of the Ceremonies may decide betwixt us. The *French* Poets, I confess, are strict Observers of these Punctilio's: They would not, for example, have suffer'd *Cleopatra* and *Octavia* to have met; or if they had met, there must have only pass'd betwixt them some cold civilities, but no eagerness of repartée, for fear of offending against the greatness of their Characters, and the modesty of their Sex. This Objection I foresaw, and at the same time contemn'd: for I judg'd it both natural and probable, that *Octavia*, proud of her new-gain'd Conquest, would search out *Cleopatra* to triumph over her; and that *Cleopatra*, thus attacqu'd, was not of a spirit to shun the encounter: and 'tis not unlikely, that two exasperated Rivals should use such Satyre as I have put into their mouths; for after all, though the one were a *Roman*, and the other a Queen, they were both Women. 'Tis true, some actions, though natural, are not fit to be represented; and broad obscenities in words, ought in good manners to be avoided: expressions therefore are a modest cloathing of our thoughts, as Breeches and Petticoats are of our bodies. If I have kept my self within the bounds of modesty, all beyond it is but nicety and affectation; which is no more but modesty deprav'd into a vice: they betray themselves who are too quick of apprehension in such cases, and leave all reasonable men to imagine worse of them, than of the Poet.

Honest *Montaigne* goes yet farther: *Nous ne sommes que ceremonie; la ceremonie nous emporte, & laissons la substance des choses: Nous nous tenons aux branches, & abandonnons le tronc*

& le corps. Nous avons appris aux Dames de rougir, oyans seulement nommer ce qu'elles ne craignent aucunement a faire: Nous n'osons appeller a droict nos membres, & ne craignons pas de les employer a toute sorte de debauche. La ceremonie nous defend d'exprimer par paroles les choses licites & naturelles, & nous l'en croyons; la raison nous defend de n'en faire point d'illicites & mauvaises, & personne ne l'en croid. My comfort is, that by this opinion my Enemies are but sucking Critiques, who wou'd fain be nibbling ere their teeth are come.

Yet, in this nicety of manners does the excellency of *French* Poetry consist: their Heroes are the most civil people breathing; but their good breeding seldom extends to a word of sense: All their Wit is in their Ceremony; they want the Genius which animates our Stage; and therefore 'tis but necessary when they cannot please, that they should take care not to offend. But, as the civilest man in the company is commonly the dullest, so these Authors, while they are afraid to make you laugh or cry, out of pure good manners, make you sleep. They are so careful not to exasperate a Critique, that they never leave him any work; so busie with the Broom, and make so clean a riddance, that there is little left either for censure or for praise: for no part of a Poem is worth our discommending, where the whole is insipid; as when we have once tasted of pall'd Wine, we stay not to examine it Glass by Glass. But while they affect to shine in trifles, they are often careless in essentials. Thus their *Hippolitus* is so scrupulous in point of decency, that he will rather expose himself to death, than accuse his Stepmother to his Father; and my Critiques I am sure will commend him for it: but we of grosser apprehensions, are apt to think that this excess of generosity, is not practicable but with Fools and Madmen. This was good manners with a vengeance; and the Audience is like to be much concern'd at the misfortunes of this admirable Heroe: but take *Hippolitus*[1] out of his Poetique Fit, and I suppose he would think it a wiser part, to set the Saddle on the right Horse, and chuse rather to live with the reputation of a plain-spoken honest man, than to die with the infamy of an incestuous Villain. In the mean time we may take notice, that where the Poet ought to have preserv'd the character as it was deliver'd to us by Antiquity, when he should have given us the picture of a rough young man, of the *Amazonian* strain, a jolly Huntsman, and both by his profession and his early rising a Mortal Enemy to love, he has chosen to give him the

[1] *Hippolitus* is a character in Racine's tragedy of *Phèdre*, which was first performed in 1677.

turn of Gallantry, sent him to travel from *Athens* to *Paris*, taught him to make love, and transform'd the *Hippolitus* of *Euripides* into Monsieur *Hippolite*. I should not have troubled my self thus far with French Poets, but that I find our *Chedreux*[1] Critiques wholly form their judgments by them. But for my part, I desire to be try'd by the Laws of my own Country; for it seems unjust to me, that the French should prescribe here, till they have conquer'd. Our little Sonnettiers who follow them, have too narrow Souls to judge of Poetry. Poets themselves are the most proper, though I conclude not the only Critiques. But till some Genius as Universal, as *Aristotle*, shall arise, one who can penetrate into all Arts and Sciences, without the practice of them, I shall think it reasonable, that the Judgment of an Artificer in his own Art should be preferable to the opinion of another man; at least where he is not brib'd by interest, or prejudic'd by malice: and this, I suppose, is manifest by plain induction: For, first, the Crowd cannot be presum'd to have more than a gross instinct, of what pleases or displeases them: every man will grant me this; but then, by a particular kindness to himself, he draws his own stake first, and will be distinguish'd from the multitude, of which other men may think him one. But, if I come closer to those who are allow'd for witty men, either by the advantage of their quality, or by common fame, and affirm that neither are they qualified to decide Sovereignly, concerning Poetry, I shall yet have a strong party of my opinion; for most of them severally will exclude the rest, either from the number of witty men, or at least of able Judges. But here again they are all indulgent to themselves: and every one who believes himself a Wit, that is, every man, will pretend at the same time to a right judging. But to press it yet farther, there are many witty men, but few Poets; neither have all Poets a taste of Tragedy. And this is the Rock on which they are daily splitting. Poetry, which is a Picture of Nature, must generally please: but 'tis not to be understood that all parts of it must please every man; therefore is not Tragedy to be judg'd by a witty man, whose taste is only confin'd to Comedy. Nor is every man who loves Tragedy a sufficient Judge of it: he must understand the excellencies of it too, or he will only prove a blind Admirer, not a Critique. From hence it comes that so many Satyrs on Poets, and censures of their Writings, fly abroad. Men of pleasant Conversation, (at least esteem'd so) and endu'd with a trifling kind of Fancy, perhaps help'd out with some smattering of Latine, are ambitious to dis-

[1] A *chedreux* was a fashionable periwig in the French style.

tinguish themselves from the Herd of Gentlemen, by their Poetry;

> *Rarus enim fermè sensus communis in illâ*
> *Fortunâ.*[1]

And is not this a wretched affectation, not to be contented with what Fortune has done for them, and sit down quietly with their Estates, but they must call their Wits in question, and needlessly expose their nakedness to publick view? Not considering that they are not to expect the same approbation from sober men, which they have found from their flatterers after the third Bottle? If a little glittering in discourse has pass'd them on us for witty men, where was the necessity of undeceiving the World? would a man who has an ill Title to an Estate, but yet is in possession of it, would he bring it of his own accord, to be try'd at *Westminster?* We who write, if we want the Talent, yet have the excuse that we do it for a poor subsistence; but what can be urged in their defence, who not having the Vocation of Poverty to scribble out of meer wantonness, take pains to make themselves ridiculous? *Horace* was certainly in the right, where he said, That *no man is satisfied with his own condition.* A Poet is not pleas'd because he is not rich; and the Rich are discontented, because the Poets will not admit them of their number. Thus the case is hard with Writers: if they succeed not, they must starve; and if they do, some malicious Satyr is prepar'd to level them for daring to please without their leave. But while they are so eager to destroy the fame of others, their ambition is manifest in their concernment: some Poem of their own is to be produc'd, and the Slaves are to be laid flat with their faces on the ground, that the Monarch may appear in the greater Majesty.

Dionysius and *Nero* had the same longings, but with all their power they cou'd never bring their business well about. 'Tis true, they proclaim'd themselves Poets by sound of Trumpet; and Poets they were upon pain of death to any man who durst call them otherwise. The Audience had a fine time on't, you may imagine; they sate in a bodily fear, and look'd as demurely as they could: for 'twas a hanging matter to laugh unseasonably; and the Tyrants were suspicious, as they had reason, that their Subjects had 'em in the wind: so, every man in his own defence set as good a face upon the business as he could: 'Twas known beforehand that the Monarchs were to be Crown'd Laureats; but when

[1] Seldom, as a rule, do they of that condition feel sympathy with their fellows at large. (Juvenal 8. 73.)

the shew was over, and an honest man was suffer'd to depart quietly, he took out his laughter which he had stifled; with a firm resolution never more to see an Emperor's Play, though he had been ten years a making it. In the mean time the true Poets were they who made the best Markets, for they had Wit enough to yield the Prize with a good grace, and not contend with him who had thirty Legions: They were sure to be rewarded if they confess'd themselves bad Writers, and that was somewhat better than to be Martyrs for their reputation. *Lucan*'s example was enough to teach them manners; and after he was put to death, for overcoming *Nero*, the Emperor carried it without dispute for the best Poet in his Dominions: No man was ambitious of that grinning honour; for if he heard the malicious Trumpetter proclaiming his name before his betters, he knew there was but one way with him. *Mecenas* took another course, and we know he was more than a great man, for he was witty too: but finding himself far gone in Poetry, which *Seneca* assures us was not his Talent, he thought it his best way to be well with *Virgil* and with *Horace*; that at least he might be a Poet at the second hand; and we see how happily it has succeeded with him; for his own bad Poetry is forgotten, and their Panegyricks of him still remain. But they who should be our Patrons, are for no such expensive ways to fame: they have much of the Poetry of *Mecenas*, but little of his liberality. They are for persecuting *Horace* and *Virgil*, in the persons of their Successors, (for such is every man, who has any part of their Soul and Fire, though in a lesse degree.) Some of their little *Zanies* yet go farther; for they are Persecutors even of *Horace* himself, as far as they are able, by their ignorant and vile imitations of him; by making an unjust use of his Authority, and turning his Artillery against his Friends. But how would he disdain to be Copyed by such hands! I dare answer for him, he would be more uneasie in their company, than he was with *Crispinus* their Forefather in the *Holy Way*; and would no more have allow'd them a place amongst the Critiques, than he would *Demetrius* the Mimique, and *Tigellius* the Buffoon;

> ——*Demetri, teq; Tigelli,*
> *Discipulorum inter jubeo plorare Cathedras.*[1]

With what scorn would he look down on such miserable Translators, who make Doggrel of his Latine, mistake his meaning,

[1] As for you, Demetrius and Tigellius, I bid you go howl amidst the chairs of your lady-pupils. (Horace, *Satires* 1. 10. 90–1.)

misapply his censures, and often contradict their own? He is fix'd as a Land-Mark to set out the bounds of Poetry,

——Saxum, antiquum ingens
Limes agro positus litem ut discerneret arvis:[1]

But other Arms than theirs, and other Sinews are requir'd, to raise the weight of such an Author; and when they would toss him against their Enemies,

Genua labant, gelidus concrevit frigore sanguis,
Tum lapis ipse, viri vacuum per inane volutus
Nec spatium evasit totum, nec pertulit ictum.[2]

For my part, I would wish no other revenge, either for my self or the rest of the Poets, from this Rhyming Judge of the Twelve-penny Gallery,[3] this Legitimate Son of *Sternhold*, than that he would subscribe his Name to his censure, or (not to tax him beyond his learning) set his Mark: for shou'd he own himself publickly, and come from behind the Lyons Skin, they whom he condemns wou'd be thankful to him, they whom he praises wou'd chuse to be condemned; and the Magistrates whom he has elected, wou'd modestly withdraw from their employment, to avoid the scandal of his nomination. The sharpness of his Satyr, next to himself, falls most heavily on his Friends, and they ought never to forgive him for commending them perpetually the wrong way, and sometimes by contraries. If he have a Friend whose hastiness in writing is his greatest fault, *Horace* wou'd have taught him to have minc'd the matter, and to have call'd it readiness of thought, and a flowing fancy; for friendship will allow a man to Christen an imperfection by the name of some neighbour virtue:

Vellem in amicitiâ sic erraremus; & isti
Errori, nomen virtus posuisset honestum.[4]

[1] A huge and ancient stone, a boundary-mark set at the field's end to divide claims to the plough-land. (Vergil, *Æneid* 12. 898.)

[2] His knees tottered; the blood froze and congealed; then the hero's stone itself, hurled through the empty void, failed to reach him, nor did the blow find its mark. (Vergil, *Æneid* 12. 905–7.)

[3] Dryden is alluding to the Earl of Rochester's (1648–1680) imitation of Horace, published anonymously and entitled *Allusion to the Tenth Satire of the First Book of Horace*, in which he was criticised; and he is pretending to be ignorant of its authorship. For Sternhold see *Dramatick Poesie*, p. 429, n. 3.

[4] I would that friends might err as lovers do (i.e. in failing to see the other's faults), and that that mistake had been blessed with an honourable name by decent, manly feeling. (*Satires* 1. 3. 41–2.)

But he would never have allow'd him to have call'd a slow man hasty, or a hasty Writer a slow Drudge, as *Juvenal* explains it:

> ——*Canibus pigris, scabieq; vetustâ*
> *Levibus, & siccæ lambentibus ora lucernæ*
> *Nomen erit, Pardus, Tygris, Leo; si quid adhuc est*
> *Quod fremit in terris violentius.*[1]

Yet *Lucretius* laughs at a foolish Lover, even for excusing the Imperfections of his Mistress:

> *Nigra* μελίχροος *est, immunda & fœtida* ἄκοσμος.
> *Balba loqui non quit,* τραυλίζει; *muta pudens est, &c.*[2]

But to drive it, *ad Æthiopem Cygnum* is not to be endur'd. I leave him to interpret this by the benefit of his French Version on the other side, and without farther considering him, than I have the rest of my illiterate Censors, whom I have disdain'd to answer, because they are not qualified for Judges. It remains that I acquaint the Reader, that I have endeavoured in this Play to follow the practise of the Ancients, who, as Mr. *Rymer* has judiciously observ'd, are and ought to be our Masters. *Horace* likewise gives it for a Rule in his Art of Poetry,

> ——*Vos exemplaria Græca*
> *Nocturnâ versate manu, versate diurnâ.*[3]

Yet, though their Models are regular, they are too little for English Tragedy; which requires to be built in a larger compass. I could give an instance in the *Oedipus Tyrannus*, which was the Masterpiece of *Sophocles*; but I reserve it for a more fit occasion, which I hope to have hereafter. In my Stile I have profess'd to imitate the Divine *Shakespeare*; which that I might perform more freely, I have dis-incumber'd my self from Rhyme. Not that I condemn my former way, but that this is more proper to my present purpose. I hope I need not to explain my self, that I have not Copy'd my Author servilely: Words and Phrases must of necessity receive a change in succeeding Ages: but it is almost a Miracle that much of his Language remains so pure; and that he who began Dramatique Poetry amongst us, untaught by

[1] "Panther," "Tiger," "Lion," or anything on earth that roars more fearsomely still—these will be the names given to dull dogs, hairless with mange of long standing, that lick at the mouth of a lamp gone dry. (8. 34–7.)

[2] The dark of hue is "honey-coloured," the unclean and musty, "careless of array." If she stammer, and cannot speak, she "lispeth"; if she be dumb, she is but "modest.". . . (4. 1160 and 1164.)

[3] Do you, for your part, apply yourselves by night and by day to the conning of Greek models. (268–9.)

any, and, as *Ben Johnson* tells us, without Learning, should by the force of his own Genius perform so much, that in a manner he has left no praise for any who come after him. The occasion is fair, and the subject would be pleasant to handle the difference of Stiles betwixt him and *Fletcher*, and wherein, and how far they are both to be imitated. But since I must not be over-confident of my own performance after him, it will be prudence in me to be silent. Yet I hope I may affirm, and without vanity, that by imitating him, I have excell'd myself throughout the Play; and particularly, that I prefer the Scene betwixt *Anthony* and *Ventidius* in the first Act, to any thing which I have written in this kind.

PROLOGUE

TO ANTHONY AND CLEOPATRA

What Flocks of Critiques hover here to-day,
As Vultures wait on Armies for their Prey,
All gaping for the Carcass of a Play!
With Croaking Notes they bode some dire event;
And follow dying Poets by the scent.
Ours gives himself for gone; y'have watch'd your time!
He fights this day unarm'd; without his Rhyme.
And brings a Tale which often has been told;
As sad as Dido'*s; and almost as old.*
His Heroe, whom you Wits his Bully call,
Bates of his mettle, and scarce rants at all:
He's somewhat lewd; but a well-meaning mind;
Weeps much; fights little; but is wond'rous kind.
In short, a Pattern, and Companion fit,
For all the keeping Tonyes of the Pit.
I cou'd name more: A Wife, and Mistress too;
Both (to be plain) too good for most of you:
The Wife well-natur'd, and the Mistress true.
Now, Poets, if your fame has been his care;
Allow him all the candour you can spare.
A brave Man scorns to quarrel once a day;
Like Hectors, in at every petty fray.
Let those find fault whose Wit's so very small,
They've need to show that they can think at all:
Errours like straws upon the surface flow;
He who would search for Pearls must dive below.
Fops may have leave to level all they can;

PROLOGUE

As Pigmies wou'd be glad to lopp a Man.
Half-Wits are Fleas; so little and so light;
We scarce cou'd know they live, but that they bite.
But, as the Rich, when tir'd with daily Feasts,
For change, become their next poor Tenants Ghests;
Drink hearty Draughts of Ale from plain brown Bowls,
And snatch the homely Rasher from the Coals:
So you, retiring from much better Cheer,
For once, may venture to do penance here.
And since that plenteous Autumn now is past,
Whose Grapes and Peaches have Indulg'd your taste,
Take in good part from our poor Poets board,
Such rivell'd Fruits as Winter can afford.

PERSONS REPRESENTED

	BY
Marc Anthony,	Mr. *Hart.*
Ventidius, his General,	Mr. *Mohun.*
Dollabella, his Friend,	Mr. *Clarke.*
Alexas, the Queens Eunuch,	Mr. *Goodman.*
Serapion, Priest of *Isis*,	Mr. *Griffon.*
Another Priest,	Mr. *Coysh.*

Servants to Anthony,

Cleopatra, Queen of *Egypt*,	Mrs. *Boutell.*
Octavia, *Anthony*'s Wife,	Mrs. *Corey.*

Charmion, } *Cleopatra*'s Maids.
Iras, }

Anthony's two little Daughters.

SCENE, Alexandria.

ALL FOR LOVE

OR, THE WORLD WELL LOST

ACT I

SCENE, *The Temple of* Isis

Enter SERAPION, MYRIS, *Priests of* Isis.

SERAPION: Portents, and Prodigies, are grown so frequent,
That they have lost their Name. Our fruitful *Nile*
Flow'd ere the wonted Season, with a Torrent
So unexpected, and so wondrous fierce,
That the wild Deluge overtook the haste
Ev'n of the Hinds that watch'd it: Men and Beasts
Were born above the tops of Trees, that grew
On th' utmost Margin of the Water-mark.
Then, with so swift an Ebb, the Floud drove backward
It slipt from underneath the Scaly Herd:
Here monstrous *Phocæ* panted on the Shore;
Forsaken *Dolphins* there, with their broad tails,
Lay lashing the departing Waves: Hard by 'em,
Sea-Horses floundring in the slimy mud,
Toss'd up their heads, and dash'd the ooze about 'em.

Enter ALEXAS *behind them.*

MYRIS: Avert these Omens, Heav'n.
SERAPION: Last night, between the hours of Twelve and One,
In a lone Isle o' th' Temple while I walk'd,
A Whirl-wind rose, that, with a violent blast,
Shook all the *Dome*: the Doors around me clapt,
The Iron Wicket, that defends the Vault,
Where the long Race of *Ptolomies* is lay'd,
Burst open, and disclos'd the mighty dead.
From out each Monument, in order plac'd,
An Armed Ghost starts up: the Boy-King last
Rear'd his inglorious head. A peal of groans
Then follow'd, and a lamentable voice
Cry'd, *Ægypt* is no more. My blood ran back,
My shaking knees against each other knock'd;

On the cold pavement down I fell intranc'd,
And so unfinish'd left the horrid Scene.

ALEXAS *showing himself*: And, Dream'd you this? or, Did invent the Story?
To frighten our *Ægyptian* Boys withal,
And train 'em up betimes, in fear of Priesthood?

SERAPION: My Lord, I saw you not,
Nor meant my words should reach your ears; but what I utter'd was most true.

ALEXAS: A foolish Dream,
Bred from the fumes of indigested Feasts,
And holy Luxury.

SERAPION: I know my duty:
This goes no farther.

ALEXAS: 'Tis not fit it should.
Nor would the times now bear it, were it true.
All Southern, from yon hills, the *Roman* Camp
Hangs o'er us black and threatning, like a Storm
Just breaking on our heads.

SERAPION: Our faint *Ægyptians* pray for *Antony*;
But in their Servile hearts they own *Octavius.*

MYRIS: Why then does *Antony* dream out his hours,
And tempts not Fortune for a noble Day,
Which might redeem, what *Actium* lost?

ALEXAS: He thinks 'tis past recovery.

SERAPION: Yet the Foe
Seems not to press the Siege.

ALEXAS: O, there's the wonder.
Mecænas and *Agrippa*, who can most
With *Cæsar*, are his Foes. His Wife *Octavia*,
Driv'n from his House, solicits her revenge;
And *Dollabella*, who was once his Friend,
Upon some private grudge, now seeks his ruine:
Yet still War seems on either side to sleep.

SERAPION: 'Tis strange that *Antony*, for some dayes past,
Has not beheld the face of *Cleopatra*;
But here, in *Isis* Temple, lives retir'd,
And makes his heart a prey to black despair.

ALEXAS: 'Tis true; and we much fear he hopes by absence
To cure his mind of Love.

SERAPION: If he be vanquish'd,
Or make his peace, *Ægypt* is doom'd to be
A *Roman* Province; and our plenteous Harvests

Must then redeem the scarceness of their Soil.
While *Antony* stood firm, our *Alexandria*
Rival'd proud *Rome* (Dominions other Seat)
And Fortune striding, like a vast *Colossus*,
Cou'd fix an equal foot of Empire here.

ALEXAS: Had I my wish, these Tyrants of all Nature
Who Lord it o'er Mankind, should perish, perish,
Each by the others Sword; but, since our will
Is lamely follow'd by our pow'r, we must
Depend on one; with him to rise or fall.

SERAPION: How stands the Queen affected?

ALEXAS: O, she dotes,
She dotes, *Serapion*, on this vanquish'd Man,
And winds her self about his mighty ruins,
Whom would she yet forsake, yet yield him up,
This hunted prey, to his pursuers hands,
She might preserve us all; but 'tis in vain——
This changes my designs, this blasts my Counsels,
And makes me use all means to keep him here,
Whom I could wish divided from her Arms
Far as the Earth's deep Center. Well, you know
The state of things; no more of your ill Omens,
And black Prognosticks; labour to confirm
The peoples hearts.

Enter VENTIDIUS, *talking aside with a Gentleman of* ANTONY'S.

SERAPION: These *Romans* will o'erhear us.
But, Who's that Stranger? By his Warlike port,
His fierce demeanour, and erected look,
He's of no vulgar note.

ALEXAS: O 'tis *Ventidius*,
Our Emp'rors great Lieutenant in the East,
Who first show'd *Rome* that *Parthia* could be conquer'd.
When *Antony* return'd from *Syria* last,
He left this Man to guard the *Roman* Frontiers.

SERAPION: You seem to know him well.

ALEXAS: Too well. I saw him in *Cilicia* first,
When *Cleopatra* there met *Antony*:
A mortal foe he was to us, and *Ægypt*.
But, let me witness to the worth I hate,
A braver Roman never drew a Sword.
Firm to his Prince; but, as a friend, not slave.

He ne'r was of his pleasures; but presides
O'er all his cooler hours and morning counsels:
In short, the plainness, fierceness, rugged virtue
Of an old true-stampt Roman lives in him.
His coming bodes I know not what of ill
To our affairs. Withdraw, to mark him better;
And I'll acquaint you why I sought you here,
And what's our present work.

[*They withdraw to a corner of the Stage; and* VENTIDIUS, *with the other, comes forwards to the front.*

VENTIDIUS: Not see him, say you?
I say, I must, and will.

GENTLEMAN: He has commanded,
On pain of death, none should approach his presence.

VENTIDIUS: I bring him news will raise his drooping Spirits,
Give him new life.

GENTLEMAN: He sees not *Cleopatra.*

VENTIDIUS: Would he had never seen her.

GENTLEMAN: He eats not, drinks not, sleeps not, has no use
Of any thing, but thought; or, if he talks,
'Tis to himself, and then 'tis perfect raving:
Then he defies the World, and bids it pass;
Sometimes he gnawes his Lip, and Curses loud
The Boy *Octavius*; then he draws his mouth
Into a scornful smile, and cries, Take all,
The World's not worth my care.

VENTIDIUS: Just, just his nature.
Virtues his path; but sometimes 'tis too narrow
For his vast Soul; and then he starts out wide,
And bounds into a Vice that bears him far
From his first course, and plunges him in ills:
But, when his danger makes him find his fault,
Quick to observe, and full of sharp remorse,
He censures eagerly his own misdeeds,
Judging himself with malice to himself,
And not forgiving what as Man he did,
Because his other parts are more than Man.
He must not thus be lost.

[ALEXAS *and the* Priests *come forward.*

ALEXAS: You have your full Instructions, now advance;
Proclaim your Orders loudly.

SERAPION: *Romans*, *Ægyptians*, hear the Queen's Command.

Thus *Cleopatra* bids, Let Labor cease;
To Pomp and Triumphs give this happy day,
That gave the World a Lord: 'tis *Antony*'s.
Live, *Antony*; and *Cleopatra* live.
Be this the general voice sent up to Heav'n,
And every publick place repeat this eccho.

VENTIDIUS *aside*: Fine Pageantry!

SERAPION: Set out before your doors
The Images of all your sleeping Fathers,
With Laurels crown'd; with Laurels wreath your posts,
And strow with Flow'rs the Pavement; Let the Priests
Do present Sacrifice; pour out the Wine,
And call the Gods to joyn with you in gladness.

VENTIDIUS: Curse on the tongue that bids this general joy.
Can they be friends of *Antony*, who Revel
When *Antony*'s in danger? Hide, for shame,
You *Romans*, your Great grandsires Images,
For fear their Souls should animate their Marbles,
To blush at their degenerate Progeny.

ALEXAS: A love which knows no bounds to *Antony*,
Would mark the Day with honours; when all Heaven
Labor'd for him, when each propitious Star
Stood wakeful in his Orb, to watch that hour,
And shed his better influence. Her own Birth-day
Our Queen neglected, like a vulgar Fate,
That pass'd obscurely by.

VENTIDIUS: Would it had slept,
Divided far from his; till some remote
And future Age had call'd it out, to ruin
Some other Prince, not him.

ALEXAS: Your Emperor,
Tho grown unkind, would be more gentle, than
T'upbraid my Queen, for loving him too well.

VENTIDIUS: Does the mute Sacrifice upbraid the Priest?
He knows him not his Executioner.
O, she has deck'd his ruin with her love,
Led him in golden bands to gaudy slaughter,
And made perdition pleasing: She has left him
The blank of what he was;
I tell thee, Eunuch, she has quite unman'd him:
Can any Roman see, and know him now,
Thus alter'd from the Lord of half Mankind,
Unbent, unsinew'd, made a Womans Toy,

Shrunk from the vast extent of all his honors,
And crampt within a corner of the World?
O, *Antony*!
Thou bravest Soldier, and thou best of Friends!
Bounteous as Nature; next to Nature's God!
Could'st thou but make new Worlds, so wouldst thou
 give 'em,
As bounty were thy being. Rough in Battel,
As the first *Romans*, when they went to War;
Yet, after Victory, more pitiful,
Than all their Praying Virgins left at home!

ALEXAS: Would you could add to those more shining Virtues,
His truth to her who loves him.

VENTIDIUS: Would I could not.
But, Wherefore waste I precious hours with thee?
Thou art her darling mischief, her chief Engin,
Antony's other Fate. Go, tell thy Queen,
Ventidius is arriv'd, to end her Charms.
Let your *Ægyptian* Timbrels play alone;
Nor mix Effeminate Sounds with *Roman* Trumpets.
You dare not fight for *Antony*; go Pray,
And keep your Cowards-Holy-day in Temples.
[*Exeunt* ALEXAS, SERAPION.

Re-enter the Gentleman of MARC ANTONY.

SECOND GENTLEMAN: The Emperor approaches, and commands,
On pain of Death, that none presume to stay.

FIRST GENTLEMAN: I dare not disobey him.
[*Going out with the other.*

VENTIDIUS: Well, I dare.
But, I'll observe him first unseen, and find
Which way his humour drives: the rest I'll venture.
[*Withdraws.*

Enter ANTONY, *walking with a disturb'd Motion, before he speaks.*

ANTONY: They tell me, 'tis my Birth-day, and I'll keep it
With double pomp of sadness.
'Tis what the day deserves, which gave me breath.
Why was I rais'd the Meteor of the World,
Hung in the Skies, and blazing as I travel'd,
Till all my fires were spent; and then cast downward
To be trod out by *Cæsar*?

VENTIDIUS *aside*: On my Soul,
'Tis mournful, wondrous mournful!

ANTONY: Count thy gains.
Now, *Antony*, Wouldst thou be born for this?
Glutton of Fortune, thy devouring youth
Has starv'd thy wanting Age.

VENTIDIUS *aside*: How sorrow shakes him!
So, now the Tempest tears him up by th' Roots,
And on the ground extends the noble ruin.

[ANTONY *having thrown himself down.*

Lye there, thou shadow of an Emperor;
The place, thou pressest on thy Mother Earth
Is all thy Empire now: now it contains thee;
Some few dayes hence, and then 'twill be too large,
When thou'rt contracted in thy narrow Urn,
Shrunk to a few cold Ashes; then *Octavia*,
(For *Cleopatra* will not live to see it)
Octavia then will have thee all her own,
And bear thee in her Widow'd hand to *Cæsar*;
Cæsar will weep, the Crocodile will weep,
To see his Rival of the Universe
Lye still and peaceful there. I'll think no more on't.

ANTONY: Give me some Musick; look that it be sad:
I'll sooth my Melancholy, till I swell,
And burst my self with sighing— [*Soft Musick.*
'Tis somewhat to my humor. Stay, I fancy
I'm now turn'd wild, a Commoner of Nature;
Of all forsaken, and forsaking all;
Live in a shady Forrest's *Sylvan* Scene,
Stretch'd at my length beneath some blasted Oke;
I lean my head upon the Mossy Bark,
And look just of a piece, as I grew from it:
My uncomb'd Locks, matted like *Misleto*,
Hang o're my hoary Face; a murm'ring Brook
Runs at my foot.

VENTIDIUS: Methinks I fancy
My self there too.

ANTONY: The Herd come jumping by me,
And fearless, quench their thirst, while I look on,
And take me for their fellow-Citizen.
More of this Image, more; it lulls my thoughts.

[*Soft Musick again.*

VENTIDIUS: I must disturb him; I can hold no longer.

[*Stands before him.*

ANTONY *starting up*: Art thou *Ventidius*?

VENTIDIUS: Are you *Antony*?
I'm liker what I was, than you to him
I left you last.

ANTONY: I'm angry.

VENTIDIUS: So am I.

ANTONY: I would be private: leave me.

VENTIDIUS: Sir, I love you,
And therefore will not leave you.

ANTONY: Will not leave me?
Where have you learnt that Answer? Who am I?

VENTIDIUS: My Emperor; the Man I love next Heaven:
If I said more, I think 'twere scarce a Sin;
Y'are all that's good, and god-like.

ANTONY: All that's wretched.
You will not leave me then?

VENTIDIUS: 'Twas too presuming
To say I would not; but I dare not leave you:
And, 'tis unkind in you to chide me hence
So soon, when I so far have come to see you.

ANTONY: Now thou hast seen me, art thou satisfy'd?
For, if a Friend, thou hast beheld enough;
And, if a Foe, too much.

VENTIDIUS *weeping*: Look, Emperor, this is no common Deaw.
I have not wept this Forty year; but now
My Mother comes afresh into my eyes;
I cannot help her softness.

ANTONY: By Heav'n, he weeps, poor good old Man, he weeps!
The big round drops course one another down
The furrows of his cheeks. Stop 'em, *Ventidius,*
Or I shall blush to death: they set my shame,
That caus'd 'em, full before me.

VENTIDIUS: I'll do my best.

ANTONY: Sure there's contagion in the tears of Friends:
See, I have caught it too. Believe me, 'tis not
For my own griefs, but thine—Nay, Father.

VENTIDIUS: Emperor.

ANTONY: Emperor! Why, that's the stile of Victory,
The Conqu'ring Soldier, red with unfelt wounds,
Salutes his General so: but never more
Shall that sound reach my ears.

VENTIDIUS: I warrant you.
ANTONY: *Actium*, *Actium*! Oh—
VENTIDIUS: It sits too near you.
ANTONY: Here, here it lies; a lump of Lead by day,
And, in my short distracted nightly slumbers,
The Hag that rides my Dreams—
VENTIDIUS: Out with it; give it vent.
ANTONY: Urge not my shame.
I lost a Battel.
VENTIDIUS: So has *Julius* done.
ANTONY: Thou favour'st me, and speak'st not half thou think'st;
For *Julius* fought it out, and lost it fairly:
But *Antony*—
VENTIDIUS: Nay, stop not.
ANTONY: *Antony*,
(Well, thou wilt have it) like a coward, fled,
Fled while his Soldiers fought; fled first, *Ventidius*.
Thou long'st to curse me, and I give thee leave.
I know thou cam'st prepar'd to rail.
VENTIDIUS: I did.
ANTONY: I'll help thee—I have been a Man, *Ventidius*.
VENTIDIUS: Yes, and a brave one; but—
ANTONY: I know thy meaning.
But, I have lost my Reason, have disgrac'd
The name of Soldier, with inglorious ease.
In the full Vintage of my flowing honors,
Sate still, and saw it prest by other hands.
Fortune came smiling to my youth, and woo'd it,
And purple greatness met my ripen'd years.
When first I came to Empire, I was born
On Tides of People, crouding to my Triumphs;
The wish of Nations; and the willing World
Receiv'd me as its pledge of future peace;
I was so great, so happy, so belov'd,
Fate could not ruine me; till I took pains
And work'd against my Fortune, chid her from me,
And turn'd her loose; yet still she came again.
My careless dayes, and my luxurious nights,
At length have weary'd her, and now she's gone,
Gone, gone, divorc'd for ever. Help me, Soldier,
To curse this Mad-man, this industrious Fool,
Who labour'd to be wretched: pr'ythee curse me.

VENTIDIUS: No.
ANTONY: Why?
VENTIDIUS: You are too sensible already
Of what y'have done, too conscious of your failings,
And like a Scorpion, whipt by others first
To fury, sting yourself in mad revenge.
I would bring Balm, and pour it in your wounds,
Cure your distemper'd mind, and heal your fortunes.
ANTONY: I know thou would'st.
VENTIDIUS: I will.
ANTONY: Ha, ha, ha, ha.
VENTIDIUS: You laugh.
ANTONY: I do, to see officious love
Give Cordials to the dead.
VENTIDIUS: You would be lost then?
ANTONY: I am.
VENTIDIUS: I say, you are not. Try your fortune.
ANTONY: I have, to th' utmost. Dost thou think me desperate,
Without just cause? No, when I found all lost
Beyond repair, I hid me from the World,
And learnt to scorn it here; which now I do
So heartily, I think it is not worth
The cost of keeping.
VENTIDIUS: *Cæsar* thinks not so:
He'l thank you for the gift he could not take.
You would be kill'd, like *Tully*, would you? do,
Hold out your Throat to *Cæsar*, and dye tamely.
ANTONY: No, I can kill myself; and so resolve.
VENTIDIUS: I can dy with you too, when time shall serve;
But Fortune calls upon us now to live,
To fight, to Conquer.
ANTONY: Sure thou Dream'st, *Ventidius*.
VENTIDIUS: No; 'tis you Dream; you sleep away your hours
In desperate sloth, miscalled *Phylosophy*.
Up, up, for Honour's sake; twelve Legions wait you,
And long to call you Chief: by painful journeys,
I led 'em, patient, both of heat and hunger,
Down from the *Parthian* Marches, to the *Nile*.
'Twill do you good to see their Sun-burnt faces,
Their skar'd cheeks, and chopt hands; there's virtue in 'em,
They'l sell those mangled limbs at dearer rates
Than yon trim Bands can buy.
ANTONY: Where left you them?

VENTIDIUS: I said, in lower *Syria*.

ANTONY: Bring 'em hither;
There may be life in these.

VENTIDIUS: They will not come.

ANTONY: Why did'st thou mock my hopes with promis'd aids,
To double my despair? They'r mutinous.

VENTIDIUS: Most firm and loyal.

ANTONY: Yet they will not march
To succor me. Oh trifler!

VENTIDIUS: They petition
You would make hast to head 'em.

ANTONY: I'm besieg'd.

VENTIDIUS: There's but one way shut up: How came I hither ?

ANTONY: I will not stir.

VENTIDIUS: They would perhaps desire
A better reason.

ANTONY: I have never us'd
My Soldiers to demand a reason of
My actions. Why did they refuse to March?

VENTIDIUS: They said they would not fight for *Cleopatra*.

ANTONY: What was't they said?

VENTIDIUS: They said, they would not fight for *Cleopatra*.
Why should they fight indeed, to make her Conquer,
And make you more a Slave? to gain you Kingdoms,
Which, for a kiss, at your next midnight Feast,
You'l sell to her? then she new names her Jewels,
And calls this Diamond such or such a Tax,
Each Pendant in her ear shall be a Province.

ANTONY: *Ventidius*, I allow your Tongue free licence
On all my other faults; but, on your life,
No word of *Cleopatra*: She deserves
More World's than I can lose.

VENTIDIUS: Behold, you Pow'rs,
To whom you have intrusted Humankind;
See *Europe*, *Africk*, *Asia* put in ballance,
And all weigh'd down by one light worthless Woman!
I think the gods are *Antony*'s, and give
Like Prodigals, this neather World away,
To none but wasteful hands.

ANTONY: You grow presumptuous.

VENTIDIUS: I take the priviledge of plain love to speak.

ANTONY: Plain love! plain arrogance, plain insolence.
Thy Men are Cowards; thou, an envious Traitor;

Who, under seeming honesty, hast vented
The burden of thy rank o'reflowing Gall.
O that thou wert my equal; great in Arms
As the first *Cæsar* was, that I might kill thee
Without a Stain to Honor!

VENTIDIUS: You may kill me;
You have done more already, call'd me Traitor.

ANTONY: Art thou not one?

VENTIDIUS: For showing you your self,
Which none else durst have done; but had I been
That name, which I disdain to speak again,
I needed not have sought your abject fortunes,
Come to partake your fate, to dye with you,
What hindred me t' have led my Conqu'ring Eagles
To fill *Octavius*'s Bands? I could have been
A Traitor then, a glorious happy Traitor,
And not have been so call'd.

ANTONY: Forgive me, Soldier:
I've been too passionate.

VENTIDIUS: You thought me false;
Thought my old age betray'd you: kill me, Sir;
Pray kill me; yet you need not, your unkindness
Has left your Sword no work.

ANTONY: I did not think so;
I said it in my rage: pr'ythee forgive me:
Why did'st thou tempt my anger, by discovery
Of what I would not hear?

VENTIDIUS: No Prince but you,
Could merit that sincerity I us'd,
Nor durst another Man have ventur'd it;
But you, ere Love misled your wandring eyes,
Were sure the chief and best of Human Race,
Fram'd in the very pride and boast of Nature,
So perfect, that the gods who form'd you wonder'd
At their own skill, and cry'd, A lucky hit
Has mended our design. Their envy hindred,
Else you had been immortal, and a pattern,
When Heav'n would work for ostentation sake,
To copy out again.

ANTONY: But *Cleopatra*—
Go on; for I can bear it now.

VENTIDIUS: No more.

ANTONY: Thou dar'st not trust my Passion; but thou may'st:

Thou only lov'st; the rest have flatter'd me.
VENTIDIUS: Heav'n's blessing on your heart, for that kind word.
May I believe you love me? Speak again.
ANTONY: Indeed I do. Speak this, and this, and this.
[*Hugging him.*
Thy praises were unjust; but, I'll deserve 'em,
And yet mend all. Do with me what thou wilt;
Lead me to victory, thou know'st the way.
VENTIDIUS: And, Will you leave this——
ANTONY: Pr'ythee do not curse her,
And I will leave her; though, Heav'n knows, I love
Beyond Life, Conquest, Empire; all, but Honor:
But I will leave her.
VENTIDIUS: That's my Royal Master.
And, Shall we fight?
ANTONY: I warrant thee, old Soldier,
Thou shalt behold me once again in Iron,
And at the head of our old Troops, that beat
The *Parthians*, cry alloud, Come follow me.
VENTIDIUS: O now I hear my Emperor! in that word
Octavius fell. Gods, let me see that day,
And, if I have ten years behind, take all;
I'll thank you for th' exchange.
ANTONY: Oh *Cleopatra*!
VENTIDIUS: Again?
ANTONY: I've done: in that last sigh, she went.
Cæsar shall know what 'tis to force a Lover,
From all he holds most dear.
VENTIDIUS: Methinks you breath
Another soul: Your looks are more Divine;
You speak a Heroe, and you move a God.
ANTONY: O, thou hast fir'd me; my Soul's up in Arms,
And Mans each part about me: once again,
That noble eagerness of fight has seiz'd me;
That eagerness, with which I darted upward
To *Cassius*'s Camp: In vain the steepy Hill
Oppos'd my way; in vain a War of Speares
Sung round my head; and planted all my shield:
I won the Trenches, while my formost Men
Lag'd on the Plain below.
VENTIDIUS: Ye Gods, ye Gods,
For such another hour.
ANTONY: Come on, My Soldier!

Our hearts and armes are still the same: I long
Once more to meet our foes; that Thou and I,
Like Time and Death, marching before our Troops,
May taste fate to 'em; Mowe 'em out a passage,
And, entring where the foremost Squadrons yield,
Begin the noble Harvest of the Field. [*Exeunt.*

ACT II

CLEOPATRA, IRAS, *and* ALEXAS.

CLEOPATRA: What shall I do, or whither shall I turn?
Ventidius has o'rcome, and he will go.
ALEXAS: He goes to fight for you.
CLEOPATRA: Then he wou'd see me, ere he went to fight:
Flatter me not: if once he goes, he's lost:
And all my hopes destroy'd.
ALEXAS: Does this weak passion
Become a Mighty Queen?
CLEOPATRA: I am no Queen;
Is this to be a Queen, to be besieg'd
By yon insulting *Roman*; and to wait
Each hour the Victor's Chain? These ills are small;
For *Antony* is lost, and I can mourn
For nothing else but him. Now come, *Octavius*,
I have no more to lose; prepare thy Bands;
I'm fit to be a Captive: *Antony*
Has taught my mind the fortune of a Slave.
IRAS: Call Reason to assist you.
CLEOPATRA: I have none.
And none would have: my Love's a noble madness,
Which shows the cause deserv'd it. Moderate sorrow
Fits vulgar Love; and for a vulgar Man:
But I have lov'd with such transcendent passion,
I soar'd, at first, quite out of Reasons view,
And now am lost above it—No, I'm proud
'Tis thus: would *Antony* could see me now;
Think you he would not sigh? though he must leave me,
Sure he would sigh; for he is noble-natur'd,
And bears a tender heart: I know him well.
Ah, no, I know him not; I knew him once,
But now 'tis past.

IRAS: Let it be past with you:
Forget him, Madam.
CLEOPATRA: Never, never, *Iras*.
He once was mine; and once, though now 'tis gone,
Leaves a faint Image of possession still.
ALEXAS: Think him unconstant, cruel, and ungrateful.
CLEOPATRA: I cannot: if I could, those thoughts were vain;
Faithless, ungrateful, cruel, though he be,
I still must love him.

Enter CHARMION.

Now, What news my *Charmion*?
Will he be kind? and, Will he not forsake me?
Am I to live, or dye? nay, Do I live?
Or am I dead? for, when he gave his answer,
Fate took the word, and then I liv'd, or dy'd.
CHARMION: I found him, Madam——
CLEOPATRA: A long Speech preparing?
If thou bring'st comfort, haste, and give it me;
For never was more need.
IRAS: I know he loves you.
CLEOPATRA: Had he been kind, her eyes had told me so,
Before her tongue could speak it: now she studies,
To soften what he said; but give me death,
Just as he sent it, *Charmion*, undisguis'd,
And in the words he spoke.
CHARMION: I found him then
Incompass'd round, I think, with Iron Statues,
So mute, so motionless his Soldiers stood,
While awfully he cast his eyes about,
And ev'ry Leaders hopes or fears survey'd:
Methought he look'd resolv'd, and yet not pleas'd.
When he beheld me strugling in the croud,
He blush'd, and bade, make way.
ALEXAS: There's comfort yet.
CHARMION: *Ventidius* fixt his eyes upon my passage,
Severely, as he meant to frown me back,
And sullenly gave place: I told my message,
Just as you gave it, broken and disorder'd;
I numbred in it all your sighs and tears,
And while I mov'd your pitiful request,
That you but only beg'd a last farewel,
He fetch'd an inward groan, and ev'ry time

I nam'd you, sigh'd, as if his heart were breaking,
But shun'd my eyes, and guiltily look'd down;
He seem'd not now that awful *Antony*
Who shook an Arm'd Assembly with his Nod,
But making show as he would rub his eyes,
Disguis'd and blotted out a falling tear.

CLEOPATRA: Did he then weep? and, Was I worth a tear?
If what thou hast to say be not as pleasing,
Tell me no more, but let me dye contented.

CHARMION: He bid me say, He knew himself so well,
He could deny you nothing, if he saw you;
And therefore——

CLEOPATRA: Thou would'st say, he wou'd not see me?

CHARMION: And therefore beg'd you not to use a power,
Which he could ill resist; yet he should ever
Respect you as he ought.

CLEOPATRA: Is that a word
For *Antony* to use to *Cleopatra*?
Oh that faint word, Respect! how I disdain it!
Disdain my self, for loving after it!
He should have kept that word for cold *Octavia.*
Respect is for a Wife: Am I that thing,
That dull insipid lump, without desires,
And without pow'r to give 'em?

ALEXAS: You misjudge;
You see through Love, and that deludes your sight:
As, what is strait, seems crooked through the Water;
But I, who bear my reason undisturb'd,
Can see this *Antony*, this dreaded Man,
A fearful slave, who fain would run away,
And shuns his Master's eyes: if you pursue him,
My life on't, he still drags a chain along,
That needs must clog his flight.

CLEOPATRA: Could I believe thee!——

ALEXAS: By ev'ry circumstance I know he Loves.
True, he's hard prest, by Intrest and by Honor;
Yet he but doubts, and parlyes, and casts out
Many a long look for succor.

CLEOPATRA: He sends word,
He fears to see my face.

ALEXAS: And would you more?
He shows his weakness who declines the Combat;
And you must urge your fortune. Could he speak

More plainly? To my ears, the Message sounds
Come to my rescue, *Cleopatra*, come;
Come, free me from *Ventidius*; from my Tyrant:
See me, and give me a pretence to leave him.
I hear his Trumpets. This way he must pass.
Please you, retire a while; I'll work him first,
That he may bend more easie.

CLEOPATRA: You shall rule me;
But all, I fear, in vain. [*Exit with* CHARMION *and* IRAS.

ALEXAS: I fear so too;
Though I conceal'd my thoughts, to make her bold:
But 'tis our utmost means, and Fate befriend it!
[*Withdraws.*

Enter Lictors *with* Fasces*; one bearing the Eagle; then enter* ANTONY *with* VENTIDIUS, *follow'd by other Commanders.*

ANTONY: *Octavius* is the Minion of blind Chance,
But holds from Virtue nothing.

VENTIDIUS: Has he courage?

ANTONY: But just enough to season him from Coward.
O, 'tis the coldest youth upon a Charge,
The most deliberate fighter! if he ventures
(As in *Illyria* once they say he did
To storm a Town) 'tis when he cannot chuse,
When all the World have fixt their eyes upon him;
And then he lives on that for seven years after,
But, at a close revenge he never fails.

VENTIDIUS: I heard, you challeng'd him.

ANTONY: I did, *Ventidius*.
What think'st thou was his answer? 'twas so tame,——
He said he had more wayes than one to dye;
I had not.

VENTIDIUS: Poor!

ANTONY: He has more wayes than one;
But he would chuse 'em all before that one.

VENTIDIUS: He first would chuse an Ague, or a Fever:

ANTONY: No: it must be an Ague, not a Fever;
He has not warmth enough to dye by that.

VENTIDIUS: Or old Age and a Bed.

ANTONY: Ay, there's his choice.
He would live, like a Lamp, to the last wink,
And crawl upon the utmost verge of life:

O *Hercules*! Why should a Man like this,
Who dares not trust his fate for one great action,
Be all the care of Heav'n? Why should he Lord it
O're Fourscore thousand Men, of whom, each one
Is braver than himself?

VENTIDIUS: You conquer'd for him:
Philippi knows it; there you shar'd with him
That Empire, which your Sword made all your own.

ANTONY: Fool that I was, upon my Eagles Wings
I bore this Wren, till I was tir'd with soaring,
And now he mounts above me.
Good Heav'ns, Is this, is this the Man who braves me?
Who bids my age make way: drives me before him,
To the World's ridge, and sweeps me off like rubbish?

VENTIDIUS: Sir, we lose time; the Troops are mounted all.

ANTONY: Then give the word to March:
I long to leave this Prison of a Town,
To joyn thy Legions; and, in open Field,
Once more to show my face. Lead, my Deliverer.

Enter ALEXAS.

ALEXAS: Great Emperor,
In mighty Arms renown'd above Mankind,
But, in soft pity to th'opprest, a God:
This message sends the mournful *Cleopatra*
To her departing Lord.

VENTIDIUS: Smooth Sycophant!

ALEXAS: A thousand wishes, and ten thousand Prayers,
Millions of blessings wait you to the Wars,
Millions of sighs and tears she sends you too,
And would have sent
As many dear embraces to your Arms,
As many parting kisses to your Lips;
But those, she fears, have weary'd you already.

VENTIDIUS *aside*: False Crocodyle!

ALEXAS: And yet she begs not now, you would not leave her,
That were a wish too mighty for her hopes,
Too presuming for her low Fortune, and your ebbing love,
That were a wish for her more prosp'rous dayes,
Her blooming beauty, and your growing kindness.

ANTONY *aside*: Well, I must Man it out; What would the Queen?

ALEXAS: First, to these noble Warriors, who attend,
Your daring courage in the Chase of Fame,
(Too daring, and too dang'rous for her quiet)
She humbly recommends all she holds dear,
All her own cares and fears, the care of you.
VENTIDIUS: Yes, witness *Actium.*
ANTONY: Let him speak, *Ventidius.*
ALEXAS: You, when his matchless valor bears him forward,
With ardor too Heroick, on his foes,
Fall down, as she would do, before his feet;
Lye in his way, and stop the paths of Death;
Tell him, this God is not invulnerable,
That absent *Cleopatra* bleeds in him;
And, that you may remember her Petition,
She begs you wear these Trifles, as a pawn,
Which, at your wisht return, she will redeem
[*Gives Jewels to the Commanders.*
With all the Wealth of *Ægypt*:
This, to the great *Ventidius* she presents,
Whom she can never count her Enemy,
Because he loves her Lord.
VENTIDIUS: Tell her I'll none on't;
I'm not asham'd of honest Poverty:
Not all the Diamonds of the East can bribe
Ventidius from his faith. I hope to see
These, and the rest of all her sparkling store,
Where they shall more deservingly be plac'd.
ANTONY: And who must wear 'em then?
VENTIDIUS: The wrong'd *Octavia.*
ANTONY: You might have spar'd that word.
VENTIDIUS: And he that Bribe.
ANTONY: But have I no remembrance?
ALEXAS: Yes, a dear one:
Your slave, the Queen——
ANTONY: My Mistress.
ALEXAS: Then your Mistress,
Your Mistress would, she sayes, have sent her Soul,
But that you had long since; she humbly begs
This Ruby bracelet, set with bleeding hearts,
(The emblems of her own) may bind your Arme.
[*Presenting a Bracelet.*
VENTIDIUS: Now, my best Lord, in Honor's name, I ask you,
For Manhood's sake, and for your own dear safety,

Touch not these poyson'd gifts,
Infected by the sender, touch 'em not,
Miriads of blewest Plagues lye underneath 'em,
And more than Aconite has dipt the Silk.

ANTONY: Nay, now you grow too Cynical, *Ventidius.*
A Lady's favors may be worn with honor.
What, to refuse her Bracelet! On my Soul,
When I lye pensive in my Tent alone,
'Twill pass the wakeful hours of Winter nights,
To tell these pretty Beads upon my arm,
To count for every one a soft embrace,
A melting kiss at such and such a time;
And now and then the fury of her love,
When——And what harm's in this?

ALEXAS: None, none my Lord,
But what's to her, that now 'tis past for ever.

ANTONY: *Going to tye it*: We Soldiers are so aukward
—help me tye it.

ALEXAS: In faith, my Lord, we Courtiers too are aukward
In these affairs: so are all Men indeed;
Ev'n I, who am not one. But shall I speak?

ANTONY: Yes, freely.

ALEXAS: Then, my Lord, fair hands alone
Are fit to tye it; she, who sent it, can.

VENTIDIUS: Hell, death; this Eunuch Pandar ruins you.
You will not see her?

[ALEXAS *whispers an Attendant, who goes out.*

ANTONY: But to take my leave.

VENTIDIUS: Then I have wash'd an *Æthiope.* Y'are undone;
Y'are in the Toils; y'are taken; y'are destroy'd:
Her eyes do *Cæsar*'s work.

ANTONY: You fear too soon.
I'm constant to my self: I know my strength;
And yet she shall not think me Barbarous, neither,
Born in the depths of *Africk*: I'm a Roman,
Bred to the Rules of soft humanity.
A guest, and kindly us'd, should bid farewel.

VENTIDIUS: You do not know
How weak you are to her, how much an Infant;
You are not proof against a smile, or glance;
A sigh will quite disarm you.

ANTONY: See, she comes!
Now you shall find your error. Gods, I thank you:

I form'd the danger greater than it was,
And, now 'tis near, 'tis lessen'd.
VENTIDIUS: Mark the end yet.

Enter CLEOPATRA, CHARMION, *and* IRAS.

ANTONY: Well, Madam, we are met.
CLEOPATRA: Is this a Meeting?
Then, we must part?
ANTONY: We must.
CLEOPATRA: Who says we must?
ANTONY: Our own hard fates.
CLEOPATRA: We make those Fates our selves.
ANTONY: Yes, we have made 'em; we have lov'd each other
Into our mutual ruin.
CLEOPATRA: The Gods have seen my Joys with envious eyes;
I have no friends in Heav'n; and all the World,
(As 'twere the bus'ness of Mankind to part us)
Is arm'd against my Love: ev'n you your self
Joyn with the rest; you, you are arm'd against me.
ANTONY: I will be justify'd in all I do
To late Posterity, and therefore hear me.
If I mix a lye
With any truth, reproach me freely with it;
Else, favour me with silence.
CLEOPATRA: You command me,
And I am dumb:
VENTIDIUS: I like this well: he shows Authority.
ANTONY: That I derive my ruin
From you alone——
CLEOPATRA: O Heav'ns! I ruin you!
ANTONY: You promis'd me your silence, and you break it
Ere I have scarce begun.
CLEOPATRA: Well, I obey you.
ANTONY: When I beheld you first, it was in *Ægypt*,
Ere *Cæsar* saw your Eyes; you gave me love,
And were too young to know it; that I setled
Your Father in his Throne, was for your sake,
I left th' acknowledgment for time to ripen.
Cæsar stept in, and with a greedy hand
Pluck'd the green fruit, ere the first blush of red
Yet cleaving to the bough. He was my Lord,
And was, beside, too great for me to rival,
But, I deserv'd you first, though he enjoy'd you.

When, after, I beheld you in *Cilicia*,
An Enemy to *Rome*, I pardon'd you.

CLEOPATRA: I clear'd my self——

ANTONY: Again you break your Promise.
I lov'd you still, and took your weak excuses,
Took you into my bosome, stain'd by *Cæsar*,
And not half mine: I went to *Ægypt* with you
And hid me from the business of the World,
Shut out enquiring Nations from my sight,
To give whole years to you.

VENTIDIUS: Yes, to your shame be't spoken. [*Aside*.

ANTONY: How I lov'd
Witness ye Dayes and Nights, and all ye hours,
That Danc'd away with Down upon your Feet,
As all your bus'ness were to count my passion.
One day past by, and nothing saw but Love;
Another came, and still 'twas only Love:
The Suns were weary'd out with looking on,
And I untyr'd with loving.
I saw you ev'ry day, and all the day;
And ev'ry day was still but as the first:
So eager was I still to see you more.

VENTIDIUS: 'Tis all too true.

ANTONY: *Fulvia*, my Wife, grew jealous,
As she indeed had reason; rais'd a War
In *Italy*, to call me back.

VENTIDIUS: But yet
You went not.

ANTONY: While within your arms I lay,
The World fell mouldering from my hands each hour,
And left me scarce a grasp (I thank your love for't.)

VENTIDIUS: Well push'd: that last was home.

CLEOPATRA: Yet may I speak?

ANTONY: If I have urg'd a falsehood, yes; else, not.
Your silence says I have not. *Fulvia* dy'd;
(Pardon, you gods, with my unkindness dy'd)
To set the World at Peace, I took *Octavia*,
This Cæsar's Sister; in her pride of youth,
And flow'r of Beauty did I wed that Lady,
Whom blushing I must praise, because I left her.
You call'd; my Love obey'd the fatal summons:
This rais'd the Roman Arms; the Cause was yours.
I would have fought by Land, where I was stronger;

You hindred it: yet, when I fought at Sea,
Forsook me fighting; and (Oh stain to Honor!
Oh lasting shame!) I knew not that I fled;
But fled to follow you.

VENTIDIUS: What haste she made to hoist her purple Sails!
And, to appear magnificent in flight,
Drew half our strength away.

ANTONY: All this you caus'd.
And, Would you multiply more ruins on me?
This honest Man, my best, my only friend,
Has gather'd up the Shipwrack of my Fortunes;
Twelve Legions I have left, my last recruits,
And you have watch'd the news, and bring your eyes
To seize them too. If you have aught to answer,
Now speak, you have free leave.

ALEXAS *aside*: She stands confounded:
Despair is in her eyes.

VENTIDIUS: Now lay a Sigh i' th' way, to stop his passage:
Prepare a Tear, and bid it for his Legions;
'Tis like they shall be sold.

CLEOPATRA: How shall I plead my cause, when you, my Judge,
Already have condemn'd me? Shall I bring
The Love you bore me for my Advocate?
That now is turn'd against me, that destroys me;
For, love once past, is, at the best, forgotten;
But oftner sours to hate: 'twill please my Lord
To ruine me, and therefore I'll be guilty.
But, could I once have thought it would have pleas'd you,
That you would pry, with narrow searching eyes
Into my faults, severe to my destruction.
And watching all advantages with care,
That serve to make me wretched? Speak, my Lord,
For I end here. Though I deserve this usage,
Was it like you to give it?

ANTONY: O you wrong me,
To think I sought this parting, or desir'd
To accuse you more than what will clear my self,
And justifie this breach.

CLEOPATRA: Thus low I thank you.
And, since my innocence will not offend,
I shall not blush to own it.

VENTIDIUS: After this,
I think she'll blush at nothing.

CLEOPATRA: You seem griev'd,
(And therein you are kind) that *Cæsar* first
Enjoy'd my love, though you deserv'd it better:
I grieve for that, my Lord, much more than you;
For, had I first been yours, it would have sav'd
My second choice: I never had been his,
And ne'r had been but yours. But *Cæsar* first,
You say, possess'd my love. Not so, my Lord:
He first possess'd my Person; you my Love:
Cæsar lov'd me; but I lov'd *Antony*.
If I endur'd him after, 'twas because
I judg'd it due to the first name of Men;
And, half constrain'd, I gave, as to a Tyrant,
What he would take by force.

VENTIDIUS: O Syren! Syren!
Yet grant that all the love she boasts were true,
Has she not ruin'd you? I still urge that,
The fatal consequence.

CLEOPATRA: The consequence indeed,
For I dare challenge him, my greatest foe,
To say it was design'd: 'tis true, I lov'd you,
And kept you far from an uneasie Wife,
(Such *Fulvia* was.)
Yes, but he'll say, you left *Octavia* for me;——
And, can you blame me to receive that love,
Which quitted such desert, for worthless me?
How often have I wished some other *Cæsar*,
Great as the first, and as the second young,
Would court my Love to be refus'd for you!

VENTIDIUS: Words, words; but *Actium*, Sir, remember *Actium*.

CLEOPATRA: Ev'n there, I dare his malice. True, I Counsel'd
To fight at Sea; but, I betray'd you not.
I fled; but not to the Enemy. 'Twas fear;
Would I had been a Man, not to have fear'd,
For none would then have envy'd me your friendship,
Who envy me your Love.

ANTONY: We're both unhappy:
If nothing else, yet our ill fortune parts us.
Speak; would you have me perish, by my stay?

CLEOPATRA: If as a friend you ask my Judgment, go;
If as a Lover, stay. If you must perish:
'Tis a hard word; but stay.

VENTIDIUS: See now th' effects of her so boasted love!

She strives to drag you down to ruine with her:
But, could she scape without you, oh how soon
Would she let go her hold, and haste to shore,
And never look behind!

CLEOPATRA: Then judge my love by this.

[*Giving* ANTONY *a Writing.*

Could I have born
A life or death, a happiness or woe
From yours divided, this had giv'n me means.

ANTONY: By *Hercules*, the Writing of *Octavius*!
I know it well: 'tis that Proscribing hand,
Young as it was, that led the way to mine,
And left me but the second place in Murder.—
See, see, *Ventidius*! here he offers *Ægypt*,
And joyns all *Syria* to it, as a present,
So, in requital, she forsake my fortunes,
And joyn her Arms with his.

CLEOPATRA: And yet you leave me!
You leave me, *Antony*; and, yet I love you,
Indeed I do: I have refus'd a Kingdom,
That is a Trifle;
For I could part with life; with any thing,
But onely you. O let me dye but with you!
Is that a hard request?

ANTONY: Next living with you,
'Tis all that Heav'n can give.

ALEXAS *aside*: He melts; We conquer.

CLEOPATRA: No: you shall go: your Int'rest calls you hence;
Yes; your dear interest pulls too strong, for these
Weak Arms to hold you here.—— [*Takes his hand.*
Go; leave me, Soldier;
(For you're no more a Lover:) leave me dying:
Push me all pale and panting from your bosome,
And, when your March begins, let one run after
Breathless almost for Joy; and cry, she's dead:
The Souldiers shout; you then perhaps may sigh,
And muster all your *Roman* Gravity;
Ventidius chides; and strait your Brow cleares up,
As I had never been.

ANTONY: Gods, 'tis too much; too much for Man to bear!

CLEOPATRA: What is't for me then,
A weak forsaken Woman, and a Lover?——
Here let me breathe my last: envy me not

This minute in your Armes: I'll dye apace:
As fast as ere I can; and end your trouble.

ANTONY: Dye! rather let me perish: loos'n'd Nature
Leap from its hinges. Sink the props of Heaven,
And fall the Skyes to crush the neather World.
My Eyes, my Soul my All!—— [*Embraces her.*

VENTIDIUS: And what's this Toy;
In ballance with your fortune, Honor, Fame?

ANTONY: What is't, *Ventidius*? it out-weighs 'em all;
Why, we have more than conquer'd *Cæsar* now:
My Queen's not only Innocent, but Loves me.
This, this is she who drags me down to ruin!
But, could she scape without me, with what haste
Would she let slip her hold, and make to shore,
And never look behind!
Down on thy knees, Blasphemer as thou art,
And ask forgiveness of wrong'd Innocence.

VENTIDIUS: I'll rather dye, than take it. Will you go?

ANTONY: Go! Whither? go from all that's excellent!
Faith, Honor, Virtue, all good things forbid,
That I should go from her, who sets my love
Above the price of Kingdoms. Give, you Gods,
Give to your Boy, your *Cæsar*,
This Rattle of a Globe to play withal,
This Gu-gau World, and put him cheaply off:
I'll not be pleas'd with less than *Cleopatra*.

CLEOPATRA: She's wholly yours. My heart's so full of joy,
That I shall do some wild extravagance
Of Love, in publick; and the foolish World,
Which knows not tenderness, will think me Mad.

VENTIDIUS: O Women! Women! Women! all the gods
Have not such pow'r of doing good to Man,
As you of doing harm. [*Exit.*

ANTONY: Our Men are Arm'd.
Unbar the Gate that looks to *Cæsar*'s Camp;
I would revenge the Treachery he meant me:
And long security makes Conquest easie.
I'm eager to return before I go;
For, all the pleasures I have known, beat thick
On my remembrance: how I long for night!
That both the sweets of mutual love may try,
And once Triumph o're *Cæsar* [ere] we dye. [*Exeunt.*

ACT III

At one door, Enter CLEOPATRA, CHARMION, IRAS, *and* ALEXAS, *a Train of* Ægyptians: *at the other,* ANTONY *and* Romans. *The entrance on both sides is prepar'd by Musick; the Trumpets first sounding on* ANTONY'S *part: then answer'd by Timbrels, &c. on* CLEOPATRA'S. CHARMION *and* IRAS *hold a Laurel Wreath betwixt them. A Dance of* Ægyptians. *After the Ceremony,* CLEOPATRA *crowns* ANTONY.

ANTONY: I thought how those white arms would fold me in,
And strain me close, and melt me into love;
So pleas'd with that sweet Image, I sprung forwards,
And added all my strength to every blow.

CLEOPATRA: Come to me, come, my Soldier, to my Arms,
You've been too long away from my embraces;
But, when I have you fast, and all my own,
With broken murmurs, and with amorous sighs,
I'll say, you were unkind, and punish you,
And mark you red with many an eager kiss.

ANTONY: My Brighter *Venus*!

CLEOPATRA: O my greater *Mars*!

ANTONY: Thou joinst us well, my Love!
Suppose me come from the *Phlegræan* Plains,
Where gasping gyants lay, cleft by my Sword:
And Mountain tops par'd off each other blow,
To bury those I slew: receive me, goddess:
Let *Cæsar* spread his subtile Nets, like Vulcan,
In thy embraces I would be beheld
By Heav'n and Earth at once:
And make their envy what they meant their sport.
Let those who took us blush; I would love on
With awful State, regardless of their frowns,
As their superior god.
There's no satiety of Love, in thee:
Enjoy'd, thou still art new; perpetual Spring
Is in thy armes; the ripen'd fruit but falls,
And blossoms rise to fill its empty place;
And I grow rich by giving.

Enter VENTIDIUS, *and stands apart.*

ALEXAS: O, now the danger's past, your General comes.
He joyns not in your joys, nor minds your Triumphs;

But, with contracted brows, looks frowning on,
As envying your Success.

ANTONY: Now, on my Soul, he loves me; truely loves me;
He never flatter'd me in any vice,
But awes me with his virtue: ev'n this minute
Methinks he has a right of chiding me.
Lead to the Temple: I'll avoid his presence;
It checks too strong upon me. [*Exeunt the rest.*

[*As* ANTONY *is going,* VENTIDIUS *pulls him by the robe.*

VENTIDIUS: Emperor.

ANTONY *looking back*: 'Tis the old argument; I pr'ythee, spare me.

VENTIDIUS: But this one hearing, Emperor.

ANTONY: Let go
My robe; or, by my Father *Hercules*——

VENTIDIUS: By *Hercules* his Father, that's yet greater,
I bring you somewhat you would wish to know.

ANTONY: Thou see'st we are observ'd; attend me here,
And I'll return. [*Exit.*

VENTIDIUS: I'm waining in his favor, yet I love him;
I love this Man, who runs to meet his ruine;
And, sure the gods, like me, are fond of him:
His Virtues lye so mingled with his Crimes,
As would confound their choice to punish one,
And not reward the other.

Enter ANTONY.

ANTONY: We can conquer,
You see, without your aid.
We have dislodg'd their Troops,
They look on us at distance, and, like Curs
'Scap'd from the Lion's paws, they bay far off,
And lick their wounds, and faintly threaten War.
Five thousand *Romans* with their faces upward,
Lye breathless on the Plain.

VENTIDIUS: 'Tis well: and he
Who lost 'em, could have spar'd Ten thousand more.
Yet if, by this advantage, you could gain
An easier Peace, while *Cæsar* doubts the Chance
Of Arms!——

ANTONY: O think not on't, *Ventidius*!
The Boy pursues my ruin, he'll no peace:
His malice is considerate in advantage;

O, he's the coolest Murderer, so stanch,
He kills, and keeps his temper.

VENTIDIUS: Have you no friend
In all his Army, who has power to move him,
Mecænas, or *Agrippa* might do much.

ANTONY: They're both too deep in *Cæsar*'s interests.
We'll work it out by dint of Sword, or perish.

VENTIDIUS: Fain I would find some other.

ANTONY: Thank thy love.
Some four or five such Victories as this,
Will save thy farther pains.

VENTIDIUS: Expect no more; *Cæsar* is on his Guard:
I know, Sir, you have conquer'd against ods;
But still you draw Supplies from one poor Town,
And of *Ægyptians*: he has all the World,
And, at his back, Nations come pouring in,
To fill the gaps you make. Pray think again.

ANTONY: Why dost thou drive me from my self, to search
For Forreign aids? to hunt my memory,
And range all o're a waste and barren place
To find a Friend? the wretched have no Friends—
Yet I had one, the bravest youth of *Rome*,
Whom *Cæsar* loves beyond the love of Women;
He could resolve his mind, as Fire does Wax,
From that hard rugged Image, melt him down,
And mould him in what softer form he pleas'd.

VENTIDIUS: Him would I see; that man of all the world:
Just such a one we want.

ANTONY: He lov'd me too,
I was his Soul; he liv'd not but in me:
We were so clos'd within each others brests,
The rivets were not found that join'd us first.
That does not reach us yet: we were so mixt,
As meeting streams, both to our selves were lost;
We were one mass; we could not give or take,
But from the same; for he was I, I he.

VENTIDIUS *aside*: He moves as I would wish him.

ANTONY: After this,
I need not tell his name: 'twas *Dollabella*.

VENTIDIUS: He's now in *Cæsar*'s Camp.

ANTONY: No matter where,
Since he's no longer mine. He took unkindly
That I forbade him *Cleopatra*'s sight;

Because I fear'd he lov'd her: he confest
He had a warmth, which, for my sake, he stifled;
For 'twere impossible that two, so one,
Should not have lov'd the same. When he departed,
He took no leave; and that confirm'd my thoughts.

VENTIDIUS: It argues that he lov'd you more than her,
Else he had staid; but he perceiv'd you jealous,
And would not grieve his friend: I know he loves you.

ANTONY: I should have seen him then ere now.

VENTIDIUS: Perhaps
He has thus long been lab'ring for your peace.

ANTONY: Would he were here.

VENTIDIUS: Would you believe he lov'd you?
I read your answer in your eyes; you would.
Not to conceal it longer, he has sent
A Messenger from *Cæsar*'s camp, with Letters.

ANTONY: Let him appear.

VENTIDIUS: I'll bring him instantly. [*Exit* VENTIDIUS.

Re-enters immediately with DOLLABELLA.

ANTONY: 'Tis he himself! himself, by holy Friendship!
[*Runs to embrace him.*
Art thou return'd at last, my better half?
Come, give me all my self.
Let me not live,
If the young Bridegroom, longing for his night,
Was ever half so fond.

DOLLABELLA: I must be silent; for my Soul is busie
About a nobler work: she's new come home,
Like a long-absent man, and wanders o'er
Each room, a stranger to her own, to look
If all be safe.

ANTONY: Thou hast what's left of me.
For I am now so sunk from what I was,
Thou find'st me at my lowest water-mark.
The Rivers that ran in, and rais'd my fortunes,
Are all dry'd up, or take another course:
What I have left is from my native Spring;
I've still a heart that swells, in scorn of fate,
And lifts me to my banks.

DOLLABELLA: Still you are Lord of all the World to me.

ANTONY: Why, then I yet am so; for thou art all.

If I had any joy when thou wert absent,
I grudg'd it to myself; methought I robb'd
Thee of thy part. But, Oh my *Dollabella*!
Thou hast beheld me other than I am.
Hast thou not seen my morning Chambers fill'd
With Scepter'd Slaves, who waited to salute me:
With Eastern Monarchs, who forgot the Sun,
To worship my uprising? menial Kings
Ran coursing up and down my Palace-yard,
Stood silent in my presence, watch'd my eyes,
And, at my least command, all started out
Like Racers to the Goal.

DOLLABELLA: Slaves to your fortune.

ANTONY: Fortune is *Cæsar*'s now; and what am I?

VENTIDIUS: What you have made your self; I will not flatter.

ANTONY: Is this friendly done?

DOLLABELLA: Yes, when his end is so, I must join with him;
Indeed I must, and yet you must not chide:
Why am I else your friend?

ANTONY: Take heed, young man,
How thou upbraid'st my love: the Queen has eyes,
And thou too hast a Soul. Canst thou remember
When, swell'd with hatred, thou beheld'st her first
As accessary to thy Brothers death?

DOLLABELLA: Spare my remembrance; 'twas a guilty day,
And still the blush hangs here.

ANTONY: To clear her self,
For sending him no aid, she came from *Egypt*.
Her Gally down the Silver *Cydnos* row'd,
The Tackling Silk, the Streamers wav'd with Gold,
The gentle Winds were lodg'd in Purple sails:
Her Nymphs, like *Nereids*, round her Couch, were plac'd;
Where she, another Sea-born *Venus*, lay.

DOLLABELLA: No more: I would not hear it.

ANTONY: O, you must!
She lay, and leant her cheek upon her hand,
And cast a look so languishingly sweet,
As if, secure of all beholders hearts,
Neglecting she could take 'em: Boys, like *Cupids*,
Stood fanning, with their painted wings, the winds
That plaid about her face: but if she smil'd,
A darting glory seem'd to blaze abroad:
That mens desiring eyes were never weary'd;

But hung upon the object: to soft Flutes
The Silver Oars kept time; and while they plaid,
The hearing gave new pleasure to the sight;
And both to thought: 'twas Heav'n, or somewhat more;
For she so charm'd all hearts, that gazing crowds
Stood panting on the shore, and wanted breath
To give their welcome voice.
Then, *Dollabella*, where was then thy Soul?
Was not thy fury quite disarm'd with wonder?
Didst thou not shrink behind me from those eyes,
And whisper in my ear, Oh tell her not
That I accus'd her of my Brothers death?

DOLLABELLA: And should my weakness be a plea for yours?
Mine was an age when love might be excus'd,
When kindly warmth, and when my springing youth
Made it a debt to Nature. Yours——

VENTIDIUS: Speak boldly.
Yours, he would say, in your declining age,
When no more heat was left but what you forc'd,
When all the sap was needful for the Trunk,
When it went down, then you constrain'd the course,
And robb'd from Nature, to supply desire;
In you (I would not use so harsh a word)
But 'tis plain dotage.

ANTONY: Ha!

DOLLABELLA: 'Twas urg'd too home.
But yet the loss was private that I made;
'Twas but my self I lost: I lost no Legions;
I had no World to lose, no peoples love.

ANTONY: This from a friend?

DOLLABELLA: Yes, *Antony*, a true one;
A friend so tender, that each word I speak
Stabs my own heart, before it reach your ear.
O, judge me not less kind because I chide:
To *Cæsar* I excuse you.

ANTONY: O ye Gods!
Have I then liv'd to be excus'd to *Cæsar*?

DOLLABELLA: As to your equal.

ANTONY: Well, he's but my equal:
While I wear this, he never shall be more.

DOLLABELLA: I bring Conditions from him.

ANTONY: Are they Noble?
Methinks thou shouldst not bring 'em else; yet he

Is full of deep dissembling; knows no Honour,
Divided from his int'rest. Fate mistook him;
For Nature meant him for an Usurer,
He's fit indeed to buy, not conquer Kingdoms.

VENTIDIUS: Then, granting this,
What pow'r was theirs who wrought so hard a temper
To honourable Terms!

ANTONY: It was my *Dollabella*, or some God.

DOLLABELLA: Not I; nor yet *Mecænas*, nor *Agrippa*:
They were your Enemies; and I a Friend
Too weak alone; yet 'twas a *Roman*'s deed.

ANTONY: 'Twas like a *Roman* done: show me that man
Who has preserv'd my life, my love, my honour;
Let me but see his face.

VENTIDIUS: That task is mine,
And, Heav'n, thou know'st how pleasing.

[*Exit* VENTIDIUS.

DOLLABELLA: You'll remember
To whom you stand oblig'd?

ANTONY: When I forget it,
Be thou unkind, and that's my greatest curse.
My Queen shall thank him too.

DOLLABELLA: I fear she will not.

ANTONY: But she shall do't: the Queen, my *Dollabella*!
Hast thou not still some grudgings of thy Fever?

DOLLABELLA: I would not see her lost.

ANTONY: When I forsake her,
Leave me, my better Stars; for she has truth
Beyond her beauty. *Cæsar* tempted her,
At no less price than Kingdoms, to betray me;
But she resisted all: and yet thou chid'st me
For loving her too well. Could I do so?

DOLLABELLA: Yes; there's my reason.

Re-enter VENTIDIUS, *with* OCTAVIA, *leading* ANTONY'S *two little Daughters.*

ANTONY: Where?—*Octavia* there! [*Starting back.*

VENTIDIUS: What, is she poyson to you? a Disease?
Look on her, view her well; and those she brings:
Are they all strangers to your eyes? has Nature
No secret call, no whisper they are yours?

DOLLABELLA: For shame, my Lord, if not for love, receive 'em

With kinder eyes. If you confess a man,
Meet 'em, embrace 'em, bid 'em welcome to you.
Your arms should open, ev'n without your knowledge,
To clasp 'em in; your feet should turn to wings,
To bear you to 'em; and your eyes dart out,
And aim a kiss ere you could reach the lips.

ANTONY: I stood amaz'd to think how they came hither.

VENTIDIUS: I sent for 'em; I brought 'em in, unknown
To *Cleopatra*'s guards.

DOLLABELLA: Yet are you cold?

OCTAVIA: Thus long I have attended for my welcome;
Which, as a stranger, sure I might expect.
Who am I?

ANTONY: *Cæsar*'s Sister.

OCTAVIA: That's unkind!
Had I been nothing more than *Cæsar*'s Sister,
Know, I had still remain'd in *Cæsar*'s Camp;
But your *Octavia*, your much injur'd Wife,
Tho' banish'd from your Bed, driv'n from your House,
In spight of *Cæsar*'s Sister, still is yours.
'Tis true, I have a heart disdains your coldness,
And prompts me not to seek what you should offer;
But a Wife's Virtue still surmounts that pride:
I come to claim you as my own; to show
My duty first, to ask, nay beg, your kindness:
Your hand, my Lord; 'tis mine, and I will have it.
[*Taking his hand.*

VENTIDIUS: Do, take it, thou deserv'st it.

DOLLABELLA: On my Soul,
And so she does: she's neither too submissive,
Nor yet too haughty; but so just a mean,
Shows, as it ought, a Wife and *Roman* too.

ANTONY: I fear, *Octavia*, you have begg'd my life.

OCTAVIA: Begg'd it, my Lord?

ANTONY: Yes, begg'd it, my Ambassadress,
Poorly and basely begg'd it of your Brother.

OCTAVIA: Poorly and basely I could never beg;
Nor could my Brother grant.

ANTONY: Shall I, who, to my kneeling Slave, could say,
Rise up, and be a King; shall I fall down
And cry, Forgive me, *Cæsar*? shall I set
A Man, my Equal, in the place of *Jove*,
As he could give me being? No; that word,

Forgive, would choke me up,
And die upon my tongue.

DOLLABELLA: You shall not need it.

ANTONY: I will not need it. Come, you've all betray'd me:
My friend too! to receive some vile conditions.
My Wife has bought me, with her prayers and tears;
And now I must become her branded Slave:
In every peevish mood she will upbraid
The life she gave: if I but look awry,
She cries, I'll tell my Brother.

OCTAVIA: My hard fortune
Subjects me still to your unkind mistakes.
But the Conditions I have brought are such
You need not blush to take: I love your Honour.
Because 'tis mine; it never shall be said
Octavia's Husband was her Brothers Slave.
Sir, you are free; free, ev'n from her you loath;
For, tho' my Brother bargains for your love,
Makes me the price and cement of your peace,
I have a Soul like yours; I cannot take
Your love as alms, nor beg what I deserve.
I'll tell my Brother we are reconcil'd;
He shall draw back his Troops, and you shall march
To rule the East: I may be dropt at *Athens*;
No matter where, I never will complain,
But only keep the barren Name of Wife,
And rid you of the trouble.

VENTIDIUS: Was ever such a strife of sullen Honour!
Both scorn to be oblig'd.

DOLLABELLA: O, she has toucht him in the tender'st part;
See how he reddens with despight and shame
To be out-done in Generosity!

VENTIDIUS: See how he winks! how he dries up a tear,
That fain would fall!

ANTONY: *Octavia*, I have heard you, and must praise
The greatness of your Soul;
But cannot yield to what you have propos'd:
For I can ne'er be conquer'd but by love;
And you do all for duty. You would free me,
And would be dropt at *Athens*; was't not so?

OCTAVIA: It was, my Lord.

ANTONY: Then I must be oblig'd
To one who loves me not, who, to her self,

May call me thankless and ungrateful Man:
I'll not endure it, no.

VENTIDIUS: I'm glad it pinches there.

OCTAVIA: Would you triumph o'er poor *Octavia*'s Virtue?
That pride was all I had to bear me up;
That you might think you ow'd me for your life,
And ow'd it to my duty, not my love.
I have been injur'd, and my haughty Soul
Could brook but ill the Man who slights my Bed.

ANTONY: Therefore you love me not.

OCTAVIA: Therefore, my Lord,
I should not love you.

ANTONY: Therefore you wou'd leave me?

OCTAVIA: And therefore I should leave you—if I could.

DOLLABELLA: Her Souls too great, after such injuries,
To say she loves; and yet she lets you see it.
Her modesty and silence plead her cause.

ANTONY: O, *Dollabella*, which way shall I turn?
I find a secret yielding in my Soul;
But *Cleopatra*, who would die with me,
Must she be left? pity pleads for *Octavia*;
But does it not plead more for *Cleopatra*?

VENTIDIUS: Justice and Pity both plead for *Octavia*;
For *Cleopatra*, neither.
One would be ruin'd with you; but she first
Had ruin'd you: the other, you have ruin'd,
And yet she would preserve you.
In every thing their merits are unequal.

ANTONY: O, my distracted Soul!

OCTAVIA: Sweet Heav'n compose it.
Come, come, my Lord, if I can pardon you,
Methinks you should accept it. Look on these;
Are they not yours? or stand they thus neglected
As they are mine? go to him, Children, go;
Kneel to him, take him by the hand, speak to him;
For you may speak, and he may own you too,
Without a blush; and so he cannot all
His Children: go, I say, and pull him to me,
And pull him to your selves, from that bad Woman.
You, *Agrippina*, hang upon his arms;
And you, *Antonia*, clasp about his waste:
If he will shake you off, if he will dash you

Against the Pavement, you must bear it, Children;
For you are mine, and I was born to suffer.
[*Here the Children go to him, &c.*

VENTIDIUS: Was ever sight so moving! Emperor!
DOLLABELLA: Friend!
OCTAVIA: Husband!
BOTH CHILDREN: Father!
ANTONY: I am vanquish'd: take me,
Octavia; take me, Children; share me all.
(*Embracing them.*)
I've been a thriftless Debtor to your loves,
And run out much, in riot, from your stock;
But all shall be amended.
OCTAVIA: O blest hour!
DOLLABELLA: O happy change!
VENTIDIUS: My joy stops at my tongue;
But it has found two chanels here for one,
And bubbles out above.
ANTONY *to* OCTAVIA: This is thy Triumph; lead me where thou wilt;
Ev'n to thy Brothers Camp.
OCTAVIA: All there are yours.

Enter ALEXAS *hastily.*

ALEXAS: The Queen, my Mistress, Sir, and yours——
ANTONY: 'Tis past. *Octavia*, you shall stay this night; To-morrow, *Cæsar* and we are one.
[*Exeunt leading* OCTAVIA. DOLLABELLA *and the Children follow.*
VENTIDIUS: There's news for you; run,
My officious Eunuch,
Be sure to be the first; haste foreward:
Haste, my dear Eunuch, haste. [*Exit.*
ALEXAS: This downright fighting Fool, this thick-scull'd Hero,
This blunt unthinking Instrument of death,
With plain dull Virtue has out-gone my Wit:
Pleasure forsook my early'st Infancy;
The luxury of others robb'd my Cradle,
And ravish'd thence the promise of a Man:
Cast out from Nature, disinherited
Of what her meanest Children claim by kind;
Yet, greatness kept me from contempt: that's gone.
Had *Cleopatra* follow'd my advice,

Then he had been betray'd, who now forsakes.
She dies for love; but she has known its joys:
Gods, is this just, that I, who know no joys,
Must die, because she loves?

Enter CLEOPATRA, CHARMION, IRAS, *Train.*

Oh, Madam, I have seen what blasts my eyes!
Octavia's here!

CLEOPATRA: Peace with that Raven's note.
I know it too; and now am in
The pangs of death.

ALEXAS: You are no more a Queen;
Egypt is lost.

CLEOPATRA: What tell'st thou me of *Egypt*?
My Life, my Soul is lost! *Octavia* has him!
O fatal name to *Cleopatra*'s love!
My kisses, my embraces now are hers;
While I——But thou hast seen my Rival; speak,
Does she deserve this blessing? Is she fair,
Bright as a Goddess? and is all perfection
Confin'd to her? It is. Poor I was made
Of that course matter, which, when she was finish'd,
The Gods threw by, for rubbish.

ALEXAS: She's indeed a very Miracle.

CLEOPATRA: Death to my hopes, a Miracle!

ALEXAS *bowing*: A Miracle;
I mean of Goodness; for in Beauty, Madam,
You make all wonders cease.

CLEOPATRA: I was too rash:
Take this in part of recompense. But, Oh, [*Giving a Ring.*
I fear thou flatter'st me.

CHARMION: She comes! she's here!

IRAS: Flie, Madam, *Cæsar*'s Sister!

CLEOPATRA: Were she the Sister of the Thund'rer *Jove*,
And bore her Brothers Lightning in her eyes,
Thus would I face my Rival.

[*Meets* OCTAVIA *with* VENTIDIUS. OCTAVIA *bears up to her. Their Trains come up on either side.*

OCTAVIA: I need not ask if you are *Cleopatra*,
Your haughty carriage——

CLEOPATRA: Shows I am a Queen:
Nor need I ask you who you are.

OCTAVIA: A *Roman*:
A name that makes, and can unmake a Queen.
CLEOPATRA: Your Lord, the Man who serves me, is a *Roman.*
OCTAVIA: He was a *Roman*, till he lost that name
To be a Slave in *Egypt*; but I come
To free him thence.
CLEOPATRA: Peace, peace, my Lover's *Juno*.
When he grew weary of that Houshold-Clog,
He chose my easier bonds.
OCTAVIA: I wonder not
Your bonds are easie; you have long been practis'd
In that lascivious art: he's not the first
For whom you spread your snares: let *Cæsar* witness.
CLEOPATRA: I lov'd not *Cæsar*; 'twas but gratitude
I paid his love: the worst your malice can,
Is but to say the greatest of Mankind
Has been my Slave. The next, but far above him
In my esteem, is he whom Law calls yours,
But whom his love made mine.
OCTAVIA *coming up close to her*: I would view nearer
That face, which has so long usurp'd my right,
To find th' inevitable charms, that catch
Mankind so sure, that ruin'd my dear Lord.
CLEOPATRA: O, you do well to search; for had you known
But half these charms, you had not lost his heart.
OCTAVIA: Far be their knowledge from a *Roman* lady,
Far from a modest Wife. Shame of our Sex,
Dost thou not blush, to own those black endearments
That make sin pleasing?
CLEOPATRA: You may blush, who want 'em.
If bounteous Nature, if indulgent Heav'n
Have giv'n me charms to please the bravest Man;
Should I not thank 'em? should I be asham'd,
And not be proud? I am, that he has lov'd me;
And, when I love not him, Heav'n change this Face
For one like that.
OCTAVIA: Thou lov'st him not so well.
CLEOPATRA: I love him better, and deserve him more.
OCTAVIA: You do not; cannot: you have been his ruine.
Who made him cheap at *Rome*, but *Cleopatra*?
Who made him scorn'd abroad, but *Cleopatra*?
At *Actium*, who betray'd him? *Cleopatra*.

Who made his Children Orphans, and poor me
A wretched Widow? only *Cleopatra*?

CLEOPATRA: Yet she who loves him best is *Cleopatra*.
If you have suffer'd, I have suffer'd more.
You bear the specious Title of a Wife,
To guild your Cause, and draw the pitying World
To favour it: the World contemns poor me;
For I have lost my Honour, lost my Fame,
And stain'd the glory of my Royal House,
And all to bear the branded Name of Mistress.
There wants but life, and that too I would lose
For him I love.

OCTAVIA: Be't so then; take thy wish. [*Exit* cum suis.

CLEOPATRA: And 'tis my wish,
Now he is lost for whom alone I liv'd.
My sight grows dim, and every object dances,
And swims before me, in the maze of death.
My spirits, while they were oppos'd, kept up;
They could not sink beneath a Rivals scorn:
But now she's gone they faint.

ALEXAS: Mine have had leisure
To recollect their strength, and furnish counsel,
To ruine her, who else must ruine you.

CLEOPATRA: Vain Promiser!
Lead me, my *Charmion*; nay, your hand too, *Iras*.
My grief has weight enough to sink you both.
Conduct me to some solitary Chamber,
And draw the Curtains round;
Then leave me to my self, to take alone
My fill of grief:
There I till death will his unkindness weep:
As harmless Infants moan themselves asleep. [*Exeunt*.

ACT IV

ANTONY, DOLLABELLA.

DOLLABELLA: Why would you shift it from your self, on me?
Can you not tell her you must part?

ANTONY: I cannot.
I could pull out an eye, and bid it go,
And t'other should not weep. Oh, *Dollabella*,

How many deaths are in this word *Depart!*
I dare not trust my tongue to tell her so:
One look of hers, would thaw me into tears
And I should melt till I were lost agen.

DOLLABELLA: Then let *Ventidius*;
He's rough by nature.

ANTONY: Oh, he'll speak too harshly;
He'll kill her with the news: Thou, only thou.

DOLLABELLA: Nature has cast me in so soft a mould,
That but to hear a story feign'd for pleasure
Of some sad Lovers death, moistens my eyes,
And robs me of my Manhood.—I should speak
So faintly; with such fear to grieve her heart,
She'd not believe it earnest.

ANTONY: Therefore; therefore
Thou only, thou art fit: think thy self me,
And when thou speak'st (but let it first be long)
Take off the edge from every sharper sound,
And let our parting be as gently made
As other Loves begin: wilt thou do this?

DOLLABELLA: What you have said, so sinks into my Soul,
That, if I must speak, I shall speak just so.

ANTONY: I leave you then to your sad task: Farewel.
I sent her word to meet you.
(*Goes to the door, and comes back.*)
I forgot;
Let her be told, I'll make her peace with mine:
Her Crown and Dignity shall be preserv'd,
If I have pow'r with *Cæsar*.——O, be sure
To think on that.

DOLLABELLA: Fear not, I will remember.
[ANTONY *goes again to the door, and comes back.*

ANTONY: And tell her, too, how much I was constrain'd;
I did not this, but with extreamest force:
Desire her not to hate my memory,
For I still cherish hers;——insist on that.

DOLLABELLA: Trust me, I'll not forget it.

ANTONY: Then that's all. (*Goes out, and returns again.*)
Wilt thou forgive my fondness this once more?
Tell her, tho' we shall never meet again,
If I should hear she took another Love,
The news would break my heart.—Now I must go;
For every time I have return'd, I feel

My Soul more tender; and my next command
Would be to bid her stay, and ruine both. [*Exit.*

DOLLABELLA: Men are but Children of a larger growth,
Our appetites as apt to change as theirs,
And full as craving too, and full as vain;
And yet the Soul, shut up in her dark room,
Viewing so clear abroad, at home sees nothing;
But, like a Mole in Earth, busie and blind,
Works all her folly up, and casts it outward
To the Worlds open view: thus I discover'd,
And blam'd the love of ruin'd *Antony*;
Yet wish that I were he, to be so ruin'd.

Enter VENTIDIUS *above.*

VENTIDIUS: Alone? and talking to himself? concern'd too?
Perhaps my ghess is right; he lov'd her once,
And may pursue it still.

DOLLABELLA: O Friendship! Friendship!
Ill canst thou answer this; and Reason, worse:
Unfaithful in th' attempt; hopeless to win;
And, if I win, undone: meer madness all.
And yet th' occasion's fair. What injury,
To him, to wear the Robe which he throws by?

VENTIDIUS: None, none at all. This happens as I wish,
To ruine her yet more with *Antony*.

Enter CLEOPATRA, *talking with* ALEXAS; CHARMION, IRAS *on the other side.*

DOLLABELLA: She comes! What charms have sorrow on that face!
Sorrow seems pleas'd to dwell with so much sweetness;
Yet, now and then, a melancholy smile
Breaks loose, like Lightning, in a Winter's night,
And shows a moments day.

VENTIDIUS: If she should love him too! Her Eunuch there!
That *porcpisce* bodes ill weather. Draw, draw nearer,
Sweet Devil, that I may hear.

ALEXAS: Believe me; try

[DOLLABELLA *goes over to* CHARMION *and* IRAS; *seems to talk with them.*

To make him jealous; jealousie is like
A polisht Glass held to the lips when life's in doubt:
If there be breath, 'twill catch the damp and show it.

CLEOPATRA: I grant you jealousie's a proof of love,
But 'tis a weak and unavailing Med'cine;
It puts out the disease, and makes it show,
But has no pow'r to cure.

ALEXAS: 'Tis your last remedy, and strongest too:
And then this *Dollabella*, who so fit
To practise on? He's handsom, valiant, young,
And looks as he were laid for Nature's bait
To catch weak Womens eyes.
He stands already more than half suspected
Of loving you: the least kind word, or glance,
You give this Youth will kindle him with love:
Then, like a burning Vessel set adrift,
You'll send him down amain before the wind,
To fire the heart of jealous *Antony*.

CLEOPATRA: Can I do this? Ah, no, my love's so true,
That I can neither hide it where it is,
Nor show it where it is not. Nature meant me
A Wife, a silly harmless houshold Dove,
Fond without art; and kind without deceit;
But Fortune, that has made a Mistress of me,
Has thrust me out to the wide World, unfurnish'd
Of falshood to be happy.

ALEXAS: Force your self.
Th' event will be, your Lover will return
Doubly desirous to possess the good
Which once he fear'd to lose.

CLEOPATRA: I must attempt it;
But Oh with what regret! [*Exit* ALEXAS.
[*She comes up to* DOLLABELLA.]

VENTIDIUS: So, now the Scene draws near; they're in my reach.

CLEOPATRA, *to* DOLLABELLA: Discoursing with my Women! Might not I
Share in your entertainment?

CHARMION: You have been
The Subject of it, Madam.

CLEOPATRA: How; and how?

IRAS: Such praises of your beauty!

CLEOPATRA: Meer Poetry.
Your *Roman* Wits, your *Gallus* and *Tibullus*,
Have taught you this from *Cytheris* and *Delia*.

DOLLABELLA: Those *Roman* Wits have never been in *Egypt*,
Cytheris and *Delia* else had been unsung:

I, who have seen——had I been born a Poet,
Should chuse a nobler name.
CLEOPATRA: You flatter me.
But, 'tis your Nation's vice: all of your Country
Are flatterers, and all false. Your Friend's like you.
I'm sure he sent you not to speak these words.
DOLLABELLA: No, Madam; yet he sent me——
CLEOPATRA: Well, he sent you——
DOLLABELLA: Of a less pleasing errand.
CLEOPATRA: How less pleasing?
Less to your self, or me?
DOLLABELLA: Madam, to both;
For you must mourn, and I must grieve to cause it.
CLEOPATRA: You, *Charmion*, and your Fellow, stand at distance.
[*aside*] Hold up, my Spirits.—Well, now your mournful matter;
For I'm prepar'd, perhaps can ghess it too.
DOLLABELLA: I wish you would; for 'tis a thankless office
To tell ill news: and I, of all your Sex,
Most fear displeasing you.
CLEOPATRA: Of all your Sex,
I soonest could forgive you, if you should.
VENTIDIUS: Most delicate advances! Woman! Woman!
Dear damn'd, inconstant Sex!
CLEOPATRA: In the first place,
I am to be forsaken; is't not so?
DOLLABELLA: I wish I could not answer to that question.
CLEOPATRA: Then pass it o'er, because it troubles you:
I should have been more griev'd another time.
Next, I'm to lose my Kingdom.——Farewel, *Egypt*.
Yet, is there any more?
DOLLABELLA: Madam, I fear
Your too deep sense of grief has turn'd your reason.
CLEOPATRA: No, no, I'm not run mad; I can bear Fortune:
And Love may be expell'd by other Love,
As Poysons are by Poysons.
DOLLABELLA: ——You o'erjoy me, Madam,
To find your griefs so moderately born.
You've heard the worst; all are not false, like him.
CLEOPATRA: No; Heav'n forbid they should.
DOLLABELLA: Some men are constant.
CLEOPATRA: And constancy deserves reward, that's certain.
DOLLABELLA: Deserves it not; but give it leave to hope.

VENTIDIUS: I'll swear thou hast my leave. I have enough:
But how to manage this! Well, I'll consider. [*Exit.*

DOLLABELLA: I came prepar'd,
To tell you heavy news; news, which I thought,
Would fright the blood from your pale cheeks to hear:
But you have met it with a cheerfulness
That makes my task more easie; and my tongue,
Which on anothers message was employ'd,
Would gladly speak its own.

CLEOPATRA: Hold, *Dollabella.*
First tell me, were you chosen by my Lord?
Or sought you this employment?

DOLLABELLA: He pick'd me out; and, as his bosom-friend,
He charg'd me with his words.

CLEOPATRA: The message then
I know was tender, and each accent smooth,
To mollifie that rugged word *Depart.*

DOLLABELLA: Oh, you mistake: he chose the harshest words,
With fiery eyes, and with contracted brows,
He coyn'd his face in the severest stamp:
And fury, shook his Fabrick like an Earthquake;
He heav'd for vent, and burst like bellowing *Ætna*,
In sounds scarce humane, " Hence, away for ever:
Let her begone, the blot of my renown,
And bane of all my hopes: [*All the time of this speech,* CLEOPATRA *seems more and more concern'd, till she sinks quite down.*
Let her be driv'n as far as men can think
From Mans commerce: She'll poyson to the Center."

CLEOPATRA: Oh, I can bear no more!

DOLLABELLA: Help, help: Oh Wretch! Oh cursed, cursed Wretch!
What have I done?

CHARMION: Help, chafe her Temples, *Iras.*

IRAS: Bend, bend her forward quickly.

CHARMION: Heav'n be prais'd,
She comes again.

CLEOPATRA: Oh, let him not approach me.
Why have you brought me back to this loath'd Being,
Th' abode of Falshood, violated Vows,
And injur'd Love? For pity, let me go;
For, if there be a place of long repose,
I'm sure I want it. My disdainful Lord

Can never break that quiet; nor awake
The sleeping Soul, with hollowing in my Tomb
Such words as fright her hence. Unkind, unkind.

DOLLABELLA *kneeling*: Believe me, 'tis against my self I speak,
That sure desires belief; I injur'd him:
My Friend ne'er spoke those words. Oh, had you seen
How often he came back, and every time
With something more obliging and more kind,
To add to what he said; what dear Farewels;
How almost vanquisht by his love he parted,
And lean'd to what unwillingly he left:
I, Traitor as I was, for love of you,
(But what can you not do, who made me false!)
I forg'd that lye; for whose forgiveness kneels
This self-accus'd, self-punish'd Criminal.

CLEOPATRA: With how much ease believe we what we wish!
Rise, *Dollabella*; if you have been guilty,
I have contributed, and too much love
Has made me guilty too.
Th' advance of kindness which I made, was feign'd,
To call back fleeting love by jealousie;
But 'twould not last. Oh, rather let me lose
Than so ignobly trifle with his heart.

DOLLABELLA: I find your breast fenc'd round from humane reach,
Transparent as a Rock of solid Crystal;
Seen through, but never pierc'd. My Friend, my Friend!
What endless treasure hast thou thrown away,
And scatter'd, like an Infant, in the Ocean,
Vain sums of Wealth which none can gather thence.

CLEOPATRA: Could you not beg
An hours admittance to his private ear?
Like one who wanders through long barren Wilds,
And yet foreknows no hospitable Inn
Is near to succour hunger,
Eats his fill, before his painful march:
So would I feed a while my famish'd eyes
Before we part; for I have far to go,
If death be far, and never must return.

VENTIDIUS, *with* OCTAVIA, *behind.*

VENTIDIUS: From hence you may discover—Oh, sweet, sweet!
Would you indeed? the pretty hand in earnest?

DOLLABELLA: I will, for this reward.—Draw it not back,

[*Takes her hand.*

'Tis all I e'er will beg.

VENTIDIUS: They turn upon us.

OCTAVIA: What quick eyes has guilt!

VENTIDIUS: Seem not to have observ'd 'em, and go on.

They enter.

DOLLABELLA: Saw you the Emperor, *Ventidius*?

VENTIDIUS: No.
I sought him; but I heard that he was private,
None with him, but *Hipparchus*, his Freedman.

DOLLABELLA: Know you his bus'ness?

VENTIDIUS: Giving him Instructions,
And Letters, to his Brother *Cæsar*.

DOLLABELLA: Well,
He must be found.

[*Exeunt* DOLLABELLA *and* CLEOPATRA.

OCTAVIA: Most glorious impudence!

VENTIDIUS: She look'd methought,
As she would say, Take your old man, *Octavia*;
Thank you, I'm better here.
Well, but what use
Make we of this discovery?

OCTAVIA: Let it die.

VENTIDIUS: I pity *Dollabella*; but she's dangerous:
Her eyes have pow'r beyond *Thessalian* Charms
To draw the Moon from Heav'n; for Eloquence,
The Sea-green Syrens taught her voice their flatt'ry;
And, while she speaks, Night steals upon the Day,
Unmark'd of those that hear: Then she's so charming,
Age buds at sight of her, and swells to youth:
The holy Priests gaze on her when she smiles;
And with heav'd hands forgetting gravity,
They bless her wanton eyes: Even I who hate her,
With a malignant joy behold such beauty;
And, while I curse, desire it. *Antony*
Must needs have some remains of passion still,
Which may ferment into a worse relapse,
If now not fully cur'd. I know, this minute,
With *Cæsar* he's endeavouring her peace.

OCTAVIA: You have prevail'd:—but for a farther purpose

[*Walks off.*

I'll prove how he will relish this discovery.
What, make a Strumpet's peace! it swells my heart:
It must not, sha'not be.

VENTIDIUS: His Guards appear.
Let me begin, and you shall second me.

Enter ANTONY.

ANTONY: *Octavia*, I was looking you, my love:
What, are your Letters ready? I have giv'n
My last Instructions.

OCTAVIA: Mine, my Lord, are written.

ANTONY: *Ventidius!* [*Drawing him aside.*

VENTIDIUS: My Lord?

ANTONY: A word in private.
When saw you *Dollabella*?

VENTIDIUS: Now, my Lord,
He parted hence; and *Cleopatra* with him.

ANTONY: Speak softly. 'Twas by my command he went,
To bear my last farewel.

VENTIDIUS *aloud*: It look'd indeed
Like your farewel.

ANTONY: More softly.—My farewel?
What secret meaning have you in those words
Of my Farewel? He did it by my Order.

VENTIDIUS *aloud*: Then he obey'd your Order. I suppose
You bid him do it with all gentleness,
All kindness, and all——love.

ANTONY: How she mourn'd,
The poor forsaken Creature!

VENTIDIUS: She took it as she ought; she bore your parting
As she did *Cæsar*'s, as she would anothers,
Were a new Love to come.

ANTONY *aloud*: Thou dost belye her;
Most basely, and maliciously belye her.

VENTIDIUS: I thought not to displease you; I have done.

OCTAVIA *coming up*: You seem disturbed, my Lord.

ANTONY: A very trifle.
Retire, my Love.

VENTIDIUS: It was indeed a trifle.
He sent——

ANTONY *angrily*: No more. Look how thou disobey'st me;
Thy life shall answer it.

OCTAVIA: Then 'tis no trifle.

VENTIDIUS *to* OCTAVIA: 'Tis less; a very nothing: you too saw it,
As well as I, and therefore 'tis no secret.
ANTONY: She saw it!
VENTIDIUS: Yes: she saw young *Dollabella*——
ANTONY: Young *Dollabella*!
VENTIDIUS: Young, I think him young,
And handsom too; and so do others think him.
But what of that? He went by your command,
Indeed 'tis probable, with some kind message;
For she receiv'd it graciously; she smil'd:
And then he grew familiar with her hand,
Squeez'd it, and worry'd it with ravenous kisses;
She blush'd, and sigh'd, and smil'd, and blush'd again;
At last she took occasion to talk softly,
And brought her cheek up close, and lean'd on his:
At which, he whisper'd kisses back on hers;
And then she cry'd aloud, That constancy
Should be rewarded.
OCTAVIA: This I saw and heard.
ANTONY: What Woman was it, whom you heard and saw
So playful with my Friend!
Not *Cleopatra*?
VENTIDIUS: Ev'n she, my Lord.
ANTONY: My *Cleopatra*?
VENTIDIUS: Your *Cleopatra*;
Dollabella's *Cleopatra*:
Every Man's *Cleopatra*.
ANTONY: Thou ly'st.
VENTIDIUS: I do not lye, my Lord.
Is this so strange? Should Mistresses be left,
And not provide against a time of change?
You know she's not much us'd to lonely nights.
ANTONY: I'll think no more on't.
I know 'tis false, and see the plot betwixt you.
You needed not have gone this way, *Octavia*.
What harms it you that *Cleopatra*'s just?
She's mine no more. I see; and I forgive:
Urge it no farther, Love.
OCTAVIA: Are you concern'd
That she's found false?
ANTONY: I should be, were it so;
For, tho 'tis past, I would not that the World

Should tax my former choice: That I lov'd one
Of so light note; but I forgive you both.

VENTIDIUS: What has my age deserv'd, that you should think
I would abuse your ears with perjury?
If Heav'n be true, she's false.

ANTONY: Tho Heav'n and Earth
Should witness it, I'll not believe her tainted.

VENTIDIUS: I'll bring you then a Witness
From Hell to prove her so. Nay, go not back;
[*Seeing* ALEXAS *just entring, and starting back.*
For stay you must and shall.

ALEXAS: What means my Lord?

VENTIDIUS: To make you do what most you hate; speak truth.
You are of *Cleopatra*'s private Counsel,
Of her Bed-Counsel, her lascivious hours;
Are conscious of each nightly change she makes,
And watch her, as *Chaldeans* do the Moon,
Can tell what Signs she passes through, what day.

ALEXAS: My Noble Lord.

VENTIDIUS: My most Illustrious Pandar,
No fine set Speech, no Cadence, no turn'd Periods,
But a plain home-spun Truth, is what I ask:
I did, my self, o'erhear your Queen make love
To *Dollabella*. Speak; for I will know,
By your confession, what more past betwixt 'em;
How near the bus'ness draws to your employment;
And when the happy hour.

ANTONY: Speak truth, *Alexas*, whether it offend
Or please *Ventidius*, care not: justifie
Thy injur'd Queen from malice: dare his worst.

OCTAVIA *aside*: See, how he gives him courage! how he fears
To find her false! and shuts his eyes to truth,
Willing to be misled!

ALEXAS: As far as love may plead for Woman's frailty,
Urg'd by desert and greatness of the Lover;
So far (Divine *Octavia!*) may my Queen
Stand ev'n excus'd to you, for loving him,
Who is your Lord: so far, from brave *Ventidius*,
May her past actions hope a fair report.

ANTONY: 'Tis well, and truly spoken: mark, *Ventidius*.

ALEXAS: To you, most Noble Emperor, her strong passion
Stands not excus'd, but wholly justifi'd.
Her Beauty's charms alone, without her Crown,

From *Ind* and *Meroe* drew the distant Vows
Of sighing Kings; and at her feet were laid
The Scepters of the Earth, expos'd on heaps,
To choose where she would Reign:
She thought a *Roman* only could deserve her;
And, of all *Romans*, only *Antony*,
And, to be less than Wife to you, disdain'd
Their lawful passion.

ANTONY: 'Tis but truth.

ALEXAS: And yet, tho love, and your unmatch'd desert,
Have drawn her from the due regard of Honor,
At last, Heav'n open'd her unwilling eyes
To see the wrongs she offer'd fair *Octavia*,
Whose holy Bed she lawlessly usurpt,
The sad effects of this improsperous War,
Confirm'd those pious thoughts.

VENTIDIUS *aside*: O, wheel you there?
Observe him now; the Man begins to mend,
And talk substantial reason. Fear not, Eunuch,
The Emperor has giv'n thee leave to speak.

ALEXAS: Else had I never dar'd t' offend his ears
With what the last necessity has urg'd
On my forsaken Mistress; yet I must not
Presume to say her heart is wholly alter'd.

ANTONY: No, dare not for thy life, I charge thee dare not,
Pronounce that fatal word.

OCTAVIA *aside*: Must I bear this? good Heav'n, afford me patience.

VENTIDIUS: On, sweet Eunuch; my dear half man, proceed.

ALEXAS: Yet *Dollabella*
Has lov'd her long, he, next my God-like Lord,
Deserves her best; and should she meet his passion,
Rejected, as she is, by him she lov'd—

ANTONY: Hence, from my sight; for I can bear no more:
Let Furies drag thee quick to Hell; let all
The longer damn'd have rest; each torturing hand
Do thou employ, till *Clĕopatra* comes,
Then joyn thou too, and help to torture her.

[*Exit* ALEXAS, *thrust out by* ANTONY.

OCTAVIA: 'Tis not well,
Indeed, my Lord, 'tis much unkind to me,
To show this passion, this extream concernment
For an abandon'd, faithless Prostitute.

ANTONY: *Octavia*, leave me: I am much disorder'd.
Leave me, I say.
OCTAVIA: My Lord?
ANTONY: I bid you leave me.
VENTIDIUS: Obey him, Madam: best withdraw a while,
And see how this will work.
OCTAVIA: Wherein have I offended you, my Lord,
That I am bid to leave you? Am I false,
Or infamous? Am I a *Cleopatra*?
Were I she,
Base as she is, you would not bid me leave you;
But hang upon my neck, take slight excuses,
And fawn upon my falshood.
ANTONY: 'Tis too much,
Too much, *Octavia*; I am prest with sorrows
Too heavy to be born; and you add more:
I would retire, and recollect what's left
Of Man within, to aid me.
OCTAVIA: You would mourn
In private, for your Love, who has betray'd you;
You did but half return to me: your kindness
Linger'd behind with her. I hear, my Lord,
You make Conditions for her,
And would include her Treaty. Wonderous proofs
Of love to me!
ANTONY: Are you my Friend, *Ventidius*?
Or are you turn'd a *Dollabella* too,
And let this Fury loose?
VENTIDIUS: Oh, be advis'd,
Sweet Madam, and retire.
OCTAVIA: Yes, I will go; but never to return.
You shall no more be haunted with this Fury.
My Lord, my Lord, love will not always last,
When urg'd with long unkindness, and disdain;
Take her again whom you prefer to me;
She stays but to be call'd. Poor cozen'd Man!
Let a feign'd parting give her back your heart,
Which a feign'd love first got; for injur'd me,
Tho' my just sense of wrongs forbid my stay,
My duty shall be yours.
To the dear pledges of our former love,
My tenderness and care shall be transferr'd,
And they shall cheer, by turns, my Widow'd Nights:

So, take my last farewel; for I despair
To have you whole, and scorn to take you half. *Exit.*

VENTIDIUS: I combat Heav'n, which blasts my best designs:
My last attempt must be to win her back;
But Oh, I fear in vain. *Exit.*

ANTONY: Why was I fram'd with this plain honest heart,
Which knows not to disguise its griefs and weakness,
But bears its workings outward to the World?
I should have kept the mighty anguish in,
And forc'd a smile at *Cleopatra*'s falshood:
Octavia had believ'd it, and had staid;
But I am made a shallow-forded Stream,
Seen to the bottom: all my clearness scorn'd,
And all my faults expos'd!—See, where he comes

Enter DOLLABELLA.

Who has prophan'd the Sacred Name of Friend,
And worn it into vileness!
With how secure a brow, and specious form
He guilds the secret Villain! Sure that face
Was meant for honesty; but Heav'n mis-match'd it,
And furnish'd Treason out with Natures pomp,
To make its work more easie.

DOLLABELLA: O, my Friend!

ANTONY: Well, *Dollabella*, you perform'd my message?

DOLLABELLA: I did, unwillingly.

ANTONY: Unwillingly?
Was it so hard for you to bear our parting?
You should have wisht it.

DOLLABELLA: Why?

ANTONY: Because you love me.
And she receiv'd my message, with as true,
With as unfeign'd a sorrow, as you brought it?

DOLLABELLA: She loves you, ev'n to madness.

ANTONY: Oh, I know it.
You, *Dollabella*, do not better know
How much she loves me. And should I
Forsake this Beauty? This all-perfect Creature?

DOLLABELLA: I could not, were she mine.

ANTONY: And yet you first
Perswaded me: how come you alter'd since?

DOLLABELLA: I said at first I was not fit to go;
I could not hear her sighs, and see her tears,

But pity must prevail: and so, perhaps,
It may again with you; for I have promis'd,
That she should take her last farewel: and, see,
She comes to claim my word.

Enter CLEOPATRA.

ANTONY: False *Dollabella*!
DOLLABELLA: What's false, my Lord?
ANTONY: Why, *Dollabella*'s false,
And *Cleopatra*'s false; both false and faithless.
Draw near, you well-join'd wickedness, you Serpents,
Whom I have, in my kindly bosom, warm'd
Till I am stung to death.
DOLLABELLA: My Lord, have I
Deserv'd to be thus us'd?
CLEOPATRA: Can Heav'n prepare
A newer Torment? Can it find a Curse
Beyond our separation?
ANTONY: Yes, if Fate
Be just, much greater: Heav'n should be ingenious
In punishing such crimes. The rowling Stone,
And gnawing Vulture, were slight pains, invented
When *Jove* was young, and no examples known
Of mighty ills; but you have ripen'd sin
To such a monstrous growth, 'twill pose the Gods,
To find an equal Torture. Two, two such,
Oh there's no farther name, two such—to me,
To me, who lock'd my Soul within your breasts,
Had no desires, no joys, no life, but you;
When half the Globe was mine, I gave it you
In Dowry with my heart; I had no use,
No fruit of all, but you: a Friend and Mistress
Was what the World could give. Oh, *Cleopatra*!
Oh, *Dollabella*! how could you betray
This tender heart, which with an Infant-fondness
Lay lull'd betwixt your bosoms, and there slept
Secure of injur'd Faith?
DOLLABELLA: If she has wrong'd you,
Heav'n, Hell, and You revenge it.
ANTONY: If she wrong'd me,
Thou wouldst evade thy part of guilt; but swear
Thou lov'st not her.
DOLLABELLA: Not so as I love you.

ANTONY: Not so! Swear, swear, I say, thou dost not love her.
DOLLABELLA: No more than Friendship will allow.
ANTONY: No more?
Friendship allows thee nothing: thou art perjur'd.——
And yet thou didst not swear thou lov'dst her not;
But not so much, no more. Oh trifling Hypocrite,
Who dar'st not own to her thou dost not love,
Nor own to me thou dost! *Ventidius* heard it;
Octavia saw it.
CLEOPATRA: They are enemies.
ANTONY: *Alexas* is not so: he, he confest it;
He, who, next Hell, best knew it, he avow'd it.
(*to* DOLLABELLA.) Why do I seek a proof beyond your self?
You whom I sent to bear my last Farewel,
Return'd to plead her stay.
DOLLABELLA: What shall I answer?
If to have lov'd be guilt, then I have sinn'd;
But if to have repented of that love
Can wash away my crime, I have repented.
Yet, if I have offended past forgiveness,
Let her not suffer: she is innocent.
CLEOPATRA: Ah, what will not a Woman do who loves!
What means will she refuse, to keep that heart
Where all her joys are plac'd! 'Twas I encourag'd,
'Twas I blew up the fire that scorch'd his Soul,
To make you jealous; and by that regain you.
But all in vain; I could not counterfeit:
In spight of all the damms, my love broke o'er,
And drown'd my heart again; Fate took th'occasion;
And thus one minutes feigning has destroy'd
My whole life's truth.
ANTONY: Thin Cobweb Arts of Falshood;
Seen, and broke through at first.
DOLLABELLA: Forgive your Mistress.
CLEOPATRA: Forgive your Friend.
ANTONY: You have convinc'd your selves,
You plead each others Cause: What Witness have you,
That you but meant to raise my jealousie?
CLEOPATRA: Our selves, and Heav'n.
ANTONY: Guilt witnesses for guilt. Hence, Love and Friendship;
You have no longer place in humane breasts,
These two have driv'n you out: avoid my sight;

I would not kill the Man whom I lov'd;
And cannot hurt the Woman; but avoid me,
I do not know how long I can be tame;
For, if I stay one minute more to think
How I am wrong'd, my Justice and Revenge
Will cry so loud within me, that my pity
Will not be heard for either.

DOLLABELLA: Heav'n has but
Our sorrow for our sins; and then delights
To pardon erring Man: sweet Mercy seems
Its darling Attribute, which limits Justice;
As if there were degrees in Infinite;
And Infinite would rather want perfection
Than punish to extent.

ANTONY: I can forgive
A Foe; but not a Mistress, and a Friend:
Treason is there in its most horrid shape,
Where trust is greatest: and the Soul resign'd
Is stabb'd by its own Guards: I'll hear no more;
Hence from my sight, for ever.

CLEOPATRA: How? for ever!
I cannot go one moment from your sight,
And must I go for ever?
My joys, my only joys are center'd here:
What place have I to go to? my own Kingdom?
That I have lost for you: or to the *Romans*?
They hate me for your sake: or must I wander
The wide World o'er, a helpless, banish'd Woman,
Banish'd for love of you; banish'd from you;
I, there's the Banishment! Oh hear me; hear me,
With strictest Justice: for I beg no favour:
And if I have offended you, then kill me,
But do not banish me.

ANTONY: I must not hear you.
I have a Fool within me takes your part;
But Honour stops my ears.

CLEOPATRA: For pity hear me!
Wou'd you cast off a slave who follow'd you,
Who crouch'd beneath your Spurn?—He has no pity!
See, if he gives one tear to my departure;
One look, one kind farewel: Oh Iron heart!
Let all the Gods look down, and judge betwixt us,
If he did ever love!

ANTONY: No more: *Alexas*!
DOLLABELLA: A perjur'd Villain!
ANTONY *to* CLEOPATRA: Your *Alexas*; yours.
CLEOPATRA: O 'twas his plot; his ruinous design
T' engage you in my love by jealousie.
Hear him; confront him with me; let him speak.
ANTONY: I have; I have.
CLEOPATRA: And if he clear me not—
ANTONY: Your Creature! one who hangs upon your smiles!
Watches your eye to say or to unsay
Whate'er you please! I am not to be mov'd.
CLEOPATRA: Then must we part? Farewel, my cruel Lord,
Th' appearance is against me; and I go
Unjustifi'd, for ever from your sight.
How I have lov'd, you know; how yet I love,
My only comfort is, I know my self:
I love you more, ev'n now you are unkind,
Than when you lov'd me most; so well, so truly,
I'll never strive against it; but die pleas'd
To think you once were mine.
ANTONY: Good Heav'n, they weep at parting.
Must I weep too? that calls 'em innocent.
I must not weep; and yet I must, to think
That I must not forgive.——
Live; but live wretched, 'tis but just you shou'd,
Who made me so: Live from each others sight:
Let me not hear you meet: Set all the Earth,
And all the Seas, betwixt your sunder'd Loves:
View nothing common but the Sun and Skys:
Now, all take several ways;
And each your own sad fate with mine deplore;
That you were false, and I could trust no more.
[*Exeunt severally.*

ACT V

CLEOPATRA, CHARMION, IRAS.

CHARMION: Be juster, Heav'n: such virtue punish'd thus,
Will make us think that Chance rules all above,
And shuffles, with a random hand, the Lots
Which Man is forc'd to draw.

CLEOPATRA: I cou'd tear out these eyes, that gain'd his heart,
And had not pow'r to keep it. O the curse
Of doting on, ev'n when I find it Dotage!
Bear witness, Gods, you heard him bid me go;
You whom he mock'd with imprecating Vows
Of promis'd Faith.——I'll die, I will not bear it.
You may hold me.——

[*She pulls out her Dagger, and they hold her.*

But I can keep my breath; I can die inward,
And choak this Love.

Enter ALEXAS.

IRAS: Help, O *Alexas*, help!
The Queen grows desperate, her Soul struggles in her,
With all the Agonies of Love and Rage,
And strives to force its passage.
CLEOPATRA: Let me go.
Art thou there, Traitor!—O
O, for a little breath, to vent my rage!
Give, give me way, and let me loose upon him.
ALEXAS: Yes, I deserve it, for my ill-tim'd truth.
Was it for me to prop
The Ruins of a falling Majesty?
To place my self beneath the mighty flaw,
Thus to be crush'd, and pounded into Atomes,
By its o'erwhelming weight? 'Tis too presuming
For Subjects, to preserve that wilful pow'r
Which courts its own destruction.
CLEOPATRA: I wou'd reason
More calmly with you. Did not you o'er-rule,
And force my plain, direct, and open love
Into these crooked paths of jealousie?
Now, what's th'event? *Octavia* is remov'd;
But *Cleopatra*'s banish'd. Thou, thou, Villain,
Hast push'd my Boat, to open Sea; to prove,
At my sad cost, if thou canst steer it back.
It cannot be; I'm lost too far; I'm ruin'd:
Hence, thou Impostor, Traitor, Monster, Devil.——
I can no more: thou, and my griefs, have sunk
Me down so low, that I want voice to curse thee.
ALEXAS: Suppose some shipwrack'd Seaman near the shore,
Dropping and faint, with climbing up the Cliff,
If, from above, some charitable hand

Pull him to safety, hazarding himself
To draw the others weight; wou'd he look back
And curse him for his pains? The case is yours;
But one step more, and you have gain'd the heighth.

CLEOPATRA: Sunk, never more to rise.

ALEXAS: *Octavia*'s gone, and *Dollabella* banish'd.
Believe me, Madam, *Antony* is yours.
His heart was never lost; but started off
To Jealousie, Love's last retreat and covert:
Where it lies hid in Shades, watchful in silence,
And list'ning for the sound that calls it back.
Some other, any man, ('tis so advanc'd)
May perfect this unfinish'd work, which I
(Unhappy only to my self) have left
So easie to his hand.

CLEOPATRA: Look well thou do't; else——

ALEXAS: Else, what your silence threatens.—*Antony*
Is mounted up the *Pharos*; from whose Turret,
He stands surveying our *Egyptian* Gallies,
Engag'd with *Cæsar*'s Fleet: now Death, or Conquest.
If the first happen, Fate acquits my promise:
If we o'ercome, the Conqueror is yours.
[*A distant Shout within.*

CHARMION: Have comfort, Madam: did you mark that Shout?
[*Second Shout nearer.*

IRAS: Hark; they redouble it.

ALEXAS: 'Tis from the Port.
The loudness shows it near: good news, kind Heavens.

CLEOPATRA: *Osiris* make it so.

Enter SERAPION.

SERAPION: Where, where's the Queen?

ALEXAS: How frightfully the holy Coward stares!
As if not yet recover'd of th' assault,
When all his Gods, and, what's more dear to him,
His Offerings, were at stake.

SERAPION: O horror, horror!
Egypt has been; our latest hour is come:
The Queen of Nations from her ancient seat,
Is sunk for ever in the dark Abyss:
Time has unrowl'd her Glories to the last,
And now clos'd up the Volume.

CLEOPATRA: Be more plain:
Say, whence thou com'st, (though Fate is in thy face,
Which from thy hagard eyes looks wildly out,
And threatens ere thou speak'st.)
SERAPION: I came from *Pharos*;
From viewing (spare me and imagine it)
Our Lands last hope, your Navy.——
CLEOPATRA: Vanquish'd?
SERAPION: No.
They fought not.
CLEOPATRA: Then they fled.
SERAPION: Nor that. I saw,
With *Antony*, your well-appointed Fleet
Row out; and thrice he wav'd his hand on high,
And thrice with cheerful cries they shouted back:
'Twas then, false Fortune, like a fawning Strumpet,
About to leave the Bankrupt Prodigal,
With a dissembled smile wou'd kiss at parting,
And flatter to the last; the well-tim'd Oars
Now dipt from every bank, now smoothly run
To meet the Foe; and soon indeed they met,
But not as Foes. In few, we saw their Caps
On either side thrown up; th' *Egyptian* Gallies
(Receiv'd like Friends) past through, and fell behind
The *Roman* rear: and now, they all come forward,
And ride within the Port.
CLEOPATRA: Enough, *Serapion*:
I've heard my doom. This needed not, you Gods:
When I lost *Antony*, your work was done;
'Tis but superfluous malice. Where's my Lord?
How bears he this last blow?
SERAPION: His fury cannot be express'd by words:
Thrice he attempted headlong to have faln
Full on his foes, and aim'd at *Cæsar*'s Galley:
With-held, he raves on you; cries, He's betray'd.
Should he now find you.——
ALEXAS: Shun him, seek your safety,
Till you can clear your innocence.
CLEOPATRA: I'll stay.
ALEXAS: You must not, haste you to your Monument,
While I make speed to *Cæsar*.
CLEOPATRA: *Cæsar!* No,
I have no business with him.

ALEXAS: I can work him
To spare your life, and let this madman perish.
CLEOPATRA: Base fawning Wretch! wouldst thou betray him too?
Hence from my sight, I will not hear a Traytor;
'Twas thy design brought all this ruine on us;
Serapion, thou art honest; counsel me:
But haste, each moment's precious.
SERAPION: Retire; you must not yet see *Antony*.
He who began this mischief,
'Tis just he tempt the danger: let him clear you;
And, since he offer'd you his servile tongue,
To gain a poor precarious life from *Cæsar*,
Let him expose that fawning eloquence,
And speak to *Antony*.
ALEXAS: O Heavens! I dare not,
I meet my certain death.
CLEOPATRA: Slave, thou deserv'st it.
Not that I fear my Lord, will I avoid him;
I know him noble: when he banish'd me,
And thought me false, he scorn'd to take my life;
But I'll be justifi'd, and then die with him.
ALEXAS: O pity me, and let me follow you.
CLEOPATRA: To death, if thou stir hence. Speak, if thou canst,
Now for thy life, which basely thou wou'dst save;
While mine I prize at this. Come, good *Serapion*.
Exeunt CLEOPATRA, SERAPION, CHARMION, IRAS.
ALEXAS: O that I less cou'd fear to lose this being,
Which, like a Snow-ball, in my coward hand,
The more 'tis grasp'd, the faster melts away.
Poor Reason! what a wretched aid art thou!
For still, in spight of thee,
These two long Lovers, Soul and Body, dread
Their final separation. Let me think:
What can I say, to save my self from death?
No matter what becomes of *Cleopatra*.
ANTONY *within*: Which way? where?
VENTIDIUS *within*: This leads to th' Monument.
ALEXAS: Ah me! I hear him; yet I'm unprepar'd:
My gift of lying's gone;
And this Court-Devil, which I so oft have rais'd,
Forsakes me at my need. I dare not stay;
Yet cannot far go hence. [*Exit*.

Enter ANTONY *and* VENTIDIUS.

ANTONY: O happy *Cæsar*! Thou hast men to lead:
Think not 'tis thou hast conquer'd *Antony*;
But *Rome* has conquer'd *Egypt*. I'm betray'd.

VENTIDIUS: Curse on this treach'rous Train!
Their Soil and Heav'n infect 'em all with baseness:
And their young Souls come tainted to the World
With the first breath they draw.

ANTONY: Th' original Villain sure no God created;
He was a Bastard of the Sun, by *Nile*,
Ap'd into Man; with all his Mother's Mud
Crusted about his Soul.

VENTIDIUS: The Nation is
One Universal Traitor; and their Queen
The very Spirit and Extract of 'em all.

ANTONY: Is there yet left
A possibility of aid from Valor?
Is there one God unsworn to my Destruction?
The least unmortgag'd hope? for, if there be,
Methinks I cannot fall beneath the Fate
Of such a Boy as *Cæsar*.
The World's one half is yet in *Antony*;
And, from each limb of it that's hew'd away
The Soul comes back to me.

VENTIDIUS: There yet remain
Three Legions in the Town. The last assault
Lopt off the rest: if death be your design,
(As I must wish it now) these are sufficient
To make a heap about us of dead Foes,
An honest Pile for burial.

ANTONY: They're enough.
We'll not divide our Stars; but side by side
Fight emulous: and with malicious eyes
Survey each other's acts: so every death
Thou giv'st, I'll take on me, as a just debt,
And pay thee back a Soul.

VENTIDIUS: Now you shall see I love you. Not a word
Of chiding more. By my few hours of life,
I am so pleas'd with this brave *Roman* Fate,
That I wou'd not be *Cæsar*, to out-live you.
When we put off this flesh, and mount together,

I shall be shown to all th' Etherial crowd;
Lo, this is he who dy'd with *Antony*.

ANTONY: Who knows but we may pierce through all their Troops,
And reach my Veterans yet? 'Tis worth the tempting,
T'o'er-leap this Gulph of Fate,
And leave our wand'ring Destinies behind.

Enter ALEXAS, *trembling.*

VENTIDIUS: See, see, that Villain;
See *Cleopatra* stampt upon that face,
With all her cunning, all her arts of falshood!
How she looks out through those dissembling eyes!
How he has set his count'nance for deceit;
And promises a lye, before he speaks!
Let me dispatch him first. [*Drawing.*

ALEXAS: O, spare me, spare me.

ANTONY: Hold; he's not worth your killing. On thy life,
(Which thou mayst keep, because I scorn to take it)
No syllable to justifie thy Queen;
Save thy base tongue its office.

ALEXAS: Sir, she's gone,
Where she shall never be molested more
By Love, or you.

ANTONY: Fled to her *Dollabella*!
Die, Traitor, I revoke my promise, die. [*Going to kill him.*

ALEXAS: O hold, she is not fled.

ANTONY: She is: my eyes
Are open to her falshood; my whole life
Has been a golden dream, of Love and Friendship.
But, now I wake, I'm like a Merchant, rows'd
From soft repose, to see his Vessel sinking,
And all his Wealth cast o'er. Ingrateful Woman!
Who follow'd me, but as the Swallow Summer,
Hatching her young ones in my kindly Beams,
Singing her flatt'ries to my morning wake;
But, now my Winter comes, she spreads her wings,
And seeks the Spring of *Cæsar*.

ALEXAS: Think not so:
Her Fortunes have, in all things, mixt with yours.
Had she betray'd her Naval force to *Rome*,
How easily might she have gone to *Cæsar*,
Secure by such a bribe!

VENTIDIUS: She sent it first,
To be more welcome after.
ANTONY: 'Tis too plain;
Else wou'd she have appear'd, to clear herself.
ALEXAS: Too fatally she has; she could not bear
To be accus'd by you; but shut her self
Within her Monument: look'd down, and sigh'd;
While, from her unchang'd face, the silent tears
Dropt, as they had not leave, but stole their parting.
Some undistinguish'd words she inly murmur'd;
At last, she rais'd her eyes; and, with such looks
As dying *Lucrece* cast,——
ANTONY: My heart forebodes.——
VENTIDIUS: All for the best:—go on.
ALEXAS: She snatch'd her Ponyard,
And, ere we cou'd prevent the fatal blow,
Plung'd it within her breast: then turn'd to me,
Go, bear my Lord (said she) my last Farewel;
And ask him if he yet suspect my Faith.
More she was saying, but death rush'd betwixt.
She half pronounc'd your Name with her last breath,
And bury'd half within her.
VENTIDIUS: Heav'n be prais'd.
ANTONY: Then art thou innocent, my poor dear Love?
And art thou dead?
O those two words! their sound shou'd be divided:
Hadst thou been false, and dy'd; or hadst thou liv'd,
And hadst been true—But Innocence and Death!
This shows not well above. Then what am I,
The Murderer of this Truth, this Innocence!
Thoughts cannot form themselves in words so horrid
As can express my guilt!
VENTIDIUS: Is't come to this? The Gods have been too gracious:
And thus you thank 'em for't.
ANTONY *to* ALEXAS: Why stay'st thou here?
Is it for thee to spy upon my Soul,
And see its inward mourning? Get thee hence;
Thou art not worthy to behold, what now
Becomes a *Roman* Emperor to perform.
ALEXAS *aside*: He loves her still:
His grief betrays it. Good! the joy to find
She's yet alive, compleats the reconcilement.
I've sav'd my self, and her. But, Oh! the *Romans*!

Fate comes too fast upon my Wit,
Hunts me too hard, and meets me at each double. [*Exit.*

VENTIDIUS: Wou'd she had dy'd a little sooner tho,
Before *Octavia* went; you might have treated:
Now 'twill look tame, and wou'd not be receiv'd.
Come, rouze your self, and lets die warm together.

ANTONY: I will not fight: there's no more work for War.
The bus'ness of my angry hours is done.

VENTIDIUS: *Cæsar* is at your Gates.

ANTONY: Why, let him enter;
He's welcom now.

VENTIDIUS: What Lethargy has crept into your Soul?

ANTONY: 'Tis but a scorn of life, and just desire
To free my self from bondage.

VENTIDIUS: Do it bravely.

ANTONY: I will; but not by fighting. O, *Ventidius*!
What shou'd I fight for now? my Queen is dead.
I was but great for her; my Pow'r, my Empire,
Were but my Merchandise to buy her love;
And conquer'd Kings, my Factors. Now she's dead,
Let *Cæsar* take the World,——
An Empty Circle, since the Jewel's gone
Which made it worth my strife: my being's nauseous;
For all the bribes of life are gone away.

VENTIDIUS: Wou'd you be taken?

ANTONY: Yes, I wou'd be taken;
But, as a *Roman* ought, dead, my *Ventidius*:
For I'll convey my Soul from *Cæsar*'s reach,
And lay down life my self. 'Tis time the World
Shou'd have a Lord, and know whom to obey.
We two have kept its homage in suspence,
And bent the Globe on whose each side we trod,
Till it was dented inwards: Let him walk
Alone upon't; I'm weary of my part.
My Torch is out; and the World stands before me
Like a black Desart, at th' approach of night:
I'll lay me down, and stray no farther on.

VENTIDIUS: I cou'd be griev'd,
But that I'll not out-live you: chuse your death;
For, I have seen him in such various shapes,
I care not which I take: I'm only troubled
The life I bear, is worn to such a rag,
'Tis scarce worth giving. I cou'd wish indeed

We threw it from us with a better grace;
That, like two Lyons taken in the Toils,
We might at least thrust out our paws, and wound
The Hunters that inclose us.

ANTONY: I have thought on't.
Ventidius, you must live.

VENTIDIUS: I must not, Sir.

ANTONY: Wilt thou not live, to speak some good of me?
To stand by my fair Fame, and guard th' approaches
From the ill Tongues of Men?

VENTIDIUS: Who shall guard mine,
For living after you?

ANTONY: Say, I command it.

VENTIDIUS: If we die well, our deaths will speak themselves,
And need no living witness.

ANTONY: Thou hast lov'd me,
And fain I wou'd reward thee: I must die;
Kill me, and take the merit of my death
To make thee Friends with *Cæsar*.

VENTIDIUS: Thank your kindness.
You said I lov'd you; and, in recompence,
You bid me turn a Traitor: did I think
You wou'd have us'd me thus? that I shou'd die
With a hard thought of you?

ANTONY: Forgive me, *Roman*.
Since I have heard of *Cleopatra*'s death,
My reason bears no rule upon my tongue,
But lets my thoughts break all at random out:
I've thought better; do not deny me twice.

VENTIDIUS: By Heav'n, I will not.
Let it not be t' out-live you.

ANTONY: Kill me first,
And then die thou: for 'tis but just thou serve
Thy Friend, before thy self.

VENTIDIUS: Give me your hand.
We soon shall meet again. Now, Farewel, Emperor.
[*Embrace.*
Methinks that word's too cold to be my last:
Since Death sweeps all distinctions, Farewel, Friend.
That's all.——
I will not make a bus'ness of a trifle:
And yet I cannot look on you, and kill you;
Pray turn your face.

ANTONY: I do: strike home be sure.
VENTIDIUS: Home, as my Sword will reach. [*Kills himself.*
ANTONY: O, thou mistak'st;
That wound was none of thine: give it me back:
Thou robb'st me of my death.
VENTIDIUS: I do indeed;
But, think 'tis the first time I e'er deceiv'd you;
If that may plead my pardon. And you, Gods,
Forgive me, if you will; for I die perjur'd,
Rather than kill my Friend. [*Dies.*
ANTONY: Farewel. Ever my Leader, ev'n in Death!
My Queen and thou have got the start of me,
And I'm the lag of Honour.—Gone so soon?
Is death no more? he us'd him carelessly,
With a familiar kindness: ere he knock'd,
Ran to the door, and took him in his arms,
As who shou'd say, Y'are welcome at all hours,
A Friend need give no warning. Books had spoil'd him;
For all the Learn'd are Cowards by profession.
'Tis not worth
My farther thought; for death, for aught I know,
Is but to think no more. Here's to be satisfi'd.
[*Falls on his Sword.*]
I've mist my heart. O unperforming hand!
Thou never cou'dst have err'd in a worse time.
My Fortune jades me to the last; and death,
Like a great Man, takes state, and makes me wait
For my admittance.—— [*Trampling within.*]
Some perhaps from *Cæsar*:
If he shou'd find me living, and suspect
That I plaid booty with my life! I'll mend
My work, ere they can reach me. [*Rises upon his knees.*

Enter CLEOPATRA, CHARMION, IRAS.

CLEOPATRA: Where is my Lord? where is he?
CHARMION: There he lies,
And dead *Ventidius* by him.
CLEOPATRA: My fears were Prophets; I am come too late.
O that accurs'd *Alexas*! [*Runs to him.*
ANTONY: Art thou living?
Or am I dead before I knew? and thou
The first kind Ghost that meets me?

CLEOPATRA: Help me seat him.
Send quickly, send for help. [*They place him in a Chair.*

ANTONY: I am answer'd.
We live both. Sit thee down, my *Cleopatra*:
I'll make the most I can of life, to stay
A moment more with thee.

CLEOPATRA: How is it with you?

ANTONY: 'Tis as with a man
Removing in a hurry; all pack'd up,
But one dear Jewel that his haste forgot;
And he, for that, returns upon the spur:
So I come back, for thee.

CLEOPATRA: Too long, you Heav'ns, you have been cruel to me;
Now show your mended Faith, and give me back
His fleeting life.

ANTONY: It will not be, my Love.
I keep my Soul by force.
Say but thou art not false.

CLEOPATRA: 'Tis now too late
To say I'm true: I'll prove it, and die with you.
Unknown to me, *Alexas* feign'd my death:
Which, when I knew, I hasted, to prevent
This fatal consequence. My Fleet betray'd
Both you and me.

ANTONY: And *Dollabella.*————

CLEOPATRA: Scarce esteem'd before he lov'd; but hated now.

ANTONY: Enough: my life's not long enough for more.
Thou sayst thou wilt come after: I believe thee;
For I can now believe whate'er thou sayst,
That we may part more kindly.

CLEOPATRA: I will come:
Doubt not, my life, I'll come, and quickly too:
Cæsar shall triumph o'er no part of thee.

ANTONY: But grieve not, while thou stay'st
My last disastrous times:
Think we have had a clear and glorious day;
And Heav'n did kindly to delay the storm
Just till our close of ev'ning. Ten years love,
And not a moment lost, but all improv'd
To th' utmost joys: What Ages have we liv'd?
And now to die each others; and, so dying,
While hand in hand we walk in Groves below,

Whole Troops of Lovers Ghosts shall flock about us,
And all the Train be ours.

CLEOPATRA: Your words are like the Notes of dying Swans,
Too sweet to last. Were there so many hours
For your unkindness, and not one for love?

ANTONY: No, not a minute.——This one kiss——more worth
Than all I leave to *Cæsar*. [*Dies.*

CLEOPATRA: O, tell me so again,
And take ten thousand kisses, for that word.
My Lord, my Lord: speak, if you yet have being;
Sigh to me, if you cannot speak; or cast
One look: Do any thing that shows you live.

IRAS: He's gone too far, to hear you;
And this you see, a lump of sensless Clay,
The leavings of a Soul.

CHARMION: Remember, Madam,
He charg'd you not to grieve.

CLEOPATRA: And I'll obey him.
I have not lov'd a *Roman* not to know
What should become his Wife; his Wife, my *Charmion*;
For 'tis to that high Title I aspire,
And now I'll not die less. Let dull *Octavia*
Survive, to mourn him dead: my Nobler Fate
Shall knit our Spousals with a tie too strong
For *Roman* Laws to break.

IRAS: Will you then die?

CLEOPATRA: Why shou'dst thou make that question?

IRAS: *Cæsar* is merciful.

CLEOPATRA: Let him be so
To those that want his mercy: my poor Lord
Made no such Cov'nant with him, to spare me
When he was dead. Yield me to *Cæsar*'s pride?
What, to be led in triumph through the Streets,
A spectacle to base *Plebeian* eyes;
While some dejected Friend of *Antony*'s,
Close in a corner, shakes his head, and mutters
A secret curse on her who ruin'd him?
I'll none of that.

CHARMION: Whatever you resolve,
I'll follow ev'n to death.

IRAS: I only fear'd
For you; but more shou'd fear to live without you.

CLEOPATRA: Why, now 'tis as it shou'd be. Quick, my Friends,

Dispatch; ere this, the Town's in *Cæsar*'s hands:
My Lord looks down concern'd, and fears my stay,
Lest I shou'd be surpriz'd;
Keep him not waiting for his love too long.
You, *Charmion*, bring my Crown and richest Jewels,
With 'em, the Wreath of Victory I made
(Vain Augury!) for him who now lies dead;
You, *Iras*, bring the cure of all our ills.

IRAS: The Aspicks, Madam?

CLEOPATRA: Must I bid you twice?

[*Exeunt* CHARMION *and* IRAS.

'Tis sweet to die, when they wou'd force life on me
To rush into the dark aboad of death,
And seize him first; if he be like my Love,
He is not frightful sure.
We're now alone, in secrecie and silence;
And is not this like Lovers? I may kiss
These pale, cold lips; *Octavia* does not see me;
And, Oh! 'tis better far to have him thus,
Than see him in her arms.——O welcome, welcome.

Enter CHARMION, IRAS.

CHARMION: What must be done?

CLEOPATRA: Short Ceremony, Friends;
But yet it must be decent. First, this Laurel
Shall crown my Hero's Head: he fell not basely,
Nor left his Shield behind him. Only thou
Cou'dst triumph o'er thy self; and thou alone
Wert worthy so to triumph.

CHARMION: To what end
These Ensigns of your Pomp and Royalty?

CLEOPATRA: Dull, that thou art! why, 'tis to meet my Love;
As when I saw him first, on *Cydnos* bank,
All sparkling, like a Goddess; so adorn'd,
I'll find him once again: my second Spousals
Shall match my first, in Glory. Haste, haste, both,
And dress the Bride of *Antony*.

CHARMION: 'Tis done.

CLEOPATRA: Now seat me by my Lord. I claim this place;
For I must conquer *Cæsar* too, like him,
And win my share o'th' World. Hail, you dear Relicks
Of my Immortal Love!

O let no Impious hand remove you hence;
But rest for ever here: let *Egypt* give
His death that peace, which it deny'd his life.
Reach me the Casket.

IRAS: Underneath the fruit the Aspick lies.

CLEOPATRA *putting aside the leaves*: Welcom, thou kind Deceiver!
Thou best of Thieves; who, with an easie key,
Dost open life, and, unperceiv'd by us,
Ev'n steal us from our selves: discharging so
Death's dreadful office, better than himself,
Touching our limbs so gently into slumber,
That Death stands by, deceiv'd by his own Image,
And thinks himself but Sleep.

SERAPION *within*: The Queen, where is she?
The Town is yielded, *Cæsar*'s at the Gates.

CLEOPATRA: He comes too late t' invade the Rights of Death.
Haste, bare my Arm, and rouze the Serpent's fury.
[*Holds out her Arm, and draws it back.*
Coward Flesh——
Wou'dst thou conspire with *Cæsar*, to betray me,
As thou wert none of mine? I'll force thee to't,
And not be sent by him,
But bring my self my Soul to *Antony*.
[*Turns aside, and then shows her Arm bloody.*
Take hence; the work is done.

SERAPION *within*: Break ope the door,
And guard the Traitor well.

CHARMION: The next is ours.

IRAS: Now, *Charmion*, to be worthy
Of our great Queen and Mistress. [*They apply the Aspicks.*

CLEOPATRA: Already, Death, I feel thee in my Veins;
I go with such a will to find my Lord,
That we shall quickly meet.
A heavy numness creeps through every limb,
And now 'tis at my head: my eye-lids fall,
And my dear Love is vanish'd in a mist.
Where shall I find him, where? O turn me to him,
And lay me on his breast. *Cæsar*, thy worst;
Now part us, if thou canst. [*Dies.*
[IRAS *sinks down at her feet, and dies;* CHARMION *stands behind her Chair, as dressing her head.*

Enter SERAPION, *two Priests,* ALEXAS *bound, Egyptians.*

2 PRIESTS: Behold, *Serapion*, what havock Death has made!
SERAPION: 'Twas what I fear'd.
Charmion, is this well done?
CHARMION: Yes, 'tis well done, and like a Queen, the last
Of her great race: I follow her. [*Sinks down; Dies.*
ALEXAS: 'Tis true,
She has done well: much better thus to die,
Than live to make a Holy-day in *Rome*.
SERAPION: See, see how the Lovers sit in State together,
As they were giving Laws to half Mankind.
Th' impression of a smile left in her face,
Shows she dy'd pleas'd with him for whom she liv'd,
And went to charm him in another World.
Cæsar's just entring: grief has now no leisure.
Secure that Villain, as our pledge of safety
To grace th' Imperial Triumph. Sleep, blest Pair,
Secure from humane chance, long Ages out,
While all the Storms of Fate fly o'er your Tomb;
And Fame, to late Posterity, shall tell,
No Lovers liv'd so great, or dy'd so well.

EPILOGUE

Poets, like Disputants, when Reasons fail,
Have one sure Refuge left; and that's to rail.
Fop, Coxcomb, Fool, are thunder'd through the Pit;
And this is all their Equipage of Wit.
We wonder how the Devil this diff'rence grows,
Betwixt our Fools in Verse, and yours in Prose:
For, 'Faith, the quarrel rightly understood,
'Tis Civil War *with their own Flesh and Blood.*
The thread-bare Author hates the gawdy Coat;
And swears at the Guilt Coach, but swears a foot:
For 'tis observ'd of every scribling Man,
He grows a Fop as fast as e'er he can;
Prunes up, and asks his Oracle the Glass,
If Pink or Purple best become his face.
For our poor Wretch, he neither rails nor prays;
Nor likes your Wit just as you like his Plays;
He has not yet so much of Mr. Bays.

EPILOGUE

He does his best; and, if he cannot please,
Wou'd quietly sue out his Writ of Ease.
Yet, if he might his own Grand Jury call,
By the Fair Sex he begs to stand or fall.
Let Cæsar's *Pow'r the Mens ambition move,*
But grace You him, who lost the World for Love.
Yet if some antiquated Lady say,
The last Age is not Copy'd in his Play;
Heav'n help the Man who for that face must drudge,
Which only has the wrinkles of a Judge.
Let not the Young and Beauteous join with those;
For shou'd you raise such numerous Hosts of Foes,
Young Wits and Sparks he to his aid must call;
'Tis more than one Man's work to please you all.

THE SPANISH FRYAR

OR,

THE DOUBLE DISCOVERY

Ut melius possis fallere, sume togam.—MA.[1]
———— Alterna revisens
Lusit, & in solido rursus fortuna locavit.—VIR.[2]

[1] The better to be able to cheat, assume the toga. (Martial, *Epigrams* 8. 48. 8.)
[2] Fortune plays a deceitful game, coming again to each side in turn; and she establishes men upon firm ground once more. (*Æneid* 11. 427.)

The Spanish Fryar or, The Double Discovery. Acted at the Duke's Theatre. [*Latin quot.*] Written by John Dryden, Servant to His Majesty. London, Printed for Richard Tonson and Jacob Tonson, at Grays-inn-gate, in Grays-inn-lane, and at the Judge's-Head, in Chancery-lane, 1681.

The Spanish Fryar was first performed at the Dorset Garden Theatre on 8 March 1680. The present text follows that of the first edition (Macdonald, 86 a). The speech headings have been expanded and, in the interests of clarity, the stage directions have occasionally been rearranged.

TO THE RIGHT HONOURABLE
JOHN, LORD HAUGHTON[1]

MY LORD,

When I first design'd this Play I found or thought I found somewhat so moving in the serious part of it, and so pleasant in the Comick, as might deserve a more than ordinary Care in both: Accordingly I us'd the best of my endeavour, in the management of two Plots, so very different from each other, that it was not perhaps the Tallent of every Writer, to have made them of a piece. Neither have I attempted other Playes of the same nature, in my opinion, with the same Judgment; though with like success. And though many Poets may suspect themselves for the fondness and partiality of Parents to their youngest Children, yet I hope I may stand exempted from this Rule, because I know my self too well to be ever satisfied with my own Conceptions, which have seldom reach'd to those Idea'*s that I had within me: and consequently, I presume I may have liberty to judge when I write more or less pardonably, as an ordinary Markes-man may know certainly when he shoots less wide at what he aymes. Besides, the Care and Pains I have bestowed on this beyond my other Tragi-comedies may reasonably make the World conclude, that either I can doe nothing tolerably, or that this Poem is not much amiss. Few good Pictures have been finish'd at one sitting; neither can a true just Play, which is to bear the Test of Ages, be produc'd at a heat, or by the force of fancie, without the maturity of judgment. For my own part, I have both so just a Diffidence of my self, and so great a Reverence for my Audience, that I dare venture nothing without a strict Examination; and am as much asham'd to put a loose indigested Play upon the Publick, as I should be to offer brass money in a Payment: For though it shou'd be taken, (as it is too often on the Stage,) yet it will be found in the second telling: And a judicious Reader will discover in his Closset that trashy stuffe, whose glittering deceiv'd him in the action. I have often heard the Stationer sighing in his shop, and wishing for those hands to take off his melancholy bargain which clapp'd its Performance on the Stage. In a Play-house every thing contributes to impose upon the Judgment; the Lights, the Scenes,*

[1] John Holles, Lord Haughton (1662–1711).

the Habits, and, above all, the Grace of Action, which is commonly the best where there is the most need of it, surprize the Audience, and cast a mist upon their Understandings; not unlike the cunning of a Juggler, who is always staring us in the face, and overwhelming us with gibberish, onely that he may gain the opportunity of making the cleaner conveyance of his Trick. But these false Beauties of the Stage are no more lasting than a Rainbow; when the Actor ceases to shine upon them, when he guilds them no longer with his reflection, they vanish in a twinkling. I have sometimes wonder'd, in the reading, what was become of those glaring Colours which amaz'd me in Bussy Damboys [1] *upon the Theatre: but when I had taken up what I suppos'd a fallen Star, I found I had been cozen'd with a Jelly: nothing but a cold dull mass, which glitter'd no longer than it was shooting: A dwarfish thought dress'd up in gigantick words, repetition in aboundance, looseness of expression, and gross Hyperboles; the Sense of one line expanded prodigiously into ten: and, to sum up all, uncorrect English, and a hideous mingle of false Poetry and true Nonsense; or, at best, a scantling of wit which lay gasping for life, and groaning beneath a Heap of Rubbish. A famous modern Poet us'd to sacrifice every year a* Statius *to* Virgil'*s Manes: and I have Indignation enough to burn a* D'amboys *annually to the memory of Johnson. But now, My Lord, I am sensible, perhaps too late, that I have gone too far: for I remember some Verses of my own* Maximin *and* Almanzor *which cry, Vengeance upon me for their Extravagance, and which I wish heartily in the same fire with* Statius *and* Chapman*: All I can say for those passages, which are I hope not many, is, that I knew they were bad enough to please, even when I writ them: But I repent of them amongst my Sins: and if any of their fellows intrude by chance into my present Writings, I draw a stroke over all those* Dalilahs *of the Theatre; and am resolv'd I will settle my self no reputation by the applause of fools. 'Tis not that I am mortified to all ambition, but I scorn as much to take it from half-witted Judges, as I shou'd to raise an Estate by cheating of Bubbles. Neither do I discommend the lofty style in Tragedy which is naturally pompous and magnificent: but nothing is truly sublime that is not just and proper. If the Ancients had judg'd by the same measures which a common Reader takes, they had concluded* Statius *to have written higher than* Virgil: *for,*

Quæ superimposito moles geminata Colosso [2]

[1] George Chapman's tragedy of *Bussy D'Ambois* was published in 1607.

[2] What is this vast bulk, doubled by the colossal figure upon it. . . .? (*Silvae* 1. 1. 1.)

carries a more thundring kind of sound than,

Tityre tu patulæ recubans sub tegmine fagi:[1]

Yet Virgil *had all the Majesty of a lawfull Prince; and* Statius *onely the blustring of a Tyrant. But when men affect a Vertue which they cannot reach, they fall into a Vice, which bears the nearest resemblance to it. Thus an injudicious Poet who aims at Loftiness runs easily into the swelling puffie style, because it looks like Greatness. I remember, when I was a Boy, I thought inimitable* Spencer *a mean Poet in comparison of* Sylvester's Dubartas:[2] *and was rapt into an ecstasie when I read these lines:*

Now, when the Winter's keener breath began
To Chrystallize the Baltick Ocean;
To glaze the Lakes, to bridle up the Floods,
And periwig with Snow the bald-pate Woods:

I am much deceiv'd if this be not abominable fustian, that is, thoughts and words ill sorted, and without the least relation to each other: yet I dare not answer for an Audience, that they wou'd not clap it on the Stage: so little value there is to be given to the common cry, that nothing but Madness can please Mad-men, and a Poet must be of a piece with the Spectators, to gain a reputation with them. But, as in a room, contriv'd for State, the height of the roof shou'd bear a proportion to the Area; so, in the Heightnings of Poetry, the strength and vehemence of Figures shou'd be suited to the Occasion, the Subject, and the Persons. All beyond this is monstrous; 'tis out of nature, 'tis an excrescence, and not a living part of Poetry. I had not said thus much, if some young Gallants, who pretend to Criticism, had not told me that this Tragi-comedy wanted the dignity of style: but as a man who is charg'd with a Crime of which he thinks himself innocent, is apt to be too eager in his own defence, so perhaps I have vindicated my Play with more partiality than I ought, or than such a trifle can deserve. Yet, whatever beauties it may want, 'tis free at least from the grossness of those faults I mention'd: What Credit it has gain'd upon the Stage, I value no farther than in reference to my Profit, and the satisfaction I had in seeing it represented with all the justness and gracefulness of Action. But as 'tis my Interest to please my Audience, so 'tis my Ambition to be read; that I am sure is the more lasting and the nobler Design: for the propriety of thoughts and

[1] Thou, Tityrus, reclining in a spreading beech-tree's shade. . . . (*Eclogues* 1. 1.)

[2] Joshua Sylvester's (1563–1618) *Du Bartas his Divine Weekes and Workes* was first published in 1598 and often reprinted.

words, which are the hidden beauties of a Play, are but confus'dly judg'd in the vehemence of Action: All things are there beheld, as in a hasty motion, where the objects onely glide before the Eye and disappear. The most discerning Critick can judge no more of these silent graces in the Action, than he who rides Post through an unknown Countrey can distinguish the scituation of places, and the nature of the soyle. The purity of phrase, the clearness of conception and expression, the boldness maintain'd to Majesty, the significancie and sound of words, not strain'd into bombast, but justly elevated, in short, those very words and thoughts which cannot be chang'd but for the worse, must of necessity escape our transient view upon the Theatre: and yet without all these a Play may take. For if either the Story move us, or the Actor help the lameness of it with his performance, or now and then a glittering beam of wit or passion strike through the obscurity of the Poem, any of these are sufficient to effect a present liking, but not to fix a lasting admiration; for nothing but Truth can long continue; and Time is the surest Judge of Truth. I am not vain enough to think I have left no faults in this, which that touchstone will not discover; neither indeed is it possible to avoid them in a Play of this nature. There are evidently two Actions in it: But it will be clear to any judicious man, that with half the pains I could have rais'd a Play from either of them: for this time I satisfied my own humour, which was to tack two Plays together; and to break a rule for the pleasure of variety. The truth is, the Audience are grown weary of continu'd melancholy Scenes: and I dare venture to prophesie, that few Tragedies except those in Verse shall succeed in this Age, if they are not lighten'd with a course of mirth. For the Feast is too dull and solemn without the Fiddles. But how difficult a task this is, will soon be try'd: for a several Genius is requir'd to either way; and without both of 'em, a man, in my opinion, is but half a Poet for the Stage. Neither is it so trivial an undertaking, to make a Tragedy end happily; for 'tis more difficult to save than 'tis to kill. The Dagger and the Cup of Poison are alwaies in a readiness; but to bring the Action to the last extremity, and then by probable means to recover all, will require the Art and Judgment of a Writer; and cost him many a pang in the performance.

And now, My Lord, I must confess that what I have written looks more like a Preface than a Dedication; and truly it was thus far my design, that I might entertain you with somewhat in my own Art which might be more worthy of a noble mind, than the stale exploded Trick of fulsome Panegyricks. 'Tis difficult to write justly on any thing, but almost impossible in Praise. I shall therefore wave so nice a subject; and onely tell you, that in recommending a Protestant Play to a Protestant Patron, as I doe my self an Honour, so I do your Noble Family a right, who have been alwaies eminent in the support and favour of our Religion and Liberties. And if the promises of your Youth, your Education at home, and your Experience abroad, deceive me not, the Principles you have embrac'd are such as will no way degenerate from your Ancestors, but refresh their memory in the minds of all true English-men, *and renew their lustre in your Person; which, My Lord, is not more the wish than it is the constant expectation of your Lordship's*

Most obedient,
faithfull Servant,
John Dryden.

PROLOGUE

Now Luck for us, and a kind hearty Pit;
For he who pleases, never failes of Wit:
Honour is yours:
And you, like Kings, at City Treats bestow it;
The Writer kneels, and is bid rise a Poet:
But you are fickle Sovereigns, to our Sorrow,
You dubb to day, and hang a man to morrow;
You cry the same Sense up, and down again,
Just like brass mony once a year in Spain*:*
Take you i' th' mood, what e'er base metal come,
You coin as fast as Groats at Bromingam*:*[1]
Though 'tis no more like Sense in ancient Plays,
Than Rome's *Religion like St.* Peter's *days.*
In short, so swift your Judgments turn and wind,
You cast our fleetest Wits a mile behind.
'Twere well your Judgments but in Plays did range,
But ev'n your Follies and Debauches change
With such a Whirl, the Poets of your age
Are tyr'd, and cannot score 'em on the Stage,
Unless each Vice in short-hand they indite,
Ev'n as notcht Prentices whole Sermons write.[2]
The heavy Hollanders *no Vices know*
But what they us'd a hundred years ago,
Like honest Plants, where they were stuck, they grow;
They cheat, but still from cheating Sires they come;
They drink, but they were christ'ned first in Mum.
Their patrimonial Sloth the Spaniards *keep,*
And Philip *first taught* Philip *how to sleep.*
The French *and we still change, but here's the Curse,*
They change for better, and we change for worse;
They take up our old trade of Conquering,
And we are taking theirs, to dance and sing:
Our Fathers did for change to France *repair,*
And they for change will try our English *Air.*
As Children, when they throw one Toy away,
Strait a more foolish Gugaw comes in play:

[1] See *Absalom and Achitophel*, p. 87, n. 1.
[2] Scott explains that "it was anciently part of the apprentice's duty to take notes of the sermon for the edification of his master or mistress."

So we, grown penitent, on serious thinking,
Leave Whoring, and devoutly fall to Drinking.
Scowring the Watch grows out of fashion wit:
Now we set up for Tilting in the Pit,
Where 'tis agreed by Bullies, chicken-hearted,
To fright the Ladies first, and then be parted.
A fair Attempt has twice or thrice been made,
To hire Night murth'rers, and make Death a Trade.
When Murther's out, what Vice can we advance?
Unless the new found Pois'ning Trick of France:
And when their Art of Rats-bane *we have got,*
By way of thanks, we'll send 'em o'er our Plot.

DRAMATIS PERSONÆ

Leonora, Queen of *Arragon*,	Mrs. *Barry*.
Teresa, Woman to *Leonora*,	Mrs. *Crofts*.
Elvira, Wife to *Gomez*,	Mrs. *Betterton*.
Torrismond,	Mr. *Betterton*.
Bertran,	Mr. *Williams*.
Alphonso,	Mr. *Wiltsheir*.
Lorenzo, his Son,	Mr. *Smith*.
Raymond,	Mr. *Gillow*.
Pedro,	Mr. *Underhill*.
Gomez,	Mr. *Nokes*.
Dominic, the Spanish Fryar,	Mr. *Lee*.

THE SPANISH FRYAR

OR, THE DOUBLE DISCOVERY

ACT I

ALPHONSO, PEDRO *meet, with Souldiers on each side, Drums, &c.*

ALPHONSO: Stand: give the Word.
PEDRO: The Queen of *Arragon.*
ALPHONSO: *Pedro?*—how goes the night?
PEDRO: She wears apace.
ALPHONSO: Then welcom day-light: We shall have warm work on't:
The *Moore* will 'gage
His utmost Forces on this next Assault,
To win a Queen and Kingdom.
PEDRO: Pox o' this Lyon-way of wooing though:
Is the Queen stirring yet?
ALPHONSO: She has not been abed: but in her Chapel
All night devoutly watch'd: and brib'd the Saints
With Vows for her Deliverance.
PEDRO: O, *Alphonso,*
I fear they come too late! her Father's crimes
Sit heavy on her; and weigh down her prayers:
A Crown usurp'd; a lawfull King depos'd;
In bondage held; debarr'd the common light;
His Children murther'd, and his Friends destroy'd:
What can we less expect then what we feel,
And what we fear will follow?
ALPHONSO: Heav'n avert it!
PEDRO: Then Heav'n must not be Heav'n: Judge the event
By what has pass'd: Th' Usurper joy'd not long
His ill-got Crown! 'Tis true, he dy'd in peace:
Unriddle that ye Pow'rs: But left his Daughter,
Our present Queen, ingag'd, upon his death-bed,
To marry with young *Bertran*, whose curs'd Father
Had help'd to make him great.
Hence, you well know, this fatal War arose;

Because the *Moore, Abdalla*, with whose Troops
Th' Usurper gain'd the Kingdom, was refus'd;
And, as an Infidel, his Love despis'd.

ALPHONSO: Well; we are Souldiers, *Pedro*: and, like Lawyers,
Plead for our Pay.

PEDRO: A good Cause wou'd doe well though:
It gives my Sword an Edge: You see this *Bertran*
Has now three times been beaten by the *Moores*:
What hope we have, is in young *Torrismond*,
Your brother's Son.

ALPHONSO: He's a successfull Warriour,
And has the Souldiers hearts: Upon the skirts
Of *Arragon*, our squander'd Troops he rallies:
Our Watchmen, from the Tow'rs, with longing Eyes
Expect his swift Arrival.

PEDRO: It must be swift, or it will come too late.

ALPHONSO: No more:——Duke *Bertran*.

Enter BERTRAN, *attended.*

BERTRAN: Relieve the Cent'rys that have watch'd all night.
[To PEDRO.] Now, Collonel, have you dispos'd your men,
That you stand idle here?

PEDRO: Mine are drawn off,
To take a short repose.

BERTRAN: Short let it be:
For, from the *Moorish* Camp, this hour and more,
There has been heard a distant humming noise,
Like Bees disturb'd, and arming in their hives.
What Courage in our Souldiers? Speak! What hope?

PEDRO: As much as when Physicians shake their heads,
And bid their dying Patient think of Heav'n.
Our Walls are thinly mann'd: our best Men slain:
The rest, an heartless number, spent with Watching,
And harass'd out with Duty.

BERTRAN: Good-night all then.

PEDRO: Nay, for my part, 'tis but a single life
I have to lose: I'll plant my Colours down
In the mid-breach, and by 'em fix my foot:
Say a short Souldier's Pray'r, to spare the trouble
Of my few Friends above: and then expect
The next fair Bullet.

ALPHONSO: Never was known a night of such distraction:
Noise so confus'd and dreadfull: Justling Crowds,

That run, and know not whither: Torches gliding,
Like Meteors, by each other in the streets.

PEDRO: I met a reverend, fat, old, gouty Fryar;
With a Paunch swoln so high, his double Chin
Might rest upon 't: A true Son of the Church;
Fresh colour'd, and well thriven on his Trade,
Come puffing with his greazy bald-pate Quire,
And fumbling o'er his Beads, in such an Agony,
He told 'em false for fear: About his Neck
There hung a Wench; the Labell of his Function;
Whom he shook off, i'faith, methought, unkindly.
It seems the holy Stallion durst not score
Another Sin before he left the world.

Enter a CAPTAIN.

CAPTAIN: To Arms, My Lord, to Arms.
From the *Moors* Camp the noise grows louder still:
Rattling of Armour, Trumpets, Drums, and Ataballes;
And sometimes Peals of Shouts that rend the Heav'ns,
Like Victory: Then Groans again, and Howlings,
Like those of vanquish'd men: But every Echo
Goes fainter off; and dyes in distant Sounds.

BERTRAN: Some false Attaque: expect on t'other side:
One to the Gunners on St. *Jago*'s Tow'r; Bid 'em, for shame,
Level their Cannon lower: On my Soul,
They 're all corrupted with the Gold of *Barbary*
To carry over, and not hurt the *Moor*.

Enter second CAPTAIN.

2 CAPTAIN: My Lord, here's fresh Intelligence arriv'd:
Our Army, led by Valiant *Torrismond*,
Is now in hot Engagement with the *Moors*;
'Tis said, within their Trenches.

BERTRAN: I think all Fortune is reserv'd for him.
He might have sent us word though;
And then we cou'd have favour'd his Attempt
With Sallies from the Town.——

ALPHONSO: It cou'd not be:
We were so close block'd up that none cou'd peepe
Upon the Walls and live: But yet 'tis time:——

BERTRAN: No, 'tis too late; I will not hazard it:
On pain of Death, let no man dare to sally.

PEDRO *aside*: Oh Envy, Envy, how it works within him!
How now! What means this Show?

ALPHONSO: 'Tis a Procession:
The Queen is going to the great Cathedral
To pray for our Success against the *Moores*.

PEDRO: Very good: She usurps the Throne; keeps the old King in Prison; and, at the same time, is praying for a Blessing: Oh Religion and Roguery, how they go together!

A Procession of Priests and Choristers in white, with Tapers, follow'd by the QUEEN *and Ladies, goes over the Stage: the Choristers singing.*

Look down, ye bless'd above, look down,
Behold our weeping Matron's Tears,
Behold our tender Virgins Fears,
And with success our Armies crown.

Look down, ye bless'd above, look down:
Oh! save us, save us, and our State restore;
For Pitty, Pitty, Pitty, we implore;
For Pitty, Pitty, Pitty, we implore.

The Procession goes off; and shout within. Then enter LORENZO, *who kneels to* ALPHONSO.

BERTRAN *to* ALPHONSO: A joyful Cry: and see your Son *Lorenzo*: Good news kind Heav'n!

ALPHONSO *to* LORENZO: O, welcome, welcome! is the General safe?
How near our Army? When shall we be succour'd?
Or, Are we succour'd? Are the *Moores* remov'd?
Answer these questions first; and then, a Thousand more:
Answer 'em all together.

LORENZO: Yes, when I have a thousand Tongues, I will.
The General's well: His Army too is safe
As Victory can make 'em: The *Moores* King
Is safe enough, I warrant him, for one.
At dawn of day our General cleft his Pate,
Spight of his woollen Night-cap: A slight wound:
Perhaps he may recover.

ALPHONSO: Thou reviv'st me.

PEDRO: By my computation now, the Victory was gain'd before the Procession was made for it; and yet it will go hard, but the Priests will make a Miracle on't.

LORENZO: Yes, Faith; we came like bold intruding Guests;
And took 'em unprepar'd to give us welcome:
Their Scouts we kill'd; then found their Body sleeping:
And as they lay confus'd, we stumbl'd o'er 'em;
And took what Joint came next; Arms, Heads, or Leggs;
Somewhat undecently: But when men want light
They make but bungling work.

BERTRAN: I'll to the Queen,
And bear the News.

PEDRO: That's young *Lorenzo*'s duty.

BERTRAN: I'll spare his trouble.——
This *Torrismond* begins to grow too fast; [*Aside.*
He must be mine, or ruin'd. [*Exit* BERTRAN.

LORENZO: *Pedro*, a word:—[*whisper.*]

ALPHONSO: How swift he shot away! I find it stung him,
In spight of his dissembling.
[*To* LORENZO.] How many of the Enemy are slain?

LORENZO: Troth, Sir, we were in hast; and cou'd not stay
To score the men we kill'd: But there they lye.
Best send our Women out to take the tale;
There's Circumcision in abundance for 'em.
[*Turns to* PEDRO *again.*

ALPHONSO: How far did you pursue 'em?

LORENZO: Some few miles.——
[*To* PEDRO.] Good store of Harlots, say you, and dog-cheap?

PEDRO: They must be had; and speedily:
I've kept a tedious Fast. [*Whisper again.*

ALPHONSO: When will he make his Entry? He deserves
Such Triumphs as were giv'n by Ancient *Rome*:
Ha, Boy, What saiest thou?

LORENZO: As you say, Sir, That *Rome* was very ancient——
[To PEDRO.] I leave the choice to you; Fair, Black, Tall, Low:
Let her but have a Nose:—and you may tell her
I'm rich in Jewels, Rings, and bobbing Pearls
Pluck'd from *Moores* ears.—

ALPHONSO: *Lorenzo?*

LORENZO: Somewhat busie
About Affairs relating to the publick.——
—A seasonable Girl, just in the nick now;—[*to* PEDRO.
[*Trumpets within.*

PEDRO: I hear the General's Trumpets: Stand, and mark

How he will be receiv'd; I fear, but coldly:
There hung a Cloud, methought, on *Bertran*'s brow.

LORENZO: Then look to see a Storm on *Torrismond*'s:
Looks fright not men: The General has seen *Moores*,
With as bad Faces; no dispraise to *Bertran*'s.

PEDRO: 'Twas rumour'd in the Camp, he loves the Queen.

LORENZO: He drinks her Health devoutly.

ALPHONSO: That may breed bad bloud 'twixt him and *Bertran*.

PEDRO: Yes, in private:
But *Bertran* has been taught the Arts of Court,
To guild a Face with Smiles: and leer a man to ruin.
O here they come.———

[*Enter* TORRISMOND *and Officers on one Side:* BERTRAN *attended on the other: they embrace:* BERTRAN *bowing low.*]

Just as I prophesy'd.——

LORENZO: Death and Hell, he laughs at him:—in 's Face too.

PEDRO: O, you mistake him: 'Twas an humble Grin;
The fawning Joy of Courtiers and of Dogs.

LORENZO *aside*: Here are nothing but Lyes to be expected: I'll e'en go lose my self in some blind Alley; and try if any courteous Damsel will think me worth the finding.

[*Exit* LORENZO.

ALPHONSO: Now he begins to open.

BERTRAN: Your Country rescu'd, and your Queen reliev'd!
A glorious Conquest; Noble *Torrismond!*
The People rend the Skyes with loud Applause;
And Heav'n can hear no other Name but yours.
The thronging Crowds press on you as you pass;
And, with their eager Joy, make Triumph slow.

TORRISMOND: My Lord, I have no taste
Of popular Applause; the noisie Praise
Of giddy Crowds, as changeable as Winds;
Still vehement, and still without a cause:
Servants to Chance; and blowing in the tyde
Of swoln Success; but, veering with its ebbe,
It leaves the channel dry.

BERTRAN: So young a Stoick!

TORRISMOND: You wrong me, if you think I'll sell one drop
Within these Veins for Pageants: But let Honour
Call for my Bloud, and sluce it into streams;
Turn Fortune loose again to my pursuit;
And let me hunt her through embattl'd Foes,

In dusty Plains, amidst the Cannons roar,
There will I be the first.

BERTRAN: I'll try him farther.—— [*Aside.*]
Suppose th' assembled States of *Arragon*
Decree a Statue to you thus inscrib'd,
To *Torrismond*, who freed his native Land.

ALPHONSO *to* PEDRO: Mark how he sounds and fathoms him, to find
The Shallows of his Soul!

BERTRAN: The just Applause
Of God-like Senates, is the Stamp of Vertue,
Which makes it pass unquestion'd through the World:
These Honours you deserve; nor shall my suffrage
Be last to fix 'em on you: If refus'd,
You brand us all with black Ingratitude;
For times to come shall say, Our *Spain*, like *Rome*,
Neglects her Champions, after Noble Acts,
And lets their Laurels wither on their heads.

TORRISMOND: A Statue, for a Battel blindly fought,
Where Darkness and Surprise made Conquest cheap!
Where Virtue borrow'd but the Arms of Chance,
And struck a random blow! 'Twas Fortune's work;
And Fortune take the praise.

BERTRAN: Yet Happiness
Is the first Fame: Vertue without Success
Is a fair Picture shown by an ill light:
But lucky men are Favorites of Heaven:
And whom should Kings esteem above Heaven's Darlings?
The Praises of a young and beauteous Queen
Shall crown your glorious Acts.

PEDRO *to* ALPHONSO: There sprung the Mine.

TORRISMOND: The Queen! That were a happiness too great!
Nam'd you the Queen, My Lord?

BERTRAN: Yes: You have seen her, and you must confess
A Praise, a Smile, a Look from her is worth
The shouts of thousand Amphitheaters.
She, she shall praise you; for I can oblige her:
To morrow will deliver all her Charms
Into my Arms; and make her mine for ever.
Why stand you mute?

TORRISMOND: Alas! I cannot speak.

BERTRAN: Not speak, My Lord! How were your thoughts employ'd?

TORRISMOND: Nor can I think; or I am lost in thought.
BERTRAN: Thought of the Queen, perhaps?
TORRISMOND: Why, if it were,
    Heav'n may be thought on, though too high to climbe.
BERTRAN: O, now I find where your Ambition drives:
    You ought not to think of her.
TORRISMOND: So I say too;
    I ought not: Madmen ought not to be mad:
    But who can help his frenzy?
BERTRAN: Fond young Man!
    The Wings of your Ambition must be clipt:
    Your shamefac'd Vertue shunn'd the Peoples Praise,
    And Senates Honours: But 'tis well we know
    What price you hold your self at: you have fought
    With some Success, and that has seal'd your Pardon.
TORRISMOND: Pardon from thee! O, give me patience Heav'n!
    Thrice vanquish'd *Bertran*; if thou darst, look out
    Upon yon slaughter'd Host, that Field of bloud:
    There seal my Pardon, where thy Fame was lost.
PEDRO: He's ruin'd, past redemption!
ALPHONSO *to* TORRISMOND: Learn respect
    To the first Prince o' th' bloud.
BERTRAN: O, let him rave!
    I'll not contend with Madmen.
TORRISMOND: I have done:
    I know 'twas Madness to declare this Truth:
    And yet 'twere Baseness to deny my Love.
    'Tis true, my hopes are vanishing as clouds;
    Lighter then childrens bubbles blown by winds:
    My merit's but the rash results of chance:
    My birth unequal: all the stars against me:
    Pow'r, promise, choice; the living and the dead:
    Mankind my foes; and onely love to friend:
    But such a love, kept at such awfull distance,
    As, what it loudly dares to tell, a Rival
    Shall fear to whisper there: Queens may be lov'd,
    And so may Gods; else, why are Altars rais'd?
    Why shines the Sun, but that he may be view'd?
    But, Oh! when he's too bright, if then we gaze,
    'Tis but to weep; and close our eyes in darkness.
[*Exit* TORRISMOND.
BERTRAN: 'Tis well: the Goddess shall be told, she shall,
    Of her new Worshipper. [*Exit* BERTRAN.

PEDRO: So, here's fine work!
He has supply'd his onely foe with arms
For his destruction. Old *Penelope*'s tale
Inverted: h' has unravell'd all by day
That he has done by night.—What, Planet-struck!

ALPHONSO: I wish I were; to be past sense of this!

PEDRO: Wou'd I had but a Lease of life so long
As till my Flesh and Bloud rebell'd this way
Against our Sovereign Lady: mad for a Queen?
With a Globe in one hand, and a Sceptre in t'other?
A very pretty Moppet!

ALPHONSO: Then to declare his Madness to his Rival!
His Father absent on an Embassy:
Himself a Stranger almost; wholly friendless!
A Torrent, rowling down a Precipice,
Is easier to be stopt, then is his Ruin.

PEDRO: 'Tis fruitless to complain: haste to the Court:
Improve your interest there, for Pardon from the Queen.

ALPHONSO: Weak remedies;
But all must be attempted. [*Exit* ALPHONSO.

Enter LORENZO.

LORENZO: Well, I am the most unlucky Rogue! I have been ranging over half the Town; but have sprung no Game. Our Women are worse Infidels then the *Moores*: I told 'em I was one of their Knight-errants, that deliver'd them from ravishment: and I think in my conscience that 's their Quarrel to me.

PEDRO: Is this a time for fooling? Your Cousin is run honourably mad in love with her Majesty: He is split upon a Rock; and you, who are in chase of Harlots, are sinking in the main Ocean. I think the Devil's in the Family. [*Exit* PEDRO.

LORENZO *solus*: My cousin ruin'd, saies he! hum! not that I wish my Kinsman's ruin; that were Unchristian: but if the General's ruin'd, I am Heir; there's comfort for a Christian. Money I have, I thank the honest *Moores* for't; but I want a Mistress. I am willing to be leud; but the Tempter is wanting on his part.

Enter ELVIRA *veil'd*.

ELVIRA: Stranger! Cavalier—will you not hear me? you *Moore-killer*, you *Matador*.——

LORENZO: Meaning me, Madam?

ELVIRA: Face about, Man; you a souldier, and afraid of the Enemy!

LORENZO *aside*: I must confess, I did not expect to have been charg'd first: I see Souls will not be lost for want of diligence in this Devil's reign:—[*to her*]—Now; Madam *Cynthia* behind a cloud; your will and pleasure with me?

ELVIRA: You have the appearance of a Cavalier; and if you are as deserving as you seem, perhaps you may not repent of your Adventure. If a Lady like you well enough to hold discourse with you at first sight; you are Gentleman enough, I hope, to help her out with an Apology: and to lay the blame on Stars, or Destiny; or what you please, to excuse the Frailty of a Woman.

LORENZO: O, I love an easie Woman: there's such a doe to crack a thick shell'd Mistress: we break our Teeth; and find no Kernel. 'Tis generous in you, to take pity on a Stranger; and not to suffer him to fall into ill hands at his first arrival

ELVIRA: You may have a better opinion of me then I deserve; you have not seen me yet: and therefore I am confident you are heart-whole.

LORENZO: Not absolutely slain, I must confess; but I am drawing on apace: you have a dangerous Tongue in your head, I can tell you that; and if your Eyes prove of as killing metal, there 's but one way with me: Let me see you, for the safeguard of my Honour: 'tis but decent the Cannon should be drawn down upon me, before I yield.

ELVIRA: What a terrible Similitude have you made, Colonel? to shew that you are inclining to the Wars: I could answer you with another in my Profession: Suppose you were in want of Money, wou'd you not be glad to take a Sum upon content in a seal'd bagg, without peeping?—but however; I will not stand with you for a sample. [*Lifts up her Veil.*

LORENZO: What Eyes were there! How keen their Glances! you doe well to keep 'em veil'd: they are too sharp to be trusted out o' th' Scabbard.

ELVIRA: Perhaps now you may accuse my forwardness; but this day of Jubilee is the onely time of freedom I have had: and there is nothing so extravagant as a Prisoner, when he gets loose a little, and is immediately to return into his Fetters.

LORENZO: To confess freely to you, Madam, I was never in love with less then your whole Sex before: but now I have seen you, I am in the direct road of languishing and sighing: and, if Love goes on as it begins, for ought I know, by to morrow morning you may hear of me in Rhyme and Sonnet. I tell you truly, I do not like these Symptoms in my self: perhaps I may go shufflingly at first; for I was never before walk'd in Trammels; yet I shall drudge and moil at Constancy, till I have worn off the hitching in my pace.

ELVIRA: Oh, Sir, there are Arts to reclaim the wildest Men, as there are to make Spaniels fetch and carry: chide 'em often, and feed 'em seldom: now I know your temper, you may thank yourself if you are kept to hard meat:——you are in for years if you make love to me.

LORENZO: I hate a formal obligation with an *Anno Domini* at end on't; there may be an evil meaning in the word Years, call'd Matrimony.

ELVIRA: I can easily rid you of that Fear: I wish I could rid my self as easily of the bondage.

LORENZO: Then you are married?

ELVIRA: If a Covetous, and a Jealous, and an Old man be a husband.

LORENZO: Three as good qualities for my purpose as I could wish: now love be prais'd.

Enter ELVIRA'S DUENNA, *and whispers to her.*

ELVIRA *aside*: If I get not home before my Husband, I shall be ruin'd. [*To him.*] I dare not stay to tell you where—farewell—cou'd I once more— [*Exit* ELVIRA.

LORENZO: This is unconscionable dealing; to be made a Slave, and not know whose livery I wear:—Who have we yonder?

[*Enter* GOMEZ.]

By that shambling in his walk, it should be my rich old Banquer, *Gomez*, whom I knew at *Barcelona*: As I live 'tis he—What, Old *Mammon* here. [*To* GOMEZ.

GOMEZ: How! young *Beelzebub*!

LORENZO: What Devil has set his Claws in thy Hanches, and brought thee hither to *Saragossa?* Sure he meant a farther Journey with thee.

GOMEZ: I alwaies remove before the Enemy: When the *Moores* are ready to besiege one Town, I shift quarters to the next: I keep as far from the Infidels as I can.

LORENZO: That's but a hair's breadth at farthest.

GOMEZ: Well, You have got a famous Victory; all true Subjects are overjoy'd at it: there are Bonfires decreed: and the times had not been hard, my Billet should have burnt too.

LORENZO: I dare say for thee, thou hast such a respect for a single Billet, thou would'st almost have thrown on thy self to save it: thou art for saving every thing but thy Soul.

GOMEZ: Well, well, You'll not believe me generous 'till I carry you to the Tavern, and crack half a Pint with you at my own charges.

LORENZO: No; I'll keep thee from hanging thy self for such an extravagance: and, instead of it, thou shalt doe me a meer verbal courtesie: I have just now seen a most incomparable young Lady.

GOMEZ: Whereabouts did you see this most incomparable young Lady? my mind misgives me plaguily.—— [*Aside.*

LORENZO: Here, man; just before this Corner-house: Pray Heaven it prove no Bawdy-house.

GOMEZ *aside*: Pray heaven he does not make it one.

LORENZO: What does thou mutter to thy self? Hast thou any thing to say against the Honesty of that house?

GOMEZ: Not I, Colonel, the Walls are very honest Stone, and the Timber very honest Wood, for ought I know. But for the Woman, I cannot say, till I know her better: describe her person; and, if she live in this quarter, I may give you tidings of her.

LORENZO: She 's of a middle Stature, dark colour'd Hair, the most bewitching Leer with her Eyes, the most roguish Cast; her Cheeks are dimpled when she smiles; and her Smiles would tempt an Hermit.

GOMEZ *aside*: I am dead, I am buried, I am damn'd.—Go on ——Colonel——have you no other Marks of her?

LORENZO: Thou hast all her Marks; but that she has a Husband; a jealous, covetous, old Huncks: speak; canst thou tell me News of her?

GOMEZ: Yes; this News, Colonel; that you have seen your last of her.

LORENZO: If thou helpst me not to the knowledge of her, thou art a circumcised *Jew*.

GOMEZ: Circumcise me no more then I circumcise you, Colonel *Hernando*: once more you have seen your last of her.

LORENZO *aside*: I am glad he knows me onely by that Name of *Hernando*, by which I went at *Barcelona*: now he can tell no tales of me to my Father.—[*To him.*] Come, thou wert ever good-natur'd, when thou couldst get by't:—Look here, Rogue, 'tis of the right damning colour:—thou art not Proof against Gold, sure!—do not I know thee for a covetous,——

GOMEZ: Jealous, old Hunncks: those were the Marks of your Mistresse's Husband, as I remember, Colonel.

LORENZO: Oh, the Devil! What a Rogue in understanding was I, not to find him out sooner! [*Aside.*

GOMEZ: Do, do, look sillily, good Colonel: 'tis a decent Melancholy after an absolute Defeat.

LORENZO: Faith, not for that, dear *Gomez*; but——

GOMEZ: But—no Pumping, My dear Colonel.

LORENZO: Hang Pumping; I was—thinking a little upon a point of Gratitude: we two have been long Acquaintance; I know thy Merits, and can make some Interest: go to; thou wert born to Authority: I'll make thee *Alcaide*, Mayor of *Saragossa*.

GOMEZ: Satisfie your self; you shall not make me what you think, Colonel.

LORENZO: Faith but I will; thou hast the Face of a Magistrate already.

GOMEZ: And you would provide me with a Magistrate's Head to my Magistrate's Face; I thank you Colonel.

LORENZO: Come, thou art so suspicious upon an idle Story—that Woman I saw, I mean that little, crooked, ugly Woman;—for t'other was a Lye;—is no more thy Wife:—As I'll go home with thee, and satisfie thee immediately, My dear Friend.

GOMEZ: I shall not put you to that trouble: no not so much as a single Visit: not so much as an Embassy by a civil, old Woman: nor a Serenade of *Twinckledum*, *Twinckledum* under my windows: Nay, I will advise you out of my tenderness to your Person, that you walk not near yon Corner-house by night; for to my certain knowledg, there are Blunderbusses planted in every loop-hole, that go off constantly of their own accord, at the squeaking of a Fiddle, and the thrumming of a Ghittar.

LORENZO: Art thou so obstinate? Then I denounce open War against thee: I'll demolish thy Citadel by force: or, at least, I'll bring my whole Regiment upon thee: my thousand Red Locusts that shall devour thee in Free-quarter.——Farwell wrought Night-cap. [*Exit* LORENZO.

GOMEZ: Farwell Buff! Free-quarter for a Regiment of Redcoat Locusts? I hope to see 'em all in the Red-sea first!—But oh, this *Jezabel* of mine! I'll get a Physician that shall prescribe her an ounce of *Camphire* every morning for her Breakfast, to abate Incontinency: she shall never peep abroad, no, not to Church for Confession; and for never going, she shall be condemn'd for a Heretick: she shall have Stripes by *Troy* weight; and Sustenance by drachms and scruples: Nay, I'll have a Fasting Almanack printed on purpose for her use; in which,

No Carnival nor Christmas shall appear;
But Lents and Ember-weeks shall fill the year.

[*Exit* GOMEZ.

ACT II

SCENE, *The Queen's Anti-chamber.*

ALPHONSO, PEDRO.

ALPHONSO: When saw you my *Lorenzo?*

PEDRO: I had a glimpse of him; but he shot by me
Like a young Hound upon a burning scent:
He's gon a Harlot-hunting.

ALPHONSO: His foreign breeding might have taught him better.

PEDRO: 'Tis that has taught him this.
What learn our Youth abroad; but to refine
The homely Vices of their native Land?
Give me an honest homespun countrey Clown
Of our own growth; his dulness is but plain;
But their's embroider'd: they are sent out Fools,
And come back Fopps.

ALPHONSO: You know what reasons urg'd me;
But now I have accomplish'd my Designs,
I shou'd be glad he knew 'em:—his wild Riots
Disturb my Soul; but they wou'd sit more close,
Did not the threaten'd down-fall of our house,
In *Torrismond*, o'erwhelm my private Ills.

Enter BERTRAN *attended; and whispering with a Courtier, aside.*

BERTRAN: I wou'd not have her think he dar'd to love her;
If he presume to own it, she's so proud
He tempts his certain ruin.

ALPHONSO *to* PEDRO: Mark how disdainfully he throws his Eyes on us.
Our old imprison'd King wore no such Looks.

PEDRO: O, would the General shake off his Dotage to th' usurping Queen,

And re-inthrone Good, Venerable *Sancho*,
I'll undertake, shou'd *Bertran* sound his Trumpets,
And *Torrismond* but whistle through his Fingers,
He draws his Army off.

ALPHONSO: I told him so:
But had an Answer louder then a Storm.

PEDRO: Now Plague and Pox on his Smock-loyalty!
I hate to see a brave bold Fellow sotted,
Made sour and senseless; turn'd to Whey by Love:
A driveling Hero; fit for a Romance.
O, here he comes; what will their greetings be!

Enter TORRISMOND *attended.* BERTRAN *and he meet and justle.*

BERTRAN: Make way, My Lords, and let the Pageant pass.

TORRISMOND: I make my way where'er I see my Foe:
But you, My Lord, are good at a Retreat:
I have no *Moores* behind me.

BERTRAN: Death and Hell!
Dare to speak thus when you come out again?

TORRISMOND: Dare to provoke me thus, insulting man?

Enter TERESA.

TERESA: My Lords, You are too loud so near the Queen:
You, *Torrismond*, have much offended her:
'Tis her Command you instantly appear,
To answer your demeanour to the Prince.
[*Exit* TERESA; BERTRAN *with his company follow her.*

TORRISMOND: O *Pedro*, O *Alphonso*, pity me!
A Grove of Pikes
Whose polish'd Steel from far severely shines,
Are not so dreadfull as this beauteous Queen.

ALPHONSO: Call up your Courage timely to your aid:
And, like a Lion press'd upon the Toyles,
Leap on your Hunters: Speak your Actions boldly;
There is a time when modest Vertue is
Allow'd to praise it self.

PEDRO: Heart, you were hot enough; too hot, but now;
Your Fury then boil'd upward to a Fome:
But since this Message came, you sink and settle;
As if cold water had been pour'd upon you.

TORRISMOND: Alas, thou know'st not what it is to love!
When we behold an Angel, not to fear,
Is to be impudent:—no I am resolv'd,

Like a led Victim, to my Death I'll goe;
And, dying, bless the hand that gave the blow. [*Exeunt.*

The SCENE *draws; and shews the* QUEEN *sitting in state,* BERTRAN *standing next to her: then* TERESA, *&c.*

She rises, and comes to the Front.

QUEEN *to* BERTRAN: I blame not you, My Lord, my Father's will,
Your own Deserts, and all my People's Voice,
Have plac'd you in the view of Sovereign Pow'r.
But I wou'd learn the cause, why *Torrismond,*
Within my Palace Walls, within my Hearing,
Almost within my Sight, affronts a Prince
Who shortly shall command him.

BERTRAN: He thinks you owe him more than you can pay;
And looks, as he were Lord of humane kind.

Enter TORRISMOND, ALPHONSO, PEDRO. TORRISMOND *bows low: then looks earnestly on the* QUEEN, *and keeps at distance.*

TERESA: Madam, The General.——

QUEEN: Let me view him well.
My Father sent him early to the Frontiers;
I have not often seen him; if I did,
He pass'd unmark'd by my unheeding Eyes.
But where's the Fierceness, the Disdainful Pride;
The Haughty Port, the Fiery Arrogance?
By all these Marks, this is not sure the man.

BERTRAN: Yet this is he who fill'd your Court with Tumult,
Whose Fierce Demeanour, and whose Insolence
The Patience of a God could not support.

QUEEN: Name his Offence, My Lord, and he shall have
Immediate punishment.

BERTRAN: 'Tis of so high a nature, shou'd I speak it,
That my Presumption then wou'd equal his.

QUEEN: Some one among you speak.

PEDRO *aside*: Now my Tongue itches.

QUEEN: All dumb! on your Allegiance, *Torrismond,*
By all your hopes, I do command you, speak.

TORRISMOND *kneeling*: O seek not to convince me of a Crime
Which I can ne'er repent, nor can you pardon.
Or, if you needs will know it, think, oh think,
That he, who thus commanded dares to speak,
Unless commanded, would have dy'd in silence.

But you adjur'd me, Madam, by my hopes!
Hopes I have none; for I am all Despair:
Friends I have none; for Friendship follows Favour.
Desert I've none; for what I did, was Duty:
Oh, that it were! that it were Duty all!

QUEEN: Why do you pause? proceed.

TORRISMOND: As one condemn'd to leap a Precipice,
Who sees before his Eyes the Depth below,
Stops short, and looks about, for some kind Shrub
To break his dreadfull Fall—so I;——
But whither am I going? if to Death,
He looks so lovely sweet in Beauties Pomp,
He draws me to his Dart.——I dare no more.

BERTRAN: He's mad beyond the Cure of Hellebore.
Whips, Darkness, Dungeons, for this Insolence.——

TORREMOND: Mad as I am, yet I know when to bear.——

QUEEN: You're both too bold. You, *Torrismond*, withdraw:
I'll teach you all what's owing to your Queen.
For you, My Lord,—
The Priest to morrow was to join our hands;
I'll try if I can live a day without you.
So both of you depart; and live in Peace.

ALPHONSO: Who knows which way she points!
Doubling and turning, like an hunted Hare.
Find out the Meaning of her mind who can.

PEDRO: Who ever found a Woman's! backward and forward, the whole Sex in every word. In my Conscience when she was getting, her Mother was thinking of a Riddle.

[*Exeunt all, but the* QUEEN *and* TERESA.

QUEEN: Hast, my *Teresa*, hast; and call him back.

TERESA: Whom, Madam?

QUEEN: Him.

TERESA: Prince *Bertran?*

QUEEN: *Torrismond*;
There is no other He.

TERESA *aside*: A rising Sun;
Or I am much deceiv'd. [*Exit* TERESA.

QUEEN: A change so swift, what heart did ever feel!
It rush'd upon me, like a mighty Stream,
And bore me in a moment far from Shore.
I've lov'd away my self: in one short hour
Already am I gon an Age of Passion.
Was it his Youth, his Valour, or Success?

These might perhaps be found in other men.
'Twas that respect; that awfull homage pay'd me;
That fearfull Love which trembled in his Eyes;
And, with a silent Earthquake, shook his Soul.
But, when he spoke, what tender words he said!
So softly, that, like flakes of feather'd Snow,
They melted as they fell.——

Enter TERESA, *with* TORRISMOND.

TERESA: He waits your pleasure.

QUEEN: 'Tis well; retire.—Oh Heav'ns, that I must speak
So distant from my heart—— [*Aside.*
[*To* TORRISMOND] How now! What Boldness brings you back again?

TORRISMOND: I heard 'twas your Command.

QUEEN: A fond mistake,
To credit so unlikely a Command.
And you return full of the same Presumption
T' affront me with your Love?

TORRISMOND: If 'tis Presumption for a Wretch condemn'd
To throw himself beneath his Judge's feet:
A Boldness, more then this, I never knew;
Or, if I did, 'twas onely to your Foes.

QUEEN: You wou'd insinuate your past Services;
And those, I grant, were great: but you confess
A Fault committed since, that cancels all.

TORRISMOND: And who cou'd dare to disavow his Crime,
When that, for which he is accus'd and seiz'd,
He bears about him still! my Eyes confess it.
My every action speaks my heart aloud.
But, oh, the Madness of my high attempt
Speaks louder yet! and all together cry,
I love and I despair.

QUEEN: Have you not heard,
My Father, with his dying voice, bequeath'd
My Crown and me to *Bertran?* And dare you,
A private man, presume to love a Queen?

TORRISMOND: That, that's the Wound! I see you set so high,
As no Desert, or Services, can reach.
Good Heav'ns, why gave you me a Monarch's Soul,
And crusted it with base Plebeian Clay!
Why gave you me Desires of such extent,

And such a Span to grasp 'em? Sure my lot
By some o'er-hasty Angel was misplac'd
In Fate's Eternal Volume!——But I rave,
And, like a giddy Bird, in dead of night,
Fly round the Fire that scorches me to death.

QUEEN: Yet, *Torrismond*, you've not so ill deserv'd,
But I may give you Counsel for your Cure.

TORRISMOND: I cannot, nay, I wish not to be cur'd.

QUEEN *aside*: Nor I, Heav'n knows!

TORRISMOND: There is a Pleasure sure
In being Mad, which none but Madmen know!
Let me indulge it: let me gaze for ever!
And, since you are too great to be belov'd,
Be greater, greater yet; and be ador'd.

QUEEN: These are the words which I must onely hear
From *Bertran*'s mouth; they shou'd displease from you;
I say they shou'd: but women are so vain,
To like the Love, though they despise the Lover.
Yet, that I may not send you from my sight
In absolute despair—I pity you.

TORRISMOND: Am I then pity'd! I have liv'd enough!
Death, take me in this moment of my Joy;
But when my Soul is plung'd in long oblivion,
Spare this one Thought: let me remember Pity;
And so deceiv'd, think all my life was bless'd.

QUEEN: What if I add a little to my Alms?
If that wou'd help, I cou'd cast in a Tear
To your Misfortunes.——

TORRISMOND: A Tear! You have o'erbid all my past Sufferings,
And all my future too!

QUEEN: Were I no Queen—
Or you of Royal Bloud——

TORRISMOND: What have I lost by my Fore-father's Fault?
Why was not I the Twenty'th by descent
From a long restive race of droning Kings?
Love! What a poor omnipotence hast thou
When Gold and Titles buy thee?

QUEEN *sighs*: Oh, my torture!——

TORRISMOND: Might I presume, but, oh, I dare not hope
That Sigh was added to your Alms for me!

QUEEN: I give you leave to guess, and not forbid you
To make the best construction for your love.
Be secret and discreet; these Fayery favours

Are lost when not conceal'd;—provoke not *Bertran.*—
Retire: I must no more but this,—Hope, *Torrismond.*
[*Exit* QUEEN.

TORRISMOND: She bids me hope; oh Heav'ns; she pities me!
And pity still foreruns approaching love;
As Lightning does the Thunder! Tune your Harps
Ye Angels to that sound; and thou, my Heart,
Make room to entertain thy flowing Joy.
Hence all my Griefs, and every anxious Care:
One word, and one kind Glance, can cure despair.
[*Exit* TORRISMOND.

SCENE, *A Chamber.*

A Table and Wine set out.

Enter LORENZO.

LORENZO: This may hit, 'tis more then barely possible: for Fryars have free admittance into every house. This *Jacobin*, whom I have sent to, is her Confessor; and who can suspect a man of such Reverence for a Pimp? I'll try for once: I'll bribe him high: for commonly none love Money better then they who have made a Vow of Poverty.

Enter SERVANT.

SERVANT: There's a huge fat religious Gentleman coming up, Sir, he saies he's but a Fryar, but he's big enough to be a Pope; his Gills are as rosie as a Turkey-Cock; his great Belly walks in state before him like an Harbinger; and his gouty Legs come limping after it: Never was such a Tun of Devotion seen.

LORENZO: Bring him in, and vanish. [*Exit* SERVANT.

Enter Father DOMINIC.

LORENZO: Welcome, Father.

DOMINIC: Peace be here: I thought I had been sent for to a dying man; to have fitted him for another world.

LORENZO: No, Faith, Father, I was never for taking such long journeys. Repose your self, I beseech you, Sir, if those spindle Legs of yours will carry you to the next Chair.

DOMINIC: I am old, I am infirm, I must confess, with Fasting.

LORENZO: 'Tis a sign by your wan Complexion, and your thin

Jouls, Father. Come—to our better Acquaintance:—here's a Sovereign Remedy for Old Age and Sorrow. [*Drinks.*

DOMINIC: The Looks of it are indeed alluring: I'll doe you reason. [*Drinks.*

LORENZO: Is it to your Palate, Father?

DOMINIC: Second thoughts, they say, are best: I'll consider of it once again. [*Drinks.*] It has a most delicious Flavour with it. Gad forgive me, I have forgotten to drink your health, Son, I am not us'd to be so unmannerly. [*Drinks again.*

LORENZO: No, I'll be sworn by what I see of you, you are not: ——To the bottom.—I warrant him a true Church-man.—Now, Father, to our business, 'tis agreeable to your calling; I do intend to doe an act of Charity.

DOMINIC: And I love to hear of Charity; 'tis a comfortable subject.

LORENZO: Being in the late Battle, in great hazard of my Life, I recommended my person to good St. *Dominic.*

DOMINIC: You cou'd not have pitch'd upon a better: he's a sure Card: I never knew him fail his Votaries.

LORENZO: Troth I e'en made bold to strike up a bargain with him, that if I scap'd with Life and Plunder, I wou'd present some Brother of his Order with part of the Booty taken from the Infidels, to be employ'd in charitable uses.

DOMINIC: There you hit him: St. *Dominic* loves Charity exceedingly: that Argument never fails with him.

LORENZO: The Spoils were mighty; and I scorn to wrong him of a Farthing. To make short my Story; I enquir'd among the *Jacobins* for an Almoner, and the general Fame has pointed out your Reverence as the Worthiest man:—here are Fifty good Pieces in this Purse.

DOMINIC: How, Fifty Pieces? 'tis too much, too much in Conscience.

LORENZO: Here; take 'em Father.

DOMINIC: No, in troth, I dare not: do not tempt me to break my Vow of Poverty.

LORENZO: If you are modest, I must force you: for I am strongest.

DOMINIC: Nay, if you compel me, there's no contending; but, will you set your strength against a decrepit, poor, old man? [*Takes the Purse.*] As I said, 'tis too great a Bounty; but St. *Dominic* shall owe you another Scape: I'll put him in mind of you.

LORENZO: If you please, Father, we will not trouble him till the next Battle. But you may doe me a greater kindness, by conveying my Prayers to a Female Saint.

DOMINIC: A Female Saint! good now, good now, how your Devotions jump with mine! I alwaies lov'd the Female Saints.

LORENZO: I mean a Female, mortal, married-woman-Saint: Look upon the Superscription of this Note; you know Don *Gomez* his wife. [*Gives him a Letter.*

DOMINIC: Who, Donna *Elvira?* I think I have some reason: I am her Ghostly Father.

LORENZO: I have some business of Importance with her, which I have communicated in this Paper; but her Husband is so horribly given to be jealous.——

DOMINIC: Ho, jealous? he's the very Quintessence of Jealousie: he keeps no Male Creature in his house: and from abroad he lets no man come near her.

LORENZO: Excepting you, Father.

DOMINIC: Me, I grant you: I am her Director and her Guide in spiritual Affairs. But he has his humours with me too: for t'other day, he call'd me False Apostle.

LORENZO: Did he so? that reflects upon you all: on my word, Father, that touches your Copy-hold. If you wou'd do a meritorious Action, you might revenge the Churche's Quarrel.—My Letter, Father——

DOMINIC: Well, so far as a Letter, I will take upon me: for what can I refuse to a man so charitably given?

LORENZO: If you bring an Answer back, that Purse in your hand has a twin-brother, as like him as ever he can look: there are Fifty Pieces lye dormant in it, for more Charities.

DOMINIC: That must not be: not a Farthing more upon my Priesthood.—But what may be the purport and meaning of this Letter; that I confess a little troubles me.

LORENZO: No harm, I warrant you.

DOMINIC: Well, you are a charitable man; and I'll take your word: my comfort is, I know not the Contents; and so far I am blameless. But an Answer you shall have: though not for the sake of your Fifty Pieces more: I have sworn not to take them: they shall not be altogether Fifty:—your Mistress,—forgive me that I should call her your Mistress, I meant *Elvira*, lives but at next door; I'll visit her immediately: but not a word more of the nine and forty Pieces.

LORENZO: Nay, I'll wait on you down Stairs.—Fifty Pounds for the postage of a Letter! to send by the Church is certainly the dearest road in Christendom. [*Exeunt.*

ACT TWO

SCENE, *A Chamber.*

GOMEZ, ELVIRA.

GOMEZ: Henceforth I banish Flesh and Wine: I'll have none stirring within these walls these twelve months.

ELVIRA: I care not; the sooner I am starv'd the sooner I am rid of Wedlock. I shall learn the knack to fast a days; you have us'd me to fasting nights already.

GOMEZ: How the Gipsey answers me! Oh, 'tis a most notorious Hilding.

ELVIRA *crying*: But was ever poor innocent Creature so hardly dealt with, for a little harmless Chat?

GOMEZ: Oh, the Impudence of this wicked Sex! Lascivious Dialogues are innocent with you!

ELVIRA: Was it such a Crime to inquire how the Battle pass'd?

GOMEZ: But that was not the business, Gentlewoman: you were not asking News of a Battle past; you were engaging for a Skirmish that was to come.

ELVIRA: An honest Woman wou'd be glad to hear, that her Honour was safe, and her Enemies were slain.

GOMEZ *in her tone*: And to ask if he were wounded in your defence; and, in case he were, to offer your self to be his Chirurgeon:—then, you did not describe your Husband to him, for a covetous, jealous, rich old Huncks.

ELVIRA: No, I need not: he describes himself sufficiently: but, in what Dream did I doe this?

GOMEZ: You walk'd in your Sleep, with your Eyes broad open, at noon of day; and dreamt you were talking to the foresaid purpose with one Colonel *Hernando*.——

ELVIRA: Who, Dear Husband, who?

GOMEZ: What the Devil have I said? You wou'd have farther Information, wou'd you?

ELVIRA: No, but my dear little old man, tell me now; that I may avoid him for your sake.

GOMEZ: Get you up into your Chamber, Cockatrice; and there immure your self: be confin'd, I say, during our Royal Pleasure: But, first, down on your marrow-bones, upon your Allegiance; and make an Acknowledgement of your Offences; for I will have ample Satisfaction. [*Pulls her down.*

ELVIRA: I have done you no Injury, and therefore I'll make you no Submission: but I'll complain to my Ghostly Father.

GOMEZ: Ay; There's your Remedy: When you receive condign

Punishment, you run with open Mouth to your Confessor; that parcel of holy Guts and Garbidge; he must chucle you and moan you: but I'll rid my hands of his Ghostly Authority one day [*Enter* DOMINIC], and make him know he's the Son of a——[*sees him*]. So;——no sooner conjure, but the Devil's in the Circle.——

DOMINIC: Son of a what, Don *Gomez?*

GOMEZ: Why, A Son of a Church, I hope there's no harm in that, Father.

DOMINIC: I will lay up your words for you till time shall serve: and to morrow I enjoyn you to Fast for Penance.

GOMEZ *aside*: There's no harm in that; she shall fast too: Fasting saves Money.

DOMINIC *to* ELVIRA: What was the reason that I found you upon your Knees, in that unseemly posture?

GOMEZ *aside*: O horrible! to find a woman upon her Knees, he says, is an unseemly posture; there's a Priest for you!

ELVIRA *to* DOMINIC: I wish, Father, you wou'd give me an opportunity of entertaining you in private: I have somewhat upon my Spirits that presses me exceedingly.

DOMINIC *aside*: This goes well: *Gomez*, stand you at distance, —farther yet,—stand out of ear-shot—I have somewhat to say to your Wife in private.

GOMEZ *aside*: Was ever man thus Priest-ridden? wou'd the Steeple of his Church were in his Belly: I am sure there's room for it.

ELVIRA: I am asham'd to acknowledg my Infirmities; but you have been alwaies an indulgent Father; and therefore I will venture, to—and yet I dare not.——

DOMINIC: Nay, if you are bashful;—if you keep your wound from the knowledge of your Surgeon;—

ELVIRA: You know my Husband is a man in years; but he's my Husband; and therefore I shall be silent: but his Humours are more intolerable then his Age: he's grown so froward, so covetous, and so jealous, that he has turn'd my heart quite from him; and, if I durst confess it, has forc'd me to cast my Affections on another man.

DOMINIC: Good:—hold, hold; I meant abominable:——pray Heaven this be my Colonel. [*Aside.*

ELVIRA: I have seen this man, Father; and have incourag'd his Addresses; he's a young Gentleman, a Souldier, of a most winning Carriage; and what his Courtship may produce at last I know not; but I am afraid of my own frailty.

DOMINIC *aside*: 'Tis he for certain:—she has sav'd the Credit of my Function, by speaking first; now must I take Gravity upon me.

GOMEZ *aside*: This Whispering bodes me no good for certain; but he has me so plaguily under the lash, that I dare not interrupt him.

DOMINIC: Daughter, Daughter, do you remember your matrimonial Vow?

ELVIRA: Yes, to my sorrow Father, I do remember it: a miserable woman it has made me: but you know, Father, a Marriage-vow is but a thing of course, which all woman take when they wou'd get a Husband.

DOMINIC: A Vow is a very solemn thing: and 'tis good to keep it:—but, notwithstanding, it may be broken, upon some occasions.—Have you striven with all your might against this frailty?

ELVIRA: Yes, I have striven; but I found it was against the stream. Love, you know, Father, is a great Vow-maker; but he's a greater Vow-breaker.

DOMINIC: 'Tis your Duty to strive alwaies: but, notwithstanding, when we have done our utmost, it extenuates the Sin.

GOMEZ: I can hold no longer.——Now, Gentlewoman, you are confessing your Enormities; I know it by that hypocritical down-cast Look: enjoin her to sit bare upon a Bed of Nettles, Father; you can doe no less in Conscience.

DOMINIC: Hold your peace; are you growing malapert? will you force me to make use of my Authority? your Wife's a well dispos'd and a vertuous Lady; I say it, *In verbo Sacerdotis.*

ELVIRA: I know not what to doe, Father; I find my self in a most desperate Condition; and so is the Colonel for Love of me.

DOMINIC: The Colonel, say you! I wish it be not the same young Gentleman I know: 'Tis a gallant young man, I must confess, worthy of any Lady's love in Christendom; in a lawfull way I mean; of such a charming behaviour, so bewitching to a Woman's eye; and furthermore, so charitably given; by all good tokens, this must be my Colonel *Hernando.*

ELVIRA: Ay, and my Colonel too, Father: I am overjoy'd; and are you then acquainted with him?

DOMINIC: Acquainted with him! why, he haunts me up and down: and, I am afraid, it is for love of you: for he press'd a Letter upon me, within this hour, to deliver to you: I confess, I receiv'd it, lest he should send it by some other; but with full resolution never to put it into your hands.

ELVIRA: Oh, dear Father, let me have it, or I shall dye.

GOMEZ: Whispering still! A Pox of your close committee! I'll listen I'm resolved. [*Steals nearer.*

DOMINIC: Nay, If you are obstinately bent to see it,—use your discretion; but for my part, I wash my hands on't.—What make you listning there? get farther off; I preach not to thee, thou wicked Eves-dropper.

ELVIRA: I'll kneel down, Father, as if I were taking Absolution, if you'll but please to stand before me.

DOMINIC: At your peril be it then. I have told you the ill Consequences; *& liberavi animam meam.*—Your Reputation is in danger, to say nothing of your Soul. Notwithstanding, when the Spiritual means have been apply'd, and fail: in that case, the Carnal may be us'd.—You are a tender Child, you are; and must not be put into Despair: your Heart is as soft and melting as your Hand.

[*He strokes her face; takes her by the hand; and gives the Letter.*

GOMEZ: Hold, hold, Father; you goe beyond your Commission: Palming is alwaies held foul play amongst Gamesters.

DOMINIC: Thus, good Intentions are misconstrued by wicked men: you will never be warn'd till you are excommunicate.

GOMEZ *aside*: Ah, Devil on him; there's his hold! If there were no more in Excommunication than the Churche's Censure, a Wise man wou'd lick his Conscience whole with a wet finger: but, if I am excommunicate, I am outlaw'd; and then there 's no calling in my Money.

ELVIRA *rising*: I have read the Note, Father, and will send him an Answer immediately; for I know his Lodgings by his Letter.

DOMINIC: I understand it not, for my part; but I wish your Intentions be honest. Remember, that Adultery, though it be a silent Sin, yet it is a crying Sin also. Nevertheless, If you believe absolutely he will dye, unless you pity him: to save a man's Life is a point of Charity; and actions of Charity do alleviate, as I may say, and take off from the Mortality of the Sin. Farewell, Daughter.—*Gomez,* cherish your vertuous Wife; and thereupon I give you my Benediction. [*Going.*

GOMEZ: Stay; I'll conduct you to the door,—that I may be sure you steal nothing by the way.—Fryars wear not their long Sleeves for nothing.—Oh, tis a *Judas Iscariot*.

[*Exit, after the* FRYAR.

ELVIRA: This Fryar is a comfortable man! He will understand nothing of the Business; and yet does it all.

Pray Wives and Virgins, at your time of need,
For a True Guide, of my Good Father's breed.

[*Exit* ELVIRA.

ACT III

SCENE, *The Street.*

LORENZO, *in Fryars habit, meeting* DOMINIC.

LORENZO: Father *Dominic*, Father *Dominic*; why in such hast, man?

DOMINIC: It shou'd seem a brother of our Order.

LORENZO: No, Faith, I am onely your brother in Iniquity: my holiness, like yours, is meer out-side.

DOMINIC: What! my noble Colonel in Metamorphosis! On what occasion are you transform'd?

LORENZO: Love; Almighty Love; that which turn'd *Jupiter* into a Town-bull, has transform'd me into a Fryar: I have had a letter from *Elvira*, in answer to that I sent by you.

DOMINIC: You see I have deliver'd my Message faithfully: I am a Fryar of Honour where I am engag'd.

LORENZO: O, I understand your Hint: the other Fifty pieces are ready to be condemn'd to Charity.

DOMINIC: But this Habit, Son, this Habit!

LORENZO: 'Tis a Habit that in all Ages has been friendly to Fornication: You have begun the Design in this Cloathing, and I'll try to accomplish it. The Husband is absent; that evil Counsellour is remov'd; and the Sovereign is graciously dispos'd to hear my grievances.

DOMINIC: Go to; go to; I find good Counsel is but thrown away upon you: Fare you well, fare you well, Son! Ah——

LORENZO: How! Will you turn Recreant at the last cast? You must along to countenance my undertaking: We are at the door, man.

DOMINIC: Well, I have thought on't; and I will not go.

LORENZO: You may stay, Father; but no Fifty pounds without it: that was onely promis'd in the Bond: but the Condition of this Obligation is such, That if the above-named Father, Father *Dominic*, do not well and faithfully perform——

DOMINIC: Now I better think on't, I will bear you company;

for the Reverence of my Presence may be a curb to your Exorbitancies.

LORENZO: Lead up your Myrmidon, and enter. [*Exeunt.*

SCENE II.

Enter ELVIRA, *in her Chamber.*

ELVIRA: He'll come, that's certain: young Appetites are sharp; and seldom need twice bidding to such a Banquet:—well; if I prove frail, as I hope I shall not till I have compass'd my Design, never Woman had such a Husband to provoke her, such a Lover to allure her, or such a Confessor to absolve her. Of what am I afraid then? not my Conscience, that's safe enough; my Ghostly Father has given it a Dose of Church Opium, to lull it: well, for soothing Sin, I'll say that for him, he's a Chaplain for any Court in Christendom.

[*Enter* LORENZO *and* DOMINIC.]

O, Father *Dominic*, what News? How, a Companion with you! What Game have you in hand, that you hunt in Couples?

LORENZO *lifting up his hood*: I'll shew you that immediately.

ELVIRA: O, my Love!

LORENZO: My Life!

ELVIRA: My Soul! [*They embrace.*]

DOMINIC: I am taken on the sudden with a grievous swimming in my Head, and such a mist before my Eyes, that I can neither hear nor see.

ELVIRA: Stay, and I'll fetch you some comfortable Water.

DOMINIC: No, no; nothing but the open Air will doe me good. I'll take a turn in your Garden: but remember that I trust you both, and do not wrong my good opinion of you.

[*Exit* DOMINIC.

ELVIRA: This is certainly the dust of Gold which you have thrown in the good man's eyes, that on the sudden he cannot see: for my mind misgives me, this Sickness of his is but Apocryphal!

LORENZO: 'Tis no Qualm of Conscience I'll be sworn: you see, Madam, 'tis Interest governs all the World: he preaches against Sin; why? because he gets by 't: he holds his tongue; why? because so much more is bidden for his silence.

ELVIRA: And so much for the Fryar.

LORENZO: Oh, those Eyes of yours reproach me justly: that I neglect the Subject which brought me hither.

ELVIRA: Do you consider the hazard I have run to see you here? if you do, methinks it shou'd inform you, that I love not at a common rate.

LORENZO: Nay, if you talk of considering, let us consider why we are alone. Do you think the Fryar left us together to tell Beads? Love is a kind of penurious God, very niggardly of his opportunities, he must be watch'd like a hard-hearted Treasurer, for he bolts out on the sudden, and, if you take him not in the nick, he vanishes in a twinkling.

ELVIRA: Why do you make such haste to have done loving me? You Men are all like Watches, wound up for striking twelve immediately; but, after you are satisfied, the very next that follows is the solitary sound of single one.

LORENZO: How, Madam! Do you invite me to a Feast, and then preach Abstinence?

ELVIRA: No, I invite you to a Feast where the Dishes are serv'd up in order: you are for making a hasty meal, and for chopping up your entertainment, like a hungry Clown: trust my management, good Colonel; and call not for your Dessert too soon: believe me, that which comes last, as it is the sweetest, so it cloies the soonest.

LORENZO: I perceive, Madam, by your holding me at this distance, that there is somewhat you expect from me: what am I to undertake or suffer e'er I can be happy?

ELVIRA: I must first be satisfied that you love me.

LORENZO: By all that's Holy: By these dear Eyes.

ELVIRA: Spare your Oaths and Protestations; I know you Gallants of the time have a mint at your tongues end to coin them.

LORENZO: You know you cannot marry me; but, By Heavens, if you were in a condition——

ELVIRA: Then you would not be so prodigal of your Promises, but have the Fear of Matrimony before your eyes: in few words, if you love me, as you profess, deliver me from this Bondage, take me out of *Egypt*, and I'll wander with you as far as Earth, and Seas, and Love can carry us.

LORENZO: I never was out at a mad Frolick, though this is the maddest I ever undertook; have with you, Lady mine; I take you at your word; and, if you are for a merry Jaunt, I'll try for once who can foot it farthest: there are Hedges in Summer, and Barns in Winter to be found: I, with my Knapsack, and you, with your Bottle at your back: we 'll leave Honour to Madmen, and Riches to Knaves; and travel till we come to the Ridge of the World, and then drop together into the next.

ELVIRA: Give me your Hand, and strike a Bargain.

[*He takes her Hand, and kisses it.*

LORENZO: In sign and token whereof the Parties interchangeably, and so forth—when should I be weary of Sealing upon this Soft wax?

ELVIRA: O, Heavens! I hear my Husband's voice.

Enter GOMEZ.

GOMEZ: Where are you, Gentlewoman? there's something in the wind I'm sure, because your Woman would have run up Stairs before me: but I have secur'd her below with a Gag in her Chaps—now, in the Devil's name, what makes this Fryar here again? I do not like these frequent Conjunctions of the Flesh and Spirit; they are boding.

ELVIRA: Go hence, good Father; my Husband you see is in an ill humour; and I would not have you witness of his folly.

[LORENZO *going.*

GOMEZ *running to the door*: By your Reverence's favour, hold a little, I must examine you something better before you go: Hi-day! who have we here? Father *Dominic* is shrunk in the wetting two yards and a half about the Belly: what are become of those two Timber-loggs that he us'd to wear for Leggs, that stood strutting like the two black Posts before a door? I am afraid some bad body has been setting him over a Fire in a great Cauldron, and boil'd him down half the quantity for a Receipt: this is no Father *Dominic*, no huge, over-grown Abbey-lubber; this is but a diminutive sucking Fryar: as sure as a Gun now, Father *Dominic* has been spawning this young, slender Anti-christ.

ELVIRA *aside*: He will be found; there's no prevention.

GOMEZ: Why does he not speak? What! Is the Fryar possess'd with a dumb Devil? If he be, I shall make bold to conjure him.

ELVIRA: He 's but a Novice in his Order, and is injoined Silence for a Penance.

GOMEZ: A Novice, quoth a; You would make a Novice of me too, if you could: but, What was his business here? answer me that, Gentlewoman, answer me that.

ELVIRA: What shou'd it be, but to give me some Spiritual Instructions?

GOMEZ: Very good; and you are like to edifie much from a dumb Preacher; this will not pass; I must examin the Contents of him a little closer; O thou Confessor! confess who thou art, or thou art no Fryar of this World: [*He comes to* LORENZO, *who struggles with him; his habit flies open, and discovers a Sword;* GOMEZ *starts back.*] As I live, this is a manifest member of the Church militant.

LORENZO *aside*: I am discover'd; now Impudence be my Refuge.—Yes, Faith 'tis I, honest *Gomez*; thou seest I use thee like a Friend; this is a familiar Visit.

GOMEZ: What! Colonel *Hernando* turn'd a Fryar! who could have suspected you for so much Godliness?

LORENZO: E'en as thou seest, I make bold here.

GOMEZ: A very frank manner of proceeding; but I do not wonder at your Visit, after so friendly an Invitation as I made you; marry, I hope you will excuse the Blunderbusses for not being in readiness to salute you; but let me know your hour, and all shall be mended another time.

LORENZO: Hang it; I hate such ripping up of old unkindness; I was upon the Frolick this evening, and came to visit thee in Masquerade.

GOMEZ: Very likely; and not finding me at home, you were forc'd to toy away an hour with my Wife, or so.

LORENZO: Right: Thou speak'st my very Soul.

GOMEZ: Why, am not I a Friend, then, to help you out? you wou'd have been fumbling half an hour for this Excuse—but, as I remember, you promis'd to storm my Citadel, and bring your Regiment of Red Locusts upon me for Free quarter: I find, Colonel, by your Habit, there are Black Locusts in the World as well as Red.

ELVIRA *aside*: When comes my share of the reckoning to be call'd for?

LORENZO: Give me thy Hand; Thou art the honestest, kind man; I was resolv'd I wou'd not out of thy house till I had seen thee.

GOMEZ: No, in my Conscience, if I had staid abroad till midnight. But, Colonel, you and I shall talk in another tone hereafter; I mean, in cold friendship, at a Bar, before a Judge, by the way of Plaintiff and Defendant: your Excuses want some grains to make 'em currant: hum and ha will not do the business—there's a modest Lady of your acquaintance, she has so much Grace to make none at all, but silently to confess the Power of Dame Nature working in her Body to Youthfull Appetite.

ELVIRA: How he got in I know not, unless it were by virtue of his Habit.

GOMEZ: Ai, ai, the Vertues of that Habit are known abundantly.

ELVIRA: I cou'd not hinder his entrance, for he took me unprovided.

GOMEZ: To resist him.

ELVIRA: I'm sure he has not been here above a quarter of an hour.

GOMEZ: And a quarter of that time wou'd have serv'd the turn: O thou epitome of thy vertuous Sex! Madam *Messalina* the Second retire to thy Appartment: I have an Assignation there to make with thee.

ELVIRA: I am all Obedience.—— [*Exit* ELVIRA.

LORENZO: I find, *Gomez*, you are not the man I thought you: we may meet before we come to the Bar, we may, and our Differences may be decided by other Weapons then by Lawyers tongues; in the mean time, no ill treatment of your Wife, as you hope to dye a natural death, and go to Hell in your Bed: *Bilbo* is the word, remember that, and tremble.—— [*He's going out.*

Enter DOMINIC.

DOMINIC: Where is this naughty Couple? where are you, in the name of Goodness? my mind misgave me; and I durst trust you no longer with your selves; here will be fine work, I'm afraid, at your next Confession.

LORENZO *aside*: The Devil is punctual, I see, he has paid me the shame he ow'd me; and now the Fryar is coming in for his part too.

DOMINIC *seeing* GOMEZ: Bless my Eyes! what do I see?

GOMEZ: Why; you see a Cuckold of this honest Gentleman's making: I thank him for his pains.

DOMINIC: I confess I am astonish'd!

GOMEZ: What, at a Cuckoldom of your own contrivance! your Head-piece and his Limbs have done my business.—Nay, do not look so strangely, remember your own words, Here will be fine work at your next Confession: What naughty Couple were they whom you durst not trust together any longer? when the hypocritical Rogue had trusted 'em a full quarter of an hour; and, by the way, horns will sprout in less time then Mushrooms.

DOMINIC: Beware how you accuse one of my Order upon light suspicions: the naughty Couple that I meant, were your

Wife and you, whom I left together with great Animosities on both sides: now, that was the occasion, mark me, *Gomez*, that I thought it convenient to return again, and not to trust your enraged Spirits too long together: you might have broken out into Revilings and matrimonial Warfare, which are Sins; and new Sins make work for new Confessions.

LORENZO *aside*: Well said, I saith, Fryar; thou art come off thy self, but poor I am left in Limbo.

GOMEZ: Angle in some other Foord, good Father, you shall catch no Gudgeons here: look upon the Prisoner at the Bar, Fryar, and inform the Court what you know concerning him; he is arraign'd here by the name of Colonel *Hernando*.

DOMINIC: What Colonel do you mean, *Gomez?* I see no man, but a Reverend Brother of our Order, whose Profession I honour, but whose person I know not, as I hope for Paradise.

GOMEZ: No, you are not acquainted with him, the more's the pity; you do not know him, under this Disguise, for the greatest Cuckold-maker in all *Spain*.

DOMINIC: O Impudence! O Rogue! O Vilain! Nay, if he be such a man, my Righteous Spirit rises at him! Does he put on Holy Garments for a cover-shame of Lewdness?

GOMEZ: Yes, and he's in the right on't, Father; when a swindging Sin is to be committed, nothing will cover it so close as a Fryar's Hood: for there the Devil plays at Bo-peep, puts out his Horns to doe a mischief, and then shrinks 'em back for safety, like a Snail into her shell.

LORENZO *aside*: It's best marching off while I can retreat with Honour; there's no trusting this Fryar's Conscience; he has renounc'd me already more heartily then e'er he did the Devil, and is in a fair way to prosecute me for putting on these Holy Robes: this is the old Church-trick, the Clergy is ever at the bottom of the Plot, but they are wise enough to slip their own Necks out of the Coller, and leave the Laity to be fairly hang'd for it.—— [*Exit* LORENZO.

GOMEZ: Follow your Leader, Fryar; your Colonel is troop'd off, but he had not gone so easily, if I durst have trusted you in the house behind me; gather up your gouty Legs, I say, and rid my house of that huge Body of divinity.

DOMINIC: I expect some Judgment shou'd fall upon you for your want of Reverence to your Spiritual Director: Slander, Covetousness, and Jealousie, will weigh thee down.

GOMEZ: Put Pride, Hypocrisie, and Gluttony into your Scale, Father, and you shall weigh against me: nay, and Sins come to be divided once, the Clergy puts in for nine parts, and scarce leaves the Laity a tythe.

DOMINIC: How darest thou reproach the Tribe of *Levi?*

GOMEZ: Marry, because you make us Lay-men of the Tribe of *Issachar*: you make Asses of us, to bear your burthens: when we are young, you put Paniers upon us, with your Church discipline; and when, we are grown up, you load us with a Wife: after that, you procure for other men, and then you load our Wives too; a fine phrase you have amongst you to draw us into Marriage, you call it Settling of a Man; just as when a fellow has got a sound Knock upon the head, they say he's settled: Marriage is a Settling blow indeed. They say every thing in the World is good for something, as a Toad, to suck up the Venom of the Earth; but I never knew what a Fryar was good for till your Pimping show'd me.

DOMINIC: Thou shalt answer for this, thou Slanderer, thy Offences be upon thy head.

GOMEZ: I believe there are some Offences there of your planting. [*Exit* DOMINIC.] Lord, Lord, that men should have sense enough to set Snares in their Warrens to catch Pol-cats, and Foxes, and yet—

Want wit a Priest-trap at their door to lay,
For holy Vermin that in houses prey. [*Exit* GOMEZ.

SCENE, *A Bed-chamber.*

QUEEN, TERESA

TERESA: You are not what you were since yesterday:
Your food forsakes you and your needfull rest:
You pine, you languish, love to be alone;
Think much, speak little; and, in speaking, sigh.
When you see *Torrismond*, you are unquiet;
But when you see him not, you are in pain.

QUEEN: O, let 'em never love, who never try'd!
They brought a Paper to me to be sign'd;
Thinking on him, I quite forgot my name;
And writ, for *Leonora, Torrismond.*
I went to bed, and to my self I thought,
That I wou'd think on *Torrismond* no more:
Then shut my Eyes; but cou'd not shut out him.
I turn'd; and try'd each corner of my Bed,

To find if Sleep were there, but Sleep was lost.
Fev'rish, for want of Rest, I rise, and walk'd;
And, by the Moon-shine, to the Windows went;
There, thinking to exclude him from my thoughts,
I cast my eyes upon the neighbouring fields,
And, e'er I was aware, sigh'd to my self,
There fought my *Torrismond.*

TERESA: What hinders you to take the Man you love?
The People will be glad, the Souldier shout;
And *Bertran*, though repining, will be aw'd.

QUEEN: I fear to try new Love,
As boys to venture on the unknown Ice,
That crackles underneath 'em, while they slide.
Oh, how shall I describe this growing ill!
Betwixt my Doubt and Love, methinks, I stand
Alt'ring, like one that waits an Ague fit;
And yet, wou'd this were all!

TERESA: What fear you more?

QUEEN: I am asham'd to say, 'tis but a fancy.
At break of day, when Dreams, they say, are true,
A drowzie slumber, rather then a sleep,
Seiz'd on my Senses, with long Watching worn.
Methought I stood on a wide River's Bank,
Which I must needs o'erpass, but knew not how:
When, on a sudden *Torrismond* appear'd,
Gave me his hand, and led me lightly o'er;
Leaping and bounding on the Billows heads,
Till safely we had reach'd the farther shore.

TERESA: This Dream portends some ill which you shall scape.
Wou'd you see fairer Visions? Take this night
Your *Torrismond* within your Arms to sleep:
And, to that end, invent some apt pretence
To break with *Bertran*: 'twould be better yet,
Cou'd you provoke him to give you th' occasion,
And then to throw him off.

Enter BERTRAN *at a distance.*

QUEEN: My Stars have sent him;
For, see, he comes: how gloomily he looks!
If he, as I suspect, have found my Love,
His Jealousie will furnish him with Fury,
And me with means to part.

BERTRAN *aside*: Shall I upbraid her? Shall I call her false?

If she be false, 'tis what she most desires.
My Genius whispers me, Be cautious, *Bertran!*
Thou walk'st as on a narrow Mountain's neck,
A dreadfull height, with scanty room to tread.

QUEEN: What Bus'ness have you at the Court, my Lord?

BERTRAN: What Bus'ness, Madam?

QUEEN: Yes, my Lord, What Bus'ness?
'Tis somewhat sure of weighty consequence
That brings you here so often, and unsent for.

BERTRAN *aside*: 'Tis what I fear'd, her words are cold enough
To freeze a man to death.——May I presume
To speak, and to complain?

QUEEN: They who complain to Princes think 'em tame:
What Bull dare bellow, or, what Sheep dares bleat,
Within the Lion's den?

BERTRAN: Yet men are suffer'd to put Heav'n in mind
Of promis'd Blessings, for they then are Debts.

QUEEN: My Lord, Heav'n knows its own time when to give;
But you, it seems, charge me with Breach of Faith.

BERTRAN: I hope I need not, Madam:
But as when men in Sickness lingring lye,
They count the tedious hours by months and years;
So every day deferr'd to Dying Lovers
Is a whole Age of pain.

QUEEN: What if I ne'er consent to make you mine?
My Father's Promise ties me not to time;
And Bonds, without a Date, they say, are void.

BERTRAN: Far be it from me to believe you bound:
Love is the freest motion of our minds:
O, cou'd you see into my secret Soul,
There you might read your own Dominion doubled,
Both as a Queen and Mistress: if you leave me,
Know I can dye, but dare not be displeas'd.

QUEEN: Sure you affect Stupidity, my Lord,
Or give me cause to think that when you lost
Three Battels to the *Moors*, you coldly stood
As unconcern'd as now.

BERTRAN: I did my best;
Fate was not in my power.

QUEEN: And with the like tame Gravity you saw
A raw young Warrier take your bafled work
And end it at a blow.

BERTRAN: I humbly take my leave; but they who blast

Your good opinion of me, may have cause
To know I am no Coward. [*He is going.*

QUEEN: *Bertran*, stay.
[*aside.*] This may produce some dismal consequence
To him whom dearer then my Life I love.
[*to him.*] Have I not manag'd my contrivance well,
To try your Love, and make you doubt of mine?

BERTRAN: Then was it but a Tryal?
Methinks I start as from some dreadfull Dream;
And often ask my self, if yet I wake.
[*aside.*] This turns too quick to be without Design;
I'll sound the bottom of't e'er I believe.

QUEEN: I find your Love; and wou'd reward it too,
But anxious Fears solicit my weak breast:
I fear my People's Faith:
That hot-mouth'd Beast that bears against the Curb,
Hard to be broken even by lawfull Kings;
But harder by Usurpers:
Judge then, my Lord, with all these Cares opprest,
If I can think of Love.

BERTRAN: Believe me, Madam,
These Jealousies, how ever large they spread,
Have but one Root, the old, imprison'd King;
Whose Lenity first pleas'd the gaping Crowd:
But when long tried, and found supinely good,
Like *Æsop*'s Logg, they leapt upon his Back:
Your Father knew 'em well; and when he mounted,
He rein'd 'em strongly and he spurr'd them hard;
And, but he durst not doe it all at once,
He had not left alive this patient Saint,
This Anvil of Affronts, but sent him hence,
To hold a peacefull Branch of Palm above,
And hymn it in the Quire.

QUEEN: You've hit upon the very String, which touch'd,
Echoes the Sound, and jars within my Soul;
There lies my Grief.

BERTRAN: So long as there's a Head,
Thither will all the mounting Spirits fly;
Lop that but off; and then——

QUEEN: My Vertue shrinks from such an horrid Act.

BERTRAN: This 'tis to have a Vertue out of season.
Mercy is good; a very good dull Vertue;
But Kings mistake its timeing; and are mild,

When manly Courage bids 'em be severe:
Better be cruel once than anxious ever:
Remove this threatning Danger from your Crown;
And then securely take the man you love.

QUEEN *walking aside*: Ha! let me think of that: the Man I love?
'Tis true, this Murther is the onely means
That can secure my Throne to *Torrismond.*
Nay more, this Execution done by *Bertran,*
Makes him the Object of the People's Hate.

BERTRAN *aside*: The more she thinks, 'twill work the stronger in her.

QUEEN *aside*: How eloquent is Mischief to persuade!
Few are so wicked as to take delight
In Crimes unprofitable, nor do I:
If then I break divine and humane Laws,
No Bribe but Love cou'd gain so bad a Cause.

BERTRAN: You answer nothing!

QUEEN: 'Tis of deep Concernment,
And I a Woman ignorant and weak:
I leave it all to you, think what you doe,
You doe for him I love.

BERTRAN *aside*: For him she loves?
She nam'd not me; that may be *Torrismond,*
Whom she has thrice in private seen this day:
Then I am fairly caught in my own Snare.
I'll think again.——Madam, it shall be done;
And mine be all the blame. [*Exit* BERTRAN.

QUEEN: O, that it were! I wou'd not doe this Crime,
And yet, like Heaven, permit it to be done.
The Priesthood grossly cheat us with Free-will:
Will to doe what, but what Heaven first decreed?
Our actions then are neither good nor ill,
Since from eternal Causes they proceed:
Our Passions, Fear and Anger, Love and Hate,
Meer sensless Engines that are mov'd by Fate;
Like Ships on stormy Seas, without a Guide,
Tost by the Winds, and driven by the Tyde.

Enter TORRISMOND.

TORRISMOND: Am I not rudely bold, and press too often
Into your presence, Madam? If I am——

QUEEN: No more; lest I shou'd chide you for your stay:

Where have you been? and, How cou'd you suppose
That I cou'd live these two long hours without you?

TORRISMOND: O, words to charm an Angel from his orb!
Welcome, as kindly Showers to long parch'd Earth!
But I have been in such a dismal place
Where Joy ne'er enters, which the Sun ne'er cheers:
Bound in with Darkness, over-spread with Damps:
Where I have seen (if I cou'd say, I saw)
The good old King majestick in his Bonds,
And 'midst his Griefs most venerably great:
By a dim winking Lamp, which feebly broke
The gloomy Vapors, he lay stretch'd along
Upon the unwholesom Earth; his Eyes fix'd upward:
And ever and anon a silent Tear
Stole down and trickl'd from his hoary Beard.

QUEEN: O Heaven, what have I done! my gentle Love,
Here end thy sad discourse, and, for my sake,
Cast off these fearfull melancholy thoughts.

TORRISMOND: My Heart is wither'd at that piteous Sight,
As early Blossoms are with Eastern blasts:
He sent for me, and, while I rais'd his Head,
He threw his aged Arms about my Neck;
And, seeing that I wept, he press'd me close:
So, leaning Cheek to Cheek and Eyes to Eyes,
We mingled Tears in a dumb Scene of Sorrow.

QUEEN: Forbear: you know not how you wound my Soul.

TORRISMOND: Can you have Grief, and not have Pity too?
He told me, when my Father did return,
He had a wondrous Secret to disclose:
He kiss'd me, bless'd me, nay, he call'd me Son;
He prais'd my Courage, pray'd for my Success:
He was so true a Father of his Countrey,
To thank me for defending ev'n his Foes,
Because they were his Subjects.

QUEEN: If they be; then what am I?

TORRISMOND: The Sovereign of my Soul, my Earthly Heaven.

QUEEN: And not your Queen?

TORRISMOND: You are so beautifull,
So wondrous fair, you justifie Rebellion:
As if that faultless Face could make no Sin,
But Heaven, with looking on it, must forgive.

QUEEN: The King must dye, he must, my *Torrismond*;
Though Pity softly plead within my Soul,

Yet he must dye, that I may make you great,
And give a Crown in dowry with my Love.

TORRISMOND: Perish that Crown—on any Head but yours;—
O, recollect your Thoughts!
Shake not his Hour-glass, when his hasty Sand
Is ebbing to the last:
A little longer, yet a little longer,
And Nature drops him down, without your Sin,
Like mellow Fruit, without a Winter Storm.

QUEEN: Let me but doe this one Injustice more:
His Doom is past; and, for your sake, he dyes.

TORRISMOND: Wou'd you, for me, have done so ill an Act,
And will not doe a good one?
Now, By your Joys on Earth, your Hopes in Heaven,
O spare this Great, this Good, this Aged King;
And spare your Soul the Crime!

QUEEN: The Crime's not mine;
'Twas first propos'd, and must be done, by *Bertran*,
Fed with false hopes to gain my Crown and Me:
I, to inhance his Ruin, gave no leave;
But barely bad him think, and then resolve.

TORRISMOND: In not forbidding, you command the Crime;
Think, timely think, on the last dreadfull day;
How will you tremble there to stand expos'd,
And formost in the rank of guilty Ghosts
That must be doom'd for Murther; think on Murther:
That Troop is plac'd apart from common Crimes;
The damn'd themselves start wide, and shun that Band,
As far more black and more forlorn then they.

QUEEN: 'Tis terrible, it shakes, it staggers me;
I knew this Truth, but I repell'd that Thought;
Sure there is none but fears a future state;
And, when the most obdurate swear they do not,
Their trembling Hearts bely their boasting Tongues.

[*Enter* TERESA.]

Send speedily to *Bertran*; charge him strictly
Not to proceed, but wait my farther Pleasure.

TERESA: Madam, he sends to tell you, 'Tis perform'd.

[*Exit* TERESA.

TORRISMOND: Ten thousand Plagues consume him, Furies drag
him,

Fiends tear him; Blasted be the Arm that strook,
The Tongue that order'd;—Onely She be spar'd
That hindred not the Deed. O, where was then
The Power that guards the Sacred Lives of Kings?
Why slept the Lightning and the Thunder-bolts,
Or bent their idle rage on Fields and Trees,
When Vengeance call'd 'em here?

QUEEN: Sleep that Thought too,
'Tis done, and since 'tis done, 'tis past recall:
And since 'tis past recall, must be forgotten.

TORRISMOND: O, never, never, shall it be forgotten;
High Heaven will not forget it, after Ages
Shall with a fearfull Curse remember ours;
And Bloud shall never leave the Nation more!

QUEEN: His Body shall be Royally interr'd,
And the last Funeral Pomps adorn his Hearse;
I will my self (as I have Cause too just)
Be the chief Mourner at his Obsequies:
And yearly fix on the revolving day
The solemn marks of Mourning, to attone
And expiate my Offences.

TORRISMOND: Nothing can,
But Bloudy Vengeance on that Traitor's Head,
Which, dear departed Spirit, here I vow.

QUEEN: Here end our Sorrows, and begin our Joys:
Love calls, my *Torrismond*; though Hate has rag'd
And rul'd the day, yet Love will rule the night.
The spitefull Stars have shed their Venom down,
And now the peacefull Planets take their turn.
This Deed of *Bertran*'s has remov'd all Fears,
And giv'n me just occasion to refuse him.
What hinders now, but that the holy Priest
In secret join our mutual Vows? and then
This night, this happy night, is yours and mine.

TORRISMOND: Be still my Sorrows; and, be loud my Joys.
Fly to the utmost Circles of the Sea,
Thou furious Tempest, that hast tost my mind,
And leave no thought, but *Leonora*, there.—
What's this I feel? a boding in my Soul
As if this day were fatal? be it so;
Fate shall but have the Leavings of my love:
My Joys are gloomy, but withall are great;
The Lion, though he sees the Toils are set,

Yet, pinch'd with raging Hunger, scowrs away,
Hunts in the Face of Danger all the day;
At night, with sullen pleasure, grumbles o'er his Prey.
[*Exeunt ambo.*

ACT IV

SCENE, *Before* GOMEZ *his Door.*

Enter LORENZO, DOMINIC, *and two* Souldiers *at a distance.*

DOMINIC: I'll not wag an ace farther: The whole World shall not bribe me to it; for my Conscience will digest these gross Enormities no longer.

LORENZO: How, thy Conscience not digest 'em! There's ne'er a Fryar in *Spain* can show a Conscience that comes near it for Digestion: it digested Pimping when I sent thee with my Letter: and it digested Perjury when thou swor'st thou didst not know me: I'm sure it has digested me Fifty pound of as hard Gold as is in all *Barbary*: Prythy, why shouldst thou discourage Fornication, when thou knowest thou lovest a sweet young Girl?

DOMINIC: Away, away; I do not love 'em;—phau; no,—[*Spits.*] I do not love a pretty Girl——you are so waggish.——
[*Spits again.*

LORENZO: Why, thy mouth waters at the very mention of them.

DOMINIC: You take a mighty pleasure in Defamation, Colonel; but I wonder what you find in running restless up and down, breaking your Brains, emptying your Purse, and wearing out your Body with hunting after unlawfull game.

LORENZO: Why there's the Satisfaction on't.

DOMINIC: This Incontinency may proceed to Adultery, and Adultery to Murther, and Murther to hanging; and there's the Satisfaction on't.

LORENZO: I'll not hang alone, Fryar; I'm resolv'd to peach thee before thy Superiours for what thou hast done already.

DOMINIC: I'm resolved to forswear it if you doe: Let me advise you better, Colonel, then to accuse a Church-man to a Church-man: in the common Cause we are all of a piece; we hang together.

LORENZO *aside*: If you don't, it were no matter if you did.

DOMINIC: Nay, if you talk of Peaching, I'll peach first, and see whose Oath will be believ'd; I'll trounce you for offering to corrupt my Honesty, and bribe my Conscience: you shall be summon'd by an host of Paratours; you shall be sentenc'd in the Spiritual Court; you shall be excommunicated; you shall be outlaw'd;——and——

[*Here* LORENZO *takes a Purse, and plaies with it, and, at last, lets the Purse fall chinking on the ground; which the* FRYAR *eyes.*

[*In another tone.*] I say a man might doe this now, if he were maliciously dispos'd, and had a mind to bring matters to extremity; but, considering that you are my Friend, a Person of Honour, and a worthy good charitable Man, I wou'd rather dye a thousand deaths then disoblige you.

[LORENZO *takes up the Purse, and poures it into the* FRYAR'S *sleeve.*

Nay, Good Sir; nay, Dear Colonel; O Lord, Sir, what are you doing now? I profess, this must not be: without this I wou'd have serv'd you to the uttermost; pray command me: a jealous, foul-mouth'd Rogue this *Gomez* is: I saw how he us'd you, and you mark'd how he us'd me too: O he's a bitter man; but we'll join our Forces; ah, shall we, Colonel? we'll be reveng'd on him with a witness.

LORENZO: But how shall I send her word to be ready at the door, (for I must reveal it in Confession to you,) that I mean to carry her away this evening, by the help of these two Souldiers? I know *Gomez* suspects you, and you will hardly gain admittance.

DOMINIC: Let me alone; I fear him not; I am arm'd with the Authority of my cloathing; yonder I see him keeping centry at his door: have you never seen a Citizen, in a cold morning, clapping his sides, and walking forward and backward a mighty pace before his Shop? but I'll gain the Pass in spight of his suspicion; stand you aside, and do but mark how I accost him.

LORENZO: If he meet with a repulse, we must throw off the Foxe's skin, and put on the Lion's; come, gentlemen, you'll stand by me

SOULDIER: Do not doubt us, Colonel.

[*They retire all three to a corner of the Stage,* DOMINIC *goes to the door where* GOMEZ *stands.*

DOMINIC: Good even *Gomez*, how does your Wife?

GOMEZ: Just as you wou'd have her, thinking on nothing, but her dear Colonel, and conspiring Cuckoldom against me.

DOMINIC: I dare say you wrong her, she is employing her thoughts how to cure you of your Jealousie.

GOMEZ: Yes, by Certainty.

DOMINIC: By you leave, *Gomez*; I have some Spiritual Advice to impart to her on that Subject.

GOMEZ: You may spare your Instructions if you please, Father, she has no farther need of them.

DOMINIC: How, no need of them! do you speak in Riddles?

GOMEZ: Since you will have me speak plainer, she has profited so well already by your Counsel, that she can say her Lesson without your teaching: Do you understand me now?

DOMINIC: I must not neglect my duty, for all that; once again, *Gomez*, by your leave.

GOMEZ: She's a little indispos'd at present, and it will not be convenient to disturb her.

[DOMINIC *offers to go by him, but t'other stands before him.*

DOMINIC: Indispos'd, say you? O, it is upon those occasions that a Confessor is most necessary; I think it was my good Angel that sent me hither so opportunely.

GOMEZ: Ay, whose good Angels sent you hither, that you best know, Father.

DOMINIC: A word or two of Devotion will do her no harm I'm sure.

GOMEZ: A little Sleep will doe her more good I'm sure: You know she disburthen'd her Conscience but this morning to you.

DOMINIC: But, if she be ill this afternoon, she may have new occasion to confess.

GOMEZ: Indeed, as you order matters with the Colonel, she may have occasion of confessing herself every hour.

DOMINIC: Pray, how long has she been sick?

GOMEZ: Lord, you will force a man to speak; why, ever since your last Defeat.

DOMINIC. This can be but some slight Indisposition, it will not last, and I may see her.

GOMEZ: How, not last! I say, It will last, and it shall last; she shall be sick these seven or eight days, and perhaps longer, as I see occasion: what; I know the mind of her Sickness a little better than you doe.

DOMINIC: I find then, I must bring a Doctor.

GOMEZ: And he'll bring an Apothecary with a chargeable long bill of *Ana*'s: those of my Family have the Grace to dye cheaper: in a word, Sir *Dominic*, we understand one anothers business here: I am resolv'd to stand like the *Swiss* of my own Family, to defend the entrance; you may mumble over your *Pater Nosters* if you please, and try if you can make my doors fly open, and batter down my walls with Bell, Book, and Candle; but I am not of opinion that you are holy enough to commit Miracles.

DOMINIC: Men of my Order are not to be treated after this manner.

GOMEZ: I wou'd treat the Pope and all his Cardinals in the same manner, if they offer'd to see my wife without my leave.

DOMINIC: I excommunicate thee from the Church, if thou dost not open, there's Promulgation coming out.

GOMEZ: And I excommunicate you from my Wife, if you go to that: there's Promulgation for Promulgation, and Bull for Bull; and so I leave you to recreate yourself with the end of an old Song——*and Sorrow came to the old Fryar*.

[*Exit* GOMEZ.

LORENZO *comes to him.*

LORENZO: I will not ask you your Success; for I over-heard part of it, and saw the Conclusion; I find we are now put upon our last Trump; the Fox is earth'd, but I shall send my two Terriers in after him.

SOULDIER: I warrant you, Colonel, we'll unkennel him.

LORENZO: And make what haste you can to bring out the Lady: what say you, Father? Burglary is but a venial Sin among Souldiers.

DOMINIC: I shall absolve them, because he is an enemy of the Church.—there is a Proverb, I confess, which saies, That Dead-men tell no Tales; but let your souldiers apply it at their own Perils.

LORENZO: What, take away a man's Wife, and kill him too! the Wickedness of this old Villain startles me, and gives me a twinge for my own Sin, though it comes far short of his: hark you, Souldiers, be sure you use as little Violence to him as is possible.

DOMINIC: Hold a little, I have thought better how to secure him, with less danger to us.

LORENZO: O Miracle, the Fryar is grown conscientious!

DOMINIC: The old King you know is just murther'd, and the persons that did it are unknown; let the Souldiers seize him for one of the Assassinates, and let me alone to accuse him afterwards.

LORENZO: I cry thee mercy with all my heart, for suspecting a Fryar of the least good nature; what, wou'd you accuse him wrongfully?

DOMINIC: I must confess, 'tis wrongfull *quoad hoc*, as to the Fact itself; but 'tis rightfull *quoad hunc*, as to this Heretical Rogue, whom we must dispatch: he has rail'd against the Church, which is a fouler Crime than the murther of a Thousand Kings; *Omne majus continet in se minus:* He that is an Enemie to the Church, is an Enemie unto Heaven; and he that is an Enemie to Heaven, wou'd have kill'd the King, if he had been in the Circumstances of doing it: so it is not wrongfull to accuse him.

LORENZO: I never knew a Church-man, if he were personally offended, but he wou'd bring in Heaven by hook or crook into his Quarrel. Souldiers, Doe as you were first order'd.

[*Exeunt* SOULDIERS.

DOMINIC: What was't you order'd 'em? Are you sure it's safe, and not scandalous?

LORENZO: Somewhat near your own Design, but not altogether so mischievous; the People are infinitely discontented, as they have reason; and Mutinies there are, or will be, against the Queen; now I am content to put him thus far into the Plot, that he should be secur'd as a Traitor; but he shall onely be Prisoner at the Souldiers' quarters; and when I am out of reach, he shall be releas'd.

DOMINIC: And what will become of me then? for when he is free he will infallibly accuse me.

LORENZO: Why then, Father, you must have recourse to your infallible Church remedies, Lie impudently, and Swear devoutly, and, as you told me but now, let him try whose Oath will be first believ'd. Retire; I hear 'em coming.

[*They withdraw.*

Enter the SOULDIERS *with* GOMEZ *strugling on their backs.*

GOMEZ: Help, good Christians, help Neighbours; my House is broken open by force; and I am ravish'd, and am like to be assassinated; what do you mean, Villains? will you carry me away like a Pedler's Pack upon your backs? will you murther a man in plain day-light?

FIRST SOULDIER: No: but we'll secure you for a Traitor; and for being in a Plot against the State.

GOMEZ: Who, I in a plot! O Lord! O Lord! I never durst be in a plot: Why, how can you in Conscience suspect a rich Citizen of so much wit as to make a Plotter? There are none but poor Rogues, and those that can't live without it, that are in Plots.

SECOND SOULDIER: Away with him, away with him.

GOMEZ: O my Gold! my Wife! my Wife! my Gold! As I hope to be saved now, I know no more of the Plot than they that made it. [*They carry him off, and exeunt.*

LORENZO: Thus far have we sail'd with a merry gale, and now we have the Cape of good Hope in sight; the Trade wind is our own if we can but double it. [*He looks out.* [*aside.*] Ah, my Father and *Pedro* stand at the corner of the street with company, there's no stirring till they are past!

Enter ELVIRA *with a Casket.*

ELVIRA: Am I come at last into your Arms?

LORENZO: Fear nothing; the Adventure's ended; and the Knight may carry off the Lady safely.

ELVIRA: I'm so overjoy'd, I can scarce believe I am at liberty; but stand panting, like a Bird that has often beaten her Wings in vain against her Cage, and at last dares hardly venture out though she sees it open.

DOMINIC: Lose no time, but make haste while the way is free for you; and thereupon I give you my Benediction.

LORENZO: 'Tis not so free as you suppose; for there's an old Gentleman of my acquaintance that blocks up the passage at the corner of the street.

DOMINIC: What have you gotten there under your Arm, Daughter? somewhat I hope that will bear your Charges in your Pilgrimage.

LORENZO: The Fryar has an Hawk's eye to Gold and Jewels.

ELVIRA: Here's that will make you dance without a Fiddle, and provide better Entertainment for us then Hedges in Summer, and Barns in Winter; here's the very Heart and Soul, and Life Bloud of *Gomez*; Pawns in abundance, old Gold of Widows, and new Gold of Prodigals, and Pearls and Diamonds of Court Ladys, till the next Bribe helps their Husbands to redeem 'em.

DOMINIC: They are the Spoils of the Wicked, and the Church endows you with 'em.

LORENZO: And, Faith, we'll drink the Churche's Health out of them. But all this while I stand on Thorns; prithe, Dear, look out, and see if the coast be free for our Escape; for I dare not peep for fear of being known.

[ELVIRA *goes to look, and* GOMEZ *comes running in upon her: she shrieks out.*

GOMEZ: Thanks to my Stars, I have recover'd my own Territories.—What do I see! I'm ruin'd! I'm undone! I'm betray'd!

DOMINIC *aside*: What a hopefull Enterprize is here spoil'd?

GOMEZ: O, Colonel, are you there? and you, Fryar? nay, then I find how the World goes.

LORENZO: Cheer up man; thou art out of jeopardy; I heard thee crying out just now; and came running in full speed with the Wings of an Eagle and the Feet of a Tyger to thy rescue.

GOMEZ: Ay, you are alwaies at hand to doe me a Courtesie with your Eagle's Feet, and your Tyger's Wings: and, What were you here for, Fryar?

DOMINIC: To interpose my Spiritual Authority in your behalf.

GOMEZ: And why did you shriek out, Gentlewoman?

ELVIRA: 'Twas for Joy at your Return.

GOMEZ: And that Casket under your Arm, for what end and purpose?

ELVIRA: Onely to preserve it from the Thieves.

GOMEZ: And you came running out of doors——

ELVIRA: Onely to meet you, sweet Husband.

GOMEZ: A fine Evidence sum'd up among you; thank you heartily; you are all my Friends: the Colonel was walking by accidentally, and, hearing my voice, came in to save me; the Fryar, who was hobling the same way too, accidentally again, and not knowing of the Colonel, I warrant you, he comes in to pray for me; and my faithfull Wife runs out of doors to meet me with all my Jewels under her Arm, and shrieks out for Joy at my return: but if my Father-in-law had not met your Souldiers, Colonel, and deliver'd me in the nick, I shou'd neither have found a Friend nor a Fryar here, and might have shriek'd out for joy my self for the loss of my Jewels and my Wife.

DOMINIC: Art thou an Infidel? Wilt thou not believe us?

GOMEZ: Such Church-men as you wou'd make any man an Infidel: Get you into your Kennel, Gentlewoman; I shall thank you within-doors for your safe custody of my Jewels and your own. [*He thrusts his Wife off the Stage.*

[*Exit* ELVIRA.

As for you, Colonel Huff-cap, we shall trie before a Civil Magistrate who's the greater Plotter of us two, I against the State, or you against the Petticoate.

LORENZO: Nay, if you will complain, you shall for some thing. [*Beats him.*

GOMEZ: Murther, murther! I give up the Ghost! I am destroy'd! help! murther! murther!

DOMINIC: Away, Colonel, let us fly for our Lives; the neighbours are coming out with Forks and Fire-shovels and Spits and other domestick Weapons; the *Militia* of a whole Alley is rais'd against us.

LORENZO: This is but the Interest of my Debt, Master Usurer, the Principal shall be paid you at our next meeting.

DOMINIC: Ah, if your Souldiers had but dispatch'd him, his Tongue had been laid a-sleep, Colonel; but this comes of not following good counsel; ah——

[*Exeunt* LORENZO *and* FRYAR *severally.*

GOMEZ: I'll be reveng'd of him if I dare; but he's such a terrible Fellow that my mind misgives me; I shall tremble when I have him before the Judge: all my Misfortunes come together: I have been robb'd, and cuckolded, and ravish'd, and beaten in one quarter of an hour; my poor Limbs smart, and my poor Head akes: ay, do, do, smart Limb, ake Head, and sprout Horns; but I'll be hang'd before I'll pity you: you must needs be married, must ye? there's for that, [*beats his own Head*] and to a fine, young, modish Lady, must ye? there's for that too; and, at threescore, you old, doting Cuckhold, take that remembrance ——a fine time of day for a man to be bound Prentice, when he is past using of his Trade; to set up an equipage of Noise, when he has most need of Quiet; instead of he being under Covert-baron, to be under Covert-feme my self; to have my Body disabl'd, and my Head fortified; and, lastly, to be crowded into a narrow Box with a shrill Trebble,

That with one Blast through the whole House does bound,
And first taught Speaking-trumpets how to sound.

[*Exit* GOMEZ.

SCENE, *The Court.*

Enter RAYMOND, ALPHONSO, PEDRO.

RAYMOND: Are these, are these, ye Powers, the promis'd joys,
With which I flatter'd my long tedious absence,

To find, at my return, my Master murther'd?
O, that I could but weep to vent my Passion!
But this dry Sorrow burns up all my Tears.

ALPHONSO: Mourn inward, Brother; 'tis observ'd at Court
Who weeps, and who wears black; and your Return
Will fix all Eyes on every Act of yours,
To see how you resent King *Sancho*'s Death.

RAYMOND: What generous man can live with that Constraint
Upon his Soul, to bear, much less to flatter
A Court like this! can I sooth Tyranny?
Seem pleas'd to see my Royal Master murther'd,
His Crown usurp'd, a Distaff in the Throne,
A Council made of such as dare not speak,
And could not if they durst; whence honest men
Banish themselves for shame of being there:
A Government that, knowing not true wisedom,
Is scorn'd abroad, and lives on Tricks at home?

ALPHONSO: Vertue must be thrown off, 'tis a coarse garment,
Too heavy for the sunshine of a Court.

RAYMOND: Well then, I will dissemble for an end
So great, so pious, as a just Revenge:
You'll join with me?

ALPHONSO: No honest man but must.

PEDRO: What Title has this Queen but Lawless Force?
And Force must pull her down.

ALPHONSO: Truth is, I pity *Leonora*'s case;
Forc'd, for her Safety, to commit a Crime
Which most her Soul abhors.

RAYMOND: All she has done, or e'er can doe, of good,
This one black Deed has damn'd.

PEDRO: You'll hardly gain your Son to our Design.

RAYMOND: Your reason for't.

PEDRO: I want time to unriddle it:
Put on your tother Face; the Queen approches.

Enter the QUEEN, BERTRAN, *and Attendants.*

RAYMOND: And that accursed *Bertran*
Stalks close behind her, like a Wiche's Fiend,
Pressing to be employ'd; stand, and observe them.

QUEEN *to* BERTRAN: Bury'd in private, and so suddenly!
It crosses my Design, which was t' allow
The Rites of Funeral fitting his Degree,
With all the Pomp of mourning.

BERTRAN: It was not safe:
Objects of pity, when the cause is new,
Would work too fiercely on the giddy Crowd:
Had *Cæsar*'s body never been expos'd,
Brutus had gain'd his Cause.
QUEEN: Then, was he lov'd?
BERTRAN: O, never man so much, for Saint-like goodness.
PEDRO *aside*: Had bad men fear'd him but as good men lov'd him,
He had not yet been sainted.
QUEEN: I wonder how the People bear his Death.
BERTRAN: Some discontents there are; some idle murmurs.
PEDRO: How, Idle Murmurs! Let me plainly speak:
The doors are all shut up; the wealthier sort,
With Arms a-cross, and Hats upon their Eyes,
Walk to and fro before their silent Shops:
Whole droves of Lenders crowd the Banquers doors,
To call in Money; those who have none, mark
Where Money goes; for when they rise 'tis Plunder:
The Rabble gather round the Man of News,
And listen with their Mouths;
Some tell, some hear, some judge of News, some make it;
And he who lies most loud, is most believ'd.
QUEEN: This may be dangerous.
RAYMOND *aside*: Pray heaven it may.
BERTRAN: If one of you must fall;
Self-preservation is the first of Laws:
And if, when Subjects are oppress'd by Kings,
They justifie Rebellion by that Law,
As well may Monarchs turn the edge of right
To cut for them, when self-defence requires it.
QUEEN: You place such Arbitrary Power in Kings,
That I much fear, if I should make you one,
You'll make your self a Tyrant; let these know
By what Authority you did this Act.
BERTRAN: You much surprize me to demand that Question:
But, since Truth must be told, 'Twas by your own.
QUEEN: Produce it; or, By Heaven, your Head shall answer
The Forfeit of your Tongue.
RAYMOND *aside*: Brave mischief towards.
BERTRAN: You bad me.
QUEEN: When, and where?

BERTRAN: No, I confess, you bad me not in words;
The Dial spoke not, but it made shrewd signs,
And pointed full upon the stroke of Murther:
Yet this you said,
You were a woman, ignorant and weak,
So left it to my care.

QUEEN: What if I said,
I was a woman ignorant and weak,
Were you to take th' advantage of my Sex,
And play the Devil to tempt me? You contriv'd,
You urg'd, you drove me headlong to your toiles;
And if, much tir'd, and frighted more, I paus'd;
Were you to make my Doubts your own Commission?

BERTRAN: This 'tis to serve a Prince too faithfully;
Who, free from Laws himself, will have that done,
Which, not perform'd, brings us to sure Disgrace;
And, if perform'd, to Ruin.

QUEEN: This 'tis to counsel things that are unjust:
First, to debauch a King to break his Laws,
(Which are his safety,) and then seek Protection
From him you have endanger'd; but, Just Heaven,
When Sins are judg'd, will damn the tempting Devil
More deep than those he tempted.

BERTRAN: If Princes not protect their Ministers,
What man will dare to serve them?

QUEEN: None will dare
To serve them ill, when they are left to Laws;
But when a Counsellor, to save himself,
Would lay Miscarriages upon his Prince,
Exposing him to publick Rage and Hate;
O, 'tis an Act as infamously base,
As should a common Souldier sculk behind,
And thrust his General in the Front of War:
It shews he onely serv'd himself before,
And had no sense of Honour, Country, King;
But center'd on himself; and us'd his Master
As Guardians do their Wards, with shows of care,
But with intent to sell the publick Safety,
And pocket up his Prince.

PEDRO *aside*: Well said, i'faith;
This Speech is e'en too good for an Usurper.

BERTRAN: I see for whom I must be sacrific'd;
And, had I not been sotted with my zeal,

I might have found it sooner.

QUEEN: From my sight!
The Prince who bears an Insolence like this
Is such an Image of the Powers above,
As is the Statue of the Thundring God,
Whose Bolts the Boys may play with.

BERTRAN: Unreveng'd
I will not fall, nor single. [*Exit* BERTRAN *cum suis.*

QUEEN *to* RAYMOND, *who kisses her hand.*

QUEEN: Welcome, welcome:
I saw you not before: one Honest Lord
Is hid with ease among a Crowd of Courtiers:
How can I be too gratefull to the Father
Of such a Son as *Torrismond?*

RAYMOND: His Actions were but Duty.

QUEEN: Yet, My Lord,
All have not paid that Debt like noble *Torrismond*;
You hear how *Bertran* brands me with a Crime,
Of which, your Son can witness, I am free;
I sent to stop the Murther, but too late;
For Crimes are swift, but Penitence is slow;
The bloudy *Bertran*, diligent in ill,
Flew to prevent the soft returns of Pity.

RAYMOND: O cursed Haste of making sure a Sin!
Can you forgive the Traytor?

QUEEN: Never, never:
'Tis written here in Characters so deep
That seven years hence, ('till then should I not meet him,)
And in the Temple then, I'll drag him thence,
Ev'n from the Holy Altar to the Block.

RAYMOND *aside*: She's fir'd, as I would wish her; aid me Justice,
As all my ends are thine, to gain this Point;
And ruin both at once:—It wounds indeed, [*To her.*
To bear Affronts too great to be forgiven,
And not have Power to punish; yet one way
There is to ruin *Bertran*.

QUEEN: O, there's none;
Except an Host from Heaven can make such haste
To save my Crown as he will doe to seize it:
You saw he came surrounded with his Friends,

And knew besides our Army was remov'd
To quarters too remote for sudden use.

RAYMOND: Yet you may give Commission
To some Bold man whose Loyalty you trust,
And let him raise the Train-bands of the City.

QUEEN: Gross feeders, Lion talkers, Lamb-like fighters.

RAYMOND: You do not know the Virtues of your City,
What pushing force they have; some popular Chief,
More noisie than the rest, but cries Halloo,
And in a trice the bellowing Herd come out;
The Gates are barr'd, the Ways are barricado'd,
And *One and All*'s the Word; true Cocks o'the Game,
That never ask for what, or whom, they fight;
But turn 'em out, and shew 'em but a Foe,
Cry Liberty, and that's a Cause of Quarrel.

QUEEN: There may be Danger, in that boist'rous Rout:
Who knows when Fires are kindled for my Foes,
But some new Blast of wind may turn those Flames
Against my Pallace Walls?

RAYMOND: But still their Chief
Must be some one whose Loyalty you trust.

QUEEN: And who more proper for that Trust then you,
Whose Interests, though unknown to you, are mine?
Alphonso, *Pedro*, haste to raise the Rabble,
He shall appear to head 'em.

RAYMOND *aside to* ALPHONSO *and* PEDRO: First sieze *Bertran*,
And then insinuate to them that I bring
Their lawfull Prince to place upon the Throne.

ALPHONSO: Our lawfull Prince.

RAYMOND: Fear not; I can produce him.

PEDRO *to* ALPHONSO: Now we want your Son *Lorenzo*: what a mighty Faction
Would he make for us of the City Wives,
With, ô, dear Husband, my sweet honey Husband,
Won't you be for the Colonel? if you love me,
Be for the Colonel; ô he's the finest man!

[*Exeunt* ALPHONSO, PEDRO.

RAYMOND *aside*: So, now we have a Plot behind the Plot;
She thinks she's in the depth of my Design,
And that it's all for her, but time shall show,
She onely lives to help me ruin others,
And last, to fall her self.

QUEEN: Now to you *Raymond*: Can you guess no reason

Why I repose such Confidence in you?
You needs must think
There's some more powerfull Cause then Loyalty:
Will you not speak to save a Lady's Blush?
Must I inform you 'tis for *Torrismond*,
That all this Grace is shown?

RAYMOND *aside*: By all the Powers, worse, worse, then what I fear'd.

QUEEN: And yet, what need I blush at such a Choice?
I love a man, whom I am proud to love,
And am well pleas'd my Inclination gives
What Gratitude would force; ô, pardon me;
I ne'er was covetous of Wealth before:
Yet think so vast a Treasure as your Son,
Too great for any private man's possession;
And him too rich a Jewel to be set
In vulgar metal, or for vulgar use.

RAYMOND: Arm me with Patience Heaven.

QUEEN: How, Patience, *Raymond!*
What exercise of Patience have you here?
What find you in my Crown to be contemn'd?
Or in my Person loath'd? Have I, a Queen,
Past by my Fellow-rulers of the World,
Whose vying Crowns lay glittering in my way,
As if the World were pav'd with Diadems?
Have I refus'd their Bloud, to mix with yours,
And raise new Kings from so obscure a race,
Fate scarce knew where to find them when I call'd?
Have I heap'd on my Person, Crown and State,
To load the Scale, and weigh'd my self with Earth,
For you to spurn the Balance?

RAYMOND: Bate the last; and 'tis what I would say;
Can I, can any Loyal Subject see
With Patience such a stoop from Sovereignty,
An Ocean pour'd upon a narrow Brook?
My Zeal for you must lay the Father by,
And plead my Countrie's Cause against my Son.
What though his Heart be great, his Actions gallant;
He wants a Crown to poise against a Crown,
Birth to match Birth, and Power to balance Power.

QUEEN: All these I have, and these I can bestow;
But he brings Worth and Vertue to my Bed;
And Vertue is the Wealth which Tyrants want:

I stand in need of one whose Glories may
Redeem my Crimes, ally me to his Fame,
Dispell the Factions of my Foes on Earth,
Disarm the Justice of the Powers above.

RAYMOND: The People never will endure this choice.

QUEEN: If I endure it what imports it you?
Goe, raise the Ministers of my Revenge,
Guide with your Breath this whirling Tempest round,
And see its Fury fall where I design;
At last a time for just Revenge is given;
Revenge the darling attribute of Heaven:
But man, unlike his Maker, bears too long;
Still more expos'd, the more he pardons Wrong;
Great in forgiving, and in suffering brave;
To be a Saint he makes himself a Slave. [*Exit* QUEEN.

RAYMOND *solus*: Marriage with *Torrismond*! it must not be;
By Heaven, it must not be; or, if it be;
Law, Justice, Honour bid farewell to Earth;
For Heaven leaves all to Tyrants.

Enter TORRISMOND, *who kneels to him.*

TORRISMOND: O, ever welcome, Sir,
But doubly now! you come in such a time,
As if propitious Fortune took a care
To swell my Tide of Joys to their full height,
And leave me nothing farther to desire.

RAYMOND: I hope I come in time, if not to make,
At least, to save your Fortune and your Honour:
Take heed you steer your Vessel right, my Son,
This Calm of Heaven, this Mermayd's melody,
Into an unseen whirl-pool draws you fast,
And in a moment sinks you.

TORRISMOND: Fortune cannot:
And Fate can scarce; I've made the Port already,
And laugh securely at the lazy storm
That wanted wings to reach me in the deep.
Your pardon, Sir; my duty calls me hence;
I go to find my Queen, my earthly Goddess,
To whom I owe my Hopes, my Life, my Love.

RAYMOND: You owe her more perhaps than you imagin;
Stay, I command you stay, and hear me first,
This hour's the very *Crisis* of your Fate,
Your Good or Ill, your Infamy or Fame;

And all the colour of your Life depends
On this important Now.

TORRISMOND: I see no danger;
The City, Army, Court espouse my Cause;
And, more then all, the Queen with publick favour
Indulges my Pretensions to her Love.

RAYMOND: Nay, if possessing her can make you happy,
'Tis granted, nothing hinders your Design.

TORRISMOND: If she can make me blest? she onely can:
Empire, and Wealth, and all she brings beside,
Are but the Train and Trappings of her Love:
The sweetest, kindest, truest of her Sex,
In whose Possession years roule round on years,
And Joys in Circles meet new Joys again:
Kisses, Embraces, Languishing and Death,
Still from each other, to each other move
To crown the various seasons of our Love:
And doubt you if such Love can make me happy?

RAYMOND: Yes, or I think you love your Honour more.

TORRISMOND: And what can shock my Honour in a Queen?

RAYMOND: A Tyrant, an Usurper?

TORRISMOND: Grant she be.
When from the Conquerour we hold our Lives,
We yield our selves his Subjects from that hour:
For mutual Benefits make mutual Ties.

RAYMOND: Why, can you think I owe a Thief my Life,
Because he took it not by lawless Force?
What, if he did not all the Ill he cou'd?
Am I oblig'd, by that, t' assist his Rapines,
And to maintain his Murthers?

TORRISMOND: Not to maintain, but bear 'em unreveng'd;
Kings Titles commonly begin by Force,
Which Time wears off and mellows into Right:
So Power, which in one Age is Tyranny,
Is ripn'd in the next to true Succession:
She's in Possession.

RAYMOND: So Diseases are:
Shou'd not a lingring Fevor be remov'd?
Because it long has rag'd within my Bloud?
Do I rebell when I wou'd thrust it out?
What, shall I think the World was made for One,
And Men are born for Kings, as Beasts for Men;
Not for Protection, but to be devour'd?

Mark those who dote on Arbitrary Power,
And you shall find 'em either hot-brain'd Youth,
Or needy Bankrupts, servil in their greatness,
And Slaves to some, to lord it o'er the rest.
O baseness, to support a Tyrant Throne,
And crush your Free-born-brethren of the World!
Nay, to become a part of Usurpation;
To espouse the Tyrants Person and her Crimes,
And, on a Tyrant, get a Race of Tyrants
To be your Country's Curse in after Ages.

TORRISMOND: I see no Crime in her whom I adore,
Or if I do, her Beauty makes it none:
Look on me as a man abandon'd o'er
To an eternal Lethargy of Love;
To pull, and pinch, and wound me, cannot cure,
And but disturb the Quiet of my Death.

RAYMOND: O, Vertue! Vertue! what art thou become?
That men should leave thee for that Toy a Woman
Made from the dross and refuse of a Man;
Heaven took him sleeping when he made her too;
Had man been waking he had ne'er consented.
Now Son, suppose
Some brave conspiracy were ready form'd
To punish Tyrants, and redeem the Land,
Cou'd you so far bely your Country's Hope,
As not to head the Party?

TORRISMOND: How cou'd my Hand rebell against my Heart?

RAYMOND: How cou'd your Heart rebell against your Reason?

TORRISMOND: No Honour bids me fight against my self;
The Royal Family is all extinct,
And she who reigns bestows her Crown on me:
So must I be ungratefull to the Living,
To be but vainly pious to the Dead;
While you defraud your Offspring of their Fate.

RAYMOND: Mark who defraud their Offspring, you or I?
For know there yet survives the lawfull Heir
Of *Sancho*'s bloud, whom when I shall produce,
I rest assur'd to see you pale with Fear
And Trembling at his Name.

TORRISMOND: He must be more then Man who makes me tremble:
I dare him to the Field with all the ods
Of Justice on his side, against my Tyrant:

Produce your lawfull Prince, and you shall see
How brave a Rebell Love has made your Son.

RAYMOND: Read that: 'tis with the Royal Signet sign'd,
And given me by the King when time shou'd serve
To be perus'd by you.

TORRISMOND *reads: I the King.*
My youngest and alone surviving Son
Reported dead t' escape rebellious rage
Till happier times shall call his Courage forth
To break my Fetters or revenge my Fate,
I will that Raymond *educate as his,*
And call him Torrismond————
If I am he, that Son, that *Torrismond,*
The World contains not so forlorn a Wretch!
Let never man believe he can be happy!
For when I thought my Fortune most secure,
One fatal moment tears me from my Joys:
And when two Hearts were joyn'd by mutual Love,
The Sword of Justice cuts upon the Knot,
And severs 'em for ever.

RAYMOND: True; it must.

TORRISMOND: O cruel man, to tell me that it must!
If you have any Pity in your Breast,
Redeem me from this Labyrinth of Fate,
And plunge me in my first Obscurity:
The Secret is alone between us two;
And though you wou'd not hide me from my self,
O, yet be kind, conceal me from the World,
And be my Father still.

RAYMOND: Your Lot's too glorious, and the Proof's too plain.
Now, in the name of Honour, Sir, I beg you
(Since I must use Authority no more)
On these old Knees I beg you, e'er I dye,
That I may see your Father's Death reveng'd.

TORRISMOND: Why, 'tis the onely bus'ness of my Life;
My Order's issued to recall the Army,
And *Bertran*'s Death resolv'd.

RAYMOND: And not the Queen's; ô She's the chief Offender!
Shall Justice turn her Edge within your Hand?
No, if she scape, you are your self the Tyrant,
And Murtherer of your Father.

TORRISMOND: Cruel Fates,
To what have you reserv'd me!

RAYMOND: Why that Sigh?

TORRISMOND: Since you must know, but break, ô break my Heart,
Before I tell my Fatal Story out,
Th' Usurper of my Throne, my House's Ruin,
The murtherer of my Father, is my Wife!

RAYMOND: O, Horrour! Horrour! after this Alliance,
Let Tygers match with Hinds, and Wolfs with Sheep,
And every Creature couple with his Foe.
How vainly Man designs when Heaven opposes!
I bred you up to Arms, rais'd you to Power,
Permitted you to fight for this Usurper,
Indeed to save a Crown, not her's, but yours,
All to make sure the Vengeance of this Day,
Which even this Day has ruin'd—one more question
Let me but ask, and I have done for ever:
Do you yet love the Cause of all your Woes,
Or, is she grown (as sure she ought to be)
More odious to your sight than Toads and Adders?

TORRISMOND: O, there's the utmost Malice of my Fate,
That I am bound to hate, and born to love!

RAYMOND: No more:—Farwell my much lamented King.
[*aside*] I dare not trust him with himself so far
To own him to the People as their King,
Before their Rage has finish'd my Designs
On *Bertran* and the *Queen*, but in Despight
Ev'n of himself I'll save him. [*Exit* RAYMOND.

TORRISMOND: 'Tis but a moment since I have been King,
And weary on't already; I'm a Lover,
And lov'd, possess; yet all these make me wretched;
And Heav'n has giv'n me Blessings for a Curse.
With what a load of Vengeance am I prest,
Yet, never, never, can I hope for Rest;
For when my heavy Burthen I remove,
The weight falls down, and crushes her I love.
[*Exit* TORRISMOND.

ACT V

SCENE, *A Bed-chamber.*

Enter TORRISMOND.

TORRISMOND: Love, Justice, Nature, Pity and Revenge
Have kindled up a Wild-fire in my Breast,
And I am all a Civil-war within!

Enter QUEEN *and* TERESA *at a distance.*

My *Leonora* there!
Mine? Is she mine? My Father's Murtherer mine?
Oh! that I could with Honour love her more,
Or hate her less with Reason! See, she weeps;
Thinks me unkind, or false, and knows not why
I thus estrange my Person from her Bed:
Shall I not tell her? no: 'twill break her Heart:
She'll know too soon her own and my Misfortunes.
[*Exit.*

QUEEN: He's gon, and I am lost; Didst thou not see
His sullen Eyes? how gloomily they glanc'd:
He look'd not like the *Torrismond* I lov'd.

TERESA: Can you not guess from whence this Change proceeds?

QUEEN: No: there's the Grief, *Teresa*: Oh, *Teresa*!
Fain would I tell thee what I feel within,
But Shame and Modesty have ty'd my Tongue!
Yet, I will tell, that thou maiest weep with me.
How dear, how sweet his first Embraces were!
With what a Zeal he join'd his Lips to mine!
And suckt my Breath at every word I spoke,
As if he drew his Inspiration thence:
While both our Souls came upward to our Mouths,
As neighbouring Monarchs at their Borders meet:
I thought: Oh no; 'Tis false: I could not think;
'Twas neither Life nor Death, but both in one.

TERESA: Then sure his Transports were not less than yours.

QUEEN: More, more! for by the high-hung Tapers light
I could discern his Cheeks were glowing red,
His very Eye-balls trembl'd with his Love,
And sparkl'd through their Casements humid Fires:
He sigh'd and kiss'd, breath'd short, and wou'd have
spoke,

But was too fierce to throw away the time;
All he cou'd say was Love, and *Leonora.*

TERESA: How then can you suspect him lost so soon?

QUEEN: Last night he flew not with a Bridegroom's haste,
Which eagerly prevents the pointed hour;
I told the Clocks, and watch'd the wasting Light,
And listned to each softly treading step,
In hope 'twas he: but still it was not he.
At last he came, but with such alter'd Looks,
So wild, so ghastly, as if some Ghost had met him;
All pale, and speechless, he survey'd me round;
Then, with a Groan, he threw himself a-bed,
But far from me, as far as he cou'd move,
And sigh'd, and toss'd, and turn'd, but still from me.

TERESA: What, all the night?

QUEEN: Even all the live-long-night.
At last: (for, blushing, I must tell thee all,)
I press'd his Hand, and laid me by his Side,
He pull'd it back, as if he touch'd a Serpent.
With that I burst into a floud of Tears,
And ask'd him how I had offended him?
He answer'd nothing, but with Sighs and Groans,
So restless past the night: and at the Dawn
Leapt from the Bed, and vanish'd.

TERESA: Sighs and Groans,
Paleness and Trembling, all are signs of Love;
He onely fears to make you share his Sorrows.

QUEEN: I wish 'twere so: but Love still doubts the worst;
My heavy Heart, the Prophetess of Woes,
Foreboads some ill at hand: To sooth my sadness
Sing me the Song which poor *Olympia* made
When false *Bireno* left her.——

A SONG.

I.

Farewell ungratefull Traytor,
Farewell my perjur'd Swain
Let never injur'd Creature
Believe a Man again.
The Pleasure of Possessing
Surpasses all Expressing,
But 'tis too short a Blessing,
And Love too long a Pain.

II.

'Tis easie to deceive us
In pity of our Pain,
But when we love you leave us
To rail at you in vain.
Before we have descry'd it
There is no Bliss beside it,
But she that once has try'd it
Will never love again.

III.

The Passion you pretended
Was onely to obtain,
But when the Charm is ended
The Charmer you disdain.
Your Love by ours we measure
Till we have lost our Treasure,
But Dying is a Pleasure,
When Living is a Pain.

Re-enter TORRISMOND.

TORRISMOND: Still she is here, and still I cannot speak;
But wander like some discontented Ghost
That oft appears, but is forbid to talke. [*Going again.*
QUEEN: O, *Torrismond*, if you resolve my Death,
You need no more but to go hence again;
Will you not speak?
TORRISMOND: I cannot.
QUEEN: Speak! oh, speak!
Your Anger wou'd be kinder than your Silence.
TORRISMOND: Oh!
QUEEN: Do not sigh, or tell me why you sigh?
TORRISMOND: Why do I live, ye Powers?
QUEEN: Why do I live, to hear you speak that word?
Some black-mouth'd Villain has defam'd my Vertue.
TORRISMOND: No! No! Pray let me go.
QUEEN *kneeling*: You shall not goe:
By all the Pleasures of our Nuptial-bed,
If ever I was lov'd, though now I'm not,

By these true Tears, which from my wounded Heart
Bleed at my Eyes.————

TORRISMOND: Rise.

QUEEN: I will never rise,
I cannot chuse a better place to dye.

TORRISMOND: Oh! I wou'd speak, but cannot.

QUEEN *rising*: Guilt keeps you silent then; you love me not:
What have I done? ye Powers, what have I done?
To see my Youth, my Beauty, and my Love
No sooner gain'd, but slighted and betray'd:
And like a Rose just gather'd from the Stalk,
But onely smelt, and cheaply thrown aside
To wither on the ground.

TERESA: For Heaven's sake, Madam, moderate your Passion.

QUEEN: Why nam'st thou Heaven? there is no Heaven for me,
Despair, Death, Hell, have seiz'd my tortur'd Soul:
When I had rais'd his groveling Fate from ground,
To Pow'r and Love, to Empire and to Me;
When each Embrace was dearer than the first;
Then, then to be contemn'd; then, then thrown off;
It calls me old, and wither'd, and deform'd,
And loathsome: Oh ! what Woman can bear Loathsome?
The Turtle flies not from his billing Mate,
He bills the closer: but ungratefull Man,
Base, barbarous Man, the more we raise our Love,
The more we pall, and cool, and kill his ardour.
Racks, Poison, Daggers, rid me but of Life;
And any Death is welcome.

TORRISMOND: Be witness all ye Powers that know my Heart,
I would have kept the fatal Secret hid,
But she has conquer'd, to her Ruin conquer'd:
Here, take this Paper, reade our Destinies;
Yet do not; but in kindness to your self,
Be ignorantly safe.

QUEEN: No! give it me,
Even though it be the Sentence of my Death.

TORRISMOND: Then see how much unhappy Love has made us.
O *Leonora!* Oh!
We two were born when sullen Planets reign'd;
When each the others Influence oppos'd,
And drew the Stars to Factions at our Birth.
Oh! better, better had it been for us
That we had never seen, or never lov'd.

QUEEN: There is no Faith in Heaven, if Heaven says so,
You dare not give it.

TORRISMOND: As unwillingly,
As I would reach out *Opium* to a Friend
Who lay in Torture, and desir'd to dye. [*Gives the Paper.*
But now you have it, spare my sight the pain
Of seeing what a world of Tears it cost you:
Go silently enjoy your part of Grief,
And share the sad Inheritance with me.

QUEEN: I have a thirsty Fevor in my Soul,
Give me but present Ease, and let me dye.
[*Exit* QUEEN *and* TERESA.

Enter LORENZO.

LORENZO: Arm, arm, my Lord, the City Bands are up,
Drums beating, Colours flying, Shouts confus'd;
All clustring in a heap, like swarming Hives,
And rising in a moment.

TORRISMOND: With design to punish *Bertran*, and revenge the King,
'Twas order'd so.

LORENZO: Then you're betray'd, my Lord.
'Tis true, they block the Castle kept by *Bertran*,
But now they cry, Down with the Palace, Fire it,
Pull out th' usurping Queen.

TORRISMOND: The Queen, *Lorenzo!* durst they name the Queen?

LORENZO: If railing and reproaching be to name her.

TORRISMOND: O Sacrilege! Say quickly who commands
This vile blaspheming Rout?

LORENZO: I'm loth to tell you,
But both our Fathers thrust 'em headlong on,
And bear down all before 'em.

TORRISMOND: Death and Hell!
Somewhat must be resolv'd, and speedily,
How sayst thou, my *Lorenzo?* darst thou be
A Friend, and once forget thou art a Son,
To help me save the Queen?

LORENZO *aside*: Let me consider; Bear Arms against my Father? he begat me; That's true; but for whose sake did he beget me? For his own sure enough: for me he knew not. Oh! but says Conscience: Fly in Nature's Face? But how if Nature fly in my Face first? Then Nature's the Aggressor: Let her look to't——He gave me Life, and he may take it back:——No, that's Boys play, say I.——'Tis Policy for Son and Father to take different sides: For then, Lands and Tenements commit no Treason. [*To* TORRISMOND] Sir, upon mature consideration, I have found my Father to be little better than a Rebel, and therefore I'll doe my best to secure him for your sake; in hope you may secure him hereafter for my sake.

TORRISMOND: Put on thy utmost speed to head the Troops
Which every moment I expect t' arrive:
Proclaim me, as I am, the lawfull King:
I need not caution thee for *Raymond*'s Life,
Though I no more must call him Father now.

LORENZO *aside*: How! not call him Father? I see Preferment alters a man strangely, this may serve me for a Use of Instruction, to cast off my Father when I am great. Methought too he call'd himself the lawfull King; intimating sweetly that he knows what's what with our Sovereign Lady: Well, if I rout my Father, as I hope in Heaven I shall, I am in a fair Way to be a Prince of the Bloud: Farwell, General; I'll bring up those that shall try what mettle there is in Orange-Tawny. [*Exit.*

TORRISMOND *at the door*: Hast there, command the Guards be all drawn up
Before the Palace gate.—By Heaven, I'll face
This Tempest, and deserve the Name of King.
O, *Leonora*, beauteous in thy Crimes,
Never were Hell and Heaven so match'd before!
Look upward, Fair, but as thou look'st on me;
Then all the Blest will begg that thou may'st live,
And even my Father's Ghost his Death forgive.
[*Exit* TORRISMOND.

SCENE *The Palace-yard.*

Drums and Trumpets within.

Enter RAYMOND, ALPHONSO, PEDRO, *and their Party.*

RAYMOND: Now, valiant Citizens, the time is come
To show your Courage and your Loyalty:
You have a Prince of *Sancho*'s Royal Bloud,
The Darling of the Heavens and Joy of Earth;
When he's produc'd, as soon he shall, among you;

Speak, what will you adventure to re-seat him
Upon his Father's Throne?

OMNES: Our Lives and Fortunes.

RAYMOND: What then remains to perfect our Success,
But o'er the Tyrant's Guards to force our way?

OMNES: Lead on, Lead on.

Drums and Trumpets on the other Side.

Enter TORRISMOND *and his Party: as they are going to fight, he speaks.*

TORRISMOND *to his*: Hold, hold your Arms.

RAYMOND *to his*: Retire.

ALPHONSO: What means this Pause?

PEDRO: Peace: Nature works within them.

[TORRISMOND *and* RAYMOND *go apart.*

TORRISMOND: How comes it, good old Man, that we two meet
On these harsh terms! thou very reverend Rebel?
Thou venerable Traitor, in whose Face
And hoary Hairs Treason is sanctified;
And Sin's black dy seems blanch'd by Age to Vertue.

RAYMOND: What Treason is it to redeem my King,
And to reform the State?

TORRISMOND: That's a stale Cheat,
The primitive Rebel, *Lucifer*, first us'd it,
And was the first Reformer of the Skyes.

RAYMOND: What if I see my Prince mistake a Poison,
Call it a Cordial? am I then a Traitor,
Because I hold his Hand or break the Glass?

TORRISMOND: How darst thou serve thy King against his Will?

RAYMOND: Because 'tis then the onely time to serve him.

TORRISMOND: I take the blame of all upon my self,
Discharge thy weight on me.

RAYMOND: O, never, never!
Why, 'tis to leave a Ship tost in a Tempest
Without the Pilot's Care.

TORRISMOND: I'll punish thee,
By Heaven, I will, as I wou'd punish Rebels,
Thou stubborn loyal Man.

RAYMOND: First let me see
Her punisht who misleads you from your Fame,

Then burn me, hack me, hew me into pieces,
And I shall dye well pleas'd.

TORRISMOND: Proclaim my Title,
To save the effusion of my Subjects Bloud; and thou shalt still
Be as my Foster-father near my Breast,
And next my *Leonora*.

RAYMOND: That word stabs me.
You shall be still plain *Torrismond* with me,
Th' Abetter, Partner, (if you like that name,)
The Husband of a Tyrant, but no King;
Till you deserve that Title by your Justice.

TORRISMOND: Then, farwell Pity, I will be obey'd.
[*To the People*.] Hear, you mistaken Men, whose Loyalty
Runs headlong into Treason: See your Prince,
In me behold your murther'd *Sancho*'s Son;
Dismiss your Arms; and I forgive your Crimes.

RAYMOND: Believe him not; he raves; his words are loose
As heaps of Sand, and scattering, wide from sense.
You see he knows not me, his natural Father;
But aiming to possess th' usurping Queen,
So high he's mounted in his Aiery hopes,
That now the Wind is got into his Head,
And turns his Brains to Frenzy.

TORRISMOND: Hear me yet, I am———

RAYMOND: Fall on, fall on, and hear him not:
But spare his Person for his Father's sake.

PEDRO: Let me come, if he be mad, I have that shall cure him.
There's no Surgeon in all *Arragon* has so much
Dexterity as I have at breathing of the Temple-vein.

TORRISMOND: My Right for me.

RAYMOND: Our Liberty for us.

OMNES: Liberty, Liberty,—— [*As they are ready to fight.*

Enter LORENZO *and his Party.*

LORENZO: On forfeit of your Lives lay down your Arms.

ALPHONSO: How, Rebel, art thou there?

LORENZO: Take your Rebel back again Father mine. The beaten Party are Rebels to the Conquerors. I have been at hard-head with your butting Citizens; I have routed your Herd; I have disperst them; And now they are retreated quietly, from their extraordinary Vocation of Fighting in the streets, to their ordinary Vocation of Cozening in their Shops.

TORRISMOND *to* RAYMOND: You see 'tis vain contending with the Truth,
Acknowledge what I am.
RAYMOND: You are my King: wou'd you wou'd be your own;
But by a fatal fondness you betray
Your Fame and Glory to th' Usurper's Bed:
Enjoy the Fruits of Bloud and Parricide,
Take your own Crown from *Leonora*'s Gift,
And hug your Father's Murtherer in your Arms.

Enter QUEEN *and* TERESA: *Women.*

ALPHONSO: No more: behold the Queen.
RAYMOND: Behold the *Basilisk* of *Torrismond,*
That kills him with her eyes. I will speak on,
My Life is of no further use to me:
I would have chaffer'd it before for Vengeance:
Now let it go for Failing.
TORRISMOND *aside*: My Heart sinks in me while I hear him speak,
And every slackn'd fiber drops its hold,
Like Nature letting down the Springs of Life:
So much the Name of Father aws me still.
Send off the Crowd:
For you, now I have conquer'd, I can hear with honour your Demands.
LORENZO *to* ALPHONSO: Now, Sir, who proves the Traitor?
My Conscience is true to me, it alwaies whispers right when I have my Regiment to back it.
[*Exeunt omnes praeter* LORENZO, RAYMOND, LEONORA.
TORRISMOND: O *Leonora!* what can Love do more?
I have oppos'd your ill Fate to the utmost:
Combated Heaven and Earth to keep you mine:
And yet at last that Tyrant, Justice! Oh——
QUEEN: 'Tis past, 'tis past: and Love is ours no more:
Yet I complain not of the Powers above;
They made m' a Miser's feast of Happiness,
And cou'd not furnish out another meal.
Now, by yon' Stars, by Heaven, and Earth, and Men
By all my Foes at once; I swear, my *Torrismond,*
That to have had you mine for one short day
Has cancell'd half my mighty sum of Woes:
Say but you hate me not.

TORRISMOND: I cannot hate you.
RAYMOND: Can you not? say that once more;
That all the Saints may witness it against you.
QUEEN: Cruel *Raymond!*
Can he not punish me but he must hate?
O, 'tis not Justice, but a brutal Rage,
Which hates th' Offender's person with his Crimes:
I have enough to overwhelm one Woman,
To lose a Crown and Lover in a day:
Let Pity lend a Tear when Rigour strikes.
RAYMOND: Then, then you should have thought of Tears and Pity,
When Vertue, Majesty, and hoary Age
Pleaded for *Sancho*'s Life.
QUEEN: My future days shall be one whole Contrition;
A Chapel will I build with large Endowment,
Where every day an hundred aged men
Shall all hold up their wither'd hands to Heaven,
To pardon *Sancho*'s Death.
TORRISMOND: See, Raymond, see: she makes a large amends:
Sancho is dead: no punishment of her
Can raise his cold stiff limbs from the dark Grave;
Nor can his blessed Soul look down from Heaven;
Or break th' eternal Sabbath of his Rest,
To see with Joy her Miseries on Earth.
RAYMOND: Heaven may forgive a Crime to Penitence,
For Heaven can judge if Penitence be true;
But Man, who knows not Hearts, should make Examples;
Which like a Warning-piece must be shot off,
To fright the rest from Crimes.
QUEEN: Had I but known that *Sancho* was his Father,
I would have pour'd a Deluge of my Bloud
To save one Drop of his.
TORRISMOND: Mark that, Inexorable *Raymond* mark!
'Twas fatal Ignorance that caus'd his Death.
RAYMOND: What if she did not know he was your Father?
She knew he was a Man, the Best of men,
Heaven's Image double stampt, as Man and King.
QUEEN: He was, he was, ev'n more than you can say,
But yet——
RAYMOND: But yet you barbarously murther'd him.
QUEEN: He will not hear me out!
TORRISMOND: Was ever Criminal forbid to plead?
Curb your ill manner'd Zeal.

RAYMOND: Sing to him *Syren*;
For I shall stop my Ears: now mince the Sin,
And mollifie Damnation with a Phrase:
Say you consented not to *Sancho*'s Death,
But barely not forbad it.

QUEEN: Hard hearted Man, I yield my guilty cause,
But all my Guilt was caus'd by too much Love.
Had I for Jealousie of Empire sought
Good *Sancho*'s Death, *Sancho* had dy'd before.
'Twas alwaies in my Power to take his Life:
But Interest never could my Conscience blind
Till Love had cast a mist before my Eyes;
And made me think his Death the onely means
Which could secure my Throne to *Torrismond*.

TORRISMOND: Never was fatal Mischief meant so kind,
For all she gave, has taken all away.
Malicious Pow'rs! is this to be restor'd?
'Tis to be worse depos'd than *Sancho* was.

RAYMOND: Heaven has restor'd you, you depose your self:
Oh! when young Kings begin with scorn of Justice,
They make an Omen to their after Reign,
And blot their Annals in the foremost page.

TORRISMOND: No more; lest you be made the first Example,
To show how I can punish.

RAYMOND: Once again:
Let her be made your Father's Sacrifice,
And after make me her's.

TORRISMOND: Condemn a Wife!
That were to attone for Parricide with Murther!

RAYMOND: Then let her be divorc'd! we'll be content
With that poor scanty Justice: Let her part.

TORRISMOND: Divorce! that's worse than Death, 'tis Death of Love.

QUEEN: The Soul and Body part not with such Pain
As I from you: but yet 'tis just, my Lord:
I am th' Accurst of Heaven, the Hate of Earth,
Your Subjects Detestation, and your Ruin:
And therefore fix this doom upon my self.

TORRISMOND: Heav'n! Can you wish it? to be mine no more!

QUEEN: Yes, I can wish it as the dearest Proof
And last that I can make you of my Love.
To leave you blest I would be more accurst

Than Death can make me; for Death ends our Woes,
And the kind Grave shuts up the mournfull Scene:
But I would live without you; to be wretched long:
And hoard up every moment of my life,
To lengthen out the Payment of my Tears,
Till ev'n fierce *Raymond*, at the last, shall say,
Now let her dye, for she has griev'd enough.

TORRISMOND: Hear this, hear this thou Tribune of the People:
Thou zealous, publick Bloud-hound hear, and melt.

RAYMOND *aside*: I could cry now, my Eyes grow womanish,
But yet my Heart holds out.

QUEEN: Some solitary Cloister will I chuse,
And there with holy Virgins live immur'd:
Course my Attire, and short shall be my Sleep,
Broke by the melancholy midnight Bell:
Now, *Raymond*, now be satisfied at last.
Fasting and Tears, and Penitence and Prayer
Shall doe dead *Sancho* Justice every hour.

RAYMOND *aside*: By your leave, Manhood! [*Wipes his Eyes.*

TORRISMOND: He weeps, now he's vanquish'd.

RAYMOND: No! 'Tis a salt rheum that scalds my Eyes.

QUEEN: If he were vanquish'd, I am still unconquer'd,
I'll leave you in the height of all my Love,
Ev'n when my Heart is beating out its way,
And struggles to you most.
Farwell, a last Farwell! My dear, dear Lord
Remember me; speak, *Raymond*, will you let him?
Shall he remember *Leonora*'s Love,
And shed a parting Tear to her Misfortunes?

RAYMOND *almost crying*: Yes, yes, he shall, pray goe.

TORRISMOND: Now, By my Soul, she shall not goe: why, *Raymond*,
Her every Tear is worth a Father's Life;
Come to my Arms, come, my fair Penitent,
Let us not think what future Ills may fall,
But drink deep Draughts of Love, and lose 'em all.

[*Exit* TORRISMOND *with the* QUEEN.

RAYMOND: No matter yet, he has my Hook within him,
Now let him frisk and flownce and run and rowle,
And think to break his hold. He toils in vain:
This Love, the Bait he gorg'd so greedily,
Will make him sick, and then I have him sure.

ACT FIVE

Enter ALPHONSO *and* PEDRO.

ALPHONSO: Brother, there's News from *Bertran*; he desires
Admittance to the King, and cryes aloud,
This day shall end our Fears of Civil War:
For his safe Conduct he entreats your Presence,
And begs you would be speedy.

RAYMOND: Though I loath
The Traitor's sight, I'll go: Attend us here.

[*Exit* RAYMOND.

Enter GOMEZ, ELVIRA, DOMINIC, *with Officers, to make the Stage as full as possible.*

PEDRO: Why, how now *Gomez*: what mak'st thou here with a whole Brother-hood of City bailifs? why, thou lookest like *Adam* in Paradise, with his guard of Beasts about him.

GOMEZ: Ay, and a man had need of them, Don *Pedro*: for here are the two old Seducers, a Wife and Priest, that's *Eve* and the Serpent, at my Elbow.

DOMINIC: Take notice how uncharitably he talks of Churchmen.

GOMEZ: Indeed you are a charitable *Belswagger*: my Wife cry'd out Fire, Fire; and you brought out your Church-buckets, and call'd for Engines to play against it.

ALPHONSO: I am sorry you are come hither to accuse your Wife, her Education has been vertuous, her Nature mild and easie.

GOMEZ: Yes! she's easie with a Vengeance, there's a certain Colonel has found her so.

ALPHONSO: She came a spotless Virgin to your Bed.

GOMEZ: And she's a spotless Virgin still for me—she's never the worse for my wearing, I'll take my Oath on't: I have liv'd with her with all the Innocence of a Man of Threescore; like a peacable Bed fellow as I am——

ELVIRA: Indeed, Sir, I have no reason to complain of him for disturbing of my Sleep.

DOMINIC: A fine Commendation you have given your self; the Church did not marry you for that.

PEDRO: Come, come, your Grievances, your Grievances.

DOMINIC: Why, Noble Sir, I'll tell you.

GOMEZ: Peace Fryar! and let me speak first. I am the Plaintiff. Sure you think you are in the Pulpit where you preach by hours.

DOMINIC: And you edifie by minutes.

GOMEZ: Where you make Doctrins for the People, and Uses and Applications for your selves.

PEDRO: *Gomez*, give way to the old Gentleman in black.

GOMEZ: No! the t'other old Gentleman in black shall take me if I do! I will speak first! nay, I will, Fryar! for all your *Verbum Sacerdotis*, I'll speak truth in few words, and then you may come afterwards, and lye by the clock as you use to doe. For, let me tell you, Gentlemen, he shall lye and forswear himself with any Fryar in all *Spain*: that's a bold word now——

DOMINIC: Let him alone: let him alone: I shall fetch him back with a *circum-bendibus* I warrant him.

ALPHONSO: Well, What have you to say against your Wife, *Gomez*?

GOMEZ: Why, I say, in the first place, that I and all men are married for our Sins, and that our Wives are a Judgment; that a Batchelour-cobler is a happier man than a Prince in Wedlock; that we are all visited with a Houshold Plague, and, *Lord have mercy upon us* should be written on all our doors.

DOMINIC: Now he reviles Marriage which is one of the seven blessed Sacraments.

GOMEZ: 'Tis liker one of the seven deadly Sins: but make your best on't, I care not: 'tis but binding a man Neck and Heels for all that! But as for my Wife, that *Crocodile* of *Nilus*, she has wickedly and traitorously conspir'd the Cuckoldom of me her anointed Sovereign Lord: and, with the help of the aforesaid Fryar, whom Heaven confound, and, with the Limbs of one Colonel *Hernando*, Cuckold-maker of this City, devilishly contriv'd to steal herself away, and under her Arm feloniously to bear one Casket of Diamonds, Pearls, and other Jewels, to the Value of 30000 Pistols. Guilty, or Not Guilty; how saiest thou Culprit?

DOMINIC: False and scandalous! Give me the Book. I'll take my corporal Oath pointblank against every particular of this Charge.

ELVIRA: And so will I.

DOMINIC: As I was walking in the Streets, telling my Beads, and praying to my self, according to my usual custom, I heard a foul Out-cry before *Gomez*' portal; and his Wife, my Penitent, making dolefull Lamentations: Thereupon, making what haste my Limbs would suffer me, that are crippl'd with often kneeling, I saw him Spurning and Fisting her most unmercifully; whereupon, using Christian Arguments with him to desist, he fell violently upon me, without respect to my Sacerdotal Orders, pusht me from him, and turn'd me about with a Finger and a Thumb, just as a Man would set up a Top. Mercy, quoth I. Damme, quoth he. And still continued Labouring me, till a good minded Colonel came by, whom, as Heaven shall save me, I had never seen before.

GOMEZ: O Lord! O Lord!

DOMINIC: Ay, and, O Lady! O Lady too! I redouble my Oath, I had never seen him. Well, this Noble Colonel, like a true Gentleman, was for taking the weaker part you may be sure—where upon this *Gomez* flew upon him like a Dragon, got him down, the Devil being strong in him, and gave him Bastinado upon Bastinado, and Buffer upon Buffet, which the poor, meek Colonel, being prostrate, suffered with a most Christian Patience.

GOMEZ: Who? he meek? I'm sure I quake at the very thought of him; why, he's as fierce as *Rhodomont*, he made Assault and Battery upon my Person, beat me into all the colours of the Rainbow. And every word this abominable Priest has utter'd is as false as the *Alcoran*. But if you want a thorough-pac'd Lyar that will swear through thick and thin, commend me to a Fryar.

Enter LORENZO, *who comes behind the Company, and stands at his Father's back unseen, over against* GOMEZ.

LORENZO *aside*: How now! What's here to doe? my Cause a trying, as I live, and that before my own Father: now Fourscore take him for an old bawdy Magistrate, that stands like the Picture of Madam Justice, with a pair of Scales in his Hand, to weigh Lechery by Ounces.

ALPHONSO: Well—but all this while, who is this Colonel *Hernando?*

GOMEZ: He's the First-begotten of *Beelzebub*, with a Face as terrible as *Demogorgon*.

[LORENZO *peeps over* ALPHONSO'*s head, and stares at* GOMEZ.]

No! I lye, I lye: He's a very proper, handsom fellow! well proportion'd, and clean shap'd, with a Face like a Cherubin.

PEDRO: What, backward and forward *Gomez?* dost thou hunt counter?

ALPHONSO: Had this Colonel any former Design upon your Wife? for, if that be prov'd, you shall have Justice.

GOMEZ *aside*: Now I dare speak; let him look as dreadfully as he will. I say, Sir, and I will prove it, that he had a leud Design upon her Body, and attempted to corrupt her Honesty. [LORENZO *lifts up his Fist clench'd at him.*
I confess my Wife was as willing—as himself; and, I believe, 'twas she corrupted him: for I have known him formerly a very civil and modest person.

ELVIRA: You see, Sir, he contradicts himself at every word: he's plainly mad.

ALPHONSO: Speak boldly man! and say what thou wilt stand by: did he strike thee?

GOMEZ: I will speak boldly: He struck me on the Face before my own threshold, that the very walls cry'd shame to him. [LORENZO *holds up again.*
'Tis true, I gave him Provocation, for the man's as peaceable a Gentleman as any is in all *Spain*.

DOMINIC: Now the Truth comes out in spight of him.

PEDRO: I believe the Fryar has bewitch'd him.

ALPHONSO: For my part, I see no wrong that has been offer'd him.

GOMEZ: How? no wrong? why, he ravish'd me with the help of two Souldiers, carried me away *vi & armis*, and would put me into a Plot against the government.
[LORENZO *holds up again.*
I confess, I never could endure the Government, because it was Tyrannical: but my Sides and Shoulders are Black and Blew, as I can strip, and show the Marks of them.
[LORENZO *again.*
But that might happen too by a Fall that I got yesterday upon the Pebbles. [*All laugh.*

DOMINIC: Fresh straw, and a dark Chamber: a most manifest Judgment, there never comes better of railing against the Church.

GOMEZ: Why, what will you have me say? I think you'll make me mad: Truth has been at my Tongue's end this half hour, and I have not power to bring it out for fear of this bloudy minded Colonel.

ALPHONSO: What Colonel?

GOMEZ: Why, my Colonel: I mean, my Wife's Colonel that appears there to me like my *malus genius*, and terrifies me.

ALPHONSO *turning*: Now you are mad indeed, *Gomez*; this is my Son *Lorenzo*.

GOMEZ: How! your Son *Lorenzo*! it is impossible.

ALPHONSO: As true as your Wife *Elvira* is my Daughter.

LORENZO: What, have I taken all this pains about a Sister?

GOMEZ: No, you have taken some about me: I am sure, if you are her Brother, my sides can shew the Tokens of our Alliance.

ALPHONSO *to* LORENZO: You know I put your Sister into a Nunnery, with a strict Command, not to see you, for fear you should have wrought upon her to have taken the Habit, which was never my Intention; and consequently, I married her without your knowledge, that it might not be in your power to prevent it.

ELVIRA: You see, Brother, I had a natural affection to you.

LORENZO: What a delicious Harlot have I lost! Now, Pox upon me, for being so near akin to thee.

ELVIRA: However, we are both beholding to Fryar *Dominic,* the Church is an indulgent Mother, she never fails to doe her part.

DOMINIC: Heaven! what will become of me?

GOMEZ: Why, you are not like to trouble Heaven; those fat Guts were never made for mounting.

LORENZO: I shall make bold to disburden him of my hundred Pistoles, to make him the lighter for his Journey: indeed, 'tis partly out of Conscience, that I may not be accessory to his breaking his Vow of Poverty.

ALPHONZO: I have no secular Power to reward the Pains you have taken with my Daughter: But I shall do't by Proxy, Fryar, your Bishop's my Friend, and is too honest to let such as you infect a Cloister.

GOMEZ: Ay, doe Father-in-law, let him be stript of his Habit, and dis-ordered—I would fain see him walk in Quirpo, like a cas'd Rabbit, without his holy Fur upon his Back, that the World may once behold the insyde of a Fryar.

DOMINIC: Farwell, kind Gentlemen: I give you all my Blessing before I go—May your Sisters, Wives, and Daughters, be so naturally lewd, that they may have no occasion for a Devil to tempt, or a Fryar to pimp for 'em.

[*Exit, with a Rabble pushing him.*

Enter TORRISMOND, LEONORA, BERTRAN, RAYMOND, TERESA, &c.

TORRISMOND: He lives! he lives! my Royal Father lives!
Let every one partake the general Joy.

Some Angel with a golden Trumpet sound,
King *Sancho* lives! and let the echoing skies
From Pole to Pole resound, King *Sancho* lives.
O *Bertran*, ô? no more my Foe, but, Brother:
One act like this blots out a thousand Crimes.

BERTRAN: Bad men, when 'tis their Interest, may doe good:
I must confess, I counsel'd *Sancho*'s Murther;
And urg'd the Queen by specious Arguments:
But still, suspecting that her Love was chang'd,
I spread abroad the Rumour of his Death,
To sound the very Soul of her Designs:
Th' Event, you know was answering to my Fears:
She threw the *Odium* of the Fact on me,
And publickly avow'd her Love to you.

RAYMOND: Heaven guided all to save the Innocent.

BERTRAN: I plead no Merit, but a bare Forgiveness.

TORRISMOND: Not onely that, but Favour: *Sancho*'s Life,
Whether by Vertue or Design preserv'd,
Claims all within my power.

QUEEN: My Prayers are heard;
And I have nothing farther to desire,
But *Sancho*'s leave to authorize our Marriage.

TORRISMOND: Oh! fear not him! Pity and he are one;
So mercifull a King did never live;
Loth to revenge, and easie to forgive:
But let the bold Conspirator beware,
For Heaven makes Princes its peculiar Care.

[*Exeunt omnes.*

EPILOGUE

By a Friend[1] *of the Author's.*

There's none I'am sure, who is a Friend to Love,
But will our Fryar's Character approve :
The ablest Spark among you sometimes needs
Such pious help for charitable Deeds.
Our Church, alas! (as Rome *objects) does want*
These Ghostly Comforts for the falling Saint :
This gains them their Whore-Converts, and may be
One Reason of the Growth of Popery.
So Mahomet's *Religion came in fashion,*
By the large leave it gave to Fornication.
Fear not the guilt, if you can pay for't well,
There is no Dives in the Roman *Hell.*
Gold opens the strait gate, and lets him in;
But want of money is a mortal sin.
For all besides you may discount to Heaven,
And drop a Bead to keep the Tallies even.
How are men cozen'd still with shows of good!
The Baud's best Mask is the grave Fryar's Hood.
Though Vice no more a Clergy-man displeases,
Than Doctors can be thought to hate Diseases :
'Tis by your living ill that they live well,
By your Debauches their fat Paunches swell.
'Tis a mock-war between the Priest and Devil,
When they think fit, they can be very civil.
As some who did French *Counsels most advance,*
To blind the World, have rail'd in print at France.
Thus do the Clergy at your Vices bawl,
That with more ease they may engross them all.
By damning yours, they do their own maintain.
A Church-man's godliness is alwaies gain.
Hence to their Prince they will superiour be;
And civil Treason grows Church-Loyalty :
They boast the gift of Heaven is in their power;
Well may they give the God they can devour.
Still to the sick and dead their claims they lay;

[1] The 'friend' was Robert Wolseley (1649–1697).

For 'tis on carrion that the Vermin prey.
Nor have they less Dominion on our Life,
They trot the Husband, and they pace the Wife.
Rouze up you Cuckolds of the Northern climes,
And learn from Sweden *to prevent such crimes.*
Unman the Fryar, And leave the holy Drone
To hum in his forsaken Hive alone;
He'll work no Honey when his sting is gone.
Your Wives and Daughters soon will leave the Cells,
When they have lost the sound of Aaron's *Bells.*

DON SEBASTIAN

KING OF PORTUGAL

A TRAGEDY

——————*Nec tarda Senectus*
Debilitat vires animi, mutatque vigorem. Virgil.[1]

[1] Nor does loitering old age sap the stoutness of our hearts or impair our bodily strength. (*Æneid* 9. 611.)

Don Sebastian, King of Portugal: A Tragedy Acted at the Theatre Royal. Written by Mr. Dryden. [*Latin quot.*] London: Printed for Jo. Hindmarsh, at the Golden Ball in Cornhil. M DC XC.

Don Sebastian was first performed at the Theatre Royal, Drury Lane, on 4 December 1689. The present text follows that of the first edition (Macdonald, 89 a). The speech headings have been expanded and, in the interests of clarity, the stage directions have occasionally been rearranged.

TO THE RIGHT HONOURABLE
PHILIP, EARL OF LEYCESTER,[1] &c.

Far be it from me, (My most Noble Lord) to think, that any thing which my meanness can produce, shou'd be worthy to be offer'd to your Patronage; or that ought which I can say of you shou'd recommend you farther, to the esteem of good men in this present Age, or to the veneration which will certainly be paid you by Posterity. On the other side, I must acknowledg it a great presumption in me, to make you this Address; and so much the greater, because by the common suffrage even of contrary parties, you have been always regarded, as one of the first Persons of the Age, and yet no one Writer has dar'd to tell you so: Whether we have been all conscious to our selves that it was a needless labour to give this notice to Mankind, as all men are asham'd to tell stale news, or that we were justly diffident of our own performances, as even Cicero *is observ'd to be in awe when he writes to* Atticus; *where knowing himself overmatch'd in good sense, and truth of knowledg, he drops the gawdy train of words, and is no longer the vain-glorious Orator. From whatever reason it may be, I am the first bold offender of this kind: I have broken down the fence, and ventur'd into the Holy Grove; how I may be punish'd for my profane attempt, I know not; but I wish it may not be of ill Omen to your Lordship; and that a crowd of bad Writers, do not rush into the quiet of your recesses after me. Every man in all changes of Government, which have been, or may possibly arrive, will agree, that I cou'd not have offer'd my Incense, where it cou'd be so well deserv'd. For you, My Lord, are secure in your own merit; and all Parties, as they rise uppermost, are sure to court you in their turns; 'tis a tribute which has ever been paid your vertue: The leading men still bring their bullion to your mint, to receive the stamp of their intrinsick value, that they may afterwards hope to pass with human kind. They rise and fall in the variety of Revolutions; and are sometimes great, and therefore wise in mens opinions, who must court them for their interest: But the reputation of their parts most commonly follows their success; few of 'em are wise, but as they are*

[1] Philip Sidney, Earl of Leicester (1619–1698) had been active in the Parliamentary cause during the Civil War, but withdrew from politics after the Restoration.

in power: Because indeed, they have no sphere of their own, but like the Moon in the Copernican Systeme of the World, are whirl'd about by the motion of a greater Planet. This it is to be ever busie; neither to give rest to their Fellow-creatures, nor, which is more wretchedly ridiculous, to themselves; Tho truly, the latter is a kind of justice, and giving Mankind a due revenge, that they will not permit their own hearts to be at quiet, who disturb the repose of all beside them. Ambitious Meteors! how willing they are to set themselves upon the Wing; and taking every occasion of drawing upward to the Sun: Not considering that they have no more time allow'd them for their mounting, than the short revolution of a day: and that when the light goes from them, they are of necessity to fall. How much happier is he, (and who he is I need not say, for there is but one Phœnix in an Age,) who centring on himself, remains immoveable, and smiles at the madness of the dance about him. He possesses the midst, which is the portion of safety and content: He will not be higher, because he needs it not; but by the prudence of that choice, he puts it out of Fortunes power to throw him down. 'Tis confest, that if he had not so been born, he might have been too high for happiness; but not endeavouring to ascend, he secures the native height of his station from envy; and cannot descend from what he is, because he depends not on another. What a glorious Character was this once in Rome*; I shou'd say in* Athens, *when in the disturbances of a State as mad as ours, the wise* Pomponius *transported all the remaining wisdom and vertue of his Country, into the Sanctuary of Peace and Learning. But, I wou'd ask the World, (for you, My Lord, are too nearly concern'd to judge this Cause) whether there may not yet be found, a Character of a Noble Englishman, equally shining with that illustrious* Roman? *Whether I need to name a second* Atticus*; or whether the World has not already prevented me, and fix'd it there without my naming. Not a second with a* longo sed proximus intervallo,[1] *not a Young* Marcellus, *flatter'd by a Poet, into a resemblance of the first, with a* frons læta parum, & dejecto lumina vultu,[2] *and the rest that follows,* si qua fata aspera rumpas Tu Marcellus eris:[3] *But a Person of the same stamp and magnitude; who owes nothing to the former, besides the Word* Roman, *and the Superstition of reverence, devolving on him by the precedency of eighteen hundred years. One who walks by him with equal paces, and shares the eyes of beholders*

[1] The nearest he, yet far behind the first. (Vergil, *Æneid* 5. 320.)

[2] But little joy showed his countenance, or the eyes with their downcast look. (*Ibid*. 6. 862.)

[3] If thou shouldst break through the bitter decrees of fate, Marcellus shalt thou be. (*Ibid*. 6. 882–3.)

with him: One, who had been first, had he first liv'd; and in spight of doating veneration is still his equal. Both of them born of Noble Families in unhappy Ages, of change and tumult; both of them retiring from Affairs of State: Yet, not leaving the Commonwealth, till it had left it self; but never returning to publick business, when they had once quitted it; tho courted by the Heads of either Party. But who wou'd trust the quiet of their lives, with the extravagancies of their Countrymen, when they were just in the giddiness of their turning; when the ground was tottering under them at every moment; and none cou'd guess whether the next heave of the Earthquake, wou'd settle them on the first Foundation, or swallow it? Both of them knew Mankind exactly well; for both of them began that study in themselves; and there they found the best part of humane composition, the worst they learn'd by long experience of the folly, ignorance, and immorality of most beside them. Their Philosophy on both sides, was not wholly speculative, for that is barren, and produces nothing but vain Ideas of things which cannot possibly be known; or if they cou'd, yet wou'd only terminate in the understanding; but it was a noble, vigorous, and practical Philosophy, which exerted it self in all the offices of pity, to those who were unfortunate, and deserv'd not so to be. The Friend was always more consider'd by them than the cause: And an Octavius, *or an* Antony *in distress, were reliev'd by them, as well as a* Brutus *or a* Cassius. *For the lowermost party to a noble mind, is ever the fittest object of good will. The eldest of them, I will suppose for his honour, to have been of the Academick Sect, neither Dogmatist nor Stoick; if he were not, I am sure he ought in common justice, to yield the precedency to his younger Brother. For stiffness of Opinion is the effect of Pride, and not of Philosophy: 'Tis a miserable Presumption of that knowledg which humane Nature is too narrow to contain. And the ruggedness of a Stoick is only a silly affectation of being a God: To wind himself up by Pulleys, to an insensibility of suffering; and at the same time to give the lye to his own Experience, by saying he suffers not, what he knows he feels. True, Philosophy is certainly of a more pliant Nature, and more accommodated to human use;* Homo sum, humani à me nihil alienum puto.[1] *A wise man will never attempt an impossibility; and such it is to strain himself beyond the nature of his Being; either to become a Deity, by being above suffering, or to debase himself into a Stock or Stone, by pretending not to feel it. To find in our selves the Weaknesses and Imperfections of our wretched Kind, is surely*

[1] I am human, and nothing that is human do I deem alien to myself. (Terence, *Heautontimorumenos* 1. 1. 25.)

the most reasonable step we can make towards the Compassion of our fellow Creatures. I cou'd give Examples of this kind in the second Atticus. *In every turn of State, without meddling on either side, he has always been favorable and assisting to opprest Merit. The Praises which were given by a great Poet to the late Queen Mother on her rebuilding* Somerset Palace,[1] *one part of which was fronting to the mean Houses on the other side of the Water, are as justly his:*

For, the distrest, and the afflicted lye
Most in his Thoughts, and always in his Eye.

Neither has he so far forgotten a poor Inhabitant of his Suburbs, whose best prospect is on the Garden of Leicester-House*; but that more than once he has been offering him his Patronage, to reconcile him to a World, of which his Misfortunes have made him weary. There is another* Sidney *still remaining, tho there can never be another* Spencer *to deserve the Favor. But one* Sidney *gave his Patronage to the applications of a Poet; the other offer'd it unask'd. Thus, whether as a second* Atticus, *or a second Sir* Philip Sidney, *the latter, in all respects, will not have the worse of the comparison; and if he will take up with the second place, the World will not so far flatter his Modesty, as to seat him there, unless it be out of a deference of Manners, that he may place himself where he pleases at his own Table.*

I may therefore safely conclude, that he, who by the consent of all men, bears so eminent a Character, will out of his inborn Nobleness, forgive the Presumption of this Address. 'Tis an unfinish'd Picture, I confess, but the Lines and Features are so like, that it cannot be mistaken for any other; and without writing any name under it, every beholder must cry out, at the first sight, this was design'd for Atticus*; but the bad Artist, has cast too much of him into shades. But I have this Excuse, that even the greater Masters commonly fall short of the best Faces. They may flatter an indifferent Beauty; but the excellencies of Nature, can have no right done to them: For there both the Pencil and the Pen are overcome by the Dignity of the Subject; as our admirable* Waller *has express'd it;*

The Hero's Race transcends the Poet's Thought.

There are few in any Age who can bear the load of a Dedication; for where Praise is undeserv'd, 'tis Satyre: Tho Satyre on Folly is now no longer a Scandal to any one Person, where a whole Age is

[1] A reference to Abraham Cowley's poem on *The Queen's repairing Somerset-House.*

dipt together; yet I had rather undertake a Multitude one way, than a single Atticus *the other; for 'tis easier to descend, than 'tis to climb. I shou'd have gone asham'd out of the World, if I had not at least attempted this Address, which I have long thought owing: And if I had never attempted, I might have been vain enough to think I might have succeeded in it: now I have made the Experiment, and have fail'd, through my Unworthiness. I may rest satisfi'd, that either the Adventure is not to be atchiev'd, or that it is reserv'd for some other hand.*

Be pleas'd therefore, since the Family of the Attici *is and ought to be above the common Forms of concluding Letters, that I may take my leave in the Words of* Cicero *to the first of them:* Me, O Pomponi, valdè pœnitet vivere: tantùm te oro, ut quoniam me ipse semper amâsti, ut eodem amore sis; ego nimirum, idem sum. Inimici mei mea mihi non meipsum ademerunt. Cura, Attice, ut valeas.[1]

Dabam Cal.
Jan. 1690.

THE PREFACE

WHETHER it happen'd through a long disuse of Writing, that I forgot the usual compass of a Play; or that by crowding it, with Characters and Incidents, I put a necessity upon my self of lengthning the main Action, I know not; but the first days Audience sufficiently convinc'd me of my error; and that the Poem was insupportably too long. 'Tis an ill ambition of us Poets, to please an Audience with more than they can bear: And, supposing that we wrote as well, as vainly we imagin our selves to write; yet we ought to consider, that no man can bear to be long tickled. There is a nauseousness in a City feast when we are to sit four hours after we are cloy'd. I am, therefore, in the first place, to acknowledg with all manner of gratitude, their civility; who were pleas'd to endure it with so much patience, to be weary with so much good-nature and silence, and not to explode an entertainment, which was design'd to please them; or discourage an Author, whose misfortunes have once more brought him against his will, upon the Stage. While I continue in these bad circumstances,

[1] As for me, Atticus, I am regretting mightily the fact that I am alive. I have only one request to make of you, that you continue to feel as warmly towards myself as you have always done. For of course I am the same as ever I was; my enemies have deprived me of my property, not of my identity. Look after yourself, dear Atticus. (*Epistulae ad Atticum* 3. 4 and 3. 5.)

(and truly I see very little probability of coming out:) I must be oblig'd to write, and if I may still hope for the same kind usage, I shall the less repent of that hard necessity. I write not this out of any expectation to be pityed; for I have Enemies enow to wish me yet in a worse condition; but give me leave to say, that if I can please by writing, as I shall endeavour it, the Town may be somewhat oblig'd to my misfortunes, for a part of their diversion. Having been longer acquainted with the Stage, than any Poet now living, and having observ'd how difficult it was to please; that the humours of Comedy were almost spent, that Love and Honour (the mistaken Topicks of Tragedy) were quite worn out, that the Theaters cou'd not support their charges, that the Audience forsook them, that young men without Learning set up for Judges, and that they talk'd loudest, who understood the least: all these discouragements had not only wean'd me from the Stage, but had also given me a loathing of it. But enough of this: the difficulties continue; they increase, and I am still condemn'd to dig in those exhausted Mines. Whatever fault I next commit, rest assur'd it shall not be that of too much length: Above twelve hundr'd lines have been cut off from this Tragedy, since it was first deliver'd to the Actors. They were indeed so judiciously lopt by Mr. *Betterton*, to whose care and excellent action, I am equally oblig'd, that the connexion of the story was not lost; but on the other side, it was impossible to prevent some part of the action from being precipitated, and coming on without that due preparation, which is requir'd to all great events: as in particular, that of raising the Mobile, in the beginning of the Fourth Act; which a Man of *Benducar's* cool Character, cou'd not naturally attempt, without taking all those precautions, which he foresaw wou'd be necessary to render his design successful. On this consideration, I have replac'd those lines, through the whole Poem, and thereby restor'd it, to that clearness of conception, and (if I may dare to say it) that lustre, and masculine vigour, in which it was first written. 'Tis obvious to every understanding Reader, that the most Poetical parts, which are Descriptions, Images, Similitudes, and Moral Sentences; are those, which of necessity were to be par'd away, when the body was swoln into too large a bulk for the representation of the Stage. But there is a vast difference betwixt a publick entertainment on the Theatre, and a private reading in the Closet: In the first we are confin'd to time, and though we talk not by the hour-glass, yet the Watch often drawn out of the pocket, warns the Actors, that their Audience is weary; in the last, every Reader is judge of his own convenience;

he can take up the book, and lay it down at his pleasure; and find out those beauties of propriety, in thought and writing, which escap'd him in the tumult and hurry of representing. And I dare boldly promise for this Play, that in the roughness of the numbers and cadences, (which I assure was not casual, but so design'd) you will see somewhat more masterly arising to your view, than in most, if not any of my former Tragedies. There is a more noble daring in the Figures and more suitable to the loftiness of the Subject; and besides this some newnesses of *English*, translated from the Beauties of Modern Tongues, as well as from the elegancies of the Latin; and here and there some old words are sprinkled, which for their significance and sound, deserv'd not to be antiquated; such as we often find in *Salust* amongst the Roman Authors, and in *Milton*'s Paradise amongst ours; though perhaps the latter instead of sprinkling, has dealt them with too free a hand, even sometimes to the obscuring of his sense.

As for the story or plot of the Tragedy, 'tis purely fiction; for I take it up where the History has laid it down. We are assur'd by all Writers of those times, that *Sebastian* a young Prince of great courage and expectation, undertook that War partly upon a religious account, partly at the sollicitation of *Muley-Mahumet*, who had been driven out of his Dominions, by *Abdelmelech*, or as others call him *Muley-Moluch*, his nigh Kinsman, who descended from the same Family of the *Xeriffs*; whose Fathers *Hamet* and *Mahomet* had conquer'd that Empire with joint Forces; and shar'd it betwixt them after their victory: That the body of *Don Sebastian* was never found in the Field of Battel; which gave occasion for many to believe, that he was not slain; that some years after, when the *Spaniards* with a pretended title, by force of Arms had Usurp'd the Crown of *Portugal*, from the House of *Braganza*, a certain Person who call'd himself *Don Sebastian*, and had all the marks of his body and features of his face, appear'd at *Venice*, where he was own'd by some of his Countrymen; but being seiz'd by the *Spaniards* was first Imprison'd, then sent to the Gallies, and at last put to Death in private. 'Tis most certain, that the *Portugueses* expected his return for almost an age together after that Battel; which is at least a proof of their extream love to his Memory; and the usage which they had from their new Conquerors, might possibly make them so extravagant in their hopes and wishes for their old Master.

This ground work the History afforded me, and I desire no better to build a Play upon it: For where the event of a great action is left doubtful, there the Poet is left Master: He may raise what he pleases on that foundation, provided he makes it of a piece, and according to the rule of probability. From hence I was only oblig'd, that *Sebastian* shou'd return to *Portugal* no more; but at the same time I had him at my own disposal, whether to bestow him in *Affrick*, or in any other corner of the World, or to have clos'd the Tragedy with his death; and the last of these was certainly the most easie, but for the same reason, the least artful; because as I have somewhere said, the poyson and the dagger are still at hand, to butcher a Heroe, when a Poet wants the brains to save him. It being therefore only necessary according to the Laws of the *Drama*, that *Sebastian* shou'd no more be seen upon the Throne, I leave it for the World to judge, whether or no I have disposed of him according to art, or have bungled up the conclusion of his adventure. In the drawing of his character I forgot not piety, which any one may observe to be one principal ingredient of it; even so far as to be a habit in him; though I show him once to be transported from it by the violence of a sudden passion, to endeavour a self murther. This being presuppos'd, that he was Religious, the horror of his incest, tho innocently committed, was the best reason which the Stage cou'd give for hind'ring his return. 'Tis true I have no right to blast his Memory, with such a crime: but declaring it to be fiction, I desire my Audience to think it no longer true, than while they are seeing it represented: For that once ended, he may be a Saint for ought I know; and we have reason to presume he is. On this supposition, it was unreasonable to have kill'd him; for the Learned Mr. *Rymer* [1] has well observed, that in all punishments we are to regulate our selves by Poetical Justice; and according to those measures an involuntary sin deserves not death; from whence it follows, that to divorce himself from the beloved object, to retire into a desart, and deprive himself of a Throne, was the utmost punishment, which a Poet cou'd inflict, as it was also the utmost reparation, which *Sebastian* cou'd make. For what relates to *Almeyda*, her part is wholly fictitious: I know it is the surname of a noble Family in *Portugal*, which was very instrumental in the Restoration of *Don John de Braganza*, Father to the most Illustrious and most Pious Princess our Queen *Dowager*. The *French* Author of a Novel, call'd *Don Sebastian*, has given that name to an *Affrican* Lady of his own invention, and makes her Sister to *Muley-Mahumet*. But I have wholly chang'd the accidents, and borrow'd nothing but the supposition, that she was belov'd by the King of *Portugal*. Tho, if I had taken

[1] See *Preface to Fables*, p. 475, n. 1.

the whole story, and wrought it up into a Play, I might have done it exactly according to the practice of almost all the Ancients; who were never accus'd of being Plagiaries, for building their Tragedies on known Fables. Thus *Augustus Cæsar* wrote an *Ajax*, which was not the less his own, because *Euripides* had written a Play before him on that Subject. Thus of late years, *Corneille* writ an *Oedipus* after *Sophocles*; and I have design'd one after him, which I wrote with Mr. *Lee*,[1] yet neither the *French* Poet stole from the *Greek*, nor we from the *French man*. 'Tis the contrivance, the new turn, and new characters, which alter the property and make it ours. The *Materia Poetica* is as common to all Writers, as the *Materia Medica* to all Physicians. Thus in our *Chronicles*, *Daniels* History is still his own, though *Matthew Paris*, *Stow* and *Hollingshed* writ before him, otherwise we must have been content with their dull relations, if a better Pen had not been allow'd to come after them, and write his own account after a new and better manner.

I must farther declare freely, that I have not exactly kept to the three Mechanick rules of unity: I knew them and had them in my eye, but follow'd them only at a distance; for the Genius of the *English* cannot bear too regular a Play; we are given to variety, even to a debauchery of Pleasure. My Scenes are therefore sometimes broken, because my Under-plot required them so to be; though the General Scene remains of the same Castle; and I have taken the time of two days, because the variety of accidents, which are here represented, cou'd not naturally be suppos'd to arrive in one: But to gain a greater Beauty, 'tis lawful for a Poet to supersede a less.

I must likewise own, that I have somewhat deviated from the known History, in the death of *Muley-Moluch*, who, by all relations dyed of a feaver in the Battel, before his Army had wholly won the Field; but if I have allow'd him another day of life, it was because I stood in need of so shining a Character of brutality, as I have given him; which is indeed the same, with that of the present Emperor *Muley-Ishmael*, as some of our *English Officers*, who have been in his Court, have credibly inform'd me.

I have been listning what objections had been made, against the conduct of the Play, but found them all so trivial, that if I shou'd name them, a true critick wou'd imagin that I play'd booty, and only rais'd up fantoms for my self to conquer. Some

[1] *Oedipus*, written in collaboration with Nathaniel Lee, was performed and published in 1679.

are pleas'd to say the writing is dull; but, *ætatem habet de se loquatur*.[1] Others that the double poyson is unnatural; let the common received opinion, and *Ausonius* his famous Epigram answer that. Lastly a more ignorant sort of Creatures than either of the former, maintain that the Character of *Dorax*, is not only unnatural, but inconsistent with it self: let them read the Play and think again, and if yet they are not satisfied, cast their eyes on that Chapter of the Wise *Montaigne*, which is intitled *de l'Inconstance des actions humaines*. A longer reply, is what those Cavillers deserve not; but I will give them and their fellows to understand, that the Earl of *Dorset* was pleas'd to read the Tragedy twice over before it was Acted; and did me the favour to send me word, that I had written beyond any of my former Plays; and that he was displeas'd any thing shou'd be cut away. If I have not reason to prefer his single judgment to a whole Faction, let the World be judge; for the opposition is the same with that of *Lucan*'s Heroe against an Army; *concurrere bellum, atque virum*.[2] I think I may modestly conclude, that whatever errors there may be, either in the design, or writing of this Play, they are not those which have been objected to it. I think also, that I am not yet arriv'd to the Age of doating; and that I have given so much application to this Poem, that I cou'd not probably let it run into many gross absurdities; which may caution my Enemies from too rash a censure; and may also encourage my friends, who are many more than I cou'd reasonably have expected, to believe their kindness has not been very undeservedly bestowed on me. This is not a Play that was huddled up in hast; and to shew it was not, I will own, that besides the general Moral of it, which is given in the four last lines, there is also another Moral, couch'd under every one of the principal Parts and Characters, which a judicious Critick will observe, though I point not to it in this Preface. And there may be also some secret Beauties in the decorum of parts, and uniformity of design, which my puny judges will not easily find out; let them consider in the last Scene of the fourth Act, whether I have not preserv'd the rule of decency, in giving all the advantage to the Royal Character; and in making *Dorax* first submit; Perhaps too they may have thought, that it was through indigence of Characters, that I have given the same to *Sebastian* and *Almeyda*; and consequently made them alike in all things but their Sex. But let them look a little deeper into the matter, and they will find that this identity

[1] He is of age; let him speak for himself. (Cf. Vulgate, *John* 9.23.)
[2] War and the hero clash together. (6. 191–2.)

of Character in the greatness of their Souls; was intended for a preparation of the final discovery, and that the likeness of their nature, was a fair hint to the proximity of their blood.

To avoid the imputation of too much vanity (for all Writers, and especially Poets will have some) I will give but one other instance, in relation to the Uniformity of the design. I have observ'd, that the *English* will not bear a thorough Tragedy; but are pleas'd, that it shou'd be lightned with underparts of mirth. It had been easie for me to have given my Audience a better course of Comedy, I mean a more diverting, than that of *Antonio* and *Morayma.* But I dare appeal even to my Enemies, if I or any man cou'd have invented one, which had been more of a piece, and more depending, on the serious part of the design. For what cou'd be more uniform, than to draw from out of the members of a Captive Court, the Subject of a Comical entertainment? To prepare this Episode, you see *Dorax* giving the Character of *Antonio*, in the beginning of the Play, upon his first sight of him at the Lottery; and to make the dependence, *Antonio* is ingag'd in the Fourth Act, for the deliverance of *Almeyda*; which is also prepar'd, by his being first made a Slave to the Captain of the Rabble.

I shou'd beg pardon for these instances; but perhaps they may be of use to future Poets, in the conduct of their Plays: At least if I appear too positive; I am growing old, and thereby, in possession of some experience, which men in years will always assume for a right of talking. Certainly, if a Man can ever have reason to set a value on himself, 'tis when his ungenerous Enemies are taking the advantage of the Times upon him, to ruin him in his reputation. And therefore for once, I will make bold to take the Counsel of my Old Master *Virgil.*

Tu, ne cede malis ; sed, contrà, audentior ito.[1]

[1] Do not thou yield to misfortune but go forth emboldened against it. (*Æneid* 6. 95.)

PROLOGUE

Spoken by a Woman

The Judge remov'd, tho he's no more My Lord,
May plead at Bar, or at the Council-Board:
So may cast Poets write; there's no Pretension,
To argue loss of Wit from loss of Pension.
Your looks are cheerful; and in all this place
I see not one, that wears a damning face.
The British *Nation, is too brave to show,*
Ignoble vengeance, on a vanquish'd foe,
At least be civil to the Wretch imploring;
And lay your Paws upon him, without roaring:
Suppose our Poet was your foe before;
Yet now, the bus'ness of the Field is o'er;
'Tis time to let your Civil Wars alone,
When Troops are into Winter-quarters gone.
Jove *was alike to* Latian *and to* Phrygian*;*
And you well know, a Play's of no Religion.
Take good advice, and please your selves this day;
No matter from what hands you have the Play.
Among good Fellows ev'ry health will pass,
That serves to carry round another glass:
When, with full bowls of Burgundy *you dine,*
Tho at the Mighty Monarch you repine,
You grant him still most Christian, in his Wine.

Thus far the Poet, but his brains grow Addle;
And all the rest is purely from this Noddle.
You've seen young Ladies at the Senate door,
Prefer Petitions, and your grace implore;
How ever grave the Legislators were,
Their Cause went ne'er the worse for being fair,
Reasons as weak as theirs, perhaps I bring;
But I cou'd bribe you, with as good a thing.
I heard him make advances of good Nature;
That he for once, wou'd sheath his cutting Satyr:
Sigh but his Peace, he vows he'll ne'er again
The sacred Names of Fops and Beaus profane.
Strike up the Bargain quickly; for I swear,
As Times go now, he offers very fair.

PROLOGUE

Be not too hard on him, with statutes neither,
Be kind; and do not set your Teeth together,
To stretch the Laws, as Coblers do their Leather.
Horses, by Papists are not to be ridden;
But sure the Muses' Horse was ne'er forbidden.
For in no Rate-Book, it was ever found
That Pegasus *was valued at Five-pound:*[1]
Fine him to daily Drudging and Inditing;
And let him pay his Taxes out, in Writing.

[1] An allusion to the Act forbidding Roman Catholics to keep a horse of more than £5 in value.

(*PERSONS REPRESENTED*)

	BY
1. Don Sebastian, King of Portugal,	Mr. *Williams.*
2. Muley-Moluch Emperor of Barbary,	Mr. *Kynaston.*
3. Dorax, a Noble Portuguese now a Renegade, formerly Don Alonzo de Sylvera Alcade or Governor of Alcazar,	Mr. *Betterton.*
4. Benducar, Chief Minister and Favourite to the Emperor,	Mr. *Sandford.*
5. The Mufti Abdalla,	Mr. *Underhill.*
6. Muley-Zeydan Brother to the Emperor,	Mr. *Powell*, Jun.
7. Don Antonio, a Young Noble amorous Portuguese, now a Slave,	Mr. *Betterton.*
8. Don Alvarez, an old Counsellor to Don Sebastian, now a Slave also,	Mr. *Boweman.*
9. Mustapha Captain of the Rabble,	Mr. *Leigh.*
10. Almeyda a Captive Queen of Barbary,	Mrs. *Barry.*
11. Morayma, Daughter to the Mufti,	Mrs. *Montfort.*
12. Johayma, Chief Wife to the Mufti,	Mrs. *Leigh.*
Two Merchants.	
Rabble.	
A Servant to Benducar.	
A Servant to the Mufti.	

Scene in the Castle of Alcazar.

DON SEBASTIAN
KING OF PORTUGAL
ACT I
SCENE I.

The Scene at Alcazar, *representing a Market-Place under the Castle.*

MULEY-ZEYDAN, BENDUCAR.

MULEY-ZEYDAN. Now *Affrica*'s long Wars are at an end;
And our parch'd earth is drench'd in Christian Blood,
My conquering Brother will have Slaves enow,
To pay his cruel Vows for Victory.
What hear you of *Sebastian*, King of *Portugal?*

BENDUCAR: He fell among a heap of slaughter'd Moors;
Though yet his mangled carcase is not found.
The Rival of our threatned Empire, *Mahumet*,
Was hot pursued; and in the general rout,
Mistook a swelling Current for a Foord;
And in *Mucazar*'s Flood was seen to rise;
Thrice was he seen; at length his Courser plung'd,
And threw him off; the Waves whelm'd over him,
And helpless in his heavy arms he drownd.

MULEY-ZEYDAN: Thus, then, a doubtful Title is extinguish'd:
Thus, *Moluch*, still the Favorite of Fate,
Swims in a sanguine torrent to the Throne.
As if our Prophet only work'd for him:
The Heavens and all the Stars are his hir'd Servants.
As *Muley-Zeydan* were not worth their care,
And younger Brothers but the draff of Nature.

BENDUCAR: Be still, and learn the soothing Arts of Court;
Adore his fortune, mix with flattering Crowds,
And when they praise him most, be you the loudest;
Your Brother is luxurious, close, and cruel,
Generous by fits, but permanent in mischief.
The shadow of a discontent wou'd ruin us;
We must be safe before we can be great:
These things observ'd, leave me to shape the rest.

MULEY-ZEYDAN: You have the Key, he opens inward to you.

BENDUCAR: So often try'd, and ever found so true,
Has given me trust, and trust has given me means
Once to be false for all. I trust not him:
For now his ends are serv'd, and he grown absolute,
How am I sure to stand who serv'd those ends?
I know your nature open, mild, and grateful;
In such a Prince the People may be blest,
And I be safe.

MULEY-ZEYDAN: My Father! [*Embracing him.*

BENDUCAR: My future King! (auspicious *Muley-Zeydan*:)
Shall I adore you? No, the place is publick;
I worship you within; the outward act
Shall be reserv'd till Nations follow me,
And Heaven shall envy you the kneeling World.
You know th' Alcald of *Alcazar*, *Dorax?*

MULEY-ZEYDAN: The gallant Renegade you mean?

BENDUCAR: The same:
That gloomy outside, like a rusty Chest,
Contains the shining Treasure of a Soul,
Resolv'd and brave; he has the Souldiers hearts,
And time shall make him ours.

MULEY-ZEYDAN: He's just upon us.

BENDUCAR: I know him from afar,
By the long stride and by the sullen port:
Retire my Lord.
Wait on your Brothers Triumph, yours is next,
His growth is but a wild and fruitless Plant,
I'll cut his barren branches to the stock,
And graft you on to bear.

MULEY-ZEYDAN: My Oracle! [*Exit* MULEY-ZEYDAN

BENDUCAR: Yes, to delude your hopes, poor credulous Fool,
To think that I wou'd give away the Fruit
Of so much toil, such guilt, and such damnation;
If I am damn'd, it shall be for my self:
This easie Fool must be my Stale, set up
To catch the Peoples eyes; he's tame and merciful,
Him I can manage, till I make him odious
By some unpopular act, and then dethrone him.

Enter DORAX

Now, *Dorax!*

DORAX: Well, *Benducar!*

BENDUCAR: Bare *Benducar!*

DORAX: Thou wouldst have Titles, take 'em then, Chief Minister,
First Hangman of the State.

BENDUCAR: Some call me Favourite.

DORAX: What's that, his Minion?
Thou art too old to be a Catamite!
Now prithee tell me, and abate thy pride,
Is not *Benducar* Bare, a better Name
In a Friend's mouth, than all those gawdy Titles,
Which I disdain to give the Man I love?

BENDUCAR: But always out of humor,——

DORAX: I have cause:
Tho all mankind is cause enough for Satyr.

BENDUCAR: Why then thou hast reveng'd thee on mankind,
They say in fight, thou hadst a thirsty Sword,
And well 'twas glutted there.

DORAX: I spitted Frogs, I crush'd a heap of Emmets,
A hundred of 'em to a single Soul,
And that but scanty weight too: the great Devil
Scarce thank'd me for my pains; he swallows Vulgar
Like whip'd Cream, feels 'em not in going down.

BENDUCAR: Brave Renegade! cou'dst thou not meet *Sebastian?*
Thy Master had been worthy of thy Sword.

DORAX: My Master? By what title,
Because I happen'd to be born where he
Happen'd to be a King? And yet I serv'd him,
Nay, I was fool enough to love him too.
You know my story, how I was rewarded,
For Fifteen hard Campaigns, still hoop'd in Iron,
And why I turn'd Mahometan: I'm grateful,
But whosoever dares to injure me,
Let that man know, I dare to be reveng'd.

BENDUCAR: Still you run off from bias; say what moves
Your present spleen?

DORAX: You mark'd not what I told you:
I kill'd not one that was his Makers Image;
I met with none but vulgar two-leg'd Brutes.
Sebastian was my aim; he was a Man:
Nay, though he hated me, and I hate him,
Yet I must do him right; he was a Man,
Above man's height, ev'n towring to *Divinity.*
Brave, pious, generous, great, and liberal:
Just as the Scales of Heaven that weigh the Seasons,

He lov'd his People, him they idoliz'd:
And thence proceeds my mortal hatred to him,
That thus unblameable to all besides
He err'd to me alone:
His goodness was diffus'd to human kind,
And all his cruelty confin'd to me.

BENDUCAR: You cou'd not meet him then?

DORAX: No, though I sought
Where ranks fell thickest; 'twas indeed the place
To seek *Sebastian*: through a track of Death
I follow'd him, by Groans of dying Foes,
But still I came too late, for he was flown
Like Lightning, swift before me to new Slaughters.
I mow'd across, and made irregular Harvest,
Defac'd the pomp of Battel, but in vain,
For he was still supplying Death elsewhere:
This mads me that perhaps ignoble hands
Have overlaid him, for they cou'd not conquer:
Murder'd by Multitudes, whom I alone
Had right to slay; I too wou'd have been slain,
That catching hold upon his flitting Ghost
I might have robb'd him of his opening Heav'n;
And drag'd him down with me, spight of Predestination.

BENDUCAR: 'Tis of as much import as *Affric*'s worth,
To know what came of him, and of *Almeyda*,
The Sister of the Vanquish'd *Mahumet*,
Whose fatal Beauty to her Brother drew
The Lands third part, as *Lucifer* did Heav'ns.

DORAX: I hope she dy'd in her own Female calling,
Choak'd up with Man, and gorg'd with Circumcision.
As for *Sebastian*, we must search the Field,
And where we see a Mountain of the Slain,
Send one to climb, and looking down below
There he shall find him at his Manly length
With his face up to Heav'n, in the red Monument,
Which his true Sword has digg'd.

BENDUCAR: Yet we may possibly hear farther news;
For while our *Affricans* pursu'd the Chace,
The Captain of the Rabble issued out,
With a black shirt-less train to spoil the dead,
And seize the living.

DORAX: Each of 'em an Hoast,

A Million strong of Vermine ev'ry Villain:
No part of Government, but Lords of Anarchy,
Chaos of Power, and priviledg'd destruction.

BENDUCAR: Yet I must tell you Friend the Great must use 'em,
Sometimes as necessary tools of tumult.

DORAX: I wou'd use 'em
Like Dogs in times of Plague, out-laws of Nature,
Fit to be shot and brain'd; without a process,
To stop infection, that's their proper death.

BENDUCAR: No more,
Behold the Emperor coming to survey
The slaves, in order to perform his Vow.

Enter MULEY-MOLUCH *the Emperor, with Attendants. The* MUFTY, *and* MULEY-ZEYDAN.

MULEY-MOLUCH: Our Armours now may rust, our idle scymitars
Hang by our sides, for Ornament not use:
Children shall beat our Atabals and Drums,
And all the noisie trades of War, no more
Shall wake the peaceful morn: the *Xeriff*'s blood
No longer in divided Channels runs,
The younger House took end in *Mahomet*.
Nor shall *Sebastian*'s formidable Name,
Be longer us'd to lull the crying babe!

MUFTY: For this Victorious day our Mighty Prophet
Expects your gratitude, the Sacrifice
Of Christian Slaves, devoted, if you won.

MULEY-MOLUCH: The purple present shall be richly paid:
That Vow perform'd, fasting shall be abolish'd:
None ever serv'd Heav'n well with a starv'd face:
Preach Abstinence no more; I tell thee, *Mufty*,
Good feasting is devout: and thou our Head,
Hast a Religious, ruddy Countenance:
We will have learned Luxury: our lean Faith
Gives scandal to the Christians; they feed high:
Then look for shoals of Converts, when thou hast
Reform'd us into feasting.

MUFTY: Fasting is but the Letter of the Law:
Yet it shows well to Preach it to the Vulgar.
Wine is against our Law, that's literal too,
But not deny'd to Kings and to their Guides,
Wine is a Holy Liquor, for the Great.

DORAX, *àside*: This *Mufti* in my conscience is some *English* Renegade, he talks so savourly of toping.

MULEY-MOLUCH: Bring forth th' unhappy Relicks of the War.

Enter MUSTAPHA *Captain of the Rabble with his followers of the Black Guard, &c. and other Moors: with them a Company of* Portuguese *Slaves without any of the chief Persons.*

MULEY-MOLUCH: These are not fit to pay an Emperors Vow;
Our Bulls and Rams had been more noble Victims;
These are but garbidge not a Sacrifice.

MUFTY: The Prophet must not pick and choose his Offrings;
Now he has giv'n the Day, 'tis past recalling:
And he must be content with such as these.

MULEY-MOLUCH: But are these all? Speak you who are their Masters.

MUSTAPHA: All upon my Honour: if you will take 'em as their Fathers got 'em, so. If not, you must stay till they get a better generation: these Christians are mere bunglers; they procreate nothing but out of their own Wives; And these have all the looks of Eldest Sons.

MULEY-MOLUCH: Pain of your lives let none conceal a Slave.

MUSTAPHA: Let every Man look to his own Conscience, I am sure mine shall never hang me.

BENDUCAR: Thou speak'st as thou wert privy to concealments: Then thou art an Accomplice.

MUSTAPHA: Nay, if Accomplices must suffer, it may go hard with me; but here's the Devil on't, there's a Great Man and a Holy Man too, concern'd with me. Now if I confess, he'll be sure to scape between his Greatness and his Holiness, and I shall be murder'd, because of my Poverty and Rascality.

MUFTI, *winking at him*: Then if thy silence save the Great and Holy,
'Tis sure thou shalt go straight to Paradise.

MUSTAPHA: 'Tis a fine place they say; but Doctor I am not worthy on't: I am contented with this homely World, 'tis good enough for such a poor rascally Musulman as I am: Besides I have learnt so much good manners, Doctor, as to let my Betters be serv'd before me.

MULEY-MOLUCH: Thou talk'st as if the *Mufty* were concern'd.

MUSTAPHA: Your Majesty may lay your Soul on't: but for my part, though I am a plain Fellow, yet I scorn to be trick'd into Paradice, I wou'd he shou'd know it. The troth on't is an't like you, His reverence bought of me the flower of all the Market; these—these are but Dogs meat to 'em, and a round price he pay'd me too I'll say that for him; but not enough for me to venture my neck for: If I get Paradice when my time comes I can't help my self; but I'll venture nothing before-hand, upon a blind Bargain.

MULEY-MOLUCH: Where are those Slaves? produce 'em.

MUFTY: They are not what he says.

MULEY-MOLUCH: No more excuses. [*One goes out to fetch them.*
Know thou may'st better dally
With a dead Prophet, than a living King.

MUFTY: I but reserv'd 'em to present thy Greatness,
An Off'ring worthy thee.

MUSTAPHA: By the same token there was a dainty Virgin, (virgin said I! but I won't be too positive of that neither) with a roguish leering eye! he paid me down for her upon the nail a thousand golden *Sultanins*; or he had never had her I can tell him that: Now is it very likely he would pay so dear for such a delicious Morsel, and give it away out of his own mouth; when it had such a farewel with it too?

Enter SEBASTIAN *conducted in mean habit, with* ALVAREZ, ANTONIO, *and* ALMEYDA: *her face veil'd with a Barnus.*

MULEY-MOLUCH: Ay; These look like the Workmanship of Heav'n:
This is the porcelain clay of human kind,
And therefore cast into these noble moulds.

DORAX, *aside while the Emperor whispers* BENDUCAR: By all my wrongs
'Tis he; damnation seize me but 'tis he!
My heart heaves up and swells; he's poyson to me;
My injur'd honour, and my ravish'd love,
Bleed at their Murderers sight.

BENDUCAR *to* DORAX *aside*: The Emperor wou'd learn these Pris'ners names;
You know 'em.

DORAX: Tell him, no.
And trouble me no more.—I will not know 'em.
Shall I trust Heav'n, that Heav'n which I renounc'd, [*Aside*
With my revenge? then, where's my satisfaction?
No, it must be my own; I scorn a Proxy.

MULEY-MOLUCH: 'Tis decreed,
These of a better aspect, with the rest
Shall share one common Doom, and Lots decide it.
For ev'ry number'd Captive put a ball

Into an Urn; three only black be there,
The rest, all white, are safe.

MUFTY: Hold Sir, the Woman must not draw.

MULEY-MOLUCH: O *Mufti*,
We know your reason, let her share the danger.

MUFTY: Our Law says plainly Women have no Souls.

MULEY-MOLUCH: 'Tis true; their Souls are mortal, set her by:
Yet were *Almeyda* here, though Fame reports her
The fairest of her Sex, so much unseen,
I hate the Sister of our Rival House,
Ten thousand such dry Notions of our *Alcoran*
Shou'd not protect her life; if not Immortal:
Die as she cou'd, all of a piece, the better,
That none of her remain.

Here an Urn is brought in: the Pris'ners approach with great concernment; and among the rest SEBASTIAN, ALVAREZ *and* ANTONIO; *who come more chearfully.*

DORAX: Poor abject Creatures how they fear to dye! [*Aside.*
These never knew one happy hour in life,
Yet shake to lay it down: is load so pleasant?
Or has Heav'n hid the happiness of Death
That Men may bear to live?—Now for our Heroes.

The Three approach.

O, these come up with Spirits more resolv'd!
Old venerable *Alvarez*, well I know him,
The Fav'rite once of this *Sebastian*'s Father;
Now Minister; (too honest for his Trade)
Religion bears him out, a thing taught young,
In Age ill practis'd, yet his prop in Death.
O, he has drawn a black; and smiles upon't,
As who shou'd say my Faith and Soul are white
Tho my Lot swarthy: Now if there be hereafter
He's blest; if not, well cheated, and dyes pleas'd.

ANTONIO, *holding his Lot in his clench'd hand*: Here I have thee,
Be what thou wilt: I will not look too soon.
Thou hast a colour; if thou prov'st not right,
I have a minute good ere I behold thee.
Now, let me rowl, and grubble thee,
Blind Men say white feels smooth, and black feels rough;
Thou hast a rugged skin; I do not like thee.

DORAX: There's th' Amorous airy spark, *Antonio*;
The wittiest Womans toy in *Portugal*.
Lord what a loss of Treats and Serenades!
The whole She Nation will b' in mourning for him.

ANTONIO: I've a moist sweaty palm; the more's my Sin;
If it be black, yet only dy'd, not odious
Damn'd Natural Ebony, there's hope in rubbing
To wash this Ethiope white.—[*Looks.*] Pox of the Proverb!
As black as Hell: another lucky saying!
I think the Devils in me:—good again,
I cannot speak one syllable, but tends
To Death or to Damnation. [*Holds up his ball.*

DORAX: He looks uneasie at his future Journey: [*Aside.*
And wishes his Boots off again; for fear
Of a bad Road, and a worse Inn at night.
Go to bed fool, and take secure repose
For thou shalt wake no more.
[SEBASTIAN *comes up to draw.*

MULEY-MOLUCH *to* BENDUCAR: Mark him who now approaches to the Lott'ry,
He looks secure of Death, superior greatness,
Like *Jove* when he made Fate, and said thou art
The Slave of my Creation; I admire him.

BENDUCAR: He looks as Man was made, with face erect,
That scorns his brittle Corps, and seems asham'd
He's not all spirit, his eyes with a dumb Pride,
Accusing Fortune that he fell not warm:
Yet now disdains to live. [SEBASTIAN *draws a black.*

MULEY-MOLUCH: He has his wish;
And I have fail'd of mine!

DORAX: Robb'd of my Vengeance, by a trivial chance! [*Aside.*
Fine work above, that their anointed care
Shou'd dye such little Death: or did his Genius
Know mine the stronger *Demon*, fear'd the grapple,
And looking round him, found this nook of fate
To skulk behind my Sword; shall I discover him?
Still he wou'd dye not mine: no,thanks to my
Revenge: reserv'd but to more royal shambles.
'Twere base too; and below those Vulgar Souls,
That shar'd his danger, yet not one disclos'd him:
But struck with Rev'rence kept an awful silence.
I'll see no more of this: Dog of a Prophet! [*Exit* DORAX.

MULEY-MOLUCH: One of these Three is a whole Hecatomb;

And therefore only one of 'em shall dye.
The Rest are but mute Cattle; and when Death
Comes, like a rushing Lion, couch like Spaniels,
With lolling tongues, and tremble at the paw,
Let Lots again decide it.

[*The Three draw again: and the Lot falls on* SEBASTIAN]

SEBASTIAN: Then there's no more to manage! if I fall
It shall be like my self; a setting Sun
Shou'd leave a track of Glory in the Skies.
Behold *Sebastian* King of *Portugal*.

MULEY-MOLUCH: *Sebastian*! ha! it must be he; no other
Cou'd represent such suff'ring Majesty:
I saw him, as he terms himself, a Sun
Strugling in dark Eclipse, and shooting day
On either side of the black Orb that veil'd him.

SEBASTIAN: Not less ev'n in this despicable now,
Than when my Name fill'd *Affricks* with affrights,
And froze your hearts beneath your torrid Zone.

BENDUCAR *to* MULEY-MOLUCH: Extravagantly brave! ev'n to an Impudence
Of Greatness.

SEBASTIAN: Here satiate all your fury;
Let fortune empty her whole Quiver on me,
I have a Soul, that like an ample Shield
Can take in all; and verge enough for more.
I wou'd have conquer'd you; and ventur'd only
A narrow neck of Land for a third World;
To give my loosen'd Subjects room to play.
Fate was not mine,
Nor am I Fate's: Now I have pleas'd my longing,
And trod the ground which I beheld from far,
I beg no pity for this mouldering Clay:
For if you give it burial there it takes
Possession of your Earth:
If burnt and scatter'd in the air: the Winds
That strow my dust, diffuse my royalty,
And spread me o'er your Clime: for where one Atome
Of mine shall light; know there *Sebastian* Reigns.

MULEY-MOLUCH: What shall I do to conquer thee?

SEBASTIAN: Impossible!
Souls know no Conquerors.

MULEY-MOLUCH: I'll show thee for a Monster through my *Affrick*.

SEBASTIAN: No thou canst only show me for a Man:
Affrick is stor'd with Monsters; Man's a Prodigy,
Thy Subjects have not seen.

MULEY-MOLUCH: Thou talk'st as if
Still at the head of Battel.

SEBASTIAN: Thou mistak'st,
For then I would not talk.

BENDUCAR: Sure he wou'd sleep.

SEBASTIAN: Till Dooms-day; when the Trumpet sounds to rise;
For that's a Soldier's call.

MULEY-MOLUCH: Thou'rt brave too late:
Thou shou'dst have dy'd in battel, like a Soldier.

SEBASTIAN: I fought and fell like one, but Death deceiv'd me,
I wanted weight of feeble Moors upon me,
To crush my Soul out.

MULEY-MOLUCH: Still untameable!
In what a ruine has thy head-strong Pride,
And boundless thirst of Empire plung'd thy People.

SEBASTIAN: What say'st thou, ha! No more of that.

MULEY-MOLUCH: Behold,
What Carcases of thine thy Crimes have strew'd,
And left our *Affric* Vultures to devour.

BENDUCAR: Those Souls were those thy God intrusted with thee,
To cherish not destroy.

SEBASTIAN: Witness, O Heaven, how much
This sight concerns me! wou'd I had a Soul
For each of these: How gladly wou'd I pay
The Ransom down: But since I have but one,
'Tis a King's life, and freely 'tis bestow'd.
Not your false Prophet, but eternal Justice
Has destin'd me the Lot, to dye for these:
'Tis fit a Sovereign so shou'd pay such Subjects;
For Subjects such as they are seldom seen,
Who not forsook me at my greatest need;
Nor for base lucre sold their Loyalty,
But shar'd my dangers to the last event,
And fenc'd 'em with their own: These thanks I pay you:
[*Wipes his Eyes.*
And know, that when *Sebastian* weeps, his Tears
Come harder than his Blood.

MULEY-MOLUCH: They plead too strongly
To be withstood: My Clouds are gath'ring too,
In kindly mixture with this Royal showr:
Be safe, and owe thy Life, not to my gift,
But to the greatness of thy mind, *Sebastian*:
Thy Subjects too shall live; a due reward
For their untainted Faith, in thy concealment.
MUFTI: Remember, Sir, your Vow. [*A general shout.*
MULEY-MOLUCH: Do thou remember
Thy Function, Mercy, and provoke not blood.
MULEY-ZEYDAN: One of his generous Fits, too strong to last.
[*Aside to* BENDUCAR.
BENDUCAR: The *Mufti* reddens; mark that holy Cheek. [*To him.*
He frets within, froths Treason at his mouth,
And churns it through his teeth; leave me to work him.
SEBASTIAN: A mercy unexpected, undesir'd,
Surprizes more: You've learnt the art to vanquish:
You cou'd not (give me leave to tell you sir)
Have giv'n me life but in my Subjects safety:
Kings, who are Fathers, live but in their People.
MULEY-MOLUCH: Still great, and grateful, that's thy character.
Unveil the Woman; I wou'd view the Face
That warm'd our *Mufti*'s Zeal:
These pious Parrots peck the fairest Fruit:
Such Tasters are for Kings.
[*Officers go to* ALMEYDA *to unveil her.*
ALMEYDA: Stand off ye Slaves, I will not be unveil'd.
MULEY-MOLUCH: Slave is thy Title: Force her.
SEBASTIAN: On your lives, approach her not.
MULEY-MOLUCH: How's this!
SEBASTIAN: Sir pardon me,
And hear me speak.——
ALMEYDA: Hear me; I will be heard:
I am no Slave; the noblest blood of *Affric*
Runs in my Veins; a purer stream than thine;
For, though deriv'd from the same Source, thy Current
Is puddl'd, and defil'd with Tyranny.
MULEY-MOLUCH: What Female Fury have we here!
ALMEYDA: I shou'd be one,
Because of kin to thee: Wou'dst thou be touch'd
By the presuming hands of sawcy Grooms?
The same respect, nay more, is due to me:
More for my Sex; the same for my descent.

These hands are only fit to draw the Curtain.
Now, if thou dar'st behold *Almeydas* face. [*Unveils herself.*

BENDUCAR: Wou'd I had never seen it! [*Aside.*

ALMEYDA: She whom thy *Mufti* tax'd to have no Soul;
Let *Affric* now be judg;
Perhaps thou think'st I meanly hope to 'scape,
As did *Sebastian* when he own'd his greatness.
But to remove that scruple know, base Man,
My murther'd Father, and my Brother's Ghost
Still haunt this Brest, and prompt it to revenge.
Think not I cou'd forgive nor dare thou pardon.

MULEY-MOLUCH: Woud'st thou revenge thee, Trait'ress, hadst thou pow'r?

ALMEYDA: Traitor, I wou'd; the Name's more justly thine:
Thy Father was not more than mine, the Heir
Of this large Empire; but with arms united
They fought their way, and seiz'd the Crown by force:
And equal as their danger was their share:
For where was Eldership, where none had right,
But that which Conquest gave? 'Twas thy ambition
Pull'd from my peaceful Father what his Sword
Help'd thine to gain: Surpriz'd him and his Kingdom,
No provocation given, no War declar'd.

MULEY-MOLUCH: I'll hear no more.

ALMEYDA: This is the living Coal that burning in me
Wou'd flame to vengeance, cou'd it find a vent.
My Brother too, that lies yet scarcely cold
In his deep watry bed: My wandring Mother,
Who in exile died.
O that I had the fruitful Heads of *Hydra*,
That one might bourgeon where another fell!
Still wou'd I give thee work; still, still, thou Tyrant,
And hiss thee with the last.

MULEY-MOLUCH: Something, I know not what, comes over me:
Whether the Toyls of Battel, unrepaird
With due repose, or other sudden qualm.
Benducar do the rest. [*Goes off, the Court follows him.*

BENDUCAR: Strange; in full health! this pang is of the Soul;
The Body's unconcern'd: I'll think hereafter.
Conduct these Royal Captives to the Castle;
Bid *Dorax* use 'em well, till further order.
[*Going off, stops.*
The inferior Captives their first owners take,

To sell, or to dispose.—You, *Mustapha*,
Set ope the Market for the sale of Slaves. [*Exit* BENDUCAR.

The Masters and Slaves come forward, and Buyers of several Qualities come in and chaffer about the several Owners, who make their Slaves do Tricks.

MUSTAPHA: My Chattels are come into my hands again, and my Conscience will serve me to sell 'em twice over; any price now, before the *Mufti* comes to claim 'em.

FIRST MERCHANT *to* MUSTAPHA: What do'st hold that old Fellow at? [*Pointing to* ALVAREZ]. He's tough, and has no service in his limbs.

MUSTAPHA: I confess he's somewhat tough; but I suppose you wou'd not boyl him. I ask for him a thousand Crowns.

FIRST MERCHANT: Thou mean'st a thousand Marvedi's.

MUSTAPHA: Prithee Friend, give me leave to know my own meaning.

FIRST MERCHANT: What virtues has he to deserve that price?

MUSTAPHA: Marry come up Sir! Virtues quoth ah! I took him in the King's Company; he's of a great Family, and rich. What other Virtues wou'dst thou have in a Noble-man?

FIRST MERCHANT: I buy him with another man's Purse, that's my comfort. My Lord *Dorax*, the Governor, will have him at any rate:—There's Hansel. Come, old Fellow, to the Castle.

ALVAREZ: To what is miserable Age reserv'd! [*Aside.*
But oh the King! And oh the fatal Secret!
Which I have kept thus long, to time it better,
And now I wou'd disclose, 'tis past my pow'r.
[*Exit with his Master.*

MUSTAPHA: Something of a Secret, and of the King I heard him mutter: A Pimp I warrant him, for I am sure he is an old Courtier. Now to put off t'other remnant of my Merchandize—stir up, Sirrah! [*To* ANTONIO

ANTONIO: Dog, what wou'dst thou have!

MUSTAPHA: Learn better manners, or I shall serve you a Dog-trick; come, down upon all four immediately; I'll make you know your Rider.

ANTONIO: Thou wilt not make a Horse of me?

MUSTAPHA: Horse or Ass, that's as thy Mother made thee:—
But take earnest in the first place for thy Sawcyness.
[*Lashes him with his Whip.*]

Be advisd, Friend, and buckle to thy Geers: Behold my Ensign of Royalty display'd over thee.

ANTONIO: I hope one day to use thee worse in *Portugal.*

MUSTAPHA: Ay, and good reason, Friend, if thou catchest me a conquering on thy side of the water, lay on me lustily, I'll take it as kindly as thou dost this.—— [*Holds up his whip.*

ANTONIO *lying down*: Hold, my dear Thrum-cap: I obey thee cheerfully, I see the Doctrine of Non-Resistance is never practis'd thoroughly but when a Man can't help himself.

Enter a Second Merchant.

SECOND MERCHANT: You, Friend, I wou'd see that Fellow do his Postures.

MUSTAPHA *bridling* ANTONIO: Now Sirrah follow, for you have rope enough: To your paces, Villain, amble, trot, and gallop:— Quick about, there.—Yeap, the more Money's bidden for you, the more your credit.

ANTONIO *follows at the end of the Bridle on his hands and feet, and does all his Postures.*

SECOND MERCHANT: He's well chin'd, and has a tolerable good back; that's half in half. [*To* MUSTAPHA] I wou'd see him strip, has he no Diseases about him?

MUSTAPHA: He's the best piece of Man's flesh in the Market, not an Eye-sore in his whole body: Feel his Legs, Master, neither Splint, Spavin nor Wind-gall.

[*Claps him on the shoulder.*

MERCHANT *feeling about him, and then putting his hand to his side*: Out upon him, how his flank heaves! The Whorson's broken-winded.

MUSTAPHA: Thick breath'd a little: Nothing but a sorry cold with lying out a nights in Trenches;—but sound Wind and Limb, I warrant him. Try him at a loose trot a little.

Puts the Bridle into his hand, he strokes him.

ANTONIO: For Heaven's sake Owner spare me; you know I am but new broken.

SECOND MERCHANT: 'Tis but a washy Jade, I see: What do you ask for this Bauble?

MUSTAPHA: Bauble, do you call him; he's a substantial true-bred Beast; bravely forehanded; mark but the cleanness of his shapes too; his Dam may be a Spanish Gennet, but a true Barb by the Sire, or I have no skill in Horse-flesh:— Marry I ask six Hundred Xeriffs for him.

Enter MUFTI.

MUFTI: What's that you are asking, Sirrah?

MUSTAPHA: Marry, I ask your Reverence Six Hundred Pardons; I was doing you a small piece of service here, putting off your Chattel for you.

MUFTI: And putting the Mony into your own Pocket.

MUSTAPHA: Upon vulgar reputation, no, my Lord, it was for your profit and emolument. What, wrong the Head of my Religion? I was sensible you wou'd have damn'd me, or any man that shou'd have injur'd you in a single Farthing; for I knew that was Sacrifice.

MUFTI: Sacriledge you mean, Sirrah,—and damning shall be the least part of your punishment; I have taken you in the manner, and will have the Law upon you.

MUSTAPHA: Good my Lord, take pity upon a poor man in this World, and damn me in the next.

MUFTI: No Sirrah, so you may repent, and escape punishment: Did not you sell this very Slave amongst the rest to me, and take Mony for him?

MUSTAPHA: Right my Lord.

MUFTI: And selling him again? Take Mony twice for the same Commodity? Oh, Villain! but did you not know him to be my Slave, Sirrah?

MUSTAPHA: Why shou'd I lye to your Honor? I did know him; and thereupon, seeing him wander about, took him up for a stray, and impounded him, with intention to restore him to the right Owner.

MUFTI: And yet at the same time was selling him to another: How rarely the Story hangs together!

MUSTAPHA: Patience, my Lord. I took him up, as your Heriot, with intention to have made the best of him, and then have brought the whole product of him in a Purse to you; for I know you wou'd have spent half of it upon your pious Pleasures, have hoarded up the other half, and given the remainder in Charities to the Poor.

MUFTI: And what's become of my other Slave? Thou hast sold him too I have a villainous suspicion.

MUSTAPHA: I know you have, my Lord; but while I was managing this young robustious Fellow, that old Spark who was nothing but Skin and Bone, and by consequence, very nimble, slipt through my fingers like an Eel, for there was no hold fast of him, and ran away to buy himself a new Master.

MUFTI *to* ANTONIO: Follow me home, Sirrah: [*To* MUSTAPHA] I shall remember you some other time.

[*Exit* MUFTI *with* ANTONIO

MUSTAPHA: I never doubted your Lordship's memory, for an ill turn: And I shall remember him too in the next rising of the Mobile, for this act of Resumption; and more especially for the Ghostly Counsel he gave me before the Emperor, to have hang'd my self in silence, to have sav'd his Reverence. The best on't is, I am beforehand with him, for selling one of his Slaves twice over.—And if he had not come just in the nick, I might have pocketed up t'other: For what should a poor Man do, that gets his living by hard labor, but pray for bad times when he may get it easily. O, for some incomparable Tumult! Then shou'd I naturally wish, that the beaten Party might prevail, because we have plundered t'other side already, and there's nothing more to get of 'em.

Both rich and poor for their own interest pray,
'Tis ours to make our Fortunes while we may;
For Kingdoms are not conquer'd every day.

[*Exit* MUSTAPHA.

ACT II

SCENE 1.

Suppos'd to be a terrace Walk, on the side of the Castle of Alcazar.

EMPEROR. BENDUCAR.

EMPEROR: And thinkest thou not it was discovered?

BENDUCAR: No:
The thoughts of Kings are like religious Groves,
The Walks of muffled Gods: Sacred retreat,
Where none but whom they please t' admit, approach.

EMPEROR: Did not my conscious Eyes flash out a Flame
To lighten those brown horrors, and disclose
The secret path I trod?

BENDUCAR: I cou'd not find it, 'till you lent a Clue
To that close Labarynth; how then shou'd they?

EMPEROR: I wou'd be loth they shou'd: it breeds contempt
For Herds to listen, or presume to pry,
When the hurt Lion groans within his Den:
But is't not strange?

BENDUCAR: To love? not more than 'tis to live; a Tax
Impos'd on all by Nature, paid in kind,
Familiar as our being.

EMPEROR: Still 'tis strange
To me: I know my Soul as wild as winds,
That sweep the Desarts of our moving Plains;
Love might as well be sow'd upon our Sands,
As in a brest so barren:
To love an Enemy, the only One
Remaining too, whom yester Sun beheld,
Must'ring her charms, and rolling as she past,
By every Squadron her alluring eyes:
To edge her Champions Swords, and urge my ruin.
The shouts of Soldiers, and the burst of Cannon,
Maintain ev'n still a deaf and murm'ring noise;
Nor is Heav'n yet recover'd of the sound
Her Battel rowsed: Yet spight of me I love.

BENDUCAR: What then controuls you?
Her Person is as prostrate as her Party.

EMPEROR: A thousand things controul this Conqueror,
My native pride to own th' unworthy passion,
Hazard of Int'rest, and my Peoples love:
To what a Storm of Fate am I expos'd!
What if I had her murder'd? 'tis but what
My Subjects all expect, and she deserves.
Wou'd not th' impossibility
Of ever, ever seeing, or possessing,
Calm all this rage, this Hurrican of Soul?

BENDUCAR: That ever, ever,
I mark'd the double, shows extream reluctance
To part with her for ever.

EMPEROR: Right thou hast me,
I wou'd, but cannot kill: I must enjoy her:
I must, and what I must be sure I will.
What's Royalty but pow'r to please my self?
And if I dare not, then am I the Slave,
And my own Slaves the Sovereigns,—'tis resolv'd.
Weak Princes flatter when they want the pow'r
To curb their People; tender Plants must bend,
But when a Government is grown to strength,
Like some old Oak, rough with its armed Bark,
It yields not to the tug, but only nods,
And turns to sullen State.

BENDUCAR: Then you resolve
T'implore her pity, and to beg relief?
EMPEROR: Death, must I beg the pity of my Slave?
Must a King beg? Yes, Love's a greater King;
A Tyrant, nay a Devil that possesses me:
He tunes the Organs of my voice, and speaks
Unknown to me within me; pushes me,
And drives me on by force.—
Say I shou'd wed her, wou'd not my wise Subjects
Take check, and think it strange? perhaps revolt?
BENDUCAR: I hope they wou'd not.
EMPEROR: Then thou doubt'st they wou'd?
BENDUCAR: To whom?
EMPEROR: To her
Perhaps, or to my Brother, or to Thee.
BENDUCAR *in disorder*: To me! me did you mention? how I tremble!
The name of Treason shakes my honest Soul.
If I am doubted, Sir,
Secure yourself this moment, take my life.
EMPEROR: No more: if I suspected thee——I wou'd.
BENDUCAR: I thank your kindness: Guilt had almost lost me! [*Aside.*
EMPEROR: But clear my doubts: think'st thou they may rebel?
BENDUCAR *aside*: This goes as I wou'd wish:—— [*to th'* EMPEROR] 'Tis possible.
A secret Party still remains, that lurks
Like Embers rak'd in ashes—wanting but
A breath to blow aside th' involving dust,
And then they blaze abroad.
EMPEROR: They must be trampled out.
BENDUCAR: But first be known.
EMPEROR: Torture shall force it from 'em.
BENDUCAR: You wou'd not put a Nation to the rack?
EMPEROR: Yes, the whole world; so I be safe, I care not.
BENDUCAR: Our Limbs and Lives
Are yours, but mixing Friends with Foes is hard.
EMPEROR: All may be foes; or how to be distinguish'd,
If some be friends?
BENDUCAR: They may with ease be winnow'd:
Suppose some one, who has deserv'd your trust,
Some one who knows Mankind, shou'd be employ'd
To mix among 'em, seem a Malcontent,

And dive into their breasts, to try how far
They dare oppose your love?

EMPEROR: I like this well: 'Tis wholesom wickedness.

BENDUCAR: Whomever he suspects, he fastens there,
And leaves no cranny of his Soul unsearch'd;
Then, like a Bee bag'd with his honey'd venome,
He brings it to your Hive: if such a Man
So able, and so honest, may be found;
If not, my project dyes.——

EMPEROR: By all my hopes thou hast describ'd thyself:—
Thou, thou alone art fit to play that Engine,
Thou only couldst contrive.

BENDUCAR: Sure I cou'd serve you:
I think I cou'd:—but here's the difficulty,
I'm so entirely yours,
That I shou'd scurvily dissemble hate;
The cheat wou'd be too gross.

EMPEROR: Art thou a Statesman
And canst not be a Hypocrite? Impossible:
Do not distrust thy Vertues.

BENDUCAR: If I must personate this seeming Villain,
Remember 'tis to serve you.

EMPEROR: No more words:
Love goads me to *Almeyda*, all affairs
Are troublesom but that; and yet that most. [*Going.*
Bid *Dorax* treat *Sebastian* like a King;
I had forgot him;—but this Love marrs all,
And takes up my whole brest. [*Exit* EMPEROR.

BENDUCAR *to the* EMPEROR: Be sure I'll tell him——
With all the aggravating Circumstances [*Alone.*
I can, to make him swell at that Command.
The Tyrant first suspected me:
Then, with a sudden gust, he whirl'd about,
And trusted me too far: Madness of Pow'r!
Now, by his own consent, I ruin him.
For, shou'd some feeble Soul, for fear or gain
Bolt out t'accuse me, ev'n the King is cozen'd,
And thinks he's in the secret.
How sweet is Treason when the Traytor's safe!

(*Sees the* MUFTI *and* DORAX *entring and seeming to confer.*)

The *Mufti*, and with him my sullen *Dorax*,
That first is mine already.

'Twas easie work to gain a cov'tous mind,
Whom rage to loose his Pris'ners had prepar'd:
Now, caught himself,
He wou'd seduce another; I must help him:
For Church-men, though they itch to govern all,
Are silly, woful, awkward Politicians;
They make lame mischief, though they mean it well:
Their Int'rest is not finely drawn, and hid,
But seams are coarsly bungled up, and seen.

MUFTI: He'll tell you more.

DORAX: I've heard enough already
To make me loath thy Morals.

BENDUCAR *to* DORAX: You seem warm:
The good Man's zeal, perhaps has gon too far.

DORAX: Not very far; not farther than zeal goes
Of course; a small days journey short of Treason.

MUFTI: By all that's Holy, Treason was not nam'd:
I spar'd the Emperors broken Vows to save
The Slaves from Death; though it was cheating Heav'n,
But I forgave him that.

DORAX: And slighted o'er [*scornfully*
The wrongs himself sustain'd in property:
When his bought Slaves were seiz'd by force, no loss
Of his consider'd, and no cost repaid.

MUFTI: Not wholly slighted o'er, not absolutely:
Some modest hints of private wrongs I urg'd.

DORAX: Two-thirds of all he said: there he began;
To shew the fulness of his heart, there ended:
Some short excursions of a broken Vow,
He made indeed, but flat insipid stuff:
But when he made his loss the Theme, he flourish'd,
Reliev'd his fainting Rhetorick with new Figures,
And thunder'd at oppressing Tyranny.

MUFTI: Why not, when Sacrilegious Pow'r wou'd seize
My Property? 'tis an affront to Heav'n,
Whose Person, though unworthy, I sustain.

DORAX: You've made such strong Alliances above,
That 'twere Profaneness in us Laiety
To offer earthly Aid.
I tell thee, *Mufti*, if the World were wise,
They wou'd not wag one finger in your quarrels.
Your Heav'n you promise, but our Earth you covet.

The *Phaetons* of mankind, who fire that World,
Which you were sent by Preaching but to warm.
BENDUCAR: This goes beyond the mark.
MUFTI: No, let him rail;
His Prophet works within him;
He's a rare Convert.
DORAX: Now his Zeal yearns
To see me burnt; he damns me from his Church,
Because I wou'd restrain him to his Duty;
Is not the care of Souls a load sufficient?
Are not your holy stipends pay'd for this?
Were you not bred apart from worldly noise,
To study Souls, their Cures and their Diseases?
If this be so, we ask you but our own:
Give us your whole Employment, all your care:
The Province of the Soul is large enough
To fill up every Cranny of your time,
And leave you much to answer, if one Wretch
Be damn'd by your neglect.
BENDUCAR *to the* MUFTI: He speaks but reason.
DORAX: Why then these foreign thoughts of State-Employments,
Abhorrent to your Function and your Breeding?
Poor droaning Truants of unpractis'd Cells,
Bred in the Fellowship of bearded Boys,
What wonder is it if you know not Men?
Yet there, you live demure, with down-cast Eyes,
And humble as your Discipline requires:
But, when let loose from thence to live at large,
Your little tincture of Devotion dies:
Then Luxury succeeds, and set agog
With a new Scene of yet untasted Joys,
You fall with greedy hunger to the Feast.
Of all your College Vertues, nothing now
But your Original Ignorance remains:
Bloated with Pride, Ambition, Avarice,
You swell, to counsel Kings and govern Kingdoms.
MUFTI: He prates as if Kings had not Consciences,
And none requir'd Directors but the Crowd.
DORAX: As private men they want you, not as Kings;
Nor wou'd you care t' inspect their publick Conscience,
But that it draws dependencies of Pow'r,
And Earthly Interest which you long to sway.
Content you with monopolizing Heav'n,

And let this little hanging Ball alone;
For give you but a foot of Conscience there,
And you, like *Archimedes*, toss the Globe.
We know your thoughts of us that Laymen are
Lag Souls, and rubbish of remaining Clay,
Which Heav'n, grown weary of more perfect work,
Set upright with a little puff of breath,
And bid us pass for Men.

MUFTI: I will not answer,
Base foul-mouth'd Renegade; but I'll pray for thee
To shew my Charity. [*Exit* MUFTI.

DORAX: Do; but forget not him who needs it most:
Allow thy self some share: He's gone too soon;
I had to tell him of his holy jugglings;
Things that wou'd startle Faith, and make us deem
Not this or that, but all Religions false.

BENDUCAR: Our Holy Oratour has lost the Cause: [*Aside.*
But I shall yet redeem it.—[To DORAX.] let him go;
For I have secret Orders from the Emperour,
Which none but you must hear: I must confess
I cou'd have wish'd some other hand had brought 'em.
When did you see your Pris'ner Great *Sebastian?*

DORAX: You might as well have ask'd me when I saw
A crested Dragon, or a Basilisk;
Both are less Poison to my Eyes and Nature.
He knows not I am I; nor shall he see me
Till time has perfected a lab'ring thought,
That rowls within my brest.

BENDUCAR: 'Twas my mistake:
I guess'd indeed that time, and his misfortunes,
And your returning duty had effac'd
The mem'ry of past wrongs; they wou'd in me;
And I judg'd you as tame and as forgiving.

DORAX: Forgive him! no, I left my foolish Faith
Because it wou'd oblige me to forgiveness.

BENDUCAR: I can but grieve to find you obstinate:
For you must see him; 'tis our Emp'rours will,
And strict Command.

DORAX: I laugh at that Command.

BENDUCAR: You must do more than see; serve, and respect him.

DORAX: See, serve him, and respect, and after all
My yet uncancell'd wrongs, I must do this!
But I forget my self.

BENDUCAR: Indeed you do.

DORAX: The Emp'rour is a stranger to my wrongs;
I need but tell my story, to revoke
This hard Commission.

BENDUCAR: Can you call me Friend,
And think I cou'd neglect to speak, at full
Th' Affronts you had from your ungrateful Master?

DORAX: And yet enjoyn'd my Service, and Attendance?

BENDUCAR: And yet enjoyn'd 'em both: wou'd that were all;
He scru'd his Face into a harden'd smile,
And said, *Sebastian* knew to govern Slaves.

DORAX: Slaves are the growth of *Africk*, not of *Europe*:
By Heav'n I will not lay down my Commission;
Not at his foot, I will not stoop so low;
But if there be a part in all his Face
More sacred than the rest, I'll throw it there.

BENDUCAR: You may; but then you lose all future means
Of Vengeance on *Sebastian*, when no more
Alcalde of this Fort.

DORAX: That thought escap'd me.

BENDUCAR: Keep your Command; and be reveng'd on both:
Nor sooth your self; you have no pow'r t' affront him;
The Emp'rours love protects him from insults.
And he, who spoke that proud ill-natur'd word,
Following the bent of his impetuous temper,
May force your reconcilement to *Sebastian*:
Nay bid you kneel, and kiss th' offending foot,
That kick'd you from his Presence.
But think not to divide their punishment;
You cannot touch a hair of loath'd *Sebastian*,
While *Muley-Moluch* lives.

DORAX: What means this Riddle?

BENDUCAR: 'Tis out: there needs no *Oedipus* to solve it.
Our Emp'rour is a Tyrant, feared and hated;
I scarce remember in his Reign, one day
Pass guiltless o'er his execrable head.
He thinks the Sun is lost that sees not bloud:
When none is shed we count it Holiday.
We, who are most in favour, cannot call
This hour our own?—you know the younger Brother,
Mild *Muley-Zeydan*;—

DORAX: Hold and let me think.

BENDUCAR: The Soldiers Idolize you,

He trusts you with the Castle,
The Key of all his Kingdom.
DORAX: Well; and he trusts you too.
BENDUCAR: Else I were mad,
To hazard such a daring Enterprize.
DORAX: He trusts us both; mark that, shall we betray him?
A Master who reposes Life and Empire
On our fidelity: I grant he is a Tyrant,
That hated name my nature most abhors;
More, as you say, has loaded me with scorn:
Ev'n with the last contempt, to serve *Sebastian*.
Yet more I know he vacates my revenge;
Which, but by this revolt I cannot compass:
But, while he trusts me, 'twere so base a part
To fawn and yet betray, I shou'd be hiss'd
And whoop'd in Hell for that Ingratitude.
BENDUCAR: Consider well what I have done for you.
DORAX: Consider thou what thou woud'st have me do.
BENDUCAR: You've too much honour for a Renegade.
DORAX: And thou too little faith to be a Fav'rite.
Is not the bread thou eat'st, the Robe thou wear'st,
Thy Wealth, and Honours, all the pure indulgence
Of him thou wou'dst destroy?
And wou'd his Creature, nay his Friend betray him?
Why then no Bond is left on human kind:
Distrusts, debates, immortal strifes ensue;
Children may murder Parents, Wives their Husbands;
All must be Rapine, Wars, and Desolation,
When trust and gratitude no longer bind.
BENDUCAR: Well have you argued in your own defence:
You, who have burst asunder all those bonds,
And turn'd a Rebel to your Native Prince.
DORAX: True, I rebell'd: but when did I betray?
Indignities, which Man cou'd not support,
Provok'd my vengeance to this noble Crime.
But he had strip'd me first of my Command,
Dismiss'd my Service, and absolv'd my Faith;
And, with disdainful Language, dar'd my worst.
I but accepted War, which he denounc'd.
Else had you seen, not *Dorax*, but *Alonzo*,
With his couch'd Lance against your foremost *Moors*:
Perhaps too turn'd the fortune of the day;
Made *Affrick* mourn, and *Portugal* triumph.

BENDUCAR: Let me embrace thee.
DORAX: Stand off Sycophant,
And keep Infection distant.
BENDUCAR: Brave and honest.
DORAX: In spight of thy Temptations.
BENDUCAR: Call 'em Trials:
They were no more: thy faith was held in Balance.
And nicely weigh'd by jealousie of Pow'r;
Vast was the trust of such a Royal Charge;
And our wise Emperour, might justly fear
Sebastian might be freed and reconcil'd,
By new Obligements to thy former love.
DORAX: I doubt thee still; thy reasons were too strong,
And driv'n too near the head, to be but Artifice.
And after all, I know thou art a Statesman,
Where truth is rarely found.
BENDUCAR: Behold the Emperour;

Enter EMPEROR, SEBASTIAN *and* ALMEYDA.

Ask him, I beg thee to be justify'd,
If he employ'd me not to foord thy Soul,
And try the footing whether false or firm.
DORAX: Death to my Eyes, I see *Sebastian* with him!
Must he be serv'd! avoid him, if we meet,
It must be like the crush of Heav'n and Earth,
T' involve us both in ruin. [*Exit* DORAX.
BENDUCAR: 'Twas a bare saving game I made with *Dorax*,
But better so than lost; he cannot hurt me,
That I precaution'd: I must ruin him.
But now this Love; Ay, there's the gath'ring storm!
The Tyrant must not wed *Almeyda*; no,
That ruins all the Fabrick I am raising.
Yet seeming to approve it, gave me time,
And gaining time gains all.
[BENDUCAR *goes and waits behind the* EMPEROUR. *The* EMPEROUR; SEBASTIAN *and* ALMEYDA *advance to the front of the Stage.*] *Guards and Attendants.*

EMPEROR *to* SEBASTIAN: I bad 'em serve you, and if they obey not,
I keep my Lions keen within their Dens,
To stop their maws with disobedient Slaves.
SEBASTIAN: If I had Conquer'd,

They cou'd not have with more observance waited:
Their eyes, hands, feet,
Are all so quick they seem t' have but one motion,
To catch my flying words. Onely the *Alcayde*
Shuns me, and with a grim Civility,
Bows, and declines my Walks.

EMPEROR: A Renegade:
I know not more of him: but that he's brave,
And hates your Christian Sect. If you can frame
A farther wish, give wing to your desires,
And name the thing you want.

SEBASTIAN: My Liberty:
For were ev'n Paradise it self my Prison,
Still I shou'd long to leap the Chrystal walls.

EMPEROR: Sure our two Souls have somewhere been acquainted:
In former beings; or, struck out together,
One spark to *Africk* flew, and one to *Portugal*.
Expect a quick deliverance: [*turning to* ALMEYDA] here's a third,
Of kindred Soul to both: pity our Stars
Have made us Foes! I shou'd not wish her death.

ALMEYDA: I ask no pity; if I thought my Soul
Of kin to thine, soon wou'd I rend my heart-strings,
And tear out that Alliance: but thou Viper
Hast cancell'd kindred, made a rent in Nature,
And through her holy bowels gnaw'd thy way,
Through thy own Bloud to Empire.

EMPEROR: This again:——
And yet she lives; and only lives t' upbraid me.

SEBASTIAN: What honour is there in a Womans death!
Wrong'd as she says, but helpless to revenge;
Strong in her Passion, impotent of Reason,
Too weak to hurt, too fair to be destroy'd.
Mark her Majestick Fabrick; She's a Temple
Sacred by birth, and built by Hands Divine;
Her Soul's the Deity, that lodges there:
Nor is the Pile unworthy of the God.

EMPEROR: She's all that thou canst say or I can think.
But the perverseness of her clam'rous Tongue
Strikes Pity deaf.

SEBASTIAN: Then onely hear her Eyes;
Though they are mute they plead; nay more, command;
For beauteous Eyes have Arbitrary Power.

All Females have prerogative of Sex,
The Shes ev'n of the salvage herd are safe;
And when they snarl or bite, have no return
But Courtship from the Male.

EMPEROR: Were She not She, and I not *Muley-Moluch*,
She's Mistress of unevitable Charms,
For all but me; nor am I so exempt,
But that—I know not what I was to say—
But I am too obnoxious to my Friends;
And sway'd by your Advice.

SEBASTIAN: Sir, I advis'd not.
By Heav'n, I never counsell'd Love but Pity.

EMPEROR: By Heav'n thou didst: deny it not, thou didst:
For what was all that Prodigality
Of praise, but to inflame me?——

SEBASTIAN: Sir,—

EMPEROR: No more:
Thou hast convinc'd me, that she's worth my Love.

SEBASTIAN: Was ever Man so ruin'd by himself! [*Aside.*

ALMEYDA: Thy Love; that odious Mouth was never fram'd
To speak a word so soft:
Name Death again, for that thou canst pronounce
With horrid grace, becoming of a Tyrant.
Love is for human hearts, and not for thine,
Where the brute Beast extinguishes the Man.

EMPEROR: Such if I were, yet rugged Lions love,
And grapple, and compel their savage Dames.—
Mark my *Sebastian*, how that sullen frown, [*She frowns.*
Like flashing Lightning, opens angry Heaven;
And while it kills delights. But yet, insult not
Too soon, proud Beauty, I confess no love.

SEBASTIAN: No, Sir, I said so, and I witness for you,
Not love; but noble pity mov'd your mind:
Int'rest might urge you too to save her life;
For those who wish her party lost, might murmur
At shedding Royal Blood.

EMPEROR: Right, thou instruct'st me;
Int'rest of State requires not Death, but Marriage;
T' unite the jarring Titles of our Line.

SEBASTIAN: Let me be dumb for ever, all I plead, [*Aside.*
Like Wild-fire thrown against the Wind, returns
With double force to burn me.

EMPEROR: Cou'd I but bend to make my beauteous Foe
The Partner of my Throne, and of my Bed.—
ALMEYDA: Still thou dissemblest, but I read thy heart,
And know the power of my own Charms; thou lov'st,
And I am pleas'd for my revenge thou dost.
EMPEROR: And thou hast cause.
ALMEYDA: I have; for I have pow'r to make thee wretched.
Be sure I will, and yet despair of freedom.
EMPEROR: Well then, I love,——
And 'tis below my greatness to disown it:
Love thee implacably, yet hate thee too;
Wou'd hunt thee bare-foot, in the mid-day Sun,
Through the parch'd Desarts, and the scorching Sands,
T' enjoy thy Love, and once enjoy'd to kill thee.
ALMEYDA: 'Tis a false Courage, when thou threat'nst me;
Thou canst not stir a hand to touch my Life:
Do not I see thee tremble while thou speak'st?
Lay by the Lions Hide, vain Conqueror,
And take the Distaff; for thy Soul's my Slave.
EMPEROR: Confusion! How thou viewest my very Heart!
I cou'd as soon,
Stop a Spring-tide, blown in, with my bare hand,
As this impetuous Love:—Yes, I will wed thee;
In spight of thee, and of my self, I will.
ALMEYDA: For what? to people *Affric* with new Monsters
Which that unnatural mixture must produce?
No, were we joyn'd, ev'n tho it were in death,
Our Bodies burning in one Funeral Pile,
The Prodigy of *Thebes* wou'd be renew'd,
And my divided flame shou'd break from thine.
EMPEROR: Serpent, I will engender Poyson with thee;
Joyn Hate with Hate, add Venom to the birth;
Our Off-spring, like the seed of Dragons Teeth,
Shall issue arm'd, and fight themselves to death.
ALMEYDA: I'm calm again; thou canst not marry me.
EMPEROR: As gleams of Sun-shine soften storms to show'rs,
So, if you smile, the loudness of my rage
In gentle Whispers shall return, but this,——
That nothing can divert my Love, but Death.
ALMEYDA: See how thou art deceiv'd, I am a Christian;
'Tis true, unpractis'd in my new Belief,
Wrongs I resent, nor pardon yet with ease:
Those Fruits come late, and are of slow increase

In haughty Hearts, like mine: Now, tell thy self
If this one word destroy not thy designs:
Thy Law permits thee not to marry me.

EMPEROR: 'Tis but a specious Tale, to blast my hopes,
And baffle my pretensions. Speak, *Sebastian*,
And, as a King, speak true.

SEBASTIAN: Then, thus adjur'd,
On a King's word 'tis truth, but truth ill tim'd;
For her dear Life is now expos'd anew;
Unless you wholly can put on Divinity,
And graciously forgive.

ALMEYDA: Now learn by this,
The little value I have left for life,
And trouble me no more.

EMPEROR: I thank thee Woman;
Thou hast restor'd me to my native Rage;
And I will seize my happiness by force.

SEBASTIAN: Know, *Muley-Moluch*, when thou dar'st attempt.——

EMPEROR: Beware, I wou'd not be provok'd to use
A Conqueror's right, and therefore charge thy silence.
If thou wou'dst merit to be thought my Friend,
I leave thee to perswade her to compliance:
If not, there's a new gust in Ravishment,
Which I have never try'd.

BENDUCAR: They must be watch'd; [*Aside.*
For something I observ'd creates a doubt.
[*Exeunt* EMPEROUR *and* BENDUCAR.

SEBASTIAN: I've been too tame, have basely born my Wrongs,
And not exerted all the King, within me;
I heard him, O sweet Heavens, he threat'ned Rape;
Nay insolently urg'd me to perswade thee,
Ev'n thee, thou Idol of my Soul and Eyes;
For whom I suffer Life, and drag this being.

ALMEYDA: You turn my Prison to a Paradise;
But I have turn'd your Empire to a Prison:
In all your Wars good fortune flew before you;
Sublime you sate in Triumph on her Wheel;
Till in my fatal Cause your Sword was drawn;
The weight of my misfortunes drag'd you down.

SEBASTIAN: And is't not strange, that Heav'n shou'd bless my Arms
In common Causes, and desert the best?

Now in your greatest, last extremity,
When I wou'd ayd you most, and most desire it,
I bring but Sighs, the succors of a Slave.

ALMEYDA: Leave then the luggage of your fate behind,
To make your flight more easie, leave *Almeyda.*
Nor think me left a base ignoble Prey,
Expos'd to this inhuman Tyrant's lust;
My Virtue is a guard beyond my strength,
And Death, my last defence, within my call.

SEBASTIAN: Death may be call'd in vain, and cannot come;
Tyrants can tye him up from your relief:
Nor has a Christian privilege to dye.
Alas thou art too young in thy new Faith;
Brutus and *Cato* might discharge their Souls,
And give 'em Furlo's for another World:
But we, like Centry's, are oblig'd to stand
In starless Nights, and wait the pointed hour.

ALMEYDA: If shunning ill be good, then Death is good
To those who cannot shun it but by Death:
Divines but peep on undiscover'd Worlds,
And draw the distant Landshape as they please:
But who has e'er return'd from those bright Regions,
To tell their Manners, and relate their Laws?
I'll venture landing on that happy shoar
With an unsully'd Body, and white Mind;
If I have err'd, some kind Inhabitant
Will pity a stray'd Soul, and take me home.

SEBASTIAN: Beware of Death, thou canst not dye unperjur'd,
And leave an unaccomplish'd Love behind:
Thy Vows are mine; nor will I quit my claim:
The tye of Minds are but imperfect Bonds,
Unless the Bodies joyn to seal the Contract.

ALMEYDA: What Joys can you possess or can I give?
Where groans of Death succeed the sighs of Love.
Our Hymen has not on his Saffron Robe;
But muffled up in Mourning, downwards holds
His dropping Torch, extinguish'd with his Tears.

SEBASTIAN: The God of Love stands ready to revive it
With his etherial breath.

ALMEYDA: 'Tis late to joyn, when we must part so soon.

SEBASTIAN: Nay rather let us haste it, ere we part:
Our Souls, for want of that acquaintance here,

May wander in the starry Walks above,
And, forc'd on worse Companions, miss ourselves.

ALMEYDA: The Tyrant will not long be absent hence;
And soon I shall be ravish'd from your arms.

SEBASTIAN: Wilt thou thy self become the greater Tyrant,
And give not love, while thou hast Love to give?
In dang'rous days, when Riches are a Crime,
The wise betimes make over their Estates:
Make o'er thy Honour, by a deed of trust,
And give me seizure of the mighty wealth.

ALMEYDA: What shall I do! O teach me to refuse!
I wou'd; and yet I tremble at the grant.
For dire presages fright my Soul by day,
And boding Visions haunt my Nightly Dreams:
Sometimes, methinks, I hear the groans of Ghosts;
Thin, hollow sounds, and lamentable screams;
Then, like a dying Eccho, from afar,
My Mothers Voice, that cries, Wed not *Almeyda!*
Forewarn'd *Almeyda*, Marriage is thy Crime.

SEBASTIAN: Some envious *Demon*, to delude our joys;
Love is not Sin, but where 'tis sinful Love.

ALMEYDA: Mine is a flame so holy, and so clear,
That the white taper leaves no soot behind;
No smoak of Lust; but chast as Sister's love,
When coldly they return a Brothers kiss,
Without the zeal that meets at lovers mouths.

SEBASTIAN: Laugh then at fond presages; I had some;
Fam'd *Nostradamus*, when he took my Horoscope,
Foretold my Father I shou'd wed with Incest:
Ere this unhappy War my Mother dy'd;
And Sisters I had none; vain Augury!
A long Religious Life, a Holy Age,
My Stars assign'd me too; impossible.
For how can Incest suit with Holiness,
Or Priestly Orders with a Princely State?

ALMEYDA: Old venerable *Alvarez*!— [*sighing*.

SEBASTIAN: But why that sigh in naming that good Man?

ALMEYDA: Your Fathers Counsellor and Confident—

SEBASTIAN: He was; and, if he lives, my second Father.

ALMEYDA: Mark'd our farewel, when going to the fight,
You gave *Almeyda* for the word of Battel.
'Twas in that fatal Moment, he discover'd
The Love that long we labour'd to conceal.

I know it; though my eyes stood full of tears,
Yet, through the mist, I saw him stedfast gaze:
Then knock'd his Aged breast, and inward groan'd;
Like some sad Prophet, that foresaw the doom
Of those whom best he lov'd, and cou'd not save.

SEBASTIAN: It startles me! and brings to my remembrance,
That, when the shock of Battel was begun,
He wou'd have much complain'd (but had not time)
Of our hid passion; then, with lifted hands,
He beg'd me by my Fathers Sacred Soul,
Not to espouse you, if he dy'd in fight:
For if he liv'd, and we were Conquerors,
He had such things to urge against our Marriage,
As, now declar'd, wou'd blunt my sword in Battel;
And dastardize my Courage.

ALMEYDA: My blood cruddles;
And cakes about my heart.

SEBASTIAN: I'll breathe a sigh, so warm into thy bosom,
Shall make it flow again. My Love, he knows not
Thou art a Christian; that produc'd his fear:
Lest thou shoud'st sooth my Soul with charms so strong,
That Heav'n might prove too weak.

ALMEYDA: There must be more:
This cou'd not blunt your Sword.

SEBASTIAN: Yes, if I drew it, with a curst intent,
To take a Misbeliever to my Bed;
It must be so.

ALMEYDA: Yet——

SEBASTIAN: No, thou shalt not plead
With that fair mouth, against the Cause of Love.
Within this Castle is a Captive Priest,
My Holy Confessor, whose free access
Not ev'n the barb'rous Victors have refus'd;
This happy hour his hands shall make us one.

ALMEYDA: I go; with Love and Fortune, two blind Guides,
To lead my way: half loth and half consenting.
If, as my Soul fore-bodes, some dire event
Pursue this Union, or some Crime unknown,
Forgive me Heav'n; and all ye Blest above,
Excuse the frailty of unbounded Love. [*Exeunt Ambo.*

SCENE 2.

Suppos'd a Garden; with Lodging Rooms behind it; or on the sides.

Enter MUFTI; ANTONIO *as a Slave*; *and* JOHAYMA *the* MUFTI'S *Wife*.

MUFTI: And how do you like him, look upon him well; he's a personable Fellow of a Christian Dog. Now I think you are fitted, for a Gardiner: Ha what say'st thou *Johayma?*

JOHAYMA: He may make a shift to sow lettice, raise Melons, and water a Garden-plat. But otherwise a very filthy Fellow; how odiously he smells of his country garlike! fugh, how he stinks of *Spain*.

MUFTI: Why honey-bird I bought him on purpose for thee; didst thou not say thou long'dst for a Christian Slave?

JOHAYMA: Ay, but the sight of that loathsom creature has almost cur'd me; And how can I tell that he's a Christian? and he were well search'd he may prove a *Jew* for ought I know. And besides I have always long'd for an Eunuch; for they say that's a Civil Creature, and almost as harmless as your self Husband: speak fellow, are not you such a kind of peaceable thing?

ANTONIO: I was never taken for one in my own Country; and not very peaceable neither, when I am well provok'd.

MUFTI: To your Occupation Dog; bind up the Jessamines in yond Arbor, and handle your pruning knife with dexterity; tightly I say, go tightly to your business; you have cost me much; and must earn it in your work; here's plentiful provision for you, rascal, sallating in the Garden, and water in the tanck, and on Holydays the licking of a platter of Rice, when you deserve it.

JOHAYMA: What have you been bred up to Sirrah, and what can you perform to recommend you to my service?

ANTONIO *making legs*: Why Madam, I can perform as much as any Man, in a fair Ladies Service. I can play upon the Flute, and Sing; I can carry your Umbrella, and fan your Ladyship, and cool you when you are too hot: in fine, no Service either by day or by night shall come amiss to me; and besides am of so quick an apprehension, that you need but wink upon me at any time, to make me understand my duty. [*She winks at him.*

ANTONIO: Very fine, she has tipt the wink already.—— [*Aside.*

JOHAYMA: The Whelp may come to something in time, when I have enter'd him into his business.

MUFTI: A very malapert Cur, I can tell him that; I do not like his fawning, you must be taught your distance Sirrah.

[*Strikes him.*

JOHAYMA: Hold, hold.—He has deserv'd it I confess; but for once let his ignorance plead his pardon; we must not discourage a beginner. Your Reverence has taught us Charity ev'n to birds and beasts: here, you filthy brute you:—take this little Alms, to buy you plaisters.

[*gives him a piece of money.*

ANTONIO: Money and a Love-pinch in the inside of my palm into the bargain. [*Aside.*

Enter a Servant.

SERVANT: Sir, my Lord *Benducar* is coming to wait on you, and is already at the Palace Gate.

MUFTI: Come in *Johayma*, regulate the rest of my Wives and Concubines, and leave the Fellow to his work.

JOHAYMA: Look how stupidly he stares about him, like a Calf new come into the World: I shall teach you Sirrah to know your business, a little better—this way you awkard rascal, here lyes the Arbour, must I be showing you eternally?

[*turning him about.*

MUFTI: Come away Minion; you shall show him nothing.

JOHAYMA: I'll but bring him into the Arbor, where a Rose-tree and a Myrtle are just falling for want of a prop; if they were bound together they wou'd help to keep up one another:—He's a raw Gardiner, and 'tis but Charity to teach him.

MUFTI: No more deeds of Charity to-day; come in, or I shall think you a little better dispos'd than I cou'd wish you.

JOHAYMA: Well, go before, I will follow my Pastor.

MUFTI: So you may cast a sheeps eye behind you: In before me. And you, Sawciness, mind your pruning knife; or I may chance to use it for you.

Exeunt MUFTI *and* JOHAYMA.

ANTONIO *alone*: Thank you for that; but I am in no such haste to be made a Musulman. For his Wedlock, with all her haughtiness, I find her coming. How far a Christian shou'd resist, I partly know; but how far a lewd young Christian can resist is another question. She's tolerable, and I am a poor Stranger, far from better Friends, and in a bodily necessity: Now have I a strange temptation to try what other Females are belonging to this Family: I am not far from the Womens apartment I am sure; and if these Birds are within distance, here's that will chuckle 'em together. [*Pulls out his Flute.*] If there be variety of Moors flesh in this Holy Market 'twere madness to lay out all my money upon the first bargain. [*He plays.*

A Grate opens and MORAYMA *the Mufti's Daughter appears at it.*

ANTONIO: Ay there's an Apparition! This is a Morsel worthy of a *Mufti*; this is the relishing bit in secret; this is the Mystery of his Alcoran, that must be reserv'd from the knowledge of the profane Vulgar. This is his Holyday Devotion; see, she beckons too.

She beckons to him.

MORAYMA: Come a little nearer and speak softly.

ANTONIO: I come, I come I warrant thee; the least twinckle had brought me to thee; such another kind syllable or two, wou'd turn me to a Meteor and draw me up to thee.

MORAYMA: I dare not speak, for fear of being over-heard; but if you think my Person worth your hazard, and can deserve my love—the rest this Note shall tell you—[*throws down a handkerchief*]. No more, my heart goes with you.

Exit from the Grate.

ANTONIO: O thou pretty little heart; art thou flown hither, I'll keep it warm I warrant it, and brood upon it in the new nest: but now for my Treasure trove, that's wrapt up in the handkerchief: No peeping here, though I long to be spelling her Arabick scrawls and pot-hooks. But I must carry off my prize, as Robbers do; and not think of sharing the booty, before I am free from danger, and out of eye-shot from the other Windows. If her wit be as poygnant as her Eyes, I am a double Slave. Our Northern Beauties are meer dough to these: Insipid white Earth, meer Tobacco-pipe-clay; With no more Soul and Motion in 'em, than a Fly in Winter.

Here the warm Planet ripens, and sublimes
The well bak'd Beauties of the Southern Climes;
Our Cupid's but a bungler in his Trade;
His keenest Arrows are in *Affrick* made.

[*Exit* ANTONIO.

ACT III

SCENE 1.

A Terrace-walk; or some other publick place in the Castle of Alcazar.

Emperor MULEY-MOLUCH; BENDUCAR.

EMPEROR: Marry'd! I'll not believe it; 'tis imposture;
Improbable they shou'd presume t' attempt,
Impossible they shou'd effect their wish.
BENDUCAR: Have patience till I clear it.
EMPEROR: I have none:
Go bid our moving Plains of Sand lye still,
And stir not, when the stormy South blows high:
From top to bottom thou hast toss'd my Soul,
And now 'tis in the madness of the Whirl,
Requir'st a sudden stop? unsay thy lye,
That may in time do somewhat.
BENDUCAR: I have done:
For, since it pleases you it shou'd be forg'd,
'Tis fit it shou'd: far be it from your Slave,
To raise disturbance in your Sacred brest.
EMPEROR: *Sebastian* is my Slave as well as thou;
Nor durst offend my love by that presumption.
BENDUCAR: Most sure he ought not.
EMPEROR: Then all means were wanting;
No Priest, no Ceremonies of their Sect;
Or, grant we these defects cou'd be supply'd,
How cou'd our Prophet do an Act so base,
So to resume his gifts, and curse my Conquests
By making me unhappy! No, the Slave
That told thee so absurd a story, ly'd.
BENDUCAR: Yet, till this moment I have found him faithful:
He said he saw it too.
EMPEROR: Dispatch; what saw he?
BENDUCAR: Truth is, considering with what earnestness,
Sebastian pleaded for *Almeyda*'s life,
Inhanc'd her beauty, dwelt upon her praise,——
EMPEROR: O stupid, and unthinking as I was!
I might have mark'd it too: 'twas gross and palpable!
BENDUCAR: Methought I trac'd a Lover ill disguis'd;
And sent my spy, a sharp observing Slave,

T' inform me better, if I guess'd aright.
He told me, that he saw *Sebastians* Page
Run cross the Marble Square; who soon return'd,
And after him there lag'd a puffing Fryar;
Close wrap'd he bore some secret Instrument
Of Christian Superstition in his hand:
My servant follow'd fast, and through a chink
Perceiv'd the Royal Captives hand in hand:
And heard the hooded Father mumbling charms,
That make those Misbelievers Man and Wife.
Which done, the Spouses kiss'd with such a fervour,
And gave such furious earnest of their flames,
That their eyes sparkled, and their mantling blood
Flew flushing o'er their faces.

EMPEROR: Hell confound 'em!

BENDUCAR: The Reverend Father, with a Holy leer,
Saw he might well be spar'd, and soon withdrew:
This forc'd my Servant to a quick retreat,
For fear to be discover'd; guess the rest.

EMPEROR: I do. My fancy is too exquisite,
And tortures me with their imagin'd bliss.
Some Earthquake shou'd have ris'n, and rent the ground,
Have swallow'd him, and left the longing Bride,
In Agony of unaccomplish'd Love. [*Walks disorderly.*

Enter the MUFTI.

BENDUCAR: In an unlucky hour [*Aside.*
That Fool intrudes, raw in this great affair,
And uninstructed how to stem the tide.

Coming up to the MUFTI, *aside.*

The Emp'ror must not marry, nor enjoy;
Keep to that point; Stand firm, for all's at stake.

EMPEROR *seeing him*: You, Druggerman of Heaven, must I attend
Your droaning Prayers? Why came you not before?
Do'st thou not know the Captive King has dar'd
To wed *Almeyda?* Cancel me that Marriage,
And make her mine; About the business, quick,
Expound thy *Mahomet*; make him speak my sense,
Or he's no Prophet here, and thou no *Mufti*,
Unless thou know'st the trick of thy vocation,
To wrest and rend the Law to please thy Prince.

MUFTI: Why, verily the Law is monstrous plain:
There's not one doubtful Text in all the Alchoran,
Which can be wrench'd in favor to your Project.

EMPEROR: Forge one, and foist it into some by-place,
Of some old rotten Roll; do't, I command thee:
Must I teach thee thy Trade?

MUFTI: It cannot be.
For Matrimony being the dearest point
Of Law, the People have it all by heart:
A Cheat on Procreation will not pass.
Besides th' offence is so exorbitant, [*In a higher tone.*
To mingle with a misbelieving Race,
That speedy Vengeance wou'd pursue your Crime,
And holy *Mahomet* launch himself from Heav'n,
Before th' unready Thunderbolt were form'd.

EMPEROR *taking him by the Throat with one hand, snatches out his Sword with the other, and points it to his Brest.*

EMPEROR: Slave, have I rais'd thee to this pomp and pow'r,
To preach against my Will? Know I am Law;
And thou, not *Mahomet*'s Messenger, but mine:
Make it, I charge thee, make my pleasure lawful:
Or first I strip thee of thy ghostly greatness,
Then send thee post, to tell thy Tale above;
And bring thy vain Memorials to thy Prophet
Of Justice done below for Disobedience.

MUFTI: For Heaven's sake hold, the respite of a moment,——
To think for you——

EMPEROR: And for thy self.——

MUFTI: For both.

BENDUCAR: Disgrace, and Death, and Avarice have lost him!
[*Aside.*

MUFTI: 'Tis true, our Law forbids to wed a Christian;
But it forbids you not to ravish her.
You have a Conqueror's right upon your Slave;
And then, the more despight you do a Christian,
You serve the Prophet more who loaths that Sect.

EMPEROR: Oh now it mends; and you talk reason, *Mufti.*
But stay! I promis'd freedom to *Sebastian*:
Now shou'd I grant it, his revengeful Soul
Wou'd ne'er forgive his violated Bed.

MUFTI: Kill him, for then you give him liberty:

His Soul is from his earthly Prison freed.

EMPEROR: How happy is the Prince who has a Churchman
So learn'd and pliant to expound his Laws!

BENDUCAR: Two things I humbly offer to your prudence.

EMPEROR: Be brief; but let not either thwart my love.

BENDUCAR: First, since our holy Man has made Rape lawful,
Fright her with that: proceed not yet to force:
Why shou'd you pluck the green distastful Fruit
From the unwilling Bough,
When it may ripen of it self and fall?

EMPEROR: Grant her a day; tho' that's too much to give
Out of a Life which I devote to Love.

BENDUCAR: Then next, to bar
All future hopes of her desir'd *Sebastian*,
Let *Dorax* be enjoyn'd to bring his head.

EMPEROR *to the* MUFTI: Go *Mufti*, call him to receive his Orders.
[*Exit* MUFTI.

I taste thy Counsel, her desire new rowz'd,
And yet unslak'd, will kindle in her fancy,
And make her eager to renew the Feast.

BENDUCAR *aside*: *Dorax*, I know before, will disobey:
There's a Foe's Head well cropt.—
But this hot love precipates my Plot;
And brings it to projection ere its time.

Enter SEBASTIAN *and* ALMEYDA *hand in hand; upon sight of the* EMPEROR, *they separate and seem disturb'd.*

ALMEYDA: He breaks, at unawares, upon our Walks,
And like a mid-night Wolf invades the Fold:
Make speedy preparation of your Soul,
And bid it arm apace: He comes for answer,
And brutal mischief sits upon his brow.

SEBASTIAN: Not the last sounding, cou'd surprize me more,
That summons drowzy Mortals to their doom,
When call'd in haste, they fumble for their Limbs,
And tremble unprovided for their charge:
My sense has been so deeply plung'd in Joys,
The Soul out-slept her hour; and, scarce awake,
Wou'd think too late, and cannot! But brave Minds
At worst can dare their Fate.——
[EMPEROR *coming up to them.*

EMPEROR: Have you perform'd
Your Embassy, and treated with success?
SEBASTIAN: I had not time.
EMPEROR: No, not for my Affairs,
But for your own too much.
SEBASTIAN: You talk in Clouds, explain your meaning, Sir.
EMPEROR: Explain yours first: What meant you hand in hand,
And when you saw me, with a guilty start,
You loos'd your hold, affrighted at my presence?
SEBASTIAN: Affrighted?
EMPEROR: Yes, astonish'd, and confounded.
SEBASTIAN: What mak'st thou of thy self, and what of me?
Art thou some Ghost, some Demon, or some God,
That I shou'd stand astonish'd at thy sight?
If thou cou'dst deem so meanly of my Courage,
Why didst thou not engage me man for man,
And try the virtue of that *Gorgon* Face,
To stare me into statue?
EMPEROR: Oh, thou art now recover'd, but by Heav'n,
Thou wert amaz'd at first, as if surpriz'd
At unexpected baseness brought to light.
For know, ungrateful man, that Kings, like Gods,
Are every where; walk in th' abyss of minds,
And view the dark recesses of the Soul.
SEBASTIAN: Base and ungrateful never was I thought;
Nor till this turn of fate, durst thou have call'd me;
But, since thou boast'st the omniscience of a God,
Say, in what cranny of *Sebastian*'s Soul,
Unknown to me, so loath'd a Crime is lodg'd?
EMPEROR: Thou hast not broke my trust repos'd in thee?
SEBASTIAN: Impos'd, but not receiv'd: Take back that falsehood.
EMPEROR: Thou art not marry'd to *Almeyda?*
SEBASTIAN: Yes.
EMPEROR: And own'st the usurpation of my Love?
SEBASTIAN: I own it in the face of Heav'n and Thee
No Usurpation; but a lawful claim,
Of which I stand possest.
EMPEROR: Sh' has chosen well,
Betwixt a Captive and a Conqueror.
ALMEYDA: Betwixt a Monster and the best of Men.
He was the envy of his neighb'ring Kings;
For him their sighing Queens despis'd their Lords,
And Virgin Daughters blush'd when he was nam'd.

To share his noble Chains is more to me,
Than all the salvage greatness of thy Throne.

SEBASTIAN: Were I to choose again, and knew my fate,
For such a night I wou'd be what I am.
The Joys I have possest are ever mine;
Out of thy reach behind Eternity;
Hid in the sacred treasure of the past;
But bless'd remembrance bring's 'em hourly back.

EMPEROR: Hourly indeed, who hast but hours to live:
O mighty purchase of a boasted bliss!
To dream of what thou hadst one fugitive night,
And never shalt have more.

SEBASTIAN: Barbarian, thou canst part us but a moment;——
We shall be one again in thy despight:
Life is but air,
That yields a passage to the whistling Sword,
And closes when 'tis gone.

ALMEYDA: How can we better dye than close embrac'd,
Sucking each others Souls while we expire?
Which so transfus'd, and mounting both at once,
The Saints deceiv'd, shall by a sweet mistake,
Hand up thy Soul for mine, and mine for thine.

EMPEROR: No, I'll untwist you:
I have occasion for your stay on earth:
Let him mount first, and beat upon the Wing,
And wait an Age for what I here detain.
Or sicken at immortal Joys above,
And languish for the Heav'n he left below.

ALMEYDA: Thou wilt not dare to break what Heav'n has joyn'd?

EMPEROR: Not break the Chain, but change a rotten link,
And rivet one to last.
Think'st thou I come to argue right and wrong?
Why lingers *Dorax* thus? Where are my Guards,

[BENDUCAR *goes out for the guards, and returns.*

To drag that Slave to death? [*Pointing to* SEBASTIAN.
Now storm and rage,
Call vainly on thy Prophet, then defie him
For wanting power to save thee.

SEBASTIAN: That were to gratifie thy Pride: I'll shew thee
How a Man shou'd, and how a King dare dye:
So even, that my Soul shall walk with ease
Out of its flesh, and shut out Life as calmly

As it does words; without a sigh, to note
One struggle in the smooth dissolving frame.

ALMEYDA *to the* EMPEROR: Expect revenge from Heav'n, inhuman Wretch;
Nor hope t' ascend *Sebastian*'s holy Bed.
Flames, Daggers, Poysons, guard the sacred steps:
Those are the promis'd Pleasures of my love.

EMPEROR: And these might fright another, but not me.
Or me, if I design'd to give you pleasure;
I seek my own, and while that lasts, you live.

Enter two of the Guards.

Go, bear the Captive to a speedy death,
And set my Soul at ease.

ALMEYDA: I charge you hold, ye Ministers of death,
Speak my *Sebastian*;
Plead for thy life: Oh ask it of the Tyrant;
'Tis no dishonor, trust me, Love, 'tis none:
I wou'd die for thee, but I cannot plead;
My haughty heart disdains it, ev'n for thee.
Still silent! Will the King of *Portugal*
Go to his death, like a dumb Sacrifice?
Beg him to save my life in saving thine.

SEBASTIAN: Farewel, my life's not worth another word.

EMPEROR *to the Guards*: Perform your Orders.

ALMEYDA: Stay, take my farewel too:
Farewel the greatness of *Almeyda*'s Soul!—
Look, Tyrant, what excess of love can do,
It pulls me down thus low, as to thy feet; [*Kneels to him.*
Nay to embrace thy Knees with loathing hands,
Which blister when they touch thee: Yet ev'n thus,
Thus far I can to save *Sebastian*'s life.

EMPEROR: A secret pleasure trickles through my Veins:
It works about the inlets of my Soul,
To feel thy touch; and pity tempts the pass;
But the tough metal of my heart resists;
'Tis warm'd with the soft fire, not melted down.

ALMEYDA: A flood of scalding Tears will make it run,
Spare him, Oh spare; can you pretend to love,
And have no pity? Love and that are Twins.
Here will I grow;
Thus compass you with these supplanting Cords,

And pull so long till the proud Fabrick falls.
EMPEROR: Still kneel, and still embrace; 'tis double pleasure,
So to be hugg'd, and see *Sebastian* dye.
ALMEYDA: Look Tyrant, when thou nam'st *Sebastian*'s death,
Thy very Executioners turn pale.
Rough as they are, and harden'd in the trade
Of Death, they start at an anointed Head,
And tremble to approach:—He hears me not;
Nor minds th' impression of a God on Kings;
Because no stamp of Heav'n was on his Soul:
But the resisting Mass drove back the Seal.
Say, though thy heart be rock of Adamant,
Yet Rocks are not impregnable to Bribes:
Instruct me how to bribe thee: Name thy price;
Lo, I resign my Title to the Crown;
Send me to exile with the Man I love,
And banishment is Empire.
EMPEROR: Here's my claim; [*Clapping his hand to his Sword.*
And this extinguish'd thine; thou giv'st me nothing.
ALMEYDA: My Father's, Mother's, Brothers death I pardon:
That's somewhat sure; a mighty Sum of Murther,
Of innocent and kindred blood stroock off.
My Prayers and Penance shall discount for these,
And beg of Heav'n to charge the Bill on me:
Behold what price I offer, and how dear
To buy *Sebastian*'s life.
EMPEROR: Let after reck'nings trouble fearful fools;
I'll stand the tryal of those trivial Crimes:
But, since thou beg'st me to prescribe my terms,
The only I can offer are thy love;
And this one day of respite to resolve.
Grant or deny, for thy next word is Fate;
And fate is deaf to Pray'r.
ALMEYDA: May Heav'n be so [*Rising up.*
At thy last breath to thine: I curse thee not,
For who can better curse the Plague or Devil,
Than to be what they are? That Curse be thine.
Now, do not speak *Sebastian*, for you need not,
But dye, for I resign your Life: Look Heav'n,
Almeyda dooms her dear *Sebastian*'s death!
But is there Heav'n, for I begin to doubt;
The Skyes are hush'd; no grumbling Thunders roul:
Now take your swing, ye impious; Sin unpunish'd;

Eternal providence seems overwatch'd,
And with a slumb'ring Nod assents to Murther.

Enter DORAX *attended by three Soldiers.*

EMPEROR: Thou mov'st a Tortoise pace to my relief.
Take hence that, once a King; that sullen pride
That swells to dumbness; lay him in the Dungeon,
And sink him deep with Irons, that when he wou'd,
He shall not groan to hearing, when I send
The next Commands are death.

ALMEYDA: Then Prayers are vain as Curses.

EMPEROR: Much at one
In a Slaves mouth, against a Monarch's Pow'r.
This day thou hast to think;
At night, if thou wilt curse, thou shalt curse kindly;
Then I'll provoke thy lips; lay siege so close,
That all thy sallying breath shall turn to Blessings.
Make haste, seize, force her, bear her hence.

ALMEYDA: Farewel, my last *Sebastian!*
I do not beg, I challenge Justice now;
O Pow'rs, if Kings be your peculiar care,
Why plays this Wretch with your Prerogative?
Now flash him dead, now crumble him to ashes;
Or henceforth live confin'd in your own Palace;
And look not idely out upon a World
That is no longer yours.

She is carried off strugling, EMPEROUR *and* BENDUCAR *follow.* SEBASTIAN *struggles in his Guards Arms, and shakes off one of them, but two others come in, and hold him; he speaks not all the while.*

DORAX: I find I'm but a half-strain'd Villain yet;
But mungril-mischievous; for my Blood boyl'd,
To view this brutal act; and my stern Soul
Tug'd at my arm to draw in her defence. [*Aside.*
Down thou rebelling Christian in my heart;
Redeem thy fame on this *Sebastian* first;
Then think on other wrongs, when thine are righted.
[*Walks a turn.*
But how to right 'em? on a Slave disarm'd,
Defenceless, and submitted to my rage?
A base revenge is vengeance on my self? [*Walks again.*

I have it; and I thank thee, honest head,
Thus present to me at my great necessity:—
[*Comes up to* SEBASTIAN.
You know me not?
SEBASTIAN: I hear men call thee *Dorax.*
DORAX: 'Tis well, you know enough for once: you speak too;
You were struck mute before.
SEBASTIAN: Silence became me then.
DORAX: Yet we may talk hereafter.
SEBASTIAN: Hereafter is not mine:——
Dispatch thy work, good Executioner.
DORAX: None of my blood were hangmen; add that falshood
To a long Bill, that yet remains unreckon'd.
SEBASTIAN: A King and thou can never have a reck'ning.
DORAX: A greater summ perhaps than you can pay.
Mean time I shall make bold t' increase your debt,
[*gives him his Sword.*
Take this, and use it at your greatest need.
SEBASTIAN: This hand and this, have been acquainted well;
[*Looks on it.*]
It shou'd have come before into my grasp,
To kill the Ravisher.
DORAX: Thou heardst the Tyrants orders; Guard thy life
When 'tis attack'd, and guard it like a man.
SEBASTIAN: I'm still without thy meaning but I thank thee.
DORAX: Thank me when I ask thanks; thank me with that.
SEBASTIAN: Such surly kindness did I never see!
DORAX *to the Captain of his Guards*: *Muza*, draw out a file, pick man by man,
Such who dare dye, and dear will sell their death.
Guard him to th' utmost; now conduct him hence,
And treat him as my Person.
SEBASTIAN: Something like
That voice methinks I shou'd have somewhere heard:
But floods of woes have hurry'd it far off;
Beyond my kenn of Soul.
[*Exit* SEBASTIAN, *with the Soldiers.*
DORAX: But I shall bring him back ungrateful Man,
I shall, and set him full before thy sight,
When I shall front thee, like some staring Ghost,
With all my wrongs about me.—What so soon
Return'd? this hast is boding.

Enter to him EMPEROR, BENDUCAR, *and* MUFTI.

EMPEROR: She's still inexorable, still Imperious;
And loud, as if like *Bacchus* born in thunder.
Be quick, ye false Physicians of my mind,
Bring speedy Death or Cure.
BENDUCAR: What can be counsell'd while *Sebastian* lives?
The Vine will cling, while the tall poplar stands:
But that cut down creeps to the next support,
And twines as closely there.
EMPEROR: That's done with ease, I speak him dead: proceed.
MUFTI: Proclaim your Marriage with *Almeyda* next,
That Civil Wars may cease; this gains the Crowd;
Then you may safely force her to your will:
For People side with violence and injustice,
When done for publick good.
EMPEROR: Preach thou that doctrine.
BENDUCAR: Th' unreasonable fool has broach'd a truth [*Aside.*
That blasts my hopes; but since, tis gone so far,
He shall divulge *Almeyda* is a Christian:
If that produce no tumult I despair.
EMPEROR: Why speaks not *Dorax*?
DORAX: Because my Soul abhors to mix with him. [*Aside.*
Sir, let me bluntly say, you went too far
To trust the Preaching pow'r on State Affairs,
To him or any Heavenly Demagogue.
'Tis a limb lopt from your Prerogative,
And so much of Heav'ns Image blotted from you.
MUFTI: Sure thou hast never heard of Holy Men
(So Christians call 'em) fam'd in State Affairs;
Such as in *Spain Ximenes Albornoz*,
In *England Woolsey*; match me these with Laymen.
DORAX: How you triumph in one or two of these,
Born to be Statesmen, hap'ning to be Church-men:
Thou callst 'em holy; so their function was;
But tell me, *Mufti*, which of 'em were Saints?
Next, Sir, to you; the summ of all is this;
Since he claims pow'r from Heav'n, and not from Kings,
When 'tis his int'rest, he can int'rest Heav'n
To preach you down; and Ages oft depend
On hours, uninterrupted, in the Chair.
EMPEROR: I'll trust his Preaching while I rule his pay.

And I dare trust my *Affricans*, to hear
Whatever he dare Preach.

DORAX: You know 'em not.
The genius of your Moors is mutiny;
They scarcely want a Guide to move their madness:
Prompt to rebel on every weak pretence,
Blustring when courted, crouching when opprest.
Wise to themselves, and fools to all the World,
Restless in change, and perjur'd to a Proverb,
They love Religion sweeten'd to the sense;
A good, luxurious, palatable faith.
Thus Vice and Godliness, prepost'rous pair,
Ride cheek by joul; but Churchmen hold the Reins.
And, when ere Kings wou'd lower Clergy greatness,
They learn too late what pow'r the Preachers have,
And whose the Subjects are; the *Mufti* knows it;
Nor dares deny what pass'd betwixt us two.

EMPEROR: No more; what ere he said was by Command.

DORAX: Why then no more, since you will hear no more;
Some Kings are resolute to their own ruin.

EMPEROR: Without your medling where you are not ask'd,
Obey your Orders, and dispatch *Sebastian*.

DORAX: Trust my revenge; be sure I wish him dead.

EMPEROR: What mean'st thou! What's thy wishing to my will;
Dispatch him, rid me of the Man I loath.

DORAX: I hear you Sir; I'll take my time and do't——

EMPEROR: Thy time? what's all thy time, what's thy whole life
To my one hour of ease? no more replies,
But see thou do'st it; Or——

DORAX: Choak in that threat: I can say Or, as loud.

EMPEROR: 'Tis well, I see my words have no effect,
But I may send a Message to dispose you. [*Is going off.*

DORAX: Expect an answer worthy of that Message.

MUFTI: The prophet ow'd him this: [*Aside.*
And thank'd be Heav'n, he has it.

BENDUCAR: By Holy Alha, I conjure you stay,
And judge not rashly of so brave a Man.
[*Draws the* EMPEROR *aside and whispers him.*]
I'll give you reasons why he cannot execute
Your Orders now, and why he will hereafter.

MUFTI: *Benducar* is a fool to bring him off, [*Aside.*
I'll work my own revenge, and speedily.

BENDUCAR: The Fort is his, the Soldiers hearts are his;

A thousand Christian Slaves are in the Castle,
Which he can free to reinforce his pow'r;
Your Troops far off, beleaguering *Larache*,
Yet in the Christians hands.

EMPEROR: I grant all this;
But grant me he must dye.

BENDUCAR: He shall; by poyson:
'Tis here, the deadly drug prepar'd in powder,
Hot as Hell fire:—then, to prevent his Soldiers
From rising to revenge their Gen'rals death,
While he is struggling with his Mortal pangs,
The Rabble on the sudden may be rais'd
To seize the Castle.

EMPEROR: Do't; 'tis left to thee.

BENDUCAR: Yet more; but clear your brow; for he observes.

[*They whisper again.*

DORAX: What will the Fav'rite prop my falling fortunes,
O prodigie of Court! [*Aside.*

EMPEROR *and* BENDUCAR *return to* DORAX.

EMPEROR: Your Friend has fully clear'd your Innocence;
I was too hasty to condemn unheard,
And you perhaps too prompt in your replies.
As far as fits the Majesty of Kings,
I ask excuse.

DORAX: I'm sure I meant it well.

EMPEROR: I know you did:—this to our love renew'd.—

[*Emperor drinks.*

Benducar, fill to *Dorax*.

[BENDUCAR *turns and mixes a powder in it.*

DORAX: Let it go round for all of us have need
To quench our heats; 'tis the kings health *Benducar*,

[*He drinks.*

And I wou'd pledge it though I knew 'twere poyson.

BENDUCAR: Another Bowl, for what the King has touch'd,

[*Drinks out of another Bowl.*

And you have pledg'd, is sacred to your loves.—

MUFTI: Since Charity becomes my calling, thus
Let me provoke your friendship: and heav'n bless it
As I intend it well.——

[*Drinks; and turning aside pours some drops out of a little Vial into the Bowl; then presents it to* DORAX.

DORAX: Heav'n make thee honest,
    On that condition we shall soon be friends. [*Drinks.*

MUFTI: Yes, at our meeting in another World; [*Aside.*
    For thou hast drunk thy passport out of this.
    Not the Nonacrian fount, nor Lethe's Lake,
    Cou'd sooner numb thy nimble faculties
    Then this, to sleep eternal.

EMPEROR: Now farewel *Dorax*; this was our first quarrel,
    And I dare prophecie will prove our last.

[*Exit* EMPEROR *with* BENDUCAR *and the* MUFTI.

DORAX: It may be so: I'm strangely discompos'd;
    Quick shootings through my limbs, and pricking pains,
    Qualms at my heart, Convulsions in my nerves,
    Shiv'rings of cold, and burnings of my entrails
    Within my little World make medley War,
    Lose and regain, beat and are beaten back;
    As momentary Victors quit their ground.
    Can it be poyson! Poyson's of one tenour,
    Or hot, or cold; this neither, and yet both.
    Some deadly Draught, some enemy of life
    Boils in my Bowels, and works out my Soul.
    Ingratitude's the growth of ev'ry Clime;
    Affrick, the Scene remov'd, is *Portugal.*
    Of all Court-service learn the common lot;
    To-day 'tis done, to-morrow 'tis forgot.
    Oh were that all! my honest Corps must lye
    Expos'd to scorn, and publick Infamy:
    My shameful Death will be divulg'd alone;
    The worth and honour of my Soul unknown. [*Exit.*

SCENE 2.

A Night Scene of the MUFTI'*s Garden where an Arbour is discover'd.*

Enter ANTONIO.

ANTONIO: She names herself *Morayma*; the *Mufti*'s only Daughter, and a Virgin! This is the time and place that she appointed in her letter, yet she comes not. Why thou sweet delicious Creature, why so torture me with thy delay! dar'st thou be false to thy Assignation? What, in the cool and silence of the night, and to a new Lover? Pox on the Hypocrite thy Father, for instructing thee so little in the sweetest point of his Religion. Hark, I hear the rustling of her Silk Mantle. Now she comes; now she comes; no, hang't, that was but the whistling of the wind through the *Orange* Trees. Now again, I hear the pit a pat of a pretty foot through the dark Alley: No, 'tis the Son of a Mare that's broken loose and munching upon the Melons:—Oh the misery of an expecting Lover! Well I'll e'en despair, go into my Arbour, and try to sleep; in a dream I shall enjoy her in despight of her. [*Goes into the Arbour and lyes down.*

Enter JOHAYMA *wrapt up in a Moorish Mantle.*

JOHAYMA: Thus far my love has carry'd me, almost without my knowledg whither I was going: Shall I go on, shall I discover my self!—What an injury am I doing to my old Husband!—Yet what injury, since he's old, and has three Wives and six Concubines besides me! 'Tis but stealing my own Tythe from him. [*She comes a little nearer the Arbour.*

ANTONIO *raising himself a little and looking*: At last 'tis she: this is no illusion I am sure; 'tis a true She-devil of Flesh and Blood; and she cou'd never have taken a fitter time to tempt me.—

JOHAYMA: He's young and handsome.——

ANTONIO: Yes, well enough I thank nature. [*Aside.*

JOHAYMA: And I am yet neither old nor ugly: sure he will not refuse me.

ANTONIO: No, thou mayst pawn thy Maiden-head upon't he wonnot. [*Aside.*

JOHAYMA: The *Mufti* wou'd feast himself upon other Women, and keep me fasting.

ANTONIO: O, the holy Curmudgeon! [*Aside.*

JOHAYMA: Wou'd Preach abstinence, and practise luxury! but I thank my Stars, I have edify'd more by his example than his precept.

ANTONIO: Most divinely argu'd; she's the best Casuist in all *Affrick.* [*Aside.*

He rushes out and embraces her.

I can hold no longer from embracing thee my dear *Morayma*: the old unconscionable Whorson thy Father, cou'd he expect cold chastity from a Child of his begetting?

JOHAYMA: What nonsense do you talk? do you take me for the *Mufti*'s Daughter?

ANTONIO: Why are you not Madam? [*throwing off her* Barnus.

JOHAYMA: I find you had an appointment with *Morayma.*

ANTONIO: By all that's good, the nauseous Wife. [*Aside.*

JOHAYMA: What you are confounded and stand mute?

ANTONIO: Somewhat nonplust I confess; to hear you deny your name so positively; why, are not you *Morayma* the *Mufti*'s Daughter? Did not I see you with him, did not he present me to you? Were you not so charitable as to give me Money? Ay and to tread upon my foot, and squeeze my hand too, if I may be so bold to remember you of past favours.

JOHAYMA: And you see I am come to make 'em good, but I am neither *Morayma* nor the *Mufti*'s Daughter.

ANTONIO: Nay, I know not that: but I am sure he is old enough to be your Father: and either Father, or Reverend Father, I heard you call him.

JOHAYMA: Once again, how came you to name *Morayma?*

ANTONIO: Another damn'd mistake of mine: For, asking one of my fellow Slaves, who were the chief Ladies about the house, he answer'd me *Morayma* and *Johayma*; but she it seems is his Daughter, with a Pox to her, and you are his beloved wife.

JOHAYMA: Say your beloved Mistris, if you please; for that's the Title I desire. This Moon-shine grows offensive to my Eyes, come, shall we walk into the Arbor? there we may rectifie all mistakes.

ANTONIO: That's close and dark.

JOHAYMA: And are those faults to Lovers?

ANTONIO: But there I cannot please my self, with the sight of your beauty.

JOHAYMA: Perhaps you may do better.

ANTONIO: But there's not a breath of air stirring.

JOHAYMA: The breath of Lovers is the sweetest air; but you are fearful.

ANTONIO: I am considering, indeed, that if I am taken with you——

JOHAYMA: The best way to avoid it, is to retire, where we may not be discover'd.

ANTONIO: Where lodges your Husband?

JOHAYMA: Just against the face of this open Walk.

ANTONIO: Then he has seen us already, for ought I know.

JOHAYMA: You make so many Difficulties, I fear I am displeasing to you.

ANTONIO *aside*: If *Morayma* comes and takes me in the arbor with her, I have made a fine exchange of that Diamond for this Pebble.

JOHAYMA: You are much fall'n off, let me tell you, from the fury of your first embrace.

ANTONIO: I confess, I was somewhat too furious at first, but you will forgive the transport of my passion; now I have consider'd it better, I have a qualm of Conscience.

JOHAYMA: Of Conscience! Why, what has Conscience to do with two young Lovers that have opportunity?

ANTONIO: Why truly Conscience is something to blame for interposing in our matters: But how can I help it, if I have a Scruple to betray my Master?

JOHAYMA: There must be something more in it; for your Conscience was very quiet when you took me for *Morayma.*

ANTONIO: I grant you, Madam, when I took you for his Daughter: For then I might have made you an honourable amends by Marriage.

JOHAYMA: You Christians are such peeking Sinners, you tremble at a Shadow in the Moon-shine.

ANTONIO: And you Affricans are such Termagants, you stop at nothing. I must be plain with you, you are married, and to a Holy Man, the Head of your Religion: Go back to your Chamber, go back, I say, and consider of it for this night; as I will do on my part: I will be true to you, and invent all the Arguments I can to comply with you; and who knows, but at our next meeting, the sweet Devil may have more power over me : I am true flesh and blood, I can tell you that for your comfort.

JOHAYMA: Flesh without blood, I think thou art; or if any, 'tis as cold as that of Fishes. But I'll teach thee, to thy cost, what Vengeance is in store for refusing a Lady, who has offer'd thee her Love:—Help, Help, there; will nobody come to my assistance?

ANTONIO: What do you mean, Madam, for Heaven's sake peace; your Husband will hear you; think of your own danger, if you will not think of mine.

JOHAYMA: Ingrateful Wretch, thou deserv'st no pity: Help, Help, Husband, or I shall be ravish'd: The Villain will be too strong for me. Help, help, for pity of a poor distressed Creature.

ANTONIO: Then I have nothing but impudence to assist me: I must drown her clamor whate'er comes on't.

He takes out his Flute, and plays as loud as he possibly can, and she continues crying out.

Enter the MUFTI *in his Night-gown, and two Servants.*

MUFTI: O thou Villain, what horrible impiety art thou committing? What ravishing the Wife of my Bosom? Take him away, ganch him, impale him, rid the World of such a Monster. [*Servants seize him.*

ANTONIO: Mercy, dear Master, Mercy: Hear me first, and after, if I have deserved hanging, spare me not: What have you seen to provoke you to this cruelty?

MUFTI: I have heard the out-crys of my Wife; the bleatings of the poor innocent Lamb: Seen nothing, say'st thou? If I see the Lamb lye bleeding, and the Butcher by her with his Knife drawn and bloody, is not that evidence sufficient of the Murther? I come too late, and the Execution is already done.

ANTONIO: Pray think in reason, Sir, is a Man to be put to death for a similitude? No Violence has been committed; none intended: The Lamb's alive; and if I durst tell you so, no more a Lamb than I am a Butcher.

JOHAYMA: How's that, Villain, dar'st thou accuse me?

ANTONIO: Be patient Madam, and speak but truth, and I'll do any thing to serve you: I say again, and swear it too, I'll do any thing to serve you.

JOHAYMA *aside*: I understand him; but I fear, 'tis now too late to save him:—Pray hear him speak, Husband; perhaps he may say something for himself; I know not.

MUFTI: Speak thou, has he not violated my Bed and thy Honor?

JOHAYMA: I forgive him freely; for he has done nothing: What he will do hereafter, to make me satisfaction, himself best knows.

ANTONIO: Any thing, any thing, sweet Madam: I shall refuse no drudgery.

MUFTI: But, did he mean no mischief? Was he endeavouring nothing?

JOHAYMA: In my Conscience, I begin to doubt he did not.

MUFTI: 'Ts impossible: Then what meant all those out crys?

JOHAYMA: I heard Musick in the Garden, and at an unseasonable time of night; and I stole softly out of my Bed, as imagining it might be he.

MUFTI: How's that *Johayma?* Imagining it was he, and yet you went?

JOHAYMA: Why not, my Lord? Am not I the Mistris of the Family? And is it not my place to see good Orders kept in it? I thought he might have allur'd some of the Shee-slaves to him; and was resolv'd to prevent what might have been betwixt him and them; when on the sudden he rush'd out upon me, caught me in his arms, with such a fury.——

MUFTI: I have heard enough, away with him.——

JOHAYMA: Mistaking me, no doubt, for one of his fellow Slaves: With that, affrighted as I was, I discover'd my self, and cry'd aloud: But as soon as ever he knew me, the Villain let me go, and I must needs say, he started back, as if I were some Serpent; and was more afraid of me than I of him.

MUFTI: O thou corrupter of my Family, that's cause enough of death; once again, away with him.

JOHAYMA: What, for an intended Trespass? No harm has been done, whatever may be. He cost you five hundred Crowns, I take it.——

MUFTI: Thou say'st true, a very considerable Sum: He shall not dye, tho he had committed folly with a Slave; 'tis too much to lose by him.

ANTONIO: My only fault has ever been to love playing in the dark, and the more she cry'd, the more I play'd; that it might be seen I intended nothing to her.

MUFTI: To your Kennel, Sirrah, mortifie your flesh, and consider in whose Family you are.

JOHAYMA: And one thing more; remember from henceforth to obey better.

MUFTI *aside*: For all her smoothness, I am not quite cur'd of my Jealousie; but I have thought of a way that will clear my doubts. [*Exit* MUFTI *with* JOHAYMA *and Servants.*

ANTONIO: I am mortify'd sufficiently already, without the help of his ghostly Counsel. Fear of Death has gone farther with me in two Minutes, than my Conscience wou'd have gone in two Months. I find my self in a very dejected condition, all over me; poor Sin lies dormant, Concupiscence is retir'd to his winter quarters; and if *Morayma* shou'd now appear, I say no more, but alas for her and me!

MORAYMA *comes out of the Arbour; she steals behind him, and claps him on the back.*

MORAYMA: And if *Morayma* shou'd appear, as she does appear, alas you say for her and you!

ANTONIO: Art thou there, my sweet temptation! my Eyes, my Life, my Soul, my all!

MORAYMA: A mighty Complement, when all these, by your own Confession, are just nothing.

ANTONIO: Nothing, till thou cam'st to new create me; thou dost not know the power of thy own Charms: let me embrace thee, and thou shalt see how quickly I can turn wicked.

MORAYMA *stepping back*: Nay, if you are so dangerous, 'tis best keeping you at a distance; I have no mind to warm a frozen Snake in my bosom; he may chance to recover, and sting me for my pains.

ANTONIO: Consider what I have suffer'd for thy sake already; and make me some amends: two disappointments in a night, O cruel Creature!

MORAYMA: And you may thank your self for both: I came eagerly to the Charge, before my time, through the back walk behind the Arbour; and you, like a fresh-water Soldier, stood guarding the Pass before: If you miss'd the Enemy, you may thank your own dulness.

ANTONIO: Nay, if you will be using stratagems, you shall give me leave to make use of my advantages, now I have you in my power: we are fairly met; I'll try it out, and give no quarter.

MORAYMA: By your favour, Sir, we meet upon treaty now, and not upon defiance.

ANTONIO: If that be all, you shall have *Carte blanche* immediately; for I long to be ratifying.

MORAYMA: No, now I think on't, you are already enter'd into Articles with my Enemy *Johayma*: Any thing to serve you Madam; I shall refuse no drudgery: whose words were those, Gentleman? was that like a Cavalier of honour?

ANTONIO: Not very heroick; but self preservation is a point above Honour and Religion too—*Antonio* was a Rogue I must confess; but you must give me leave to love him.

MORAYMA: To beg your life so basely; and to present your Sword to your Enemy; Oh Recreant!

ANTONIO: If I had died honourably, my fame indeed wou'd have sounded loud, but I shou'd never have heard the blast: Come, don't make your self worse-natur'd than you are: to save my life, you would be content I shou'd promise any thing.

MORAYMA: Yes, if I were sure you wou'd perform nothing.

ANTONIO: Can you suspect I wou'd leave you for *Johayma?*

MORAYMA: No; but I can expect you wou'd have both of us: Love is covetous, I must have all of you; heart for heart is an equal truck. In short, I am younger; I think handsomer; and am sure I love you better, she has been my step-mother these fifteen years: you think that's her face you see, but 'tis only a dawb'd Vizard: she wears an Armour of proof upon 't: an inch thick of Paint, besides the Wash: her Face is so fortifi'd that you can make no approaches to it, without a Shovel; but for her constancy, I can tell you for your comfort, she will love till death, I mean till yours: for when she has worn you out, she will certainly dispatch you to another world, for fear of telling tales; as she has already serv'd three Slaves, your Predecessors of happy memory in her favours. She has made my pious Father a three-pil'd Cuckold to my knowledg: and now she wou'd be robbing me of my single Sheep too.

ANTONIO: Prithee prevent her then; and at least take the shearing of me first.

MORAYMA: No; I'll have a Butchers pen'worth of you; first secure the Carcase, and then take the fleece into the bargain.

ANTONIO: Why sure, you did not put your self and me to all this trouble, for a dry come off: by this hand——[*Taking it.*

MORAYMA: Which you shall never touch; but upon better assurances than you imagine. [*Pulling her hand away.*

ANTONIO: I'll marry thee, and make a Christian of thee thou pretty damn'd Infidel.

MORAYMA: I mean you shall: but no earnest, till the bargain be made before witness: there's love enough to be had, and as much as you can turn you to; never doubt it, but all upon honourable terms.

ANTONIO: I vow and swear by Love; and he's a Deity in all Religions.

MORAYMA: But never to be trusted in any: he has another name too, of a worse sound. Shall I trust an Oath, when I see your Eyes languishing, your Cheeks flushing, and can hear your heart throbbing? No, I'll not come near you: He's a foolish Physitian who will feel the pulse of a Patient, that has the Plague-spots upon him.

ANTONIO: Did one ever hear a little Moppet, argue so perversly against so good a Cause! Come, prithee, let me anticipate a little of my Revenue.

MORAYMA: You wou'd fain be fingring your Rents before-hand; but that makes a man an ill Husband ever after. Consider, Marriage is a painful Vocation, as you shall prove it; manage your Incomes as thriftily as you can, you shall find a hard task on't, to make even at the years end, and yet to live decently.

ANTONIO: I came with a Christian intention, to revenge my self upon thy Father; for being the head of a false Religion.

MORAYMA: And so you shall; I offer you his Daughter for your Second: but since you are so pressing, meet me under my Window, to-morrow night, body for body, about this hour; I'll slip down out of my Lodging, and bring my Father in my hand.

ANTONIO: How, thy Father!

MORAYMA: I mean all that's good of him; his Pearls, and Jewels, his whole contents, his heart, and Soul; as much as ever I can carry. I'll leave him his Alchoran that's revenue enough for him; every page of it is Gold and Diamonds. He has the turn of an Eye, a demure Smile, and a godly Cant, that are worth Millions to him. I forgot to tell you, that I will have a Slave prepar'd at the Postern gate, with two Horses ready sadled: no more, for I fear, I may be miss'd; and think I hear 'em calling for me,——if you have constancy and Courage.——

ANTONIO: Never doubt it: and love, in abundance to wander with thee all the World over.

MORAYMA: The value of twelve hundred thousand Crowns in a Casket!——

ANTONIO: A heavy burden Heaven knows! but we must pray for patience to support it.

MORAYMA: Besides a willing Titt that will venture her Corps with you:—Come, I know you long to have a parting blow with me; and therefore to shew I am in Charity——

[*He kisses her.*

ANTONIO: Once more, for pity; that I may keep the flavour upon my lips till we meet again.

MORAYMA: No; frequent Charities make bold Beggars: and besides I have learn'd of a Falconer, never to feed up a Hawk when I wou'd have him fly: that's enough—but if you will be nibling, here's a hand to stay your stomach.

[*Kissing her hand.*

ANTONIO: Thus Conquer'd Infidels, that Wars may cease,
Are forc'd to give their hands, and sign the Peace.

MORAYMA: Thus Christians are outwitted by the Foe;
You had her in your Pow'r, and let her go.
If you release my hand, the fault's not mine;
You shou'd have made me seal, as well as sign.

She runs off, he follows her to the door; then comes back again, and goes out at the other.

ACT IV

SCENE I.

BENDUCAR'S *Pallace in the Castle of* Alcazar.

BENDUCAR: My future Fate, the colour of my life, [*Solus.*
My all depends on this important hour:
This hour my Lott is weighing in the Scales,
And Heav'n, perhaps, is doubting what to do.
Almeyda and a Crown, have push'd me forward;
'Tis fix'd, the Tyrant must not ravish her:
He and *Sebastian* stand betwixt my hopes;
He most; and therefore first to be dispatch'd.
These and a thousand things are to be done
In the short compass of this rowling Night,
And nothing yet perform'd,
None of my Emissaries yet return'd.

Enter HALY—*First Servant.*

Oh *Haly*, thou hast held me long in pain.
What hast thou learnt of *Dorax?* is he dead?
HALY: Two hours I warily have watch'd his Palace;
All doors are shut, no Servant peeps abroad;
Some Officers with striding hast pass'd in,
While others outward went on quick dispatch;
Sometimes hush'd silence seem'd to reign within;
Then Cries confus'd, and a joint clamour follow'd;
Then Lights went gliding by, from room to room,
And shot like thwarting Meteors cross the house:
Not daring farther to enquire: I came
With speed, to bring you this imperfect news.
BENDUCAR: Hence I conclude him either dead or dying:
His mournful Friends, summon'd to take their leaves,
Are throng'd about his Couch, and sit in Council.
What those Caballing Captains may design,
I must prevent, by being first in Action.
To *Muley Zeydan* fly with speed, desire him
To take my last instructions; tell th' importance
And hast his presence here. [*Exit* HALY.
How has this Poison lost its wonted way?
It shou'd have burnt its passage, not have linger'd

In the blind Labyrinths and crooked turnings
Of human Composition; now it moves
Like a slow Fire that works against the Wind,
As if his stronger Stars had interpos'd.

Enter HAMET.

Well *Hamet*, are our Friends the Rabble rais'd?
From *Mustafa*, what Message?

HAMET: What you wish:
The streets are thicker in this noon of Night,
Than at the Mid-day Sun: a drowzy horrour
Sits on their Eyes, like fear not well awake.
All crowd in heaps, as at a Night Alarm
The Bees drive out upon each others backs,
T' imboss their Hives in clusters; all ask news:
Their busie Captain runs the weary round
To whisper Orders; and commanding silence
Makes not noise cease; but deafens it to murmurs.

BENDUCAR: Night wasts apace: when, when will he appear?

HAMET: He only waits your Summons.

BENDUCAR: Hast their coming.
Let secrecy and silence be enjoin'd
In their close march: what news from the Lieutenant?

HAMET: I left him at the Gate, firm to your Interest,
T' admit the Townsmen at their first appearance.

BENDUCAR: Thus far 'tis well: go hasten *Mustafa*.

[*Exit* HAMET.

Enter ORCHAN *the Third Servant*.

O, *Orchan*, did I think thy diligence
Wou'd lag behind the rest? what from the *Mufti?*

ORCHAN: I sought him round his Palace; made enquiry
Of all the Slaves: in short, I us'd your name
And urg'd th' importance home; but had for answer
That since the shut of Evening none had seen him.

BENDUCAR: O the curst fate of all Conspiracies!
They move on many Springs, if one but fail
The restiff *Machine* stops.—In an ill hour he's absent;
'Tis the first time, and sure will be the last
That e'er a *Mufti* was not in the way,
When Tumult and Rebellion shou'd be broach'd.
Stay by me; thou art resolute and faithful;
I have Employment worthy of thy Arm. [*Walks.*

ACT FOUR

Enter MULEY-ZEYDAN.

MULEY-ZEYDAN: You see me come impatient of my hopes,
And eager as the Courser for the Race:
Is all in readiness?
BENDUCAR: All but the *Mufti.*
MULEY-ZEYDAN: We must go on without him.
BENDUCAR: True we must;
For 'tis ill stopping in the full Career,
How e'er the leap be dangerous and wide.
ORCHAN *looking out*: I see the blaze of Torches from afar;
And hear the trampling of thick beating feet;
This way they move.
BENDUCAR: No doubt the Emperour.
We must not be surpriz'd in Conference.
Trust to my management the Tyrants death;
And hast your self to join with *Mustafa.*
The Officer who guards the Gate is yours;
When you have gain'd that Pass, divide your Force;
Your self in Person head one chosen half,
And march t' oppress the Faction in Consult
With dying *Dorax*: Fate has driv'n 'em all
Into the Net: you must be bold and sudden:
Spare none, and if you find him strugling yet
With pangs of Death, trust not his rowling Eyes
And heaving gasps; for Poison may be false,
The home-thrust of a friendly Sword is sure.
MULEY-ZEYDAN: Doubt not my Conduct: they shall be surpriz'd;
Mercy may wait without the Gate one Night,
At Morn I'll take her in.——
BENDUCAR: Here lies your way,
You meet your Brother there.
MULEY-ZEYDAN: May we ne'er meet:
For, like the Twins of *Leda,* when I mount
He gallops down the Skies.—— [*Exit* MULEY-ZEYDAN.
BENDUCAR: He comes: now Heart
Be rib'd with Iron for this one attempt:
Set ope thy Sluces, send the vigorous bloud
Through every active Limb for my relief:
Then, take thy rest within thy quiet Cell,
For thou shalt drum no more.

Enter MULEY-MOLUCH *and Guards attending him.*

MULEY-MOLUCH: What news of our Affairs, and what of *Dorax?*
Is he no more? say that, and make me happy.

BENDUCAR: May all your Enemies be like that Dog,
Whose parting Soul is lab'ring at the Lips.

MULEY-MOLUCH: The People, are they rais'd?

BENDUCAR: And Marshall'd too;
Just ready for the March.

MULEY-MOLUCH: Then I'm at ease.

BENDUCAR: The Night is yours, the glitt'ring Hoast of Heav'n
Shines but for you; but most the Star of Love,
That twinckles you to fair *Almeyda*'s Bed.
Oh there's a joy, to melt in her embrace,
Dissolve in pleasures;
And make the gods curse Immortality,
That so they could not dye.
But haste, and make 'em yours.

MULEY-MOLUCH: I will; and yet
A kind of weight hangs heavy at my Heart;
My flagging Soul flyes under her own pitch;
Like Fowl in air too damp, and lugs along,
As if she were a body in a body,
And not a mounting substance made of Fire.
My Senses too are dull and stupifi'd,
Their edge rebated; sure some ill approaches,
And some kind Spirit knocks softly at my Soul,
To tell me Fate's at hand.

BENDUCAR: Mere Fancies all.
Your Soul has been beforehand with your Body,
And drunk so deep a Draught of promis'd bliss,
She slumbers o'er the Cup; no danger's near,
But of a Surfeit at too full a Feast.

MULEY-MOLUCH: It may be so; it looks so like the Dream
That overtook me at my waking hour
This Morn; and Dreams they say are then divine,
When all the balmy Vapors are exhal'd,
And some o'er-pow'ring God continues sleep.
'Twas then methought *Almeyda*, smiling, came
Attended with a Train of all her Race,
Whom in the rage of Empire I had murther'd.
But now, no longer Foes, they gave me Joy
Of my new Conquest, and with helping hands

Heav'd me into our Holy Prophet's arms,
Who bore me in a purple Cloud to Heav'n.

BENDUCAR: Good Omen, Sir, I wish you in that Heaven
Your Dream portends you.
Which presages death.—— [*Aside.*

MULEY-MOLUCH: Thou too wert there;
And thou methought didst push me from below,
With thy full force to Paradise.

BENDUCAR: Yet better.

MULEY-MOLUCH: Ha! What's that grizly Fellow that attends thee?

BENDUCAR: Why ask you Sir?

MULEY-MOLUCH: For he was in my Dream;
And help'd to heave me up.

BENDUCAR: With Pray'rs and Wishes;
For I dare swear him honest.

MULEY-MOLUCH: That may be;
But yet he looks Damnation.

BENDUCAR: You forget,
The Face wou'd please you better: Do you love,
And can you thus forbear?

MULEY-MOLUCH: I'll head My people,
Then think of dalliance, when the danger's o'er.
My warlike Spirits work now another way;
And my Soul's tun'd to Trumpets.

BENDUCAR: You debase your self,
To think of mixing with th' ignoble Herd.
Let such perform the servile Work of War,
Such who have no *Almeyda* to enjoy.
What shall the People know their God-like Prince
Skulk'd in a nightly Skirmish? Stole a Conquest,
Headed a Rabble, and profan'd his Person,
Shoulder'd with Filth, born in a tide of Ordure,
And stifled with their rank offensive Sweat?

MULEY-MOLUCH: I am off again: I will not prostitute
The Regal Dignity so far, to head 'em.

BENDUCAR: There spoke a King.
Dismiss your Guards to be employ'd elsewhere
In ruder Combats: You will want no Seconds
In those Alarms you seek.

MULEY-MOLUCH: Go joyn the Crowd; [*To the Guards.*
Benducar, thou shalt lead 'em, in my place.
[*Exeunt Guards.*

The God of Love once more has shot his Fires
Into my Soul; and my whole Heart receives him.
Almeyda now returns with all her Charms;
I feel her as she glides along my Veins,
And dances in my Blood: So when our Prophet
Had long been ham'ring in his lonely Cell,
Some dull, insipid, tedious Paradise,
A brisk Arabian Girl came tripping by;
Passing she cast at him a side-long glance,
And look'd behind in hopes to be pursu'd:
He took the hint, embrac'd the flying Fair;
And having found his Heav'n, he fix'd it there.

[*Exit* MULEY-MOLUCH.

BENDUCAR: That Paradise thou never shalt possess.
His death is easie now, his Guards are gone;
And I can sin but once to seize the Throne.
All after Acts are sanctify'd by pow'r.

ORCHAN: Command my Sword and Life.

BENDUCAR: I thank thee *Orchan*,
And shall reward thy Faith: This Master Key
Frees every Lock, and leads us to his Person:
And shou'd we miss our blow, as Heav'n forbid,
Secures retreat: Leave open all behind us;
And first set wide the *Mufti*'s Garden Gate,
Which is his private passage to the Palace:
For there our Mutineers appoint to meet,
And thence we may have aid. Now sleep ye Stars
That silently o'erwatch the fate of Kings;
Be all propitious Influences barr'd,
And none but murd'rous Planets mount the Guard.

[*Exit with* ORCHAN.

A Night Scene of the MUFTI'S *Garden.*

Enter the MUFTI *alone, in a Slave's habit, like that of* ANTONIO.

MUFTI: This 'tis to have a sound Head-piece; by this I have got to be chief of my Religion; that is, honestly speaking, to teach others what I neither know nor believe my self. For what's *Mahomet* to me, but that I get by him? Now for my Policy of this night: I have mew'd up my suspected Spouse in her Chamber. No more Embassies to that lusty young Stallion of a Gardiner. Next my habit of a Slave; I have made my self as like him as I can, all but his youth and vigor; which when I had, I pass'd my time as well as any of my Holy Predecessors. Now walking under the Windows of my Seraglio, if *Johayma* look out, she will certainly take me for *Antonio*, and call to me; and by that I shall know what Concupiscence is working in her; she cannot come down to commit Iniquity, there's my safety; but if she peep, if she put her Nose abroad, there's demonstration of her pious Will: And I'll not make the first precedent for a Church-man to forgive Injuries.

Enter MORAYMA *running to him with a Casket in her hand, and embracing him.*

MORAYMA: Now I can embrace you with a good Conscience; here are the Pearls and Jewels, here's my Father.

MUFTI: I am indeed thy Father; but how the Devil didst thou know me in this disguise? And what Pearls and Jewels dost thou mean?

MORAYMA *going back*: What have I done, and what will now become of me!

MUFTI: Art thou mad, *Morayma?*

MORAYMA: I think you'll make me so.

MUFTI: Why, what have I done to thee? Recollect thyself, and speak sense to me.

MORAYMA: Then give me leave to tell you, you are the worst of Fathers.

MUFTI: Did I think I had begotten such a Monster? Proceed my dutiful Child, proceed, proceed.

MORAYMA: You have been raking together a mass of Wealth, by indirect and wicked means; the Spoils of Orphans are in these Jewels, and the Tears of Widows in these Pearls.

MUFTI: Thou Amazest me!

MORAYMA: I wou'd do so. This Casket is loaded with your Sins; 'tis the Cargo of Rapines, Simony, and Extortions; the Iniquity of thirty Years Muftiship, converted into Diamonds.

MUFTI: Wou'd some rich rayling Rogue would say as much to me, that I might squeeze his Purse for scandal.

MORAYMA: No Sir,. you get more by pious Fools than Raylers, when you insinuate into their Families, manage their Fortunes while they live, and beggar their Heirs by getting Legacies when they dye. And do you think I'll be the receiver of your Theft? I discharge my Conscience of it: Here take again your filthy Mammon, and restore it you had best to the true Owners.

MUFTI: I am finely documented by my own Daughter.

MORAYMA: And a great credit for me to be so: Do but think how decent a Habit you have on, and how becoming your Function to be disguis'd like a Slave, and eaves-dropping under the Womens Windows, to be saluted, as you deserve it richly, with a Piss-pot: If I had not known you casually by your shambling gate, and a certain reverend awkardness that is natural to all of your Function, here you had been expos'd to the laughter of your own Servants; who have been in search of you through your whole Seraglio, peeping under every Petticoat to find you.

MUFTI: Prithee Child reproach me no more of human Failings; they are but a little of the pitch and spots of the World that are still sticking on me; but I hope to scour 'em out in time: I am better at bottom than thou think'st; I am not the Man thou tak'st me for.

MORAYMA: No, to my sorrow Sir you are not.

MUFTI: It was a very odd beginning, tho methought, to see thee come running in upon me with such a warm embrace; prithee what was the meaning of that violent hot Hug?

MORAYMA: I am sure I meant nothing by it, but the zeal and affection which I bear to the Man of the World, whom I may love lawfully.

MUFTI: But thou wilt not teach me at this age the nature of a close Embrace?

MORAYMA: No indeed; for my Mother in Law complains, that you are past teaching: But if you mistook my innocent Embrace for Sin, I wish heartily it had been given where it wou'd have been more acceptable.

MUFTI: Why, this is as it shou'd be now: Take the Treasure again, it can never be put into better hands.

MORAYMA: Yes, to my knowledg but it might. I have confess'd my Soul to you, if you can understand me rightly; I never disobey'd you till this night; and now since, through the violence of my Passion, I have been so unfortunate, I humbly beg your pardon, your blessing, and your leave, that upon the first opportunity I may go for ever from your sight; for Heaven knows, I never desire to see you more.

MUFTI *wiping his Eyes*: Thou mak'st me weep at thy unkindness; indeed dear Daughter we will not part.

MORAYMA: Indeed dear Daddy but we will.

MUFTI: Why if I have been a little pilfering, or so, I take it bitterly of thee to tell me of it; since it was to make thee rich; and I hope a Man may make bold with his own Soul, without offence to his own Child: Here take the jewels again, take 'em I charge thee upon thy Obedience.

MORAYMA: Well then, in vertue of Obedience I will take 'em; but on my Soul, I had rather they were in a better hand.

MUFTI: Meaning mine, I know it.

MORAYMA: Meaning his whom I love better than my life.

MUFTI: That's me again.

MORAYMA: I wou'd have you think so.

MUFTI: How thy good nature works upon me; well I can do no less than venture damning for thee, and I may put fair for it, if the Rabble be order'd to rise to Night.

Enter ANTONIO *in an* Affrican *rich habit.*

ANTONIO: What do you mean my Dear, to stand talking in this suspicious place, just underneath *Johayma*'s Window? [*to the* MUFTI] You are well met Comerade, I know you are the friend of our flight? are the horses ready at the postern gate?

MUFTI: *Antonio*, and in disguise! now I begin to smell a rat.

ANTONIO: And I another, that out-stinks it; false *Morayma*, hast thou thus betray'd me to thy Father!

MORAYMA: Alas, I was betray'd my self. He came disguis'd like you, and I poor Innocent ran into his hands.

MUFTI: In good time you did so; I laid a trap for a Bitch Fox, and a worse Vermine has caught himself in it: You wou'd fain break loose now, though you left a limb behind you; but I am yet in my own Territories and in call of Company, that's my comfort.

ANTONIO *taking him by the throat*: No; I have a trick left to put thee past thy squeeking: I have giv'n thee the quinzey; that ungracious tongue shall Preach no more false Doctrin.

MORAYMA: What do you mean? you will not throttle him? consider he's my Father.

ANTONIO: Prithee let us provide first for our own safety; if I do not consider him, he will consider us with a vengeance afterwards.

MORAYMA: You may threaten him for crying out, but for my

sake give him back a little cranny of his Wind-pipe, and some part of Speech.

ANTONIO: Not so much as one single Interjection: Come away Father-in-Law, this is no place for Dialogues, when you are in the Mosque you talk by hours, and there no Man must interrupt you; this is but like for like, good Father-in-Law; now I am in the Pulpit, 'tis your turn to hold your tongue. [*He struggles.*]

Nay if you will be hanging back, I shall take care you shall hang forward.

[*Pulls him along the Stage; with his Sword at his reins.*]

MORAYMA: T' other way to the Arbour with him; and make hast before we are discover'd.

ANTONIO: If I only bind and gag him there, he may commend me hereafter for civil usage; he deserves not so much favour by any action of his life.

MORAYMA: Yes, pray bate him one, for begetting your Mistress.

ANTONIO: I wou'd, if he had not thought more of thy Mother than of thee; once more, come along in silence, my Pythagorean Father-in-Law.

JOHAYMA *at the Balcony*: A Bird in a Cage may peep at least; though she must not fly; what bustle's there beneath my Window? *Antonio* by all my hopes, I know him by his habit; but what makes that Woman with him, and a Friend, a Sword drawn, and hasting hence? this is no time for silence: Who's within, call there, where are the Servants? why *Omar*, *Abedin*, *Hassan* and the rest, make hast and run into the Garden; there are Thieves and Villains; arm all the Family, and stop 'em.

ANTONIO *turning back*: O that Schriech Owl at the Window! we shall be pursu'd immediately; which way shall we take?

MORAYMA *giving him the Casket*: 'Tis impossible to escape them; for the way to our Horses lyes back again by the House, and then we shall meet 'em full in the teeth; here take these Jewels; thou may'st leap the Walls and get away.

ANTONIO: And what will become of thee then poor kind Soul?

MORAYMA: I must take my fortune; when you are got safe into your own Country, I hope you will bestow a sigh on the memory of her who lov'd you!

ANTONIO: It makes me mad, to think how many a good night will be lost betwixt us! take back thy Jewels; 'tis an empty

Casket without thee; besides I shou'd never leap well with the weight of all thy Father's sins about me, thou and they had been a bargain.

MORAYMA: Prithee take 'em, 'twill help me to be reveng'd on him.

ANTONIO: No; they'll serve to make thy peace with him.

MORAYMA: I hear 'em coming; shift for your self at least; remember I am yours for ever.

[*Servants crying* this way, this way, *behind the Scenes.*]

ANTONIO: And I but the empty shadow of my self without thee! farewel Father-in-Law, that shou'd have been, if I had not been curst in my Mothers belly—Now which way fortune.—

[*Runs amazedly backwards and forwards.*]

SERVANTS *within*: Follow, follow, yonder are the villains.

ANTONIO: O, here's a gate open; but it leads into the Castle; yet I must venture it. [*Going out.*

[*A shout behind the Scenes where* ANTONIO *is going out.*]

ANTONIO: There's the Rabble in a Mutiny; what is the Devil up at Midnight!—however 'tis good herding in a Crowd. [*Runs out.*

[MUFTI *runs to* MORAYMA *and lays hold on her, then snatches away the Casket.*]

MUFTI: Now, to do things in order, first I seize upon the Bag, and then upon the Baggage: for thou art but my flesh and blood, but these are my Life and Soul.

MORAYMA: Then let me follow my flesh and blood, and keep to yourself your Life and Soul.

MUFTI: Both or none; come away to durance.

MORAYMA: Well, if it must be so, agreed; for I have another trick to play you; and thank your self for what shall follow. [*Enter Servants.*

JOHAYMA *from above*: One of them took through the private way into the Castle; follow him be sure, for these are yours already.

MORAYMA: Help here quickly *Omar*, *Abedin*; I have hold on the Villain that stole my jewels; but 'tis a lusty Rogue, and he will prove too strong for me; what, help I say, do you not know your Masters Daughter?

MUFTI: Now if I cry out they will know my voice; and then I am disgrac'd for ever: O thou art a venomous Cockatrice!

MORAYMA: Of your own begetting. [*The Servants seize him.*

FIRST SERVANT: What a glorious deliverance have you had Madam from this bloody-minded Christian!

MORAYMA: Give me back my Jewels, and carry this notorious Malefactor to be punish'd by my Father. I'll hunt the other dry-foot.

[*Takes the Jewels and runs out after* ANTONIO *at the same Passage.*]

FIRST SERVANT: I long to be hanselling his hide, before we bring him to my master.

SECOND SERVANT: Hang him, for an old Covetous Hypocrite: he deserves a worse punishment himself for keeping us so hardly.

FIRST SERVANT: Ay, wou'd he were in this Villains place; thus I wou'd lay him on, and thus. [*Beats him.*

SECOND SERVANT: And thus wou'd I revenge my self of my last beating. [*He beats him too, and then the rest.*

MUFTI: Oh, oh, oh!

FIRST SERVANT: Now supposing you were the *Mufti*, Sir.— [*Beats him again.*

MUFTI: The Devil's in that supposing Rascal; I can bear no more; and I am the *Mufti*: Now suppose your selves my Servants, and hold your hands; an anointed halter take you all.

FIRST SERVANT: My Master! You will pardon the excess of our zeal for you, Sir, indeed we all took you for a Villain, and so we us'd you.

MUFTI: Ay so I feel you did; my back and sides are abundant testimonies of your zeal. Run Rogues, and bring me back my Jewels, and my Fugitive Daughter: run I say.

[*They run to the Gate and the first Servant runs back again.*]

FIRST SERVANT: Sir, the Castle is in a most terrible combustion; you may hear 'em hither.

MUFTI: 'Tis a laudable commotion: The voice of the Mobile is the voice of Heaven. I must retire a little, to strip me of the Slave, and to assume the *Mufti*; and then I will return: for the piety of the People must be encouraged; that they may help me to recover my Jewels, and my Daughter.

[*Exit* MUFTI *and Servants.*

ACT FOUR

Scene changes to the Castle-yard, and discovers ANTONIO, MUSTAPHA, *and the Rabble shouting, They come forward.*

ANTONIO: And so at length, as I inform'd you, I escap'd out of his covetous clutches; and now fly to your illustrious feet for my protection.

MUSTAPHA: Thou shalt have it, and now defie the *Mufti.* 'Tis the first Petition that has been made to me since my exaltation to Tumult; in this second Night of the Month *Abib*, and in the year of the *Hegyra*; the Lord knows what year; but 'tis no matter; for when I am settled, the Learned are bound to find it out for me: for I am resolv'd to date my Authority over the Rabble, like other Monarchs.

ANTONIO: I have always had a longing to be yours again; though I cou'd not compass it before, and had design'd you a Casket of my Masters jewels too; for I knew the Custom, and wou'd not have appear'd before a Great Person, as you are, without a present: But he has defrauded my good intentions, and basely robb'd you of 'em, 'tis a prize worth a Million of Crowns, and you carry your Letters of mark about you.

MUSTAPHA: I shall make bold with his Treasure, for the support of my New Government. [*The People gather about him.* What do these vile ragga-muffins so near our Person? your savour is offensive to us; bear back there, and make room for honest Men to approach us; these fools and knaves are always impudently crowding next to Princes, and keeping off the more deserving, bear back I say.— [*They make a wider Circle.* —That's dutifully done; now shout to show your Loyalty. [*A great shout.*] Hear'st thou that, Slave *Antonio?* these obstreperous Villains shout, and know not for what they make a noise. You shall see me manage 'em, that you may judge what ignorant Beasts they are. For whom do you shout now? who's to Live and Reign? tell me that, the wisest of you?

FIRST RABBLE: Even who you please Captain.

MUSTAPHA: La you there; I told you so.

SECOND RABBLE: We are not bound to know who is to Live and Reign; our business is only to rise upon command, and plunder.

THIRD RABBLE: Ay, the Richest of both Parties; for they are our Enemies.

MUSTAPHA: This last Fellow is a little more sensible than the rest; he has enter'd somewhat into the merits of the Cause.

FIRST RABBLE: If a poor Man may speak his mind, I think, Captain, that your self are the fittest to Live and Reign, I mean not over, but next and immediately under the People; and thereupon I say, *A Mustapha, A Mustapha.*

[*All Cry*]: *A Mustafa, a Mustafa!*

MUSTAPHA: I must confess the sound is pleasing, and tickles the ears of my Ambition; but alas good People, it must not be: I am contented to be a poor simple Vice Roy; But Prince *Muley-Zeydan* is to be the Man: I shall take care to instruct him in the arts of Government; and in his duty to us all: and therefore mark my Cry: *A Muley-Zeydan, A Muley-Zeydan!*

[*All Cry*]: *A Muley-Zeydan, a Muley-Zeydan.*

MUSTAPHA: You see Slave *Antonio*, what I might have been.
ANTONIO: I observe your Modesty.
MUSTAPHA: But for a foolish promise I made once to my Lord *Bendúcar*, to set up any one he pleas'd.

Re-enter the MUFTI *with his Servants.*

ANTONIO: Here's the Old Hypocrite again; now stand your ground, and bate him not an inch. Remember the Jewels, the Rich and Glorious Jewels; they are destin'd to be yours, by virtue of Prerogative.
MUSTAPHA: Let me alone to pick a quarrel, I have an old grudge to him upon thy account.
MUFTI, *making up to the Mobile*: Good people, here you are met together.
FIRST RABBLE: Ay, we know that without your telling, but why are we met together, Doctor? for that's it which no body here can tell.
SECOND RABBLE: Why to see one another in the Dark; and to make Holy-day at Midnight.
MUFTI: You are met, as becomes good Musulmen, to settle the Nation; for I must tell you, that though your Tyrant is a lawful Emperor, yet your lawful Emperor is but a Tyrant.
ANTONIO: What stuff he talks!
MUSTAPHA: 'Tis excellent fine matter indeed, Slave *Antonio*; he has a rare tongue; Oh, he wou'd move a Rock of Elephant!
ANTONIO *aside*: What a Block have I to work upon. [*to him*] But still remember the Jewels, Sir, the Jewels.

MUSTAPHA: Nay that's true on t'other side: the Jewels must be mine; but he has a pure fine way of talking; my Conscience goes along with him, but the Jewels have set my heart against him.

MUFTI: That your Emperor is a Tyrant is most manifest; for you were born to be *Turks*, but he has play'd the *Turk* with you; and is taking your Religion away.

SECOND RABBLE: We find that in our decay of Trade; I have seen for these hundr'd years, that Religion and Trade always go together.

MUFTI: He is now upon the point of Marrying himself, without your Sovereign consent; and what are the effects of Marriage?

THIRD RABBLE: A scoulding, domineering Wife, if she prove honest; and if a Whore, a fine gawdy Minx, that robs our Counters every Night, and then goes out, and spends it upon our Cuckold-makers.

MUFTI: No, the natural effects of Marriage are Children: Now on whom wou'd he beget these Children? Even upon a Christian! Oh horrible; how can you believe me, though I am ready to swear it upon the *Alcoran!* Yes, true Believers, you may believe me that he is going to beget a Race of Misbelievers.

MUSTAPHA: That's fine, in earnest; I cannot forbear hearkening to his enchanting Tongue.

ANTONIO: But yet remember.——

MUSTAPHA: Ay, Ay, the Jewels! Now again I hate him; but yet my Conscience makes me listen to him.

MUFTI: Therefore to conclude all, Believers, pluck up your Hearts, and pluck down the Tyrant: Remember the Courage of your Ancestors; remember the Majesty of the People; remember your selves, your Wives and Children; and lastly, above all, remember your Religion, and our holy *Mahomet*; all these require your timous assistance; shall I say they beg it? No, they claim it of you, by all the nearest and dearest Tyes of these three P's, Self-Preservation, our Property, and our Prophet. Now answer me with an unanimous chearful Cry, and follow me, who am your Leader, to a glorious Deliverance.

[*All cry,* A Mufti, A Mufti, *and are following him off the Stage.*]

ANTONIO: Now you see what comes of your foolish Qualms of Conscience: The Jewels are lost, and they are all leaving you.

MUSTAPHA: What am I forsaken of my Subjects? Wou'd the Rogue purloin my liege People from me! I charge you in my own Name come back ye Deserters; and hear me speak.

FIRST RABBLE: What will he come with his Balderdash, after the *Mufti*'s eloquent Oration?

SECOND RABBLE: He's our Captain, lawfully pick'd up, and elected upon a Stall; we will hear him.

OMNES: Speak Captain, for we will hear you.

MUSTAPHA: Do you remember the glorious Rapines and Robberies you have committed? Your breaking open and gutting of Houses, your rummaging of Cellars, your demolishing of Christian Temples, and bearing off in triumph the superstitious Plate and Pictures, the Ornaments of their wicked Altars, when all rich Moveables were sentenc'd for idolatrous, and all that was idolatrous was seiz'd? Answer first for your remembrance, of all these sweetnesses of Mutiny; for upon those Grounds I shall proceed.

OMNES: Yes we do remember, we do remember.

MUSTAPHA: Then make much of your retentive Faculties. And who led you to those Hony-Combs? Your *Mufti?* No, Believers, he only preach'd you up to it; but durst not lead you; he was but your Counsellor, but I was your Captain; he only lood you, but 'twas I that led you.

OMNES: That's true, that's true.

ANTONIO: There you were with him for his Figures.

MUSTAPHA: I think I was, Slave *Antonio*. Alas I was ignorant of my own Talent.—Say then, Believers, will you have a Captain for your *Mufti*, Or a *Mufti* for your Captain? And further to instruct you how to Cry, Will you have a *Mufti*, or no *Mufti?*

OMNES: No *Mufti*, no *Mufti*.

MUSTAPHA: That I laid in for 'em, Slave *Antonio*.—Do I then spet upon your Faces? Do I discourage Rebellion, Mutiny, Rapine, and Plundering? You may think I do, Believers, but Heaven forbid: No, I encourage you to all these laudable Undertakings; you shall plunder, you shall pull down the Government; but you shall do this upon my Authority, and not by his wicked Instigation.

THIRD RABBLE: Nay, when his turn is serv'd, he may preach up Loyalty again, and Restitution, that he might have another Snack among us.

FIRST RABBLE: He may indeed; for 'tis but his saying 'tis Sin, and then we must restore; and therefore I wou'd have a new

Religion, where half the Commandments shou'd be taken away, the rest mollifi'd, and there should be little or no Sin remaining.

OMNES: Another Religion, a new Religion, another Religion.

MUSTAPHA: And that may easily be done, with the help of a little Inspiration: For I must tell you, I have a Pigeon at home, of *Mahomet*'s own breed; and when I have learnt her to pick Pease out of my Ear, rest satisfi'd till then, and you shall have another. But now I think on't, I am inspir'd already, that 'tis no Sin to depose the Mufti.

ANTONIO: And good reason; for when Kings and Queens are to be discarded, what shou'd Knaves do any longer in the pack?

OMNES: He is depos'd, he is depos'd, he is depos'd!

MUSTAPHA: Nay, if he and his Clergy will needs be preaching up Rebellion, and giving us their Blessing, 'tis but justice they shou'd have the first fruits of it.—Slave *Antonio*, take him into custody; and dost thou hear, Boy, be sure to secure the little transitory Box of Jewels: If he be obstinate, put a civil Question to him upon the Rack, and he squeaks I warrant him.

ANTONIO *seizing the* MUFTI: Come my *quondam*-Master, you and I must change Qualities.

MUFTI: I hope you will not be so barbarous to torture me, we may preach Suffering to others, but alas, holy Flesh is too well pamper'd to endure Martyrdom.

MUSTAPHA: Now, late *Mufti*, not forgetting my first Quarrel to you, we will enter our selves with the Plunder of your Palace: 'tis good to sanctify a Work, and begin a God's name.

FIRST RABBLE: Our Prophet let the Devil alone with the last *Mob*.

MOB: But he takes care of this himself.

As they are going out enter BENDUCAR *leading* ALMEYDA: *He with a Sword in one hand;* BENDUCAR'S *Slave follows, with* MULEY-MOLUCH'S *Head upon a Spear.*

MUSTAPHA: Not so much hast Masters; come back again; you are so bent upon mischief, that you take a man upon the first word of Plunder. Here's a sight for you: the Emperour is come upon his head to visit you. [*Bowing.*] Most Noble Emperour, now I hope you will not hit us in the teeth, that we have pull'd you down, for we can tell you to your face, that we have exalted you. [*They all shout.*

BENDUCAR *to* ALMEYDA *apart*: Think what I am, and what your self may be,
In being mine: refuse not proffer'd Love,
That brings a crown.

ALMEYDA *to him*: I have resolv'd,
And these shall know my thoughts.

BENDUCAR *to her*: On that I build.——

[*He comes up to the Rabble.*]

Joy to the People for the Tyrant's Death!
Oppression, Rapine, Banishment, and Bloud
Are now no more ; but speechless as that tongue
That lyes for ever still.
How is my grief divided with my joy,
When I must own I kill'd him! bid me speak,
For not to bid me, is to disallow
What for your sakes is done.

MUSTAPHA: In the name of the People, we command you speak: But that pretty Lady shall speak first; for we have taken somewhat of a likeing to her Person, be not afraid Lady to speak to these rude Ragga-muffians: there's nothing shall offend you, unless it be their stink, and please you.

[*Making a Legg.*

ALMEYDA: Why shou'd I fear to speak who am your Queen?
My peacefull Father sway'd the Scepter long;
And you enjoy'd the Blessings of his Reign,
While you deserv'd the name of *Affricans.*
Then not commanded, but commanding you,
Fearless I speak: know me for what I am.

BENDUCAR: How she assumes! I like not this beginning. [*Aside.*

ALMEYDA: I was not born so base, to flatter Crowds,
And move your pitty by a whining tale:
Your Tyrant would have forc'd me to his Bed;
But in th' attempt of that foul brutal Act,
These Loyall Slaves secur'd me by his death.

[*Pointing to* BENDUCAR.

BENDUCAR: Makes she no more of me then of a Slave? [*aside.*
Madam, I thought I had instructed you [*to* ALMEYDA.
To frame a Speech more suiting to the times:
The Circumstances of that dire design,
Your own despair, my unexpected ayd,
My Life endanger'd by his bold defence,
And after all, his Death, and your Deliv'rance,
Were themes that ought not to be slighted o're.

MUSTAPHA: She might have pass'd over all your petty businesses, and no great matter: but the Raising of my Rabble is an Exploit of consequence; and not to be mumbled up in silence for all her pertness.

ALMEYDA: When force invades the gift of Nature, Life,
The eldest Law of nature bids defend:
And if in that defence, a Tyrant fall,
His death's his Crime, not ours,
Suffice it that he's Dead: all wrongs dye with him;
When he can wrong no more I pardon him:
Thus I absolve my self; and him excuse.
Who sav'd my life, and honour; but praise neither.

BENDUCAR: 'Tis cheap to pardon, whom you would not pay;
But what speak I of payment and reward?
Ungratefull Woman, you are yet no Queen;
Nor more than a proud haughty *Christian* slave:
As such I seize my right. [*Going to lay hold on her*

ALMEYDA *drawing a Dagger*: Dare not to approach me;
Now, *Affricans*,
He shows himself to you; to me he stood
Confest before, and own'd his Insolence
T' espouse my person, and assume the Crown,
Claym'd in my Right; for this he slew your Tyrant;
Oh no, he only chang'd him for a worse;
Imbas'd your Slavery by his own vileness,
And loaded you with more ignoble bonds:
Then think me not ungratefull, not to share,
Th' Imperial Crown with a presuming Traytor.
He says I am a *Christian*; true I am,
But yet no Slave: If *Christians* can be thought,
Unfit to govern those of other Faith,
'Tis left for you to judge.

BENDUCAR: I have not patience; she consumes the time
In Idle talk, and owns her false Belief:
Seize her by force, and bear her hence unheard.

ALMEYDA *to the People*: No, let me rather dye your sacrifice
Than live his Tryumph;
I throw my self into my Peoples armes;
As you are Men compassionate my wrongs,
And as good men Protect me.

ANTONIO *aside*: Something must be done to save her.
[*to* MUSTAPHA] This is all address'd to you, Sir: She singles you out with her eye, as Commander in chief of the mobility

MUSTAPHA: Think'st thou so Slave *Antonio?*

ANTONIO: Most certainly Sir; and you cannot in honour but protect her. Now look to your hits, and make your fortune.

MUSTAPHA: Methought indeed she cast a kind leer towards me: Our Prophet was but just such another Scoundrell as I am, till he rais'd himself to power, and consequently to Holyness, by marrying his masters Widow: I am resolved I'lle put forward for my self: for why should I be my Lord *Benducars* Fool and Slave, when I may be my own fool and his Master?

BENDUCAR: Take her into possession, *Mustapha.*

MUSTAPHA: That's better Counsell than you meant it: Yes I do take her into possession, and into protection too: what say you, Masters, will you stand by me?

OMNES: One and all; One and all.

BENDUCAR: Hast thou betray'd me Traytor?
Mufti speak to mind 'em of Religion.

[MUFTI *shakes his head.*

MUSTAPHA: Alas the poor Gentleman has gotten a cold, with a Sermon of two hours long, and a prayer of four: and besides, if he durst speak, mankind is grown wiser at this time of day, than to cut one anothers throats about Religion. Our *Mufti* is a Green coat, and the *Christians* is a black coat; and we must wisely go together by the ears, whether green or black shall sweep our spoils. [*Drums within and shouts.*

BENDUCAR: Now we shall see whose numbers will prevail:
The Conquering Troups of *Muley-Zeydan*, come
To crush Rebellion, and espouse my Cause.

MUSTAPHA: We will have a fair Tryall of Skill for 't, I can tell him that. When we have dispatch'd with *Muley-Zeydan*, your Lordship shall march in equall proportions of your body, to the four gates of the City; and every Tower shall have a Quarter of you. [ANTONIO *draws them up and takes* ALMEYDA *by the hand. Shouts again, and Drums.*]

Enter DORAX *and* SEBASTIAN *attended by* Affrican *Soldiers and Portugueses.* ALMEYDA *and* SEBASTIAN *run into each others armes, and both speak together.*

SEBASTIAN *and* ALMEYDA: My *Sebastian!* My *Almeyda!*

ALMEYDA: Do you then live?

SEBASTIAN: And live to love thee ever.

BENDUCAR: How! *Dorax* and *Sebastian* still alive!
The Moors and Christians joyn'd! I thank thee Prophet.

DORAX: The Citadell is ours; and *Muley-Zeydan*

Safe under Guard, but as becomes a Prince.
Lay down your armes: such base Plebeian bloud
Would only stain the brightness of my Sword,
And blunt it for some nobler work behind.

MUSTAPHA: I suppose you may put it up without offence to any man here present? For my part, I have been Loyall to my Soveraign Lady: though that Villain *Benducar*, and that Hypocrite the *Mufti*, would have corrupted me; but if those two scape publick Justice, then I and all my late honest Subjects here, deserve hanging.

BENDUCAR *to* DORAX: I'm sure I did my part to poyson thee,
What Saint soe're has sodder'd thee again.
A Dose less hot had burst through ribs of Iron.

MUFTI: Not knowing that, I poyson'd him once more,
And drench'd him with a draught so deadly cold
That, had'st not thou prevented, had congeal'd
The channell of his bloud, and froze him dry.

BENDUCAR: Thou interposing Fool, to mangle mischief,
And think to mend the perfect work of Hell.

DORAX: Thus, when Heaven pleases, double poysons cure.
I will not tax thee of Ingratitude
To me thy Friend, who hast betray'd thy Prince:
Death he deserv'd indeed, but not from thee.
But fate it seems reserv'd the worst of men
To end the worst of Tyrants.
Go bear him to his fate.
And send him to attend his Masters Ghost.
Let some secure my other poys'ning Friend,
Whose double diligence preserv'd my life.

ANTONIO: You are fall'n into good hands, Father-in-law; you sparkling Jewels, and *Morayma*'s eyes may prove a bette bail than you deserve.

MUFTI: The best that can come of me, in this condition, is t have my life begg'd first, and then to be begg'd for a Foc afterwards. [*Exit* ANTONIO *with the* MUFTI, *and, at th same time*, BENDUCAR *is carry'd of*

DORAX *to* MUSTAPHA: You and your hungry herd depart ur touch'd;
For Justice cannot stoop so low, to reach
The groveling sin of Crowds: but curst be they
Who trust revenge with such mad Instruments,
Whose blindfold bus'ness is but to destroy:
And like the fire Commission'd by the Winds,

Begins on sheds, but rouling in a round,
On Pallaces returns. Away ye skum,
That still rise upmost when the Nation boyls:
Ye mungrill work of Heaven, with humane shapes,
Not to be damn'd, or sav'd, but breath, and perish,
That have but just enough of sense, to know
The masters voice, when rated, to depart.

[*Exeunt* MUSTAPHA *and* Rabble.

ALMEYDA *kneeling to him*: With gratitude as low, as knees can pay
To those blest holy Fires, our Guardian Angells,
Receive these thanks; till Altars can be rais'd.

DORAX *raising her up*: Arise fair Excellence, and pay no thanks,
Till time discover what I have deserv'd.

SEBASTIAN: More then reward can answer.
If *Portugall* and *Spain* were joyn'd to *Affrique*,
And the main Ocean crusted into Land,
If Universall Monarchy were mine,
Here should the gift be plac'd.

DORAX: And from some hands I shou'd refuse that gift:
Be not too prodigall of Promises;
But stint your bounty to one only grant,
Which I can ask with honour.

SEBASTIAN: What I am
Is but thy gift, make what thou canst of me.
Secure of no Repulse.

DORAX *to* SEBASTIAN: Dismiss your Train.
[*To* ALMEYDA] You, Madam, please one moment to retire.

[SEBASTIAN *signes to the Portugueses to go off.* ALMEYDA *bowing to him, goes off also. The* Affricans *follow her.*]

DORAX *to the Captain of his Guard*: With you one word in private. [*Goes out with the Captain.*

SEBASTIAN *Solus*: Reserv'd behaviour, open Nobleness,
A long misterious Track of a stern bounty.
But now the hand of Fate is on the Curtain,
And draws the Scene to sight.

Re-enter DORAX, *having taken off his Turbant and put on a Peruque Hat and Crevat.*

DORAX: Now do you know me?

SEBASTIAN: Thou shouldst be *Alonzo.*

DORAX: So you shou'd be *Sebastian:*
But when *Sebastian* ceas'd to be himself,
I ceas'd to be *Alonzo.*
SEBASTIAN: As in a Dream
I see thee here, and scarce believe mine eyes.
DORAX: Is it so strange to find me, where my wrongs,
And your Inhumane Tyranny have sent me?
Think not you dream: or, if you did, my Injuries
Shall call so loud, that Lethargy should wake;
And Death should give you back to answer me.
A Thousand Nights have brush'd their balmy wings
Over these eyes, but ever when they clos'd,
Your Tyrant Image forc'd 'em ope again,
And dry'd the dewes they brought.
The long expected hour is come at length,
By manly Vengeance to redeem my fame;
And that once clear'd, eternall sleep is welcome.
SEBASTIAN: I have not yet forgot I am a King;
Whose Royall Office is redress of Wrongs:
If I have wrong'd thee, charge me face to face;
I have not yet forgot I am a Soldier.
DORAX: 'Tis the first Justice thou hast ever done me.
Then, though I loath this Womans War of tongues,
Yet shall my Cause of Vengeance first be clear:
And, Honour, be thou Judge.
SEBASTIAN: Honour befriend us both.
Beware, I warn thee yet, to tell thy griefs
In terms becoming Majesty to hear:
I warn thee thus, because I know thy temper
Is Insolent and haughty to Superiours:
How often hast thou brav'd my peacefull Court,
Fill'd it with noisy brawls, and windy boasts;
And, with past service, nauseously repeated,
Reproach'd ev'n me thy Prince?
DORAX: And well I might, when you forgot reward,
The part of Heav'n in Kings: for punishment
Is Hangmans work, and drudgery for Devils.
I must and will reproach thee with my service,
Tyrant, (it irks me so to call my Prince.)
But just resentment and hard usage coyn'd
Th' unwilling word; and grating as it is
Take it, for 'tis thy due.
SEBASTIAN: How Tyrant?

DORAX: Tyrant.
SEBASTIAN: Traytour? that name thou canst not Eccho back:
That Robe of Infamy, that Circumcision
Ill hid beneath that Robe, proclaim thee Traytor:
And, if a Name
More foul than Traytor be, 'tis Renegade.
DORAX: If I'm a Traytor, think and blush, thou Tyrant,
Whose Injuries betray'd me into treason,
Effac'd my Loyalty, unhing'd my Faith,
And hurryed me from hopes of Heav'n to Hell.
All these, and all my yet unfinish'd Crimes,
When I shall rise to plead before the Saints,
I charge on thee, to make thy damning sure.
SEBASTIAN: Thy old presumptuous Arrogance again,
That bred my first dislike, and then my loathing.
Once more be warn'd, and know me for thy King.
DORAX: Too well I know thee; but for King no more:
This is not *Lisbonne*, nor the Circle this,
Where, like a Statue, thou hast stood besieg'd,
By Sycophants and Fools, the growth of Courts:
Where thy gull'd eyes, in all the gawdy round,
Met nothing but a lye in every face;
And the gross flattery of a gaping Crowd,
Envious who first should catch, and first applaud
The Stuff of Royall Nonsence: when I spoke,
My honest homely words were carp'd, and censur'd,
For want of Courtly Stile: related Actions,
Though modestly reported, pass'd for boasts:
Secure of Merit if I ask'd reward,
Thy hungry Minions thought their rights invaded,
And the bread snatch'd from Pimps and Parasits.
Enriquez answer'd, with a ready lye,
To save his King's, the boon was begg'd before.
SEBASTIAN: What sayst thou of *Enriquez?* now by Heaven
Thou mov'st me more by barely naming him,
Than all thy foul unmanner'd scurril taunts.
DORAX: And therefore 'twas to gaul thee, that I nam'd him:
That thing, that nothing, but a cringe and smile;
That Woman, but more dawb'd; or if a man,
Corrupted to a Woman: thy Man Mistress.
SEBASTIAN: All false as Hell or thou.
DORAX: Yes; full as false
As that I serv'd thee fifteen hard Campaignes,

And pitch'd thy Standard in these Forreign Fields:
By me thy greatness grew; thy years grew with it,
But thy Ingratitude outgrew 'em both.

SEBASTIAN: I see to what thou tend'st, but tell me first
If those great Acts were done alone for me;
If love produc'd not some, and pride the rest?

DORAX: Why Love does all that's noble here below;
But all th' advantage of that love was thine.
For, coming fraughted back, in either hand
With Palm and Olive, Victory and Peace,
I was indeed prepar'd to ask my own:
(For *Violante*'s vows were mine before:)
Thy malice had prevention, ere I spoke;
And ask'd me *Violante* for *Enriquez*.

SEBASTIAN: I meant thee a reward of greater worth.

DORAX: Where justice wanted, could reward be hop'd?
Could the robb'd Passenger expect a bounty,
From those rapacious hands who stript him first?

SEBASTIAN: He had my promise, e're I knew thy love,

DORAX: My Services deserv'd thou should'st revoke it.

SEBASTIAN: Thy Insolence had cancell'd all thy Service:
To violate my Laws, even in my Court,
Sacred to peace, and safe from all affronts;
Ev'n to my face, as done in my despight,
Under the wing of awfull Majesty
To strike the man I lov'd!

DORAX: Even in the face of Heaven, a place more Sacred,
Would I have struck the man, who propt by power,
Would Seize my right, and rob me of my Love:
But, for a blow provok'd by thy Injustice,
The hasty product of a just despair,
When he refus'd to meet me in the field,
That thou should'st make a Cowards Cause thy own!

SEBASTIAN: He durst; nay more desir'd and begg'd with tears,
To meet thy Challenge fairly: 'twas thy fault
To make it publique; but my duty, then,
To interpose; on pain of my displeasure,
Betwixt your Swords.

DORAX: On pain of Infamy
He should have disobey'd.

SEBASTIAN: Th' Indignity thou didst, was meant to me;
Thy gloomy eyes were cast on me with scorn,
As who should say the blow was there intended;

But that thou didst not dare to lift thy hands
Against Annointed power: so was I forc'd
To do a Soveraign justice to myself;
And spurn thee from my presence.

DORAX: Thou hast dar'd
To tell me, what I durst not tell my self:
I durst not think that I was spurn'd, and live;
And live to hear it boasted to my face.
All my long Avarice of honour lost,
Heap'd up in Youth, and hoarded up for Age;
Has honours Fountain then suck'd back the stream?
He has; and hooting Boys may dry-shod pass,
And gather pebbles from the naked Foord.
Give me my Love, my Honour; give 'em back:—
Give me revenge; while I have breath to ask it.—

SEBASTIAN: Now, by this honour'd Order which I wear,
More gladly would I give, than thou dar'st ask it:
Nor shall the Sacred Character of King
Be urg'd, to shield me from thy bold appeal.
If I have injur'd thee, that makes us equall:
The wrong, if done, debas'd me down to thee.
But thou hast charg'd me with Ingratitude:
Hast thou not charg'd me; speak?

DORAX: Thou know'st I have:
If thou disown'st that Imputation, draw,
And prove my Charge a lye.

SEBASTIAN: No; to disprove that lye, I must not draw:
Be conscious to thy worth, and tell thy Soul
What thou hast done this day in my defence:
To fight thee, after this, what were it else,
Than owning that Ingratitude thou urgest?
That *Isthmus* stands betwixt two rushing Seas;
Which, mounting, view each other from afar;
And strive in vain to meet.

DORAX: I'le cut that *Isthmus*.
Thou know'st I meant not to preserve thy Life,
But to reprieve it, for my own revenge.
I sav'd thee out of honourable malice:
Now draw; I should be loath to think thou dar'st not:
Beware of such another vile excuse.

SEBASTIAN: O patience Heaven!

DORAX: Beware of Patience too;
That's a Suspicious word: it had been proper

Before thy foot had spurn'd me; now 'tis base:
Yet, to disarm thee of thy last defence,
I have thy Oath for my security:
The only boon I begg'd was this fair Combat:
Fight or be Perjur'd now; that's all thy choice.

SEBASTIAN *drawing*: Now I can thank thee as thou wouldst be thank'd:
Never was vow of honour better payd,
If my true Sword but hold, than this shall be.
The sprightly Bridegroom, on his Wedding Night,
More gladly enters not the lists of Love.
Why 'tis enjoyment to be summon'd thus.
Go: bear my Message to *Enriquez* ghost;
And say his Master and his Friend reveng'd him.

DORAX: His Ghost! then is my hated Rivall dead?

SEBASTIAN: The question is beside our present purpose;
Thou seest me ready; we delay too long.

DORAX: A minute is not much in eithers Life,
When there's but one betwixt us; throw it in,
And give it him of us, who is to fall.

SEBASTIAN: He's dead: make hast, and thou mayst yet o're take him.

DORAX: When I was hasty, thou delay'st me longer.
I prethee let me hedge one moment more
Into thy promise: for thy life preserv'd:
Be kind: and tell me how that Rivall dy'd,
Whose Death next thine I wish'd.

SEBASTIAN: If it would please thee thou shouldst never know:
But thou, like Jealousy, enquir'st a truth,
Which, found, will torture thee: He dy'd in Fight:
Fought next my person; as in Consort fought;
Kept pace for pace, and blow for every blow;
Save when he heav'd his Shield in my defence;
And on his naked side receiv'd my wound.
Then, when he could no more, he fell at once:
But rowl'd his falling body cross their way;
And made a Bulwark of it for his Prince.

DORAX: I never can forgive him such a death!

SEBASTIAN: I prophecy'd thy proud Soul could not bear it.
Now, judge thy self, who best deserv'd my Love.
I knew you both; and (durst I say) as Heaven
Foreknew among the shining Angell host
Who would stand firm, who fall.

DORAX: Had he been tempted so, so had he fall'n;
And so, had I been favour'd, had I stood.
SEBASTIAN: What had been is unknown; what is appears:
Confess he justly was preferr'd to thee.
DORAX: Had I been born with his indulgent Stars,
My fortune had been his, and his been mine.
O, worse than Hell! what Glory have I lost,
And what has he acquir'd, by such a death!
I should have fallen by *Sebastian*'s side;
My Corps had been the Bulwark of my King.
His glorious end was a patch'd work of fate,
Ill sorted with a soft effeminate life:
It suited better with my life than his
So to have dy'd: mine had been of a piece,
Spent in your service, dying at your feet.
SEBASTIAN: The more effeminate and soft his life,
The more his fame, to struggle to the field,
And meet his glorious fate: Confess, proud Spirit,
(For I will have it from thy very mouth)
That better he deserv'd my love than thou.
DORAX: O, whither would you drive me! I must grant,
Yes I must grant, but with a swelling Soul,
Enriquez had your Love with more desert:
For you he fought, and dy'd; I fought against you;
Through all the mazes of the bloudy field,
Hunted your Sacred life; which that I miss'd
Was the propitious errour of my fate,
Not of my Soul; my soul's a Regicide.
SEBASTIAN *more calmly*: Thou might'st have given it a more gentle name:
Thou meant'st to kill a Tyrant, not a King:
Speak didst thou not, *Alonzo?*
DORAX: Can I speak!
Alas, I cannot answer to *Alonzo*:
No, *Dorax* cannot answer to *Alonzo*:
Alonzo was too kind a name for me.
Then, when I fought and conquer'd with your Armes,
In that blest Age I was the man you nam'd:
Till rage and pride debas'd me into *Dorax*;
And lost like *Lucifer*, my name above.
SEBASTIAN: Yet, twice this day I ow'd my life to *Dorax*.
DORAX: I sav'd you but to kill you; there's my grief.
SEBASTIAN: Nay, if thou can'st be griev'd, thou can'st repent:

Thou coud'st not be a Villain, though thou woud'st:
Thou own'st too much, in owning thou hast err'd;
And I too little, who provok'd thy Crime.

DORAX: O stop this headlong Torrent of your goodness:
It comes too fast upon a feeble Soul,
Half drown'd in tears, before; spare my confusion:
For pitty spare, and say not, first, you err'd.
For yet I have not dar'd, through guilt and shame,
To throw my self beneath your Royall feet.
[*Falls at his feet.*
Now spurn this Rebell, this proud Renegade:
'Tis just you should, nor will I more complain.

SEBASTIAN: Indeed thou shoud'st not ask forgiveness first,
But thou preventst me still, in all that's noble.
[*Taking him up.*
Yet I will raise thee up with better news:
Thy *Violante*'s heart was ever thine;
Compell'd to wed, because she was my Ward,
Her Soul was absent when she gave her hand:
Nor could my threats, or his pursuing Courtship,
Effect the Consummation of his Love:
So, still indulging tears, she pines for thee,
A Widdow and a Maid.

DORAX: Have I been cursing Heav'n while Heav'n blest me?
I shall run mad with extasy of joy:
What, in one moment, to be reconcil'd
To Heaven, and to my King, and to my Love!
But pitty is my Friend, and stops me short,
For my unhappy Rivall: poor *Enriquez*!

SEBASTIAN: Art thou so generous too, to Pitty him?
Nay, then I was unjust to love him better.
Here let me ever hold thee in my arms: [*Embracing him.*
And all our quarrells be but such as these,
Who shall love best, and closest shall embrace:
Be what *Enriquez* was; be my *Alonzo*.

DORAX: What, my *Alonzo* say'd you? my *Alonzo*!
Let my tears thank you; for I cannot speak:
And if I cou'd,
Words were not made to vent such thoughts as mine.

SEBASTIAN: Thou canst not speak, and I can ne're be silent.
Some Strange reverse of Fate must, sure attend
This vast profusion, this extravagance
Of Heaven, to bless me thus. 'Tis Gold so pure

It cannot bear the Stamp, without Allay.
Be kind, ye Powers, and take but half away:
With ease the gifts of Fortune I resign;
But, let my Love, and Friend, be ever mine. [*Exeunt.*

ACT V

The Scene is a Room of State.

Enter DORAX *and* ANTONIO.

DORAX: Joy is on every face, without a Cloud:
As, in the Scene of opening Paradice,
The whole Creation danc'd at their new being:
Pleas'd to be what they were; pleas'd with each other.
Such Joy have I, both in my self, and Friends:
And double Joy, that I have made 'em happy.

ANTONIO: Pleasure has been the bus'ness of my life;
And every change of Fortune easy to me,
Because I still was easy to my self.
The loss of her I lov'd would touch me nearest;
Yet, if I found her, I might love too much;
And that's uneasy Pleasure.

DORAX: If she be fated
To be your Wife, your fate will find her for you:
Predestinated ills are never lost.

ANTONIO: I had forgot
T' enquire before, but long to be inform'd,
How, poison'd and betray'd, and round beset,
You could unwind your self from all these dangers;
And move so speedily to our relief!

DORAX: The double poisons, after a short Combat,
Expell'd each other in their Civill War,
By natures benefit: and rows'd my thoughts
To Guard that life which now I found Attack'd.
I summon'd all my Officers in hast,
On whose experienc'd Faith I might rely:
All came; resolv'd to dye in my defence,
Save that one Villain who betray'd the Gate.
Our diligence prevented the surprize
We justly fear'd: so, *Muley-Zeydan* found us
Drawn-up in Battle, to receive the charge.

ANTONIO: But how the *Moors* and *Christian* slaves were joyn'd,
You have not yet unfolded.

DORAX: That remains.
We knew their Int'rest was the same with ours:
And though I hated more than Death, *Sebastian*,
I could not see him dye by Vulgar hands:
But prompted by my Angell, or by his,
Freed all the Slaves, and plac'd him next my self,
Because I would not have his Person known.
I need not tell the rest, th' event declares it.

ANTONIO: Your Conquest came of course; their men were raw,
And yours were disciplin'd: one doubt remains,
Why you industriously conceal'd the King,
Who, known, had added Courage to his Men?

DORAX: I would not hazard civill broils, betwixt
His Friends and mine: which might prevent our Combat:
Yet, had he fall'n, I had dismiss'd his Troops;
Or, if Victorious, order'd his escape.
But I forgot a new increase of Joy,
To feast him with surprize; I must about it:
Expect my swift return. [*Exit* DORAX.

Enter a Servant to ANTONIO.

SERVANT: Here's a Lady at the door, that bids me tell you, she is come to make an end of the game, that was broken off betwixt you.

ANTONIO: What manner of Woman is she? Does she not want two of the four Elements? has she any thing about her but ayr and fire?

SERVANT: Truly, she flys about the room, as if she had wings instead of legs; I believe she's just turning into a bird: a house-bird I warrant her: and so hasty to fly to you, that, rather than fail of entrance, she wou'd come tumbling down the Chimney, like a Swallow.

Enter MORAYMA.

ANTONIO *running to her and Embracing her*: Look if she be not here already: what, no deniall it seems will serve your turn? why! thou little dun, is thy debt so pressing?

MORAYMA: Little Devill if you please: Your lease is out, good Mr. Conjurer; and I am come to fetch you Soul and Body; not an hour of lewdness longer in this world for you.

ANTONIO: Where the Devill hast thou been? and how the Devill didst thou find me here?

MORAYMA: I follow'd you into the Castle-yard; but there was nothing but Tumult, and Confusion: and I was bodily afraid of being pick'd up by some of the Rabble: considering I had a double charge about me,—my Jewells, and my Maydenhead.

ANTONIO: Both of 'em intended for my Worships sole use and Property.

MORAYMA: And what was poor little I among 'em all?

ANTONIO: Not a mouthfull a piece: 'twas too much odds in Conscience!

MORAYMA: So seeking for shelter, I naturally ran to the old place of Assignation, the Garden-house: where for want of instinct you did not follow me.

ANTONIO: Well for thy Comfort, I have secur'd thy Father; and I hope thou hast secur'd his effects for us.

MORAYMA: Yes truly I had the prudent foresight to consider that when we grow old, and weary of Solacing one another, we might have, at least, wherewithal to make merry with the World; and take up with a worse pleasure of eating and drinking, when we were disabled for a better.

ANTONIO: Thy fortune will be e'en too good for thee: for thou art going into the Country of Serenades, and Gallantries; where thy street will be haunted every Night, with thy foollish Lovers, and my Rivals; who will be sighing, and singing under thy inexorable windows, lamentable ditties, and call thee cruell, & Goddess, & Moon, and Stars, and all the Poeticall names of wicked rhyme: while thou and I, are minding our bus'ness, and jogging on, and laughing at 'em; at leisure minutes, which will be very few, take that by way of threatning.

MORAYMA: I am afraid you are not very valiant, that you huff so much before hand: but, they say, your Churches are fine places for Love-devotion: many a she-Saint is there worship'd.

ANTONIO: Temples are there, as they are in all other Countries, good conveniences for dumb enterviews: I hear the Protestants an't much reform'd in that point neither; for their Sectaries call their Churches by the naturall name of Meeting-houses. Therefore I warn thee in good time, not more of devotion than needs must, good future spowse; and allways in a veile; for those eyes of thine are damn'd enemies to mortification.

MORAYMA: The best thing I have heard of Christendom, is that we women are allow'd the priviledge of having Souls; and I assure you, I shall make bold to bestow mine, upon some Lover, when ever you begin to go astray, and, if I find no Convenience in a Church, a private Chamber will serve the turn.

ANTONIO: When that day comes, I must take my revenge and turn Gardener again: for I find I am much given to Planting.

MORAYMA: But take heed, in the mean time, that some young *Antonio* does not spring up in your own Family; as false as his Father, though of another mans planting.

Re-enter DORAX *with* SEBASTIAN *and* ALMEYDA. SEBASTIAN *enters speaking to* DORAX, *while in the mean time* ANTONIO *presents* MORAYMA *to* ALMEYDA.

SEBASTIAN: How fares our Royall Prisoner, *Muley-Zeydan?*

DORAX: Dispos'd to grant whatever I desire,
To gain a Crown, and Freedom: well I know him,
Of easy temper, naturally good,
And faithfull to his word.

SEBASTIAN: Yet one thing wants,
To fill the measure of my happiness
I'm still in pain for poor *Alvarez*'s life.

DORAX: Release that fear; the good old man is safe:
I pay'd his ransome:
And have already order'd his Attendance.

SEBASTIAN: O bid him enter for I long to see him.

Enter ALVAREZ *with a Servant, who departs when* ALVAREZ *is enter'd.*

ALVAREZ *falling down and embracing the* KINGS *knees*: Now by my Soul, and by these hoary hairs,
I'm so ore-whelm'd with pleasure, that I feel
A latter spring within my with'ring limbs,
That Shoots me out again.

SEBASTIAN *raising him*: Thou good old Man,
Thou hast deceiv'd me into more, more joys;
Who stood brim-full before.

ALVAREZ: O my dear Child!
I love thee so, I cannot call thee King,
Whom I so oft have dandled in these arms!
What, when I gave thee lost to find thee living!
'Tis like a Father, who himself had scap'd

A falling house, and after anxious search,
Hears from afar, his only Son within:
And digs through rubbish, till he drags him out
To see the friendly light.
Such is my hast, so trembling is my joy
To draw thee forth from underneath thy Fate.

SEBASTIAN: The Tempest is ore-blown; the Skies are clear,
And the Sea, charm'd into a Calm so still,
That not a wrinkle ruffles her smooth face.

ALVAREZ: Just such she shows before a rising storm:
And therefore am I come, with timely speed,
To warn you into Port.

ALMEYDA: My Soul fore-bodes [*Aside.*
Some dire event involv'd in those dark words;
And just disclosing, in a birth of fate.

ALVAREZ: Is there not yet an Heir of this vast Empire,
Who still Survives, of *Muley-Moluchs* branch?

DORAX: Yes such an one there is, a Captive here,
And Brother to the Dead.

ALVAREZ: The Power's above
Be prais'd for that: My prayers for my good Master
I hope are heard.

SEBASTIAN: Thou hast a right in Heav'n,
But why these prayers for me?

ALVAREZ: A door is open yet for your deliv'rance,
Now you my Country-men, and you *Almeyda*,
Now all of us, and you (my all in one)
May yet be happy in that Captives life.

SEBASTIAN: We have him here an honourable Hostage
For terms of peace: what more he can Contribute
To make me blest, I know not.

ALVAREZ: Vastly more:
Almeyda may be settled in the Throne;
And you review your Native Clime with fame:
A firm Alliance, and eternal Peace,
(The glorious Crown of honourable War,)
Are all included in that Princes life:
Let this fair Queen be giv'n to *Muley-Zeydan*;
And make her love the Sanction of your League.

SEBASTIAN: No more of that: his life's in my dispose;
And Pris'ners are not to insist on terms.
Or if they were, yet he demands not these.

ALVAREZ: You shou'd exact 'em.

ALMEYDA: Better may be made;
These cannot: I abhor the Tyrants race;
My Parents Murtherers, my Throne's Usurpers.
But, at one blow to cut off all dispute,
Know this, thou busy, old, officious Man,
I am a Christian; now be wise no more;
Or if you woud'st be still thought wise, be silent.
ALVAREZ: O! I perceive you think your Int'rest touch'd:
'Tis what before the Battail I observ'd:
But I must speak, and will.
SEBASTIAN: I prethee peace;
Perhaps she thinks they are too near of bloud.
ALVAREZ: I wish she may not wed to bloud more near.
SEBASTIAN: What if I make her mine?
ALVAREZ: Now Heav'n forbid!
SEBASTIAN: Wish rather Heav'n may grant.
For, if I cou'd deserve, I have deserv'd her:
My toyls, my hazards, and my Subjects lives,
(Provided she consent) may claim her love;
And, that once granted, I appeal to these,
If better, I cou'd chuse a beauteous Bride.
ANTONIO: The fairest of her Sex.
MORAYMA: The pride of Nature.
DORAX: He only merits her; she only him.
So payr'd, so suited in their minds and Persons,
That they were fram'd the Tallyes for each other.
If any Alien love had interpos'd
It must have been an eyesore to beholders,
And to themselves a Curse.
ALVAREZ: And to themselves
The greatest Curse that can be, were to joyn.
SEBASTIAN: Did I not love thee, past a change to hate,
That word had been thy ruine; but no more,
I charge thee on thy life, perverse old man.
ALVAREZ: Know, Sir, I wou'd be silent if I durst:
But, if on Shipbord, I shou'd see my Friend,
Grown frantique in a raging Calenture,
And he, imagining vain flowery fields,
Wou'd headlong plunge himself into the deep,
Shou'd I not hold him from that mad attempt,
Till his sick fancy were by reason cur'd?
SEBASTIAN: I pardon thee th' effects of doting Age:
Vain doubts, and idle cares, and over-caution;

The second Non-age of a Soul, more wise;
But now decay'd, and sunk into the Socket,
Peeping by fits and giving feeble light.

ALVAREZ: Have you forgot?

SEBASTIAN: Thou mean'st my Fathers Will,
In bar of Marriage to *Almeyda*'s bed:
Thou seest my faculties are still entire,
Though thine are much impair'd, I weigh'd that Will,
And found 'twas grounded on our diff'rent Faiths;
But, had he liv'd to see her happy change,
He wou'd have cancell'd that harsh Interdict,
And joyn'd our hands himself.

ALVAREZ: Still had he liv'd and seen this change,
He still had been the Same.

SEBASTIAN: I have a dark remembrance of my Father;
His reas'nings and his Actions both were just;
And, granting that, he must have chang'd his measures.

ALVAREZ: Yes, he was just, and therefore cou'd not change.

SEBASTIAN: 'Tis a base wrong thou offer'st to the Dead.

ALVAREZ: Now Heav'n forbid,
That I shou'd blast his pious Memory:
No, I am tender of his holy Fame:
For, dying he bequeath'd it to my charge.
Believe I am; and seek to know no more,
But pay a blind obedience to his will.
For to preserve his Fame I wou'd be silent.

SEBASTIAN: Craz'd fool, who woud'st be thought an Oracle.
Come down from off thy Tripos, and speak plain:
My Father shall be justify'd, he shall:
'Tis a Son's part to rise in his defence;
And to confound thy malice, or thy dotage.

ALVAREZ: It does not grieve me that you hold me craz'd;
But, to be clear'd at my dead Masters cost,
O there's the wound! but let me first adjure you,
By all you owe that dear departed Soul,
No more to think of Marriage with *Almeyda*.

SEBASTIAN: Not Heav'n and Earth combin'd can hinder it.

ALVAREZ: Then, witness Heav'n and Earth, how loath I am
To say, you must not, nay you cannot wed.
And since not only a dead Fathers fame,
But more a Ladies honour must be touch'd,
Which nice as Ermines will not bear a Soil;

Let all retire; that you alone may hear
What ev'n in whispers I wou'd tell your ear.
[*All are going out.*

ALMEYDA: Not one of you depart; I charge you stay.
And, were my voice a Trumpet loud as Fame,
To reach the round of Heav'n, and Earth, and Sea,
All Nations shou'd be Summon'd to this place,
So little do I fear that Fellows charge:
So shou'd my honour like a rising Swan,
Brush with her wings, the falling drops away,
And proudly plough the waves.

SEBASTIAN: This noble Pride becomes thy Innocence:
And I dare trust my Fathers memory,
To stand the charge of that foul forging tongue.

ALVAREZ: It will be soon discover'd if I forge:
Have you not heard your Father in his youth,
When newly marry'd, travel'd into *Spain*,
And made a long abode in *Phillip*'s Court?

SEBASTIAN: Why so remote a question, which thy self
Can answer to thy self? for thou wert with him,
His Fav'rite, as I oft have heard thee boast:
And nearest to his Soul.

ALVAREZ: Too near indeed, forgive me Gracious Heaven
That ever I should boast I was so near,
The Confident of all his young Amours.
And have not you, unhappy beauty, [*To* ALMEYDA] heard,
Have you not often heard, your Exil'd Parents
Were refug'd in that Court, and at that time?

ALMEYDA: 'Tis true: and often since, my Mother own'd
How kind that Prince was, to espouse her cause;
She Counsell'd, nay, Enjoin'd me on her blessing
To seek the Sanctuary of your Court:
Which gave me first encouragement to come,
And, with my Brother, beg *Sebastians* aid.

SEBASTIAN *to* ALMEYDA: Thou help'st me well, to justify my War:
My dying Father swore me, then a Boy;
And made me kiss the Cross upon his Sword,
Never to sheath it, till that exil'd Queen
Were by my Arms restor'd.

ALVAREZ: And can you finde
No mistery, couch'd in this excess of kindness?
Were Kings e're known, in this degenerate Age,

So passionately fond of noble Acts,
Where Interest shar'd not more than half with honour?

SEBASTIAN: Base groveling Soul, who know'st not honours worth;
But weigh'st it out in mercenary Scales;
The Secret pleasure of a generous Act,
Is the great minds great bribe.

ALVAREZ: Show me that King, and I'le believe the Phœnix.
But knock at your own breast, and ask your Soul
If those fair fatall eyes, edg'd not your Sword
More than your Fathers charge, and all your vows?
If so; and so your silence grants it is,
Know King, your Father had, like you, a Soul;
And Love is your Inheritance from him.
Almeyda's Mother too had eyes, like her,
And not less charming, and were charm'd no less
Than your's are now with her, and her's with you.

ALMEYDA: Thou ly'st Impostor, Perjur'd Fiend thou ly'st.

SEBASTIAN: Was't not enough to brand my Father's fame,
But thou must load a Ladies memory?
O Infamous base, beyond repair.
And, to what end this ill concerted lye,
Which, palpable and gross, yet granted true,
It barrs not my Inviolable vows.

ALVAREZ: Take heed and double not your Fathers crimes;
To his Adult'ry, do not add your Incest.
Know, she is the product of unlawfull Love:
And 'tis your Carnall Sister you wou'd wed.

SEBASTIAN: Thou shalt not say thou wert Condemn'd unheard.
Else, by my Soul, this moment were thy last.

ALMEYDA: But think not Oaths shall justify thy charge;
Nor Imprecations on thy cursed head,
For who dares lye to Heaven, thinks Heaven a Jest.
Thou hast confess'd thy self the Conscious Pandar
Of that pretended passion:
A Single Witness, infamously known,
Against two Persons of unquestion'd fame.

ALVAREZ: What Int'rest can I have, or what delight
To blaze their shame, or to divulge my own?
If prov'd you hate me, if unprov'd Condemn?
Not Racks or Tortures could have forc'd this secret,
But too much care, to save you from a Crime,

Which would have sunk you both. For let me say,
Almeyda's beauty well deserves your love.

ALMEYDA: Out, base Impostor, I abhor thy praise.

DORAX: It looks not like Imposture: but a truth,
On utmost need reveal'd.

SEBASTIAN: Did I expect from *Dorax*, this return?
Is this the love renew'd?

DORAX: Sir, I am silent;
Pray Heav'n my fears prove false.

SEBASTIAN: Away; you all combine to make me wretched.

ALVAREZ: But hear the story of that fatall Love;
Where every Circumstance shall prove another;
And truth so shine, by her own native light,
That if a Lye were mixt, it must be seen.

SEBASTIAN: No; all may still be forg'd, and of a piece.
No; I can credit nothing thou can'st say:

ALVAREZ: One proof remains; and that's your Fathers hand:
Firm'd with his Signet; both so fully known,
That plainer Evidence can hardly be,
Unless his Soul wou'd want her Heav'n awhile,
And come on Earth to swear.

SEBASTIAN: Produce that Writing.

ALVAREZ *to* DORAX: *Alonzo* has it in his Custody.
The same, which when his nobleness redeem'd me,
And in a friendly visit own'd himself,
For what he is, I then deposited:
And had his Faith to give it to the King.

DORAX *giving a seal'd Paper to the* KING: Untouch'd, and Seal'd as when intrusted with me,
Such I restore it, with a trembling hand,
Lest aught within disturb your peace of Soul.

SEBASTIAN *tearing open the Seals*: Draw near *Almeyda*, thou art most concern'd
For I am most in Thee.
Alonzo, mark the Characters:
Thou know'st my Fathers hand observe it well:
And if th' Impostors Pen have made one slip,
That shows it Counterfeit, mark that and save me.

DORAX: It looks, indeed, too like my Masters hand:
So does the Signet; more I cannot say;
But wish 'twere not so like.

SEBASTIAN: Methinks it owns
The black Adult'ry, and *Almeyda*'s birth;

But such a mist of grief comes o're my eyes,
I cannot, or I wou'd not read it plain.

ALMEYDA: Heav'n cannot be more true, than this is false.

SEBASTIAN: O coud'st thou prove it with the same assurance!
Speak, hast thou ever seen my Fathers hand?

ALMEYDA: No; but my Mothers honour has been read
By me, and by the world, in all her Acts;
In Characters more plain, and legible
Than this dumb Evidence, this blotted lye.
Oh that I were a man, as my Soul's one,
To prove thee, Traytor, and Assassinate
Of her fair fame: thus wou'd I tear thee thus:—
[*Tearing the Paper.*
And scatter, o're the field, thy Coward limbs,
Like this foul offspring of thy forging brain.
[*Scatt'ring the Paper*

ALVAREZ: Just so shalt thou be torn from all thy hopes.
For know proud Woman, know in thy despight,
The most Authentique proof is still behind.
Thou wear'st it on thy finger: 'Tis that Ring,
Which match'd with that on his, shall clear the doubt.
'Tis no dumb forgery: for that shall speak;
And sound a rattling peal to eithers Conscience.

SEBASTIAN: This Ring indeed, my Father, with a cold
And shaking hand, just in the pangs of Death,
Put on my finger; with a parting sigh,
And wou'd have spoke; but faulter'd in his speech,
With undistinguish'd sounds.

ALVAREZ: I know it well:
For I was present: Now, *Almeyda*, speak:
And, truly tell us, how you come by yours?

ALMEYDA: My Mother, when I parted from her sight,
To go to *Portugall* bequeath'd it to me,
Presaging she shou'd never see me more:
She pull'd it from her finger, shed some tears,
Kiss'd it, and told me 'twas a pledge of Love;
And hid a Mistery of great Importance
Relating to my Fortunes.

ALVAREZ: Mark me now,
While I disclose that fatall Mistery.
Those rings, when you were born, and thought anothers,
Your Parents, glowing yet in sinfull love,
Bid me bespeak: a Curious Artist wrought 'em:

With joynts so close, as not to be perceiv'd;
Yet are they both each others Counterpart.
Her part had *Juan* inscrib'd, and his had *Zayda*,
(You know those names are theirs:) and in the midst,
A heart divided in two halves was plac'd.
Now if the rivets of those Rings, inclos'd,
Fit not each other, I have forg'd this lye:
But if they joyn, you must for ever part.

[SEBASTIAN *pulling off his Ring.* ALMEYDA *does the same, and gives it to* ALVAREZ, *who unscrues both the Rings & fits one half to the other.*]

SEBASTIAN: Now life, or death.

ALMEYDA: And either thine, or ours.
I'm lost for ever. ——————— [*Swoons*

[*The Women and* MORAYMA, *take her up and carry her off.* SEBASTIAN *here stands amaz'd without motion, his eyes fixt upward.*]

SEBASTIAN: Look to the Queen my Wife; For I am past
All pow'r of Aid, to her or to my self.

ALVAREZ: His Wife, said he, his Wife! O fatall sound!
For, had I known it, this unwelcome news
Had never reach'd their ears.
So they had still been blest in Ignorance,
And I alone unhappy.

DORAX: I knew it, but too late: and durst not speak.

SEBASTIAN *starting out of his amazement*: I will not live: no not a moment more;
I will not add one moment more to Incest.
I'le cut it off, and end a wretched being.
For, should I live, my Soul's so little mine,
And so much hers, that I should still enjoy.
Ye Cruell Powers,
Take me as you have made me, miserable;
You cannot make me guilty; 'twas my fate
And you made that, not I. [*Draws his Sword.*

[ANTONIO *and* ALVAREZ *lay hold on him, and* DORAX *wrests the Sword out of his hand.*]

ANTONIO: For Heav'ns sake hold, and recollect your mind.

ALVAREZ: Consider whom you punish, and for what;
Your self? unjustly: You have charg'd the fault,
On Heav'n that best may bear it.
Though Incest is indeed a deadly Crime,

You are not guilty, since, unknown 'twas done,
And, known, had been abhorr'd.

SEBASTIAN: By Heaven, y're Traytours all, that hold my hands,
If death be but cessation of our thought,
Then let me dye, for I would think no more.
I'le boast my Innocence above;
And let 'em see a Soul they cou'd not sully:
I shall be there before my Fathers Ghost;
That yet must languish long, in frosts and fires,
For making me unhappy by his Crime:
Stand off, and let me take my fill of death;

[*Struggling again.*

For I can hold my breath in your despight,
And swell my heaving Soul out, when I please.

ALVAREZ: Heav'n comfort you!

SEBASTIAN: What are thou giving comfort!
Wou'dst thou give comfort, who hast giv'n despair?
Thou seest *Alonzo* silent; he's a man.
He knows, that men abandon'd of their hopes
Shou'd ask no leave, nor stay for sueing out
A tedious Writ of Ease, from lingring Heaven,
But help themselves, as timely as they cou'd,
And teach the fates their duty.

DORAX *to* ALVAREZ *and* ANTONIO: Let him go;
He is our King; and he shall be obey'd.

ALVAREZ: What to destroy himself? O Parricide!

DORAX: Be not Injurious in your foolish zeal,
But leave him free; or by my sword I swear,
To hew that Arm away, that stops the passage
To his Eternal rest.

ANTONIO *letting go his hold*: Let him be Guilty of his own death if he pleases: for I'le not be guilty of mine by holding him. [*The* KING *shakes off* ALVAREZ.

ALVAREZ *to* DORAX: Infernal Fiend,
Is this a Subjects part?

DORAX: 'Tis a Friends Office.
He has convinc'd me that he ought to dye,
And, rather than he should not, here's my sword
To help him on his Journey.

SEBASTIAN: My last, my only Friend, how kind art thou
And how Inhuman these!

DORAX: To make the trifle death, a thing of moment!

SEBASTIAN: And not to weigh th' Important cause I had,
To rid my self of life?

DORAX: True; for a Crime,
So horrid in the face of Men and Angells,
As wilfull Incest is!

SEBASTIAN: Not wilfull neither.

DORAX: Yes, if you liv'd and with repeated Acts,
Refresh'd your Sin, and loaded crimes with crimes,
To swell your scores of Guilt.

SEBASTIAN: True; if I liv'd.

DORAX: I said so, if you liv'd.

SEBASTIAN: For hitherto 'twas fatall ignorance:
And no intended crime.

DORAX: That you best know.
But the Malicious World will judge the worst.

ALVAREZ: O what a Sophister has Hell procur'd,
To argue for Damnation!

DORAX: Peace, old Dotard.
Mankind that always judge of Kings with malice,
Will think he knew this Incest, and pursu'd it.
His only way to rectify mistakes,
And to redeem her honour, is to dye.

SEBASTIAN: Thou hast it right, my dear, my best *Alonzo!*
And that, but petty reparation too;
But all I have to give.

DORAX: Your pardon, Sir;
You may do more, and ought.

SEBASTIAN: What, more than death?

DORAX: Death? Why that's Childrens sport: a Stage-Play, Death.
We Act it every Night we go to bed.
Death to a Man in misery is sleep.
Wou'd you, who perpetrated such a Crime,
As frighten'd nature, made the Saints above
Shake Heav'ns Eternal pavement with their trembling,
To view that act, wou'd you but barely dye?
But stretch your limbs, and turn on t'other side,
To lengthen out a black voluptuous slumber,
And dream you had your Sister in your arms.

SEBASTIAN: To expiate this, can I do more then dye?

DORAX: O yes: you must do more; you must be damn'd:
You must be damn'd to all Eternity.
And, sure, self-Murder is the readiest way.

SEBASTIAN: How, damn'd?

DORAX: Why is that News?
ALVAREZ: O, horrour! horrour!
DORAX: What, thou a Statesman,
And make a bus'ness of Damnation?
In such a World as this, why 'tis a trade.
The Scriv'ner, Usurer, Lawyer, Shop-keeper,
And Soldier, cannot live, but by damnation.
The Polititian does it by advance:
And gives all gone before-hand.
SEBASTIAN: O thou hast giv'n me such a glimpse of Hell,
So push'd me forward, even to the brink,
Of that irremeable burning Gulph,
That looking in th' *Abyss*; I dare not leap.
And now I see what good thou meanst my Soul,
And thank thy pious fraud: Thou hast indeed,
Appear'd a Devill, but didst an Angells work.
DORAX: 'Twas the last Remedy, to give you leisure;
For, if you cou'd but think, I knew you safe.
SEBASTIAN: I thank thee, my *Alonzo*: I will live:
But never more to *Portugall* return:
For, to go back and reign, that were to show
Triumphant Incest, and pollute the Throne.
ALVAREZ: Since Ignorance——
SEBASTIAN: O, palliate not my wound:
When you have argued all you can, 'tis Incest:
No, 'tis resolv'd: I charge you plead no more;
I cannot live without *Almeyda*'s sight,
Nor can I see *Almeyda* but I sin.
Heav'n has inspir'd me with a Sacred thought,
To live alone to Heav'n: and dye to her.
DORAX: Mean you to turn an Anchorite?
SEBASTIAN: What else?
The world was once too narrow for my mind,
But one poor little nook will serve me now;
To hide me from the rest of humane kinde.
Affrique has desarts wide enough to hold
Millions of Monsters, and I am, sure, the greatest.
ALVAREZ: You may repent, and wish your Crown too late.
SEBASTIAN: O never, never: I am past a Boy,
A Scepter's but a play thing, and a Globe
A bigger bounding Stone. He who can leave
Almeyda, may renounce the rest with ease.
DORAX: O Truly great!

A Soul fix'd high, and capable of Heav'n.
Old as he is your Uncle Cardinall,
Is not so far enamour'd of a Cloyster,
But he will thank you, for the Crown you leave him.

SEBASTIAN: To please him more, let him believe me dead:
That he may never dream I may return.
Alonzo, I am now no more thy King,
But still thy Friend, and by that holy Name,
Adjure thee, to perform my last request.
Make our Conditions with yon Captive King,
Secure me but my Solitary Cell;
'Tis all I ask him for a Crown restor'd.

DORAX: I will do more:
But fear not *Muley-Zeydan*; his soft mettall
Melts down with easy warmth; runs in the mould,
And needs no farther forge. [*Exit* DORAX.

Re-enter ALMEYDA, *led by* MORAYMA, *and follow'd by her Attendants.*

SEBASTIAN: See where she comes again.
By Heav'n when I behold those beauteous eyes,
Repentance laggs and Sin comes hurrying on.

ALMEYDA: This is too cruell!

SEBASTIAN: Speak'st thou of Love, of Fortune, or of Death,
Or double Death? for we must part *Almeyda*.

ALMEYDA: I speak of all.
For all things that belong to us are cruell.
But what's most cruell, we must love no more.
O 'tis too much that I must never see you,
But not to love you is impossible:
No, I must love you: Heav'n may bate me that,
And charge that Sinfull Sympathy of Souls
Upon our Parents, when they lov'd too well.

SEBASTIAN: Good Heav'n, thou speakst my thoughts, and I speak thine.
Nay then there's Incest in our very Souls
For we were form'd too like.

ALMEYDA: Too like indeed,
And yet not for each other.
Sure when we part (for I resolv'd it too
Tho' you propos'd it first,) however distant,
We shall be ever thinking of each other.
And, the same moment for each other pray.

SEBASTIAN: But if a wish shou'd come athwart our prayers!
ALMEYDA: It would do well to curb it: if we cou'd.
SEBASTIAN: We cannot look upon each others face,
But, when we read our love, we read our guilt.
And yet methinks, I cannot chuse but love.
ALMEYDA: I wou'd have ask'd you, if I durst for shame,
If still you lov'd? you gave it Air before me.
Ah why were we not born both of a Sex;
For then we might have lov'd, without a Crime.
Why was not I your Brother? though that wish
Involv'd our Parents guilt, we had not parted;
We had been Friends, and Friendship is not Incest.
SEBASTIAN: Alas, I know not by what name to call thee!
Sister and Wife are the two dearest Names;
And I wou'd call thee both; and both are Sin.
Unhappy we! that still we must confound
The dearest Names, into a common Curse.
ALMEYDA: To love, and be belov'd, and yet be wretched!
SEBASTIAN: To have but one poor night of all our lives;
It was indeed a glorious, guilty night:
So happy, that, forgive me Heav'n, I wish
With all its guilt, it were to come again.
Why did we know so soon, or why at all,
That Sin cou'd be conceal'd in such a blisse?
ALMEYDA: Men have a larger priviledge of words,
Else I shou'd speak: but we must part, *Sebastian*,
That's all the name that I have left to call thee.
I must not call thee by the name I wou'd;
But when I say *Sebastian*, dear *Sebastian*,
I kiss the name I speak.
SEBASTIAN: We must make hast, or we shall never part.
I wou'd say something that's as dear as this;
Nay, wou'd do more than say: one moment longer,
And I shou'd break through Laws Divine, and Humane;
And think 'em Cobwebs, spred for little man,
Which all the bulky herd of nature breaks.
The vigorous young world, was ignorant
Of these restrictions, 'tis decrepit now;
Not more devout, but more decay'd, and cold.
All this is impious; therefore we must part:
For, gazing thus, I kindle at thy sight,
And, once burnt down to tinder, light again
Much sooner then before.

Re-enter DORAX.

ALMEYDA: Here comes the sad denouncer of my fate,
To toul the mournfull knell of Separation:
While I, as on my Death-bed, hear the sound,
That warns me hence for ever.

SEBASTIAN *to* DORAX: Now be brief,
And I will try to listen.
And share the minute that remains, betwixt
The care I owe my Subjects and my Love.

DORAX: Your fate has gratify'd you all she can;
Gives easy misery, and makes Exile pleasing.
I trusted *Muley-Zeydan*, as a friend,
But swore him first to Secresy: he wept
Your fortune, and with tears, not squeez'd by Art,
But shed from nature, like a kindly shower:
In short, he proffer'd more than I demanded;
A safe retreat, a gentle Solitude,
Unvex'd with noise, and undisturb'd with fears:
I chose you one.——

ALMEYDA: O do not tell me where:
For if I knew the place of his abode,
I shou'd be tempted to pursue his steps,
And then we both were lost.

SEBASTIAN: Ev'n past redemption.
For, if I knew thou wert on that design,
(As I must know, because our Souls are one,)
I shou'd not wander, but by sure Instinct
Shou'd meet thee just half-way, in pilgrimage
And close for ever: for I know my love
More strong than thine, and I more frail than thou.

ALMEYDA: Tell me not that: for I must boast my Crime,
And cannot bear that thou shoud'st better love.

DORAX: I may inform you both: for you must go,
Where Seas, and winds, and Desarts will divide you.
Under the ledge of *Atlas*, lyes a Cave,
Cut in the living Rock by Natures hands:
The Venerable Seat of holy Hermites,
Who there, secure in separated Cells,
Sacred ev'n to the Moors, enjoy Devotion:
And from the purling Streams, and savage fruits,
Have wholesome bev'rage, and unbloudy feasts.

SEBASTIAN: 'Tis pennance too Voluptuous, for my Crime.

DORAX: Your Subjects, conscious of your life, are few:
But all desirous to partake your Exile:
And to do office to your Sacred Person.
The rest who think you dead, shall be dismiss'd,
Under safe Convoy till they reach your Fleet.

ALMEYDA: But how am wretched I to be dispos'd?
A vain Enquiry, since I leave my Lord:
For all the world beside is Banishment!

DORAX: I have a Sister, Abbesse in *Tercers's*,
Who lost her Lover on her Bridall day.

ALMEYDA: There, fate provided me a fellow-Turtle;
To mingle sighs with sighs, and tears with tears.

DORAX: Last, for my self, if I have well fulfill'd
My sad Commission, let me beg the boon,
To share the sorrows of your last recess:
And mourn the Common losses of our loves.

ALVAREZ: And what becomes of me? must I be left,
(As Age and time had worn me out of use?)
These Sinews are not yet so much unstrung,
To fail me when my Master shou'd be serv'd:
And when they are, then will I steal to death:
Silent, and unobserv'd, to save his tears.

SEBASTIAN: I've heard you both: *Alvarez* have thy wish.
But thine *Alonzo*, thine, is too unjust.
I charge thee with my last Commands, return,
And bless thy *Violante* with thy vows.
Antonio, be thou happy too, in thine.
Last, let me swear you all to Secresy;
And to conceal my shame, conceal my life.

DORAX, ANTONIO, MORAYMA: We swear to keep it secret.

ALMEYDA: Now I wou'd speak the last farewell, I cannot.
It wou'd be still farewell a thousand times:
And, multiply'd in Eccho's, still farewell.
I will not speak; but think a thousand thousand;
And be thou silent too, my last *Sebastian*;
So let us part in the dumb pomp of grief.
My heart's too great; or I wou'd dye this moment:
But Death I thank him, in an hour, has made
A mighty journey, and I hast to meet him.

[*She staggers and her Women hold her up.*

SEBASTIAN: Help to support this feeble, drooping flower:
This tender Sweet, so shaken by the storm.
For these fond arms must, thus be stretch'd in vain,

And never, never must embrace her more.
'Tis past:——my Soul goes in that word;—farewell.

[ALVAREZ *goes with* SEBASTIAN *to one end of the Stage. Women with* ALMEYDA *to the other*. DORAX, *coming up to* ANTONIO *and* MORAYMA, *who stand on the Middle of the Stage.*

DORAX: Hast to attend *Almeyda*: for your sake
Your Father is forgiven: but to *Antonio*
He forfeits half his Wealth: be happy both:
And let *Sebastian* and *Almeyda*'s Fate,
This dreadfull Sentence to the World relate,
That unrepented Crimes of Parents dead,
Are justly punish'd on their Childrens head.

PROLOGUE

Sent to the Authour by an unknown hand,[1] *and propos'd to be spoken By Mrs.* Montford *drest like an Officer.*[2]

Bright Beauties who in awfull Circle sit,
And you grave Synod of the dreadfull Pit,
And you the Upper-Tire of pop-gun wit.

Pray ease me of my wonder if you may
Is all this Crowd barely to see the play,
Or is't the Poets Execution-day?

His breath is in your hands I will presume
But I advise you to deferr his doom:
Till you have got a better in his room.

And don't maliciously combine together,
As if in spight and spleen you were come hither,
For he has kept the Pen tho' lost the feather.

And on my Honour Ladies I avow,
This Play was writ in Charity to you,
For such a dearth of Wit who ever knew?

Sure 'tis a Judgment on this Sinfull Nation
For the abuse of so great Dispensation:
And therefore I resolve'd to change Vocation.

For want of Petti-coat I've put on buff,
To try what may be got by lying rough:
How think you Sirs, is it not well enough?

Of Bully Criticks I a Troup wou'd lead;
But one reply'd, thank you there's no such need,
I at Groom-Porters Sir can safer bleed.

[1] The 'unknown hand' was Sir Henry Sheeres (*d.* 1710).
[2] The humour of the prologue turns upon the unwillingness of the nobility to accompany William III with the army into Ireland.

Another who the name of danger loaths,
Vow'd he would go, and swore me Forty Oaths,
But that his Horses were in body-cloaths.

A third cry'd, Dammy bloud, I'de be content
To push my Fortune, if the Parliament
Would but recall Claret from Banishment.

A Fourth (and I have done) made this excuse
I'de draw my Sword in Ireland *Sir to chuse;*
Had not their Women gouty leggs and wore no shoes?

Well, I may march thought I and fight and trudge,
But of these blades the Devill a man will budge,
They there would fight e'n just as here they judge.

Here they will pay for leave to find a fault,
But when their Honour calls they can't be bought,
Honour in danger, bloud and wounds is sought.

Lost Virtue whither fled, or where's thy dwelling,
Who can reveal, at least 'tis past my telling,
Unless thou art Embarkt for Iniskelling.

On Carrion tits those Sparks denounce their rage
In boot of wisp and Leinster freese engage,
What would you do in such an Equipage?

The Siege of Derry *does you Gallants threaten:*
Not out of Errant shame of being beaten,
As fear of wanting meat or being eaten.

Were Wit like honour to be won by fighting
How few just Judges would there be of writing,
Then you would leave this Villanous back-biting.

Your Talents lye how to express your spight,
But where is he knows how to praise aright,
You praise like Cowards but like Criticks fight.

Ladies be wise, and wean these yearling Calves
Who in your Service too are meer faux-braves,
They Judge and write and fight, and—Love by halves.

EPILOGUE

To Don Sebastian, King of Portugall. Spoken betwixt ANTONIO *and* MORAYMA.

MORAYMA: *I Quak'd at heart for fear the Royal Fashion*
Shou'd have seduc'd Us two to Separation:
To be drawn in, against our own desire,
Poor I to be a Nun, poor You a Fryar.

ANTONIO: *I trembled when the Old Mans hand was in,*
He would have prov'd we were too near of kin:
Discovering old Intrigues of Love, like t'other,
Betwixt my Father and thy sinfull Mother;
To make us Sister Turk and Christian Brother.

MORAYMA: *Excuse me there; that League shou'd have been rather*
Betwixt your Mother and my Mufti-*Father;*
'Tis for my own and my Relations Credit
Your Friends shou'd bear the Bastard, mine shou'd get it.

ANTONIO: *Suppose us two* Almeyda *and* Sebastian
With Incest prov'd upon us:—

MORAYMA: *Without question*
Their Conscience was too queazy of digestion.

ANTONIO: *Thou woud'st have kept the Councell of thy Brother*
And sinn'd till we repented of each other.

MORAYMA: *Beast as you are on Natures Laws to trample;*
'Twere fitter that we follow'd their Example
And since all Marriage in Repentance ends,
'Tis good for us to part while we are Friends.
To save a Maids remorses and Confusions
E'en leave me now before We try Conclusions.

ANTONIO: *To copy their Example first make certain*
Of one good hour like theirs before our parting;
Make a debauch o're Night of Love and Madness;
And marry when we wake in sober sadness.

MORAYMA: *I'le follow no new Sects of your inventing,*
One Night might cost me nine long months repenting;
First wed, and if you find that life a fetter,
Dye when you please, the sooner Sir the better:
My wealth wou'd get me love e're I cou'd ask it:
Oh there's a strange Temptation in the Casket:
All these Young Sharpers wou'd my grace importune,
And make me thundring Votes of lives and fortune.